50ˢ

All-American Ads

I'm going to name him Champ, Dad!

Yes — pups, people or products — names play a very important part in our everyday lives.

Today, our standard of living is greatly enriched by our system of competing brand names.

What do these names mean to you? A great deal, because they really make you — and every consumer — the *boss*.

When a manufacturer proudly signs his name to his product, he knows that he has to win your faith in that name.

Only through satisfying you, can he be sure that you will buy again — *and again!*

That's the main reason why manufacturers of branded and advertised products carry on continuous programs of research and product improvement. That's why winning your favor is the full time job of thousands of scientists and testing engineers, and the sole purpose of laboratories and experimental plants in every division of industry where trade-marking is practiced.

Yes, in the factories of the brand-makers, yours is the final word. Your free choice of branded products makes you the boss *of the greatest manufacturing system in the world.*

Brand Names Foundation
INCORPORATED

A NON-PROFIT EDUCATIONAL FOUNDATION · 37 WEST 57TH STREET, NEW YORK 19, N. Y.

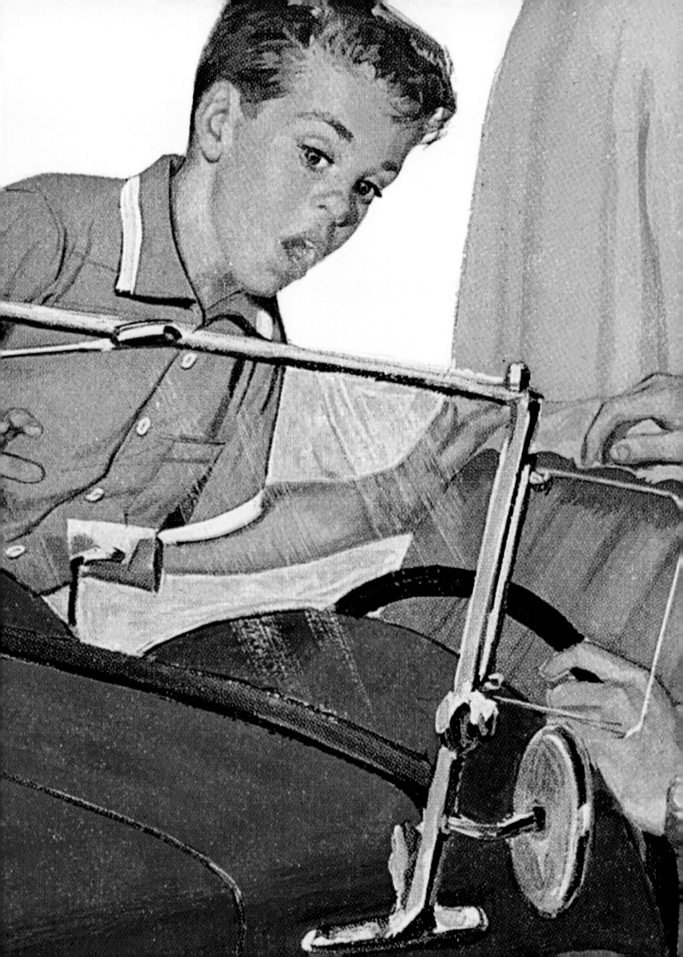

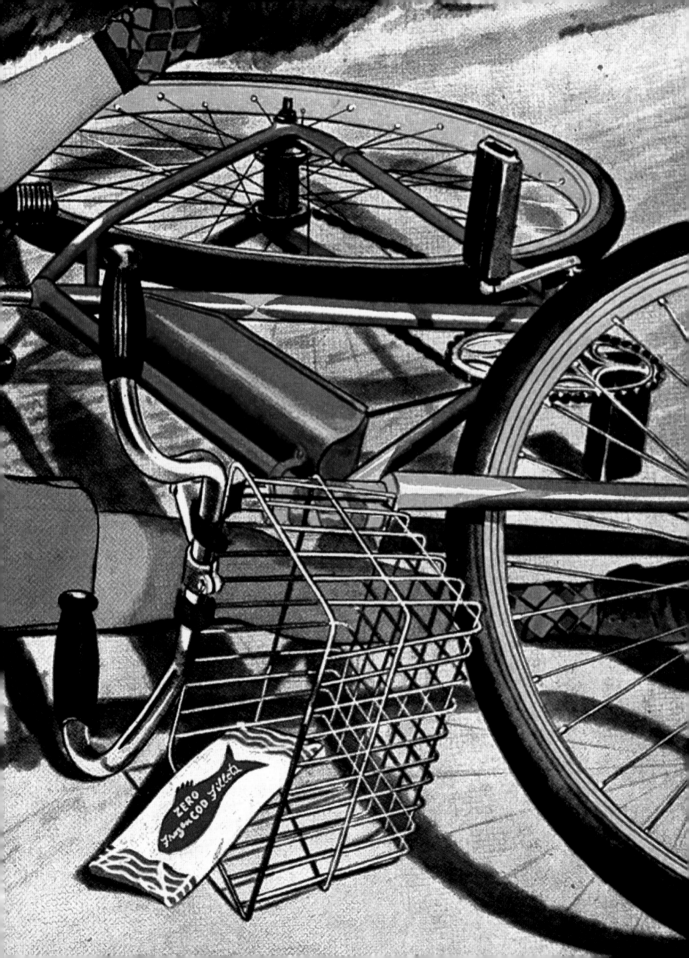

ZERO Fresh COD fillets

Acknowledgements

Produced in record speed, this volume of historical material would never have been completed without the help of Cindy Vance of Modern Art & Design, who went above and beyond the call of duty by putting an inordinate amount of hours and dedication into the project. In addition to preparing the document for printing, she infused the book with her own insight and design, as well as materials from her and her husband Steve's collections.

Also instrumental in providing the raw material for this book are the various hunters and gathers of printed ephemera. Gary Fredericks, on top of being a terrific guy, has generously provided me with visual material for this and many of my projects over the years, and it would have been tough to complete this book in a timely manner without his unselfish help. The depth of this project would never have been achieved without the assistance of Ralph Bowman, who also deserves a big handshake for letting me traverse the canyons of his warehouse, as well as Jeff and Pat Carr, who likewise have been overly generous with their help. Thanks also to Jerry Aboud, who provided the book with some key visuals, and to the countless others who had the foresight to save paper material which has served as the basis for this retelling of history.

Thanks once again to the folks at Artworks—Blue, Liz and Adrian—for countless hours of scanning and photographing, and to Jan Strnad for his swift editing skills. And finally, thanks to Benedikt and Angelika Taschen for their insight, support, and friendship. "Trust Makes the Difference."

Jim Heimann

Imprint

© 2001 TASCHEN GmbH
Hohenzollernring 53, D–50672 Köln
www.taschen.com

Art Direction & Design: Jim Heimann, L.A.
Digital Composition & Design: Cindy Vance, Think Modern Design, L.A.
Cover Design: Sense/Net, Andy Disl, Cologne
Production: Tina Ciborowius, Cologne
German translation: Stefan Barmann, Cologne
French translation: Simone Manceau, Paris

Printed in Germany
ISBN 3–8228–1158–0

Cover: *Arrow Shirts, 1950*
Endpapers: *Van Heusen Shirts, 1950*
page 2-3: *Lucky Strike Cigarettes, 1950*
page 4-5: *Grumann Aircraft Engineering Co., 1954*
page 6-7: *Oldsmobile, 1957*
page 8-9: *Wollensak Electric Eye-Matic, 195?*
page 10-11: *The Thing From Another World*
page 12-13: *Riegel Fabric, 1955*
page 14-15: *DuPont Cellophane, 195?*
page 16-17: *Hewitt Robins, 195?*
page 18-19: *Koroseal, 1953*
page 20-21: *SAS Scandinavian Airlines, 1958*

50's

All-American Ads

Edited by Jim Heimann
with an introduction by Jim Heimann

TASCHEN

KÖLN LONDON MADRID NEW YORK PARIS TOKYO

Entertainment
500

Fashion & Beauty
538

Food & Beverage
616

Industry
684

Interiors
772

Travel
834

RICAN

The 1950s

From Poodles To Presley, Americans Enter The Atomic Age

by Jim Heimann

The atomic bomb changed everything. By 1950, Americans were slowly accepting the fact that something fundamentally different was going on in society. Despite the victories of World War II and a post-war prosperity that brought a rush of unheralded consumerism, atomic power had many Americans wondering what the future held. At the end of the summer in the year 1949, the explosion of a Russian atomic bomb confirmed that the United States was no longer the sole possessor of the mightiest nuclear device in the world and Americans responded in different ways. Some bought Geiger counters to mine for uranium. Others started digging bomb shelters in their backyards to protect them from a nuclear blast. But regardless of their action, for most Americans the advent of the bomb signaled an end to an age of innocence and a time to buy, buy, buy.

The early 1950s witnessed the continued paranoia that accompanied the possession of nuclear warheads. The U.S. government, in an attempt to keep one step ahead of the Russians, initiated an arms race. If the Reds had an atomic bomb, America needed a more powerful one. The resulting H-bomb put the U. S. that one strategic step ahead. This rush to create the world's top nuclear power ushered in the atomic age which was quickly joined by other sobriquets for new technological developments. Soon advertising copy was peppered with references to the jet age and the space age. A new category of advertising emerged addressing the Cold War. The tanks and jeeps of World War II were replaced by nuclear subs and guided missiles. It was in this atmosphere that Madison Avenue, in attempting to put a positive spin on the atom and doomsday predictions, embraced nuclear power and applied it to advertising. The "peaceful atom" was now working for Americans. In one amazing ad, a mushroom cloud is accompanied by copy which claims that "Even this cloud has a silver lining." Advertisers appropriated space helmets and rockets to sell cereal. Car designers came up with exaggerated tail fins for automobiles to express this new accelerated speed. And the American public ate it up.

Unlike previous decades in which the Depression and World War II condoned frugality and rationing, American consumers of the 1950s were experiencing an unprecedented phenomenon. A generation born before and during the Depression were of an age where their earning power created a pocket of wealth. This, combined with a declining number of individuals to share it and the resumption of American industry's aggressive consumer economy after World War II, set the stage for a buying binge that Americans would indulge in for the foreseeable future. With a productivity rate of two percent per year between 1945 and 1955 Americans were buying 75 % of the cars and appliances on the earth. Despite the shadow of atomic obliteration hanging over the American consciousness, advertisers continued to barrage the public, a new "mass market," with products that were newer, better and faster. And Americans felt entitled to it. Striving to lead normal productive lives after saving the world from Axis aggression, the American public looked beyond their pre-World War II days and gazed to the future – and the future looked great. At least as seen through the eyes of television, magazines and advertising.

Bolstered by the media, consumers obliged this onslaught of advertising by buying the endless array of products. Home

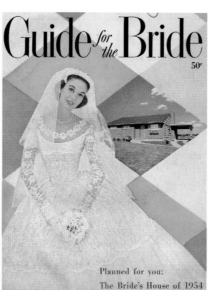

Striving to lead normal productive lives after saving the world from Axis aggression the American public looked beyond their pre-World War II days and gazed to the future. And the future looked great.

ownership, which most Americans considered their birthright, along with disposable income were the foundation for much of this consumption in the 1950s. Prompted by post-war housing shortages, the drift away from the city and into the suburbs was well on its way by the beginning of the decade with 23.6 million Americans owning their own homes. By 1960, there were 32.8 million homeowners. This suburban trend was firmly established with the construction of sprawling suburbs such as Levittown, New York, a former potato field that was developed into a mass of 17,447 houses in 1951. With all of these detached, single family dwellings came the need to furnish and maintain them. Within ten years the sale of lawn and porch furniture sales jumped from 53.6 million dollars to 145.2 million dollars, while automatic washer sales almost doubled from 1.7 million to 2.6 million.

After home ownership, the automobile was next in line for Americans unabated consumption. The introduction of the 1955 models in the fall of 1954 set off a buying frenzy. Redesigned to reflect the era's preoccupation with speed, the new line of cars had sleek styling and lots of chrome. Chevro-

lets in particular received much of the attention with their range of colors and dynamic new look. The hint of luxury was implied in marketing the cars and buyers were promised a bit of the future as well. An ad for the Ford Lincoln asked buyers "Why be tied down to yesterday?" while copy for the Buick Roadmaster suggested that everywhere you went a red carpet would be rolled out upon your arrival. The status associated with automobiles was unavoidable. Cars reflected an economic standard and a place in society for their owners. They also could be seen as reflections of their driver's personality.

As the decade progressed, the extremes of car design were taken to their limits. Fins got larger, chrome embellished almost every surface and the size of the cars expanded to near-impossible lengths. The advertising which accompanied these behemoths bordered on pretension. The doomed Ford Edsel claimed "They'll know you've arrived when you drive up in an Edsel." The Buick Limited was "The car conceived and created to change your ideas of luxury motoring." The ad copy for the Pontiac declared "A bold new car for a bold new generation." The trend in massive cars would last into the

early 1960s when smaller compact imports including the Volkswagen, an odd little German car which appeared at the end of the decade, would profoundly change the future of American car buying. Until then, America basked in an era unmatched in automobile production.

Serious consumption was joined by whimsical buying in a move that seemed to counter the harsh realities of nuclear annihilation. Americans wholeheartedly embraced a whole range of fads in the 1950s buying unnecessary objects out of sheer compulsion. Coonskin caps, chlorophyll-infused products, Capri pants, bongos, shrunken heads, hula hoops, flying saucers, Tupperware, and purple people eaters were bought with abandon. For one short period in the mid 1950s anything that was pink was in. Pink refrigerators, pink stoves, pink lipstick, pink dress shirts and pink typewriters. Ads for GE's pink light bulbs boasted that they would flatter complexions and furnishings. Copy for Royal portable typewriters gushed that finally you had choice in the color of your typewriter. The Russian threat would just have to wait until Americans could stock up on pink toilet paper.

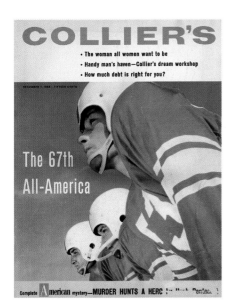

In the 1950s, the public was badgered to consume, and no one wanted to be old fashioned. Replacing the old with the new was considered a good thing. Advertisements reinforced the idea that to be modern was to be hip. In design and architecture, modern usually meant European Modernism. But modern also came to mean that objects were manufactured, not hand made, and most had a planned obsolescence built in. The American public trusted that industry had their best interests in mind and that they were being led to a better future by accepting everything modern. As long as things looked newer, exciting and better, consumption rolled swiftly along.

Television, the new media giant that was a plaything in the 1930s and introduced to the public in the 1940s, had become in the '50s an all-consuming monolith absorbing the attention of every man, woman and child across the country. In just five years, the sale of TV sets climbed from 3.1 million in 1950 to more than 32 million by mid-decade. Game shows, cartoons, variety shows, Westerns, cop shows and an endless variety of sit-at-home entertainment entranced American viewers night after night. Technological

advances rapidly increased the size of TV sets and advertisers prompted consumers to go for the 21-inch set that was the price of the 17-inch set. Ads for Crosley televisions emphasized family viewing with "full room vision." Within a few years, this trend was reversed and sets were being downsized for portability. "The personal TV for take it with you use" was how GE advertised the new portable. By 1959, Americans were staring at the "boob tube" for an average of six hours a day, seven days a week. Its across-the-board appeal would directly compete with and disable the motion picture industry. Eventually it also would erode the world of print, signaling the slow decline of American magazine advertising.

Music in the early 1950's was affected by the changing tastes of the post-war period. The slow elimination of the Big Band sound which had dominated the music world for almost two decades was replaced in the charts by a range of tunes that were a mixture of sweet vocals, ballads, a bit of hillbilly/country and mood music. Liberace, dressed in a tuxedo while playing at his candlelit grand piano, exemplified this musical malaise. Making up to a million dollars a

year, he catered to these sappy tastes. Just as popular was Mitch Miller, and his *Sing Along with Mitch* albums which sold 1.75 million records in fifteen months. With the jukebox fading and replaced by the potent combination of TV, the portable record player and the compact 45-rpm record, the music scene was ripe for a change. By far the defining moment in this musical hodgepodge was the eruption of rock and roll in the mid 1950s. Led by black artists who defined the roots of rock, it was Elvis Presley who captured the attention of the huge teenage population and changed the direction of American music for generations to come. His first three singles sold over a million copies and he had amassed 120 million in record and merchandising sales by 1960. Elvis as a phenomenon was quickly followed by other teenage idols. Their popularity was boosted by TV programs such as Dick Clark's American Bandstand, the top rated teenage program that could make or break a rising star. The world of rock and roll was largely ignored by print advertisers in mass market magazines. Radio was the primary advertising conduit, though a growing number of teen and fan magazines began to fill the void.

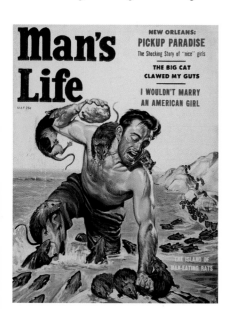

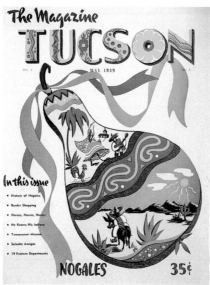

As an antidote to the conformity portrayed on television and the reality of the blandness of suburban living, some Americans would actively challenge the norm by nonconformist behavior. In a prelude to the turbulent sixties individuals such as author Jack Kerouac would personify the anti-social behavior that became the backbone of Beat culture, providing the straight world with the Beat Generation. James Dean became the cinema version of the lonely, alienated and misunderstood youth. Juvenile delinquents were the polar opposite of the squeaky-clean football players and cheerleaders America liked to think were the backbone of the country. Teenagers meanwhile reveled in the symbolic trappings of rebellion in an affront to their parents middle class values. Hot rods and customized cars represented the free expression of car design disengaged from Detroit's assembly line product. Jazz, which had simmered and evolved into an abstract and free form expression, perfectly matched the mood of this underground swell of new hipsters and was an alternative to the cloying pop music of the masses. These undercurrents of social change paralleled the optimistic picture painted in the advertisements of magazines and the mainstream press and anticipated the social upheaval the next decade would bring.

The '50s could be distilled into a world of pink and charcoal gray. The blandness of the man in the gray flannel suit versus the pink pouting lips of sex goddess Marilyn Monroe. The black and white McCarthy hearings and pink poodles advertising liquor. The dull conformity of the suburbs versus the wild bongo rhythms of the beatniks. The unabashed consumerism of the 1950s expressed in the advertisements of the decade reflected the extremes of a modern affluent generation and would lead Americans into the turbulent 1960s rejecting and reflecting on the tidal wave of 1950s consumerism.

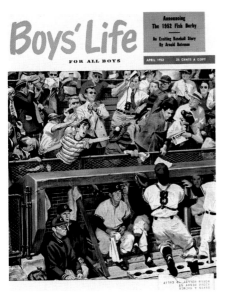

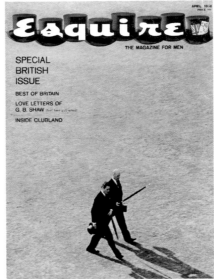

Cool cookery for summer • Family fun at Western beaches

Die Fünfziger

Mit pinkfarbenen Pudeln und Presley ins Atomzeitalter

Von Jim Heimann

Mit der Atombombe wandelte sich alles. Um 1950 akzeptierten die Amerikaner allmählich, dass sich in der Gesellschaft etwas fundamental veränderte. Ungeachtet der Siege im Zweiten Weltkrieg und einer Nachkriegsprosperität, die einen ungeahnten Konsumrausch mit sich brachte, fragten sich viele, was die Zukunft bereithalte. Durch die Explosion einer russischen Atombombe im Spätsommer 1949 bestätigte sich, dass die Vereinigten Staaten nicht länger im Alleinbesitz des stärksten Sprengkörpers der Welt waren. Und auf diese Erkenntnis reagierten die Amerikaner auf unterschiedliche Weise. Manche kauften Geigerzähler, um nach Uranvorkommen zu suchen. Andere schachteten bei sich zu Hause Luftschutzbunker aus, um sich vor einem nuklearen Sprengsatz zu schützen. Doch was auch immer sie taten: Für die meisten Amerikaner signalisierte die Bombe das Ende eines Zeitalters der Unschuld und einer Epoche des Kaufens, Kaufens, Kaufens.

Die frühen Fünfziger erlebten die fortwährende Paranoia, die mit dem Besitz nuklearer Sprengköpfe einherging. In dem Bestreben, den Russen einen Schritt voraus zu bleiben, setzte die US-Regierung ein Wettrüsten in Gang. Wenn die Roten eine Atombombe hatten, so benötigte Amerika eine stärkere. Die daraufhin entwickelte Wasserstoffbombe brachte den USA einen Vorsprung um diesen einen strategischen Schritt. Der Kampf um die nukleare Vormachtstellung mündete in das so genannte Atomzeitalter, das bald im Zuge anderer technischer Neuentwicklungen um weitere Etikettierungen ergänzt wurde. So waren die Werbebotschaften rasch mit Anspielungen auf das Düsenzeitalter und das Weltraumzeitalter gespickt. Eine neue Kategorie von Werbung entstand, die auf den Kalten Krieg abhob. An die Stelle der Panzer und Jeeps aus dem Zweiten Weltkrieg traten Atom-U-Boote und ferngesteuerte Raketen. In diesem Klima versuchte man in der Madison Avenue, nuklearer Bedrohung und Weltuntergangsverheißungen eine positive Wendung zu geben, indem man sich die Atomenergie werbewirksam zu Eigen machte. Jetzt arbeitete das »friedliche Atom« für die Amerikaner. In einer erstaunlichen Werbung ziert einen Atompilz der Spruch: »Auch diese Wolke ist ein Silberstreif am Horizont«. Die Werbeleute bemühten Raumhelme und Raketen, um Frühstücksflocken zu verkau-

fen. Autodesigner warteten mit übertriebenen Heckflossen auf, um der neuen beschleunigten Geschwindigkeit Ausdruck zu verleihen. Und die amerikanische Öffentlichkeit biss an.

Anders als in früheren Jahrzehnten, in denen aufgrund der Depression oder des Zweiten Weltkriegs Sparsamkeit und Rationierung auf der Tagesordnung standen, erlebten die amerikanischen Verbraucher in den Fünfzigern ein beispielloses Phänomen. Eine Generation, die vor und während der Depression zur Welt gekommen war, war nun in einem Alter, in dem ihre Kaufkraft ein Vermögen ausmachte. In Kombination mit der abnehmenden Zahl derjenigen, die es sich teilen mussten, und der nach dem Zweiten Weltkrieg wieder einsetzenden aggressiven Konsumgüterproduktion der amerikanischen Industrie bereitete dies den Boden dafür, dass die Amerikaner auf absehbare Zeit dem Kaufrausch frönten. Mit einer jährlichen Produktivitätssteigerung von zwei Prozent zwischen 1945 und 1955 kauften die Amerikaner 75 % der Autos und Geräte auf der ganzen Welt. Ungeachtet des Schattens atomarer Auslöschung, der auf dem amerikanische Bewußtsein lastete, bombardierten

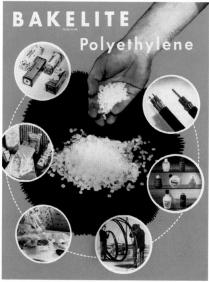

Die USA hatten die Welt aus dem Würgegriff der Achsenmächte befreit. Im Bemühen, ein normales Leben zu führen, blickte die amerikanische Bevölkerung nun über ihre Vorkriegstage hinaus und schaute in die Zukunft. Und die sah großartig aus.

die Werber das Publikum – einen neuen »Massenmarkt« – mit Produkten, die neuer, besser und schneller waren. Und die Amerikaner hatten nach ihrem Empfinden einen Anspruch darauf. Die USA hatten die Welt aus dem Würgegriff der Achsenmächte befreit. Im Bemühen, ein normales Leben zu führen, blickte die amerikanische Bevölkerung nun über ihre Vorkriegstage hinaus und schaute in die Zukunft. Und die sah großartig aus. Zumindest mit Blick auf das Fernsehen, auf Magazine und die Werbung.

Von den Medien ermuntert, honorierten die Verbraucher den Werbefeldzug und kauften eine nimmer endende Reihe von Produkten. Die Konsumwelle in den Fünfzigern gründete im Immobilienbesitz, den die meisten Amerikaner für ihr angeborenes Recht hielten, sowie im Anstieg des verfügbaren Einkommens. Die von der Nachkriegswohnungsnot verursachte Abwanderung aus den Innenstädten in die Vorstädte war zu Beginn des Jahrzehnts in vollem Schwange: 23,6 Millionen Amerikaner nannten ein Haus ihr Eigen. Um 1960 gab es bereits 32,8 Millionen Hausbesitzer. Endgültig etablierte sich dieser Trend zum Suburbanen mit dem Bau ausufernder Vorstädte wie Levittown, New

York, ein ehemaliger Kartoffelacker, auf dem 1951 die Unmenge von 17.447 neu gebauten Häusern stand. Diese ganzen freistehenden Einfamilienheime wollten möbliert und erhalten werden. Binnen zehn Jahren stieg der Verkauf von Garten- und Terrassenmöbeln von 53,6 auf 145,2 Millionen Dollar an, während der Absatz von Waschmaschinen von 1,7 auf 2,6 Millionen Stück hochschnellte.

Nach dem Eigenheim kam im ungebremsten Konsum das Auto dran. Die Einführung der 1955er Modelle im Herbst 1954 löste ein Kauffieber aus. Im Design sollte sich jetzt die zeitgemäße Idee von Geschwindigkeit spiegeln, so dass die neue Autolinie in schnittigem Styling und mit jeder Menge Chrom daherkam. Viel Aufsehen erweckten vor allem die Chevrolets mit ihrer Farbskala und neuen dynamischen Erscheinung. Die Autowerbung winkte mit Luxus und versprach den Käufern ein Stück Zukunft. Eine Reklame für den Ford Lincoln stellte den Käufern die Frage »Warum an Gestern gefesselt bleiben?«, während die für den Buick Roadmaster suggerierte, wo immer man hinfahre, werde einem bei der Ankunft ein roter Teppich ausgerollt. An das Auto knüpfte sich unumgänglich der soziale Status. Zugleich

ließ es sich als Ausdruck der Persönlichkeit seines Fahrers betrachten.

Mit Voranschreiten des Jahrzehnts drang das Autodesign an die extremsten Grenzen vor. Die Flossen wurden immer voluminöser, jede nur denkbare Fläche zierte Chrom, und die Länge der Karosserien dehnte sich ins nahezu Unmögliche. Die Werbungen für derlei Ungetüme strahlten ebenfalls etwas Vermessenes aus. Der inzwischen längst von der Bildfläche verschwundene Ford Edsel versprach: »Sie werden wissen, dass du angekommen bist, wenn du in einem Edsel vorfährst« und der Slogan für Pontiac lautete: »Ein kühnes neues Auto für eine kühne neue Generation«. Der Trend zu massiven Limousinen sollte bis in die frühen Sechziger anhalten, als kleinere Importwagen auf dem Markt auftauchten und die Zukunft des Fahrzeugmarktes in Amerika in eine andere Richtung lenkten – darunter auch der sonderbare kleine Käfer aus Deutschland, der zum Ende des Jahrzehnts eingeführt wurde.

Angesichts der reellen Drohung nuklearer Vernichtung setzte man nicht mehr nur auf die sicheren Werte, sondern gab sich auch dem Lustkauf hin. Nach Herzenslust schwelgten die Amerikaner in den Fünfzi-

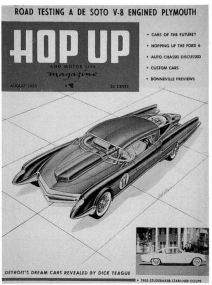

gern in einer ganzen Welt von Gimmicks und kauften schier zwanghaft überflüssiges Zeug. Waschbärkappen, Caprihosen, Bongos, Schrumpfköpfe, Hula-Hoop-Reifen, Fliegende Untertassen und Tupperware fanden reißenden Absatz. Für einen kurzen Zeitraum Mitte der fünfziger Jahre war alles in, was pink war: Kühlschränke, Elektroherde, Lippenstifte, Smokinghemden und Schreibmaschinen. Die Werbung für General Electric's pinkfarbene Glühbirnen behauptete vollmundig, deren Licht schmeichele dem Teint und der Wohnungseinrichtung. Der Text für Royal Reiseschreibmaschinen schwärmte davon, endlich könne man sich die Farbe seiner Schreibmaschine selber aussuchen. Die russische Bedrohung würde einfach warten müssen, bis die Amerikaner ihre Vorräte an pinkfarbenem Toilettenpapier aufgefüllt hätten.

Unter dem allgemeinen Trommeln zum Konsum wollte in den fünfziger Jahren keiner mehr altmodisch sein. Das Alte durch das Neue zu ersetzen, galt als eine gute Sache. Die Werbungen verstärkten die Vorstellung, modern sein bedeute hip sein. In Design und Architektur wurde unter »modern« für gewöhnlich der europäische Modernis-

mus verstanden. Doch jetzt bezeichnete »modern« auch Gegenstände, die fabrikmäßig hergestellt wurden. Die amerikanische Bevölkerung vertraute darauf, dass die Industrie ihr Bestes im Sinn habe und sie in eine bessere Zukunft führen würde, wenn sie nur alles Moderne annähme. Und solange die Dinge neuer und aufregender aussahen, wurde munter weiterkonsumiert.

Das Fernsehen, der neue Medienriese, der in den Dreißigern noch ein Spielzeug gewesen war und in den Vierzigern an die Öffentlichkeit gebracht wurde, war in den Fünfzigern zu einem Monolithen geworden, der die Aufmerksamkeit sämtlicher Männer, Frauen und Kinder im Lande okkupierte. In fünf Jahren kletterte der Verkauf von Fernsehgeräten von 3,1 Millionen auf über 32 Millionen im Jahr 1955. Spieleshows, Zeichentrickfilme, Sketchsendungen, Western, Polizeiserien und ein endloses Allerlei an Pantoffelunterhaltung berieselten Abend für Abend die amerikanische Zuschauerschaft. Technische Fortschritte ließen die Fernsehgeräte rasch größer werden, und die Werber bewogen die Verbraucher, sich zum Preis des 17-Zollers den 21-Zoll-Apparat zuzulegen. Die Werbung für Crosley Fernsehgeräte

betonte das Betrachten im Familienkreis bei »raumfüllender Sicht«. Binnen weniger Jahre kehrte sich dieser Trend um, und die Geräte wurden der Tragbarkeit halber verkleinert. »Dein persönliches TV zum Mitnehmen«, bewarb General Electric den neuen Tragbaren. Um 1959 starrten die Amerikaner durchschnittlich sechs Stunden pro Tag in die »Glotze«, und zwar an sieben Tagen die Woche. Der breitenwirksame Reiz des Fernsehens sollte unmittelbar mit der Filmindustrie konkurrieren und diese schließlich aus dem Rennen werfen. Das Fernsehen begann auch das Verlagswesen zu schwächen und den Niedergang der amerikanischen Magazinwerbung einzuläuten.

Auf die Musik der frühen fünfziger Jahre wirkten sich die gewandelten Geschmäcker der Nachkriegszeit aus. Der Big-Band-Sound, der in der Musik fast zwei Jahrzehnte lang den Ton angegeben hatte, verklang allmählich und wich in den Charts einem Strauß bunter Melodien, in dem sich süßlicher Gesang, Balladen, ein bisschen Hillbilly oder Country mit »Stimmungsmusik« mischte. Liberace, im Smoking am kerzenbeleuchteten Flügel spielend, verkörperte diese musikalische Malaise. Bei einem Jahresverdienst

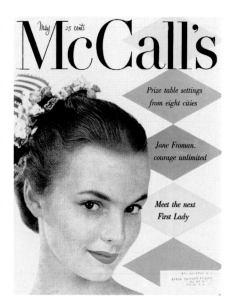

von bis zu einer Million Dollar bediente er schwelgerische Gemüter. Ebenso populär waren Mitch Miller und seine Alben *Sing Along with Mitch*, von denen in 15 Monaten 1,75 Millionen Aufnahmen verkauft wurden. Als die Jukebox gegenüber der wirkungsmächtigen Kombination von Fernseher, tragbarem Plattenspieler und 45er-Scheiben ins Hintertreffen geriet, war die Musikszene reif für eine Veränderung. Am folgenreichsten war natürlich der Ausbruch des Rock and Roll in den Mittfünfzigern. Im Gefolge schwarzer Künstler, die die Wurzeln des Rock gelegt hatten, war es Elvis Presley, der das breite Teenagervolk für sich gewann und der amerikanischen Musik auf Generationen hinaus eine neue Richtung wies. Von seinen ersten drei Singles wurden über eine Million Exemplare abgesetzt, und 1960 hatte er mit dem Verkauf von Schallplatten und Fanartikeln 120 Millionen Dollar eingefahren. Rasch folgten dem Phänomen Elvis weitere Teenageridole. Ihre Popularität wurde von Fernsehprogrammen wie Dick Clarks *American Bandstand* angekurbelt, dem meistgesehenen Teenagerprogramm, das ein aufgehendes Sternchen auch sogleich zum Verglühen bringen konnte. Die Welt des Rock and Roll

wurde von den Printwerbern weitgehend ignoriert. Wichtigster Werbekanal war das Radio, wiewohl eine wachsende Zahl von Teen- und Fanmagazinen die Lücke zu füllen begann.

Als Gegengift zur Konformität, die das Fernsehen zeichnete, und zur farblosen Realität des Vorstadtlebens machten sich einige Amerikaner daran, die Norm durch ungebührliches Betragen aktiv herauszufordern. In einem Vorspiel zu den turbulenten Sechzigern verkörperte ein Autor wie Jack Kerouac das antisoziale Verhalten, das zum Leitfaden der Beatkultur wurde. James Dean war die Kinoversion der einsamen, entfremdeten und unverstandenen Jugend. Jugendliche Straftäter bildeten das Gegenmodell zu den adretten Footballspielern und Cheerleadern, in denen Amerika gerne das Rückgrat der Nation sah. Unterdessen hoben die Teenager im Ansturm gegen die Werte ihrer Eltern die symbolischen Zeichen der Rebellion aufs Panier. Heiße Öfen und umfrisierte Autos standen für einen freien Ausdruck des Fahrzeugdesigns, das sich vom Fließbandprodukt aus Detroit emanzipierte. Der Jazz, der sich in einem gehörigen Gärprozess zur abstrakten, freien Ausdrucksform entwickelt

hatte, traf genau die Stimmung dieser neuen Hipster und bot eine Alternative zur abgedroschenen Popmusik der Massen. Solche zeitgleich zu dem optimistischen Mainstream vorhandenen Unterströmungen gesellschaftlicher Verhältnisse wiesen auf die sozialen Bewegungen und Unruhen voraus, die das nächste Jahrzehnt verhieß.

In einem Bild von der Lebenswelt der Fünfziger müssten Pink und Mausgrau in Kontrast gesetzt werden. Die Farblosigkeit des Herrn im grauen Flanellanzug gegen den rosaroten Schmollmund der Sexgöttin Marilyn Monroe. Die schwarzweißen McCarthy-Anhörungen gegen den pinkfarbenen Pudel, der für Likör wirbt. Die dumpfe Eintönigkeit der Vorstädte gegen die wilden Bongorhythmen der Beatniks. Der grenzenlose Konsumwahn, der sich in der Werbung dieses Jahrzehnts ausdrückt, spiegelt die Extreme einer modernen wohlhabenden Generation, die die Amerikaner in die turbulenten Sechziger führen sollte, in denen solch ungebremste Konsumbegeisterung zurückgewiesen und kritisch beleuchtet wurde.

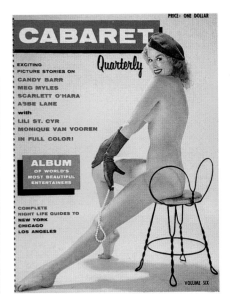

Les Années 50

Elvis et petits caniches roses : les Américains entrent dans l'ère atomique

de Jim Heimann

La bombe atomique a tout changé. Vers 1950, les Américains se font lentement à l'idée qu'un changement fondamental se produit dans leur société. Malgré les victoires de la Seconde Guerre mondiale et une prospérité qui entraîne le pays dans un consumérisme sans précédent, le danger atomique pousse nombre d'Américains à s'interroger sur l'avenir. A la fin de l'été 1949, l'explosion d'une bombe atomique russe confirme que les Etats-Unis ne sont plus l'unique détenteur du dispositif nucléaire le plus puissant du monde. Les habitants réagissent de différentes manières. Certains se munissent de compteurs Geiger pour faire de la prospection d'uranium. D'autres se mettent à creuser des abris anti-atomiques au fond de leur jardin. Mais indépendamment de ces actions, pour la plupart des Américains l'arrivée de la bombe annonce la fin de l'innocence et la venue d'une époque où chacun ne pense plus qu'à acheter, acheter, encore acheter.

Le début des années 50 témoigne de cette paranoïa qui monte avec la propagation des ogives nucléaires. Afin de garder l'avantage sur les Russes, le gouvernement américain se lance dans la course aux armements. Si les Rouges possèdent une bombe atomique, l'Amérique doit en avoir une encore plus puissante. Le résultat, c'est la bombe H et une avance stratégique pour les USA. Cette obsession à devenir la première puissance nucléaire donne naissance au terme d'ère atomique, ainsi qu'à d'autres sobriquets accompagnant les avancées technologiques successives. Très vite, les affiches publicitaires s'émaillent de références à l'ère des supersoniques, à celle de l'espace. D'autres s'inspirent de la guerre froide. Les tanks et les Jeeps de la dernière guerre sont remplacés par des sous-marins nucléaires et des missiles téléguidés. C'est dans cette atmosphère que Madison Avenue, pour tenter d'insuffler un tour positif aux prédictions catastrophiques concernant l'atome, s'empare de l'énergie nucléaire et la lance dans la publicité. « L'atome de la paix » travaille dorénavant pour les Américains. Sur une réclame étonnante, un champignon nucléaire est accompagné d'une légende affirmant que « même ce nuage possède un manteau d'argent ». Les annonceurs s'approprient casques d'astronautes et fusées spatiales pour vendre des céréales. Les fabricants de voitures les dotent d'ailerons fuselés qui s'inspirent de cette vitesse fantastique. Le public américain est aux anges.

Contrairement aux décennies précédentes, où la Crise de 29 puis la Seconde Guerre mondiale avaient imposé frugalité et rationnement, les consommateurs des années 50 vivent un phénomène sans précédent. Une génération née avant et pendant la Crise a atteint l'âge où son pouvoir d'achat la place en position de richesse. Ce phénomène, le fait qu'un nombre moindre d'individus y participe, et l'extraordinaire reprise économique de l'industrie américaine après la guerre, incitent les Américains à dépenser sans compter. Avec un taux de productivité de deux pour cent par an, entre 1945 et 1955, ils achètent 75% des voitures et des appareils fabriqués sur la terre. Ignorant l'inquiétude nucléaire qui plane, les annonceurs continuent d'inonder le public, nouveau « marché de grande distribution », de produits toujours plus nouveaux, plus pratiques et plus rapides. Et les Américains pensent qu'ils l'ont bien mérité. Les Etats-Unis avaient sauvé le monde du déluge de feu et de cendres. S'efforçant de reprendre une vie normale, la population américaine voulait oublier la guerre et regardait à pré-

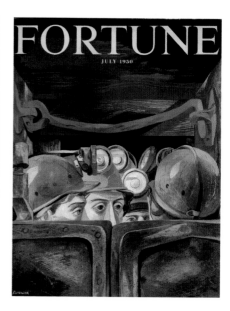

Les Etats-Unis avaient sauvé le monde du déluge de feu et de cendres. S'efforçant de reprendre une vie normale, la population américaine voulait oublier la guerre et regardait à présent vers l'avenir. Un avenir qui s'annonçait formidable.

sent vers l'avenir. Un avenir qui s'annonçait formidable.

Du moins vu à travers le regard de la télévision, des magazines et de la publicité. Encouragés par les médias, les consommateurs obéissent à ces attaques publicitaires et achètent tout ce qui leur est incessamment proposé. Devenir propriétaire, ce que la plupart des Américains considèrent comme un droit, et jouir de revenus disponibles, tels sont les principaux axes de la consommation des années 50. Conséquence du manque de logements après la guerre, s'éloigner de la ville en direction de la banlieue s'inscrit alors comme réalité sociale et 23,6 millions d'Américains deviennent propriétaires de leur domicile. En 1960, ils sont 32,8 millions. Cette migration entraîne la construction de banlieues interminables telles que Levittown, New York, ancien champ de pommes de terre, qui en 1951, se couvre de 17 447 maisons. Tous ces pavillons individuels, il faut les meubler et les maintenir en bon état. Dans les dix ans qui suivent, la vente de meubles de jardin et de véranda passe de 53,6 à 145,2 millions de dollars. Celle des machines à laver automatiques double presque, passant de 1,7 à 2,6 millions.

Après l'acquisition du logement, l'automobile occupe la deuxième place dans cette consommation constante des Américains. La mise en vente des modèles 1955, à l'automne 1954, provoque une véritable frénésie. Redessinées pour refléter le désir de vitesse de l'époque, ces voitures arborent des lignes fuselées et se parent de chromes. Les Chevrolet suscitent un intérêt particulier par leur gamme de couleurs et leur allure dynamique. Pour la commercialisation, on parle aux acheteurs de luxe et d'avenir. Une publicité pour la Ford Lincoln leur pose la question : « Pourquoi rester attaché au passé ? », tandis que celle de la Buick Roadmaster vous assure que, où que vous alliez, on déroulera le tapis rouge, rien que pour vous. Impossible d'éviter la relation entre automobile et statut social. La voiture reflète le niveau économique et financier de son propriétaire. Elle est sans doute aussi l'écho de sa personnalité.

A mesure que la décennie avance, toutes les possibilités du design sont explorées. Les ailerons se gonflent, le chrome vient souligner presque chaque surface et la taille des voitures atteint des longueurs à la limite du possible. La publicité qui accompagne

ces mastodontes n'est pas sans prétention. La malheureuse Ford Edsel proclame : « Ils sauront que c'est vous, quand vous arriverez dans votre Edsel ». La Buick Limited s'affirme « la voiture conçue et créée pour changer vos idées en matière de luxe ». La Pontiac enfin se déclare « une voiture intrépide pour une génération qui l'est tout autant ». Ce goût pour la voiture massive va se perpétuer jusqu'au début des années soixante, où l'importation de modèles compacts comme la Volkswagen, petite allemande apparue à la fin de la décennie, viendra profondément changer les perspectives des acheteurs américains. Jusque-là, en ce qui concerne la production automobile, l'Amérique profite d'un succès inégalé.

Cette consommation sérieuse s'accompagne d'un goût pour les achats de fantaisie, sans doute en réponse à l'angoisse d'une catastrophe nucléaire. Dans les années 50, les Américains s'adonnent à toute une série d'engouements qui les poussent irrépressiblement à acheter des choses parfaitement inutiles. Ils dépensent sans compter pour des casquettes en peau de raton-laveur, des produits à la chlorophylle, des pantalons Toréadors, des bon-

gos, des têtes Jivaros, des hula-hoops, des soucoupes volantes, des Tupperware, et autres mangeurs de têtes. Vers 1955, pendant une courte période, tout ce qui est rose est à la mode. Réfrigérateurs roses, fourneaux roses, rouges à lèvres roses, chemises roses et machines à écrire roses. Des publicités soutiennent que les ampoules roses de la General Electric mettent en valeur le teint et l'ameublement. Celles pour les machines à écrire portatives Royal stipulent que le choix de la couleur vous revient. La menace russe devra attendre que les Américains aient le temps de stocker leur papier toilette rose.

Dans ces années ivres de consommation, personne n'oserait se laisser dépasser par la mode. Il faut à tout prix remplacer le vieux par le neuf. La publicité renforce l'idée qu'être moderne, c'est être à la page. En matière de design et d'architecture, il n'est de Modernisme qu'européen. Mais ne sont modernes que les objets manufacturés, et non fabriqués à la main, dont la plupart sont conçus avec une obsolescence calculée. Le public américain est persuadé que la production industrielle est animée des meilleures intentions, comme de leur ouvrir

la voie vers un monde meilleur, à condition d'accepter tout ce qui est moderne. Aussi longtemps que les choses semblent nouvelles, étonnantes et meilleures, la consommation a le vent en poupe.

La télévision, media gigantesque, gadget des années 30 introduit au public dans les années 40, devient au cours des années cinquante un monolithe qui absorbe l'attention de tous, hommes, femmes et enfants, d'un bout à l'autre du pays. En cinq ans, la vente des postes passe de 3,1 millions en 1950 à plus de 32 millions vers 1955. Jeux télévisés, dessins animés, variétés, westerns, films policiers, toute une gamme de divertissements à consommer chez soi captive chaque soir l'attention d'innombrables spectateurs. Très vite, le progrès technologique agrandit la taille des écrans et les annonceurs incitent les consommateurs à acquérir un 55 cm pour le prix d'un 44 cm. Pour les télévisions Crosley, la publicité insiste sur la vie de famille avec « un écran visible de toute la pièce ». Quelques années plus tard, cette tendance s'inverse au profit de la TV petit format, donc transportable. « Une TV personnelle, pour votre seul usage », propose la General Electric. Vers

1959, les Américains regardent « la télé » en moyenne six heures par jour, sept jours par semaine. Cette attirance sans limite est une concurrence directe pour l'industrie cinématographique qu'elle met en difficulté. De plus, elle représente un danger pour la presse écrite, et l'on note un certain déclin de la publicité dans les magazines.

La musique aussi, au début des années 50, connaît une évolution dans les goûts. Les grands orchestres qui avaient régné sur le monde de la musique pendant presque deux décennies sont lentement éliminés par toutes sortes de compositions mêlant douces mélodies, ballades, hillbilly/country et « musique d'ambiance ». Liberace, en smoking, jouant sur son piano à queue éclairé d'une bougie, illustre bien ce malaise musical. Gagnant jusqu'à un million de dollars par an, il satisfait ce goût de niaiseries. Mitch Miller est tout aussi populaire et ses albums Sing Along with Mitch (Chantez avec Mitch) se vendent à 1,75 millions d'exemplaires en quinze mois. Le juke-box perd du terrain. Il est remplacé par la combinaison TV, tourne-disque portatif et disque compact 45 tours. Ainsi paré, le monde de la musique est prêt au changement. A l'évi-

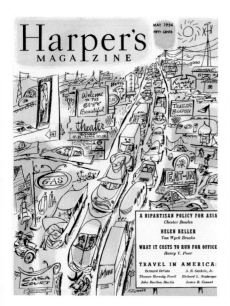

dence, dans tout ce fatras, le moment décisif est l'irruption du rock vers le milieu des années 50. Précédé par les artistes noirs qui en définissent les racines, c'est Elvis Presley qui séduit une énorme masse d'adolescents et donne une nouvelle orientation à la musique américaine pour des générations à venir. Ses trois premiers singles se vendent à plus d'un million d'exemplaires. En 1960, il a amassé 120 millions de dollars en vente de disques et de produits dérivés. Le phénomène qu'il représente est rapidement suivi par d'autres idoles des jeunes. Leur popularité est amplifiée par des programmes télévisés comme l'American Bandstand de Dick Clark, le programme pour jeunes le plus regardé, capable de fabriquer ou de briser une carrière. Dans la presse écrite grand public, le monde du rock est largement ignoré par les annonceurs. La radio est le principal canal publicitaire, même si un nombre croissant de magazines destinés aux jeunes et aux fans commence à occuper l'espace.

En guise d'antidote au conformisme tel qu'il apparaît à la télévision et à la réalité terne de la banlieue, certains Américains cherchent à défier la norme et adoptent un comportement anticonformiste. En prélude aux turbulentes années 60, des gens comme l'écrivain Jack Kerouac représentent déjà le comportement antisocial qui va s'inscrire au centre de la culture Beat, et choquer la petite bourgeoisie. James Dean incarne la version cinématographique de la jeunesse qui se sent isolée, aliénée et incomprise. Les délinquants sont à l'opposé des joueurs de foot et des cheerleaders propres sur eux que les Américains aiment à considérer comme les représentants typiques de leur pays. Pendant ce temps, les adolescents affichent avec délectation les signes extérieurs de la rébellion et s'opposent aux valeurs petites-bourgeoises de leurs parents. Les moteurs gonflés et les voitures personnalisées manifestent une grande liberté par rapport à ce qui se pratique à Detroit, sur les chaînes de montage. Le jazz, qui a longtemps couvé avant de se transformer en une expression libre et abstraite, rassemble parfaitement les tendances underground de ces nouveaux jeunes à la coule et propose une alternative à la fade musique pop des masses. Ces courants sous-jacents se développent parallèlement à l'image optimiste renvoyée par la publicité des magazines et de la presse grand public. Ils sont les signes avant-coureurs de la dégradation et du bouleversement social qui vont marquer la décennie suivante.

Les années 50s pourraient se distiller en un monde rose et gris charbon. L'inconsistance de l'homme en costume flanelle gris opposée aux lèvres sensuelles du sex-symbol Marilyn Monroe. Les auditions en noir et blanc des procès maccarthistes, face aux caniches roses vantant des boissons alcoolisées. Le triste conformisme des banlieues opposé aux rythmes endiablés du bongo sous les doigts des Beatniks. Le consumérisme sans vergogne des années 50 qui s'exprime dans la publicité reflète les extrêmes de cette génération de l'abondance qui, pendant les années 60, allaient amener les Américains à rejeter et à repenser cette marée de consumérisme qui avait submergé les années 50.

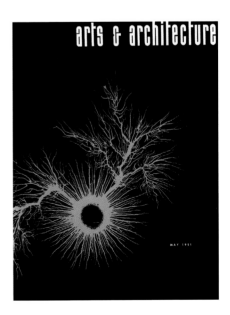

Refreshingly yours

from the land of sky blue waters!

Hamm's BEER

Isn't this a cool, refreshing idea? . . . a frosty-
cold glass of Hamm's beer, from the enchanted land of
sky blue waters! Hamm's crisp, clean-cut taste is
your kind of flavor . . . try it! Tonight!

Hamm's Beer, 1955

Traditionally the Finest

All along the New England shore,
you'll find a special kind of hospitality . . . a hospitality steeped in traditions
older than America itself, and further enriched by the bounties of the sea. Here, where good food
and beverages are a part of the art of living, MILLER HIGH LIFE . . . the *Champagne of Bottle Beer*
. . . is an accepted favorite. Golden and gleaming in its distinguished crystal-clear bottle,
MILLER HIGH LIFE is at home in New England homes . . . *and wherever quality gets the call.*

Proudly highlight your hospitality by serving MILLER HIGH LIFE . . .
the genuine Milwaukee beer that's brewed and bottled by the Miller Brewing Company ONLY
. . . and ONLY in Milwaukee, Wisconsin

Miller HIGH LIFE
The Champagne of Bottle Beer

Photography—Leslie Gill
Skirt and Blouse—Jeanne Campbell
Cook-N-Wagon—Tulsa, Oklahoma

Hamm's Beer, 1959 ◀◀ Goebel Beer, 1951 ◀ Miller Beer, 1953

WHAT'LL YOU HAVE?

Pabst Blue Ribbon

Between Rounds...

. . . treat your friends to a round of smooth, sociable, satisfying Pabst
Blue Ribbon. Each foam-capped glass opens up a whole new world
of beer enjoyment for you . . . gives you a refreshed feeling you've
never known before with any beer. Discover Pabst Blue Ribbon
soon! Find out what you've been missing!

Try this . . . for one week . . . make Pabst
Blue Ribbon your beer. When you find out
how much you've been missing—your one
week's trial of Pabst Blue Ribbon will
stretch into a lifetime of beer enjoyment.

DRINK PABST BLUE RIBBON . . . *taste that smoother, smoother flavor!*

FOLLOW PABST BLUE RIBBON BOXING BOUTS . . . EVERY WEDNESDAY NIGHT ON TELEVISION . . . CBS NETWORK, Copr. 1953, Pabst Brewing Company, Milwaukee, Wis. Trade Marks Reg. U. S. Pat. Off.

Pabst Blue Ribbon Beer, 1953

"*Blatz is Milwaukee's Finest Beer* ...

It's Milwaukee's <u>favorite</u> beer.
I'm from Milwaukee,
I ought to know!"

says *Liberace*

Famed Milwaukee-born piano virtuoso
Columbia recording artist

● "Milwaukee is my home town," says Liberace, shown here with his valuable collection of one-of-a-kind piano miniatures. "Many people I meet on tour are surprised to learn that Blatz, in Milwaukee, outsells every other brand by a wide margin!"

● "Blatz tastes so good it's Milwaukee's favorite beer. That's quite a testimonial coming from the people living right in the beer capital of America. Make your next glass of beer *Blatz*. You'll find it everywhere. It'll be *your* favorite, too."

Today, taste  **Milwaukee's <u>finest</u> beer!**

© 1952, Blatz Brewing Co., Est. 1851 in Milwaukee, Wis.

There's nothing like it
...absolutely nothing

Some sort of recreation belongs in every one of your busy days. But, just some sort of beer isn't enough to make the most of recreation. Budweiser and good living have been partners for nearly a century. The reason why? That distinctive taste that smacks of quality in every sip! Live life, every golden minute of it. Enjoy Budweiser, every golden drop of it.

ANHEUSER-BUSCH, INC.
ST. LOUIS

Budweiser
LAGER BEER

Budweiser Beer, 1950

Beer—the healthful refresher
brewed with the Goodness of Malt

The Malt in beer helps build and sustain high energy.

You'll find the goodness of Malt in many fine foods and beverages.

INVIGORATING! That's the word for wholesome, refreshing, beer or ale brewed with Barley Malt. For Malt puts more than Fun-Flavor in your favorite brew...gives you nature's own minerals, B-complex vitamins, protein, maltose and dextrins. Enjoy Malt in beer and in good food every day.

Barley and Malt INSTITUTE
228 NORTH LA SALLE, CHICAGO 1, ILLINOIS

Barley and Malt Industry, 1959

New—
Party Brew!

So smooth—so different!
Looks inviting...tastes exciting!

Goetz Country Club Malt Liquor

Mmm—just wait until you taste it! Smooth, sparkling Country Club Malt Liquor . . . far more refreshing than any brew you have ever tasted before.

It's so *different!* Ideal for "special" occasions. Wonderful way to add a new note of hospitality to *any* get-together!

Serve Country Club Malt Liquor, clear and cold, from its distinctive container . . . and watch this bright-spirited brew bring extra zest and enjoyment to your next party!

M. K. Goetz Brewing Company, Kansas City—St. Joseph, Missouri

SINCE 1859 . . . BREWERS OF MELLOW COUNTRY CLUB BEER

Country Club Malt Liquor, 1955

NATIONAL BREWING COMPANY • BALTIMORE, MD. • DETROIT, MICH. • ORLANDO, FLA.

Wet, cold and
delicious...

When you're thirsty, *really* thirsty . . . reach for a bottle of National Bohemian Beer. Here's a taste that's earning its way across the country. Today . . . there are three National Brewing Company plants, in Maryland, in Michigan, in Florida. Soon you'll be able to enjoy National Bohemian Beer, "wet, cold and delicious" . . . wherever you live.

'Oh boy, what a beer!"

Mr. Boh

NATIONAL BOHEMIAN *Light Beer*

National Bohemian Beer, 1957

▶ *Ballentine Beer, 1957*

"Amateur Magician," by John Gannam. Number 47 in the series "Home Life in America."

Beer belongs...enjoy it

In this home-loving land of ours ... in this America of kindliness, of friendship, of good-humored tolerance ... perhaps no beverages are more "at home" on more occasions than good American beer and ale.

For beer and ale are the kinds of beverages Americans like. They belong—to pleasant living, to good fellowship, to sensible moderation. And our right to enjoy them, this too belongs—to our own American heritage of personal freedom.

AMERICA'S BEVERAGE OF MODERATION
United States Brewers Foundation ... Chartered 1862

United States Brewers Foundation, 1950

Sketched by Bouché at the West Side Tennis Club

Court Favorite: Gin-and-Tonic with Schweppes

COMMANDER EDWARD WHITEHEAD —Schweppes' bearded ambassador to the United States—has just conducted an interesting experiment at Forest Hills. He tried to find somebody who had never tasted a gin-and-tonic made with Schweppes. He found one, too—a confirmed addict of elderberry wine. She wouldn't try a gin-and-tonic, even when the Commander

explained to her that it is *the coolest drink in the world.*

Why so cool? For two reasons. Gin-and-Tonic is served deliciously *iced* and, more important, Schweppes gives Gin-and-Tonic its cool *taste.* Thanks to Schweppes, a wonderfully fresh sensation strikes the palate and soothes the fevered brow.

You'll find Gin-and-Tonic so easy

to make. Just mix ice and gin with Schweppes in a highball glass. Stir affectionately—and there you are!

You don't have to dip into capital to be a Schweppesman nowadays, because Schweppes is being bottled in these United States. You can now get Schweppes in handy six-bottle cartons at your grocer's *for about the same price as domestic mixers!*

Schweppes, 1953

"Cooling Off In The Country," by Douglas Crockwell. Number 44 in the series "Home Life in America."

Beer belongs...enjoy it

In this home-loving land of ours ... in this America of kindliness, of friendship, of good-humored tolerance ... perhaps no beverages are more "at home" on more occasions than good American beer and ale.

For beer and ale are the kinds of beverages Americans like. They belong—to pleasant living, to good fellowship, to sensible moderation. And our right to enjoy them, this too belongs—to our own American heritage of personal freedom.

AMERICA'S BEVERAGE OF MODERATION
The United States Brewers Foundation ... Chartered 1862

At mealtime, too!

Barley & Malt Institute, 1959 ◀ *United States Brewers Foundation, 1950*

 "Home from Hunting," by Douglas Crockwell. Number 48 in the series "Home Life in America."

Beer belongs...enjoy it

In this home-loving land of ours ... in this America of kindliness, of friendship, of good-humored tolerance ... perhaps no beverages are more "at home" on more occasions than good American beer and ale.

For beer and ale are the kinds of beverages Americans like. They belong—to pleasant living, to good fellowship, to sensible moderation. And our right to enjoy them, this too belongs—to our own American heritage of personal freedom.

AMERICA'S BEVERAGE OF MODERATION
United States Brewers Foundation ... Chartered 1862

United States Brewers Foundation, 1950

WHAT

D'YA HEAR

•

IN THE BEST OF

CIRCLES?

"*Schaefer all around!*"

Good music. Good friends. Schaefer.

Here's a beer with cello-mellow flavor...

never sharp, never flat, a smooth **round** taste.

That's why folks call it — REAL BEER!

he F. & M. Schaefer Brewing Co., New York and Albany, N. Y.

Schaefer Beer

▶ *Owens-Illinois Glass Bottles, 1957*

"My beer is Rheingold —the Dry beer!"

says MADELYN DARROW
MISS RHEINGOLD 1958

MISS RHEINGOLD PHOTOGRAPHED WITH BMW ISETTA "300" BY PAUL HESSE · COSTUME BY BERNARD NEWMAN OF BERGDORF GOODMAN

Rheingold
EXTRA DRY
Lager Beer

It's beer as beer should taste!

Always refreshing – never filling

Seasons change, but never Rheingold Extra Dry. For Rheingold's *real-beer* taste never changes. Every glass of Rheingold is always the same. The same refreshing dryness, never sweet, never bitter, makes Rheingold New York's largest-selling beer—year after year.

Rheingold Beer, 1958

World's largest selling beer *Schlitz*

THE BEER THAT MADE
MILWAUKEE FAMOUS

So Light, So Refreshing

Once more, America has paid its highest tribute to the matchless
quality of Schlitz Beer. During the past year, Schlitz again led all
the nation's breweries in sales. Throughout the world, people
enjoyed more bottles and cans of Schlitz — *millions more* — than
any other beer, at *any* price.

© 1956 – Jos. Schlitz Brewing Company, Milwaukee, Wis., Brooklyn, N. Y., Los Angeles, Calif.

Schlitz Beer, 1956

Your thirst can "feel" the difference!

No harsh bitterness! Your taste can
actually "feel" the difference between
Schlitz and any other beer. A soothing,
cooling, refreshing difference you can
really feel as well as taste. What a wonderful feeling! No other beer refreshes
like Schlitz.

In the Schlitz original HALF-QUART can
(packed 24 to the case), also in the convenient
6-pak with the handy handle that makes it
so easy to carry.

If you like beer you'll love Schlitz

The Beer that Made Milwaukee Famous

© 1955 – Jos. Schlitz Brewing Company, Milwaukee, Wis., Brooklyn, N. Y., Los Angeles, Cal.

Schlitz Beer, 1953

"I'm glad they
still brew a beer
like this!"

BREWED IN THE GREAT TRADITION

Miller HIGH LIFE

ONLY IN MILWAUKEE

Miller Beer, 1957

53

Schlitz Beer, 1951

Schlitz Beer, 1952

Schlitz Beer, 1951

Schlitz Beer, 1950 ▶ *Schlitz Beer, 1951* ▶▶ *Budweiser Beer, 1956*

PRODUCED IN LIMITED QUANTITY

BY THE   MASTER VINTNERS OF ASTI CELLARS

ASTI

ASTI
CALIFORNIA
Riesling
SELECTED AND BOTTLED BY
ITALIAN SWISS COLONY
Asti Sonoma County
CALIFORNIA

FINE CALIFORNIA *Wines* FROM THE

VINEYARDS OF WORLD-FAMOUS WINE DISTRICTS

Asti Wine, 1952

▶ *Creme de Menthe, 1957*

Open Hearth Dining by—
Great Western

Sizzling kabobs . . . crackling logs on an open hearth . . . flickering firelight . . . needs but one thing more to make your next open hearth dining party one to remember . . . Great Western Wine. Burgundy, Sauternes, Rhine Wine or Chablis, depending on your preference, are all superb New York State Dinner Wines. Say Great Western— it should be on the tip of your tongue.

This fitting pouring stand, made especially for Great Western, is available. Name and address of distributor on request.

OTHER GREAT NEW YORK STATE WINES BY GREAT WESTERN . . .

PORT   AMERICAN SHERRY   TAWNY PORT   ROSÉ
TOKAY   CLARET   SWEET OR DRY VERMOUTH

By the Producers of Great Western . . . America's Largest Selling Champagne

Send to our Wine Counselor, Mrs. Charles D. Chamalin, for our special free booklet on wining and dining: "Open Hearth Dining."

Original Entrance to the Oldest and Largest Champagne Cellars in America in Continuous Use Since 1860

Great Western
WINES SINCE 1860

COPYRIGHT 1955 BY THE PLEASANT VALLEY WINE COMPANY, RHEIMS, HAMMONDSPORT, N. Y. DEPT. 13

Great Western Wine, 1955

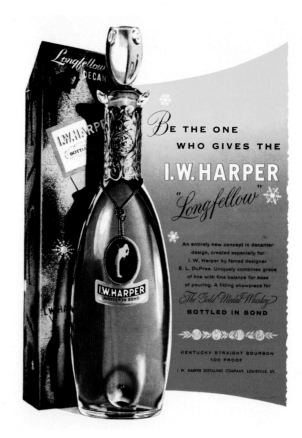

Be the one
WHO GIVES THE
I. W. HARPER
"Longfellow"

An entirely new concept in decanter design, created especially for I. W. Harper by famed designer E. L. DuPree. Uniquely combines grace of line with fine balance for ease of pouring. A fitting showpiece for

The Gold Medal Whiskey
BOTTLED IN BOND

KENTUCKY STRAIGHT BOURBON
100 PROOF
I. W. HARPER DISTILLING COMPANY, LOUISVILLE, KY.

I. W. Harper Bourbon, 1955

Transatlantic travelers come home with glowing reports of a marvelous new drink

IRISH COFFEE

Americans stopping at the famous Shannon Airport first discovered the unique delight of Irish Coffee. Now, more and more smart spots are serving this fabulous drink . . . more and more people are making it at home. In San Francisco, for example, Irish Coffee is becoming as popular as the Dry Martini.

The magic of Irish Coffee lies in the fact that the coffee, the John Jameson and cream combine in some mysterious way to create a seductive new flavour. It is what scientists call synergistic action, which means that the cooperative action of the ingredients is infinitely more delightful than any of them taken independently. Skeptical about that synergistic action? Well, try Irish Coffee. And do insist on John Jameson. It is *all* pot still whiskey—every drop matured 7 years in oak casks.

How to make IRISH COFFEE

Into a pre-warmed stemmed 7-ounce goblet or a coffee cup, put jigger of John Jameson Irish Whiskey and 1 to 2 teaspoons of sugar. Fill to within ½ inch of top with strong black coffee. Instant coffee may used if desired. Stir until sugar is dissolved. Top to brim with chilled whipped cream, so that cream floats on top. Do not stir after adding cream. The true delight of Irish Coffee is obtained by drinking the hot coffee and John Jameson through the cream. P. S. It is important to use all pot still Irish whiskey—and that means John Jameson.

JOHN JAMESON

BLENDED IRISH WHISKEY • 86 PROOF
Imported by
W. A. TAYLOR & COMPANY, NEW YORK, N. Y.
Sole Distributors for the U.S.A.

John Jameson Irish Whiskey, 1955

CUERVO TEQUILA MARTINISMANSHIP

LEMON AND SALT IN A MARTINI?—CARAMBA!

Look not askance . . . this is martini with Cuervo Tequila, so pleasurably dry it invites a break with tradition. Mix Cuervo with just the right dash of dry vermouth, stir over cubed ice and pour. But wait . . . the secret of your artistry is here revealed. Now quarter a slice of lemon and salt each section lightly. Place a quarter section in each cocktail before serving, as you would an olive. That's all, except of course, to experience a Cuervo martini—supremely smooth, uncommonly dry. *Magnifico!* No tequila-come-lately, Cuervo has its own tradition as *el licor mexicano más celebrado,* the choice of aficionados the world over. Try tequila martini soon. Say Cuervo (kwair-vo) . . . there is a difference. And don't forget the lemon-and-salt!

JOSE CUERVO TEQUILA

SOLE U.S. IMPORTERS   YOUNG'S MARKET COMPANY, LOS ANGELES, CALIFORNIA

86 PROOF

Jose Cuervo Tequila, 1959   ▶ *Courvoisier Cognac, 1952*

Moet Champagne, 1952

Pol Roger Champagne, 1957

Piper-Heidsieck Champagne, 1958 ◄   *Mumms Champagne, 1955*

Great Western Champagne, 1958   ► *Calvert Whiskey, 1950*

ENJOY THE
KING
OF BLENDS

ASK FOR
KING
IT'S REALLY LIGHT

MAKES YOUR DRINKS REALLY SMOOTH AND MIL

A FINER BLEND FROM OLD KENTUCKY

WED·IN·THE·WOOD is a time-honored Glenmore method. It means that after blending, instead of being bottled immediately, Old Thompson is put back into charred oaken barrels to assure uniform high quality. This method costs us more, but it's worth it because of the distinctive flavor it gives to Old Thompson.

GLENMORE'S

OLD THOMPSON BRAND ®

Blended Whiskey

86.8 PROOF · 4/5 QUART

GLENMORE DISTILLERIES COMPANY · OWENSBORO, KENTUCKY
BLENDED & BOTTLED BY · WED·IN·THE·WOOD · COMPANY

THE STRAIGHT WHISKIES IN THIS PRODUCT ARE FOUR YEARS OR MORE OLD, 35% STRAIGHT WHISKIES, 65% GRAIN NEUTRAL SPIRITS

© G. D. CO.

GLENMORE DISTILLERIES COMPANY · LOUISVILLE, KENTUCKY

King Blended Whiskey, 1952 ◄ *Old Thompson Whiskey, 1950*   ► *Charter Oak Bourbon, 1950*

Wolfschmidt has the secret of Christmas cheer

It's in this brilliantly styled Cocktail Pitcher brimming with wonderful Wolfschmidt Vodka. The secret, of course, is our exclusive refining process that makes Wolfschmidt cleaner, clearer—a happy companion to almost anything liquid. And this gay sparkling Wolfschmidt Cocktail Pitcher carries its usefulness to every season. It comes beautifully gift wrapped at no extra cost. An exciting gift for personal and business friends . . . for their Christmas stockings . . . or stocking for the New Year. Jolly thought: why not a case? Merry Wolfschmidt!

GENERAL WINE & SPIRITS CO., N.Y. 22, N.Y. • MADE FROM GRAIN, 100 OR 80 PROOF. PRODUCT OF U.S.A.

Wolfschmidt Vodka, 1958

▶ *Seagram's Gin, 1957*   ▶▶ *Black & White Scotch Whiskey, 1950*

For men among men, Hiram Walker makes a whiskey among whiskies—Imperial

Man, this is whiskey!

Imperial Whiskey, 1956

Calvert Reserve Whiskey, 1951

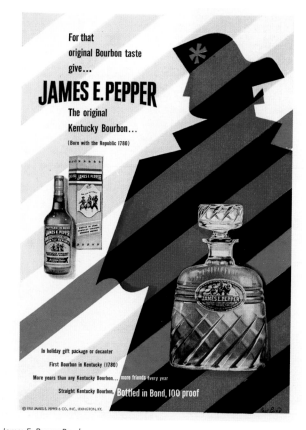

For that original Bourbon taste give...

JAMES E. PEPPER

The original Kentucky Bourbon...

(Born with the Republic 1780)

In holiday gift package or decanter
First Bourbon in Kentucky (1780)
More years than any Kentucky Bourbon... more friends every year
Straight Kentucky Bourbon, **Bottled in Bond, 100 proof**

James E. Pepper Bourbon, 1951

For People of Inherent Good Taste

His gracious manner and respected presence tell you—here is a man of inherent good taste. And *he* will tell you that such taste responds to the two great whiskies shown here with a warmth no others awaken. Kentucky Tavern, a classic native sour mash Bourbon made to the same family formula for three generations; and King's Ransom, known round the world for the vigor of its hearty Scotch character.

Each is a proud offering of the House of Glenmore, where perfection of product is tradition. We commend them to you, confident that you, too, will find in each the ultimate fulfillment of that tradition.

For Your Considered Selection

KENTUCKY TAVERN — Kentucky Straight Sour Mash Bourbon, Bottled-in-Bond, 100 Proof
KING'S RANSOM — Famed "Round the World" Blended Scotch Whisky — 94 Proof — Imported solely by Glenmore Distilleries

Glenmore Distillers

▶ *Heublein Cocktails, 1957*

EDWARD G. ROBINSON, DISTINGUISHED STAR OF STAGE AND SCREEN.

dward G. Robinson never gets tough with his guests

No considerate host disregards the preference of his guests. If a man wants a Dry Martini, don't force something else on him.
Serve Martinis—Martinis you can be proud of—Heublein's. They're made of choicest liquors, perfectly proportioned, expertly mixed.
Uniformly excellent, first to last. You can pour Martinis on-the-rocks right from the Heublein bottle (easy as whiskey) because
they're full strength. Or stir with ice and serve in traditional cocktail glasses. Cheers! G. F. HEUBLEIN & BRO., HARTFORD, CONN.

EXTRA DRY MARTINIS, 75 PROOF · MANHATTANS, 65 PROOF · VODKA MARTINIS, 70 PROOF

DAIQUIRIS, 60 PROOF · OLD FASHIONEDS, 70 PROOF · AND 5 OTHER POPULAR KINDS.

HEUBLEIN COCKTAILS

FULL-STRENGTH · READY-TO-SERVE

REFLECTION ... of PERFECTION
Seagram's 7 Crown

"IT LEAVES YOU BREATHLESS!" says Benny Goodman

Smooth, flawless Smirnoff gives you everything you ask for in a vodka. And nothing you *don't* want! Having virtually no taste of its own, it never "takes over" in your drinks. It has no "breath"... leaves no whisper of liquor on your lips. Let nobody tell you all vodkas are the same. Make sure you get the one and only *Smirnoff*. Just mention our name!

the vodka of vodkas

Smirnoff
THE GREATEST NAME IN **VODKA**

80 AND 100 PROOF. DISTILLED FROM GRAIN. STE. PIERRE SMIRNOFF FLS. (DIVISION OF HEUBLEIN). HARTFORD, CONN.

Smirnoff Vodka, 1958

WHAT DOES SMIRNOFF VODKA TASTE LIKE? "Nobody ever tasted Smirnoff," says Wally Cox, "because it doesn't hardly *have* a taste. It's just sort of willing!" When you mix a jigger of Smirnoff Vodka in orange juice, *it tastes like orange juice*; when you pour Smirnoff in ginger ale, *it tastes like ginger ale!* You don't have to learn new recipes to make delicious drinks with Smirnoff Vodka. Just use Smirnoff instead of gin in your dry martini, collins or tonic—or add a jigger of Smirnoff to any fruit juice or soft drink you like. It's a revelation!

the vodka of vodkas

Smirnoff
THE GREATEST NAME IN **VODKA**

80 AND 100 PROOF. DISTILLED FROM GRAIN. STE. PIERRE SMIRNOFF FLS (DIVISION OF HEUBLEIN). HARTFORD, CONNECTICUT.

Smirnoff Vodka, 1957

GOLDEN JIGGER
and pouring lip impart grace and ease to serving—simply remove jigger, tip, and pour.

Genuine OLD FITZGERALD *in the* Candlelight Decanter

Bonded Bourbon by Stitzel-Weller... none finer to gladden the throat of man! *Decanter* by the famous Walter Landor... to add high-fashion flair to an old-fashioned whiskey! Its convenience and decorative after-uses make doubly welcome your gift of OLD FITZGERALD... *the final choice of mature tastes.*

Candlelight Decanter costs no more than regular fifth.

Your Key to Hospitality

KENTUCKY STRAIGHT BOURBON WHISKEY • BONDED 100 PROOF • STITZEL-WELLER DISTILLERY, ESTABLISHED LOUISVILLE, KY., 1849

Seagram's 7 Crown, 1950 ◀   *Old Fitzgerald Bourbon Whiskey, 1955*

same fine Old Forester   in striking new decanter

NO BETTER WAY TO GIVE THE BEST

The finest of fine bonded bourbons, in this exquisite decanter by famed Raymond Loewy. Truly the gift to be given with pride, for there is nothing better in the market. Same price as standard fifth.

Old Forester

KENTUCKY STRAIGHT BOURBON WHISKY • BOTTLED IN BOND • 100 PROOF • BROWN-FORMAN DISTILLERS CORPORATION • AT LOUISVILLE IN KENTUCKY

Old Forester Bourbon, 1955

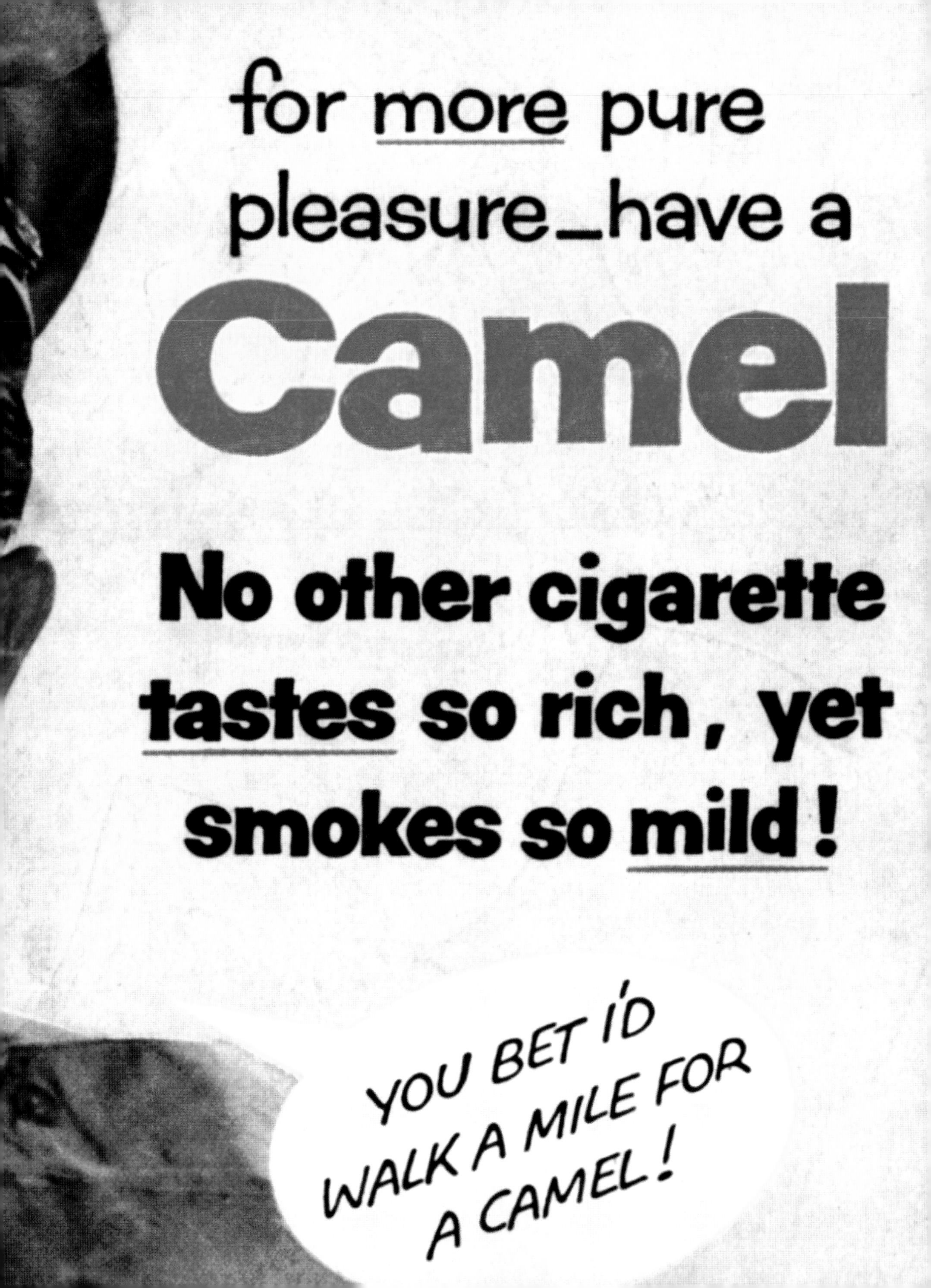

for more pure pleasure_have a
Camel
No other cigarette tastes so rich, yet smokes so mild!
YOU BET I'D WALK A MILE FOR A CAMEL!

You'll get more pure pleasure out of Camels!

Try Camels, the best-liked cigarette of all. You'll see why Camels give more pleasure—to more smokers today—than any other brand.

Only CAMELS taste so rich... yet smoke so mild!

Camel Cigarettes, 1956 ◄ *Camel Cigarettes, 1956*

NOSE, THROAT,

and Accessory Organs not Adversely Affected by Smoking Chesterfields

FIRST SUCH REPORT EVER PUBLISHED ABOUT ANY CIGARETTE

A responsible consulting organization has reported the results of a continuing study by a competent medical specialist and his staff on the effects of smoking Chesterfield cigarettes.

A group of people from various walks of life was organized to smoke only Chesterfields. For six months this group of men and women smoked their normal amount of Chesterfields – 10 to 40 a day. 45% of the group have smoked Chesterfields continually from one to thirty years for an average of 10 years each.

At the beginning and at the end of the six-months period each smoker was given a thorough examination, including X-ray pictures, by the medical specialist and his assistants. The examination covered the sinuses as well as the nose, ears and throat.

The medical specialist, after a thorough examination of every member of the group, stated: "It is my opinion that the ears, nose, throat and accessory organs of all participating subjects examined by me were not adversely affected in the six-months period by smoking the cigarettes provided."

ASK YOUR DEALER FOR CHESTERFIELD – EITHER WAY YOU LIKE 'EM

★ CONTAINS TOBACCOS OF BETTER QUALITY & HIGHER PRICE THAN ANY OTHER KING-SIZE CIGARETTE

Buy CHESTERFIELD _Much Milder

Chesterfield Cigarettes, 1952

IT'S A PSYCHOLOGICAL FACT: PLEASURE HELPS YOUR DISPOSITION

How's *your* disposition today?

EVER YIP LIKE A TERRIER when the store sends you the wrong package? That's only natural when little annoyances like this occur. But — it's a psychological fact that pleasure helps your disposition! That's why everyday pleasures — like smoking, for instance — mean so much. So if you're a smoker, it's important to smoke the *most pleasure-giving cigarette* — Camel.

R. J. Reynolds Tobacco Co., Winston-Salem, N. C.

For more pure pleasure — have a Camel

"*I've tried 'em all— but it's Camels for me!*" *Rock Hudson*

YOU CAN SEE RUGGED ROCK HUDSON STARRING IN U-I'S "NEVER SAY GOODBYE"

No other cigarette is so rich-tasting yet so mild!

ROCK HUDSON AGREES with Camel smokers everywhere: there *is* more pure pleasure in Camels! More flavor, genuine mildness! Good reasons why today more people smoke Camels than any other cigarette

Remember this: pleasure helps your disposition. And for *more* pure pleasure — have a Camel!

Camel Cigarettes, 1956

How MILD can a Cigarette be?

MAKE THE 30-DAY CAMEL MILDNESS TEST—SEE WHY...

MORE PEOPLE SMOKE CAMELS
than any other cigarette!

MAN'S IDEA OF A MOVIE HERO
And the women agree! 6 feet 4 inches, John Wayne has smashed his way to fame in dozens of knock-down-and-drag-out—hard-riding...glorious motion pictures!

"The roles I play in movies are far from easy on my voice— I can't risk throat irritation. So I smoke Camels—they're <u>mild</u>"

John Wayne

POPULAR, HANDSOME HOLLYWOOD STAR

"I've been around movie sets long enough to know how important cigarette mildness is to an actor. So when it came to deciding what cigarette was just right for my throat — I was very particular. I made a *sensible* test—my own 30-Day Camel Mildness Test!

"I gave Camels a real tryout for 30 days. The most pleasure I ever had from smoking. My own 'T-Zone' told me just how mild and good tasting a cigarette can be! I found out for myself why *more people smoke Camels than any other cigarette!*"

R. J. Reynolds Tobacco Company, Winston-Salem, N. C.

Make your own 30-Day Camel MILDNESS Test in your "T-Zone"

(T for Throat, T for Taste)

Not one single case of throat irritation *due to smoking*
CAMELS!

Yes, these were the findings of noted throat specialists after a total of 2,470 weekly examinations of the throats of hundreds of men and women who smoked Camels — and only Camels — for 30 consecutive days.

Camel Cigarettes, 1951

▶ *L & M Cigarettes, 1953*

So Good to your TASTE

So Quick on the DRAW !

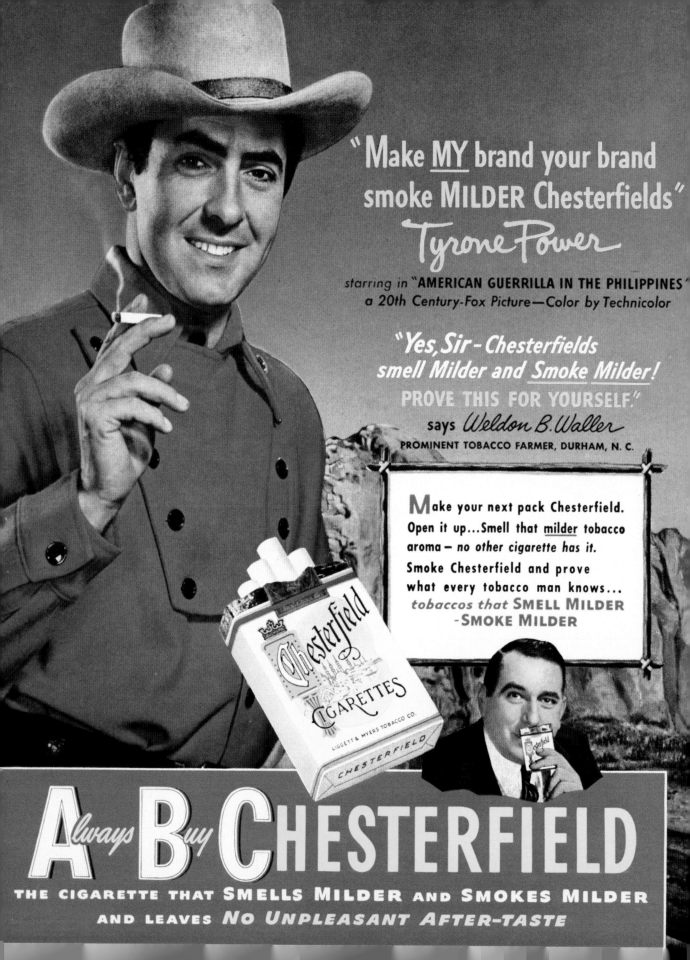

L & M Cigarettes, 1958

Chesterfield Cigarettes

Chesterfield Cigarettes, 1950 ◀ Chesterfield Cigarettes, 1952

Cigars

Lucky Strike Cigarettes, 1951

Lucky Strike Cigarettes, 1951

Lucky Strike Cigarettes, 1950

Lucky Strike Cigarettes, 1950 ▶ *Old Gold Cigarettes, 1950*

No song and dance
about medical claims...

Old Gold's specialty is to give
you a TREAT instead of a TREATMENT!

du Maurier Cigarettes, 1958

Winston Cigarettes, 1956

Spring Cigarettes, 1959

Chase National Bank, 1952　　▶ *Old Gold, 1952*　▶▶ *Old Gold, 1953*

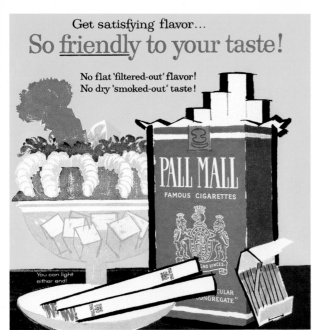

Get satisfying flavor…
So <u>friendly</u> to your taste!

No flat 'filtered-out' flavor!
No dry 'smoked-out' taste!

See how PALL MALL's greater length of fine tobaccos filters the smoke and makes it mild – but does not filter out that satisfying flavor!

FOR FLAVOR AND MILDNESS, FINE TOBACCO FILTERS BEST

1 You get greater length of the finest tobaccos money can buy 2 Pall Mall's greater length filters the smoke <u>naturally</u> 3 Filters it over, under, around and through Pall Mall's fine tobaccos!

Outstanding…and they are <u>Mild</u>!

Product of The American Tobacco Company—"Tobacco is our middle name"

Pall Mall Cigarettes, 1958

GET SATISFYING FLAVOR…
SO *FRIENDLY* TO YOUR TASTE!

Pall Mall's greater length filters the smoke —does not filter out the Pall Mall flavor!

1 Don't give up flavor to get mildness.
2 For flavor and mildness fine tobacco filters best.
3 Pall Mall tobaccos are the finest quality money can buy.

OUTSTANDING…AND THEY ARE <u>MILD</u>!

Product of The American Tobacco Company—"Tobacco is our middle name"

Pall Mall Cigarettes, 1958

This Christmas, give yourself (and your friends) <u>satisfying</u> flavor…so <u>friendly</u> to your taste!

No flat "filtered-out" flavor! No dry "smoked-out" taste!

Product of The American Tobacco Company—"Tobacco is our middle name"

Outstanding…and they are <u>Mild</u>!

Pall Mall Cigarettes, 1958

You can light either end!

Get satisfying flavor…So <u>friendly</u> to your taste!

NO FLAT "FILTERED-OUT" FLAVOR!

NO DRY "SMOKED-OUT" TASTE!

Outstanding… and they are <u>Mild</u>!

See how Pall Mall's famous length of fine tobacco travels and gentles the smoke—makes it mild—but does not filter out that <u>satisfying</u> flavor!

HERE'S WHY SMOKE "TRAVELED" THROUGH FINE TOBACCO TASTES BEST

1 You get Pall Mall's famous length of the finest tobaccos money can buy. 2 Pall Mall's famous length travels and gentles the smoke <u>naturally</u>… 3 Travels it over, under, around and through Pall Mall's fine tobaccos!

Product of The American Tobacco Company—"Tobacco is our middle name"

Pall Mall Cigarettes, 1959

▶ *Pall Mall Cigarettes, 1958*

PALL MALL

FAMOUS CIGARETTES

PER ASPERA AD ASTRA

·IN HOC SIGNO VINCES·

"WHEREVER PARTICULAR
PEOPLE CONGREGATE"

PALL MALL

PALL MALL

YOU
CAN LIGHT
EITHER
END!

says: **ARLENE DAHL**

"I love to see a man smoke a Cigarillo"

and her husband, **LEX BARKER,** *says:*

"Cigarillos have just what it takes
to please me...Full delicious tobacco
taste, yet mild...Stylish, manly shape
and cigarette convenience...And they
cut down chain smoking."

For Limited Time Only
To get this custom-built
holder for Robt. Burns
Cigarillos, worth twice the
cost, send 10 Robt. Burns
Cigarillo bands and 50¢ to
P. O. Box 192, Midtown
Sta., New York 18, N. Y.

*Arlene Dahl, starring in Pine-Thomas production,
"Caribbean Gold", Paramount Picture, color by Technicolor.
Lex Barker, starring in "Tarzan's Savage Fury", RKO release.*

Robt. Burns
Cigarillos 5¢ EACH

IF IT'S NOT A <u>ROBT. BURNS</u>**, IT'S NOT** <u>THE CIGARILLO</u>

Robt. Burns Cigarillos, 1952

MRS. HUMPHREY BOGART SAYS :
(Lauren Bacall)

"I love to see a man smoke a Cigarillo"

Lauren Bacall, speaking
for style-wise women
everywhere, endorses
The New Idea in Smoking from
the feminine point of view...
As for men, they go in a big
way for delicious smoking
pleasure in a shape, trim and
handy as a cigarette...
The *perfect mild* smoke.

*Convenient as a cigarette.
Fits neatly between the smoker's lips,
or into a holder.*

*Humphrey Bogart and his wife, Lauren Bacall, co-stars
of Santana Pictures, are both ardent, expert sailors.*

Robt. Burns *Cigarillos* 5¢ EACH

"IN A CLASS BY ITSELF"

Robt. Burns Cigarillos, 1951

UNMISTAKABLY ASCOT!

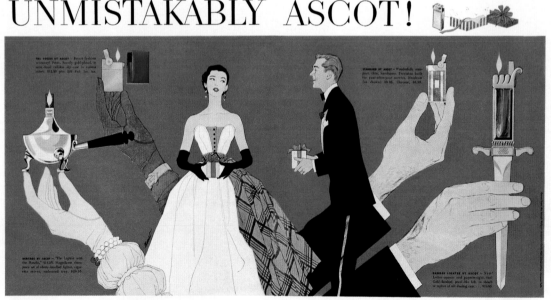

You cannot give a more beautiful gift than the fabulous *Ascot* lighter

   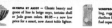

Ascot Lighters, 1952

Philip Morris Cigarettes, 1952

Pall Mall Cigarettes, 1950

Marlboro Cigarettes, 1950

▶ Old Gold Cigarettes

we love you...

for the largest sales
in Old Gold's history

And the winner is...

Yes, You Need Never Feel Over-Smoked

Tobacco companies promised many things, but this ad went beyond the soothing throat and the glamour-of-smoking pitches that were a staple among advertisers. Using infants to suggest an innocent cigarette could cure just about anything, including uptight homemakers, was about as low as you could go. Child abuse? Come on, Mom. Just light up and calm those jangled nerves with a cigarette.

Nie wieder Nikotinkater

Tabakfirmen versprachen vieles, doch diese Reklame ging über die unter Werbern gängigen Verkaufsargumente von kehlenschonendem oder glamourösem Rauchgenuß weit hinaus. Kleinkinder zu benutzen, um zu suggerieren, eine unschuldige Zigarette könne so gut wie alles kurieren, auch gebeutelte Hausfrauen – niederträchtiger ging es kaum. Kindesmißhandlung? Sei doch nicht so, Mama. Steck dir eine an und beruhige die strapazierten Nerven mit einer Zigarette.

Non, vous ne serez jamais trop enfumés

Les compagnies de tabac promettent sans compter, mais cette réclame dépasse les bienfaits pour la gorge et les charmes du tabagisme, rengaines des annonceurs. Tout est permis, même l'utilisation d'enfants en bas âge pour suggérer que la cigarette soigne tout, y compris la ménagère à cran. Maltraitance ? Voyons, Maman. Et si tu t'en grillais une pour te calmer les nerfs ?

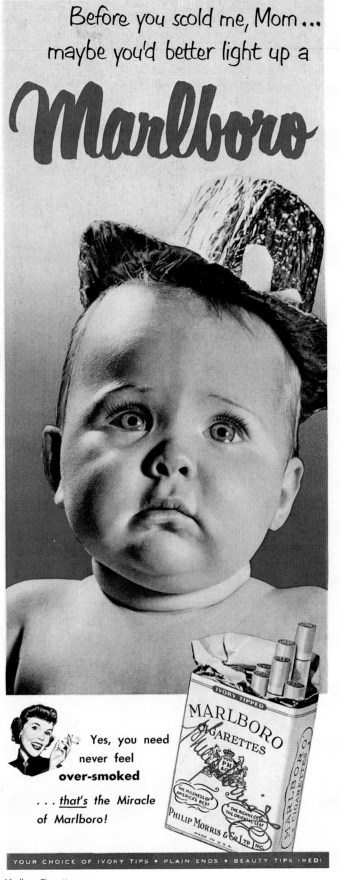

Marlboro Cigarettes, 1950

Westinghouse Atomic Reactor, 1956

FIRST ATOM SUB GOES TO SEA
Atomic Engine Drives Revolutionary Submarine "Nautilus"

Martin Aircraft, 1951 ◀ *Westinghouse Atomic Reactor, 1956*

Target for Tomorrow!

Photo-mapped today by the U.S. Air Force!

Swift, unarmed, these "recon" planes carry eleven probing "eyes" through fire and flak on a final camera run. Their mission: get enemy information and *get it back!*

Like the lone Indian scout of old, the reconnaissance officer of today guards the safety of the entire command in daring sorties into enemy territory. He brings back knowledge to assist commanders in deciding *where—when—how* to strike.

Sometimes his plane comes in low, through deadly enemy ground fire—sometimes high, up to 40,000 feet, a target for bristling enemy fighters. But, high or low, night or day, these "recon" missions are tough. And so are the men who fly them!

Only a few young men stand a chance of qualifying. And these the U. S. Air Force chooses carefully from the nation's best . . . trains them in the finest aviation schools under experienced officers.

Selection of Airmen is just as important, for they must keep planes and equipment in tip-top shape. They are trained in Air Force technical schools for important assignments in 42 different career fields.

No wonder your U. S. Air Force is able to demand and receive, from Officers and Airmen alike, *superior performance at all times and under all conditions!*

U. S. AIR FORCE

EYES FRONT: Ground crews prepare to remove exposed film from nose cameras of an RB-45 just back from its "recon" mission, rush them off for developing.

TOP VIEW: Skilled photo-interpreters of ground and air, using modern stereoscopic techniques, assess the pictures for detailed information on the enemy.

STRIKE: Bombers take over. Now they know *when*, *where* and *how* to strike a devastating blow at enemy installations—thanks to good reconnaissance!

U.S. Air Force, 1951

RED 1...Scramble

A telephone jangles harshly in the ready room. "Enemy aircraft, zero nine zero, 30,000. *Scramble!*" Pilots and radar-observers burst out across the flight line, buckling on gear as they race to the waiting planes. In a matter of minutes the sleek jets are thundering skyward to the attack.

Meanwhile, ground radar is tracking the intruder, guiding our defenders to the rapidly-moving, yet unseen target. The seconds tick off. Then their own radar 'scopes pick up the hot scent, and the swift fighters close in for the kill.

Fox-and-hounds in the dark at six hundred miles an hour is no game for beginners. The steel-nerved team of pilots and radar-observers and skilled ground crews who man our all-weather interceptor bases know every play in the book, and how to use it.

Men do not master these complex duties in a day, a month, or a year. That is why your Air Force must go on painstakingly selecting, training, proving and seasoning qualified personnel for these key posts in the nation's air defenses. For whether it's only in practice or whether it's in deadly earnest ...when Combat Alert says "*Scramble*," it's time for action on the double-quick!

U. S. AIR FORCE

READY! Skilled watchers at a well-hidden Air Defense Direction Center track the invader by ground radar and guide our all-weather fighters toward the intruder.

AIM! The radar-observer, at his 'scope in the rear seat, navigates the plane to the target. The pilot takes over, pin-pointing the enemy in his radar sights.

FIRE! On target! Still guided only by radar, the pilot fires a long burst, pulls up sharply to avoid crashing into the enemy bomber he has successfully intercepted!

U.S. Air Force, 1951

Checkmate !

Battle by bitter battle our combat soldiers checkmate a strong, fanatical enemy. Once again the American fighting man is leaving his mark on the history books of the world—*the mark of a man.*

Outstanding among these men is the paratrooper—the combat soldier who flies to work—dropping out of the skies in the enemy's rear or on the flanks to deliver the blow that leads to victory.

From the moment that he collapses his chute, he is on his way. Surprise is his ally ... speed and firepower his weapons ... raw courage his stock in trade ... success his mission.

This fighting man knows that he carries in his pack the hopes of a free world. He knows that if *tomorrow* we are to live in freedom ... *today* we must fight the enemy of freedom—*today* we must fight those who make a mockery of individual rights.

He cannot fight on alone. He needs your help. He needs men, *brave* men, who will volunteer to serve alongside him. Men who can make a success of any mission. Men who will fight for freedom.

U. S. ARMY
VISIT YOUR NEAREST U. S. ARMY AND U. S. AIR FORCE RECRUITING STATION

THE MARK OF A MAN
This is the paratrooper's badge that marks a man of the Airborne. It is the mark of a real combat soldier—a man among men.

U.S. Army, 1951

1 LAUNCHED FROM NAVY JET FIGHTER.

2 SPARROW AUTOMATICALLY GUIDED TO TARGET

3 DESTROYS ENEMY IN A MATTER OF SECONDS

Carrier Based Jets to have Radar Guided Missiles

NAVY'S AIR-TO-AIR SPARROW 1 IN PRODUCTION

THE STORY BEHIND THE STORY:

■ On May 12, newspapers from coast to coast carried headlines like the ones above, announcing the Navy's newest weapon of defense–Sparrow 1–and the beginning of volume production for operational use in the fleets.

■ Ahead of these headlines were 7 years of intensive cooperative effort shared by the Navy's Bureau of Aeronautics and Sperry.

■ The rocket-powered, radar-guided Sparrow 1, coming off the production lines here and at the new Sperry Farragut plant in Bristol, Tennessee, meets these requirements–and more. It embodies the proved features of more than 100 different missiles designed, constructed and tested during a 7-year period — and the finest brains of an organization that has devoted more than 40 years creating and manufacturing automatic flight control and fire control systems.

■ Originally designated project HOT SHOT, Sparrow began back in 1947 when the Bureau of Aeronautics assigned to Sperry the full responsibility of creating an entirely new air-to-air missile system. It had to be light and compact — so multiple units could be carried by fighter-type jets. It had to be deadly accurate — capable of outmaneuvering the swiftest bombers an enemy could produce. And it had to be practical–suitable for large-scale production.

SPERRY GYROSCOPE COMPANY
DIVISION OF THE SPERRY CORPORATION · GREAT NECK, N.Y.

Sperry Gyroscope Company, 1954

AMERICA'S NEWEST WINGS FOR ATOMIC DEFENSE...
"DELTA WINGS," BORN AND BUILT BY CONVAIR'S

Engineering to the Nth power

WATER-BASED FIGHTER
Convair's twin-jet "Sea-Dart" (XF2Y-1) expands the air defense perimeter of fleets at sea and bases ashore

LAND-BASED INTERCEPTOR
From this experimental design comes Convair's supersonic F-102 to spearhead U.S. defenses

HERE'S A TRIANGLE WITH MORE THAN THREE POINTS

Convair was the first to engineer, build and *fly* the triangular shaped solution to the problem of human flight in the vicinity of the speed of sound ... and beyond. Through the versatile skills of Convair engineering, the delta configuration has already given America its first land-based, supersonic interceptor...and the world's first water-based very-high-speed jet fighter. Adaptations of the delta to bomber and transport designs are now under way. Proof again, that Convair engineering achieves the maximum of air power...Engineering to the *Nth* Power!

CONVAIR SAN DIEGO & POMONA, CALIFORNIA
FORT WORTH & GRANGERFIELD, TEXAS

Convair, 1953
▶ *National Plumbing Seals, 1956*

When the moon is but a stop on the milk run...

National Oil Seals will protect the bearin

When inter-planetary trips become commonplace, surface travel in the family car may move normally 200 m.p.h., farm implements may become complete food processing plants, Farmer Jones may do his plo with atomic power. Contributing to mechanical progre such as this will be new oil seal designs, new sealing member compounds which will permit a higher orde bearing performance. National Oil Seal engineers hav many of these new oil seals on the drawing boards and in production now. For this reason, you can look to National for "years-ahead" performance in your products of today as well as anticipate "years-ahead" performance in your products of tomorrow.

NATIONAL MOTOR BEARING CO., INC.

General Offices: Redwood City, California
Plants: Redwood City and Los Angeles, California;
Van Wert, Ohio

NATIONAL
OIL AND FLUID **SEALS**

Original equipment on all cars, trucks, buses, tractors,
in fact wherever shafts turn.

IMPORTANT TIP TO CAR OWNERS: It is difficult to remove an oil seal without damaging it beyond further safe use. Sensitive sealing members must provide perfect closure around shafts to retain lubricant in bearings. Insist on new seals every time one is removed from any equipment. The cost is slight...the protection worth many dollars. Make sure you get genuine parts designed especially for the job.

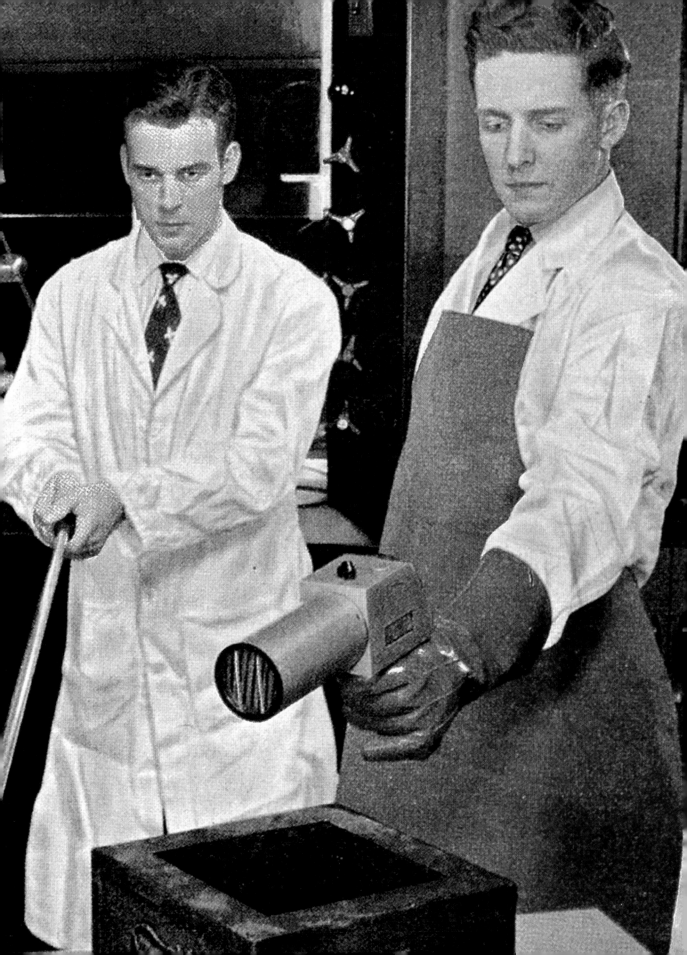

CONVAIR-*Astronautics*: shedding light on the mysteries of space

"…The time is bound to come when man will venture ever deeper into space—
not to win wars on earth but to battle the limitless challenge of the universe."

— *General Thomas S. Power, Commander in Chief, Strategic Air Command.*

CONVAIR
A DIVISION OF GENERAL DYNAMICS CORPORATION

Chrysler Corporation, 1951 ◀   *Convair, 1958*　　　　　　　　　　　　　　　　　　　▶ *North American Aviation, 1955*

F7U-3 Cutlass, new Chance Vought general purpose fighter now in service with the U.S. Navy. Swift and versatile, it is armed with cannons and rockets, can carry bombs and guided missiles. Twin turbojet J46 engines, equipped with afterburners, supply the Cutlass with more than 12,000 pounds of thrust.

70% of our planet is
deep water

...and here's how your New Air Navy will use it for America's defense

Keeping the world's sea lanes open to our own forces and denying their use to any aggressor is the primary mission of the United States Navy.

These sea lanes are a two-way lifeline. Over them we transport the strategic materials vital to our industrial life, and send forth the supplies and troops essential to the existence of our overseas bases.

To control the seas a strong nation must control the skies above the seas...this is the job of your New Air Navy.

High-flying, hard-hitting jet fighters, like Chance Vought's Cutlass, are designed to range from the Navy's roving task forces, sweeping the skies and extending the striking power of our surface fleets.

They are an "insurance policy" against attack upon our far-flung bases...an advance guard against attack at home.

Your New Air Navy plays a vital role in the use of deep water as part of America's defense.

NAVY FLIERS CHALLENGE THE JET FRONTIER
Action, adventure...fellowship, prestige...and priceless training that fits you for the challenge of the new jet age...all wait for you as a Navy flier. If you are unmarried, and between the ages of 18-25, visit your nearest Naval Air Station or write NAVCAD, Washington 25, D.C.

CHANCE VOUGHT AIRCRAFT
INCORPORATED · DALLAS, TEXAS

Voight Aircraft, 1955

No. 35 in a series:

First production model of

U. S. Navy's new fighter

surpasses speed of sound—

during routine delivery flight

—the Douglas F4D Skyray

The pilot was seeking no record. But suddenly, his *production model* Douglas F4D Skyray was flying faster than the speed of sound *in level flight!*

Though this supersonic show of speed was unscheduled, it came as no surprise. Skyray is holder of the world's official

F.A.I. sea-level speed record at 753.4 m.p.h. Designed for interceptor duty with the U. S. Navy, it is powered by a Pratt & Whitney J-57 engine with afterburner. Agile as well as fast, Skyray has a very high rate of climb and low landing speeds—operates with ease from air-

craft carriers . . . to strengthen the fleet air arm.

The outstanding performance of F4D Skyray is another example of Douglas leadership in aviation. Faster and farther with a bigger payload is always the basic rule of Douglas design.

Be a Naval Aviator, write Nav. Cad., Washington 25, D. C.

Depend on DOUGLAS First in Aviation

Douglas Aviation, 1954

No. 27 in a series

First carrier-based airplane

to hold a world's speed record

753.4 m.p.h.

the U. S. Navy's

Douglas F4D Skyray

Streaking each mile in *less* than 5 seconds, during four passes at a 3-kilometer course, a Douglas F4D Skyray returned the official world speed record to the United States.

Two weeks later, Skyray blazed into a 100-kilometer course, cracked all records

by an even wider margin. Now in production for the Navy, this delta wing jet interceptor adds terrific climb and firepower to its speed—plus the ease of handling needed in carrier landings. The Douglas F4D Skyray has now passed its initial carrier tests, in service will guard

our fleets against the fastest of modern jet bombers.

Performance of the Navy's F4D Skyray is another example of Douglas leadership in aviation. Faster and farther with a bigger payload is always the basic rule of Douglas design.

Be a Naval Aviator— write Nav. Cad. Washington 25, D. C.

Depend on DOUGLAS First in Aviation

Douglas Aviation, 1954

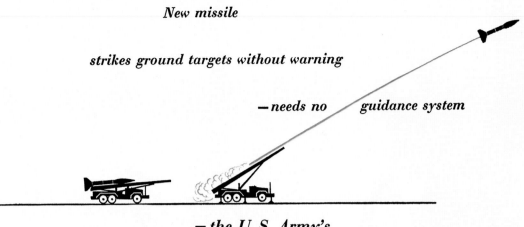

New missile

strikes ground targets without warning

—needs no   guidance system

—the U. S. Army's

Douglas-designed HONEST JOHN

Add to the U. S. Army's ever-growing arsenal of rocket weapons a new ground-to-ground missile . . . the Douglas-designed Honest John.

Developed in co-operation with Army Ordnance—and already being delivered to troop units—Honest John is a free flight rocket without complicated guid-

ance system, and designed to supplement artillery in the medium to heavy range. Honest John is extremely mobile, moves quickly into position on a special truck which also serves as transport *and* launcher. Highly accurate, this rocket can handle either an atomic warhead, or a single high explosive round equalling

the explosive force of hundreds of rounds of artillery shells.

Design of Honest John and other missiles is further evidence of Douglas leadership in its field. Now that the time to produce missiles in quantity has become a reality, Douglas manufacturing skill is ready and able for the job.

Depend on DOUGLAS   **First in Aviation**

En Garde!

ON GUARD FOR AMERICA'S AIR DEFENSE

THE F-102 IS A RAPIER in the hand of the U.S. Airman.

At its controls, he flashes through the skies at supersonic speeds, day or night in any weather. With it, he can seek out the invader . . . strike and destroy him.

Built for the U.S. Air Force, Convair's F-102 interceptor is delta-winged and jet-powered, designed for the men who are *on guard for America's air defense.*

Advanced aircraft like the F-102 are the result of engineering that aims at the maximum . . . the Nth degree of air power . . .

Engineering to the Nth power

CONVAIR

A DIVISION OF GENERAL DYNAMICS CORPORATION

Wear the wings of the U.S. Air Force. If you are 19 to 26, you may qualify for cadet training. Write to: Aviation Cadet, Headquarters United States Air Force, Washington 25, D.C.

Convair builds the world's
most advanced aircraft through...

Engineering
to the <u>Nth</u> power

NAVY'S XFY-1
TAKES OFF AND LANDS
ON A DIME

Here's a new kind of aircraft
for America's aviation arsenal...the
Convair XFY-1, a vertical takeoff,
delta wing Navy fighter. Powered by
a turbojet engine, it is one of the
world's fastest propeller driven planes.

The XFY-1 is as responsive as a
hummingbird over a rose bud.
It rises nose-up like a guided missile
...flies like a fighter at speeds
beyond 500 mph...hovers
motionless...darts forward, and
sideways...backs down on its tail
to a feather-light landing.

This remarkable aeronautical
achievement is another result of
Convair's engineering for the
maximum degree of performance...
the Nth degree of air power...
Engineering to the Nth power

CONVAIR
A DIVISION OF
GENERAL DYNAMICS CORPORATION

ANY SHIP BECOMES
AN AUXILIARY AIRCRAFT CARRIER
WITH THE XFY-1 ON DECK!

ANY FIELD, EVEN A BACKYARD,
IS AN AIRBASE FOR THE XFY-1!

ANY PLACE WHERE FIGHTER-BOMBERS
ARE NEEDED, THE XFY-1 CAN OPERATE!

NAVY

NAVY

CONVAIR

READY AS

A RIFLE BULLET

America has an arsenal

of operational missiles.

Their 'readiness' is a tribute

to the ability of private

industry to lend full support to

government and military effort.

A high percentage of the

rocket power plants for these

missiles was developed and

produced by Aerojet-General,

a subsidiary of The General

Tire and Rubber Company.

AEROJET-GENERAL

CORPORATION,

AZUSA AND SACRAMENTO,

CALIFORNIA

FIRE

General Tire

pioneer

in

Wanted...
More Men Like Mike !

—men who want to *go* places, and have plenty of the stuff it takes to *get* there!

Mike could be any one of a thousand typical young career men who are going places in today's Army. He could be you!

Mike lived a lively American boyhood. An average student, a popular athlete, he finished high school in '46, decided to start building a career in the Army.

Careful studies of Mike's personal aptitudes led to his selection for technical training in tanks and other armored vehicles. He took to it like a duck to water!

Finishing technical school as a Private, First Class, Mike progressed steadily in skill, efficiency and rank. Each year he took a 30-day vacation trip, with pay.

Mike studied, worked, watched his chances. Finished his first "hitch" as a Sergeant. During leave he went home and married his high school sweetheart.

Now, only four years after enlisting, Mike is a Sergeant, First Class, with an assured career ahead. He wouldn't trade places, or future opportunities, with anybody!

The young man of today who wants to get ahead can continue his education and start building a career at the same time, in the new U. S. Army. More than 200 courses of specialized training for many different career fields are taught in the various Army schools. Each man's abilities are charted, to place him where he should develop rapidly. Working with career-minded young men like himself on the frontiers of military science, he can serve his country with true professional pride. Today's U.S. Army is providing excellent career opportunities for America's finest young men.

RECRUITING

U.S. ARMY

U.S. AIR FORCE

U. S. ARMY

VISIT YOUR NEAREST U. S. ARMY AND U. S. AIR FORCE RECRUITING STATION

General Tire, 1958 ◄ *U.S. Army*

INVISIBLE JET FIGHTER MAKES TEST FLIGHT

This Grumman jet fighter is invisible. She is electrons. Yet day after day, she makes supersonic flights through an electronic sky.

Actually she is an electronic brain by name of REAC (Reeves Electronic Analog Computer) directed by a group of brilliant human brains. The latter convert the mathematics of the aircraft into a language they and she understand. They "tell" her everything they know about the new fighter design through wired panels and curves wired on revolving drums.

The cockpit with its human pilot is plugged in. At a signal he takes off and climbs to fifty thousand feet. The electronic

air is smooth up to the transonic range where sound waves pile up until the air misbehaves. Once through, the air is smooth again, and they are ready to test a combat maneuver at supersonic speed.

"Now decelerate."

The pilot extends speed brakes. All eyes watch the instruments, and the reactions recorded on moving graph paper.

These performance data, gained months before actual flight tests, help check designs created with results from other Grumman research. One reason Grumman planes are ready in quantity when needed.

GRUMMAN AIRCRAFT ENGINEERING CORPORATION · BETHPAGE · LONG ISLAND · NEW YORK

Designers and builders of the Cougar jet fighter, the S2F-1 sub-killer, the Albatross amphibian, metal boats, and Aerobilt truck bodies.

Grumman Aircraft Engineering Corporation, 1954

This is part of a REAC formula worked out in the Grumman "Brain Room". Unlike digital computers which work directly with numbers, this analog computer works with forces of motion by reproducing them in volts.

The computer is "told" the facts of the problem through miniature switchboards. A different problem can be made known to the computer quickly, simply by changing boards.

Some data, like wind tunnel results, are fed into the computer from revolving drums. The computer gets its information electrically from copper wires glued over penciled curves.

These are typical REAC answers. Engineers translate these squiggles into design information. Sometimes thousands of such answers may be required to solve any one of the many design problems.

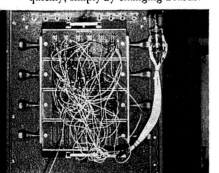

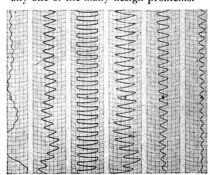

PRIZE CATCH!

Raytheon's sonar detection system hooks underwater prowlers

The so-called silent world is actually rife with noise. Fish, porpoises, whales—or the cautious "breathing" of a prowling sub—all are identified by the new underwater sound equipment pioneered by Raytheon.

A major contract for this radically new sonar system was recently placed with Raytheon by the Navy for its expanded atomic submarine program. This sensitive system – still highly classified – performs search, attack and communications functions.

Here, as in other areas of advanced electronics, the 39,000 men and women of Raytheon are contributing to U.S. strength and security.

RAYTHEON MANUFACTURING COMPANY, Waltham, Mass.

Excellence in Electronics   **RAYTHEON**

ENGINEERS and SCIENTISTS: for challenging opportunities with a growing company in all phases of electronics, write E. H. Herlin, Professional Personnel Coordinator.

Raytheon, 1959

best—but it takes years to design and build them. To keep them best, there must be uninterrupted development and production. Only such a sustained program can make and keep American Air Power an effective instrument for world peace.

9. **Chance Vought's "Regulus,"** a powerful, new Navy guided missile, can be launched and directed against surface targets from submarines (as shown in this artist's concept), or from ships or shore bases.

Can U.S. Air Power Prevent a War?

The answer lies in how consistently America pursues a sound peacetime Air Power policy

REGULUS, NIKE, MATADOR—new names for new kinds of aerial weapons, target-seeking guided missiles. Some have already begun to serve our armed forces. More will follow as development continues. American Air Power, of which missiles are a part, has now become so important that its strength or weakness can mean the difference between winning, losing, or *preventing* another world war.

To succeed in *preventing* war, our Air Power must be strong enough to discourage aggression before it starts. This means we must develop and build military aircraft in *every* category, including guided missiles, that are ready for instant retaliation—aircraft that are second to none in *performance* and strong enough in *numbers* to do the job.

Because of enormous technical problems, it has taken years to bring the guided missiles to their present stage of usefulness. And more time, plus consistent research, development and production, will be needed to improve and perfect them. With the U. S. exposed to possible atomic attack, the need for this effort is more urgent than ever.

That is why the Armed Forces—the Air Force, Navy, Marine Corps and Army—must have the support of every citizen for a realistic, continuous Air Power program. Only through such a program can the nation meet, and even forestall, emergencies—and at the same time avoid the waste and cost of stop-and-go aircraft production programs.

UNITED AIRCRAFT CORPORATION
EAST HARTFORD, CONNECTICUT

Pratt & Whitney jet and piston engines, Hamilton Standard propellers and aircraft equipment, Chance Vought aircraft and guided missiles, and Sikorsky helicopters. In Canada: Canadian Pratt & Whitney Aircraft Co., Ltd.

Engineers: We need additional experienced engineers. If you are not in defense work, write our Personnel Dept., stating complete qualifications.

Raytheon, 1959

"Living Minerals"

From modern research.... new horizons for industry

You are seeing the "flower" of life itself—a tiny piece of potash magnified many times. Like all *Living Minerals,* potash is part of the living earth. It gives life and growth to plants, animals and all mankind. It helps provide new products for industry, new living benefits for us all. Mining, processing and marketing such *Living Minerals* is the vital job of International Minerals.

Almost as it comes from the ground, potash is a basic ingredient of all chemical fertilizers. As an ore, it is a source of potassium and magnesium chemicals used in TV tubes,

medicine, glassware, metals and cosmetics. A few of the many products from potash are shown at left.

Here at International Minerals, eager young scientists daily discover new uses for many *Living Minerals:* phosphates, feldspar, bentonites, mica, uranium, fluorides and barite. May we help your company develop new products from *Living Minerals?*

International
MINERALS
CHEMICALS

INTERNATIONAL MINERALS & CHEMICAL CORPORATION
Chicago 6, Illinois

International Chemicals, 1958

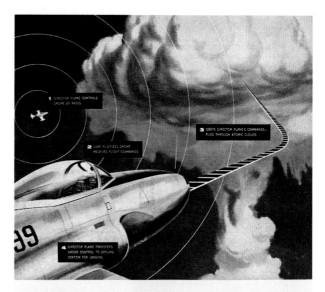

1 DIRECTOR PLANE CONTROLS DRONE BY RADIO

2 USAF PILOTLESS DRONE RECEIVES FLIGHT COMMANDS

3 OBEYS DIRECTOR PLANE'S COMMANDS - FLIES THROUGH ATOMIC CLOUDS

4 DIRECTOR PLANE TRANSFERS DRONE CONTROL TO GROUND STATION FOR LANDING

Pilotless Jets Penetrate Atomic Cloud in Tests

BRING BACK DATA PREVIOUSLY IMPOSSIBLE TO SECURE

THE STORY BEHIND THE STORY:

■ Mix the drama of atomic tests and pilotless flight and it's page one news. Such was the case when the U. S. Air Force thrust pilotless jet drones into the heart of atomic clouds and landed them safely—with their cargo of mice and monkeys—for scientific study by the Atomic Energy Commission.

The story behind the testing of the effect of radiation on animals is one of pilotless flight, "beep" pilots and precise

Sperry controls. Lockheed QF-80 drones, specially equipped with Sperry remote flight control systems, fly through atomic clouds guided by radio and radar.

■ These drones are flown remotely by skilled USAF pilots who use "beep" boxes to command them – either from director planes in the air or control stations on the ground for take-off and landing. Under their radio commands the drone takes off, at the proper speed retracts its landing gear, climbs to the desired altitude, banks and turns and keeps the airspeed necessary to arrive at

an exact point in the atomic cloud at a prescribed second.

■ This remarkable flight control system brings the drone through the awesome turbulence of the atomic cloud under complete control—on course and altitude. Returning to its airbase, the radiation-saturated drone lands as precisely as though a veteran pilot were at its controls.

■ Sperry is an old hand at pilotless flight. It developed the first guided missile—an aerial torpedo for the Navy — back in 1915. And since 1912, Sperry has been the leader in developing automatic flight controls for *piloted* flight. Sperry automatic pilots are installed on military and commercial planes the world over.

SPERRY
GYROSCOPE COMPANY
DIVISION OF THE SPERRY CORPORATION • GREAT NECK, N.Y.

Sperry Gyroscope Company, 1954

▶ *Convair, 1959*

Engineers: North American offers unusual opportunities. Write Engineering Personnel Office, Los Angeles or Downey, California; or Columbus, Ohio.

THE PEACEFUL ATOM...IT'S WORKING FOR YOU!

North American Aviation early saw the need for development and application of the atom to peaceful purposes. Using its own funds, the company set up an organization staffed by leading atomic scientists and engineers. This Nuclear Engineering and Manufacturing organization conducts work for the Atomic Energy Commission and has initiated many new developments in nuclear applications.

This continuing effort has produced several types of research reactors. Two important examples of these, produced for the Atomic Energy Commission, are now in operation. One is being used by the company for advanced developmental study of other reactor designs, and general nuclear research is being done with the other. Other North American designed reactors for industrial and medical research will soon be in operation.

Still another example of North American's advance in this field is the "Sodium Reactor Experiment," a new reactor concept in atomic power. This development is being jointly financed by the Atomic Energy Commission and the company. From this will come many answers to the problem of producing economical electricity from the atom.

ENGINEERING AHEAD FOR A BETTER TOMORROW

NORTH AMERICAN AVIATION, INC.

Union Carbide, 1959 ◄ *North American Aviation, 1955*

You'd fly like this

without the vital accessories created by AiResearch to make possible today's high-speed, high-altitude flight

NEW "LUNGS" FOR THE LUXURY AIRLINERS!

When you're flying at 20,000 feet and you sit there warm and comfortable, breathing clean fresh air, you reap the benefit of years of painstaking development work by AiResearch engineers.

"Living room" comfort in the newest high-altitude airliners like the Super Constellation, the Martin 404 and the Convair 340 is the work of AiResearch.

The air you breathe is scooped up from the outside, compressed and refrigerated or heated —

delivered inside the cabin at just the right temperature.

On supersonic jets and turboprops even greater problems of air conditioning are conquered by AiResearch equipment.

Every American-built, highspeed, high-altitude airplane flies with the aid of products manufactured by AiResearch.

Would you like to work with us? Qualified engineers, scientists and skilled craftsmen are needed now at AiResearch.

In a modern airliner at 20,000 feet or higher, you are not only comfortable, but you fly *safer* and *faster*. Vital "lung" in the pressurizing system is the AiResearch cabin supercharger. Together with the AiResearch refrigeration unit, it keeps the plane air conditioned in the air or on the ground.

AiResearch Manufacturing Company

A DIVISION OF THE GARRETT CORPORATION
LOS ANGELES 45, CALIFORNIA • PHOENIX, ARIZONA

DESIGNER AND MANUFACTURER OF AIRCRAFT EQUIPMENT IN THESE MAJOR CATEGORIES

Air Turbine Refrigeration   Heat Transfer Equipment   Electric Actuators   Gas Turbines   Cabin Superchargers   Pneumatic Power Units   Electronic Controls   Cabin Pressure Controls   Temperature Controls

AiResearch Manufacturing Company, 1952

▶ *Republic Aviation, 1954*

Anaconda engineers Teflon Hose assemblies for the space age

The complete line, Anaconda MIL SPEC hose assemblies, standard or custom-engineered. Here's the lightweight, flexible hose designed for demanding space age assignments. This smooth bore Teflon* hose is covered by a high tensile stainless steel braid for added strength and meets specification MIL-H-25579. Ideal for conveying corrosives and dependable at temperatures from −65°F to 450°F.

TEFLON HOSE ASSEMBLIES BY ANACONDA ARE NOW USED BY LEADING AIRFRAME, POWER-PLANT, GSE AND ELECTRONICS MANUFAC-TURERS FOR: chemical lines, pneumatic lines, vent lines, jet fuel lines, lubrication lines, ballistics lines, instrumentation lines.

Complete engineering assistance available. For more information, write: Anaconda Metal Hose Division, Anaconda American Brass Company, P. O. Box 791, Waterbury 20, Connecticut. In Canada: Anaconda American Brass Ltd., Montreal 2, Quebec.

*Teflon is a DuPont trademark

Circle Number 54 on Reader-Service Card

ANACONDA®
METAL HOSE DIVISION

Anaconda Metal Hose

HAND IN HAND....

FS-124

NA TO

Peace . . . strength . . . freedom . . . are symboli-cally emphasized by the growing number of NATO countries who operate F-84 Thunderjets.

Belgium, Denmark, France, Greece, Italy, Netherlands, Norway and Turkey . . . in association with the USAF and Republic Aviation . . . are devel-oping these strong defenses against aggression.

REPUBLIC · AVIATION
FARMINGDALE, LONG ISLAND, N. Y.

Makers of the Mighty Thunderbolt · Thunderjet · XF-91 · F84F

Republic Aviation, 1952

No. 28 in a series:

Stiletto-shaped twin jet

Skyrocket—set world records in '53 of 1327 mph, 83,235 feet altitude

joins Douglas family of

high-speed research aircraft

Skystreak—world speed record 1948, 650 mph

—the supersonic Douglas X-3

Now to the record-breaking Sky-streak, the Douglas Skyrocket and the record-holding carrier-based Sky-ray, add this important experimental plane—the Douglas X-3.

Performance is secret, but a little can be told. Longer, heavier than a DC-3 transport, X-3 flies on wings smaller than a DC-3's tail—using conventional jet engines for *sustained* flight. X-3 has already contributed basic facts on insulation, refrigeration, and the use of heat-resistant *titanium*, while its payload of research instru-ments has been used to study the stresses and strains of flight at super-sonic speeds.

Design of X-3 is another example of Douglas leadership in aviation. *Faster and farther with a bigger pay-load is a basic Douglas rule.*

Enlist to fly with the U.S. Air Force

Depend on DOUGLAS **First in Aviation**

Voight Aircraft, 1954 ◄ *Douglas, 1954*

Today's Navy...power for peace

Your New Navy stands today as a nuclear-age bulwark of freedom, a powerful deterrent to aggression.

Leadership, manpower and mobility form the taut core of this strength. But to be an *effective force* the Navy must have *effective weapons.*

Chance Vought, with 40 years in the high performance military aircraft field, is dedicated to the complex science of developing and producing those vital weapons.

Record-breaking *Crusader* jet fighters, now in squadron status, and *Regulus* guided missiles, on station and ready for use when needed, represent a portion of Vought's growing contribution to Navy strength—a strength that means power for peace throughout the world.

CHANCE VOUGHT AIRCRAFT
INCORPORATED · DALLAS, TEXAS

Voight Aircraft ► *Sperry Gyroscope Company, 1954*

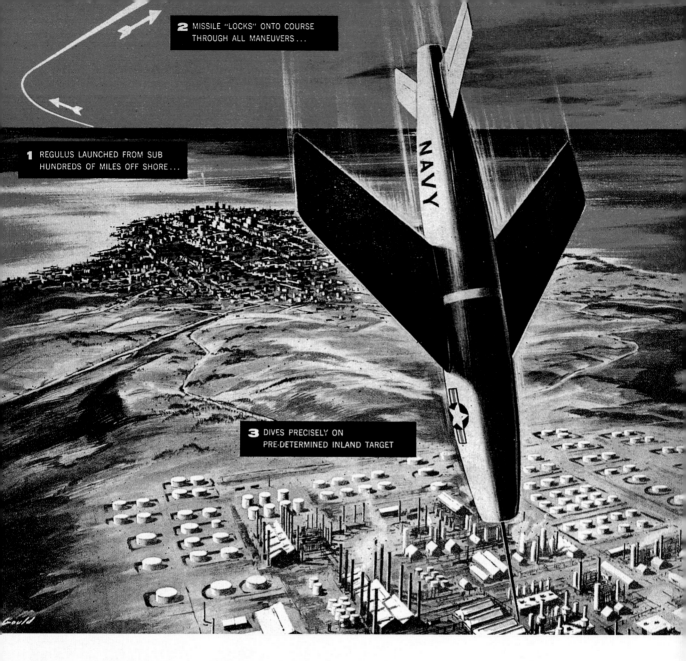

2 MISSILE "LOCKS" ONTO COURSE
THROUGH ALL MANEUVERS...

1 REGULUS LAUNCHED FROM SUB
HUNDREDS OF MILES OFF SHORE...

3 DIVES PRECISELY ON
PRE-DETERMINED INLAND TARGET

Sub-Launched Missile Gives Navy New Striking Power

CONTROL OF REGULUS HELD "UNCANNY"..."BIRDS" CAN BE RETRIEVED DURING TESTS

THE STORY BEHIND THE STORY:

■ When a guided missile launched from a submarine hundreds of miles off shore can be held to an accurate course at speeds approaching Mach 1, and precisely aimed at a specific inland target—that's news, *bad* news for a possible enemy. And, when costly models of the missile can be recovered and re-used time after time for evaluation and training, that's news, too — *good* news for American taxpayers.

■ On both counts, the Navy's Regulus, developed by Chance Vought Aircraft, Inc., is constantly in the headlines.

■ Providing the stability that holds Regulus on its course with a vise-like grip —and assuring recovery during tests—is a specially-designed Automatic Pilot, created by Sperry. Like its relative, the famous Sperry Gyropilot* Flight Control favored by the military and leading airlines, this electronic "brain" is sensitive to the slightest signal change in the flight path. Under its command, powerful servos or "muscles" of the control system

make instant corrections — fly Regulus unfailingly through intricate maneuvers at all speeds and at all altitudes.

■ There's a mighty difference between the automatic controls created by Sperry for this newest guided missile of the Navy, and those provided by Sperry for the Navy's first guided missile back in World War I days. But they're alike in this respect: Both resulted from an unmatched combination of skillful engineering *plus* specialized experience in electronics and gyroscopics, and precision in production.

*T M REG. U.S. PAT. OFF.

SPERRY *GYROSCOPE COMPANY*

DIVISION OF THE SPERRY CORPORATION

ALONG THE AVENUES
OF SPACE

tomorrow's spacecraft seek the mastery of a
universe. En route, environmental conditions will
be severe, imposing stringent requirements for

- Outstanding Reliability
- Personnel Safety
- High Performance
- Precision Control

To meet these demands, Aerojet has brought into
reality a variety of advanced liquid rocket concepts...
ABLESTAR, the first rocket engine to be restarted
in space...simple pressure-fed engines for
on-board propulsion...pulse rockets for attitude
control, variable thrust, and multiple restart.

Aerojet's leadership in liquid rocket power helps
propel America's space program from concept
to conquest.

LIQUID ROCKET PLANT

Aerojet-General®
C O R P O R A T I O N
Sacramento, California

A
SUBSIDIARY
OF

THE **GENERAL** TIRE

AND
RUBBER
COMPANY

Boron-fueled missile flies three times the speed of sound!

One of the most significant "breakthroughs" in modern science is the continuing discovery of new uses for the versatile, *high-energy* element Boron.

A ramjet missile burning one of these new Boron fuels has flown more than *three* times the speed of sound—or faster than 2,000 miles per hour!

Another form of this same atomic element, Boron, in Richfield Boron Gasoline dramatically increases the power and mileage of your motor car.

It's the West's *only* Boron motor fuel—and is guaranteed OVER 100 OCTANE!

Richfield Boron has the special ability to quench the red-hot carbon deposits in a car's combustion chamber that cause pre-ignition and knock—rob your engine of power and performance.

And because every drop burns cleanly and completely, you enjoy far more miles to each gallon.

So for *real driving economy*—YOUR BEST BUY IS BORON! With your very first tankful you get the ultimate in motoring pleasure and performance. Try Richfield Boron today—exclusively at Richfield stations throughout most Western states.

RICHFIELD BORON. GASOLINE
OVER 100 OCTANE

Richfield Boron Gasoline, 1959

New Boron fuels may enable Jets like the B-58 to circle the world non-stop!

Unlocking secrets of the versatile, atomic element Boron has already resulted in remarkable scientific advances.

Boron, for example, is a key factor in exotic fuels that could vastly increase the speed and range of supersonic jets like the B-58...even *double* the efficiency of jet engines!

In another form, this same high-energy element in Richfield Boron Gasoline steps up the power and mileage of your car with your very first tankful!

It's the *only* Boron motor fuel you can buy in the West ...and it's OVER 100 OCTANE.

Richfield Boron has the special ability to quench those red-hot carbon deposits in your car's combustion chamber that cause pre-ignition—that rob your engine of power and performance.

And because every drop burns cleanly and completely, you get *more miles* to each gallon.

Ask any user. He'll tell you Richfield Boron is your BEST GASOLINE BUY for smooth, knock-free performance...for *real driving economy!* Exclusively at Richfield stations throughout most Western states.

RICHFIELD BORON. GASOLINE
OVER 100 OCTANE

Richfield Boron Gasoline, 1959

World's largest Boron mine yields element vital in advanced fuels for jets and motor cars!

Millions have been spent to develop the world's largest Boron mine in California's Mojave desert. Here is the world's prime source of this versatile, atomic element—Boron.

Increasing quantities of Boron are now being utilized in new *high-energy* fuels to power jets, missiles and rockets to almost unbelievable speeds and altitudes.

In another form, this same Boron element in Richfield Boron Gasoline steps up the power and mileage of your car with your very first tankful.

Richfield Boron has the special ability to prevent pre-ignition in high-compression engines. And every drop burns exceptionally clean to give more miles to each gallon. If you want smoother, knock-free power in traffic or on the open road, YOUR BEST BUY IS BORON!

Throughout most Western states this is the only motor fuel that gives you BOTH—over 100 octane *and* Boron.

All cars that run on regular gasoline will perform their thrifty best on *improved* Richfield Hi-Octane Regular.

Thus, whatever make or model you drive, one of Richfield's two great "years-ahead" gasolines meets its every requirement for *maximum* performance and *real* driving economy.

RICHFIELD BORON. GASOLINE
OVER 100 OCTANE

Aerojet General Corporation, 1952 ◄ *Richfield Boron Gasoline, 1959*

Sprints from deck to stratosphere

HIS BEAT is the oceans of the world. His job, to challenge unknown intruders on our defense perimeters. A Navy pilot is a seagoing sentry on 24-hour duty.

A major role in this job of positive interception —and as far from our shores as possible—is being assigned to the Douglas F4D Skyray. Less than a minute after leaving the deck, Skyray can soar past the 10,000-ft. mark. Seconds later it's hissing through the stratosphere . . . 35,000 feet up . . . at the ready with rockets and cannons.

This rate of climb comes as no surprise. Skyray also holds the world's official F.A.I. sea level speed records for the 3- and 100-kilometre courses.

Douglas F4D Skyray—fastest carrier-based interceptor. Performance of agile Skyray continues the Douglas tradition of "faster and farther with a bigger payload." Yet performance figures are meaningless without a skilled pilot at the controls. If you are interested in a career as a Naval Aviator, write Nav. Cad. Washington 25, D. C.

Depend on *DOUGLAS*   First in Aviation

Douglas Aviation, 1956   ► *Richfield Boron, 1959*   ►► *General Electric, 1953*

Boron is factor in tremendous cruising range of *USS Nautilus*

Almost daily, in America's research laboratories, scientists are discovering new uses for the unusually versatile element Boron.

For example, Boron contributes to the life of the nuclear core in the *USS Nautilus* and is a factor in the tremendous cruising range of America's first atomic submarine on such voyages as its historic run under the North Pole.

This same atomic element, Boron, in Richfield Boron Gasoline gives your car extra power and mileage!

Richfield Boron is the West's *only* Boron motor fuel. It is guaranteed OVER 100 OCTANE.

Richfield Boron has the special ability to quench those red-hot carbon deposits in your car's combustion chamber that cause pre-ignition—rob your engine of power and performance.

And because every drop burns cleanly and completely, you get more miles to each gallon.

For smooth, knock-free performance and *real driving economy* —YOUR BEST BUY IS BORON! Exclusively at Richfield stations throughout most Western states.

RICHFIELD BORON.
GASOLINE

OVER **100** OCTANE

ON SHORT RUNWAYS, AIR FORCE PILOTS CAN SAVE THEIR BRAKES AND TIRES BY RELEASING SPECIAL LANDING PARACHUTE FROM THE TAIL OF THE B-47.

POWERED AND PROTECTED BY G.E
THE B-47 IS OUR FASTEST BOMBER

Six G-E Jet Engines Power Boeing Bomber: G-E Armament System Protects It

The Air Force's B-47, fastest known bomber in the world, is a sleek, swept-wing aircraft, powered by six mighty G-E jet engines. A medium bomber of 600 mph class, it can fly 3000 miles, at an altitude of over seven miles. For protection against enemy attack, it is being equipped with a General Electric radar-controlled gunfire system which can operate even at night or in poor visibility. The complex plane is manned by three highly trained Air Force officers—pilot, co-pilot, and navigator-bombardier.

The Air Force called upon General Electric to supply the power and armament systems for the B-47 because military men recognized G.E.'s long history of engineering leadership. For instance, General Electric has supplied armament systems for several other types of military aircraft before the Boeing B-47, turbo-superchargers for piston-engine planes since 1921, and jet engines since 1942. And, of course, the Air Force knew that General Electric would have the production help of thou-

sands of "small-business" subcontractors and suppliers. Our nation's defense is our most important problem, and it takes all kinds of businesses, large and small, all working together, assure our continued freedom. General Electric Company, Schenectady 5, N. Y.   230

You can put your confidence in—

GENERAL ⊛ ELECTRIC

UNITED STATES AIR FORCE

1903—Wright Brothers make first powered flight at Kitty Hawk

1910—Eugene Ely takes off from deck of converted battleship

1918—American pilots engage in daring aerial combat over France

1919—Navy flying boat makes first successful trans-Atlantic flight

1921—G-E supercharged Air Corps plane sets altitude record

1942—G-E powered Bell P-59, first US jet, test-flown at Muroc, Calif.

1944—Boeing B-29 uses first G-E electronic gunfire system

1953—G-E powered North American F-86 outscores MIG

50TH ANNIVERSARY OF POWERED FLIGHT — PROGRESS — SECURITY

G-E ENGINEERS rely upon their experience, ingenuity, and mechanical aids such as the digital computer to accomplish such engineering triumphs as jet engines and radar fire-control systems.

DIGITAL

PRODUCTION of complex equipment depends upon advanced engineering techniques and skilled use of modern, costly machinery. Often, a new machine must be designed for one specific job.

A-OK
FOR TOMORROW'S MISSILE DEMANDS

MIDVAC STEELS OPEN NEW HORIZONS FOR DESIGN ENGINEERS

Where maximum reliability in high temperature ranges and minimum rejects are required . . . plus larger sizes for the new missiles, Midvac Steels have answered and are ready to solve the problems of many engineers. These ultra-clean steels are now available in ingots up to 60 inches in diameter, weighing 80,000 pounds.

Produced by consumable electrode vacuum melting Midvac Steels have improved workability and ingot soundness not attainable by other methods of melting. Segregation of inclusions is reduced and better mechanical properties are assured in all super alloy steels.

Whether it be a large rocket motor, missile case, nuclear reactor part or an "extra-size" commercial product Midvac Steels offer the same high reliability. For complete data and technical booklet write to . . .

MIDVALE-HEPPENSTALL COMPANY
NICETOWN, PHILADELPHIA, PA.
SUBSIDIARY OF HEPPENSTALL COMPANY, PITTSBURGH, PA.

Midvac Steels ◇MH◇

VACUUM AND CONSUMABLE ELECTRODE STEELS · BACK-UP ROLL SLEEVES · FORGED STEEL ROLLS · FORGINGS
RINGS · PRESSURE VESSELS · INDUSTRIAL KNIVES · DIE BLOCKS · MATERIALS HANDLING EQUIPMENT

Hitco, 1952 ◄ *Midvac Steel, 1952*

Speed

Brown and Root's record
of early project completion
means a bonus of unexpected production;
which in analysis,
presents a reduction in
plant cost.

BROWN & ROOT, INC.
Engineers · Constructors
POST OFFICE BOX 3, HOUSTON 1, TEXAS

No. One Wall Street, New York 3, New York

Brown & Root de Mexico, S.A. de C.V., Mexico City, Mexico

Brown & Root Construcciones, S.A., Caracas, Venezuela

Brown & Root, Ltd., Edmonton, Alberta, Canada

Brown & Root, S.A., Panama City, Panama

CABLE ADDRESS—BROWNBILT

Brown & Root, Inc., 1957

10 years of post-war progress in military aviation

These are some of the aircraft and missiles developed and built by Douglas within the past decade to provide solutions for almost every logistic and tactical problem confronting our military establishment.

But more important to our national defense than the aircraft themselves, is the experienced personnel that brings them into being. At Douglas this experience dates back 35 years, and is spread among thousands of men and women whose com-

bined talents made possible: Globemaster's lift of 50,000-lb. payloads; Skyray's record of 753.4 m.p.h.; Skyrocket's speed of 1327 m.p.h.; new military horizons opened by such jets as the A3D, B-66 and A4D; guided missiles like Nike and rockets like Honest John.

This vast arsenal of experience made possible the Douglas concept of more performance per pound of plane; which is another way of saying—*more defense for your tax dollar.*

AD Skyraiders
Called world's most versatile aircraft

C-118A—R6D
Air Force and Navy versions of the DC-6A

F4D Skyray
Only carrier plane to hold speed record

C-124 Globemaster
Biggest production transport, 25-ton payload

Nike / Rocket
Supersonic anti-aircraft missile already in service

D558-2 Skyrocket
First plane to fly double speed of sound

A4D Skyhawk
Can take off from small carrier with A-bomb

Honest John
Delivers atomic or high explosive warhead

A3D Skywarrior
Navy's largest carrier-based bomber

RB-66
Versatile Air Force reconnaissance bomber

YC-124B
First military transport to use turboprop power

X-3
Jet research plane, performance classified

F3D Skyknight
Twin-jet, radar-guided night fighter

Depend on
DOUGLAS
First in Aviation

Douglas Aviation, 1951

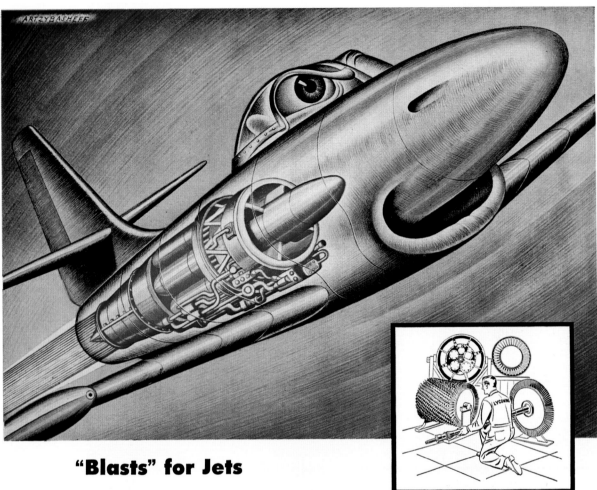

"Blasts" for Jets

To gun a jet to incredible speeds . . . to power it through the intricate twists and turns of combat . . . to "pour it on" in climbs, in dives, in instantaneous bursts of speed—the mighty engine of a jet plane demands parts that are tough, precise and unfailing. To assure such vital performance, General Electric looks to Lycoming as a leading supplier of the major components that go into its superb J-47 jet engine.

Whether you require precision parts of *any* kind . . . or need high-volume production, product development—or a *complete* air-cooled power plant—Lycoming's extensive research facilities and well-rounded experience stand ready to serve you. *Whatever* your problem—look to Lycoming!

For a more complete story on Lycoming's varied abilities and facilities, write—on your company letterhead—for the interesting, illustrated booklet "Let's Look at Lycoming."

For major engine parts that put the "blast" in jets,

Lycoming is one of

General Electric's

leading sources of

precision production.

AIR-COOLED ENGINES FOR AIRCRAFT AND INDUSTRIAL USES • PRECISION-AND-VOLUME-MACHINE PARTS • GRAY-IRON CASTINGS • STEEL-PLATE FABRICATION

LOOK TO **LYCOMING** FOR RESEARCH
FOR PRECISION PRODUCTION

LYCOMING-SPENCER DIVISION · AVCO MANUFACTURING CORPORATION · WILLIAMSPORT, PA.
BRIDGEPORT-LYCOMING DIVISION · STRATFORD, CONN.

This one was only a test (atomic detonation in Nevada).

Big reason for better roads

"It has been determined as a matter of Federal policy," reports the President's Advisory Committee on a National Highway Program, "that at least 70 million people would have to be evacuated from target areas in case of threatened or actual enemy attack. No urban area in the country today has highway facilities equal to this task."

But such highways are coming: the 41,000-mile National System of Interstate and Defense Highways.

This tremendous network of no-stop freeways offers other vital defense benefits, too. Obviously, it will speed the movement of men and materiel. But more importantly, it will encourage the decentralization of our industries. Already more and more plants are following these fine new roads out of congested cities, out into the wide countryside just minutes away by swift, safe freeways.

WHAT EVERY CITIZEN SHOULD KNOW

Don't allow the Interstate-Defense Highway Program to bog down. Find out how it will serve you, how much it will actually cost, how long it will take to finish. Send today for a free copy of an informative booklet, "The Road Ahead." Write Dept. 12T, Caterpillar Tractor Co., Peoria, Illinois, U.S.A.

CATERPILLAR
REG. U.S. PAT. OFF.

Diesel Engines • Tractors • Motor Graders • Earthmoving Equipment

THE WORLD'S NO. 1 ROAD BUILDING EQUIPMENT

Atomic Energy...

...or Medicine

*Fabricated by
an equipment builder
using the Lukenomics principle.*

Here's a sample of Lukenomics coordination at work. For high purity in Chloromycetin—vital new antibiotic—acid adjustment tanks and fermentation units were built of Lukens Inconel-Clad Steel with specially polished interiors. *Bonus* results: low initial cost, minimum maintenance, special resistance to corrosion threats of salt and other chemicals. And—by use of *clad*—the builder also saved critical amounts of one of today's scarce metals.

. . . whatever your business, if it depends on a production or process operation, consider this: *in the current emergency, how long can you keep on producing?* Here's an idea that may help.

There are progressive *equipment builders* who specialize today in delivering new production potentials despite current shortages. Coordination of the major factors in equipment design, including problem exploration, is the key.

This coordination of effort we call Lukenomics. Through it, such equipment builders combine their specialized experience, and that of competent designers and engineers, with Lukens' knowledge of materials, their production and use.

We can put you in touch with such builders. Write today, outlining your problem. Manager, Marketing Service, Lukens Steel Company, 476 Lukens Building, Coatesville, Pa.

Promote steel production generally—speed sale of your scrap.

LUKENS L

LUKENS STEEL COMPANY

OVER 140 YEARS EXPERIENCE AS THE WORLD'S LEADING PRODUCER OF SPECIALTY STEEL PRODUCTS

STEEL PLATE   **CLAD STEELS**   **HEADS**   **STEEL PLATE SHAPES**

Even this cloud

as a silver lining

Enrico Fermi atomic power plant *is under way near Detroit through the joint efforts of 18 electric companies. A group of equipment manufacturers and the Atomic Energy Commission are also associated in the project.*

Dresden, Illinois, plant *is being developed by 7 electric light and power companies, their equipment manufacturers, and with the co-operation of the AEC.*

Yankee atomic-electric plant *is being developed by 12 New England electric companies. A number of equipment manufacturers and the AEC are participating.*

What will atomic-electric power plants look like?

Among the atomic-electric power plants now under way, three will look like the drawings above when completed.

Although they appear somewhat alike, each involves different methods, different materials, a different type of atomic reactor

or "furnace." That's because the electric companies, the equipment manufacturers and the U. S. Atomic Energy Commission — who are all participating in atomic development — are searching for the best ways to produce electricity, using atomic energy as fuel.

The development of atomic-powered electric plants is the latest stage in bringing plentiful electricity to America. You can be sure that electric company skills and experience, acquired in 75 years of service, are being applied to this great new job.

America's Independent Electric Light and Power Companies*

Company names on request through this magazine

Inco Nickel Company ◄ *Atomic Electric Power, 1957*   ► *American Bosch Arma Corporation, 1959*

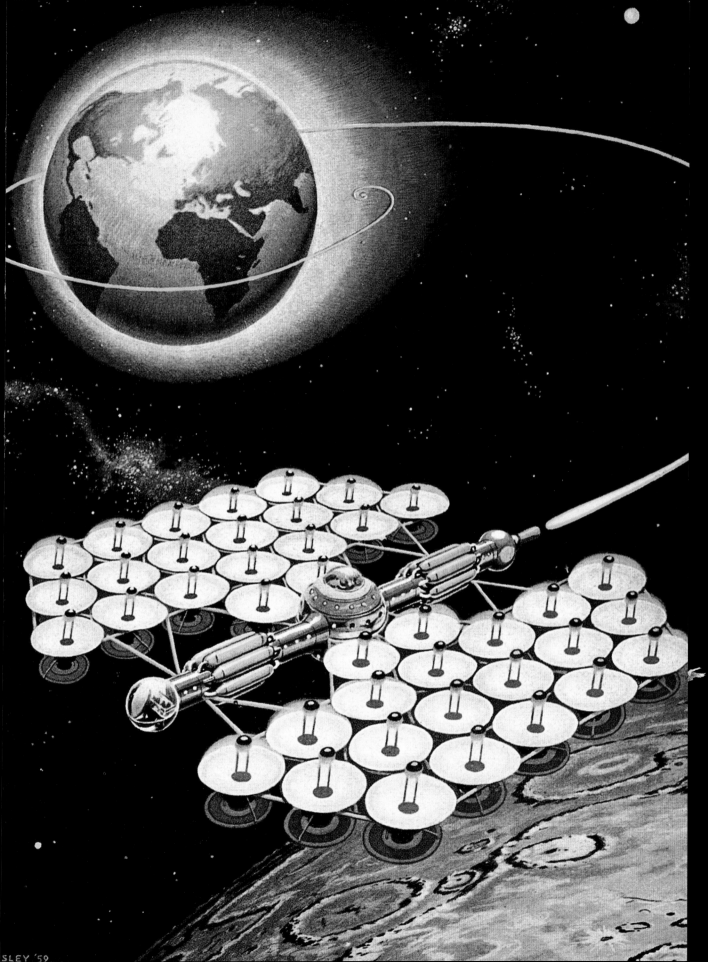

Margin for Error . . . *None!*

You swing into your final approach. At precisely the right instant the Landing Signal Officer flags you to cut your power—and you're aboard! ☆ Such skill and precision is indicative of that which is required today in *every* phase of the aircraft industry. The bearings in modern jet turbines, for instance, must be held to accurate tolerances measured in millionths of an inch. That's why the leading jet turbine manufacturers specify Bower aircraft bearings first. Their exceptional high quality and unerring precision allow Bower bearings to stand unbelievable turbine speeds and temperatures—that match the supersonic speeds of today's jet aircraft—*with a minimum of lubrication.* ☆ Whatever *you* produce, if it uses bearings, specify Bower! Choose from a complete line of tapered, straight and journal roller bearings for every field of transportation and industry.

BOWER ROLLER BEARING DIVISION
FEDERAL-MOGUL-BOWER BEARINGS, INC., DETROIT 14, MICH.

IDEALLY SUITED TO HIGH-SPEED OPERATION

Built to hold their precision indefinitely, these aircraft bearings are recommended wherever superior quality and high-speed operation are required. For some applications, a special alloy steel—developed jointly by Bower and several aircraft companies—is used.

 BOWER

ROLLER BEARINGS

Bower Roller Bearings, 1953 ◀ *Bower Roller Bearings, 1957*

FLYING SAUCERS...REAL!

One type of instrument a weather balloon carries aloft is the radiosonde. What this inexpensive little weather observer can do is just short of magic . . . for it reports continuously—by radio—the temperature, pressure, and humidity of the upper air.

Key parts of radiosonde are temperature and humidity elements and a disc-shaped, pressure-responsive diaphragm that supplies the all-important pressure "reference".

United States Gauge has a special gift for making aneroid diaphragms or cells—a distinction acquired over many years, and narrowed to ± two-millibar accuracy by uncompromising requirements for similar cells in complex parachute control and navigation instruments.

U. S. Gauge makes radiosonde diaphragms from Ni-Span C—an alloy with a constant thermal modulus—to cancel temperature effects. Compensating thermal influence of the instrument components within the diaphragm design was another—and tough—problem. USG licked it—hopes to tackle one for you.

If you require diaphragms like those we've described . . . if you have any product in need of accurate temperature or pressure-sensing elements or instruments, let USG creative instrumentation go to work for you. United States Gauge, Division of American Machine and Metals, Inc., Sellersville, Pa.

PRODUCTS OF UNITED STATES GAUGE . . . Absolute Pressure Gauges Aircraft Instruments • Air Volume Controls • Altitude Gauges • Boiler Gauges Chemical Gauges • Mercury Gas and Vapor Dial Thermometers • Glass Tube and Industrial Thermometers • Flow Meters • Inspectors' Test Gauges Precision Laboratory Test Gauges • Marine, Ship and Air-Brake Gauges Voltmeters • Ammeters • Welding Gauges

OTHER DIVISIONS OF AMERICAN MACHINE AND METALS, INC. AT SELLERSVILLE, PA.: GOTHAM INSTRUMENTS, AND AUTOBAR SYSTEMS

Creative Instrumentation

UNITED STATES GAUGE

USG

GARCIA

United States Gauge, 1953

▶ *Thiskol Chemical Corporation, 1957*

FRONTIERS UNLIMITED

for solid propellant rocketry

From the deadly **FALCON** to the space-sounding **NIKE-CAJUN**; the short range **LACROSSE** to the massive **RV-A-10**; the powerful **MATADOR** booster, the formidable **NIKE HERCULES**—THIOKOL solid propellant rocket engines have proven their remarkable versatility, ruggedness and power.

Their future possibilities appear almost unlimited. THIOKOL solid propellant propulsion systems can be specifically designed to fit a wide range of rocket power requirements.

THIOKOL rocket engines are simple and low cost in construction. Needing no complex launching techniques, they are ready for instant action even under extreme environmental conditions. This is why military and civilian contractors have specified THIOKOL solid propellant systems for many of our nation's top rockets and guided missiles.

If you are a mechanical, electronic, chemical or aeronautical engineer, a chemist or physicist interested in joining the expanding field of solid propellant rocketry, you are invited to send your inquiries to THIOKOL CHEMICAL CORP., Redstone Div., Huntsville, Ala.; Longhorn Div., Marshall, Texas; Elkton Div., Elkton, Md.; and Utah Div., Brigham City, Utah.

Thiokol ® CHEMICAL CORPORATION

780 North Clinton Avenue, Trenton 7, N. J.

® Registered trademark of the THIOKOL Chemical Corporation for its liquid polymers, rocket propellants, plasticizers and

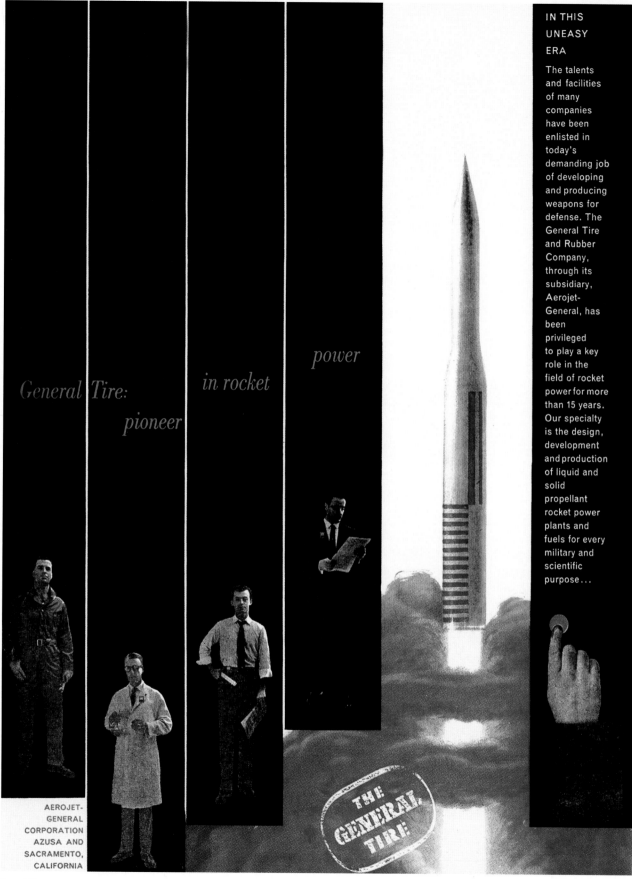

General Tire: pioneer in rocket power

AEROJET-
GENERAL
CORPORATION
AZUSA AND
SACRAMENTO,
CALIFORNIA

THE GENERAL TIRE

General Tire, 1955

► *General Tire, 1958*

General Tire:

pioneer in

rocket power

DESTINATION: *known*

earth-shaking...ear-shattering...
eye-searing, these are words that
partially describe the terrifying
take-off of today's
rocket powered missiles.
Aerojet-General is a pioneer in this
vital new field and the nation's leading
producer of both liquid and solid
propellant rocket power plants.
Aerojet-General is a subsidiary of
The General Tire and Rubber Company.

ENGINEERING BEYOND THE EXPECTED

0'59 PB

AWAKE IN THE DEEP

Soon American seamen aboard swift, nuclear-powered submarines will patrol "Awake in the Deep"...armed with the U.S. Navy's devastating POLARIS fleet ballistic missile. Should they be forced to enter unfriendly waters on a mission of retaliation, a Packard Bell "Digitizer" will play a leading role in the missile's underwater or surface launching. This is one of a series of electronic production and pre-launch check-out devices developed by Packard Bell Electronics for the Missiles and Space Division of Lockheed Aircraft. It is a militarized version of commercial equipment created through company sponsored research...another Packard Bell achievement based upon 34 years of "Engineering Beyond The Expected" for the home, industry and national defense.

To engineers of exceptional ability and earning power
Packard Bell offers *opportunities beyond the expected*, too.

 Packard Bell Electronics

LOS ANGELES 64, CALIFORNIA

Packard Bell Electronics, 1959

▶ *Transitron Electronic Corporation, 1959*

wherever there's electronics...

there's Transitron

From below the sea, launched from a nuclear submarine, the Polaris missile will streak hundreds of miles through the skie[s] directly to its target. Transitron's tiny, super-reliable semiconductors play a major part in launching and guiding Polaris through water sky and to final destination. At Transitron, more than 4000 skilled employees are working constantly and exclusively to develop high qualit[y] silicon and germanium semiconductors. In missiles as in radar, computers, atomic subs, communications, jets and thousands of other militar[y] and commercial applications — wherever there's electronics . . . there's Transitron, leading the field in advanced semiconductor reliabilit[y]

TRANSISTORS · DIODES · RECTIFIERS · SWITCHES · REGULATORS · REFERENCES

Transitron

electronic corporation · wakefield, massachusetts

SALES OFFICES IN PRINCIPAL CITIES THROUGHOUT THE U. S. A. · CABLE ADDRESS: TRELCO

CITATION

TO A LADY WITH 20mm CLAWS

Her ancestors were Grumman Wildcats and Hellcats. Two-thirds of the Jap plane tally was theirs in World War II. They were first getting there, first in combat.

Same with her. She was on the job in Korea December 10, 1950. And then she really flew and fought with Marine Fighter Squadron 311. She racked up 1,002 hours, a total of 445 combat missions. She dropped over 400,000 pounds of bombs. She fired so much ammo, almost 100,000 rounds, she wore out sixteen 20 mm cannons.

Then, as if not content with that record, she transferred to Navy. From the carrier deck of the U.S.S. Boxer, she flew 63 more successful sorties in over 160 combat hours.

And so, because the Marines respect a lady and a fighter, they gave a citation to Grumman Panther jet fighter WL-2, the oldest, toughest combat plane of her kind in Korea.

"...Her Purple Hearts are the scars inflicted by enemy fire, and of these she had her full share. Her record is more than an example of exceptional performance of duty; it is a tribute to those loyal and competent workmen who brought this aircraft into being, and to the individual Marines who maintained her and took her into battle. Her record of service has been in keeping with the highest traditions of the United States Naval Service."

For all the Grumman people who contributed to Panther jets and swept-wing Cougar jets—thanks.

GRUMMAN AIRCRAFT ENGINEERING CORPORATION • BETHPAGE • LONG ISLAND • NEW YORK
DESIGNERS AND BUILDERS ALSO OF THE COUGAR JET FIGHTER (IN FORMATION ON THE LEFT), THE ALBATROSS TRIPHIBIAN, AND THE S2F-1 SUB-KILLER

The famed Air-Ground Team of the U. S. Marine Corps can offer you a rewarding career.

Grumman Citation

LOCKHEED X-7 RAMJET
BLASTS U.S. MISSILES AHEA

...y's most arresting new weapons for the ...n's "Perimeter of Defense" are the ramjet-...red interceptor missiles. Capable of speeds ...he rumsonic realm—far faster than today's ...rsonic jets—these missiles are guided in ...t. Spotted at strategic points in our continental ...nse system, interceptor missiles will guard the ...: wherever invaders might venture.

...heed Missile Systems Division designed and ...t the X-7 to expedite interceptor missile de-...pment. Engineered as a ramjet test vehicle, ...X-7 tests the mettle of powerful new engines.

... sophisticated telemetering instrumentation, ...loped by Lockheed scientists, is crammed into

every available space in the X-7 "flying laboratory." In stratospheric flight, the X-7 transmits as many as 100 measurements—speed, altitude, aerodynamic behavior—almost simultaneously down to earth monitoring stations.

Here, Missile Systems Division engineers analyze results of hundreds of flights to insure the performance of present-day engines—and to amass data vital to the development of radically new ramjet engines. After flight the X-7 is lowered gently to earth by parachute—saving millions of dollars for the taxpayers and countless hours of manufacturing time.

At Lockheed Missile Systems Division more than

5,000 engineers, scientists and technicians working on high-priority missile programs. I ities at Van Nuys, California, are in full opera New missile research laboratories are at Palo California, and additional engineering and m facturing facilities are being built at Sunnyva few miles away.

Lockheed's continuing contributions to fu missile developments have created many nev gineering and scientific career openings. If value the opportunity to rise in your professi live and work in pleasant and healthful surro ings, write: Research & Engineering Staff, 1 heed Missile Systems Division, Sunnyvale, C

LOCKHEED MISSILE SYSTEMS DIVISION · Van Nuys, Palo Alto, Sunnyvale, California

Lockheed, 1956

Behind the scenes on the B-47

Here is the Boeing B-47—the sleek jet-propelled bomber that eats up distance at a rate of more than 10 miles per minute.

Operating such a swift air giant demands a range of controls that must represent the last word in quality.

Boeing looks to Foote Bros. for the production of actuators and power units which are aiding in the amazing performance of this master of the skies.

On many of America's leading aircraft and aircraft engines, you will find equipment manufactured by Foote Bros. —chosen because of the years of experience of this company in producing gears and actuators light in weight, achieving new extremes in accuracy, capable of traveling at high speed, designed to fit a confined space envelope.

FOOTE BROS. GEAR AND MACHINE CORPORATION
Dept. A · 4545 South Western Boulevard · Chicago 9, Ill.

Landing Gear Actuator—One of the Units Produced by Foote Bros. for the Boeing B-47.

FOOTE BROS.

Better Power Transmission Through Better Gears

Foote Bros., 1956

Grumman Aircraft, 1953

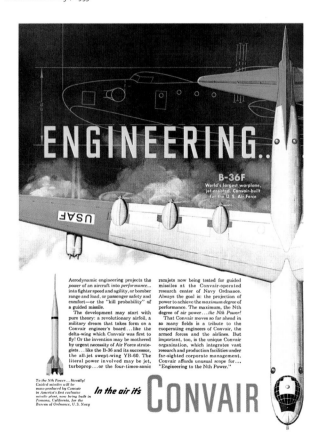

Convair

Torrington Bearings, 1950

And the winner is...

Based On Principles Learned At Hiroshima And Nagasaki

Could your house survive a five megaton H-bomb? You bet, if your family residence was constructed of blast-resistant concrete. Built from technology "based on principles learned at Hiroshima and Nagasaki," this home for the paranoid Cold War years offered a worrisome nation some momentary mental relief from that awful Russian menace. Build your house out of concrete, the ad implies, and that gnawing Communist aggression could be dismissed along with the hard realities of nuclear power. Right.

Mit der Erfahrung von Hiroshima und Nagasaki

Könnte Ihr Haus einer Fünf-Megatonnen-Wasserstoffbombe standhalten? Gewiss doch, wenn Ihr Eigenheim aus bomben-sicherem Beton gebaut wurde. Auf dem Stand der Technik »mit der Erfahrung von Hiroshima und Nagasaki« bot dieses für die paranoiden Jahre des Kalten Krieges entwickelte Haus einer verängstigten Nation so etwas wie zeitweilige seelische Erleichterung von der gräulichen russischen Bedrohung. Bau dein Haus aus Beton, deutet diese Werbung an, und die zersetzende kommunistische Aggression lässt sich mitsamt den harten Realitäten atomarer Macht aus der Welt schaffen. Dann mal ran.

Selon des principes découlant de Hiroshima et Nagasaki

Votre maison peut-elle survivre à une bombe H de cinq mégatonnes? Sans problème, si elle est construite avec du béton anti-explosions. Conçue selon des principes « découlant de Hiroshima et Nagasaki », cette maison propose à une nation inquiète, en ces années de Guerre Froide et de paranoïa régnante, un réconfort moral momentané face à la terrible menace russe. Bâtissez votre maison en béton, suggère la réclame, et l'obsession de l'agression communiste pourrait s'envoler, tout comme la sinistre réalité de l'énergie nucléaire. Bravo.

Houses for the Atomic Age!

Now you can protect precious lives with

An all-concrete blast-resistant house

Here's a house with all the advantages of any concrete house—PLUS protection from atomic blasts at minimum cost.

A firesafe, attractive, *low-annual-cost* house, it provides comfortable living—PLUS a refuge for your family in this atomic age.

The blast-resistant house design is based on principles learned at Hiroshima and Nagasaki and at Eniwetok and Yucca Flats. It has a reinforced concrete first floor and roof and reinforced concrete masonry walls. The walls, the floor and the roof are tied together securely with reinforcement to form a rigidly integrated house that the engineers calculate will resist blast pressures 40% closer to bursts than conventionally-built houses.

Anywhere in the concrete basement of the house would be much safer than above ground but a special shelter area has been provided in this basement to protect occupants from blast pressures expected at distances as close as 3,600 feet from ground zero of a bomb with an explosive force equivalent to 20,000 tons of TNT. This shelter area affords protection from radiation, fire and flying debris as well. And the same shelter area also can serve as a refuge from the lesser violence of tornadoes, hurricanes and earthquakes.

The safety features built into this blast-resistant house are estimated by the architect and engineer to raise the cost less than 10%.

Concrete always has been known for its remarkable strength and durability. That's why it can be used economically to build houses with a high degree of safety from atomic blasts.

Like all concrete structures, blast-resistant concrete houses are moderate in first cost, require little maintenance and give long years of service. The result is *low-annual-cost* shelter. Write for folder.

PORTLAND CEMENT ASSOCIATION
Dept. A6-9, 33 West Grand Avenue, Chicago 10, Illinois
A national organization to improve and extend the uses of portland cement and concrete through scientific research and engineering field work.

Interiors of a blast-resistant house have all the charm and livability of conventional houses.

Portland Cement Association, 1955

Lincoln, 1950

Nash, 1950

Oldsmobile, 1952 ◄ *Mercury, 1950*

Lincoln, 1950 ► *Lincoln, 1950* ►► *Pontiac, 1950* ►►► *Pontiac, 1951*

Exciting to look at—thrilling to drive!

Lincoln for 1951

*All Lincoln cars equipped with improved HYDRA-MATIC transmission at extra cost.

THERE'S A NEW and exciting Lincoln for you to see! A sleek, debonair car with the look of an adventurer... with a giant heart and a gypsy spirit ...as your first ride will prove!

For under its gleaming hood is the great Lincoln V-type 8-cylinder engine, eager as a thoroughbred colt! Anxious to take you places.

And how you *will* go places. With this mighty Lincoln engine coupled with HYDRA-MATIC*, you've got the freedom and power of an eagle in soaring flight—right under your very toe!

And *inside* this dramatically new Lincoln, there's exciting news as well! Tailor-fashioned upholsteries...a new kind of smart and modern motorcar decor...and Fiberglas soundproofing. Yet all of this car luxury costs less than you imagine!

Arrange with your Lincoln dealer for your personal driving experience in a glamorous new Lincoln or the magnificent new Lincoln Cosmopolitan, finest of 1951's fine cars. These cars enhance the great and growing Lincoln reputation for creating the best of everything in automobiles. If you've looked forward to the day when your car will be the one most exciting to look at—most thrilling to drive—the new Lincolns await your inspection.
Lincoln Division • Ford Motor Company

Lincoln—Nothing could be finer

Dollar for Dollar you can't beat a

Pontiac

All it needs is _you_ behind the wheel!

Dollar for Dollar you can't beat a
Pontiac

Wonderful—in Sunlight or Moonlight!

first
in No-Shift Driving at lowest prices

Drive a Chevrolet with Powerglide Automatic Transmission* and you'll agree it's first and finest for *no-shift driving* at lowest cost. All you have to do is steer, accelerate and stop. There's no clutch pedal—no gears to shift in normal driving. And you glide through all speed ranges with a smooth, unbroken flow of power.

CHEVROLET

and finest
in Valve-in-Head road action with economy

Your own tests will tell you the only way to equal Chevrolet's brand of thrills and thrift is to *buy a Chevrolet!* For here's a combination of acceleration, hill-climbing ability, dependability and economy exclusive to this one low-priced car. That's true whether you choose a Chevrolet with the 105-h.p. Valve-in-Head Engine and Powerglide Automatic Transmission,* or a Chevrolet with the highly improved standard Valve-in-Head Engine and Synchro-Mesh Transmission.

Combination of Powerglide Automatic Transmission and 105-h.p. Engine optional on De Luxe models at extra cost.

CHEVROLET

at lowest cost
only low-priced car with all these fine car features

Most pleasing of all, Chevrolet brings you feature after feature of the highest-priced cars at lowest prices. For example, Body by Fisher for the finest beauty, comfort and safety. Center-Point Steering and the Unitized Knee-Action Ride for outstanding steering-ease and riding-ease. Curved Windshield with Panoramic Visibility and Proved Certi-Safe Hydraulic Brakes for maximum safety-protection. Buy Chevrolet and you buy the car that's *first and finest at lowest cost!*

CHEVROLET

AMERICA'S BEST SELLER ... AMERICA'S BEST BUY

Chevrolet, 1950

This year it's clear...

Kaiser's the car!

1951 Kaiser DeLuxe 4-door sedan...one of 6 body styles and 12 models. Hydra-Matic Drive available in all models at extra cost. Styled by DARRIN

1951 Kaiser... the only car with
Anatomic Design !

1951 Kaiser sedan Wins World's Highest Honor

Grand Prix D'Honneur at Cannes, France

From the sensational new Safety-Cushion Padded Instrument Panel to the smart, continental High-Line rear Fenders, the beautiful KAISER is the *all-new* car for 1951. You look out through the biggest of all windshields, unhampered by thick corner posts, for the widest vision in any car. Wide doors, curving high into the roof, let you step in without knocking off your hat. The Tuck-Away Tire Well gives you extra trunk space because the spare tire is stored under the luggage compartment ... not in it!

The great Kaiser Supersonic Engine is the most efficient engine on the highway today. Inside and out, Kaiser's the *all-new* car for 1951. See it—drive it at your Kaiser-Frazer dealer's today!

Built to Better the Best on the Road!

Kaiser, 1950

It's in the '51 FORD—
new FORDOMATIC
AUTOMATIC TRANSMISSION

FORD

Now Borg-Warner and the Ford Motor Company, working hand in hand, bring you Fordomatic Drive ... the newest of all automatic transmissions.

Today you enjoy the crowning benefit of the Borg-Warner-Ford association that began long before the famed Model "T". It's *Fordomatic Drive*, the no-shift transmission that creates a new standard of driving enjoyment. Engine power is translated into a new kind of ride, luxurious in its hushed smoothness. 92% of the work of driving is done for you. It's pleasure all the way. Command with the gas pedal—Fordomatic response is positive, *instant*, whether you want to take off, cruise, or climb hills.

There's sure, solid braking by the engine for safe hill descents. Rocking in mud or snow is even easier than with standard transmissions. And to top it all—you get real gas economy.

Fordomatic gives you traditional Ford quality, the result of specialized Ford skills. In addition, you benefit from famous B-W engineering and production that have served the fast-growing auto industry steadily since its infancy. Today, in 19 out of the 20 makes of cars you'll find B-W parts such as transmissions, overdrives, clutches, universal joints, propeller shafts, radiators, and timing chains.

 new "JET-AWAY" PERFORMANCE
You sweep out smooth and fast with Fordomatic Drive. No hesitation, no need to race the engine. For steep grades, for fast passing, this new drive lets you summon a super-power range at a touch of the gas.

new FULL MILEAGE FROM EVERY GALLON
Fordomatic automatically selects the right drive ratio for you on the instant to give you maximum driving efficiency and economy at all times.

 DANGER STEEP HILL

 new SAFETY DOWN HILLS
With this drive, the engine can actually help to slow the car on down-grades. For extra safety, get from "low" to "low" at any time you desire.

ALMOST EVERY AMERICAN BENEFITS EVERY DAY FROM THE 185 PRODUCTS MADE BY
BORG-WARNER

These units from BORG-WARNER, Executive Offices, 310 S. Michigan Ave., Chicago: BORG & BECK • BORG-WARNER INTERNATIONAL • BORG-WARNER SERVICE PARTS • CALUMET STEEL • DETROIT GEAR • DETROIT VAPOR STOVE • FRANKLIN STEEL • INGERSOLL STEEL • LONG MANUFACTURING • LONG BELL LUMBER LTD. • MARBON • MARVEL-SCHEBLER PRODUCTS • MECHANICS UNIVERSAL JOINT • MORSE CHAIN • MOTOR GEAR, LTD. • NORGE • NORGE-HEAT • PESCO PRODUCTS • ROCKFORD CLUTCH • SPRING DIVISION • WARNER AUTOMOTIVE PARTS • WARNER GEAR • WARNER GEAR CO., LTD.

Handsome on the Highway...
Husky and Smooth in the Hills!

Take a good long look at the Fords go by. There's "Fashion" written in every low, lovely line! Outside, inside... from sparkling-fresh, baked-on body colors to smartly tailored upholstery... Ford's America's best-dressed car!

What's more, Ford's heavy-gauge all-steel "Lifeguard" Body and sturdy box-section frame are built for rugged service. You get smooth riding comfort on any road, with the famous "Mid Ship" Ride, on Sofa-Wide seats for six.

You'll enjoy the instant response of Ford's new "hushed" 100 h.p. V-8 engine or its quality companion, the advanced 95 h.p. Six! And Ford's durability and running economy make it as thrifty to drive as it is to buy!

Yes, for beauty, comfort and performance... for long life and economy, as well... Ford's the one *for* car in its field! A "Test Drive" will show you why. You'll see, hear and feel the difference!

"Test Drive" the Big New FORD

Ford, 1950

Won't you join the Jury?

It's only human to get a glow when others view your car with admiring eyes. The satisfaction of Plymouth owners doesn't end here. For they know that their car contains admirable traits you can't see in a glance— advanced engineering, quality materials, honest craftsmanship, and an enduring performance that constantly sustains their judgment in choosing a Plymouth.

PLYMOUTH

Chrysler Corporation's No. 1 Car

New Yorker DeLuxe 4-door Sedan

Now on display

AMERICA'S **FIRST FAMILY** OF FINE CARS

New Yorker DeLuxe Convertible— *New Yorker and New Yorker DeLuxe in 9 body styles*

A stunning new mood in **Highway Fashion!**

Never before has such a brilliant array of fine motor cars been introduced to the American public . . . styled to create a glamorous new mood in Highway Fashion . . . and embodying the kind of engineering the world associates with Chrysler performance and safety!

And here is a *range* of cars unequalled anywhere. The beautiful Windsor line . . . lowest-priced of all Chryslers. The spectacular New Yorker . . . whose performance has all America talking. The matchless Imperial . . . custom-built for those who demand the absolute finest. All in a variety of body models, colors, and interior trim combinations to suit every need and every wish.

. . . and now on display at your nearby Chrysler dealer's!

The beautiful 1953 **CHRYSLER**

Custom Imperial 4-door Sedan—*Imperial line also includes the Town Limousine*

Windsor Club Coupe—*Windsor and Windsor DeLuxe in 7 body styles*

Plymouth, 1953 ◄ *Chrysler, 1952*

167

The most important new car in America... *Henry J*

"It fills the needs, the wants, the purchasing power of all America as no other car has done in the last ten years, and has the full generous proportions to which Americans are accustomed. It is the car that every American family can afford to buy, to operate, to maintain, and be proud to own."

(signed) HENRY J. KAISER

Henry J Sedan....See it today at your Kaiser•Frazer dealer!

smart!

The Henry J's a honey! Smart to look at... smart to own! Note the "low waistline"... speed-style radiator grille... fluted upswept fenders... fashioned flanges at wheel cut-outs. Extra-wide doors, front seat 5 feet wide! And the rear seat folds forward, giving you 55 cubic feet of storage space!

tough!

The Henry J's tough as an elephant yet nimble as a kitten! Husky Double-Channel Frame... the rear axle, Hypoid-geared, as in most expensive car! Largest vision area in any low-priced car! Short turning radius, Triple-Control Steering, oversized brakes make it far *safer*, much easier to handle, to park!

thrifty!

The Henry J means less to pay every way. You get up to 30 to 35 miles per gallon from the quiet, responsive Supersonic Engine (choice of 4 or 6 cylinders). Lower maintenance... repair bills... insurance... operating cost! Your savings, in just two years, can more than total the down payment on the Henry J!

Built to Better the Best on the Road!

costs less to buy ... less to drive ... less to maintain!

© 1950 KAISER-FRAZER SALES CORPORATION

Kaiser•Frazer Sales Corporation, *Willow Run, Michigan*

Henry J, 1950

---

the **car for today**! ...The *Henry J*

America's most important new car!

The *Henry J* DeLuxe sedan....See it today at your Kaiser•Frazer dealer's!

smart !

Timely as this very second, with a new Windsweep design that's as smart as it's practical and as comfortable as it's smart... with new speed-style radiator grille and fluted upswept fenders... roomy, double-purpose interior that converts to give you 51 cubic feet of storage space!

tough !

Yes, tough as an ox! Husky Double-Channel Frame reinforced like a steel bridge... shorter turning radius for easiest parking... Triple-Control Steering and oversized brakes for easiest, safest handling! Ruggedly built for long-lasting service.

thrifty !

Up to 30-35 miles a gallon from its smooth, responsive Supersonic Engines (Henry J—4 cylinder; Henry J DeLuxe—6 cylinder). Saves on maintenance... repairs... operating cost... yes, even insurance! Come in and let us prove its amazing economy—now!

and **nimble as a kitten!**

Built to Better the Best on the Road!

costs less to buy ... less to drive ... less to maintain!

© 1950 KAISER-FRAZER SALES CORPORATION

Kaiser•Frazer Sales Corporation, *Willow Run, Michigan*

Henry J, 1950

▶ *Henry J, 1951* ▶▶ *Chevrolet, 1953*

Meet America's smartest new car!

The *Henry J* sedan $**1299.**

Delivered at Willow Run, with Federal taxes
paid. Only white sidewall tires, de luxe bumper
guards, wheel rings, and local tax (if any) additional.
Price subject to change without notice.

Kaiser★Frazer's *Henry J* receives

the famous Fashion Academy Gold Medal Award

for its "smart fashion appeal"

Beauty already hailed by millions...now
officially recognized as supreme! The roomy front seat
of the Henry J provides living-room comfort...its
double-purpose interior affords luggage space galore!

for its "superb performance"

Its Supersonic Engine gives you faster getaway, more
responsive power. Its short turning radius, Triple-Control
Steering and oversized brakes make it the perfect car for
today...the ideal car for the *busy* life!

for its "unprecedented economy"

The lowest cost, lowest down payment,
lowest monthly payments of any full-size car in America! And
it gives you up to 30 to 35 miles per gallon! Lower maintenance, repair
bills, operating costs. See your Kaiser-Frazer Dealer today!

The *Henry J* costs less to buy...
less to drive...less to maintain!
Built to Better the Best on the Road!

©1951 KAISER-FRAZER SALES CORP., WILLOW RUN, MICHIGAN

Here's what's NEW in motor cars for 1951...
all in America's Largest and Finest Low-priced Car!

plus Chevrolet's time-proved POWER *Glide* automatic transmission*

Look—and see! All these *new* things, all these *pleasing* things, all these *proved* things you and your family want in an automobile, are yours in the '51 Chevrolet—*America's largest and finest low-priced car!* You'll find it's outstanding—in size, in styling, in comfort, in

Valve-in-Head engine performance, and in time-proved *no-shift* driving or *standard* driving—all at lowest cost. See it, drive it, and you'll *know* it's the smartest buy of the year! Chevrolet Motor Division, *General Motors Corporation,* Detroit 2, Michigan.

Combination of Powerglide automatic transmission and 105-h.p. engine optional on De Luxe models at extra cost.

The *Smart New* Styleline De Luxe 4-Door Sedan

NEW *America-Preferred Bodies by Fisher*

ith new and even more strikingly beautiful lines, ntours and colors . . . with extra-sturdy Fisher nisteel construction . . . Curved Windshield and noramic Visibility . . . the smartest, safest, ost comfortable edition of Chevrolet's America-referred Bodies by Fisher.

NEW *Modern-Mode Interiors*

With upholstery and appointments of outstanding quality, in beautiful two-tone color harmonies . . . with an even more attractive steering wheel embodying a new full-circle horn ring (in De Luxe models) . . . and with extra-generous head, leg and elbow room for driver and all passengers.

NEW *Improved Center-Point Steering*

(and Center-Point Design) Making steering even easier at low speeds or while parking . . . just as Chevrolet's famous Unitized Knee-Action Gliding Ride is comfortable beyond comparison in its price range . . . additional reasons why more people buy Chevrolets than any other car.

NEW *American Beauty Design*

Brilliant new styling . . . featuring entirely new grille, parking lights, fender moldings and rear-end design . . . imparting that longer, lower, wider big-car look which sets Chevrolet above and apart from all other motor cars in its field.

NEW *More Powerful Jumbo-Drum Brakes*

(with Dubl-Life rivetless brake linings) Largest brakes in the entire low-price field . . . with both brake shoes on each wheel self-energizing for forward and reverse operation of car . . . providing maximum stopping-power with up to 25% less driver effort.

NEW *Safety-Sight Instrument Panel*

Safer, more convenient, more efficient . . . having an overhanging upper crown to eliminate reflections in windshield from instrument lights . . . and with plain easy-to-read instruments in two large clusters directly in front of the driver.

CHEVROLET

More people buy Chevrolets than any other car!

These keys unlock GREATER VALUES FOR YOU IN '52!

HERE are the five new cars General Motors offers you for '52.

Each has a famous name of its own: Chevrolet, Pontiac, Oldsmobile, Buick, Cadillac.

Each has its own personality in styling, appointments, features, power.

But all enjoy an advantage which stems from the research into better ways to do things—the testing of everything from the integrity of metal to the soundness of design—the broad knowledge of engineering and manufacturing methods which General Motors provides.

The results, as you will discover, are comfort, convenience, performance unknown a few years ago.

Each year witnesses new advances—and we believe you will find these newest cars, now readied for the market, the finest we have built thus far.

We invite you to see them now at your local GM dealer's—and you will know why "your key to greater value" appears on the key of every car.

"MORE AND BETTER THINGS FOR MORE PEOPLE" — **GENERAL MOTORS** — *Your Key to Greater Value — The Key to a General Motors Car*

General Motors, 1952

Dreams- on wheels

OUR General Motors engineers are practical men. But they have dreams, too—dreams of exciting new cars that some day might be built with new processes, new materials and new techniques now being developed. And, because you can't tell about pet ideas until you try them, we gave our staff the go-ahead.

Here are the results—five glamorous hand-built "running" models, fabricated of steel and Fiberglas and plastic. All combine many never-seen-before advances, all are different. More

than a million people have already acclaimed them at our recent Motorama Shows from coast to coast.

We feel these dream cars serve a useful purpose. By finding out which features you, the public, like best in these far-in-advance models, we can set our sights on the long task of including them on production cars.

We show them here as another example of the forward-looking engineering that has long made the key to a General Motors car, your key to greater value.

GENERAL MOTORS "More and better things for more people"

WILDCAT by Buick

LE MANS by Cadillac

CORVETTE by Chevrolet

PARISIENNE by Pontiac

STARFIRE by Oldsmobile

GM ENGINEERING ...PERFECTS TODAY'S PROGRESS ...PATTERNS TOMORROW'S PROMISE

General Motors, 1953

"Merry Christmas, Grandma...we came in our new PLYMOUTH!"

Plymouth, 1950

Stretch Out and See

NEW SPACE-PLANNED DESIGN— No unused space—this is the new lean-luck-and-take-it-easy Mercury that puts every inch of car to work. And looks? "Forerunner" styling is yours ahead.

Why It Challenges Them All

NEW SEA-TINT* GLASS reduces heat, glare, and eyestrain. New larger windows permit safety-sure visibility all around. *Every view* proves that Mercury is new—in looks, in power, in extra value.

WE BUILT A NEW CAR and made this challenge: Match Mercury if you can. Now we know we've got the sweetest thing on wheels since the ladies began to drive.

For all America is falling in love with a car.

No wonder. It's big and beautiful, inside, outside, and all over. With a host of Future Features—Forerunner styling, Jet-scoop hood, suspension-mounted brake pedal, Interceptor instrument panel, higher horsepower V-8 engine—the new Mercury is the most challenging car that ever came down the *American Road*.

See it, drive it. You'll fall in love, too. And with Mercury's famous economy—*proved* in official tests— this is a love affair you can afford.

MERCURY DIVISION - FORD MOTOR COMPANY

The New 1952 MERCURY
WITH MERC-O-MATIC DRIVE

3-WAY CHOICE—Mercury presents three dependable, performance-proved drives: silent-ease, standard transmission; thrifty Touch-O-Matic Overdrive,* and Merc-O-Matic,* greatest of all automatic drives.
*Optional at extra cost

Mercury, 1952

Announcing
THE NEW
1951 STUDEBAKER

A grand new
Studebaker Champion

in the lowest price field!
One of the 4 lowest price
largest selling cars in America!

A brand new
high-efficiency V-8
Studebaker Commander

A truly great car that sparkles
with brilliant new performance!

STOP in and see these styled ahead, engineered ahead, enduringly built new 1951 Studebakers! They're attractively priced! They're amazingly saving of gasoline! They don't require premium fuels! They're on view for you right now—at all Studebaker dealers' showrooms!

Studebaker Automatic Drive or overdrive available on all models at extra cost

Studebaker...the thrifty one for '51

PAUL HESSE PHOTO—1951 STUDEBAKER COMMANDER STATE 4-DOOR SEDAN. WHITE SIDEWALL TIRES AND WHEEL TRIM RINGS OPTIONAL ON ALL MODELS AT EXTRA COST.

©1951, THE STUDEBAKER CORPORATION, SOUTH BEND 27, INDIANA, U. S. A.

Studebaker, 1950

Ford, 1951

Lincoln, 1952

Aero Willys, 1952

Chevrolet, 1953 ▶ *Continental Mark II, 1956* ▶▶ *Seiberling, 1953*

There's a difference, too, that <u>can't</u> be seen

You know, instinctively, that the straightforward lines, the distinctive styling, of the Continental *Mark II* will not fall victim to changeful fashion.

But you must *experience*, rather than see, another difference that sets the Continental apart. That is its exhilarating, spirited performance. Here, you sense, is strength and sinew to weather roads and miles and elements.

The quiet competence of this superlative motor car is one of the most gratifying facts of Continental ownership.

Continental
Mark II

Continental Division · Ford Motor Company

Cuts 92% of your driving motions! New Fordomatic Drive* does your gear shifting for you. It's America's newest, finest, most flexible automatic transmission!

*Optional at extra cost

Stretch your driving dollars—with Ford's Automatic Mileage Maker! You get high-compression performance with regular gasoline! A new Waterproof Ignition System prevents engine "shorts" from moisture.

No car is better finished, better built! There's quality that lasts in the quiet elegance of Ford's new Luxury Lounge Interior, in the soundness of Ford's coachwork!

All the best
FOR THE YEARS AHEAD

Enjoy "Fashion-Car" styling—from the new recessed headlights to new Jet-Styled Windsplits. Ford's designed to stay "right" in the years ahead!

"Test Drive" the '51 Ford ... at your Ford Dealer's today. And as you drive it, remember that this car is built for the years ahead! With 43 "Look Ahead" features, it was planned and engineered to stay young in performance, to stay in style, to stay thrifty —for years to come!

Feel the safety of an extra-heavy steel Luxury Lifeguard Body! And Ford's new Double-Seal King-Size Brakes keep out dirt and water—give smooth, safe stops in any weather!

Relax with Ford's new Automatic Ride Control! It adjusts your ride to any road automatically! The going stays easy, level— no pitch, no jounce, no roll!

YOU CAN PAY MORE BUT YOU CAN'T BUY BETTER!
'51 Ford

Ford, 1951

It's New! Only Hudson has...
Miracle H-Power

Tune in THE BILLY ROSE SHOW
ABC-TV Network

Sensational new H-145 engine in the fabulous
NEW HUDSON HORNET

There's never been anything like it! And the beauty is, you needn't take our word for it!

All you need do is drive the fabulous new Hudson Hornet—experience the thrilling get-up-and-go of Miracle H-Power—found only in Hudson.

Then notice that the sensational new high-compression H-145 engine that supplies this *performance unlimited* is as quiet and smooth as a sea gull in a glide!

Remember that this amazing H-145 engine is simple in design for low upkeep cost and trouble-free operation. And—it is built to outlast any other engine on the market!

The spectacular new Hudson Hornet itself is breath-takingly beautiful—gracefully streamlined, with a new high note in luxury inside!

And—it is "step-down" designed—lowest built for the world's best and safest ride!

See your Hudson dealer—see for yourself that there's never been anything like Miracle H-Power and the fabulous new Hudson Hornet!

Important today— perhaps VITAL tomorrow

All Hudsons give high-compression performance on REGULAR GAS!

Hudson... most DURABLE car your money can buy!

Hudson, 1951

"Nothing like it for Long Life!"

Here's the one for the long run— mile after mile—year after year... it's engineered to last!

New 1951 MERCURY
Nothing like it on the Road!

3-WAY CHOICE! *With Mercury for 1951, you have a triple choice for "the drive of your life"—Mercury's new, simpler, smoother, more efficient automatic transmission, Merc-O-Matic Drive, or thrifty Touch-O-Matic Overdrive are optional at extra cost; and in addition, there's the silent-ease synchronized standard transmission.*

From the stitches in its seats to the head bolts on its power plant, Mercury is *precision-built* for the years ahead of it. For long-run investment, you're smart to put your money in this penny-pincher!

Mercury stays new longer—keeps upkeep low and trade-in value high—goes easy on gas—gives you what you want and deserve from a 1951 car.

You get a great new car that *looks* the part. There's a sweep of motion in its line and a sense of power in its look. But Mercury's beauty goes far deeper than that—it's built into every part of the car!

Drive a Mercury first chance you get. Test the whisper-hustle of its great 8-cylinder, V-type engine. Check the broader, softer seating—the new increased visibility—the extra roominess. Then you be the judge.

You'll decide Mercury's got what you want—and you'll enjoy it for many years to come!

MERCURY DIVISION • FORD MOTOR COMPANY

Mercury, 1951

THE MOST BEAUTIFUL THING ON WHEELS

DOLLAR FOR DOLLAR
you can't beat a
PONTIAC

WHEN DAYS SEEM MADE FOR EXTRA ZEST AND EXCITEMENT
PONTIAC FITS INTO THE PICTURE WONDERFULLY—
A STRIKING BEAUTY, A SUPERB PERFORMER, A GREAT VALUE!

Pontiac, 1950 ▶ Cadillac, 1951 ▶▶ Willys, 1951 ▶▶▶ Willys, 1951

FURS BY REVILLON

Its grace and beauty have captured the hearts of wo
everywhere—but only the woman who has *driven* i
know how satisfying this great Cadillac is to her *pra*
side. Those miles and miles of confident, trouble
motoring have taught her how wonderfully dependable and
from maintenance expense it is . . . and she's reminded of its rem
able gasoline economy every time she glances at the fuel gauge.
if she looks a little smug now and then—well, she actually pai
for her *Cadillac* than many of her friends paid for *other* makes of

Cadillac

CADILLAC MOTOR CAR DIVISION • GENERAL MOTORS CORPORATI

Goes a long, long way on a gallon

WILLYS *makes sense*

—IN DESIGN   —IN ECONOMY   —IN USEFULNESS

*"We needn't stop for gas
...I filled it last week"*

WILLYS *makes sense*

—IN ECONOMY —IN EASE OF DRIVING —IN COMFORT

The New DeSoto Fire Dome 8

With its mighty 160 h.p. V-Eight Engine...Power Steering...Power Braking...and No-Shift Driving...it is the most revolutionary new car of 1952. See and *drive* it!

Drive... AS NEVER BEFORE!

This Fire Dome engine with famous dome-shaped combustion chambers gets more power from every drop of fuel. Terrific acceleration and cruising performance *on regular gas.* ★★★★ Smart, practical Air-Vent Hood directs stream of cool air to carburetor for maximum engine power.

Steer... WITHOUT EFFORT!

Power Steering is easy as dialing a telephone . . . you can turn wheel with one finger. Hydraulic power does the work. Parking is *easy!*

DE SOTO DIVISION, CHRYSLER CORPORATION

White sidewall tires, when available, are optional equipment.

DeSoto, 1952

NOW—a fine car that meets every test of modern living

Lincoln for 1952

IN TWO INCOMPARABLE SERIES—
THE *Cosmopolitan*—THE *Capri*

NEW GLASS-WALL VISIBILITY—There's a new way of life in America reflected in today's glass walled rooms for modern living. Lincoln, too, surrounds you with glass—3271 square inches. With chair-high seats and down-sweep hood, even the daintiest woman driver can see the right front fender—see the road in front and way ahead. Every line has a reason.

NEW VERSATILE SMARTNESS—This is beauty with purpose. Right for trip or town, a business car, a family car—with more leg room, more head room, almost 30 cu. ft. in the luggage compartment. Yet Lincoln is smartly sized to thread through traffic, park easily. At your garage. The one fine car deliberately designed for modern living.

NEW FLIGHT-LIKE POWER—There's ready-to-fly excitement in Lincoln's completely new, overhead-valve, high-compression, V-8 engine—premium product of the company that has built more V-8's than all other makers combined. With HYDRA-MATIC Transmission (as standard equipment), and new ball-joint front suspension (first on a standard U.S. car), steering and handling are astonishingly effortless.

LINCOLN DIVISION—FORD MOTOR COMPANY

Lincoln, 1952

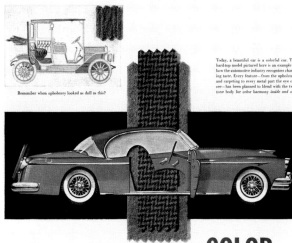

Remember when upholstery looked as dull as this?

Horsepower of another COLOR

A basic business premise with Chatham is to match every change in its customers' product with an improvement of its own. When color became an important selling feature of fine cars, Chatham upholstery immediately reflected the swing to color. This awareness of the customers' market existed long before Chatham became a great mill. It began with the founder when he established his small family enterprise 75 years ago, and is still going strong today as a matter of family pride with the fourth generation of Chatham sons. *And family pride is a very good guarantee of quality.*

This Chatham upholstery fabric and bolster fabric were especially designed to match the colors of the car illustrated above. They're only one of Chatham's many smart new patterns in nylon, wool and nylon mixtures, worsted, and woolen broadcloths—fabrics which leading automotive manufacturers prefer for their sturdiness and colorful style.

CHATHAM *upholstery*

Chatham Manufacturing Company, Elkin, North Carolina • Automotive Fabrics Representative: Getsinger-Fox Company, Detroit

Chatham Upholstery, 1958

SMART YET CASUAL—LIKE THE MODERN HOSTESS. Clean-lined, without gingerbread, the new Lincoln is proof that a fine car can be as handsomely functional as the new-day homes—and new-day living. Inside, you find superb fittings—and the seats are high, the hood is low; you can see the road directly ahead, you can see the world all around through 3,721 square inches of glass (sea-tint glass available).

VERSATILE AS A LIVING ROOM DESIGNED FOR LIVING. Lincoln is luxurious yet maneuverable, beautiful yet *powerful.* New V-8 engine, with overhead valves, 7.5 to 1 compression ratio—plus new, improved dual range HYDRA-MATIC Transmission. And, with new ball-joint front wheel suspension, first on a U.S. production car, handling becomes astonishingly easy.

IN TWO INCOMPARABLE SERIES—
THE COSMOPOLITAN—THE CAPRI

Now—LINCOLN

makes your driving as modern as your living

It is completely new. It is almost incredibly new. But more than this—it is an entirely new *approach* to fine automobiles, designed for those whose concept of luxury motoring does not include the common, the ponderous, or the unwieldy.

Lincoln for 1952 is for those who ask their car to match their new perspective on living. Though it may well be the most luxurious automobile on the *American Road,* it is magnificently functional.

There is a reason for every dimension. There is a purpose behind each line. The new Lincoln is spirited, compact, and surpassingly efficient.

There is only one way to know this new kind of motoring—this fine car that is like a feather in traffic, an arrow on the road. That way is to try it and to drive it. See the new Lincoln Cosmopolitan and Capri at your dealer's showroom. Lincoln—*the one fine car deliberately designed for modern living.*

LINCOLN DIVISION—FORD MOTOR COMPANY

Lincoln, 1952

Magic in Motion

The New Aero Willys

LOAFS AT 60 · CRUISES AT 75 · WITH POWER TO SPARE

NEW 90 H.P. · 6 CYLINDER HURRICANE ENGINE

DRIVER SEES ALL FOUR FENDERS

61-INCH-WIDE SEATING

Willys Dealers Invite You To Experience an "Airborne" Ride

Come . . . take the wheel of the most astonishing car you ever drove! A car that responds like magic to your toe on the gas, your touch of the wheel. A car with a ride so smooth, soft and silent you can underestimate your speed on bad roads and good. The only car that challenges the largest cars on comfort and spaciousness . . . the smallest on ease of handling . . . and with overdrive* under comparable conditions surpasses every other six-passenger car on miles per gallon. See a Willys dealer this day!

A Willys First—Gas filler cap near center at rear, easy to reach from either side of the car—a real time-saver.

7.6 Compression and F-head design step up power and stretch mileage in the new Hurricane 6 Engine.

Unmatched Visibility . . . driver can see all four fenders . . . a safer, panoramic view all around the car.

Luxurious Spaciousness . . . seating space 61 inches wide, front and rear . . . and 24 cu. ft. of luggage space.

Aero Willys, 1952

Star of the silky way

Buick Roadmaster, 1953

HIS one had to be good. It's our Golden Anniversary ROADMASTER.

upon it we lavished our skills, our [t]nts and our time to make it the st in a fifty-year line of fine cars.

[wh]en you drive it, you will come to know [how] good a fifty-year best really is.

[yo]u'll know it in the swift and soaring [pow]er response of its V8 Engine. The [grea]t Fireball V8. The first such V8 with [8.5] to 1 compression, with vertical [val]ves, with 12-volt electrical system, [wit]h a host of modern engineering [feat]ures.

You'll know it in the silken velocity of its getaway — with Twin-Turbine Dynaflow adding far swifter, quieter acceleration to infinite smoothness.

You'll know it, too, in the velvety luxury of its bettered ride, in the new ease of its handling, in the more precise control it gives you, in the more reassuring comfort you feel.

For Buick engineers pulled all the stops on this 1953 ROADMASTER. They widened the front tread — compacted the frame—shortened the turn radius—recalibrated the four coil springs—increased the braking power — made

Power Steering standard equipment, and even added Power Brakes* to lighten the task of quick, sure stopping.

But why say more?

It is for you, the beneficiary of all this engineering excellence, to discover the great and gorgeous going of the swiftest, the smoothest, the silkiest, the most silent automobile yet built in half a century of Buick building.

Your Buick dealer will be happy to introduce you two. Why not visit him soon?

BUICK *Division of* GENERAL MOTORS

Optional at extra cost.

Then—
Now—
Tomorrow

1903

1953

When better
automobiles are built
BUICK will build them

Custom Built **ROADMASTER** *by Buick*

Johnny and Lucille, Oldsmobile's singing sweethearts, invite you to ride the "Rocket" . . . to drive Oldsmobile's sensational new Super "88"!

TRY **160 H.P.** "ROCKET" ACTION

. . .in the New Super "88"

You're got to drive it to believe it! Never before has Oldsmobile had such an exciting performance story to tell! For here is a *new* kind of "Rocket" Engine car—*dramatically new* with the flashing 160-h.p. "Rocket" . . . now paired with smooth new Hydra-Matic Super Drive*! The result is performance that truly *stands out* even in this era of high-powered motor cars! GM Hydraulic Steering, the Autronic-Eye*, and many other new features add to your motoring comfort and safety. Drive Oldsmobile's Super "88" . . . you'll never settle for anything else!

*Hydra-Matic Super Drive, GM Hydraulic Steering, Autronic-Eye and white sidewall tires (when available) optional at extra cost. Equipment, accessories and trim, subject to change without notice.

A General Motors Value

"ROCKET" POWERED **OLDSMOBILE**

Oldsmobile, 1952

THE BIG **4-Power Package** OF 1953 !

Take command of the power sensation of the year—Oldsmobile's brilliant new Super "88"! Take a look at the bold new front end, the sweeping fender lines, the long, level rear-deck . . . *that's Power Styling!* Now take the wheel and feel the smooth, swift response of the higher-compression, higher-power, higher-voltage engine . . . *that's the new "Rocket"!* Take a curve or a corner—park and maneuver with incredible ease . . . *that's GM Power Steering*! And it takes just a touch of your toe to bring you to a smoother, quicker, safer stop . . . *with Pedal-Ease Power Brakes*! Plus Frigidaire Car Conditioning*, Autronic-Eye*! Drive the power-great Super "88" soon, at your Oldsmobile Dealer's.

*Optional at extra cost.

Car illustrated above: Oldsmobile Super "88" 4-Door Sedan. A General Motors Value.

1 Power Steering
2 Power Styling
3 Power Brakes
4 "Rocket" Engine

OLDSMOBILE

Oldsmobile, 1953

A GENERAL MOTORS VALUE.

Starfire—the "show car" that can be your car! *Starfire*—with a long, rakish, waist-high silhouette . . . smartly curving panoramic windshield and spectacular sweep-cut rear fenders . . . saddle-stitched leather interior in dramatic new two-tone patterns. *Starfire*—with the surging might of a new 185-horsepower "Rocket" Engine! See and drive this glamorous new Oldsmobile convertible—the "Dream Car" Ninety-Eight *Starfire*—at your Oldsmobile dealer's now.

OLDSMOBILE'S FABULOUS NEW "*Starfire*"

NOW IN PRODUCTION !

"Be careful—drive safely!"

Oldsmobile, 1954

Sports Classic

Soft, pliant, leather—in matching shades or solid colors—enhances the ultra-smart interior of the Ninety-Eight Convertible.

At the country club . . . down at the beach . . . out on the open road . . . Oldsmobile's lithe and lovely Ninety-Eight Convertible fits right into the picture! Like all Oldsmobiles, it's designed for delightful driving . . . a breezy beauty that's loaded with looks and packed with power! You touch the accelerator—and the mightiest "Rocket" Engine of all time surges into action. Take a corner—and Power Steering* takes over 80% of the turning effort. And to stop—just pivot on your heel and the gentle brawn of Power Brakes* halts you in a hurry! So if you've a yen for real motoring pleasure . . . for the thrills of a "Rocket Ride" . . . stop in today at your Oldsmobile dealer's. Make a date with a "Rocket 8"!

*Optional at extra cost

Car illustrated above: Ninety-Eight Convertible Coupé. A General Motors Value.

"ROCKET" ENGINE **OLDSMOBILE**

Oldsmobile, 1953 ▶ Oldsmobile, 1955

ummer classic

Car illustrated above:
Ninety-Eight Convertible
A General Motors Value.

Tops for the "top-down" days ahead . . . the Classic Ninety-Eight Convertible by Oldsmobile.
It's youthful, gay, carefree—and styled to *look* the part. Rakish lines and bold contours are
gracefully proportioned to achieve true Classic design. What's more, this spirited beauty
acts the part, with the smooth, hushed response of the mighty "Rocket" Engine, with
effortless Power Steering* and Pedal-Ease Power Brakes*. You're cordially invited to
drive this Classic Convertible. Visit your Oldsmobile Dealer soon.

*Optional at extra cost.

"ROCKET" ENGINE

OLDSMOBILE

LINCOLN

for the fine art of modern living

MAKING AN ENTRANCE IN MODERN STYLE. Lincoln's 3,271 square inches of glass give modern, glass-wall visibility. Modern Fiberglas insulation hushes your ride. And Lincoln's completely new overhead valve V-8 engine is effortlessly controlled with new HYDRA-MATIC Transmission and new ball-joint front wheel suspension.

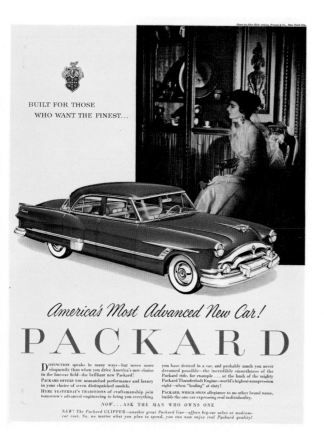

EXHIBITING THE SPACIOUSNESS OF MODERN LIVING. And magnificent Lincoln expresses it in motion. There is driving luxury with divan-width seats, deep-pile carpeting, and sparkling new appointments. And you can enrich the interior from an almost wanton selection of colorful fabrics and leathers.

Standard equipment, accessories, and trim illustrated are subject to change without notice. Sea-tint glass and white side-wall tires optional at extra cost.

If you know that good design reflects the era in which it is created...then you know that now the motor car has caught up with this century.

For Lincoln has been designed as a modern masterpiece in motion. It is the one fine car that superbly captures the spirit of modern living... that breaks with the heavy decor of the past...

that departs from impractical frills and furbelows.

Here is beauty—graceful, clean and alive ... devoted to the cause of comfort and the joy of driving. It is expressed in striking, relaxing interiors ... in a practical luggage compartment, nearly 30 cubic feet big. It is the beauty of incomparable performance with sports car nimbleness

blended with big car stability for the first time.

To appreciate the new Lincoln Cosmopolitan or Capri, you must do more than see it at your dealer's showroom. Be sure to ask him for a demonstration drive with *the one fine car deliberately designed for modern living.*

LINCOLN DIVISION — FORD MOTOR COMPANY

Lincoln, 1952

Standard equipment, accessories, and trim illustrated are subject to change without notice. Sea-tint glass and white side-wall tires optional at extra cost.

LINCOLN —a wonderful lesson in modern living

THE American motorist is going to school—and Lincoln is doing the teaching. It is demonstrating that driving, like modern schooling, is more fun in an atmosphere of relaxation and open-space beauty.

For this is the one fine car that has superbly captured today's fun-of-living spirit ... setting into motion a great new trend in motor cars.

The grandeur of its sweeping lines ... the wide, roomy seats have but one purpose: to set you in a glorious mood for driving. The glass-wall visibility ... the low, compact hood ... and the astonishing ease

of steering and braking—all serve one function: to make you the most relaxed driver on the road. This is a big car that handles with majestic ease. It has a completely new engine with more power than you may ever need ... quick and catlike ... and as quiet as midnight on the open road.

Your dealer is now showing the Lincoln Cosmopolitan and Capri in exciting models and color styles. See these great cars — now. Drive one. Find out how much more you get out of life from *the one fine car deliberately designed for modern living.*

LINCOLN DIVISION—FORD MOTOR COMPANY

NEW SCHOOL OF DESIGN sets the pattern for the modern school ... for the modern Lincoln. Lincoln has strikingly beautiful interiors ... almost 30 cubic feet of luggage compartment ... and a high-compression overhead valve V-8, the premium product of the world's greatest builders of V-8s. New dual range HYDRA-MATIC Transmission, and exclusive ball joint front wheel suspension, first on any American production car, make handling astonishingly easy.

Lincoln, 1952

BUILT FOR THOSE
WHO WANT THE FINEST...

Gown by John Hirst; setting, Proms & Co., New York City

America's Most Advanced New Car!

PACKARD

DISTINCTION speaks in many ways—but never more eloquently than when you drive America's new choice in the fine-car field—the brilliant new Packard!

PACKARD OFFERS you unmatched performance and luxury in your choice of seven distinguished models.

HERE YESTERDAY'S TRADITIONS of craftsmanship join tomorrow's advanced engineering to bring you everything

you have desired in a car, and probably much you never dreamed possible—the incredible smoothness of the Packard ride, for example ... or the hush of the mighty Packard Thunderbolt Engine—world's highest-compression eight—when "loafing" at sixty!

PACKARD, WHICH OWES ALLEGIANCE to no other brand name, builds the one car expressing *real* individuality.

NOW ... ASK THE MAN WHO OWNS ONE

NEW! The Packard CLIPPER—another great Packard line—offers big-car value at medium-car cost. So, no matter what you plan to spend, you can now enjoy real Packard quality!

Packard, 1953

The New Standard of the American Road

Merely Terrific!

And it hangs onto its value better than any other car on the American Road

"TERRIFIC" is the word for the '53 Ford.

A glance will tell you it's *your* dream car—come true! For this new Ford with its longer, lower, wider look is undoubtedly the style-setter of the '53 season. Here's beauty that's terrific...*merely terrific!*

When you take off for the open spaces you'll thrill to the wonderful "Go" of Ford's famous V-8 engine. And with Fordomatic Drive the shifting is done for you ... and a sight better than you can do it by hand.

On highways or byways you'll find "top level" comfort with Ford's new *Wonder Ride*...a new ride so

harmonized that you enjoy new freedom from jolt, pitch and roll—new smoothness, quiet and stability.

See this Ford and Value Check the #1 "Worth More" features. Test Drive it. Then you'll see why Ford is worth more when you buy it ... worth more when you sell it. You'll agree it's the New Standard of the American Road.

Fordomatic Drive, white sidewall tires, optional at extra cost. Equipment, accessories and trim subject to change without notice.

See it ... Value Check it ... Test Drive it

Great TV! Ford Theatre, NBC-TV, Thursday evenings.

'53 FORD

Ford, 1953

PRESENTING THE BEAUTIFUL NEW
1953 Dual-Streak Pontiac

PONTIAC MOTOR DIVISION · GENERAL MOTORS CORPORATION

A GENERAL MOTORS MASTERPIECE

Here, in the greatest Pontiac ever built, is the perfect expression of the Pontiac idea—to produce the finest, most beautiful, most luxurious car that can possibly be built to sell at a price just above the lowest.

This wonderful 1953 Dual-Streak Pontiac is completely new in every styling detail, inside and out. It has a longer wheelbase for a smooth, easy ride. It has sweeping vision with its one-piece curved windshield and wrap-around rear window. Pontiac's famous Dual-Range* power train makes it a spectacular performer anywhere, any time.

New and fresh as this car is, it has a wonderful tradition built into every line and part—the tradition of Pontiac's *thorough goodness*; the tradition of Pontiac's remarkable year-after-year dependability and economy. This 1953 Pontiac is magnificent new proof that *dollar for dollar you can't beat a Pontiac*. See it at your nearest Pontiac dealer.

*Optional at extra cost.

Pontiac, 1953

Nash, 1953

► Lincoln, 1953

WHY BE TIED DOWN T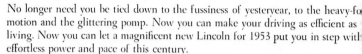

No longer need you be tied down to the fussiness of yesteryear, to the heavy-fo[...]
motion and the glittering pomp. Now you can make your driving as efficient as [...]
living. Now you can let a magnificent new Lincoln for 1953 put you in step with [...]
effortless power and pace of this century.

For now with Lincoln, everything you touch turns to astonishing power. You to[...]
the wheel, and two tons of flawless engineering turn with incredible ease—than[...]
the unique combination of power steering and exclusive ball-joint front wheel [...]
pension. You touch the brake, and again two tons do your bidding, as power aids [...]
braking. You even touch buttons on your seat, and power moves you not only forw[...]
or backward, but also up or down as you wish. The seat even adjusts to your pos[...]

Standard equipment, accessories, and trim illustrated are subject to change without notice.
Power steering, power elevator seats, power brakes, white side-wall tires optional at extra cost.

LINCOLN

THE ONE FINE CAR DESIGNED FOR MODERN LIVING
—POWERED TO LEAVE THE PAST FAR BEHIND

Crowning achievement of Ford Motor Company's 50th
Anniversary—"50 Years Forward on the American Road"

YESTERDAY ?

And then--then you touch the accelerator and the new V-205 engine is at your command. That's V-205 for 205 horsepower in the new V-8 power plant that brought Lincoln first, second, third *and* fourth places in the stock car division of the Mexican Pan-American Race, called the toughest automobile competition in the world.

And all of this power is contained in the shape of things to come--the Lincoln design that breaks sharply with the past. Clean lined, without gingerbread or superfluous brightwork, it is a superb achievement in functional design, dramatized by the most dazzling colors and fabrics that ever took to the road. Come accept Lincoln's invitation to depart from the past. Your Lincoln dealer awaits you with a Lincoln Cosmopolitan or Capri.

LINCOLN DIVISION — FORD MOTOR COMPANY

Fifty Years Forward on the American Road

You "belong" in a '53 FORD

And, with its 41 "worth more" features, you'll find it is worth more when you buy it . . . worth more when you sell it!

One of the nicest things about owning a Ford in that it is accepted *everywhere!* Likewise, Ford owners are known and respected for their good taste and sound business judgment for selecting the car that is not only beautifully built and finished but one that returns more of its initial cost when sold!

Of course, this is perfectly natural when you realize what a '53 Ford *really is and does.*

Consider the Crestmark Body, for example. Only a few short years ago it would have been difficult to produce a body like it for a car selling at such a low price. The tools, the methods, the

materials simply weren't that far advanced. Think of that when you feel the elegant softness of any Ford seat cushion. (It comes from a new use of springing plus a thick pad of foam rubber.) Think of it again when you realize that Ford upholstery materials and exterior finishes are the most beautiful money can buy. Then open the door—it stays open in your choice of two positions. Now, slam the door —notice the solid "snick" of the latch —like closing the breech of a shotgun. Here's quality—Ford quality that tips its hat to no one!

Finally, remember Ford Crestmark bodies are insulated bodies—"hull

tight" . . . to seal out weather and dust!

But Ford Crestmark bodies are not the whole story by a long shot. There are 41 "Worth More" features—all the way from your choice of high-compression Strato-Star V-8 or Mileage Maker Six engines to a ride that reduces front-end road shock up to 80%, a ride that's a perfect wonder in smoothness and stability.

Why not let your Ford Dealer give you a complete fill-in? He wants you to see—to value check—to test drive the '53 Ford.

FORD . . . worth more when you buy it . . . when you sell it, too!

Ford, 1953

Its beauty is just the beginning

This joyous thing of exquisite grace is the Skylark — Buick's stunning new luxury sports car.

Yet the gorgeous beauty of this motorcar is just the beginning of the deep excitement.

For it's a Buick. And in any Buick, the real heart-lift you get is from the manner of its going — impeccably smooth, gentle of ride, superbly easy to handle, trigger-quick in response.

In other Buicks — SPECIAL, SUPER and ROADMASTER — many of these advances are yours either as standard equipment, or as options at moderate extra cost.

Upon the Skylark, we have lavished practically every modern automotive advance — including the world's newest V8 Engine, Twin-Turbine Dynaflow, Power Steering, Power Brakes, hydraulic control of the radio antenna, windows, top, and front-seat adjustment.

But in *all* Buicks — even the low-priced SPECIAL — you get the Buick Million Dollar Ride, Buick room, Buick comfort, Buick Fireball power—the highest horsepowers and compression ratios, Series for Series, in all Buick history.

Your Buick dealer is waiting to seat you at the wheel of the car that will do fullest justice to your dreams and your purse. See him this week.

BUICK *Division of* GENERAL MOTORS

When better automobiles are built Buick will build them

The greatest **BUICK** in 50 great years

Buick, 1953

Cadillac

Jewels by Harry Winston

Authoritative records of used car values reveal that a Cadillac may be expected to return a greater share of its owner's investment at the time of re-sale than any other car built in America. . . . This is true not only after a Cadillac's *first* year of service—but after its *second,* and *third and fourth* years, as well. . . . This is, we think, a wholly understandable circumstance. . . . It is obvious, for instance, that a Cadillac's beauty and character and stature are little dimmed by the miles and the years. Its

performance, as owners can testify, is a constant joy throughout its life span. And its luxury and dependability and economy continue over almost any period of time its owner may elect to enjoy them. . . . If you are one of the many who are presently contemplating the move up to Cadillac, please reflect on these important facts. For they prove beyond doubt that, in addition to all of its other wonderful qualities, a Cadillac car is *one of the soundest investments in the automotive world!*

CADILLAC MOTOR CAR DIVISION · GENERAL MOTORS CORPORATION

Cadillac, 1953

Cadillac

Jewels by Van Cleef & Arpels

Wanted . . . By Almost Half the People!

According to a recent widespread survey—almost half the motor car owners in the United States would own a Cadillac, if they had their unrestricted choice. Cadillac was, in fact, voted the favorite by more than *five to one* over any other motor car built in America—a degree of leadership that is probably without parallel in all our industrial history. We regret, sincerely, that all who expressed their desire to own a Cadillac

cannot do so. But we believe, with equal sincerity, that a great many have needlessly denied themselves the pleasure. Cadillac's relatively modest price, its unusual operating economy and long life, make it a *far* more practical and sensible possession than many motorists realize. Why not visit your dealer soon— and see for yourself? You might be surprised to find you're closer to the "Standard of the World" than you ever imagined.

CADILLAC MOTOR CAR DIVISION ★ GENERAL MOTORS CORPORATION

Cadillac, 1950 ▶ *Cadillac, 1950* ▶▶ *Cadillac, 1953* ▶▶▶ *Cadillac, 1953*

Cadillac

Jewels by Harry Winston

It is in the record that men and women who move up to Cadillac are almost certain to stay with Cadillac. According to a recent nation-wide survey, almost nine out of ten of those who have purchased Cadillacs during recent years have already decided that their next cars will bear the same honored and distinguished name. This is but logical—for, beyond Cadillac, there is only the future. Those who want the finest want—the Standard of the World!

CADILLAC MOTOR CAR DIVISION
GENERAL MOTORS CORPORATION

Jewels by Harry

ere are few occasions in a motorist's life that are so surprising or
ightful as his first ride behind the wheel of a new Cadillac. For, in
t single journey, he discovers power and responsiveness—and handling ease
d comfort—he never imagined possible in a motor car. It is, in essence, an
cation in all the good things of motordom. If you are still looking forward to
extraordinary experience, we urge you to visit your Cadillac dealer soon. The
is waiting for you now—waiting to give you the most revealing ride of your life!

Cadilla

DILLAC MOTOR CAR DIVISION ★ GENERAL MOTORS CORPORATION

Jewels by Harry Winston

It Will Add to Your Happiness!

There is a great *plus* value that comes with a Cadillac which is very difficult for anyone to evaluate—except a Cadillac owner. To put it briefly, a Cadillac adds a goodly measure of happiness to a family's daily existence. It is not just the satisfaction which comes from fine performance and extraordinary comfort and out-standing safety and handling ease—thrilling though these things can be. It is more a sense of pride and family well-being—a joy of possession—and a consciousness of membership in the world's most distinguished group of motor car owners. Although difficult to explain and define—Cadillac owners from all sections of the country can testify that it is very real and very valuable—a most moving reason for moving up to Cadillac. And remember—all this is in *addition* to the innumerable *practical* reasons for owning a Cadillac. It's too much to miss—any longer. Better see your Cadillac dealer right away. He'll be delighted to see you.

You get "Worth More" Performance

Ford is the only car in its field to offer the smooth, responsive performance of a V-8 engine. And for those who prefer Sixes, Ford's the most modern of all

You get a "Worth More" Ride

Ford's smooth, level ride reduces front end road shock alone by as much as 80% ... proves it doesn't take big, heavy car weight to give day-long riding comfort

Safest place to put your new-car dollars

You get "Worth More" Convenience

Ford has the biggest luggage compartment in its field. Deck lid opens at a key turn on counterbalancing hinges

You get "Worth More" Economy

Both V-8 and Six have Ford's gas-saving Automatic Power Pilot for high-compression performance with regular gas

Ford is worth more when you buy it and when you sell it ... your soundest new car investment.

If you could take the time to compare Ford with the highest priced cars, you'd find that Ford matches them in feature after feature...but sells at half the price. Then if you could check the used car markets around the country you'd find that year-old Fords return a higher proportion of their original cost in resale than any other car in America. These two facts alone would make Ford your safest new car investment.

But there's much more to Ford's "worth more" story.

Take the special pleasure you'll get from Ford's smooth, responsive "go." Take the day-long comfort you'll find in Ford's new ride. And consider Ford's fine-car look that makes it truly "at home" wherever you may wish to drive it. You'll agree Ford is not only worth more when you buy it and when you sell it...it's worth more all the time you drive it, too.

But visit your Ford Dealer and see for yourself what Ford quality really adds up to. Test Drive the model of your choice. You'll reach just one conclusion: Ford is the safest place to put your new-car dollars.

You get "Worth More" Styling

Note Ford's long, low graceful lines ... the huge amount of window area. And Ford's modern color finishes are baked on to stay beautiful

You get "Worth More" Ease-of-Handling

Master-Guide power steering (available on V-8 models) gives you easier, safer control ... makes parking almost effortless ... retains the natural "feel" of steering on straightaways

FORD America's "Worth More" Car!

Ford, 1953

It's like money in the bank! Even when you're not using it, nice to know it's there ... this surge of

extra **Power**

CORONET V-EIGHT CLUB COUPE

In the new 140-h.p. Red Ram V-Eight engine, Dodge engineers have provided you with a magnificent reserve of acceleration and performance. You take to the highway with greater confidence, greater safety.

And with this surging Red Ram power, you enjoy nimble change-of-pace of new Gyro-Torque Drive. A new road-hugging, curve-holding ride. A new sense of driving mastery.

If your active life demands an Action Car ... this sleek, trim Dodge is for you. "Road Test" it ... soon.

New-All New '53 Dodge

Specifications and equipment subject to change without notice.

The Action Car For Active Americans

Dodge, 1953

Nash Presents for 1954 New Continental Dream Cars

Styled by Pinin Farina

Something new and wonderful is waiting for you now at your Nash dealer's. For Pinin Farina has done it again—sparked a new continental style.

Never have you seen such beauty, such sleek racing lines ... such smart interiors ... such seating space, such visibility!

Come try everything! New Nash Power Brakes! New Power Steering, New Power-Lift Windows! New high-compression dual-carburetor power! New travel comfort, in Airliner Reclining Seats!

Yes, come and try a new way of life on wheels. Spend an hour with your Pinin Farina styled "dream car." You will never want to give it back!

Announcing

The All-New Rambler Four-Door Sedan—Yes, the Nash Rambler you asked for is here! The new four-door sedan ... now in seating space and luggage space ... and offering the Rambler's flashing performance, easy handling and gasoline economy. Nash Reclining Seats and Twin Beds are available. Price includes continental tire mount and many other custom accessories.

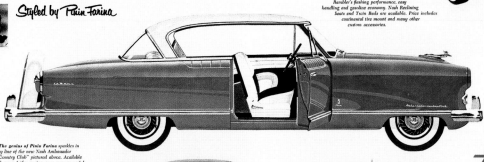

At your Nash dealer's now you'll see the greatest advance of the past 10 years ... developments that make Nash your safest investment today, your soundest resale value tomorrow!

The genius of Pinin Farina sparkles in every line of the new Nash Ambassador "Country Club" pictured above. Available with super Jetfire engine, even more powerful for 1954 ... or the "Le Mans" Dual Jetfire engine of international racing fame.

Terrific new Dual Powerflyte engine for the Nash Statesman—same famous economy. In all Nash Airflytes you have a choice of three transmissions, including Dual-Range Hydra-Matic Drive.

Wire wheel trim, hood ornament, white sidewall tires optional at extra cost.

The Nash Rambler "Country Club" combines the open air fun of a convertible with the safety and comfort of a sedan. It's America's smartest custom compact "hardtop" with continental tire mount and many custom accessories at no extra cost.

1954 Nash Airflytes

Built with the "Double Lifetime" ...Your Safest Investment Today ...Your Soundest Resale Value Tomorrow

AMBASSADOR • STATESMAN
RAMBLER

Nash Motors, Division Nash-Kelvinator Corporation, Detroit, Mich.

Nash, 1954

Mercury, 1955

Body by Fisher, 1955

Pontiac, 1955

▶ *Budd Transportaion, 1953*

It rolls out the red carpet wherever you go

YOU find an exultant satisfaction at the wheel of a 1954 ROADMASTER that you find in precious few other motorcars.

When you take that wheel — or relinquish it to an attendant — you do so with a special pride.

For this great Buick is an impressive automobile — in size and length and breadth and beauty.

It has, as you can see, a serene look of luxury and the unmistakable mark of true style modernity. Both are recognized immediately by all who see it.

Then, of course, there is the royal treatment you enjoy *underway* in ROADMASTER.

It's in the easy cruising sweep of its great 200-horsepower V8 engine — and in the incredibly smooth delivery of this power through Twin-Turbine Dynaflow.

It's in the wondrous visibility provided by the back-swept windshield — and the advanced comfort of high-air ventilation.

It's in the masterful levelness of ride that comes from a blending of engineering features found in no other car in the world.

And it's in the literally luxurious handling you find at your finger tips with Buick Safety Power Steering. It's in the added convenience, optional at extra cost, of Power Brakes, power-positioned front seat, power-operated radio antenna.

You need but one look at, one ride in, one arrival with ROADMASTER to know what tremendous satisfaction is to be had here.

Your Buick dealer will gladly arrange matters. See him soon.

BUICK *Division of* GENERAL MOTORS

When better automobiles are built BUICK will build them

MILTON BERLE
STARS FOR BUICK
See the
Buick-Berle Show
Tuesday evenings

ROADMASTER *Custom Built by* BUICK

Pontiac, 1954

Chrysler, 1954

Buick Roadmaster, 1954 ◀   *Buick Roadmaster, 1954*

Buick Roadmaster, 1954

Low...and behold! A new concept of low-cost motoring!

The Bel Air Sport Coupe—one of 14 new Fisher Body beauties in three new series.

Chevrolet, 1955

Here is excitement on wheels . . .
the newest, freshest thing you ever laid eyes on.
And it's even more exciting to drive
than to look at!

the motoramic Chevrolet for 1955!

Take a good look and you'll know that the Motoramic Chevrolet is far more than just a new model. Take the wheel and you'll realize that it's more, even, than a completely new car!

For this is the Chevrolet that began with a whole new idea—the idea that a low-priced car can be made to look, ride and perform like the very finest and highest-priced automobiles.

Big order? You bet! So big that only the world's leading car builders could have filled it. Chevrolet and General Motors alone have the resources and the facilities it takes to put this great new idea on wheels.

Everything's new in the Motoramic Chevrolet—from its tubeless tires to its lower top! Your Chevrolet dealer will be happy to show it to you. . . . Chevrolet Division of General Motors, Detroit 2, Michigan.

GREAT NEW V8—TWO NEW 6's! New "Turbo-Fire V8" delivers 162 h.p. with an ultra-high compression ratio of 8 to 1. Two new 6's, too—the new "Blue-Flame 136" with Powerglide (optional at extra cost) and the new "Blue-Flame 123."

SWEEP-SIGHT WINDSHIELD WITH FOUR-FENDER VISIBILITY! Chevrolet's new Sweep-Sight Windshield curves around to vertical corner pillars. And you can see all four fenders from the driver's seat!

OVERDRIVE JOINS THE POWER TEAMS! Take your choice. There's new Overdrive teamed with the new V8 or the new "Blue-Flame 123." There's Powerglide teamed with the

new V8 or the new "Blue-Flame 136." (Powerglide and Overdrive are extra-cost options.) And there's a new standard transmission teamed with the new V8 or the "Blue-Flame 123."

WONDERFUL NEW GLIDE-RIDE FRONT SUSPENSION! New spherical joints flex freely to cushion road shocks. New Anti-Dive Braking Control, exclusive with Chevrolet, assures "heads up" stops.

A VENTILATING SYSTEM THAT REALLY WORKS! Chevrolet's new High-Level Ventilating System takes in air at hood-high level, away from road heat, fumes and dust.

NEW OUTRIGGER REAR SPRINGS! Rear springs are longer—and they're

attached at the outside of the frame to give you greater stability in cornering.

EVEN AIR CONDITIONING, IF YOU WISH! Air is heated or cooled by a single highly efficient unit. This is only one of the wonderful extra-cost options you can get!

MORE THAN A NEW CAR . . .
A NEW CONCEPT OF LOW-COST MOTORING

Chevrolet

The sports-car styled 1954 Buick SPECIAL Convertible—lowest-priced of Buick's four great Se now V8 powered for record-high performance, compression ratio, fuel eco

Thing of beauty and a joy for budgets

STUDY this one well, good friend — then ready yourself for the high-voltage news.

This automobile—this gorgeous grace of glass and color and flowing line pictured here — is the 1954 Buick SPECIAL Convertible.

It is Buick's lowest-priced Convertible.

MILTON BERLE STARS FOR BUICK See the Buick-Berle Show Tuesday Evenings

It sells for just a few dollars more than similar models of the so-called "low-price three."

But from that point on, it differs every step of the way.

It's styled to the breath of Spring and the lift of a breeze.

It's pulsed with a completely new V8 that's in the record books as the highest-powered engine ever placed in a Buick of this budget-priced Series.

It's cradled on a chassis of 122 inches, where four coil springs, and a steadying torque-tube, and a sensational new front-end geometry give you a ride and handling ease that come pretty near to bliss.

And it's new, this Buick—completely new, like every 1954 Buick.

New in style, body, interior. New in the backswept expanse of its panoramic windshield. New in the wider swing-open of its doors. New in the better fuel economy of its Power-Head Pistons. New in a long list of advancements that add to comfort, convenience and safety.

Your Buick dealer cordially invites you to drop in and see this stunning new Buick and judge for yourself what a thrill and a buy it is in every way.

BUICK Division of GENERAL MOTORS

When better automobiles are built Buick will build them

BUICK
the Beautiful Buy

Buick, 1954

Dollar for Dollar

You Can't Beat a

PONTIAC

STAR CHIEF CONVERTIBLE
A General Motors Masterpiece

National Open Champion!

Here is the car that is sparking the new trend to convertibles—that long, low Silver Streaked style-setter up above. And here's what makes it the all-out favorite of roving, sun-loving Americans from coast to coast.

In the Pontiac manner, this rakish beauty offers more smart distinction, more tasteful luxury, more spacious comfort and more dashing performance than a like amount of money ever covered before.

And that phrase applies without a change to every other Pontiac model. The prideful satisfaction of impressive size and beauty . . . the ever-new thrill of abundant, surging power . . . the happy confidence inspired by unquestioned dependability—*all* the special qualities of fine-car ownership are yours in a Pontiac. Yet the price of this distinguished car is within a few dollars of the very lowest on any new car!

Drop in for a test of Pontiac's great all-around performance, and check on the actual figure required to put a big, luxurious Silver Streak in your driveway. You can count on it—you will be delightfully surprised.

Cadillac FOR 1955 . .

THIS is the most significant announcement in Cadillac history!

For it introduces to the world's motorists our greatest achievement in fifty-three years of motor car production—the '55 Cadillac!

It is, beyond question, the most magnificent Cadillac of all time!

It is, as you can readily see, magnificent in beauty. Its new, jewel-like grille assembly . . . its new sculptured side treatment . . . its graceful new roof line . . . all add immeasurably to Cadillac's world-famous styling.

It is magnificent, too, in performance. There's a great new 250-h.p. engine . . . a refined Hydra-Matic Drive . . . advanced Cadillac Power Steering . . . and, as an option at extra cost, improved Cadillac Power Braking.

And it is magnificent in luxury. Its interiors are almost unbelievably beautiful . . . and each is offered in a wide selection of gorgeous new fabrics and leathers.

This, in summary, is the new Standard of the World—and it awaits your inspection now in your dealer's showroom. Stop in soon—for a personal appraisal of this Cadillac masterpiece.

The spectacular Eldorado—featuring a 270-h.p. Cadillac engine.

CADILLAC MOTOR CAR DIVISION   •   GENERAL MOTORS CORPORATION

The magnificent Cadillac Series Sixty Special—new masterwork of the industry's master crafts

Presents the Most Beautiful and Fines Performing Cars in Its History!

The dramatic Cadillac Coupe de Ville—offering the most colorful and breath-taking interiors of all time.

The inspiring Cadillac Convertible—an exciting a brilliant expression of the new Cadillac styling.

The fortunate woman who enjoys possession of a 1954 Cadillac would find it
difficult, indeed, to single out the one
quality of the car which she finds most
rewarding. Cadillac's new performance,
for instance, is a constant joy through
every mile . . . its great beauty is a source
of unending pride and satisfaction . . its
marvelous luxury delights her every time
she glances about the car's interior . . . and
its remarkable economy is a continuing
compliment to her practical wisdom. For,
truly, this magnificent motoring creation
is superlative in every respect. If you have
not as yet discovered this for yourself, you
should visit your Cadillac dealer without
delay. You'll be welcome at any time.

* * *

*Dress designed by Hattie Carnegie expressly
for the Cadillac Convertible.*

Cadillac

CADILLAC MOTOR CAR DIVISION • GENERAL MOTORS CORPORATION

Unretouched photograph of Plymouth Belvedere Sport Coupe • Enjoy "That's My Boy," "Shower of Stars," and "Climax!" on CBS-TV

SO BIG...SO POWERFUL...SO EXCITING ...ALL-NEW PLYMOUTH '55

Biggest car of the low-price 3.... A completely new car ... powerful new V-8 and 6 engines...new Metal-in-Motion Styling...
new chassis....Plymouth is the car to measure against. This year, of all years, look at all 3. When you do, you'll change to Plymouth!

Here at last is a completely new car—a car in which *nothing has been borrowed from the past!*

No limit has been set upon the funds, brains or talent needed for the development of this car. Enough new ideas have gone into it for a dozen ordinary "new models."

Why did we "start from scratch" with this automobile?

The answer lies in the spirit and nature of the American people. We as a nation are dynamic, searching, young in heart . . . never really satisfied with anything short of the best. For us a car that is simply a good car, that will satisfy most needs, is not enough.

So we have built our car. Its greatly increased power and size . . . its fleet and forward-thrusting lines . . . all are in the young-hearted tempo of our times.

In this, America's shining new "portrait in steel," you'll see a reflection. And that reflection will be you.

The New Hy-Fire V-8 Engine The newest, most advanced eight in the lowest-price field, with the Polysphere combustion chamber. Flashing new power . . . more "go" per gallon . . . aviation performance on regular-grade gasoline. . . . Or, you may choose Plymouth's new economical high-horsepower PowerFlow 6, a rugged engine of notable simplicity and smoothness . . . based on a design famous for thrift and reliability

PowerFlite No-Clutch Transmission with New Flite-Control Drive Selector Finest of fully automatic transmissions. New, convenient drive selector *on instrument panel*—exclusively Plymouth's in the lowest-price field!

Full-Time Power Steering does 80% of the work for you, and—unlike the "other two"—does it 100% of the time!

Power Brakes make driving easier for you. New, wider pedal is *suspended*, both on power and regular brakes, for easier action and added foot room.

New Easy-Glide Power Seats The front seat moves forward and up or backward and down at the touch of a button. Completely effortless.

New Easy-Lift Power Windows Raised or lowered with a flick of a switch! Operated from the driver's seat or individually.

New Full-View Windshield is a true swept-back wrap-around. Your range of vision extends to the sides, where you need it. No blind spots from posts slanting forward at eye level as in other makes.

New Metal-in-Motion Styling Trim, taut-muscled, "forward" lines reflect the dynamic spirit of a nation that's young in heart!

Luxurious New Interiors Fabrics are excitingly modern. Glamorous color styling harmonizes with brilliant exteriors. Beautiful new instrument panel with no-glare finish.

Extra Overhead Strength from new box-girder body construction. Much larger streamlined trunk, fully lined to protect your bags.

New Airtemp Air Conditioning for complete all-weather comfort.

PowerFlite, Power Steering, Power Brakes, Power Seats, Power Window Lifts, Air Conditioning, Automatic Overdrive all available at low extra cost.

Now on display at your
Plymouth dealer's . . .
a great new car for the
YOUNG IN HEART

Plymouth, 1955

You get the solid quality of Body by Fisher.

Pontiac combines glamour and utility to bring you the scene-stealing Safari

Here's the glamorous new successor to the station wagon—the adventure-loving Safari by Pontiac.

One breathtaking look tells you that here is a fresh and exciting new kind of car—long, sleek, low as a sedan . . . beautiful far beyond the ordinary wagon.

In steel and glass and in spirit . . . the Safari gives driving new life and zest.

In performance, the Safari stands alone. Under all load conditions, exclusive Wide-Track Wheel design provides geared-to-the-road stability and resistance to lean, sway and crosswinds you'll find in no conventional wagon.

And you can choose from the industry's two most modern V-8 power plants—the Tempest 420, for the ultimate in action, or the

420E, which puts the accent on economy by delivering small car mileage on regular gas—yet with V-8 power and pep.

The ladies in particular will appreciate the Safari's superb handling ease; smooth, sure Air-Cooled True-Contour Brakes; luxurious—but rugged—interiors and roll-down rear windows with no top gate to tug with. The rear window is dash-controlled, electrically operated on Catalina 9-passenger Safari (optional at extra cost on others).

Choose from three glamorous Safaris—the Catalina 6 or 9-passenger or the superb Bonneville 6-passenger. Whatever your choice—admiring glances will be a constant reminder that you're stealing the scene with America's most glamorous wagon!

Your Pontiac dealer invites you to drive this truly remarkable car!

PONTIAC!

America's Number ① Road Car

3 Totally New Series • Catalina • Star Chief • Bonneville

THE ONLY CAR WITH *WIDE-TRACK* WHEELS

The wheels are moved out 5 inches for the widest, steadiest stance in America—lower center of gravity for better grip on the road, safer cornering, smoother ride, easier handling. Pontiac gives you roadability no narrow gauge car can offer!

PONTIAC MOTOR DIVISION • GENERAL MOTORS CORPORATION

Cadillac, 1954 ◄   Pontiac, 1954

► Buick, 1955

What's up in styling? power?

New Safety. *When you want quick action to get out of a traffic tight-spot, you just push the accelerator pedal the last half inch beyond full throttle—and the way those variable pitch propellers in Dynaflow Drive go to work is hard to believe.*

erformance?

Thrill of the year is Buick

O F COURSE there's a fresh, new-day note to its styling, from that gleaming Wide-Screen Grille to the smart sweep of that new tail assembly.

Of course there's new power beneath that graceful bonnet—a new high of 188 hp in the low-price SPECIAL — a new high of 236 hp in the CENTURY, SUPER and ROADMASTER.

But the big thrills go even deeper in these 1955 Buicks.

We took a tip from aeronautics

When we tell you these eager new Buicks use the modern airplane's principle of "variable pitch" propulsion, we mean that literally.

As any aeronautical engineer will tell you, one of the greatest boons to aviation has been a propeller that uses one "pitch" of its blades for take-off and fast climbing — another "pitch" for gas-saving in the cruising range.

And now Buick engineers have applied this pitch-changing principle to Dynaflow Drive.*

A new sensation in driving

What happens when the little blades of the "stator" — deep inside a Dynaflow Drive — change their pitch like the blades of a plane propeller?

The answer is waiting for you now — in the handsomest, ablest and highest-powered Buicks that ever greeted a new year.

So what are you waiting for? Better get behind the wheel of a 1955 Buick—and be up to date on the greatest advance in years.

BUICK *Division of* GENERAL MOTORS

*Standard on Roadmaster, optional at extra cost on other Series.

WHEN BETTER AUTOMOBILES ARE BUILT
BUICK WILL BUILD THEM

re miles per gallon

s spectacular new Dynaflow
elopment, added to other advances
ecent years, gives you up to
more miles per gallon than Buicks
e in 1948.

—and a new high in V8 power

236 hp in the ROADMASTER
236 hp in the SUPER
236 hp in the CENTURY
188 hp in the SPECIAL

STEEP
HILL

It's Pontiac's year to star!

Sensational news...from performance to price tag!

Trust car-wise America to get the point about the '55 Pontiac —and get it fast! This All-New General Motors Masterpiece has adorned streets and driveways for just a few weeks—yet public opinion has already marked it as the sum of all that's new and news for 1955.

Drive it, and you'll go all the way with that widespread opinion, too.

You'll note heads turning to admire its lower, future-fashioned lines, panoramic windshield and Vogue Two-Tone styling. You'll feel the thrilling surge of Strato-Streak V-8 power . . . the all-new ease of control from new recirculating ball steering and front suspension . . . the restful ride and stability from new parallel rear springs and more rigid frame. You're handling a pace setter in

every department—and you know it from the instant you settle down in the wider front seat.

Yet the price is still next door to the very lowest. That's the crowning sensation of the sensational car on display at your Pontiac dealer—the year's boldest advance in beauty, luxury, power. See and drive it today!

PONTIAC MOTOR DIVISION OF GENERAL MOTORS CORPORATION

 Over three and a half million test miles prove this 180-HP Strato-Streak V-8 foremost in performance, economy and dependability.

SEE THE RED BUTTONS SHOW, FRIDAYS—NBC-TV

'55 Pontiac
WITH THE 180-HP STRATO-STREAK V-8

Pontiac, 1955

It's Pontiac's year to star!

Room for everything - except improvement!

The statement above neatly sums up what we have done to make this all-new General Motors Masterpiece the highway star of the year.

You'll agree, it looks the part. Pontiac's low future-fashioned contour, twin-streaked hood and Vogue Two-Tone styling are new to motoring—as is the mode-of-tomorrow décor of the roomier interiors.

At the wheel you'll learn that it acts the part, as well. Strato-Streak V-8 performance is just as sensational as it sounds. Recirculating ball steering, bigger brakes, parallel

rear springs and front suspension work equal wonders in handling and riding ease. Driving becomes a fresh and thrilling experience again!

That's Pontiac for '55—a car that overtakes tomorrow in every department of motoring . . . styled, powered and appointed to challenge any car at any price on any count —yet priced within a few dollars of the very lowest. See it, drive it, buy it—own all that's new and best for '55.

Pontiac Motor Division of General Motors Corporation
SEE THE RED BUTTONS SHOW, FRIDAYS—NBC-TV

 Pontiac station wagons for '55 feature a wide vision, wrap-around rear window as well as a new panoramic windshield.

'55 Pontiac
WITH THE 180-HP STRATO-STREAK V-8

Pontiac, 1955

THE 1955 NEWS STORY ON FINE CAR PERFORMANCE

There's a strong statement that needs to be made right now. This year Lincoln has been built to give you performance that cannot be approached by any other fine car on the road.

First, there is Lincoln's new Turbo-Drive—the most significant forward step in no-shift transmissions in 15 years. At last—completely *smooth* shifting plus instant acceleration, giving you both in combination for the first time.

The next news comes from a dramatic engineering achievement—the new, high

torque Lincoln V-8 engine. Here is an efficient power plant with more than just high horsepower and high compression ratio. Teamed with the new Turbo-Drive, this new engine gives you performance that is matchless—not just at expressway speeds but in *all* speeds.

You move effortlessly through traffic. You pass other cars as if they weren't there. Hills are leveled. Curves are straightened. This is performance—this is *action*—out of the engineer's dreambook.

Won't you visit your Lincoln dealer

soon? See for yourself Lincoln's dramatic new styling for 1955. Then take a Lincoln or Lincoln Capri out on the road. You'll quickly understand why it's the car for modern living—for *magnificent driving!*

LINCOLN DIVISION • FORD MOTOR COMPANY

NEW 1955
LINCOLN
for modern living
for magnificent driving

Lincoln, 1955

ALL
AROUND
NEW!

ALL THE WAY THROUGH!

New 1955 Ninety-Eight Deluxe Holiday Coupé. A General Motors Value.

...Powered by "ROCKET" 202

Headed straight for highest honors! It's the new "Go-Ahead" look . . . Oldsmobile's styling exclusive for '55! Here's grace and glamour to raise your spirits . . . a "flying color" flair that's Oldsmobile's alone! What's more, the new "Rocket" 202 Engine steps ahead in power and performance! By all means see and drive this all-around-new "Rocket" Oldsmobile . . . at your dealer's now!

 Higher power (202 hp.), higher compression (8.5:1), higher torque—the greatest "Rocket" on record!

Ninety-Eight
OLDSMOBILE

Oldsmobile, 1955 ▶ *Plymouth, 1954*

New 1954 Plymouth offers you Hy-Style Beauty

Hy-Drive No-Shift Driving...New Power Steering

Great New Value!

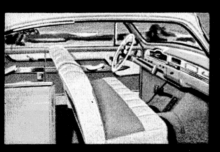

NEW HY-STYLE design features glowing new colors, sweeping lines accented with brilliant chrome; a car that's inches longer with a lower, wider look; new Color-Tuned interiors; three new lines of cars, the Plaza, the Savoy, the Belvedere.

NEW HY-DRIVE is the newest, smoothest, least expensive no-shift drive in the low-price field! A special power-multiplying feature gives you fast, positive getaway. From start to stop, Hy-Drive is smooth; no lag or jerk at any speed!

NEW POWER STEERING makes parking and driving practically effortless, yet you always have the sensation of sure, safe control. For a demonstration of these and other new features we hope you'll see your Plymouth dealer soon!

Tune in Medallion Theatre weekly on CBS-TV. See TV page of your newspaper for time and station.   Power Steering and Hy-Drive—also Automatic Overdrive—optional at extra cost.

PLYMOUTH

Chrysler Corporation's
No. 1 Car

American Motors Announces

YOU'RE LOOKING AT IT NOW—the *first* new car from dynamic American Motors!

Not just a new car, but a complete *new idea* in automobiles, to meet the new motoring wants of millions.

Here's the new idea in
luxury . . . the rakish flair of the continental sports car, with color-smart interiors like you've never seen before!

Here's the new idea in performance.
The liveliest, easiest-to-handle car you've ever had your hands on. A Rambler that darts through traffic . . . turns in the shortest radius, parks easier and out-maneuvers any sedan built in America today . . . and that out-distances them all on a tankful of gasoline!

Here are whole new ideas in
comfort and safety. *Complete "All-Season" Air Conditioning* Airliner Reclining Seats. A new kind of Deep Coil Ride that smooths out the bumps as it hugs the road. A new kind of safety construction . . . Double Strength Unit Body.

See and try
this newest idea in automobiles—for never before has a car so fine *been priced so low.* Now on display at all Hudson Dealers and Nash Dealers throughout America.

NEW IDEA! *You never saw such luxury in a car priced so low. Genuine leathers and exquisite nylon jacquards, color-keyed from roof lining to two-tone carpet.*

NEW IDEA! *It's All-Season Air Conditioning*—greatest health, comfort, safety feature of fifty years. No cold in winter! No heat in summer! No traffic roar or dust—constant fresh, filtered air. Needs no trunk space. A Rambler so equipped costs less than an ordinary car!*

**Patents applied for*

NEW IDEA! *You're cradled in deep, Airliner Reclining Seats that adjust to let you rest on the roughest roads. Make up into Twin Travel Beds in most models.*

New Idea! On Television: "Disneyland" . . . great new all-family entertainment. ABC Network, see TV listings for time, station.

JEWELRY BY VAN CLEEF & ARPELS • GOWNS BY CEIL CHAPMAN

NEW IDEA *in "get up and go" . . . smart as tomorrow from its rakish sports car grille to its dashing continental rear tire mount, the new Rambler is easiest to handle in city traffic and on the highway.*

Rambler, 1955

Whole **New Idea** in Automobiles

It's the Country Club in Coral and Snowberry White! *One of Rambler's 22 rainbow-gay color combinations—in smart sedans, hardtop convertibles, station wagons.*

NEW IDEA! *Here's spectacular performance in a car that turns in a 38-foot circle. Unique, new Deep Coil Ride keeps you grooved to curves. Pictured here is the Rambler "Cross Country"—the New Idea in station wagons.*

THE 1955

Rambler

American Motors Corporation, Detroit, Michigan

W AT *Nash* DEALERS AND HUDSON DEALERS EVERYWHERE

▶ *Buick Roadmaster, 1955*

That wealthy look at a healthy saving!

THE 870 CATALINA

Pontiac's mighty, new Strato-Streak V-8 and all-new shockproof chassis deliver a completely new kind of performance, control and roadability.

From instrument panel to rear window, Pontiac provides the roominess and luxury of costly cars.

When you buy a Pontiac, fine things happen immediately.

Your pride gets a lift. You own one of America's most desired possessions—the objective, and the envy, of everyone with eyes for clean, modern beauty, rakish smartness and the splendor of luxury fabrics artfully keyed' to the two-toned colors of the spacious bodies.

Motoring becomes exciting again. You drive the ablest performer you have ever headed down a highway—alive with new alertness . . . sweeping uphill or down with the same effortless ease . . . responding with crisp, compelling power to every call for action.

And you have the pleasant knowledge that you have also pampered your purse. Pontiac prices are practical for every new-car buyer! Take a ride and look at the price tag for '55's finest value!

PONTIAC MOTOR DIVISION OF GENERAL MOTORS CORPORATION

'55 Pontiac
STRATO-STREAK V-8

SEE THE RED BUTTONS SHOW, FRIDAYS—NBC-TV

STEALING THE SHOW
from the
HIGH-PRICED CARS

SHOW-CAR STYLING

Sweep-Sight windshield

Four-Fender visibility

High-Level ventilation

Entirely new ride

Ball-Race steering

Tubeless tires

two new **6**'s

New
Standard
Transmission

New
Touch-Down
Overdrive*

Super-Smooth
Powerglide*

3 MODERN DRIVES

MOTORAMIC

CHEVROLET

*Overdrive and Powerglide extra-cost options

The Bel Air Sport Coupe

You're looking at the profile of the greatest show stealer since "The Great Profile" himself—the new Chevrolet!

Time was, you know, when the high-priced cars took the bows for styling, performance, and the rest. But not *this* year. No, sir! The Motoramic Chevrolet's getting the big hand everywhere—at the auto shows, in the showroom, and on the road. And almost everybody from bankers to bobby soxers seems to love it.

But then, why shouldn't they? Where could you find a handsomer and livelier performer? (And we mean at *any* price!) You can tell just by its long, low, "let's go"

look that the Motoramic Chevrolet is strictly top billing.

And when you drive it, the curtain goes up on an exciting new drama starring *you!* Just give the nod to Chevrolet's new 162-h.p. "Turbo-Fire V8" or one of the two new "Blue-Flame" 6's, and you'll see what we mean. Then Chevrolet brings you all the luxuries a first-nighter could ask for—plus a full program of extra-cost options, even to air conditioning on V8 models.

The next performance starts any time you drop in. No ticket needed.

SEE YOUR CHEVROLET DEALER

MORE THAN A NEW CAR...A NEW CONCEPT OF LOW-COST MOTORING!

Chevrolet, 1955

With Flying Colors..

1955 Oldsmobile Super "88" Holiday Coupé. A General Motors Value.

OLDSMOBILE **88**
ROCKETS INTO 1955 !

NEW!

NEW!

ALL-AROUND-NEW!

Flashing into the future with flying colors . . . *Oldsmobile for '55!* . . . *more spectacular, more colorful, more powerful* than ever! In three exciting series (Ninety-Eight, Super "88", "88"), every one of them new, all-around-new, *all the way through!* And Oldsmobile's owner-proved "Rocket"—the engine that blazed the way into the Power Era—is all-new, too! New 202 horsepower, new higher torque, new higher compression ratio—new combustion chambers! Every new Oldsmobile has that commanding new "Go-Ahead" look—bold, sweeping front-end design—dramatic new "flying color" patterns—dazzling new styling from front to rear—the newest *new ideas on wheels!* More than ever, Oldsmobile is out ahead to *stay ahead!* See your dealer now . . . see these magnificent new "Rocket" Oldsmobiles for 1955!

Pontiac, 1955 ◄ Oldsmobile, 1955

When better automobiles are built Buick will build them

Why not make a smart move – just for the fun of it?

It makes good sense, if you like the finer things in life, to go looking where the cream lies thickest.

In motoring, that means a meeting with ROADMASTER—and for a very sound reason.

This top-of-the-line Buick is the very cream of the most successful line of Buicks in all history — with sales now soaring to an all-time best-seller high.

That brings to the buyer of a ROADMASTER many things not to be had in other fine cars of similar stature.

For the advantages that are bringing such soaring success to *all* Buicks are merely the beginnings for ROADMASTER.

Here, the great Buick ride of all-coil springing is made measurably better by larger tires, by

bigger brakes, by special cushioning in the car's interior.

Here, exclusive fabrics and finish are fully in keeping with the custom production status of this luxurious automobile.

And here, as you would expect, is a long list of items provided as standard equipment at no extra cost—including Buick's much-wanted Safety Power Steering.

But this year, the move to ROADMASTER is a smarter move than ever in the fine-car field— because here you get the most modern automatic transmission yet developed.

It is the new Variable Pitch Dynaflow—smo to the absolute—improved in gasoline mileas thrilling beyond all previous experience w you call for action. And it is given life by highest horsepower ever placed in a Buick.

So may we suggest that you look i ROADMASTER—just for the fun and satisfact it can bring you? Your Buick dealer will gla arrange matters—and show you the sensi price that Buick's volume production perm for this custom-built automobile.

BUICK *Division of* GENERAL MOTO

ROADMASTER

Custom-Built by Buick

Milton Berle Stars for Buick
See the Buick-Berle Show
Alternate Tuesday Evenings

Packard Clipper, 1955

Buick Roadmaster, 1955 ◄   *Mercury, 1955*

De Soto, 1955   ► *Plymouth, 1955* ►► *Plymouth, 1956*

The car that's going places with the Young in Heart!

Aerodynamic Plymouth '56

All-new Plymouths in 29 models. Choice of engines—new Hy-Fire V-8 or PowerFlow 6

Driving Takes Wings

Settle yourself behind the Push-Button controls of the all-new Plymouth '56.
Look proud, because every eye is turned on this big, beautiful triumph of
jet-age design.... Then a gentle toe-touch on the throttle! Feel that forward push
against your back ... see how Plymouth leaves other cars behind?

That's Plymouth's magnificent new Hy-Fire V-8 ... plus *90-90 Turbo-Torque*
getaway and PowerFlite, for top thrust at take-off ... swift, safe passing.
Or, for maximum economy, choose the new, increased-horsepower PowerFlow 6.

Get the news: PLYMOUTH NEWS CARAVAN with John Cameron Swayze, NBC-TV. SHOWER OF STARS and "CLIMAX!" CBS-TV.

PUSH-BUTTON DRIVING

What it means to you. First on Plymouth in the low-
price 3! A touch of a button selects your driving range.
Easy as pressing a light switch. Then PowerFlite fully
automatic transmission takes over. Here's new driving ease!

Unretouched photograph of Plymouth "6" Belvedere 4-door Sedan

THE BIGGEST IS THE MOST GLAMOROUS, TOO!

...WEST...MOST MODERN...OF THE LOW-PRICE 3

Biggest car in the lowest-price field . . . 17 feet of beauty!

Brilliant new 6-cylinder PowerFlow 117, with exclusive Chrome-Sealed Action. Exciting new 167-hp Hy-Fire V-8, highest standard horsepower in its field.

Glamorous new Full-View Windshield . . . a true swept-back wrap-around, with greatest visibility of any low-price car. All Power Driving Aids.

PowerFlite . . . finest no-clutch transmission made, with PowerFlite Range Selector on the instrument panel.

It seems spun out of fire and flowing lines — the 1955 Plymouth. You see it everywhere — proudly thrusting through the night, or jewel-brilliant in the sun. For America recognizes that the beautiful '55 Plymouth is unmistakably one of the great cars of automotive history.

This big beauty was deliberately created to revolutionize the lowest-price field. It is lithe, eager, *new*. Nothing borrowed. No hand-me-down styling. No compromises. Just the endur-

ing beauty of perfect taste—yours now, in *the biggest car of the low-price 3.*

Inner value is well mated to outer grace in the new Plymouth. You sense that . . . in the hushed power, the nimble handling, of this superb car . . . This year, of all years, *look at all 3.* Study Plymouth's engineering and craftsmanship. Then we believe, you'll join the big swing to Plymouth

PowerFlite and all Power Driving Aids available at low extra cost. Enjoy "PLYMOUTH NEW CARAVAN" on NBC-TV and "SHOWER OF STARS" and "CLIMAX!" on CBS-TV.

ALL-NEW PLYMOUTH '55

See it...drive it...today at your Plymouth dealer's...a great new car for the YOUNG IN HEART

Now, in America, a refreshing new concept in fine motor cars

The excitement it stirs in your heart when you see the Continental *Mark II* lies in the way it has dared to depart from the conventional, the obvious.

And that's as we intended it. For in designing and building this distinguished motor car, we were thinking, especially, of those who admire the beauty of honest, simple lines . . . and of those who most appreciate a car which has been so conscientiously crafted.

The man who owns a Continental *Mark II* will possess a motor car that is truly distinctive and will *keep* its distinction for years to come.

Continental
Mark II

Continental Division · Ford Motor Company

Plymouth, 1955 ◀ *Continental Mark II, 1955*

Hard top, soft top or open—the Thunderbird is the star in *any* setting!

And now: the latest version
of America's most exciting car:
Ford THUNDERBIRD for '56

Ready to give you a new lease on driving fun, this newest version of America's favorite dream car is more stunning in style . . . more thrilling in power . . . more luxurious in comfort.

Here, poised for flight you see what many people hardly dreamed possible: a more beautiful, more powerful, more distinctive Thunderbird.

The graceful contours of its long, low lines . . . the unique flair of its new spare-tire mounting . . . the dazzling sheen of its new two-tone colors are but a hint of its newness.

It is when you put the selector in drive position and nudge the gas pedal of a Fordomatic model that the new Thunderbird will really take you by the heart. Nestled beneath that sleek hood lies a new 225-h.p. Thunderbird Y-8, ready to revise all your ideas of how a car should respond.

Now, you may choose hard top, soft top or both. There's a glass-fibre hard top and a foldaway fabric top. Now, the interiors are richer—more beautiful than ever. Now, you get the added protection of Ford's exclusive Lifeguard design. Now, the ride is smoother—the cornering is flatter than ever. And, as always, you may have optional power steering, brakes, windows and seat. Ask your Ford Dealer just how soon *you* can start enjoying the better things of driving.

The 1956 Thunderbird's brand-new rear spare-tire mounting folds back handily, as quick as a wink. It adds as greatly to your luggage space as it does to the over-all beauty of the car.

Ford Thunderbird, 1955

▶ *Chevrolet, 1956*

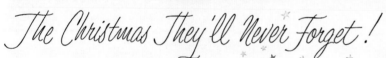

The Christmas They'll Never Forget!

Cadillac

YOUR CADILLAC DEALER

Cadillac, 1955

Behold the Incomparable

PACKARD

America's only fine car with...

Torsion-Level Ride — the new suspension principle that outmodes coil and leaf springs

Up to 310 Horsepower — giving you mightier wheel-driving force than any other car

Electronic Touch-Button Drive — the only electronically operated finger-touch control

Twin-Traction Safety Differential — for dramatically safer road-grip the year round

The fastest increase in resale value of any car — up as much as 9.6% in the past year

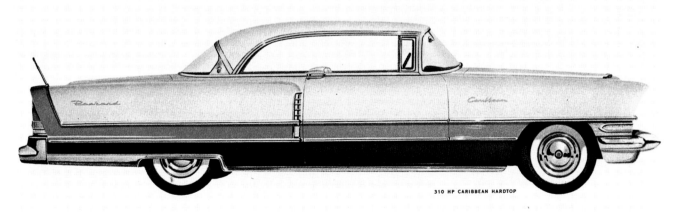

310 HP CARIBBEAN HARDTOP

ASK THE MAN WHO OWNS *the New* ONE

PACKARD DIVISION — STUDEBAKER-PACKARD CORPORATION — Where Pride of Workmanship *Still* Comes First

Packard, 1956

▶ *Chevrolet, 1956*

19 sure cures for Spring Fever
...all easy to take !

Those fresh and frisky '56 Chevrolets

THE BEL AIR SPORT COUPE—*Another hardtop honey! With windows down, it's wide open for fun!*

THE BEL AIR CONVERTIBLE—*Loves to go—and looks it. Horsepower ranges clear up to 225!*

THE BEL AIR NOMAD—*Sweet and low. This 6-passenger beauty is Chevrolet's last word in wagons!*

THE "TWO-TEN" SPORT SEDAN—*Four doors and no sideposts in this stylish new Chevy.*

THE "TWO-TEN" BEAUVILLE—*This 4-door wagon holds a whole baseball team, or ½-ton of cargo.*

THE "TWO-TEN" SPORT COUPE—*Made to have fun with—and it's Chevrolet's lowest priced hardtop!*

THE "TWO-TEN" HANDYMAN—*Looking for a 2-door station wagon that seats six and handles big loads?*

THE "TWO-TEN" DELRAY CLUB COUPE—*Its all-vinyl interior thrives on hard use. Washes clean.*

THE "ONE-FIFTY" 4-DOOR SEDAN—*Notice the tasteful chrome trim in Chevrolet's lowest priced series.*

THE BEL AIR SPORT SEDAN—One of Chevrolet's two new 4-door hardtops. Body by Fisher, of course.

THE HOT ONE'S EVEN HOTTER

CHEVROLET

Traffic-test it—it's a beautiful thing to handle!

Are you feeling slightly day-dreamy these days? Find yourself thinking of far-away places where tall trees hem in the highway and sunlight skips merrily along a chuckling mountain stream? That's spring fever, friend.

It's curable, though—and we don't mean with sulphur and molasses. You just pick yourself out a frisky new Chevrolet and go find that mountain stream. Or, if you can't get away for the trip, just *owning* a new Chevrolet will do the trick.

Sunday sightseeing around town and afternoon jaunts in the countryside are shiny new adventures when you're driving one of these fun-loving new Chevies.

In all, Chevrolet offers 19 sure cures for spring fever—all with Body by Fisher and horsepower ranging up to 225 for safer, happier traveling. We'll be happy to fill the prescription whenever you stop in. Why not make it soon?

SEE YOUR CHEVROLET DEALER

THE BEL AIR 4-DOOR SEDAN—Chevrolet brings you the security of safety door latches in all models!

THE BEL AIR 2-DOOR SEDAN—A beautiful thing to handle! Ball-Race steering makes turning easier.

THE BEL AIR BEAUVILLE—Seats nine passengers, or converts quickly to roomy cargo carrier.

THE "TWO-TEN" 4-DOOR SEDAN—As you can see, the "Two-Ten" series has its own sassy new styling.

THE "TWO-TEN" TOWNSMAN—Plenty of room for six—plus big load space in this 4-door wagon.

THE "TWO-TEN" 2-DOOR SEDAN—Directional signals are standard in all new Chevrolets.

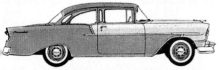

THE "ONE-FIFTY" 2-DOOR SEDAN—Your choice of V8 or 6 power in every new Chevrolet.

THE "ONE-FIFTY" UTILITY SEDAN—The entire rear compartment is load space.

THE "ONE-FIFTY" HANDYMAN—Rear seat folds flat for extra carrying capacity in this 2-door wagon.

THERE'S MORE BEHIND THE DOOR OF A PONTIAC

And a very important "more" it is—this famous Fisher Body
coach emblem. For—like such dramatic style advances as the four-door
hardtop and the panoramic windshield—it represents those added
values of exterior line and color—of interior luxury—of sturdier,
safer construction which only generations of experience and the
latest tools and techniques can build into a car body.

We hear it from thousands:
"Best Ride yet"

Ever since the 1956 Buicks made their bow some months back, we've been getting the rosiest reports!

And it's happening right across the country. The fine comments keep coming in, while Buick sales keep climbing up.

Sure, it's to be expected. New car, new compliments.

But never before, believe us, anything like this!

For this wave of raves about the '56 Buick goes for something beyond the bold, bright sweep-ahead styling that graces and identifies the best Buick yet.

It moves on beyond the might of new 322-cubic-inch V8 engines that hit the record book with the highest horsepowers and compression ratios in Buick annals.

It even reaches beyond the spectacular new double-action getaway and stepped-up gas mileage of Variable Pitch Dynaflow*—where the thrills come thick even *before* you switch the pitch.

This rising enthusiasm for this year's Buick is, more and more, for the way this beauty *rides* . . .

For the way it corners and tracks and hugs the road with a truer "sense of direction" than any Buick before it . . .

For the way it brings boulevard smoothness to roads that need renewing—for the

way its coil springs at all four wheels smother ruts and ripples—for the way its deep-oil shock absorbers snub out jars and jounce—for the way its big broad chassis lances along with swift and sure precision to keep a firm and level buoyancy for the car body and its passengers.

We could give you reasons by the dozens for this Buick's great ride.

But why take anyone's word for the feel of a car that is ride-engineered like no other car in the world?

Just drop in on us and take the wheel yourself. That way you'll know that here, literally, is the best ride yet.

Join Buick's "Thrill-A-Minute Club" Just drop in, drive a 1956 Buick, and discover the new thrills in ride, handling, power and switch-pitch performance to be had in the Best Buick Yet.

Best Buick yet

See Your Buick Dealer

SEE JACKIE GLEASON ON TV Every Saturday Evening

Buick, 1956

JUST PRESS HERE
—for Zoom Service

(That's how you switch the pitch for the most thrilling safety-surge in America today!)

It happens like this:

You want to enter an opening in fast-moving traffic. Or to pass in fewer seconds for safety's sake. Or get out of an emergency. Or breast a mountain.

So you dip the gas pedal of your new Buick to switch the pitch and—*zoom*.

You're on your merry way, quick and sure as greased lightning with the chains off.

But even before you do that—even before you switch the pitch in Buick's advanced new Variable Pitch Dynaflow*—you make another great discovery:

Smack in the very first inch of gas pedal travel—right where you save gas every foot of the way—there's a brisk and

breezy new getaway response. It gives you new control over the countless events that arise in everyday driving. And it's winning races all over America.

So you owe it to yourself to call on your Buick dealer soon and try Dynaflow's new zoom service, new gas savings.

Try it, along with the mightiest V8 engine in Buick annals—322 cubic inches of high-compression efficiency.

Try Buick's sweet new ride, cushioned by new vertical shock absorbers containing triple the former volume of oil.

Try Buick's rock-firm stability on curves—its "sense of direction" steering—its lighthearted handling—the full sweep of excitement awaiting you here.

When you do, you'll also learn that this best of all Buicks, this most beautiful of all Buicks, can be yours at a surprisingly low figure. And that, sir, is a promise.

Can you make it real soon?

BUICK *Division of* GENERAL MOTORS

New Advanced Variable Pitch Dynaflow is the only Dynaflow Buick builds today. It is standard on Roadmaster, Super and Century—optional at modest extra cost on the Special.

When better automobiles are built Buick will build them

Best Buick yet

SEE JACKIE GLEASON ON TV Every Saturday Evening

Buick, 1956

Bel Air 2-Door Sedan—one of 20 frisky new Chevrolet models.

It's a beautiful thing to handle!

Pick out a '56 Chevy owner—one who recently switched from another make of car—and ask, in a comparative kind of way, about Chevrolet handling and safety. Easier to park? Quicker reflexes in traffic? Holds the road better taking corners and curves?

We'll bet you get 100 percent affirmative answers. Because we know for a fact that Chevrolet's one of the few cars being built today with such handling ease, pep and roadability. Chevy proved that by breaking the Pikes Peak record. And proved it again by taking top honors in its field at the NASCAR Daytona Beach time trials.

What's the secret? Lively horsepower up to 225—plus a beautiful combination of road-car qualities that other cars don't have. Drive a Chevy and see what we mean. . . . Chevrolet Division of General Motors, Detroit 2, Michigan.

The Hot One's Even Hotter!

CHEVROLET
America's largest-selling car—2 million more on the road

Body By Fisher, 1958 ◀ *Chevrolet, 1956*

Frisky is the word for Chevy! Here's the Bel Air 4-door Sedan with Body by Fisher

velvet smooth
and full of spunk!

This sweet, smooth and sassy new Chevrolet has its own special way of going. It's spirited, sure . . . but a honey to handle. And if the roads out your way suddenly seem newer, that's Chevy's new ride!

We might as well own up to it—there's a certain restless energy about the new Chevrolet. It's not the stay-at-home type at all. Even when it's parked in the driveway, you can tell it's poised to travel.

The plain fact is, this beauty's full

of vim, vigor and V8 action! (Horsepower, you know, ranges up to 245*.) But for all its fresh and frisky ways, Chevy's a real solid citizen on the highway.

It's a honey to handle—sure-footed on curves, beautifully smooth on roads that have seen better days, always quick and quiet in its response to your touch.

You'd have to go a long way to find a car that offers more pure pleasure. But it's just a short trip to your Chevrolet dealer's. . . . Chevrolet Division of General Motors, Detroit 2, Michigan.

CHEVROLET
1 USA
57 CHEVROLET

Optional at extra cost. 270-h.p. high-performance V8 engine also available at extra cost.

Chevrolet, 1951 ▶ *Nash, 1956* ▶▶ *Chevrolet, 1957*

Nash Thought of the Children, too, in the World's Finest Travel Car!

Photographed in Disneyland

We didn't stop with giving Nash the swiftest, boldest speedlines and the hottest new V-8. We added a "baker's dozen" of exclusive benefits for children's comfort and parents' peace of mind.

We put the biggest, safest room on the road into the world's strongest, safest construction . . . an instant "nap couch" nearly 3 feet wide for two youngsters, plus "sit-up" room for parents . . . a "game table" rear arm rest . . . a new kind of low-cost air conditioning.

We built the broadest windshield and rear window for wide young eyes . . . developed a whole new springing system to banish "back-seat bounce".

Bring the family and travel-test this new Nash. And try to match these wonderful travel features in any other car! See your Nash dealer.

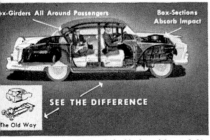

Advanced Over Old-Type bolted body and frame (left), in Nash (above), the Double Safety of the single, all-welded unit extends big box-girders around your precious cargo. Lasts twice as long, means higher resale value.

Just Tap the "Go" Pedal of the new 220 H.P. Jetfire V-8 and the Rocky Mountains seem Florida-flat. Breath-taking getaway with Twin Ultramatic Drive. Brand-new Statesman overhead valve engine, too.

No Freeze, No Sneeze, No Sizzle with amazing, lower-priced All-Season Air Conditioning. One control warms you in winter, gives you refrigerated, dry, cool comfort in summer. Filters and ventilates all year 'round.

New Speedline-Styled Nash Ambassador Four-Door Sedan, above, photographed in Disneyland.

WORLD'S FINEST TRAVEL CAR

Nash '56

TOPS IN RESALE VALUE

SEE THE ALL-NEW RAMBLER, TOO, AT YOUR NASH DEALER

 AMERICAN MOTORS MEANS MORE FOR AMERICANS

See Disneyland—great TV for all the family over ABC network.

In the market for a car that's sweet, smooth, and sassy?

Chevy's got 20 to pick from!

*Here's the whole beautiful line-up of '57 Chevrolets. And every last
one — from the "One-Fifty" 2-Door Sedan to the dashing new
Corvette — brings you a special, spirited way of going that's Chevy's alone!*

1. The "One-Fifty" Utility Sedan.
2. The "Two-Ten" Beauville.
3. The "Two-Ten" Townsman.
4. The "Two-Ten" 4-Door Sedan.
5. The "One-Fifty" 2-Door Sedan.
6. The Bel Air 4-Door Sedan.
7. The "Two-Ten" Sport Sedan.
8. The "One-Fifty" Handyman.
9. The "Two-Ten" 2-Door Sedan.
10. The "One-Fifty" 4-Door Sedan.
11. The Bel Air Nomad.
12. The "Two-Ten" Sport Coupe.
13. The Bel Air Convertible.

14. The Bel Air 2-Door Sedan.
15. The "Two-Ten" Handyman.
16. The "Two-Ten" Delray Club Coupe.
17. The Corvette Sports Car.
18. The Bel Air Sport Sedan.
19. The Bel Air Sport Coupe.
20. The Bel Air Townsman.

See your favorite "number" at your Chevrolet dealer's. . . . Chevrolet Division of General Motors, Detroit 2, Michigan.

CHEVROLET

1 USA

'57 CHEVROLET

Gowns by Amelia G[...]

Owners tell us that one of the most rewarding aspects of Cadillac ownership is the remarkable *friendliness* which they encounter at the wheel. Wherever they travel, they find that the "car of cars" introduces them in a very special manner—and seems to inspire the confidence and respect of those about them. This unique Cadillac virtue comes, of course, as something extra when you make your de-

cision for Cadillac. It comes in addition to the car's great beauty—its outstanding performance—and its marvelous comfort and handling ease. We suggest that you visit your dealer soon for a personal appraisal of this glorious list of Cadillac virtues—and to learn why this is such a wonderful season to make the move, both for delivery and economy.
CADILLAC MOTOR CAR DIVISION • GENERAL MOTORS CORPORATION

Cadillac

It Gives a Man a New Outlook...

...when he first views the world through the windshield of his own Cadillac car. In fact, we have it on the word of Cadillac owners themselves that it constitutes one of the most edifying experiences of a motorist's life. There is, for instance, the wholly new sense of pride he feels as he sits in possession of a motor car that is so widely respected and admired. There is the entirely new feeling of confidence and mastery he enjoys as he puts the car through its brilliant paces for the very first time. There is the priceless satisfaction of knowing that he is surrounded by every luxury and safeguard known to automotive science. And, finally, there is his deep inner pleasure in realizing that he has made one of motordom's soundest investments. And, of course, these wonderful sentiments will be all the more pronounced for the lucky motorist who makes the move to Cadillac in 1957. Why not visit your dealer for a preview journey and see for yourself? You're welcome to try the view from the driver's seat at any time.

CADILLAC MOTOR CAR DIVISION • GENERAL MOTORS CORPORATION

Cadillac, 1956 ◀ *Cadillac, 1956*

▶ *Mercury, 1954*

As you would expect, it's Oldsmobile—pioneer in hardtop styling—that brings you the *first luxury hardtop with four doors.*

This Ninety-Eight DeLuxe Holiday Sedan is smart as a convertible, yet offers full four-door sedan convenience *and room.* No center posts mar the flow of lines—and there's no folding the front seat forward ever!

From the smallest detail right on to the challenging performance of the "Rocket" 202 Engine, this is a car for the person who favors the exceptional. Come try it at your Oldsmobile dealer's . . . now!

NINETY-EIGHT DELUXE
HOLIDAY SEDAN

Oldsmobile, 1955

Star Chief Four-door Catalina

Born to Go Together!

STRATO-STREAK V-8 **+** **STRATO-FLIGHT HYDRA-MATIC**	Wheeling this big beauty down the road you're in command of a *very special* kind of performance—performance reserved exclusively for the pleasure of Pontiac owners! Why so special? Well, first of all, under that broad, gleaming hood there's the industry's most advanced high-torque, high-compression engine—the brilliant new 227-h.p. Strato-Streak V-8. Most cars would be satisfied to stop right there—but not Pontiac! A new transmission was developed to refine all that

power—and refined it is, with the oil-smooth Strato-Flight Hydra-Matic*, tailor-made for Strato-Streak power—*and nothing else!*

The result? America's newest, smoothest, most modern performance team and *the greatest "go" on wheels!*

Why not come in and take up our invitation to try it? And don't hesitate to ask about prices. When you do, we're betting you and Pontiac will be going steady! *An extra-cost option

SEE YOUR PONTIAC DEALER

 *You can actually buy a big, glamorous Pontiac 860 for less
than you would pay for 43 models of the low-priced three!*

The '56 Strato-Streak

PONTIAC

WITH STRATO-FLIGHT HYDRA-MATIC

Pontiac Bonneville, 1958

Every 1959 Oldsmobile has the smart new "Linear Look"—trim, light, wide-open, spacious! Inside and out it's aglow with bright ideas—safer brakes, improved visibility, smoother ride, more luggage room. Yes, and a brand-new Rocket Engine, too! An engine that is incredibly smooth, the most efficient Rocket yet. Think a moment. Isn't it time to step up to an Olds—*acknowledged leader in the medium price class!* Talk it over with your local quality dealer.

OLDSMOBILE DIVISION,
GENERAL MOTORS CORPORATION

Oldsmobile, 1959

"Guests of Honor" Wherever They Go !

Not long after a motorist takes delivery of his first Cadillac car, he makes a truly wonderful and thrilling discovery.

No matter where he travels at the wheel of his Cadillac, he finds that he is accorded an *extra* measure of courtesy and respect.

And this discovery will be all the more rewarding for the man or woman who makes the move to Cadillac in 1955. For the "car of cars" now offers more of everything to inspire respect and admiration.

Its world-famous beauty, for example, is more majestic and distinctive than *ever* before. Its celebrated interior luxury and elegance are far more wonderful to behold . . . and to enjoy. And its performance is, from every standpoint, the finest in Cadillac history!

If you haven't as yet inspected and driven the magnificent 1955 Cadillac—you ought to do so soon at your Cadillac dealer's.

You'll be most welcome at any time you find convenient.

CADILLAC MOTOR CAR DIVISION ★ GENERAL MOTORS CORPORATION

Cadillac, 1955

The 1958 Fords are out ...

Rent one from Avis today

When you rent a car from Avis you get the best . . . in equipment and in service. Waiting for you will be a car you are proud to drive . . . sparkling on the outside, faultlessly clean on the inside. And it will be a new car.

Avis is always among the first to get new models from auto manufacturers. For instance, you can rent a sleek, beautiful 1958 Ford from Avis today. Or you can choose other fine makes of new cars.

Yet it costs no more to go first class with Avis. For instance, two travelers can enjoy the convenience of a spick-and-span Avis car for two days in Chicago, drive 200 miles, at a cost of only $18 each; or for three people, just $12 each!

Next trip go first class . . . *all the way.* Have an Avis car waiting for you. To reserve a car anywhere in the world, call the nearest of more than 1000 Avis stations. Look under "A" in the phone book.

Copyright 1961, Avis Inc.   184 High Street, Boston 10, Mass.

AVIS

RENT-a-CAR

GO FIRST CLASS . . . ALL THE WAY

Avis Rent-A-Car & Ford, 1958   ▶ Pontiac, 1958   ▶▶ Pontiac, 1956

A BOLD NEW CAR FOR A BOLD NEW GENERATION

BOLD PONTIAC

PONTIAC MOTOR DIVISION OF GENERAL MOTORS CORPORATION

The Most Sweeping

Pontiac has it in the

OVER SIX DOZEN "FIRSTS", INCLUDING...

STAR FLIGHT BODY DESIGN—*a Pontiac Exclusive—longer and lower than ever before—
the year's most distinctive new automotive styling.*

THE "OFF THE SHOULDER" LOOK INTERIOR STYLING—*a fashion "first" for '57—perfectly
color-matched with the exterior of your choice.*

NEW WORLD-RECORD V-8 ENGINE—*270 h.p. in Star Chief and Super Chief, 252 h.p. in the Chieftain—
with smoother Strato-Flight Hydra-Matic.*

CLOUD-SOFT, LEVEL-LINE RIDE—*the ride sensation of the year—a new suspension system
based on a big, road-hugging 124- or 122-inch wheelbase.*

Change of All!

Surprise Package OF '57!

In the boldest new-car move of the year, Pontiac for '57 leaves them all behind—in beauty, in performance, in ride!

Here's the year's most clear-cut break with the commonplace. It's a fresh, new styling story told in crisp, dramatic lines—giving the cue for a trend that's sure to follow!

And its newness goes all the way through: Brand-new power even more efficient than its predecessor that broke over 50 stock car records and led all eights in miles per gallon . . . Strato-Flight Hydra-Matic* that's nothing short of perfection . . . new suspension ideas and pre-

cision handling that crack the whip over the wildest roads imaginable. And it comes to you proved as no other car in history, because a proto-type of this big, eye-opening dazzler strutted its easy way through 100,000 miles of the most rugged road tests the engineers could devise!

Be among the first to bring yourself up to date on the car that caught them all napping.

Drive this '57 Pontiac and sample in a single memorable mile all that's been proved by 100,000 miles of testing!   *An extra-cost option

PONTIAC MOTOR DIVISION OF GENERAL MOTORS CORPORATION

IT'S AMERICA'S NUMBER ① ROAD CAR!

WHO SAYS TOMORROW NEVER COMES?

Don't miss Plymouth's two great new TV programs: "The Lawrence Welk Show" and "The Ray Anthony Show."

YOU'RE LOOKING AT IT!

This is the car you might have expected in 1960, yet it's here today—the *only* car that dares to break the time barrier.

Plymouth has reached far into the future to bring you 1960-new Flight-Sweep Styling, and a *car-full* of exciting features ... revolutionary new Torsion-Aire ride ... terrific new power for safety with the fabulous Fury "301" V-8 engine, super-powered to 235 hp ... super-safe Total Contact Brakes ... exhilarating sports-car handling.

1960 is as near as your Plymouth dealer. Drive this *great* automobile *today!*

SUDDENLY, IT'S 1960 ➤ PLYMOUTH

Plymouth, 1959

▶ *Cadillac, 1956*

Cadillac presents
the greatest advancements it has ever achieved
in motor car styling and engineering ! ➤➤➤

The Sixty Special

Cadillac for 1957...brilliant

Cadillac, 1956

Embodied in the beautiful cars on these pages are the most important and most significant automotive advancements we have ever been privileged to present to the motoring public.

Entirely new in design and engineering, and bringing to the world's highways a wholly new standard of quality and excellence—Cadillac for 1957 represents one of the greatest achievements of all time.

Cadillac's renowned stylists have created a brilliant new type of beauty . . . majestically graceful in every line and contour . . . wonderfully exciting in spirit and in concept . . . and with a dramatically new balance of chrome and glass and steel.

Cadillac's master coachcrafters have brought a new measure of luxury and excitement to the car's interiors . . . with gorgeous new fabrics and leathers . . . with inspiring new colors and patterns . . . and with marvelous new appointments and conveniences on every hand

ew in beauty, brilliantly new in performance!

The Eldorado Biarritz

And Cadillac's world-famous engineers have introduced a sensational new concept of automotive performance . . . with two great new Cadillac engines . . . with an even smoother, more responsive Hydra-Matic Drive . . . with greatly improved power steering and power braking . . . with a revolutionary new frame design . . . and with a host of other equally vital engineering advancements.

These dramatic Cadillac achievements are being presented for 1957 in ten individual body styles, including the breath-taking Eldorado series. Each is a Cadillac masterpiece . . . a brilliant tribute to the men who design and build the Standard of the World.

We extend you our cordial invitation to see . . . to inspect . . . and to drive the new 1957 Cadillac at your very earliest convenience.

It will be the most enlightening experience of your motoring life.

★ YOUR CADILLAC DEALER ★

The Bel Air Sport Coupe shows the solid quality of its Body by Fis[her]

It likes to flex those big new muscles!

The Sweet, Smooth and Sassy '57 Chevrolet...

[N]ew muscles under the hood—with [a] choice of *five* precision-balanced new [p]owerplants—to move you along in [ea]ger and effortless smoothness. New [m]uscles to grip the road even more [ti]ghtly and lay into the curves even [m]ore solidly. New muscles to give [yo]u a new lift in driving!

[He]re's a car designed to put the sparkle back into [dri]ving, a car that gives you that glad-to-be-alive [fee]ling the moment you nudge the throttle! Part of

the pleasure is performance—and part is the wonderful sense of security that comes from Chevy's superb road-holding and precision control.

How do you like to drive? There's a Chevy combination to suit every motoring mood, from the thrifty Six to the terrific Corvette V8, from the sports car *close-ratio* stick shift to the free-flight feeling of either of Chevrolet's two automatic drives.* Whenever the miles seem dull and motoring a chore, remember this: There's a sure cure just as close as your nearest Chevrolet dealer! . . . Chevrolet Division of General Motors, Detroit 2, Michigan.

Corvette engine, close-ra[tio] transmission, Powerglide [and] Turboglide automatic tra[ns]missions optional at extra c[ost]

Pick a mount with the **DE SOTO** brand, pardner!

Fireflite 2-door Sportsman in Fiesta Red and White

Choose any car in the De Soto corral, and, pardner, you've got yourself a thoroughbred. From hooded headlamps to upswept tail fins, De Soto Flight Sweep styling is the new shape of motion. New Torsion-Aire ride makes bumpy roads seem like super-highways . . . and super-highways seem like clouds. Add up all the great features of De Soto, and you've got the most exciting car in the world today. Drive a De Soto before you decide on any car. You'll be glad you did. De Soto Division, Chrysler Corporation.

Wide new price range . . . starts close to the lowest!

FIRESWEEP – big-value newcomer for 1957 – priced just above the lowest. 245 hp.

FIREDOME – medium-priced pacemaker – exciting style and performance. 270 hp.

FIREFLITE – high-powered luxury for 1957 – the last word in design and power. 295 hp.

Fireflite 4-door sedan in Muscatel Maroon and Sunburst Yellow

Fireflite convertible in Sunburst Yellow, Tamarack Green

Firesweep Sportsman in Samoa Green

DE SOTO...*the most exciting car in the world today!*

Chevrolet, 1957 ◄ *De Soto, 1957*

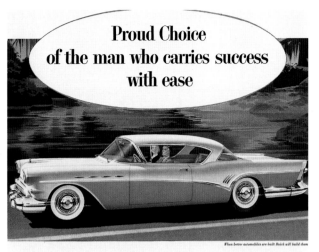

Proud Choice of the man who carries success with ease

When better automobiles are built Buick will build them

It is generally true that the more a man makes his own way in the world — the more confidence he carries into everything he does.

In his selection of fine cars, for example, he can afford to look beyond the obvious impression price makes — and go directly to the spirited satisfaction the car itself can offer.

This, we believe, is the basic reason for ROADMASTER's growing preference among fine-car buyers.

It is, you see, a car with a lift and life and luxury unlike any other in the world.

The answer is as simple as this:

As the top car of a completely new line of Buicks, ROADMASTER begins with the many advances found in all Buicks — then moves on to a summit of its own.

That's true of its distinctive beauty — the richness of its décor within — the exclusive style notes throughout.

It's true of its distinctive handling, the levelness of its stopping.

It's true of its power — the mightiest engine ever in a Buick.

Most definitely, it is true in the silken sweep of its performance.

For only ROADMASTER, of all the world's fine cars, has the velvet responsiveness of an advanced new Variable Pitch Dynaflow to take you from curbside to cruising in one infinitely smooth build-up of power.

Only ROADMASTER gives you such instantaneous obedience in "Drive" — and only here can

you switch the pitch for an all-out safety-surge of power should the need and good judgment demand it.

So this is a magnificent and spirited companion for your travels by every measure you can put to it. And you should sample it for yourself soon.

Your Buick dealer will be happy to arrange matters whenever you say. Call him this week.

BUICK Division of GENERAL MOTORS

SAFETY NEWS
Only Buick has the
SAFETY MINDER

— a simple device that's a great boon to your safety. You merely preset the miles-per-hour you want. When you reach that pace, a warning buzzer sounds. Drop below that pace and the buzzer stops.

ROADMASTER
Custom Built by Buick

Buick Roadmaster, 1957

There's just no end to the distinctive newness of this long, low, lovely Lincoln

Lincoln Premiere Two-Door Hardtop

First you see dramatic new beauty from distinctive Quadra-Lite Grille to canted rear blades.

Then, every mile you drive brings a new revelation of handling ease that's uniquely, wonderfully Lincoln's. The newness never ends, that's why more and more fine car owners are changing to this finest Lincoln ever.

From the first moment you relax behind the wheel, you find how magnificently Lincoln's crisp, new styling fulfills itself — in action.

No other fine car is so effortless to drive. The most complete array of power luxuries in any car brings a new, easy mastery to every driving situation.

A new Turbo-Drive transmission puts this most powerful Lincoln of all time instantly and smoothly at your command . . . and Lincoln's exclusive new Hydro-Cushion suspension system relaxes you

along your way as no other car can.

See all this exciting newness at your Lincoln dealer's — drive it where you will. Then and only then will you know why the trend among discerning fine car buyers is unmistakably to Lincoln.

LINCOLN DIVISION, FORD MOTOR COMPANY

LINCOLN
Unmistakably . . . the finest in the fine car field

Lincoln, 1957

Congratulations to the man who drives the exclusive Imperial

IMPERIAL
Finest expression of The Forward Look ➤

Six months ago, when the magnificent new Imperial swept on the scene, buyers of vision — like yourself — instantly recognized a great car. You, who own or have ordered or will order Imperials, are the leaders in a remarkable switch in America's fine car tastes.

Now the car of your choice is the most sought-after and talked about of all

the fine cars. Its beauty and power and flawless engineering have excited a nation . . . and have set a historic new high in month-to-month sales records. You knew it would. We knew it would. Now all the world knows it did. Congratulations!

IMPERIAL . . . FINEST PRODUCT OF CHRYSLER CORPORATION

Imperial, 1957

SUPER 88 HOLIDAY SEDAN

Check the Score... AND YOU'LL GO OVER TO OLDS!

You're in for a whole series of pleasant surprises when you first check the score on Olds ownership.

Very likely, you'll find the price less than you imagined — most people do! And when it comes to value, it's great to see how much more Oldsmobile offers for your every dollar. *Performance* values in the Rocket Engine. *Engineering* values that spell greater comfort, safety and driving ease. *Styling* values, inside and out,

that mean you'll drive your Oldsmobile with pride. And most important, *lasting value* . . . that holds a real pay-off for you at resale time!

Talk it over with your Oldsmobile dealer. He'll show you that *there's a Rocket for every pocket* . . . and that this is the right time to make that wonderful move to Olds!

OLDSMOBILE DIVISION, GENERAL MOTORS CORPORATION

OLDSMOBILE
SEE YOUR AUTHORIZED OLDSMOBILE QUALITY DEALER

Oldsmobile, 1951

Want a car that takes off like a torpedo?

Want a car with modern push-button drive selector?

Want a car with the finest brakes yet developed?

Want a car that rides like a dream?

Want a car that's safe and solid under the style?

Want the smartest car on the road?

DRIVE A DE SOTO

BEFORE YOU DECIDE

Push-button drive control is at your fingertips to the left. Positive mechanical control. Absolutely foolproof. So easy, so natural. Try it today.

PRICE a De Soto before you decide! Your De Soto dealer will give you a most attractive trade-in allowance! De Soto dealers present **Groucho Marx** in "You Bet Your Life" on NBC radio and TV • **DE SOTO DIVISION, CHRYSLER CORPORATION**

DE SOTO—OFFICIAL PACE CAR 1956 INDIANAPOLIS 500-MILE RACE.

De Soto, 1956

There Are Some Secrets a Man Can't Keep ...

...when he is seen in the driver's seat of a new 1957 Cadillac. And not the least among these is the fact that he is a man of unusual practical wisdom. For it is widely recognized that when a motorist selects the "car of cars", he selects one of the soundest of all motor car purchases. The original cost of a new Cadillac, for instance, is remarkably modest—in view of the great beauty and luxury and performance it represents. Cadillac's marvelous economy of operation and its extraordinary dependability are without counterpart on the world's highways. And Cadillac's unsurpassed resale value assures its owner a greater return on his investment than any other automobile in the land. If you would like to enjoy these many practical benefits in *your* next motor car—then you are looking for Cadillac! The car is waiting for you in your dealer's showroom—and this is the perfect moment to make the move quickly and economically. CADILLAC MOTOR CAR DIVISION • GENERAL MOTORS CORPORATION

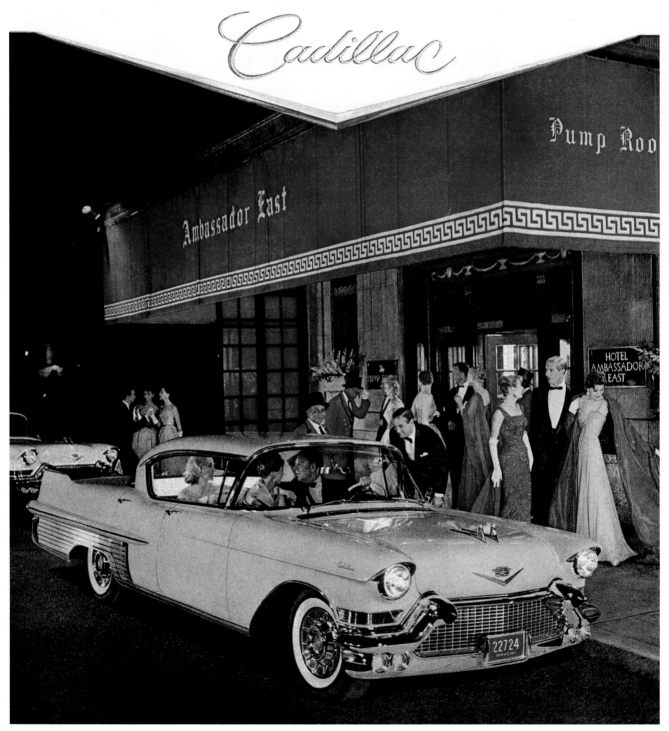

Cadillac, 1956

▶ *Buick, 1959*　▶▶ *Imperial, 1956*

THERE'S NOTHING LIKE A NEW CAR... AND NOTHING LIKE THE '60 BUICK LE SABRE 4-DOOR SEDAN YOU SEE HERE.

BUICK'S ALL-TIME BEST

There is more than mechanical excellence behind the greatness of this Buick. There is more than the Buick brakes, unsurpassed on any American car today. There is more than the smoothest automatic transmission made. More than the wonderful silence of this car in motion. More than the room, and the solid, confident feeling of an important and wholly road-worthy automobile.

More than all these is the deep-down satisfaction you get from the fact that this car's name is BUICK... and everybody knows what that stands for.

BUICK MOTOR DIVISION, GENERAL MOTORS CORPORATION

THE TURBINE DRIVE BUICK '60

BUICK LESABRE—The lowest-priced Buick **BUICK INVICTA**—The high-performance Buick **BUICK ELECTRA**—The finest Buick of all

Beauty shared by no other car—biggest size and value increase in the industry

EXCLUSIVE DREAM-CAR DESIGN. Here is clean-lined beauty, a massive grace, that is Mercury's alone. Notice the distinctive Jet-Flo bumpers, V-angle tail-lights.

FAMILY-CAR BIG
There's stretch-out comfort for six. This year's Mercury is bigger in 8 vital dimensions inside, 4 outside. There are inches of spare headroom, hip room, shoulder room, and leg room.

PRICED FOR EASY BUYING
Never before has so much bigness and luxury cost so little. See for yourself. Ask your BIG M dealer for the fun-to-read figures, today.

ONLY MERCURY OFFERS YOU THESE 6 DREAM-CAR FEATURES
- Exclusive Dream-Car Design
- Exclusive Floating Ride, with 4 new bump-smothering features
- Exclusive Power-Booster Fan in Montclair Series
- New Merc-O-Matic Keyboard Control
- Power seat that "remembers"
- New Thermo-Matic Carburetor

THE BIG MERCURY for '57 with DREAM-CAR DESIGN
MERCURY DIVISION · FORD MOTOR COMPANY

Mercury, 1957

MORE LIGHT, AIR, GLASS, GLAMOR! Mercury's new station wagons give 9½ feet of picture-window vision on each side, thanks to THE BIG M's exclusive hardtop design. And the back window rolls down into the tail gate, eliminating the old-style lift gate! Illustrated above: The Colony Park.

FIRST TRUE PASSENGER CAR RIDE: Mercury's sensational Floating Ride, with special Air-Cushion Suspension, brings true passenger car comfort to station wagons.

UNIQUE ALL-CLEAR LOADING PLATFORM. With no overhanging lift gate, and lower tail gate, loading is easier than ever!

True hardtop design, true passenger car ride, new giant capacity, 6 wonderful models to choose from

Now at last you can move up to a completely new class of station wagons—and get the luxury you've looked for! The new Mercury fleet brings you *more beauty*, with true hardtop design and dream-car styling . . . *more size* (87.4 cu. ft. of cargo capacity) . . . *more comfort* with the first "sedan" ride in station wagons . . . *more power* (up to 290 hp in the Turnpike Cruiser V-8 engine) . . . and far *more loading convenience*. Six models available: deluxe 9-passenger Colony Park, 6- and 9-passenger Voyagers, and three 6- and 9-passenger Commuters in Mercury's lowest-priced series.

THE BIG MERCURY for '57 with DREAM-CAR DESIGN

Mercury, 1957

New luxury and distinction—the Bel Air Impala Sport Coupe.

Almost too new to be true!   '58 CHEVROLET

The bold new Bel Air 4-Door Sedan.

The stylish new Nomad Station Wagon.

Here's styling that sets a new style! The beautiful '58 Chevrolet is nine inches longer, four inches wider and up to 2½ inches lower.

CHEVROLET

FORWARD FROM FIFTY

From dual headlights to gull-wing rear fenders, these are truly impressive cars. Interiors, wheelbases, grilles, styling accents, fabrics and appointments — everything is new, luxurious, exciting!

Never, *never* has a car been so wonderfully new in so many different ways! Here are radical departures in style, power and ride . . . all wrapped up in the longest, lowest, widest Chevrolet that ever said, "C'mon, let's get going!"

Here are just *some* of the real surprises that await you in Chevrolet's three new series, its new line of station wagons, its eye-brightening array of 17 all-new models:

A revolutionary new V8! So new it even looks different on the outside—that's Chevy's Turbo-Thrust V8*! Combustion chambers are *in the block*—a radical design development that results in super-smooth performance and high efficiency. Horsepower ranges up to 280. There are three new versions of the famous Turbo-Fire V8, too, including Ramjet Fuel Injection*, and more power for the super-thrifty Blue-Flame Six.

New body-frame construction! The secret of Chevy's road-hugging lowness is the new X-design Safety-Girder frame. There's extra safety in the lower center of gravity . . . and new locked-together strength in the way this new frame is wedded to Chevrolet's new Body by Fisher.

All-new 4-coil suspension! Here's a fabulous combination of super-soft coil springs *and* the super stability of Chevy's exclusive four-link rear suspension. Unquestionably, the finest standard suspension in Chevrolet's field!

You can even ride on air! Level Air suspension* puts air springs at *every* wheel for the ultimate in thistledown comfort. It changes every concept of motoring smoothness—and the car stays level, regardless of load changes front or rear! . . . See the year's newest car at your Chevrolet dealer's. . . . Chevrolet Division of General Motors, Detroit 2, Michigan.
*Extra-cost option

Chevrolet, 1957

▶ *Chevrolet, 1957*   ▶▶ *Buick, 1957*

'58 CHEVROLET

The 1958 Chevrolet Impala in Anniversary Gold, a new color created in commemoration of General Motors 50th Anniversary Year.

FIRST BIG FAMILY CAR —
WITH A SPORTS CAR HEART

It's big, bold, buoyant

THE AIR BORN

RETCH OUT IN LOUNGE-CAR COMFORT—Immaculately
ored seats are more than 5 feet wide and sofa-soft. Headroom,
room, legroom and footroom for all 6 riders, including those
he middle.

THRILL TO THE B-12000 ENGINE—Most advanced Bui
V8 yet. 12,000 pounds of thrust behind every power stroke. Pl
nodal-point mounting and center-of-percussion balance for sof
ness, sweetness, silence.

PICTURE a cruiser that's nimble as a PT boat.

A bomber deft as a jet fighter.

Picture a big and spacious automobile with the heart and soul, the sparkle and spirit, the control, obedience, response and maneuverability of the sportiest sports car ever.

We're talking about the bold and buoyant Buick for '58 —and until you drive it you don't know what driving is.

For here in this straight-from-tomorrow Buick you boss a B-12000 engine as modern as the look of the car itself.

Here, behind this fresh face of fashion, you pilot a Flight Pitch Dynaflow* literally born of aircraft design.

Here, in this fabulous B-58 Buick you glide, soar, float— with a Miracle Ride plus Buick's Air-Poise Suspension.*

Here, in brief, you discover totally new concepts in driving delight—extending from noise and vibration suppression to ingeniously air-cooled aluminum brakes* . . .

Because this, you discover, is a car born of more aircraft principles—including greater use of aluminum —than any other car yet built . . .

This, you finally realize, is the first big car that's really light on its feet.

There's a Buick — a roomy and radiant B-58 Buick — ready at your Buick dealer's—*today.*

Drive it and give the red-blooded *you* a break.

BUICK *Division of* GENERAL MOTORS

*Flight Pitch Dynaflow standard on LIMITED and ROADMASTER 75, optional at extra cost on other Series. Air-Poise Suspension optional at extra cost on all Series. Aluminum Front Brakes standard on all Series except SPECIAL. Safety-Buzzer standard on LIMITED and ROADMASTER 75, optional at extra cost on other Series.

See TALES OF WELLS FARGO, Monday Nights, N
and THE PATRICE MUNSEL SHOW, Friday Nights

When better automobiles are built Buick w

B-58 BUICK

TINGLE TO FLIGHT PITCH DYNAFLOW—"Low" is replaced by automatic downhill engine braking. "Drive" gives you the astonishing performance of triple turbines <u>plus</u> "a million ways to switch the pitch."

ENJOY IT ALL TO THE HILT with the one and or Safety-Buzzer.* Decide on a safe, sane miles-per-hour. figure to view in the "window." If you exceed that pace—bu Drop below it and the buzzing stops.

Announcing the great new *58 FORD*

PROVED AND APPROVED AROUND THE WORLD

A new car rolled out of Detroit one day last July, bound for the greatest adventure in motor car history. The car: the 58 Ford. The assignment: to test the performance and dependability of this new car around the world . . . if possible.

The route was the most rugged that could be laid out. After London and Paris came the Alps; after Rome came Yugoslavia's rockbound seacoast; after Istanbul came the camel-tracks of Iran and Afghanistan; then the Khyber Pass through the Himalayas, the bullock-trails of India, the jungle roads east to Vietnam. Weather: worse than you'll ever encounter— 122° heat, sandstorms, and 24-hour-a-day rains.

The 58 Ford rolled beautifully, easily through the severest road test ever given a car *before* its American announcement. The Ford *endured*— and came through still glittering and fresh.

Acclaimed from Buckingham Palace to the Taj Mahal, it showed camels how to cross deserts and elephants how to move through jungles. It was *proved* and *approved* by everyone from natives who had never seen an American car before to famous stylists and nabobs who have seen every car built.

Never before has such a trip been made. This round-the-world performance test became a victory parade, from London to Saigon and back to Detroit. Again, in the Ford tradition, the 58 Ford has broken a trail far out beyond competition.

see the following pages →

Lukens Steel Company ◄   *Ford, 1957*

This is the EDSEL

"A remarkable new automobile   joins the Ford family of fine cars"

Originality is written in the vertical grille, the elegant sweeping lines and the clean flight deck of this Edsel Citation 2-door Hardtop

There has never been a car like the Edsel. It is a magnificent automobile. Behind it lie all the resources of Ford Motor Company, all the experience and engineering skill.

The results are clear. The Edsel is powered by the newest V-8 engines in the world—the Edsel 400 and the Edsel 475. Their specifications: 400 and 475 pound-feet of torque; 303 and 345 horsepower; 361 and 410 cubic inches of displacement; 10.5 to 1 compression ratio. It is unlikely you have ever driven a car with so much usable power.

The Edsel's big, safe brakes do not need periodic adjustment. In the course of daily driving, they adjust automatically.

The Edsel shifts itself. In an Edsel equipped with Teletouch Drive, you just touch a button on the steering wheel hub. Teletouch Drive does the rest—smoothly, surely, safely, *electrically.*

The Edsel's list of available new features is long. Examples: contour seats; a dial that lets you select temperature, quantity and direction of air with one twist of the wrist; a warning signal that flashes when you exceed your pre-set speed limit; another that flashes when oil is one quart low; a release that enables you to open the luggage compartment from the driver's seat. You will find there are many things that make the Edsel different from any car you have ever driven. More exciting, more sure, more safe.

What does an Edsel cost? Edsel prices range from just above the lowest to just below the highest. You can afford an Edsel. And you can choose from four series, 18 models. Your Edsel Dealer invites you to see and drive the Edsel—soon.

EDSEL DIVISION · FORD MOTOR COMPANY

EDSEL
NOW AT YOUR EDSEL DEALER

Edsel, 1951

TRY SPRINGTIME *in this Sweet Stepper*

LET THERE BE new lilt in your heart with this bright and blossoming season.

Let there be new sparkle in your eyes, new tingle in your pulse, new freshness in your spirits.

Let there be a new Buick in your life.

That does it — *beautifully.*

For you, behind the wheel of this big bold automobile, feel a tonic in your senses.

You feel it in the sweet new styling, the gay new colors, the tasteful newness — certainly.

But ah!—how you feel it in the *going!*

That's where Buick's newness comes to flower—in performance, in command response, in the joy of driving.

You, in this nimble stepper, boss a brand-new engine with the most exuberant vigor in all Buick history.

You, in this stalwart beauty, have on tap the new *instant obedience* of today's spectacular Variable Pitch Dynaflow.*

You, in *any* new Buick, go joyously along in the dream car of the year *to drive.*

Go ahead and try it.

Try Springtime in a Buick, with its eye-brightening colors and the boundless spirit of eagles under its broad bonnet.

Try it, too, for a buy second to none. See your Buick dealer now—and see how wonderful *this* Spring can be.

BUICK *Division of* GENERAL MOTORS

New Advanced Variable Pitch Dynaflow is the only Dynaflow Buick builds today. It is standard on Roadmaster, Super and Century—optional at modest extra cost on the Special.

Try the "Built-In Conscience" Buick's Exclusive

SAFETY-MINDER

It buzzes when you reach the miles-per-hour you preset for yourself. You won't want to drive without it. (Standard on ROADMASTER, optional at extra cost on other Series.)

DROP IN FOR A WONDERFUL SPRING TONIC AT YOUR BUICK DEALER'S

See those Gay New Colors — New radiant hues that glint and gleam like sunshine on dew! NOW

Feel that Great New Zing — The high-spirited performance of new V8 power, and the *instant* response of today's Dynaflow!

Price those Spring-Sale Buys — Riviera hardtops —Sedans—Convertibles—Estate Wagons—and the fabulous CABALLERO—all at easy-to-take prices. (If you can afford any new car, you can afford a Buick today.)

Come Swing into Spring and Prove it Yourself—
BIG THRILL'S BUICK
SPECIAL · CENTURY · SUPER · ROADMASTER

When better automobiles are built

Buick Roadmaster

MIGHTY CHRYSLER NEW YORKER 4-DOOR HARDTOP

Enjoy Chrysler's bold new look of success!

Thousands are hailing the success of Chrysler's new Flight-Sweep styling . . . the brilliance of Chrysler's forward-thinking engineering!

In every way you can judge an automobile today, The Mighty Chrysler is literally beyond compare. Its almost unbelievable roadability, comfort and restfulness are years ahead of contemporary engineering. See the glamorous Chrysler New Yorker at your Chrysler Dealer's, also the Chrysler Saratoga, and the all-new Chrysler Windsor—now in a lower-priced field!

TREMENDOUS—Four-beam dual headlighting!

SERENE—New Torsion-Aire Ride!

EFFORTLESS—New Constant-Control power steering!

CONVENIENT—New Pushbutton TorqueFlite!

SUPERSCENIC—New Compound-Curved windshields!

EXCLUSIVE—New Auto-Pilot!*

*Optional at extra cost.

THE **MIGHTY CHRYSLER**

GLAMOUR CAR OF THE FORWARD LOOK

Chrysler, 1958

WHY PAY UP TO $200 EXTRA for so-called new air springs (they've been tried in buses for several years), when Dodge Torsion-Aire suspension is standard equipment at no extra cost on all Swept-Wing 58 models? That's a question Dodge dealers are asking new car prospects, and backing it up with a "test flight" in the new Dodge. Most noticeable difference between the two rides—Torsion-Aire vs. air springs—is the distinct freedom from lean or sway on turns with Torsion-Aire, which uses torsion bars in front. "Air springs may be some improvement over old coil springs," states Indianapolis (Ind.) Dodge dealer H. E. Fadley, "but they don't begin to match the level, smooth ride of Torsion-Aire. Why pay more and get less?" A lot of buyers seem to agree.

SWEPT-WING 58 by DODGE

Dodge, 1957

⤴ Introducing NEW SWEPT·WING 58
(So advanced it leaves the rest behind !)

A MOST UNUSUAL NEW CAR is now enjoying enthusiastic reception all over America. It is very low, very daring, beautifully proportioned. The manufacturer, Dodge Division of Chrysler Corporation, has designated the car "Swept-Wing 58" with the statement: "This is the successor to the 1957 Swept-Wing Dodge which launched a 'buying revolution' against the high, boxy design carried over by other cars in the field. In Swept-Wing 58, owners will have the most advanced 1958 car on the road in style, ride and true greatness of handling." While horsepower and torque ratings on the new Ram-Fire V-8 engine have not been disclosed, it is announced that electronic fuel injection will be available in limited quantity. A remarkable automatic transmission (TorqueFlite) combines both a fluid torque converter (for smoothness) and 3-speed gear ranges (agility and economy). Driver controls all ranges by pushbutton, a Dodge "trademark" since introducing it to the industry in 1956. Torsion-Aire ride, which virtually eliminates road-sway and brake dip, is standard equipment on all models. Other significant advances include a new Constant-Control power steering system, and a "Sure-Grip" differential for better traction on snow and ice. Among those who have previewed the Swept-Wing 58, most frequent comments concerned the luxurious new grille and a vast new "picture window" windshield which curves up, back and around. The sports-car lowness of design also made a strong impression. A Dodge spokesman pointed out: "We honestly feel that the Swept-Wing 58 has no counterpart. To own it is a new adventure." All body styles are now on display at Dodge dealerships. Dealers report large crowds from announcement day on.

Costumes by Bonnie Cashin for Philip Sills

SWEPT·WING 58 *by* DODGE

Buick, 1958

▶ *Buick, 1957*   ▶▶ *Cadillac, 1958*

Just born—and bound to make history!

the first big car that's light on its feet—

YOU LOOK at it—and you see "BIG" written all over this bold and beautiful 1958 Buick.

You drive it—and you know that never in all your born days have you known a car so nimble, so eager, so light on its feet.

It took plenty to bring you this easiest-handling, sweetest-riding Buick ever built.

It took a brilliant new engine—the B-12000—which packs 12,000 pounds of punch behind every piston's power stroke.

It took a brilliantly engineered transmission—Flight Pitch Dynaflow*—that swings its blades through infinite angles of pitch to give precise response to every ounce of pedal pressure.

It took the wonders of the 1958 Buick Miracle Ride—plus the perfection of Buick Air-Poise Suspension*—and Buick Air-Cooled Aluminum Brakes*—and a combination of other modern advances you'll find nowhere but in a 1958 Buick.

But surely you can't be content just to sit there and *read* about all these wonders! Hurry in to your Buick dealer's and *see* and *feel* what he has in store for you!

BUICK *Division of* GENERAL MOTORS

Flight Pitch Dynaflow standard on LIMITED and ROADMASTER 75, optional at extra cost on other Series. Air-Poise Suspension optional at extra cost on all Series. Aluminum Brakes standard on all Series except SPECIAL.

Big·Bold·Buoyant
the *AIR BORN B-58 BUICK*

A BOLD NEW CAR FOR A BOLD NEW GENERATION

PONTIAC

OLDSmobility

A new, 'free-and-easy' way
of going places and doing things in this <u>mobile</u> era!

Scan this sparkling span of lighthearted beauty—Oldsmobile for '58! Nearly eighteen feet of sheer excitement . . . captured in a tasteful new mobile look. There's new magic in its motion, too, with the "big-economy-news" Rocket Engine . . . and exclusive New-Matic Ride*, Oldsmobile's *true* air suspension. So come take a test ride at your dealer's soon. See how Olds for '58 makes real driving pleasure the rule on any road!

OLDSMOBILE DIVISION, GENERAL MOTORS CORPORATION

*Optional at extra cost.

OLDSMOBILE

FORWARD FROM FIFTY . . . INTO THE ROCKET AGE

Oldsmobile, 1958

Sports Car Thrills on a Luxury Car Level. An exciting new personality has arrived in the select world of performance-bred sport machines. Born of bold Pontiac advances in basic automotive engineering . . . outfitted to a man's taste in elegance . . . the pure pleasures of a new kind of motoring await you now in this latest and greatest of fine cars.

BOLD NEW Bonneville *BY PONTIAC*

AMERICA'S NUMBER ① ROAD CAR

This bird's-eye view of the Bonneville Convertible portrays the extra sports-car smartness conferred by front and rear bucket seats, optional at slight added cost. Leather upholstery, color-matched to exterior trim, is standard with either conventional or bucket seats. Front bucket seats and leather-upholstered interior are also available at extra cost in the distinguished new Sport Coupe.

Pontiac Bonneville, 1958

The car conceived and created to change your ideas of luxury motoring

This is sweeping line and commanding length. This is unusual richness of interior cushioning and appointment. This is uncompromising precision. This is the LIMITED.

It is the car we conceived and created to outmode the present measure of fine cars. It is the car you will drive with a new sense of magnificence that grows out of its performance, its comfort, its excellence of construction. Your Buick dealer cordially invites you to see the distinguished LIMITED—and to take a personal demonstration behind its wheel. See him for an appointment.

PROUDLY PRESENTED, PROUDLY POSSESSED

The LIMITED *by Buick*

Pontiac, 1958 ◄ *Buick, 1958*

► *Thunderbird, 1958*

THU

America's most individual car—an automotive jewel that's pure Thunderbird in design, spirit and performance...with full fine-car room, comfort and luxury for four

new version of a great classic...the <u>4-passenger</u>

NDERBIRD

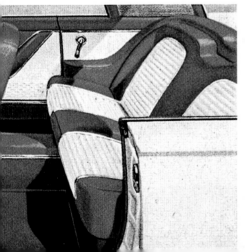

Another first from Ford! In the 1958 Thunderbird, Ford has created a wholly new size and type of fine car. It gives you Thunderbird compactness, Thunderbird handling and traditional Thunderbird performance— yet, miraculously, it now gives you full fine-car room and comfort for *four* people! It brings you interior appointments that are unbelievably imaginative and luxurious. Now, happily, you can share your Thunderbird thrills with deserving friends. Now it's *twice the fun* to own the car that became an American classic the very day it was introduced. For details about America's most excitingly different car,

turn the page, please

FIRST STATION WAGONS TO COMBINE

Mercury gives you superior performance in station wagons. You get new Marauder engines with as much as 330 hp — 4450 pounds of solid, road-hugging luxury — all wrapped up in Clean Line Modern Styling.

NOW YOU CAN ENJOY STATION-WAGON TRAVEL. This yea Mercury set out to give you station wagons that would mov as easily as passenger cars. And the results actually beat an other car you could name. You get a 312- or 330-hp Maraude V-8—either one with brand-new Cool-Power Design. An that means a new high in efficiency and economy—a new kin of response and maneuverability never before achieved i a station wagon.

You move safely past trucks—enter fast-moving traffi with an effortless ease that tops any passenger car but Mercury. And there are dozens of wonderful new driving aid like the push-button magic of Merc-O-Matic Keyboard Control

The magnificent Colony Park (*foreground*), the luxurious Voyager (*left*), the value-leading Commuter (*top right*)— Mercury's 3 series. Your choice of 6 models.

SPIRITED PERFORMANCE WITH BEAUTY AND SIZE

ND YOU TRAVEL IN STYLE! Clean Line Modern Styling, ercury's reflection of the taste and tempo of our times. Lines as an as a bridge—free from useless chrome or wings or things. And like all good modern design, it's supremely functional. e airy, spacious hardtop design gives you the widest, most nderful view on wheels. There's no liftgate to get in the y when loading; a rear window that disappears into the gate takes its place. And any Big M station wagon for 1958 es you the largest, most usable cargo area you can find— ger in all the dimensions that count.

No wonder Big M station wagons lead their field in sales. We ite you to see *all* the reasons at your Mercury dealer's

1958 MERCURY

MEA S THE MOST FOR YOUR MONEY

Pick-up Truck:
1764-lb. payload.

Panel Delivery:
1830-lb. payload,
170 cu. ft. capacity.

Turns on a dime...parks on a dime...runs on pennies

In but a matter of months, businessmen have found the Volkswagen Truck so sound an investment that, today, it has become the fastest growing seller in the U.S.A. Ask your dealer to show you comparative operating costs. He can prove that Volkswagen trucks deliver the goods . . . for less.

 VOLKSWAGEN

The engineered dependability of every Volkswagen is backed up by famous VW Service and Genuine VW Spare Parts in all 49 states. For free full-color brochure, "Go Places with Volkswagen Trucks," write P. O. Box 2506, N. Y. 17, N. Y.

Mercury, 1958 ◄   Volkswagen, 1958

Mercedes, 1958

Mercedes, 1958

YOU'LL GET A REAL CHARGE *out of the way this*
'58 CHEVROLET *responds to your touch, the slightest hint of*
command. Here's vigorous new V8 performance that's enough to perk up anybody's pride. Here's the kind of eager-to-please handling and polo pony response that lets you know you're the boss, right from the start!

That's a wonderful feeling, you know. But it doesn't happen by chance; it's a careful blend of qualities that demands real engineering talent.

Very few cars in any price range even come close to Chevy's precise, clean ease of handling, the beautifully balanced way it clings to any road, the crisp accuracy of its steering, the supple surefootedness of its Full Coil suspension.

There's never been another list of tremendous advances like the '58

Chevrolet's Level Air 100 percent air springs*, its low-slung X-built frame, its unprecedented Turbo-Thrust V8 engines*, its totally new bodies. But the biggest advance in the new Chevrolet is the whole new feeling of ease and competence and security. You won't know how significant *that* is till you try it—and that's something you ought to do this week! . . . *Chevrolet Division of General Motors, Detroit 2, Michigan.*

*Optional at extra cost.

CHEVROLET

Classic elegance in motorcars: The Lincoln Landau. Gown by Traina-Norell.

THE CLASSIC FINE CAR
that brings Continental luxury within the reach of every fine car buyer

THE NEW LINCOLN
styled and crafted in the classic Continental tradition

Inspiration for The New Lincoln: the new Continental Mark III. Mark III prices are just slightly above the fine car field.

The New Lincoln—styled and crafted in the Continental tradition—has created a new standard by which all fine cars must now be measured.

For the first time, every fine car owner has the opportunity to know Continental standards of luxury, driving qualities and craftsmanship.

The man who owns a Lincoln drives a car of classic beauty. And as he drives, he knows the pleasure of being surrounded by classic elegance in interiors.

The Lincoln owner knows an engine built to a whole new standard of precision tolerances . . . and in the Continental ideal of luxurious, *effortless* driving—every power assist known.

We invite your inspection of the first distinctively new choice in fine cars in many, many years.

LINCOLN DIVISION, FORD MOTOR COMPANY

Chevrolet, 1958

Lincoln, 1958

▶ *Body By Fisher, 1959*

281

A BOLD NEW CAR FOR A BOLD NEW GENERATION

PONTIAC

PONTIAC MOTOR DIVISION OF GENERAL MOTORS CORPORATION

Gives you the POWER TO TAKE IT EASY

It's the '57 Century—the dream car to drive!

You want both hustle and muscle in the car you drive—right?

Well then, the '57 Buick CENTURY is your car for sure.

This most completely changed Buick in history gives you twinkle-toe nimbleness—plus the brilliant performance of a great new V8 engine.

This engine has a wonderful reserve of power that lets you handle all your normal driving situations as effortlessly as a sprinter taking a stroll.

Exclusive with Buick—SAFETY-BUZZER—
the "built-in complaint" that buzzes when you reach the miles-per-hour you want to stay under, keeps silent when you drop below that pace.

So you—and the car and the engine—take it sweet and easy—climb tall hills in a breeze, practically *laze* along when you cruise on the level.

And you do it all smooth as sunrise—with response quick as light—thanks to today's *instant* new Dynaflow.*

Want to discover this performance—and learn why this glamorous '57 Buick is called the dream car *to drive?*

See your Buick dealer first thing tomorrow.

BUICK Division of GENERAL MOTORS

*New Advanced Variable Pitch Dynaflow is the only Dynaflow Buick builds today. It is standard on Roadmaster, Super and Century—optional at modest extra cost on the Special. Safety Buzzer standard on Roadmaster, optional at extra cost on other Series.

SEE THE WORLD'S HEAVYWEIGHT TITLE FIGHT
Monday, July 29 — NBC-TV Network. Check your local newspaper for Time and Channel.

Big Thrills Buick

Special · Century · Super · Roadmaster and Roadmaster 75

When better automobiles are built Buick will build them

Buick, 1957

THE MOST BEAUTIFUL WEDDING OF THE YEAR

Please turn the page...

Ford, 1958

NOTHING GOES WITH SPRINGTIME LIKE A BRIGHT NEW CHEVY!

Here are cars to rejoice in...sports-minded, fun-hearted and beautiful as all outdoors. The way they perform, ride and handle makes for the happiest driving you've ever known. Got spring fever? Trade it for that Chevrolet feeling!

There's something about these new Chevies that was made to order for the warm, wonderful days ahead.

You can see it in the eagerness of their low-thrusting silhouettes. You can feel it in the spirited way they take to an open stretch of highway, in the nimble way they negotiate a winding country road.

These are cars to rejoice in—the surest, happiest cure ever invented for an old-fashioned case of spring fever. And the treatment starts with your first close-up look at the gull-wing glamor of that all-new Body by Fisher.

Every one of these new Chevrolet passenger cars is lower, wider and more luxurious in every detail. And every clean-etched line has a freshness you'll find on no other car in Chevy's field.

Once you're behind the wheel you'll find plenty of other exclusives that make driving more restful and zestful. Give some rein to the radically new Turbo-Thrust V8,* for instance, and see how it loves to shrink the miles out where they're long and lonesome. Or follow your wanderlust down a dipping backwoods road—and feel the putting-green smoothness of Chevrolet's new kind of ride.

Your local dealer will be glad to fill you in on all the details—including prices as low as Chevy's roofline!... Chevrolet Division of General Motors, Detroit 2, Michigan.
*Optional at extra cost.

CHEVROLET

The dashing Corvette—America's only authentic sports car.

The Bel Air Sport Sedan—Body by Fisher, of course.

The Bel Air Sport Coupe—every window of every Chevrolet is Safety Plate Glass.

The Impala Sport Coupe—only Chevy's got this kind of gull-wing glamor!

The Impala Convertible—supremely smart... superbly appointed.

Pontiac, 1958 ◀   Chevrolet, 1958

▶ Ford, 1958

Married in style and luxury! The 59 Thunderbird and the new Ford Galaxie

ANNOUNCING — THI

Brilliant wedding of Thunderbird elegance and
the world's most beautifully proportioned cars

The 59 Fords awarded the Gold Medal
of the Comite Francais de L'Elégance
for beautiful proportions
at the Brussels World's Fair.

Just married in style to the Thunderbird! It'
smartest, richest and most exciting of 59 Fords—the
gant new Galaxie. A bright new personality in c
and more! The Galaxie is a full "fine car" 6-passenge
pression of Thunderbird grace—spirit—style and lu
in an altogether-new line of Fords.

It's Thunderbird in looks! The Galaxie, as y
quickly see, is as wonderfully all-the-way Thunde
as a low-priced Ford can be. The smart straight

NEW FORD *Galaxie*

...axie roof and dramatic see-it-all rear window say ...underbird *unmistakably*. So do the clean, crisp, low-...ept body lines. Here is the most perfect match yet of ...Thunderbird's silhouette—the most modern and most ...nted "new look" in cars today!

...s **Thunderbird in luxury!** New Galaxie appoint-...nts—like the plush, deep-pile carpets—are so very ...underbird in taste. And just like the Thunderbird, the ...laxie seats you in the tailored elegance of specially

quilted and pleated fabrics. There's Thunderbird V-8 power, too. A surpassing luxury that tells you how superbly these newlyweds "GO" together.

Reception now—you are invited. Why not come in —this very week—see the new Galaxie and all the mem-bers of the year's most beautiful wedding. The experi-ence, we bet, will please you proud. It might even set you to planning a second honeymoon—most elegantly— in the car that's Thunderbird in everything *except price!*

Reception starting this week at your Ford Dealer's

SUPREMACY

In no other field of commerce has a single product stood so pre-eminently alone—for so long a time—as has the Cadillac car. For more than half a century, its name has been a living symbol of automotive goodness. And the Cadillac of 1958 has underscored this supremacy with revealing emphasis. To inspect it is to behold a motor car of incredible beauty. To drive it is to command the very finest in automotive performance. And to own it is to possess the most rewarding of personal possessions. This is a wonderful time to do all three —and your dealer is waiting with details on each of Cadillac's Fleetwood-crafted models, including the Eldorado Brougham.

Every Window of Every Cadillac is Safety Plate Glass • Gown by Henri Bendel

FORWARD FROM FIFTY

CADILLAC MOTOR CAR DIVISION • GENERAL MOTORS CORPORATION

Cadillac

Dodge, 1958 ◄   *Cadillac, 1958*

Announcing

THE MARK IV
Continental

The fourth and finest in the Distinguished Series of the world's most admired car.

LINCOLN DIVISION · FORD MOTOR COMPANY

Mark IV Continental, 1958

We deliberately designed it to be the world's finest automobile

Beyond a doubt, this newest of fine cars goes well beyond the familiar concepts of luxury and performance. Indeed, that was our goal in creating the LIMITED. Thus, its interior presents a degree of elegance and comfort that sets a new level of magnificence. Its performance exceeds existing standards—to the point of providing a wholly new experience in ease of handling and serenity of ride. Even in the matter of its extra length, the LIMITED goes beyond the call of familiar dimensions. You will find this superbly crafted automobile a most satisfying possession —and your Buick dealer will be understandably proud to introduce you to it.

BUICK *Division of* GENERAL MOTORS

PROUDLY PRESENTED, PROUDLY POSSESSED —

The LIMITED *by Buick*

Buick, 1958

Now there's a full series of elegant Impalas, including the new Sport Sedan shown here.

ALL NEW ALL OVER AGAIN!

It's shaped to the new American taste with a lean, clean silhouette, crisp new contours, beautifully restrained accents. It brings you more spaciousness and comfort with a new Body by Fisher. It has a bright new sheen—a new kind of finish that keeps its luster without waxing for up to three years. New bigger brakes. Vast new areas of visibility. New Hi-Thrift 6. New handling ease and road steadiness. It's new right down to the tires!

Never before has an automobile manufacturer made such sweeping changes two years in a row. And never before has any car been new like this one.

The 1959 Chevrolet is your kind of car. Shaped to reward your new taste in style. Designed to anticipate your desire for greater roominess and comfort. Engineered to bring you greater safety, economy, ease of handling and smoothness of ride.

Chevrolet's new Slimline design brings entirely new poise and proportion to automobile styling. Inside the new and roomier Body by Fisher you'll find truly tasteful elegance. And you'll see more through the new Vista-Panoramic windshield that curves overhead. It's more than 50 per cent larger!

There's much, much more. A new steering ratio makes handling easier. New suspension engineering gives you a more stable ride. (Level Air suspension* is now even softer!) There's a sweet new edition of Turboglide*. A new Hi-Thrift 6 that goes and goes on a gallon. New Safety-Master brakes. And with all that's new, you'll find those fine old Chevrolet virtues of economy and practicality. See this fresh new Chevy at your Chevrolet dealer's. . . . Chevrolet Division of General Motors, Detroit 2, Michigan.

*Optional at extra cost

CHEVROLET

What America wants, America gets in a Chevy!

The new Bel Air 2-Door Sedan—like all '59 Chevies—rolls on stronger, safer Tyrex cord tires.

'59 CHEVROLET

Chevrolet, 1959

The Lincoln Premiere Landau

MOST DRAMATIC DEBUT OF 1959 ∵
NEWEST EDITION OF THE LINCOLN LOOK

A masterpiece at rest... A miracle in motion

This is the Lincoln for 1959. The lineage of its glorious past is apparent—struck beautifully into metal and glass. But there is more, much more, to see, to feel, to behold.

Here, indeed, is the timeless Lincoln look. And, this *look* is just one reason why Lincoln is such a practical investment now, and worth so much more for all the years ahead. It is reassuring, as well, to know that Lincoln shares its appearance and dimensions with no other motorcar.

Of all the 1959 cars, Lincoln is the widest, deepest and most comfortable inside—unquestionably the most handsomely appointed. And Lincoln, powered by America's most agile engine, handles with incredible ease.

What's more its unique uniframe construction brings a new stability, safety and silence to motoring. If you yearn for the distinctive, yet wish to invest shrewdly, the Lincoln must inevitably be your motorcar choice for 1959.

The Lincoln lines are completely original—unshared with any other car.

THE 1959 LINCOLN LOOK

Classic beauty— unexcelled craftsmanship.

LINCOLN DIVISION • FORD MOTOR COMPANY

Good looks never carried so much weight!

Chevrolet Task·Force 59 Trucks

Here's the handsomest thing that ever happened to hauling—the new El Camino, combining the stunning style of a '59 Chevrolet passenger car with the cargo capacity of a pickup. It's another example of the added prestige Chevrolet trucks bring to your business—from the Sunday-go-to-meeting look of the new Fleetside pickups (available with new two-toning as an extra-cost option) to the built-for-stamina styling of heavy-duty models. Your dealer's waiting now to show you the entire new Chevrolet Task-Force 59 lineup—the best yet of the best sellers—with *new might, new models, new money-saving power.*

CHEVROLET DIVISION OF GENERAL MOTORS, DETROIT 2, MICHIGAN

Chevrolet Trucks, 1959

So totally new... so typically Olds!

OLDSMOBILE FOR '59 introduces the new "Linear Look" ...the start of a completely new styling cycle! It's the most spacious Rocket Olds ever built...for passengers and luggage! Rides and drives like a dream! Wonderfully smooth...unbelievably silent! It's a traffic-stopper! It's a beauty! And there's one at your Olds Dealer's...waiting for you to claim it!

OLDSMOBILE DIVISION, GENERAL MOTORS CORPORATION

1959 Ninety-Eight Holiday SportSedan

Oldsmobile, 1959

OLDSMOBILE FOR '59 brings you the "Linear Look" ... alive with advanced ideas! Everything is new! The view is Vista-Panoramic ... there's more passenger room and luggage space, too. Rocket Engine power is quieter and smoother ... the ride is best described as a "Glide". To step out of the ordinary, step into a '59 Olds at your dealer's today!

OLDSMOBILE DIVISION, GENERAL MOTORS CORPORATION

Oldsmobile, 1959

▶ *Thunderbird, 1959*

FORD THUNDERBIRD '59

The car everyone would love to own!

Introducing the "Linear Look"...

OLDSMOBILE for '59

So totally new...so typically Olds!

Here you see the start of a new styling cycle! Sweeping expanses of glass enhance Oldsmobile's new inner spaciousness. For in every '59 Olds there's *new roominess*... here, there, everywhere... from leg room to luggage space! New Rocket Engines, too, newly engineered for quietness, smoothness *and economy*! And everywhere you look on *every* '59 Olds you'll find the *added values* you asked for . . . from new Magic-Mirror Finishes to safety-cooled Air-Scoop Brakes on *all four* wheels. See the quality leader of the medium price class—the exciting '59 Oldsmobile!

OLDSMOBILE DIVISION, GENERAL MOTORS CORPORATION

Ninety-Eight Holiday SceniCoupe—features new heat-resistant rear window, combining cool comfort with maximum visibility. Sceni-Coupe styling also available in Dynamic 88 and Super 88 Series.

Super 88 Holiday SportSedan—full family size with 4-door convenience plus the flair of a sports car. Also available in the Dynamic 88 (right rear) and Ninety-Eight Series.

Discover the added values in OLDSmobility...
at your local quality dealer's!

Oldsmobile, 1959

Start of a New Styling Cycle...

OLDSMOBILE FOR '59

Oldsmobile's 1959 Ninety-Eight Holiday SceniCoupe—with rear window of tinted, heat-resistant glass.

The car that conquers "Inner" Space!

You wished for it! You asked for it! It's here! Wonderful new spaciousness . . . everywhere . . . in the new Ninety-Eight by Olds! Even your outlook is bigger . . . broader . . . from vistas of glass that accent a rakish "Linear Look."

Here, too, you command the hushed quiet of the most responsive Rocket Engine of all. You relax as you drive with instantly obedient, effortless Roto-Matic Power Steering. Here's new luxury . . . in lines . . . looks . . . action!

See the '59 Ninety-Eight by Olds . . . at your dealer's, Oldsmobile Division, General Motors Corporation.

DISCOVER THE ADDED VALUES IN OLDSmobility... AT YOUR LOCAL QUALITY DEALER'S!

Oldsmobile's Ninety-Eight Holiday SportSedan—a 4-door family model with the flair and fun of a sports car . . . highlighted by a wrap-around rear window and Vista-Panoramic Windshield.

Oldsmobile, 1959

299

THE CAR: BUICK '59

ELECTRA 225 IN THE EYE-STOPPING NEW 4-DOOR HARDTOP

LE SABRE
The thriftiest Buick

INVICTA
The most spirited Buick

ELECTRA
The most luxurious Buick

Here it is...and now you know! Know why we have called this THE CAR. Know that a new generation of great Buicks is truly here. From just this one view you can see that here is not just new design...but a splendidly right design for this day and age. A car that is lean and clean and stunningly low...and at the same time great in legroom and easy to get into and out of. From anywhere you look, here is a classic modern concept that is Buick speaking a new language of today. A language of fine cars priced within reach of almost everyone. A language of quality and comfort and quiet pride...a language of performance satisfactions without equal.

New Bodies by Fisher • New Easy Power Steering* • New Twin-Turbine and Triple-Turbine automatic transmissions* • New Wildcat Engines • New Equipoise Ride New, improved, exclusive aluminum front brake drums and fin-cooled rear brakes
*OPTIONAL AT EXTRA COST ON CERTAIN MODELS.

A NEW CLASS OF FINE CARS WITHIN REACH OF 2 OUT OF 3 NEW CAR BUYERS

Buick, 1959

YOUR EYES, YOUR HEART, YOUR GOOD SENSE TELL YOU IT'S...

THE CAR
BUICK '59

A new class of fine cars within reach of 2 out of 3 new car buyers

1. Enjoy the finest ride in Buick history, finest in any car today. New Equipoise Chassis, soft, quiet, sure-footed. Quality feel matches quality look...

2. Stop with the surest-stopping, longest-wearing brakes in America today. New fin-cooled rear brakes, exclusive aluminum front brakes...

3. Admire new "classic modern" beauty. Lean, clean, low. Easy to get in, roomy to be in. Big new Vista-Panoramic windshields. And a stunning new kind of 4-door hardtop design...

4. Feel the sense of command behind new control-center instrument panel. New constant-speed electric windshield wipers on all models.

5. Discover the smooth power-flow of Buick Wildcat engine and Twin-Turbine transmission*. No gears to change, no sense of power-pause. Truly automatic. Improved fuel economy...

6. Steer more easily, more surely than ever in your life with Buick's new Easy Power Steering*, best combination yet of true "road feel" and ease of control!

Buick, 1959

Life's a lot more fun when you own a Buick!

There has never been anything like it before! Wherever you go in your Buick, it tells you wonderful things. And it says wonderful things about you. It tells you about the power, the handling, the ride, the operating silence of a truly great automobile. And it proclaims your good judgment, your good taste, to the whole wide world. For the car you have chosen is the most supremely fine Buick ever built. And the most excitingly beautiful Buick in nearly 60 proud years.

LE SABRE INVICTA ELECTRA
The thriftiest Buick — The most spirited Buick — The most luxurious Buick

New Equipoise ride • New super-quiet Bodies by Fisher • New Magic-Mirror finishes • New fin-cooled rear brakes, aluminum front brake drums Safety-plate glass all around • Thriftier, more powerful Wildcat engines • New Buick Easy Power Steering* • Exclusive Twin-turbine and Triple-turbine transmissions*
(*Optional at extra cost on certain models.)

A new class of fine cars within reach of 2 out of 3 new car buyers

BUICK MOTOR DIVISION, GENERAL MOTORS CORPORATION

THE CAR:
BUICK '59

Buick, 1959

When better automobiles are built Buick will build them

Just one Big Thrill from end to end

LET'S SAY you've just taken your first drive in a '56 Buick—and *you're* telling the story.

Where would you start? With that new Variable Pitch Dynaflow*?

Fair enough—for *that* brings a new thrill no other car can even come close to.

How did it feel when you pressed that pedal and found yourself taking off in a single, smooth and unbroken sweep—with no lag between standstill and go—no gear-to-gear "bump" as you moved up to cruising pace?

Did you get a kick out of gliding through traffic like a skier on slopes?

Were you thrilled as you rolled the highway at only part throttle—where folks do most of their driving—and where Dynaflow brings you its biggest boost in gas mileage?

And did you feel a joyous satisfaction when you switched the pitch for Dynaflow's all-out surge of full power to pull you safely out of a tight spot on the highway?

But wait. How about all those other new Buick lifts?

How about the fun of bossing Buick's big, new, walloping 322-cubic-inch V8 engine—now lofted to new highs in power and compression . . .

The honey-comfort of Buick's great new ride—now made even sweeter and more buoyant by new deep-oil shock-absorber cushioning added to Buick's famed all-coil springing . . .

The bliss and bounty of Buick's new handling ease —and new road steadiness—and new Safety Power Steering†—and new luxury of fabrics, appointments and colors . . .

The happy thrill of knowing you can get all these

Buick blessings at a satisfying price—all the way from the thrifty, bedrock-priced SPECIAL, to the fast-stepping CENTURY, to the spirited SUPER—and on to the custom-built ROADMASTER.

Looks like *we've* told the story, after all.

But *your* time is coming—if you'll just go take your ride and make your deal, at your Buick dealer's. See him this week, for sure.

BUICK *Division of* GENERAL MOTORS

*New Advanced Variable Pitch Dynaflow is the only Dynaflow Buick builds today. It is standard on Roadmaster, Super and Century—optional at modest extra cost on the Special.
†Standard on Roadmaster and Super, optional at extra cost on other Series.

AT A NEW LOW PRICE—4-Season Comfort in your new Buick
with FRIGIDAIRE CONDITIONING

See Jackie Gleason
on TV every
Saturday Evening

Best Buick yet

Buick

LE SABRE Convertible

*Whatever car you have in mind . . .
you're better off with a Buick!*

Almost any new American car you're thinking of buying falls within reach of today's Buick price range. And when this same money pays for a Buick, today more than ever before it brings you things you just can't buy elsewhere!

It pays for a very special feeling of wisdom and pride. It pays for the magic in the Buick name itself—a sense of quality, tradition, reliability. And it pays—in ways you can touch and feel—for the most exciting beauty, the most advanced performance ever built into Buick cars.

If you're thinking of buying a car, don't fail to see your Quality Buick Dealer. He has some wonderful new surprises for your money.

New Magic-Mirror finishes • New super-quiet Bodies by Fisher • Safety PLATE Glass all around • New Equapoise ride • New fin-cooled brakes, front and rear • Aluminum front brake drums • Thriftier, higher compression, more powerful Wildcat engines • New electric windshield wipers • New Buick Easy Power Steering* • Exclusive Twin-Turbine and Triple-Turbine transmissions* • New Automatic heat and fresh air control*

*Optional at extra cost on certain models.

LeSABRE *The thriftiest Buick*   INVICTA *The most spirited Buick*   ELECTRA *The most luxurious Buick*

BUICK MOTOR DIVISION, GENERAL MOTORS CORPORATION

THE CAR:
BUICK '59

Buick, 1959

Gas goes a whole lot farther…

Savings reach new heights in this new Ford Ranch Wagon . . . designed for families living it up on a budget. All six Ford Wagons—Standard Six or Thunderbird V-8—use *regular* gas, save you up to $40 a year on fuel alone! America's wagon specialists have designed them *new*, like a hardtop. Living room comfortable . . . with sofa-soft seats for up to nine. A stratospheric 92 cu. ft. of cargo space is push-button easy to load with single-operation tailgate. Biggest, most elegant Ford wagons ever. Want a lift?

THE SMARTLY STYLED CUSTOM 300 TUDOR SEDAN . . . LOWEST PRICED OF THE POPULAR THREE.

New award-winning proportions • New hardtop styling for picture-window view • All seats face comfortably forward • Safety Glass all around • New Diamond Lustre finish never needs waxing • Aluminized mufflers for twice the life • Full-flow oil filtration takes you 4000 miles without an oil change.

WORLD'S MOST BEAUTIFULLY PROPORTIONED CARS

Ford, 1959   ▶ Cadillac, 1959 ▶▶ Cadillac, 1959

Sedan de Ville

THE FLEETWOOD SIXTY SPECIAL

A NEW

THE 1959 *Cadillac*

By appointment to the world's most discriminating motorists

THE ELDORADO BIARRITZ

REALM OF MOTORING MAJESTY

single glance tells you these are the newest and most magnificent Cadillac cars ever created. Dazzling in their beauty, [gr]ace and elegance, and inspiring in their Fleetwood luxury [an]d decor—they introduce a new realm of motoring majesty. [An]d a single journey at the wheel will reveal still another fact [—]that these are the finest performing Cadillacs ever produced. [W]ith a spectacular new engine, more responsive Hydra-Matic

drive and improved qualities of ride and handling, they provide a totally new sense of mastery over time and distance. This brilliant new Cadillac beauty and performance are offered in thirteen individual body styles. To inspect and to drive any of them is to acknowledge Cadillac a new measure of supremacy. We invite you to do both—soon!

CADILLAC MOTOR CAR DIVISION • GENERAL MOTORS CORPORATION

THE SIXTY-TWO COUPE

STARFIRE 98 HOLIDAY CO

...enjoying the luxury of a Starfire 98 !

ngratulations are in order! And the owner of this newest Oldsmobile
asterpiece is sure to receive his share!

re is distinction. The exclusive Accent-Styled Body by Fisher com-
ands immediate attention, instant recognition. You travel in all the
mfort and luxury that the most exacting craftsmanship can provide.

owpiece that it is, the Starfire 98 reveals its enthusiastic personality on
e road. The Rocket T-400 Engine is ever ready with a more-than-

confident answer to all the demands of modern travel. And naturally, a
complement of power assists, including Jetaway Hydra-Matic, Saf
Power Steering and Power Brakes, is standard equipment.

For that very special assurance that goes with driving the finest, cons
your Oldsmobile Quality Dealer at your earliest convenience. It is
pleasure to assist in your choice of body model, finish and appointmer
OLDSMOBILE DIVISION, General Motors Corporation.

 OLDSMOBILE

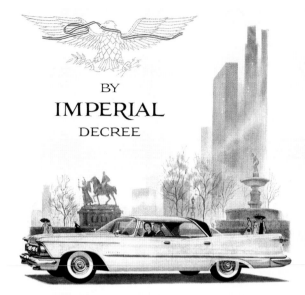

The most distinguished motorcar of our time...

CONTINENTAL
Mark IV

LINCOLN DIVISION · FORD MOTOR COMPANY

"When a man of rank appears, he deserves to have his merits handsomely allowed"

SAMUEL JOHNSON

Continental Mark IV, 1959

IMPERIAL
DECREE

...heads will turn

Until more people are able to control their curiosity and admiration, heads will turn to follow your Imperial out of sight. When you park, people will gather . . . to peer through windows.

You will accept these small and pleasant intrusions as conditions of Imperial ownership.

But, as long-term *personal* satisfactions, accept the power of a new engine which develops greater thrust with fewer engine revolutions. Accept the common sense of Auto-Pilot which may be specially installed to mind speed and accelerator for you.

Adjust yourself to the silent comfort of Imperial's Royal Coach Body . . . cushioned from stress by refinements in our time-tested torsion bar suspension.

All these excellences . . . and others you'll discover each time you drive . . . are decreed by Imperial's careful, unhurried crafting . . . in the industry's most functional and efficient plant.

Your Imperial dealer has one of these excellent cars for you to inspect. Drive it . . . as his guest. Watch the heads turn.

The 1959

IMPERIAL
...excellence without equal

Imperial, 1959

Like all '59 Chevies, this Impala Sport Coupe is new right down to its safer Tyrex cord tires.

FRESH, FINE AND FASHIONABLE !

Chevy's Slimline design says new in a way all its own. And beneath the beauty there's new engineering that goes down deep. Here's all the car anyone could ask for!

From the clean thrust of its grille to the jaunty flare of its rear deck, this '59 Chevrolet is shaped to the new American taste. And you'll find its beauty has a practical slant too— with more seating room, new areas of visibility and a longer lasting Magic-Mirror acrylic finish.

Once you're on the road you'll discover dozens of deep-down engineering benefits—from easier steering to safer stopping. Your Chevrolet dealer's waiting now with the car that can give your pride a big lift at a low price. . . . Chevrolet Division of General Motors, Detroit 2, Mich.

'59 CHEVROLET

CHEVROLET

What America wants, America gets in a Chevy!

The Bel Air 2-Door Sedan—Fisher Body beauty and Safety Plate Glass all around.

Cadillac, 1959 ◄◄   *Oldsmobile, 1957* ◄   *Chevrolet, 1959*

TAKE A NIGHT-FLIGHT IN THE TURBINE DRIVE BUICK "60"

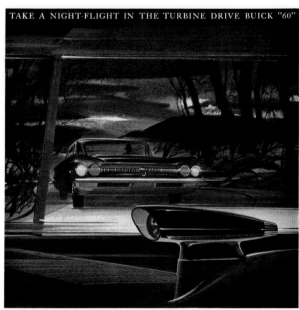

1960 BUICK *with* GUIDE-MATIC

Ease your way through the night behind the wheel of the Turbine Drive Buick "60" and discover the new assurance that comes from driving with Guide-Matic. It's so easy to relax while the Guide-Matic Power Headlight Control selects the right light for passing, for turning, for city or turnpike cruising. And, you'll notice Guide-Matic always remembers, even when you could forget.

Most of all you'll want to try Safety Salute and see how it helps make courtesy contagious. For with Guide-Matic's exclusive Safety Salute, you can urge other nighttime drivers to *dim-down* their brights at the instant you're dimming your own.

Why be without the final touch of safety and convenience when factory-installed Guide-Matic is one of the lower cost options you can buy?

SAFETY SALUTE works like this . . . energized by the lights from an on-coming car, Guide-Matic fades down your bright beams ⊙⊙ 1 ⊙⊙ to a soft glow, signaling the other driver to dim his brights ⊙⊙ 2 ⊙⊙. An instant later, the inboard beams turn off ⊙● 3 ●⊙ . . . restating . . . with greater urgency . . . a safety message that can't be ignored. Once you've passed in perfect safety, all four lamps instantly switch back to ⊙⊙ 4 ⊙⊙ bright.

Look for Safety Salute tonight, try Guide-Matic tomorrow.

GUIDE-MATIC
POWER HEADLIGHT CONTROL

DEVELOPED BY GUIDE LAMP DIVISION · GENERAL MOTORS CORPORATION · ANDERSON, INDIANA

Buick, 1959   ► *Imperial, 1959*

Presenting ... the NEW 1959

IMPERIAL

...excellence without equal

The 1959 Imperial LeBaron Silvercrest four door hardtop . . . fresh from Imperial's all-new plant to host this year's Imperial Ball

Today, America has a new measurement for excellence in motoring.

IMPERIAL FOR 1959 . . . a car whose great dignity is matched by an eagerness of spirit . . . whose luxury and elegance are made richer by a gracious practicality.

A car in which careful interior redesign has provided more space for passengers . . . a car which makes available for the first time front seats that swivel doorward to make entry and exit easy.

IMPERIAL FOR 1959 . . . a car whose farsighted engineering concepts combine spectacular handling ease with a firm sense of absolute control . . . whose newly designed engine develops enormous power with fewer engine revolutions . . . so it need never race or strain or raise its voice.

A car which can be equipped with Auto-Pilot, to remind you of the speed limit, and to maintain a steady turnpike pace, hour on hour, up hill and down, without a touch of the accelerator.

IMPERIAL FOR 1959 . . . whose spacious Royal Coach Body gives you new dimensions of comfort and enjoyment. A car that comes to you in all its carefully crafted excellence from America's newest automotive plant . . . designed for the utmost in quality control.

IMPERIAL FOR 1959 . . . excellence without equal. A boastful statement? The car is ready for your inspection at Imperial showrooms. See it. Drive it. And then decide,

NINETY-EIGHT HOLIDAY SPORTSEDAN

3 WIDE SEATS, 5 BIG DOORS—Lots of room for the biggest families. The tailgate is a fifth-door with positive outside key lock, so children can't open from inside. Rear passengers step in easily without having to scramble over tailgate or seats. Easier to load, too.

EASY TO ENTER. Rambler's high, wide doors let you step in, not stoop in. Interior is completely new for 1960—stunning new fabrics, colors. The new instrument panel is beautiful, too, and provides greater safety . . . easy-to-see dials and easy-to-reach controls.

NEW 1960 RAMBLER CUSTOM CROSS COUNTRY—America's biggest selling compact station wagon now even smarter, thriftier, easier to park. Six or Rebel V-8.

At top right is the brilliant new Rambler Custom Four-Door Sedan for '60.

THE WORLD'S LARGEST BUILDER OF COMPACT CARS ANNOUNCES
The New Standard of Basic Excellence...
NEW RAMBLER FOR '60

NEW 1960 RAMBLER CUSTOM FOUR-DOOR SEDAN offers big room for six 6-footers in a car that's even easier to turn, park and garage. Six or Rebel V-8 for balanced performance, economy.

Ahead by 10 years and 25 billion owner-driven miles

A new motoring concept is at your Rambler dealer's today—the new standard of basic excellence. Come discover what it means to you.

Come see America's most advanced Compact* cars—proved by 10 years and 25 billion happy owner miles. See styling that is entirely new and classically Rambler in its fresh, clean design. See completely new models no American car has offered before. See brand-new features—new improvements for 1960.

See the new cars with better balance: fine performance balanced with top economy . . . big car room balanced with small car handling . . . high quality balanced with low price.

Try exclusive Personalized Comfort—separate front seats that glide back and forth individually . . . reclining seatbacks . . . adjustable headrests.

Visit your Rambler dealer. See and drive the new Rambler—discover the new standard of basic excellence.

ONLY RAMBLER GIVES YOU THE BEST OF BOTH: Big car room and comfort / Small car economy and handling ease

NEW 1960 AMBASSADOR V-8 BY RAMBLER—the compact luxury car in the medium price field offers new improved fuel economy on regular gasoline.

Rambler, 1959

How GM engineers explore new horizons

Here you see the XP-300 and Le Sabre. The press likes to call them "cars of the future."

Thousands of people have flocked to see them, and the question most often asked is, "When will you build cars like these for the public?"

Well, the answer is—these aren't intended to show exactly what future cars will be like. They were built and rebuilt over a period of several years, to give our engineers and designers the chance to test out fresh ideas, and get these ideas beyond the blueprint and laboratory stage.

You never know, till you get far-in advance ideas to the point where you can road-test them and let folks look at them, how practical they'll be—and how the public will take them.

We can promise you that, as time goes on, some of these features will begin to appear on cars in regular production.

We say that because it has happened before. Many of today's commonplace features on General Motors cars came right out of "tries" like these in early years.

So Le Sabre and XP-300 are the latest examples of how far we go to make the key to a GM car your key to greater value.

335-Horsepower Performance from a 550-Pound Motor—GM engineers solved the problem of putting a very high-powered engine in small space by developing an entirely new light alloy engine for both of these cars. The engine is a supercharged V-8 having 10 to 1 compression ratio and operating on premium-grade fuel for all normal driving—premium fuel plus supercharged fuel suitable for supercharged engines at higher speeds. Engines are supercharged by a blower GM engineers developed for Diesel engines.

XP-300

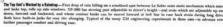

The Top that's Worked by a Raindrop—First drop of rain falling on a sensitized spot between Le Sabre seats starts mechanism which raises and locks top, rolls up side windows. XP-300 has steering post adjustable to driver's height—and seats which are adjustable up and down, forward and backward, and whose contour backs can be moved forward at belt line to ease back strain during long drive. Both have built-in jacks for easy tire changing. Typical of the many GM engineering experiments in these cars—to advance even further passenger comfort and driving ease.

Your Key to Better Engineering—the Key to a General Motors Car

From just such continuous GM engineering experiments as are now being tested in XP-300 and Le Sabre come the superior performance, handling ease and beauty of the 1952 Chevrolets, Pontiacs, Oldsmobiles, Buicks and Cadillacs. Further proof that a key to a GM car is your key to better engineering—and thus to greater value.

GENERAL MOTORS
"MORE AND BETTER THINGS FOR MORE PEOPLE"

CHEVROLET · PONTIAC
OLDSMOBILE · BUICK · CADILLAC
All with Body by Fisher

GMC TRUCK & COACH

Hear HENRY J. TAYLOR on the air every Monday evening over the ABC Network, coast to coast

Oldsmobile, 1959 ◄ *General Motors, 1952* ► Chevrolet Corvette

"REALLY, OLD BOY, YOU AREN'T SUPPOSED TO BUILD THAT SORT OF THING IN AMERICA, Y'KNOW."

The unforgivable thing, of course, is this: The new Corvette not only looks delightful and rides like the Blue Train—but it also is quite capable of macerating the competition out on the road circuits.

This dual nature is the classic requirement before you can call a pretty two-seater a *sports car*. And properly so, for this is an honorable name, and only a vehicle with race-bred precision of handling, cornering and control can make a mortal driver feel quite so akin to the gods.

Unlike the gentleman above, who has been a little slow in catching up with current events, most sports car people are becoming aware that the Corvette is truly one of the world's most remarkable cars. Because it does two disparate things outstandingly well: It provides superbly practical motoring, with every luxury and convenience your heart might covet, and accompanies this with a soul-satisfying ferocity of performance.

We could recite the full specifications. But if you are the kind of driver who is meant for a Corvette, you'll want to find out firsthand—and that, sir, would be our pleasure! . . . *Chevrolet Division of General Motors, Detroit 2, Michigan.*

CORVETTE

by Chevrolet

SPECIFICATIONS: *283-cubic-inch V8 engine with single four-barrel carburetor, 220 h.p. (four other engines* range to 283 h.p. with fuel injection). Close-ratio three-speed manual transmission standard, with special Powerglide automatic drive* available on all but maximum-performance engines. Choice of removable hard top or power-operated fabric top, Power-Lift windows.* Instruments include 6000 r.p.m. tachometer, oil pressure gauge and ammeter.* *Optional at extra cost.*

The Plymouth Cranbrook Sedan and the Plymouth Savoy,
shown at the Greenbrier, White Sulphur Springs, W. Va.

The architecture of an automobile can kindle a light in its owner's eyes and warm

the pride of possession. As, indeed, the balanced new beauty of the Plymouth does

And beneath this beauty, unseen, is the integrity of the engineering that created it . . .

a low-priced car, built so well, to look so well, to serve so long and well.

PLYMOUTH

Plymouth

ENJOY GREAT TV ENTERTAINMENT FROM PLYMOUTH! The laugh and love hit of the year, "DATE WITH THE ANGELS," with Betty White, and Lawrence Welk's "TOP TUNES AND NEW TALENT."

His love of sports cars...

Her love of beauty and comfort...

are "married" in the years-ahead *Plymouth*

3 full years ahead of the "other two" with revolutionary new Torsion-Aire Ride . . . choice of five great power plants including the terrific new FURY V-800 engine . . . new sports car handling . . . Flight-Sweep Styling, the new shape of motion. *At your Plymouth dealer's!*

Plymouth

▶ *Dodge, 1959*

The new Mercedes-Benz 220SE Coupe...and why aren't you in the picture?

This Mercedes-Benz Invites You to Europe as its Guest

More than 60,000 owners of Mercedes-Benz motorcars in this country can tell you about substantial savings in fuel, in routine maintenance, in repairs. They will happily confide that, instead of trading in every two or three years, they prefer to keep on enjoying their Mercedes-Benz and keep their money in the bank.

But you can enjoy still another advantage in Mercedes-Benz. Arrange with your dealer to take delivery in Europe...the dollar savings can pay for a glorious vacation.

We suggest you visit him, and ask for the figures. And while you are there, take a drive behind the three-pointed silver star!

Mercedes-Benz Sales, Inc.
(A Subsidiary of Studebaker Corporation)
South Bend, Indiana

Mercedes

▶ *Cadillac Eldorado*   ▶▶ *Sky Chief, 1954*

320   Automobiles

This is the Eldorado—a new adventure in automotive design and engineering—with brilliant and dramatic styling . . . hand-crafted, imported leather interiors . . . "disappearing" top . . . and a sensational 270-h.p. engine. In all that it is, and does, and represents . . . it is the finest fruit of Cadillac's never-ending crusade to build greater quality into the American motor car.

Now in limited production • Price on request

Eldorado

BY CADILLAC

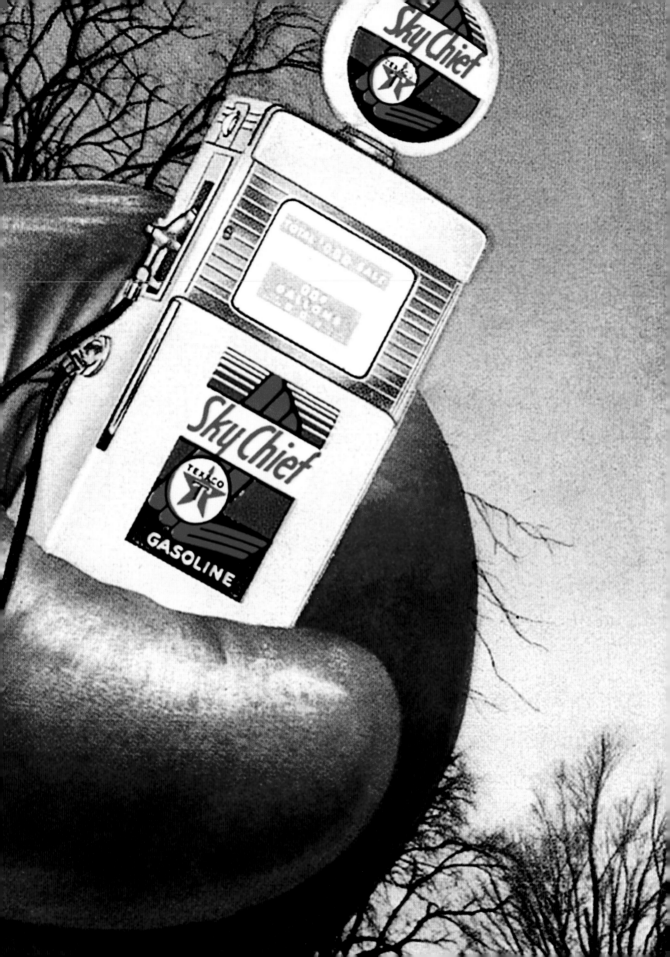

Page-ing all drivers!

SPARKY

Patti Page, star of "The New Olds Show," and "Sparky," AC's famous horse who plugs better performance on "Zorro," sing about AC Hot Tip Spark Plugs — the original equipment plugs that give your car "like new" smoothness and pep. See both shows on ABC-TV every week.

WHEN YOU REPLACE SPARK PLUGS... ★

ASK FOR AC...USED ON MORE

NEW CARS THAN ANY OTHER BRAND!

*To maintain top performance, we recommend Spark Plug replacement at least every 10,000 miles.

AC HOT TIP **SPARK PLUGS**

AC SPARK PLUG ✻ THE ELECTRONICS DIVISION OF GENERAL MOTORS

AC Spark Plugs, 1958

Wonderful Start!

OAKWOOD HIGH SCHOOL DRIVER TRAINING

AC

Lesson number one: a new set of ACs can save three times their cost in gasoline!

First solo! It's a great day for any driver . . . and it's a great day, too, when a new set of AC Hot Tip Spark Plugs goes under the hood of your car.

Here's why: the long, thin, recessed "Hot Tip" insulator heats faster to burn away carbon, oil and combustion deposits as fast as they form. This assures efficient fuel combustion.

This exclusive AC anti-fouling action can save as much as one gallon of gasoline out of every ten you buy. In an average year's driving this kind of gas saving will pay for a new set of ACs three times over.

AC Hot Tip Spark Plugs are standard factory equipment on more new cars than any other make. Let your AC dealer install a new set in your car every 10,000 miles.

AC ⚛ THE ELECTRONICS DIVISION OF GENERAL MOTORS

Watch Walt Disney Studios' ZORRO every week on ABC-TV

ACTION starts with

HOT TIP

SPARK PLUGS

FORWARD FROM FIFTY

AC Spark Plugs, 1957

Now, to protect your engine against winter...to keep it clean and easy to start...drive into

that clean, friendly Gulf Station for *Gulfpride, the clean-working oil.*

Gulfpride The World's Finest Motor Oil

Super-refined by Gulf's exclusive Alchlor Process. Gives you the most complete engine protection you can buy.

Gulf Oil, 1957

NEW! **A special-grade oil that help you 3 ways in winter!**

1. **FASTER STARTS:** Makes your engine *easier* to start—even at temperatures well below zero! Saves tempers, saves batteries! (Fact: special-grade Gulfpride H.D. Light actually flows at 35° below zero!)

2. **ALL-WEATHER PROTECTION:** Gulfpride H.D. Light has the tough protective film that means *constant* protection from cold start to full engine heat. Safeguards your engine on long trips and on winter's warmest days.

3. **KEEPS ENGINES CLEAN:** Protects against sludge deposits, corrosion, rust and wear—problems that are at their worst in cold weather.

The World's Finest Motor Oil

Gulf Oil Corporation · Gulf Refining Company

Ask for new **Gulfpride H.D. Light** *for winter!*

Gulf Oil

FOR YOUR WINTER OIL... CHANGE TO QUAKER STATE MOTOR OIL

Whether *your* winter driving is through ice and snow or in southern sunshine—Quaker State Motor Oil is tailor-made for *your* car. Skillfully refined from 100% Pure Pennsylvania Grade Crude Oil, Quaker State is the product of continuous research, engine-testing and 50 years of specialization in automotive lubrication. It gives your car complete lubrication and long-lasting protection.

QUAKER STATE OIL REFINING CORPORATION, OIL CITY, PA.
Member Pennsylvania Grade Crude Oil Association

Quaker State Motor Oil, 1953

for the look of luxury . . . the feel of luxury . . . luxury itself

Genuine UPHOLSTERY *Leather*

for your car
. . . your office
. . . your home

genuine leather gives pride of possession

No other material for the upholstery of your car . . . your furniture . . . can match the luxury of Genuine Leather. The luxury of color—fashion right and in exciting variety. The luxury of texture—so pleasing to the touch, so comfortable. The luxury of long wear—for with normal use and simple care leather actually improves in appearance. The luxury of the *genuine*—a source of pride in its possession and evidence of your sound sense of value.

When you buy your next car . . . furniture for home or office . . . be sure the upholstery is Genuine Leather and enjoy the luxury that leather alone affords.

● *Many cars are now available with leather trim; standard in convertibles, optional in closed cars. Write to us for the names of the manufacturers.*

THE UPHOLSTERY LEATHER GROUP · TANNERS' COUNCIL OF AMERICA · 141 EAST 44TH ST., NEW YORK 17, N. Y.

The Upholstery Leather Group, 1952 ▶ *Kelly Tires, 1953* ▶▶ *Mobilgas, 1950*

TOURIST FAVORITES: HISTORIC MOUNT VERNON . . . DEPENDABLE KELLY T

Wherever you go...GO WORRY-FREE ON KELLYS

The miles seem far shorter, the roads far smoother, when you go *worry-free* on safe, dependable Kelly Tires! For famous Kelly "know-how" really pays off!

GREATER SAFETY! Kellys are sure-footed, quick-stopping — quality-built throughout to stay safer longer!

GREATER MILEAGE! Kelly's tougher, slower-wearing Armorubber tread is good for extra thousands of safe miles!

GREATER ECONOMY! The "bonus" mileage built into longer-wearing Kelly Tires means far lower long-run cost!

Don't wait for tire troubles! See your friendly Kelly Dealer today—get *full* credit for *all* unused mileage on a trade-in for *worry-free* Kellys! It's the best tire deal in town!

Proved and Improved for 59 years

ALL TANGLED UP IN GASOLINE CLAIMS?

HERE'S A TIP...

No other gasoline has yet equalled this power and mileage record—

22.3 MILES PER GALLON AVERAGE

IN THE 1953 Mobilgas Economy Run 25 new U.S. stock cars, using Mobilgas or Mobilgas Special, averaged an amazing 22.3 miles per gallon over a punishing 1206-mile route.

Proof!...it takes perfect balance of high volatility, high power and high mileage ingredients to deliver top economy and performance! Fill up at your Mobilgas dealer today!

Mobilgas
SOCONY-VACUUM

GET HIGH QUALITY ECONOMY GASOLINE

Mobilgas, 1953

Hatful of Pep!

AND in your car famous Fire-Chief is a
tankful of pep. Ready to give you quick starts . . .
fast warm-ups . . . smooth getaways.
Fire-Chief is *regular priced*, too. So step up
your driving pleasure. Fill up at your Texaco Dealer
. . . the best friend your car ever had.

TEXACO
FIRE-CHIEF
GASOLINE

THE TEXAS COMPANY
TEXACO DEALERS IN ALL 48 STATES
Texaco Products are also distributed in Canada and Latin America

TUNE IN: On television—the TEXACO STAR THEATER starring MILTON BERLE—every Tuesday night. On radio—
Metropolitan Opera Broadcasts—every Saturday afternoon. See newspaper for time and station.

Texaco, 1951

Introducing...
From Sinclair's Space-Age Research

NEW 3-STAGE GASOLINE

OVER 100-OCTANE
NO INCREASE IN PRICE

New Sinclair Power-X Gives You 100-Octane Performance in All 3 Driving Stages

1 **STARTING** Power-primed with rocket fuel, new Power-X Gasoline is over 100-octane! You start quick as a click in any weather...and your engine warms up smooth and sweet. No stalling, no skipping.

2 **ACCELERATION** 12,000 pounds thrust at the touch of your toe! No need for fancy super-priced gasolines. With new Power-X, you get lightning getaway...reserve power for smoother, safer driving.

3 **MILEAGE** Those extra octanes mean extra economy, too...more miles in every thrifty gallon. And there's no increase in price! Watch for the new Power-X at your neighborhood Sinclair Dealer's Station.

NO PRICE INCREASE

SINCLAIR POWER-X OVER 100 OCTANE

SINCLAIR

WATCH FOR THE ARRIVAL OF NEW POWER-X GASOLINE IN YOUR COMMUNITY

Sinclair Refining Company, 600 Fifth Avenue, New York 20, N. Y.

Sinclair, 1959

▶ *Diamond Chemicals* ▶▶ *Conoco, 1950*

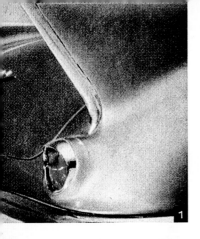

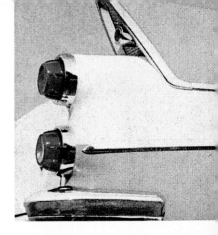

Diamond's Guide to Car Watching
(can you identify them?*)

Here are the southern exposures of nine northbound 57's. Dramatically different as these new cars are, they have one thing in common. On each is some chrome plating that started with DIAMOND Chromic Acid. DIAMOND ALKALI is one of the world's largest producers of chromium chemicals, and DIAMOND research has recently developed a new additive for chrome platers which reduces plating time and cost, gives a harder, brighter finish.

Progress like this helps explain why DIAMOND's "Chemicals you live by" are preferred by so many industries, found in so many places.
DIAMOND ALKALI COMPANY, Cleveland 14, Ohio.

Diamond Chemicals

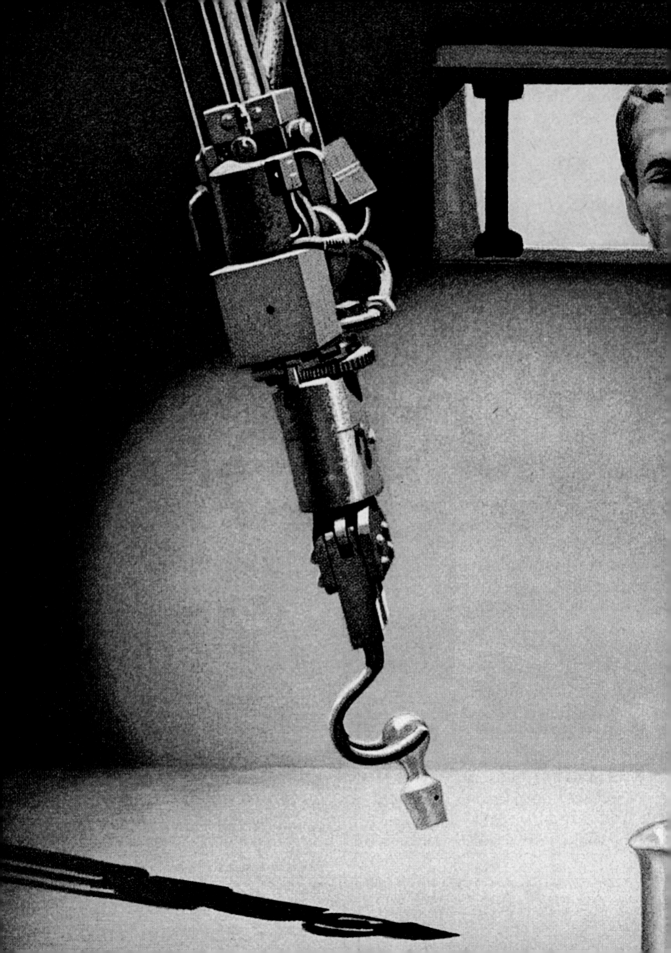

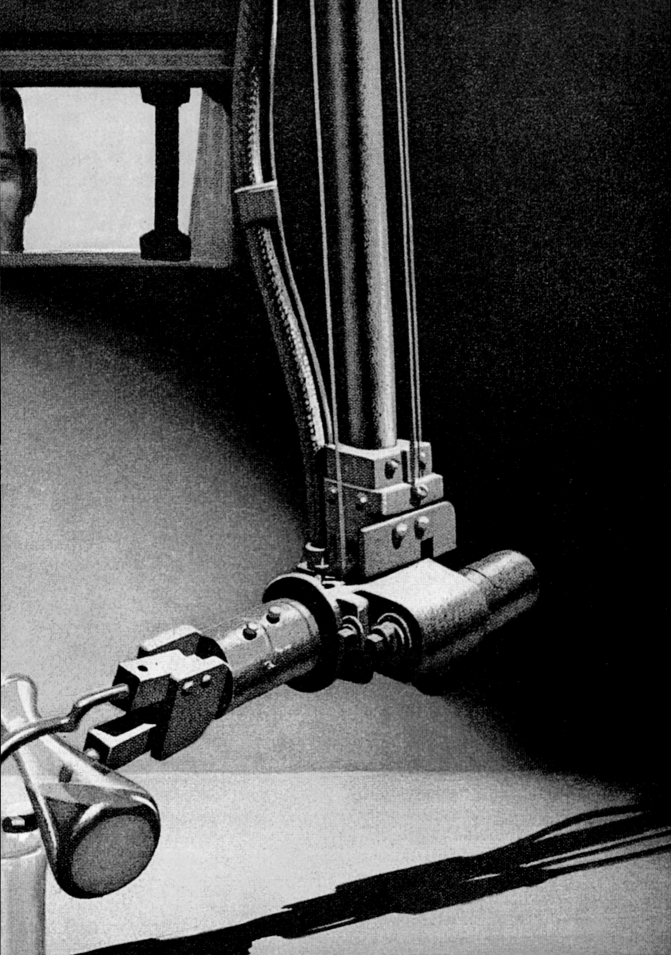

Your engine makes this much Acid every day

...And it's Acid Action—not friction— that causes 90% of engine wear

New Alkaline Shell X-100 Motor Oil counteracts Acid Action

If you are a typical motorist, in a normal day's driving:—a pint or more of acid is formed and passes through your car's engine, and it's acid action, not friction, that causes 90% of your engine wear. To neutralize the harmful effect of this acid, Shell Research has produced an alkaline motor oil—Shell X-100. Fortified with alkaline "X" safety factors, it neutralizes the acid action, prolonging the life of your engine.

The new Shell X-100 is a Premium Motor Oil. It is a Heavy Duty Motor Oil. In addition, it contains positive cleansing factors that help protect hydraulic valve lifters and other vital parts from fouling deposits.

Shell X-100 is the finest motor oil money can buy. Let your Shell dealer give your engine the protection of this new alkaline Shell X-100 Motor Oil today.

It's Incomparable!

SHELL
X-100
MOTOR OIL
PREMIUM-HEAVY DUTY

Shell Motor Oil, 1951 ◀ *Shell Motor Oil, 1952*

Havoline Motor Oil, 1950

Havoline Motor Oil, 1956

Olin Aluminum

J-Wax, 1956

Your engine makes this much **acid** every day

...And it's Acid Action – not friction that causes 90% of engine wear!

ARTZYBASHEFF

NEW *alkaline* Shell X-100 Motor Oil
neutralizes Acid Action

It's not *friction* but *acid action* that causes 90% of engine wear! To neutralize the harmful effect of the pint or more of acid formed in average daily driving, Shell Research has produced an *alkaline* motor oil— Shell X-100. Fortified with alkaline "X" safety factors, it neutralizes the acid action, prolonging the life of your engine.

The new Shell X-100 is a Premium Motor Oil. It is a Heavy Duty Motor Oil. In addition, it possesses cleansing factors which help prevent deposits that would foul your engine.

Shell X-100 is the finest motor oil money can buy. Let your Shell dealer give your engine the protection of this new alkaline Shell X-100 Motor Oil today.

SHELL X-100 MOTOR OIL

SHELL

It's Incomparable!

Shell Motor Oil, 1952

▶ *Borg-Warner, 1955*

And the winner is...

Because It Always Says A Lot About You

They'll know you've arrived all right. Arrived in one of the worst-received cars of the twentieth century. The Edsel, one of Ford's most unpopular vehicles, was a giant dud with consumers who abandoned the car wholesale. Marketed for the young executive, it ended up being the butt of jokesters who said it looked like an Oldsmobile sucking a lemon.

Sag mir, was du fährst, und ich sage dir, wer du bist

Sie werden wissen, dass du gut angekommen bist. In einem der unbeliebtesten Autos des zwanzigsten Jahrhunderts. Der Edsel, eines von Fords unpopulärsten Fahrzeugen, war ein gigantischer Flop; die Verbraucher verschmähten ihn vollständig. Eigentlich für junge Führungskräfte auf den Markt gebracht, wurde er rasch zum Gespött von Witzbolden, die sagten, er sehe aus wie ein zitronenlutschendes Oldsmobile.

Puisqu'elles en disent tant sur vous

Ils sauront que vous êtes bien arrivés. Et dans une des voitures les plus mal reçues du siècle. La Edsel, une des productions les moins populaires de Ford, une nullité totale massivement désertée par les consommateurs. Destinée aux jeunes cadres, elle devient la cible des plaisantins qui la comparent à une Oldsmobile suçant un citron.

They'll know you've *arrived*

when you drive up in an Edsel

Step into an Edsel and you'll learn where the excitement is this year.

Other drivers spot that classic vertical grille a block away—and never fail to take a long look at this year's most exciting car.

On the open road, your Edsel is watched eagerly for its already-famous performance.

And parked in front of your home, your Edsel always gets even more attention—because it always says a lot about you. It says you chose elegant styling, luxurious comfort and such exclusive features as Edsel's famous Teletouch Drive—only shift that puts the buttons where they belong, on the steering-wheel hub.

Your Edsel also means you made a wonderful buy. For of all medium-priced cars, this one really new car is actually priced the lowest.* See your Edsel Dealer this week.

Based on comparison of suggested retail delivered prices of the Edsel Ranger and similarly equipped cars in the medium-price field.

Above: Edsel Citation 2-door Hardtop. Engine: the E-475, with 10.5 to one compression ratio, 345 hp, 475 ft.-lb. torque. Transmission: Automatic with Teletouch Drive. Suspension: Ball-joint with optional air suspension. Brakes: self-adjusting.

EDSEL DIVISION · FORD MOTOR COMPANY

1958 EDSEL

Of all medium-priced cars, the one that's really new is the lowest-priced, too!

Edsel, 1958

THE King James Version MAKES THE HOME COMPLETE

"*Your Majesty, we present you with this Book, the most valuable thing this world affords.*"

With these words the King James Bible was bestowed upon Elizabeth II at her coronation. The copy was specially printed and bound for the occasion by Oxford.

Oxford University Press

"So lifelike you feel you're right there

with 3 dimension pictures!"

New sensational Revere 3 Dimension Camera enables you to take amazingly lifelike pictures as easy as pie! Just press the button as you do with any ordinary camera. What you see, you catch in thrilling three dimensions. Everything has shape, form, depth! Full color scenes seem to spring to life with breath-taking 3 dimensional realism. So truly lifelike, viewers exclaim it's like being right there!

See the two lenses? They're perfectly matched and act like your eyes. Simply press the button and they take two separate views of each scene. When viewed, they blend into 3-dimensions. Inexpensive, too! Get 29 stereos from regular 35mm. roll; 20 from special stereo film.

Even beginners get fine results from their first roll, as simple is Revere to operate! Guesswork is eliminated. Even focusing for distance is automatic with the built-in range finder. Too, stereos are now mounted by your film processor and are returned to you ready to show!

Every picture a thrill! Sheer enjoyment when you view stereo through the new Revere Viewer. Advance design brings out the best in every shot. Ask your dealer to show you the new Revere Stereo Camera and Viewer.
REVERE CAMERA COMPANY, CHICAGO 16, ILLINOIS

For a new adventure in photography...

Revere 33
STEREO CAMERA

In pursuit of happiness Revere adds 3 years, pleasure

Top Value Stamps, 1956 ◄   Revere Stereo Camera, 1952

Reader's Digest invites you to accept this 576-page book for 10¢
TO COVER POSTAGE

576 pages
49 illustrations
in color

Yours to keep—no more to pay!

This exciting volume regularly sells for $2.32. But we offer it to you—to keep—for only 10¢ to introduce you to Reader's Digest Condensed Books.

Just fill out the Shipping Label below and mail it with 10¢. We'll gum the label on the shipping carton containing your copy of this book and ship it to you at once.

What you get for 10¢

You get these 5 great current books condensed in one volume:

BOON ISLAND. Kenneth Roberts recreates the true story of a ship wrecked off the Maine coast in 1710, and of 14 survivors who battled for their lives against a winter sea. Publisher's price $3.75
BELOVED. Latest novel by Vina Delmar. The dramatic love story of a brilliant Confederate leader and his beautiful but scandalously unstable Creole wife. Publisher's price $3.95
CAPTAIN OF THE QUEENS. These adventures of Harry Grattidge, who rose from being the most knocked-about apprentice into sailing this ship to become master of the *Queen Elizabeth*. Publisher's price $4.50
THE LAST HURRAH. Close-up of a colorful, rascally politician, a charmer in spite of his unforgivable shenanigans, and the inner story of his last campaign. By Edwin O'Connor. Publisher's price $4.00
IN MY FATHER'S HOUSE. Grace Nies Fletcher. Recalls her youth in a parsonage, full of both faith and humor. Publisher's price $3.50
Total Original Prices $19.70

From all the outstanding new books Reader's Digest editors select the best: novels, biographies and important non-fiction—then skillfully condense them, keeping all the essential narrative, style and flavor.

FOUR or more condensations are collected in each volume of Reader's Digest Condensed Books, illustrated in color, beautifully printed and bound, these volumes (of some 500 pages each) are available to Club members only for just $2.32 plus postage. None of these condensations appears in Reader's Digest magazine.

Conditions of this offer

After shipping your trial book, we will enroll you as a TRIAL member of the Reader's Digest Condensed Book Club. If, after reading this introductory volume, you decide not to continue as a member, you may keep the volume and cancel your membership with no obligation simply by sending us a post card. If you decide to remain a member, do nothing, and succeeding volumes will be shipped to you as issued—one every 3 months. You pay $2.32 plus 12¢ postage for each, after delivery. You may cancel at any time. Because our supply of introductory books is limited, we cannot extend this offer beyond October 31. So please hurry. Mail Shipping Label with 10¢ today. (Offer limited to new trial members only.)

What some famous readers say

J. Edgar Hoover says: "Reader's Digest Condensed Books enable one to profit by many worthwhile works I might otherwise be forced to pass over."

Olivia de Havilland comments!! "Every page of Reader's Digest Condensed Books holds the magic of broad horizons and deep insights, of distinguished writing expertly selected and distilled."

Quentin Reynolds adds: "Even we authors admit that in Reader's Digest Condensed Books the pace of a story is quickened and unimportant trivia are eliminated. Between the hard covers of these handsome volumes are printed the most interesting books of our time."

TO GET YOUR
$2.32 BOOK FOR 10¢
fill in and mail
Shipping Label with 10¢

Send to Reader's Digest Condensed Book Club, Pleasantville, N. Y. As a TRIAL member you will receive this 576-page book to keep for 10¢. Books are issued one every 3 months. If you do not cancel by November 15, the next volume will be automatically sent you for $2.32 plus postage. You may still cancel your membership at any time thereafter. (Offer good only in U.S. and Possessions; limited to new trial members only.)

SHIPPING LABEL

FROM: READER'S DIGEST CONDENSED BOOK CLUB
PLEASANTVILLE, NEW YORK
RETURN POSTAGE GUARANTEED

To: Your Name_____
Address_____
City_____State_____

CONTENTS—BOOK
POSTMASTER: THIS PARCEL MAY BE OPENED
FOR POSTAL INSPECTION IF NECESSARY

Reader's Digest, 1956   ► Argus, 1956

Here's proof that luxuries needn't be expensive !

Argus C-3—only **$66.50** _complete_ with case and flash

No other 35mm camera in all the world offers you so many luxury features for the money! The Argus C-3 has a color-corrected f:3.5 Cintar lens; gear-controlled shutter with speeds up to 1/300 second; easy-to-use Color-matic settings; lens-coupled rangefinder; built-in flash synchronization—the flashgun plugs right into the camera. And the C-3 is the only American-made camera that offers you a selection of interchangeable lenses that make it versatile as cameras costing hundreds of dollars more! See the amazing Argus C-3 at your dealer's today.

These two interchangeable lenses make the C-3 perform like cameras costing hundreds of dollars more !

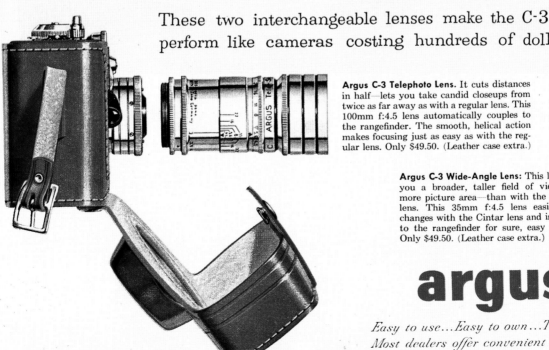

Argus C-3 Telephoto Lens. It cuts distances in half—lets you take candid closeups from twice as far away as with a regular lens. This 100mm f:4.5 lens automatically couples to the rangefinder. The smooth, helical action makes focusing just as easy as with the regular lens. Only $49.50. (Leather case extra.)

Argus C-3 Wide-Angle Lens: This lens gives you a broader, taller field of view—87% more picture area—than with the standard lens. This 35mm f:4.5 lens easily interchanges with the Cintar lens and is coupled to the rangefinder for sure, easy focusing. Only $49.50. (Leather case extra.)

argus ®

Easy to use...Easy to own...That's Argus!
Most dealers offer convenient credit terms

BAUSCH & LOMB BALOMATIC

the slide projector with HIGH PICTURE FIDELITY

Always stays in focus ... runs by itself !

Now Bausch & Lomb gives you *High Picture Fidelity*. Now you can project color slides with all the detail of the scenes you originally captured on film. The magic moments of your memories spring to life with full brilliance, astounding clarity and faithful color, just as high fidelity sound faithfully reproduces the beauty of great music. In addition, your slides *always stay in focus*, slide after slide after slide. No annoying slide "pop" ... no fuzzy images. You have *true* automatic operation because you never have to get up to re-focus! Balomatic runs through your slide collection *all by itself*. You watch big, life-sized pictures, *not* the projector! Serve your guests refreshments ... your slide show goes right along without you. Best relaxation a slide showman ever had!

The Balomatic—developed by world famous Bausch & Lomb optical scientists, creators of CinemaScope lenses and the finest optical instruments—*operates* just as beautifully as it *looks*. You project with 500-watt illumination; all controls grouped together on illuminated panel; 100% automatic with 4-to-60 second timing; finger-tip automatic and optional remote control; precise B & L Balcoted 5″ lens; non-spill slide trays that store and protect 40 slides—35 mm, 828 and Super Slides in any kind of 2x2 mount.

Choose from three Balomatic models. Prices start at $84.50 ... available at low monthly terms. Your dealer is featuring *High Picture Fidelity* Balomatics today ... visit him and see for yourself. Bausch & Lomb Optical Co., Rochester 2, New York.

BAUSCH & LOMB BALOMATIC

Basch & Lomb Balomatic, 1958

▶ *Keystone, 1956*

how much should you pay
for a fine 16mm movie camera?

Keystone K-51
16mm Magazine Movie Camera
with f2.5 coated lens
$139.50

Keystone K-56
16mm Magazine Turret
Movie Camera with ultra-fast
f1.9 coated lens
$189.50
(Telephoto lens optional at extra cost)

Keystone A-15
16mm Rollfilm Turret
Movie Camera with
ultra-fast f1.5 coated lens
$199.50
(Telephoto lens optional at extra cost)

photographed in Bermuda

Just the price of a Keystone . . . and no more. For no other camera at any price
give you finer results or better value. With Keystone, you get the clear, sharp detail
and picture brilliance you have a right to expect . . . the precision engineering and simplicity
operation you have a right to demand. For versatility, ease and high-level performance,
look to Keystone 16mm movie cameras. Preferred by people
who can afford to pay more . . . but who know they don't have to.

K **Keystone**

REGISTERED IN YOUR NAME WITH A LIFETIME GUARANTEE

one K-161M Magna-Scope Projector
ls 60" screen from a distance of 20 feet. "Long-Throw"
or extra large rooms is optional. **$169.50**

Best pictures you ever took

...ALL FINISHED IN 60 SECONDS

● Her first corsage! Moments like this only come once — and only with a Polaroid Land Camera can you be *sure* of capturing them forever. Your pictures are developed in one minute — right inside the camera. If a shot isn't just what you want, you can snap it again right away . . . before the chance for a once-in-a-lifetime picture is lost forever.

Here's picture-taking as it should have been all along! You show your pictures to family and friends on the spot — while everyone's there to share in the fun. You enjoy the satisfaction of watching your skill improve picture by picture . . . minute by minute. You'll get the best pictures you've ever taken, and get them right away, when they mean the most.

You and your friends will want plenty of copies and enlargements of the pictures you take — and with a Polaroid Camera that's easy! Extra prints are made directly from your picture. No need to hunt up old negatives.

If you've never seen this camera in action you've got an exciting 60 seconds coming to you. Drop in at your photo dealer today — he'll be glad to give you a demonstration.

Your Polaroid pictures are guaranteed If you're ever dissatisfied with the results from any roll, just send the pictures to Polaroid and you'll get a new roll free. Polaroid Corporation, Cambridge 39, Mass.

60 seconds after you snap the shutter, lift out a beautiful finished print like this.

Why wait days when a minute does it?

POLAROID® *Land* CAMERAS

Polaroid Pathfinder Model 110

Polaroid Model 95

Polaroid Land Cameras, 1953

No more guessing about light!

No more figuring correct distance!

Amazing new movie camera takes perfect pictures automatically!

The modern magic of electronics takes over! With Revere ELECTRIC EYE-MATIC you simply aim, shoot . . . and get perfect color movies without a thought to exposure.

Whatever the light condition, the Exposure Computor Lens electronically adjusts the iris opening, like the reflex action in the pupil of your eye. All done by energy of light, without aid of batteries. What's more, a setting scale, viewed right through the viewfinder, electronically computes and indicates the "f" exposure being used. You actually see it swing back and forth as you shoot under varying light conditions, outdoors or indoors. It even signals when there is insufficient light.

Added flexibility! In addition to its fully automatic operation you can also add your own personal touches to moviemaking. The exclusive Semi-Auto Dial permits you to take special effects, professional fades and unusual dramatic scenes. No other camera is so versatile and automatic! See the Revere ELECTRIC EYE-MATIC Cameras at your authorized Revere dealer now! REVERE CAMERA COMPANY, CHICAGO 16, ILLINOIS.

Always ready for instant use ...just aim and shoot!

Capture the action the moment it happens. Sweep from sunlight to shade without re-setting! Lens adjusts instantly and automatically. No over-exposure or under-exposure because of extraneous light. Each of the many rectangular ultra sensitive cells of the Exposure Computor Lens measures the light only in the area seen by the camera. Too, it is placed above the natural grip so it cannot be accidentally blocked by the fingers.

MODELS
CA-1 and CA-3

MODELS
CA-2 and CA-4

Revere
ELECTRIC EYE-MATIC
f/1.8 8MM MOVIE CAMERAS

Your choice of four different models

CA-1 ELECTRIC EYE-MATIC 8MM SPOOL CAMERA
Easy drop-in film spool loading; fast f/1.8 Wollensak Wocoted lens; continuous run and single frame; large picture window view-finder; powerful long run motor and many other sensational features.   F.E.T. inc., **$139.50**

CA-2 ELECTRIC EYE-MATIC 8MM SPOOL TURRET CAMERA
All the features of above plus fast f/1.8 3-lens turret system for taking normal, wide angle and telephoto shots.   F.E.T. inc., **$169.50**

CA-3 ELECTRIC EYE-MATIC 8MM MAGAZINE CAMERA
Same as Model CA-1 with convenience of quick magazine loading. Includes "Mechanical Heart-Beat" to signal proper film advance. F.E.T. inc., **$169.50**

CA-4 ELECTRIC EYE-MATIC 8MM MAGAZINE TURRET CAMERA
The ultimate in 8mm automatic movie cameras. Combines convenience of magazine load with fast f/1.8 3-lens Turret System for normal, wide angle and telephoto shots. All features of above models.   F.E.T. inc., **$199.50**

Polaroid Land Cameras, 1953

Kodak, 1956

S & H Green Stamps, 1956

"Even I was amazed!" says Susan Smart*

YOU CHOOSE FROM MORE THAN 1000 SMART STOCKING GIFTS
AT *Woolworth's* TOILETRIES COUNTERS

FOR HER... FOR HIM
From
WOOLWORTH'S

What is as enchanting as a gift of beauty? And where, but at Woolworth's would you find so complete, so wondrous an array of cosmetics and toiletries! Within just a few feet (what a blessing at Christmas-shopping time!), you'll find beauty aids to leave a woman dazzling from top to toe... toiletries to warm a manly heart. You'll choose from a who's-who assortment of the most wanted brands. Best of all, you can examine *all* the brands... take your own sweet time to compare and select. Should you want advice, ask the friendly Woolworth salesgirl. She's *always* happy to help!

A stocking-full of glamour is such fun!

And I have such fun choosing these gifts at Woolworth's. There are whole counters of toiletries that cost little, make a big impression. Colorful cosmetic gifts galore . . . so easy to choose from the compact array of fine brands and new-fashion shades. For a man's stocking . . . grooming aids by the score. In just a few steps . . . in no time at all, my stocking gift shopping is done at Woolworth's!

Merry, Merry Christmas to All!

Susan Smart
Your Woolworth Shopping Reporter

High on my list - these Eight gift stars from Woolworth's

1. BEAUTIFUL HANDS deserve lanolin-rich *Sofskin Cream* . . . a true beauty treatment. Woolworth's has Sofskin for stocking gifts or as a generous gift-by-itself.
10c, 33c, 59c, 98c†

2. ALWAYS A FAVORITE with Woolworth shoppers, this *Gillette Super-Speed Razor Set* is right for him or her. Razor and Blue Blade dispenser in smart plastic travel case. $1 set

3. WOOLWORTH'S GIFT SIZE of *Mennen Skin Bracer* saves money. And its wake-up tingle, he-man aroma make it a favorite after-shave lotion. Gift boxed 59c† Smaller unboxed size 29c†

4. A TOP-NOTCH GIFT...*Vitalis Hair Tonic.* Used with a 60-second workout, it keeps hair and scalp handsome, healthy. Buy it for him at Woolworth's. 27c, 49c†

5. FOR DAILY ENJOYMENT, *Lady Esther 4-Purpose Cream.* As a quick daily home facial it benefits skin 4 ways. An ideal Woolworth stocking gift.
29c, 55c, 83c†

6. DOUBLY WELCOME . . . a *Cutex Make-Up Duet.* Nail Brilliance in miracle Spillpruf bottle and creamy Stay Fast indelible lipstick. A Woolworth gift buy!
59c set†

7. FRAGRANT SALUTE to Christmas . . . purse-size *Darcel Stick Cologne* in handsome brass containers. Woolworth's has a joy-inspiring choice of floral scents. 39c†

8. A SURE HIT . . . the one-step home permanent, *Shadow Wave.* Sure because you've no timing, no rinsing, no neutralizer, no hair-type worries. Woolworth's has kits, $2.00†; refills, $1.25†

DARCEL STICK COLOGNES

F. W. WOOLWORTH CO.

† *Prices plus tax.*

F.W. Woolworth Co., 1952

353

View-Master 3-D adds DEPTH to pictures like this

"I'm clicking with 3-D* now!"

"The View-Master Personal Stereo Camera turned photography into an exciting adventure for me! There's nothing like the thrill you get out of taking and seeing beautiful color pictures of your family and friends in the amazing 'come to life' realism of View-Master 3-Dimension.

"And stereo pictures are so easy to take with the View-Master Personal Camera! People with little or no experience take excellent 3-D pictures the very first time ...there's no focusing...no fussing with gadgets. Just one simple setting and snap the picture. It's that easy!

"But the most amazing thing is that the View-Master 3-D pictures actually cost less than black and white snapshots made with a box camera! These pictures can be viewed in View-Master Stereoscopes or projected in the new View-Master 'Stereo-matic' Projector. Before you buy *any* camera be sure to see the View-Master and the exciting 3-D pictures it takes."

View-Master Personal Stereo Camera...$149.00

*VIEW-MASTER® Personal® STEREO CAMERA

Write Sawyer's Inc., Box 490, Portland 7, Oregon, for free sample 3-D picture Reel.

THE NEW VIEW-MASTER *Stereo-matic* 500" 3-D PROJECTOR
For finest 3-Dimension projection. Ask your View-Master dealer for a demonstration. $177.50

Prices slightly higher in Canada
® Sawyer's Inc., Portland 7, Oregon
Trade Mark Reg. U. S. Pat. Off. Marca Registrada

DARKNESS MEANS...DANGER

PROTECT YOURSELF

Tonight.. be safe with an OLIN "Matched Pair" flashlight

NEW LOW PRICES
2-cell: only $1.35 less batteries
3-cell: only $1.55 less batteries
(For EXTRA RANGE and POWER)

$1.35 LESS BATTERIES

$1.55 LESS BATTERIES

BOND No. 102 Fresh SUPER POWER BATTERY

WINCHESTER No. 1511 Fresh HI-POWER Super BATTERY

Available only in

WINCHESTER and BOND lines

OF OLIN INDUSTRIES, INC., Electrical Division, New Haven 4, Conn.

View Master Stereo Camera, 1953

Winchester Batteries, 1950

▶ *Motorola, 1956*

General Electric, 1952

$25,000.00 IN PRIZES

FUNNY FACE CONTEST

Can you "Tape Up" funnier faces than these?

← SEE OPPOSITE PAGE FOR BIG PRIZES

EASY—just clip out eyes, ears, nose, etc. from panel below.
ARRANGE features on outline face on entry blank to make a funny face.
TAPE them down with "Scotch" cellophane tape.
FILL OUT entry blank and mail. It's fun—do it today!

TO INTRODUCE AMAZING NEW FORMULA

SCOTCH BRAND Cellophane Tape

STICKS AT A FEATHER TOUCH!

Sticks 6 times tighter!

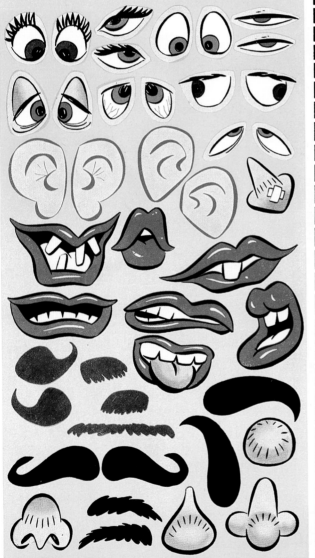

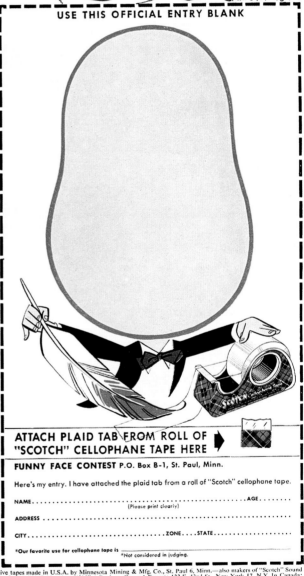

USE THIS OFFICIAL ENTRY BLANK

ATTACH PLAID TAB FROM ROLL OF "SCOTCH" CELLOPHANE TAPE HERE ➤

FUNNY FACE CONTEST P.O. Box B-1, St. Paul, Minn.

Here's my entry. I have attached the plaid tab from a roll of "Scotch" cellophane tape.

NAME . . . . AGE . . . .
(Please print clearly)

ADDRESS . . . .

CITY . . . . ZONE . . . . STATE . . . .

*Our favorite use for cellophane tape is . . . . *Not considered in judging.

Scotch Cellophane Tape, 1953

▶ *Norcross Greeting Cards, 1957*

A NORCROSS VALENTINE...

says what's in your *heart* the *way* you *want* to say it. To be sentimental . . . or old-fashioned or serious—or just for fun—say it with Norcross Valentines!

Be sure to see the beautiful selection at your Norcross dealer's, especially the *exclusive* Norcross King-Size and Queen-Size cards, the best of all ways to say "Be My Valentine." Look for these famous cards displayed in their special racks.

No matter which you choose . . . Norcross Valentines always please. No matter who's your "Valentine" you'll find just the *right* greeting at your Norcross dealer's *now*.

NORCROSS VALENTINES

Say the things you want to say

FOR A GRAND PAIR —
Brother and His Wife
A VALENTINE

For a
VERY NICE GIRL

Hi Sweetie!

You 'n me know   What day this is...

FOR A
Grand Person

A Valentine
Message

A Valentine for the
WORLD'S BEST
POP!

A Valentine for a MOTHER
who's an ANGEL

..from
someone who AIN'T

A perfect saint is what I ain't
My halo isn't showin'...

FOR SOMEONE I LIKE!

A
VALENTINE

ACROSS
THE MILES
on
Valentine's
Day.

Love to my WIFE
on Valentine's Day!

MM-MM
What a gal!

Hi Sis
Some compliments are half-hearted
But it isn't hard to see—

That this compliment
for YOU, Sis—

A Valentine
Sweetheart

Do I love you?
Well, if loving
Means you're always in my heart—
If it means I think of you, dear
When you're near or we're apart
And if loving you means wishing
Life's best and finest, too
On Valentine's Day
and all days—

For my HUBBY

My
Valentine

First things
first
I always say
So I'm letting my work pile high

A VALENTINE PAPER DOLL

For a
Nice Little
Girl

NORCROSS, INC.

Norcross Valentines say the things you want to say

WHETHER your wish is sentimental, secret — or just for fun — Norcross Valentines "say the things you want to say."

A colorful collection of new designs—full of Cupid's charm—is waiting for you. Pick your favorites *now* . . . at better greeting card shops and department stores everywhere.

They'll *know* your heart's in it . . . when you send Norcross Valentines!

N
NORCROSS
GREETING CARDS
Say the things you want to say

Norcross Greeting Cards, 1958

Scripto Satellite Ball Pen, 1958

Hallmark Christmas Cards now present the paintings of the Right Honourable Winston S. Churchill, O.M., C.H., M.P.

In addition to bringing you the work of the foremost artists of America, Hallmark Cards now offer you reproductions in full color of the paintings of Mr. Churchill, world-renowned statesman and artist

Now, for the first time, you can send Christmas Cards distinguished by the paintings of Winston Churchill, Britain's great statesman, who has become the most famous amateur painter in the world. Carefully selected from over 200 originals, his paintings are reproduced on Hallmark Cards for 1950 in full, rich color.

On occasions when Mr. Churchill has submitted paintings under an assumed name (so as not to influence the judges), his canvases have been selected and honored by the Royal Academy of London. For in each stroke of the brush—each rich flash of color —you will find the same warmth and understanding that has made Winston Churchill's name great among people of good will the whole world over.

So, this year, *even more than ever*, you will want to visit the fine store where you buy your Hallmark Cards. Browse through the wide selection, the most beautiful, most memorable collection of Christmas Cards

you've ever seen. As you do, you can visualize the delight and appreciation of all who will receive your Hallmark greetings.

Here, on easy-to-see displays, you will find Hallmark Christmas Cards distinguished by Mr. Churchill's paintings and name. His "Chartwell in Winter," the charming Churchill country estate after a heavy snowfall . . . his vivid portrayal of the "Fox Hunt" . . . his serene "Mill Pond and Cottage" . . . and others as well.

And you will find, too, the work of such celebrated American artists as Grandma Moses and Norman Rockwell, to name but two. Each card a perfect reflection of your own good taste as you convey the sentiments of the season. Each one with the "Hallmark" on the back that says "you cared enough to send the very best."

At Christmas, As Always, Remember

Hallmark Cards

when you care enough to send the very best

CARDS TO SELECT INDIVIDUALLY. Ask to see the *Hallmark Gallery Artists Collection* . . . Look at these masterpieces and select the card just right for each person on your list. You will find a wide selection featuring the work of Mr. Churchill . . . cards painted especially by Grandma Moses, Norman Rockwell and many other world famous artists.

WINSTON CHURCHILL CARDS IN BOXES. Among the wide selection of Hallmark Boxed Collections—a convenient and economical way to buy your cards—you will find two special boxes featuring the distinguished paintings of Winston Churchill. 12 assorted cards are $1.00. Or, if you prefer your cards all alike, boxes of 25 are priced at only $2.00.

WINSTON CHURCHILL CARDS FOR IMPRINTING. Included in the famous Hallmark Albums — where you select from hundreds of cards for imprinting with your name—any Mr. Churchill's English countrysides, a hunting scene, sunny landscapes. For a wide and wonderful selection of truly distinctive Christmas Cards, see these fine Hallmark Albums.

In Canada . . . it's Coutts *Hallmark Cards*

Hallmark Cards, 1950

▶ *Dixon Ticonderoga Pencils, 1950*   ▶▶ *Parker 61 Pen, 1957*

Mary had a little friend
Besides the lamb you know.
And everywhere that Mary went
This other friend would go.

She carried it to class each day
Along with books and rule.
And so did all the other kids
Who went to Mary's school.

At home, she saw it all the time
For it was loved by Mother.
And Daddy's office had it, too,
For he would use no other.

Ticonderoga is this friend,
A Pencil without master.
Its rounded edges, *LeadFast* point,
Make writing smoother, faster.

Ticonderoga's famous name
Is doubly exciting.
It added much to history
And to the ease of writing.

DIXON
Ticonderoga
HE NATION'S FIRST PENCIL

now with gleaming metal tip!

Joseph Dixon Crucible Co., Dept. 52-19, Jersey City 3, N. J.
Canadian Plant: Dixon Pencil Co., Ltd., Newmarket, Ont.

Sheaffer's, 1950

Sheaffer's, 1953

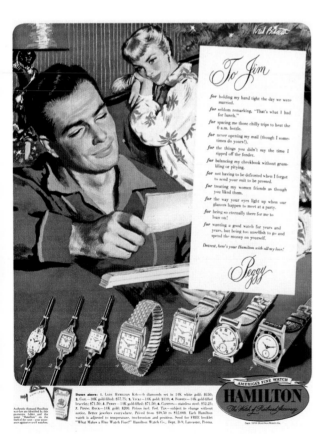

Hamilton Watch Co., 1950

Hamilton Watch Co., 1950

GRUEN
THE NEWEST LOOK IN TIME!

brings you
THE CONTINENTAL

an entirely new concept
in watch design
from stem to strap

from $ 71.50

...ake room on your wrist for tomorrow! Gruen . . . the Newest Look in Time . . . has swept aside the conventional to bring you the breathtakingly new Continental Collection.

Here, for the first time, are watches that capture the clean, uncluttered look of modern fashion with crisp, unbroken lines . . . with broad, gleaming gold bezels that frame dials of simple magnificence . . . with recessed stems . . . with chamois-soft, gold flecked bands that seem to flow from the watches themselves. And a hundred distinctions more!

Your neighborhood Gruen jeweler will be proud to show you the great new Continental Collection. So, before you buy any watch, be sure to see Gruen . . . the Newest Look in Time!

GRUEN THE PRECISION WATCH®—OFFICIAL WATCH OF TRANS WORLD AIRLINES—THE GRUEN WATCH CO . TIME HILL . CINCINNATI 6 OHIO IN CANADA, TORONTO, ONT.

Gruen Watches, 1955

General Electric, 1955

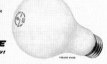

Westinghouse, 1956

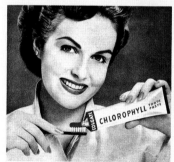

Avon, 1957 ◄ *Colgate Toothpaste, 1952*

Westinghouse, 1952

Colgate, Toothpaste 1956

Crest Toothpaste, 1959

Gleem Toothpaste, 1956

Gleem Toothpaste, 1958

Fresh Deodorant, 1957

Scottissue Bathroom Tissue, 1956

Waldorf Bathroom Tissue, 1958

Soft-Weve Bathroom Tissue, 1953

▶ *Vinylite Plastic, 1951*

FOR THE ENJOYMENT OF LOVELIER, MORE RADIANT HAIR ... MORE OFTEN

The Lady Sunbeam is so simple to use—just set the dial for any drying air temperature you want—hot, medium, warm or cool. Scientifically designed vinyl cap fits easily over your hair and concentrates drying air where hair is heaviest. Drying air comes from heat-control unit through durable, flexible hose. The Lady Sunbeam Hair Dryer eliminates the tiring arm raising and head turning necessary with ordinary hand held dryers—and annoying, uncomfortable hot air on neck and shoulders from professional type dryers. Cap has no electric wires. Only $24.95*

Only *Lady Sunbeam*
gives you all these advantages
● Greater convenience

ARE YOU A SUN LOVER? Like to soak up Old Sol? Remember, hair and scalp can get so much sun they feel almost dry enough to blow off. So get extra protection with Vitalis care.

AVIDLY AQUATIC? Dunking daily can make your scalp feel like a regular "Sahara." But with that scalp-stimulating Vitalis "60-second workout," you can always duck in without drying out.

SHOWER FIEND? A needle spray can chase heat and humidity—but also bring on dry hair and scalp. To prevent dryness, depend on Vitalis—it contains pure vegetable oil, not greasy liquid petrolatum.

Don't let **Sun, Water, Wind** wreck your hair

FRESH AIR FAN? If you're strictly a convertible man, watch out for that air in your hair. Keep your top down with Vitalis—it controls perfectly, makes hair look neat, natural, never "slicked down."

Guard hair and scalp with
Vitalis
and the
"60-Second Workout"

A Product of Bristol-Myers

Summer sun, wind and water leave your hair dry and brittle, your scalp parched and flaky. So more than ever, summer's the time for Vitalis care... time to give your hair and scalp 60 seconds of *top* protection every day.

50 seconds' massage—feel the difference in your scalp. Vitalis stimulates scalp, prevents dryness, routs flaky dandruff, helps check excessive falling hair.

10 seconds' combing—try the difference in your hair. Neater, handsomer—set to stay all day. So get Vitalis soon—at any drug counter or barber shop.

Vitalis, 1951

You can have a smoother, richer tan . . . faster with SKOL's exclusive new formula

GREATEST ADVANCE IN SUNTAN PRODUCT HISTORY!

Now—Have a Richer Tan
in a single day—

with SKOL'S revolutionary new "RICH-TAN" Formula

This summer put a glow in your tan that will make all your other tans seem dull! The secret is in SKOL's exclusive new "Rich-Tan" formula. This new kind of tan magic actually "lights up" your tan with vibrant life and luster . . . gives you a *richer* tan, *faster—more safely than ever before.*

New control factor

SKOL's new formula controls the reaction of your skin to the sun. It makes your skin more "receptive" to beautiful tanning . . . lets you tan more deeply without burning.

And you tan faster

With SKOL's new "Rich-Tan" formula you can get a tan in just a few hours!

Use SKOL's new "Rich-Tan" formula this summer. Discover how rich and deep and smooth your tan can really be.

This formula is the exclusive property of SKOL and cannot be used by any other manufacturer.

Now! SKOL's wonderful "Rich-Tan" Formula in 4 popular forms

SKOL Tanning Oil . . . Gives skin faster . . . prevents dryness. Also in Aerosol can.
SKOL Tanning Foam . . . Rich cream that softens, smooths. Effective for dry skin.
SKOL Tanning Cream . . . Greaseless cream with a special skin softening ingredient.

Regular SKOL . . . Not oily. Doesn't pick up sand. Goes on evenly. The world's largest selling tanning lotion! Available in plastic bottle or in handy new squeeze-spray plastic.

Skol Tanning Lotion, 1956

ALL NEW SCHICK

SCHICK
FIRST IN ELECTRIC SHAVING

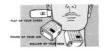
Power-Shave

FOR A NEW KIND OF SHAVE, DEEP DOWN WHERE YOUR BEARD BEGINS

NEW FULL-CONTACT HEAD—TWICE AS BIG—SHAVES YOU FASTER!

The size of that FULL-CONTACT HEAD! Biggest news since Schick invented electric shaving. Twice as big a shaving head—and all of it designed to shave on every curve of your face—flats, rounds, and hollows. New Schick doesn't curve away like most other electrics that shave more air than hair. Powershave is *naturally* faster!

BUILT-IN WHISKER GUIDES—POP WHISKERS OUT—SHAVE YOU CLOSER!

Leave it to Schick to discover the safe, sure way to closer shaves . . . with hundreds of amazing WHISKER GUIDES built into the shaving edges! Not an attachment as on shavers that roll whiskers flat. Schick's built-in WHISKER GUIDES smooth skin down and pop whiskers out, for a new kind of shave, deep down where your beard begins!

TWICE AS POWERFUL ON YOUR BEARD—YET GENTLE ON YOUR SKIN!

With a big new motor, twice as powerful as ever before, here's a he-man shaver to mow down toughest beards. Prove it yourself, on *your* beard! Ask to test the new Schick Powershave. Most stores offer a 14-day FREE HOME TRIAL! Choice of four handsome colors: Desert Tan, Forest Green, Royal Black, Glacier White.

© 1957, Schick Incorporated, Lancaster, Pa.

Lady Sunbeam, 1957 ◄ *Schick, 1957*

Let 10 Days Prove This One Shaves Close!

Try the New Schick "20's" exclusive Comb-Action. Get clean shaves — or get your money back!

There's a world of difference in electric shavers — even between old and new models of the same make. So why not find out—without risking a penny—how much these differences can mean to you? For instance, there are tiny, beveled comb-edges on the New Schick "20." No other shaver has them—yet whiskers must be individually lined up for truly clean shaves. The New Schick "20" does this, as no other shaver can—and delivers whiskers to shaving edges for a clean sweep precisely at skinline!

And what sweet shaving edges they are! Honed, self-sharpening — powered by the world's mightiest rotary motor of

its size — they fairly sing their way through the toughest beard. From the moment you snap that handy Stop-Start Button, they take every type of whisker in stride—closely, cleanly, comfortably!

Even those hard-to-get-into places around nose, lips and chin can't confuse the New Schick "20." Its Hi-Velocity Heads are scientifically sized and shaped to get in anywhere—and come out with the whiskers!

Those are some of the reasons why close shaves are no idle boast for the New Schick "20." They are also reasons why more men use Schick Electric Shavers than any other make.

They are reasons why we invite you to go to any Schick dealer — or Schick Electric Shaver Shop—and ask for the New Schick "20" on 10-days' trial. If, after 10 days, its close shaves don't still delight you—return it—and every penny will be cheerfully refunded.

The New Schick "20" complete with Caddie Case (ideal for bathroom shelf or travel bag) is only $24.50. Other fine Schick Electric Shavers as low as $19.95. **Schick Electric Shaver Shops** in principal cities. Address listed under "Shavers" in classified telephone directories. Schick Incorporated, Stamford, Conn.

NEW SCHICK COLONEL HAS MANY NEW SCHICK "20" FEATURES!

- NEW finger-fitting design
- NEW single-bead version of "20's" famous comb-action
- NEW AC-DC real rotary motor
- NEW handy Caddie Case
- SAME 10-day, no-risk trial! $19.95

"THE LOW-PRICED LUXURY SHAVER"

NEW Schick "20"

MORE MEN USE SCHICK ELECTRIC SHAVERS THAN ANY OTHER MAKE

...better-built for closer shaves

Schick Electric Shaver, 1952

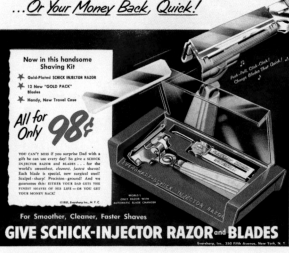
Schick Injector Razor, 1951

The PRACTICAL GIFT with THE LUXURY TOUCH

REMINGTON Contour De Luxe

GIVE A REMINGTON *The Shaver Men Prefer*

Watch his eyes light up when he sees this streamlined beauty! He knows nothing can match the Remington Contour DeLuxe for sheer shaving perfection. And you'll both be proud of its graceful lines and rich, ivory look, highlighted with gleaming chrome, resting in that handsome jewelry case.

It's a gift he'll use every day . . . a gift to make shaving a pleasure instead of a chore. The Remington Contour shaves faster and smoother, without nicks or cuts . . . without muss or bother. Even the toughest beard—even the tenderest face—feels smooth and

refreshed after the gentle massage-like action of a Remington Contour shave.

In performance, in quality, and in styling, there's no shaving instrument to compare with a Remington Contour DeLuxe Electric Shaver. It's the perfect combination of usefulness and elegance. Give the gift that combines the things you want to give with those he likes to receive. Give the best —the Remington Contour at your dealer's, or at any of our 108 Shaver Headquarters.

A PRODUCT OF *Remington Rand*.

The only electric shaver with attached single-hinge hair pocket—swings back for quicker, easier cleaning.

Remington Electric Shaver, 1950

Eversharp Hydro-magic Razor, 1954   ▶ *Schick Electric Razor, 1951*

Want a closer shave?
—Follow the Crowd!

For a shave that leaves <u>nothing</u> on your face but smoothness — for an easier, faster shave — follow the hundreds of thousands who turned so quickly to the new Schick "20."

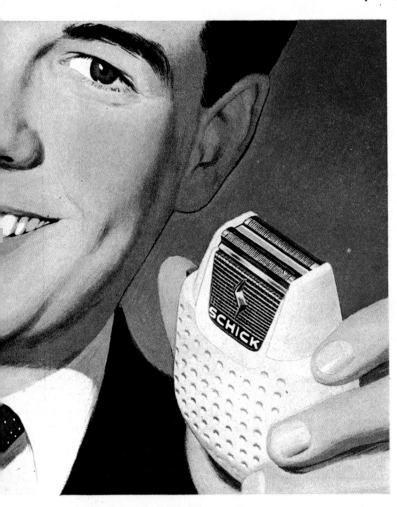

Think you know how close a shave can be?

Just wait till you follow legions of other men — and try the wonderfully different Schick "20."

Wait till you hold this balanced new shape — lightest electric shaver out — and feel it nestle in your fingers.

And — just wait till you learn how *easily* your whiskers glide off with this revolutionary new electric shaver.

For Schick's brand-new Hi-Velocity Heads get whiskers off as *fast* as you can move the "20" over your face. They get 'em right down at skinline — because these heads have Schick's exclusive comb edges plus interceptor bars for skin-close shaving.

And — they're driven by Schick's *real* rotary motor — most powerful built by Schick. Press the Stop-Start Button — and it purrs into action, moving the heads through your whiskers as though nothing were there.

In a few flying moments — you're shaved. *Close? Clean?* Check your face in a magnifying mirror — you'll see the smoothest skin you've ever shown the world.

What's more, the "20" comes to you in its very own Caddie Case, designed to fit your bathroom shelf or suitcase. So get set for a really close shave. Get a new Schick "20" at the nearest dealer's. The Schick Super and Colonel are there, too. Schick Incorporated, Stamford, Conn. Service offices in principal cities.

Schick "20" — $24.50 • Schick Super — $22.50 • Schick Colonel — $17.50

THESE HI-VELOCITY HEADS • THIS REAL ROTARY MOTOR ↙

Make the Schick "20" "The Finest Shaving Instrument of All Time"

New high-speed, precision-made shearing heads, of exclusive Schick design. Sharpened and honed. Comb edges guide whiskers into slots. Interceptor bars pick up short stubble. All for fast, close, skinline shaving.

Schick's real rotary motor. Precision-built. Smooth. Quiet. A powerhouse. The most powerful motor Schick ever built. AC or DC. Stop-Start Button snaps it on or off.

Schick "20"

MORE MEN USE SCHICK ELECTRIC SHAVERS THAN ANY OTHER MAKE

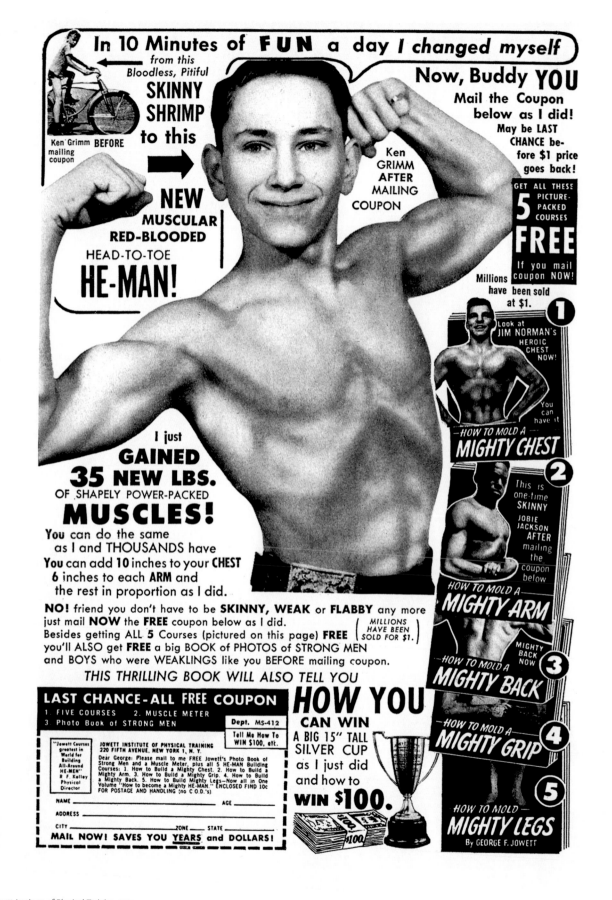

Jowett Institute of Physical Training, 1954

Don't Be Half A Man!

Let Me PROVE I Can Make You A REAL HE-MAN from Head to Toe—in Just 15 Minutes A Day!

7

Charles Atlas

RONALD REAGAN
starring in
"BEDTIME FOR BONZO"
a Universal-International
Picture

"JERIS rates cheers
for greaseless good grooming
and healthier, handsomer hair"

says *Ronald Reagan*

BILLY ECKSTINE
Famous singing
Star of
"THE BIRD CAGE"
and featured on
many MGM
record hits.

JERIS gets my applause

for GLOSSY GOOD GROOMING, and HEALTHIER, HANDSOMER HAIR,

says Billy Eckstine

ONLY DANDRUFF-DESTROYING* JERIS HAS THIS FRESH, CLEAN-SCENTED MASCULINE FRAGRANCE

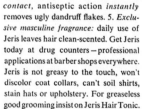

Of all the hair tonics on the market, JERIS and only JERIS brings you all these hair benefits: 1. *Glossy good grooming.* 2. *Healthier, handsomer hair.* 3. *Scalp-stimulation:* Daily JERIS massage helps promote healthy hair growth, relieves dry scalp, excessive falling hair. 4. *Destroys dandruff germs* on contact,* antiseptic action *instantly* removes ugly dandruff flakes. 5. *Exclusive masculine fragrance:* daily use of Jeris leaves hair clean-scented. Get Jeris today at drug counters — professional applications at barber shops everywhere. Jeris is not greasy to the touch, won't discolor coat collars, can't soil shirts, stain hats or upholstery. For greaseless good grooming insist on Jeris Hair Tonic.

JERIS KILLS DANDRUFF GERMS* ON CONTACT.
*Pityrosporum ovale, which many authorities recognize as the cause of infectious dandruff is destroyed by Jeris Antiseptic Hair Tonic.

JERIS
ANTISEPTIC HAIR TONIC

Women go for men with Handsome Hair!

For smooth, smart, suave, well groomed hair that women love and men admire, depend on Murray's famous hair preparations. Enjoy more popularity and romance, look better, feel more confident.
Keep your hair neat, handsome, natural looking all day long. Ask for Murray's today. On sale everywhere.

Hair-Glo: A Medium weight dressing. Keeps hair looking natural.

Pomade: Makes it easy to control hair hard to manage.

Heads you win.. Hearts you win with Murray's.

Murray's
for well groomed hair

ACCEPT NO SUBSTITUTE

Murray's **SUPERIOR PRODUCTS COMPANY** Chicago 17, Illinois

© 1950

Jeris Antiseptic Hair Tonic, 1951 ◀ *Jeris Antiseptic Hair Tonic, 1950*   *Murray's Hair Products, 1950*

Top Left — Prell

at last !

A LIQUID SHAMPOO

that's **EXTRA RICH !**

IT'S LIQUID
PRELL

FOR
'Radiantly Alive' Hair

Only new Liquid Prell has this unique, *extra-rich* formula . . . that's why only Liquid Prell leaves your hair looking 'Radiantly Alive'! And how you'll love its mounds of richer, more effective lather . . . the way Liquid Prell leaves your hair whisper-soft yet so obedient. Treat yourself to this luxurious shampoo today—there's radiant beauty in every drop!

JUST POUR IT . . . and you'll see the glorious difference!

Never too thin or watery—never too messy or wasteful—like so many ordinary liquid shampoos.

Never too thick, with a "fibbing" ingredient that can dull hair like so many cream shampoos.

Extra-Rich Liquid Prell has just the right consistency. It won't run and it never leaves a dulling film.

And you'll love **PRELL CONCENTRATE**—leaves hair extra clean . . . extra radiant!

Not a cream—not a liquid—but a clear shampoo concentrate that contains more cleansing ingredients, ounce for ounce, than any other type of shampoo! That's why fabulous Prell Concentrate leaves your hair *extra clean, extra radiant!*

Prell Shampoo, 1956

Top Right — Party Curl

New! party curl

HOME PERMANENT *by* Lilt

Prettiest curls at the party!

Lovely day after day!

Nearly twice as fast as any leading children's home permanent!

3 REASONS WHY PARTY CURL PLEASES EVERY LITTLE GIRL . . .

1. So much easier to *have* than any other children's home permanent. Neutralizes automatically . . . no pincurls.
2. *Prettiest Hair in the Neighborhood!* Party Curl curls have that envied natural look—are far, far softer!
3. *Doesn't have to be set between shampoos!* Perfectly formed curls can be brushed into place like naturally curly hair.

3 REASONS WHY PARTY CURL MAKES A HIT WITH MOTHER . . .

1. So much easier to *give!* From start to finish it's nearly twice as fast as any leading children's home permanent.
2. A perfectly-groomed little girl! Hair is easy to comb—always has a gleaming-smooth, cared-for appearance.
3. *Lasts and lasts!* Party Curl keeps hair looking better day after day!

$1.50 (plus tax)

party curl

Children's Home Permanent
by Lilt

NEWEST and BEST HOME PERMANENT FOR CHILDREN'S HAIR

119

Lilt Home Permanent, 1954

Bottom Left — Helene Curtis Shampoo Whip

new shampoo sensation actually shines hair

gets it so clean you can feel the difference!

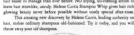

Now bring out the *full* beauty of your hair with a revolutionary shampoo that works in a completely new way! Helene Curtis Shampoo Whip bombards hair and scalp with billions of lively, lanolin-loaded bubbles that *rush* dirt and dandruff away—even in hardest water. Actually *shines* hair. Leaves it so gloriously fresh and clean you can *feel* the difference. So sunbeam bright . . . so enchantingly soft . . . you'll take new, exciting pride in your hair.

It's the world's first whipped LOTION-LATHER shampoo—wonderfully *good* for your hair and scalp. A marvelous beauty treat—with amazing new *atomized* lanolin, that penetrates like magic mist to EVERY part of hair and scalp. MORE lanolin by far than ordinary shampoos.

And because of miraculous LOTION-LATHER, *this* shampoo leaves hair easier to manage than ever before. NO drying, oil-robbing action to leave hair strawlike, unruly. Helene Curtis Shampoo Whip gives hair rich glowing beauty never before possible without costly special after-rinse.

This amazing new discovery by Helene Curtis, leading authority on hair, makes ordinary shampoos old-fashioned. Try it today, and you will throw away your old shampoos.

Just press nozzle — and out billows rich **ACTUAL LATHER** (like whipped cream)

Helene Curtis SHAMPOO WHIP

Not a Soap, Creme or Liquid but a revolutionary new Helene Curtis discovery—the World's first whipped LOTION-LATHER shampoo!

SO ECONOMICAL! HALF-YEAR SUPPLY . . . $1

New! Bombards dirt and dandruff with billions of microscopic bubbles!

Gets hair so clean you can feel the difference.

New! Guaranteed—for more applications for one dollar than *any* previous shampoo!

Wonderful for the WHOLE family!

New! Atomized-lanolin gets hair fabulously soft, magically obedient!

Far MORE lanolin than any ordinary shampoo.

Helene Curtis Shampoo Whip, 1950

Bottom Right — Halo

Hair with the fresh young HALO look

is softer, brighter

Whistle Clean

HALO SHAMPOO

—for clear, liquid Halo . . . unlike most shampoos . . . contains no greasy oils or soap. Nothing to interfere with cleaning action or dull your hair with heavy, dirt-catching film. Mild, gentle Halo leaves hair softer, brighter . . . whistle clean!

Halo Shampoo, 1956

▶ *L.B. Hair Products, 1959*

AT LAST YOU CAN HAVE
Shades LIGHTER
Smoother
Softer... SKIN

It's True
FAIRER LOVELINESS CAN BE YOURS

WITH SAFE...SCIENTIFIC
BLACK AND WHITE
BLEACHING CREAM
THAT IS
Not 1 Not 2
BUT NOW
3 TIMES STRONGER
THAN BEFORE

For those breathless moments when you're together—be a vision of loveliness to dazzle his eyes. Be sure your skin always looks light, smooth, soft. Black and White Bleaching Cream is your beauty guarantee.

Yes, your skin can look shades lighter, smoother, softer! For now, famous Black and White Bleaching Cream is 3 times stronger than before—to give you the complexion you've longed for. This amazing cream's "special ingredient" works directly on the color in your skin to make it shades lighter—and this direct bleaching action goes right into the layer in your skin where skin color is regulated. So start using it today. Black and White Bleaching Cream's amazing action—a result of regular dressing table use as directed—will help you have shades lighter, smoother, softer skin. Modern science knows no faster method of lightening skin. It's hard to believe this cream that does so much costs so little. Buy a jar today.

BLACK AND WHITE
Triple Strength BLEACHING CREAM *Triple Strength*

Black and White Bleaching Cream, 1950

The Softer Dressing For Softer Hair

JUST FEEL
How <u>Soft</u> It Is

Royal Crown Hair Dressing brings out the natural beauty of your hair. Thanks to a special softening ingredient that makes your hair velvety soft and easy to manage, so easy to arrange in any style you like. It's extra white, can't stain clothing or bed clothes.

For true hair beauty use Royal Crown Hair Dressing, the softer dressing for softer hair, and you will thrill to the glorious soft beauty of your hair.

Its purity and quality guarantee you complete satisfaction or your money back. Ask for the famous red and green can. Sold everywhere in 10c & 25c sizes.

Royal Crown Hair Dressing, 1950

> ## Good news for women with dark, oily skin!

A delight to use
...won't rub off
on clothing or pillow

Watch day-by-day improvement
...skin grows lighter, clearer
...ugly shine disappears

Announcing new

NADINOLA

DE LUXE

GREASELESS BLEACH CREME

Famous "double-strength" bleach now in marvelous new formula
. . . non-oily, non-greasy, delightful to use

Now treat yourself to a delightful new kind of cream that women everywhere have been waiting for—the exciting new *greaseless* bleaching cream *de luxe*, made by the makers of famous NADINOLA.

This soft velvety new cream contains no oil or grease . . . shows an amazing bleaching and clearing action for lighter lovelier skin beauty. And it's such a joy to use—spreads lightly over the skin, disappears when you smooth it in, leaves no oily coat, no messiness to soil clothing or bed linen.

Yet even after Nadinola *De Luxe* has vanished deep into your skin, its marvelous beautifying action goes on and on! Day by day, you can watch your skin grow lighter, clearer, smoother, softer.

NADINOLA *De Luxe* is a special new type of bleaching cream that works quickly to give you beauty benefits no ordinary cream can

furnish. Use it to counteract *oily shine* and see your skin quickly become clearer, more attractive. Use it to help loosen and remove blackheads and to help clear up pimples externally caused. Most often, you see remarkable improvement after only a week or so of use, your skin feeling softer, looking smoother and younger and much clearer.

You can't lose—Money-Back Guarantee!
We know you'll be delighted with Nadinola *De Luxe* Greaseless Bleach Cream and so it's fully guaranteed. Just buy a jar today. If it doesn't do everything we say, every cent you pay for it will be refunded.

So don't make beauty wait! Get Nadinola *De Luxe* right away at your drug store or toilet counter. Only 75c for a great big jar—enough to last you for many weeks. Be sure to ask for Nadinola *De Luxe*. NADINOLA, Paris, Tennessee.

Now every woman can be helped to a lighter, lovelier complexion by

NADINOLA

RESULTS GUARANTEED FROM JUST ONE JAR!

The original, genuine, ever famous NADINOLA Bleaching Cream for those who prefer the extra richness of fine oils in their skin cream @ 60c and $1

Nadinola Bleach Creme, 1950

AVON GIFTS

A joy to select . . . a joy to give . . . a joy
to receive. Original, appealing, charmingly
packaged gifts of cosmetics and
fragrances for everyone in the family.

AVON cosmetics
NEW YORK · MONTREAL

AVAILABLE ONLY THROUGH YOUR AVON REPRESENTATIVE WHO CALLS AT YOUR HOME.

Avon, 1959

Beautiful Hair

B R E C K

THERE ARE THREE BRECK SHAMPOOS
FOR THREE DIFFERENT HAIR CONDITIONS

When you buy a shampoo, keep in mind one thought – the
condition of your hair. It is either dry, oily or normal. For each
of these hair conditions, there is a different Breck Shampoo.
One Breck Shampoo is for dry hair. Another Breck Shampoo is
for oily hair. A third Breck Shampoo is for normal hair.
A Breck Shampoo is mild and gentle in action and not
drying to the hair. The Breck Shampoo for your individual
hair condition leaves your hair clean, soft and beautiful.

The Three Breck Shampoos are available at Beauty Shops, Drug Stores, Department Stores and wherever cosmetics are sold.

JOHN H BRECK INC · MANUFACTURING CHEMISTS · SPRINGFIELD 3 MASSACHUSETTS
NEW YORK · CHICAGO · SAN FRANCISCO · LOS ANGELES · OTTAWA CANADA
Copyright 1956 by John H. Breck Inc.

Breck Shampoo, 1957

T

NEW **T**USSY ROTO-MAGIC DEODORANT

ROLLS ON ANTI-PERSPIRANT PROTECTION

A new Tussy Deodorant
in lotion form.

- Checks perspiration
  24 hours.
- Stops odor all day, too.
- Won't acid-damage
  skin or clothes.
- In an unbreakable case.
- Dries quickly.
  No sticky underarms.
- The perfect family
  deodorant. $1.00 plus tax

TUSSY roto-magic deodorant

On Canadian counters see   © Tussy, 655 Park Avenue, New York

Tussy Deodorant, 1957

Du Barry discovered it!

"THE MISSING PINK"

Du Barry, 1958

Hollywood's favorite

Lustre-Creme Shampoo...

Never Dries— it Beautifies!

Elizabeth Taylor
co-starring in M-G-M's
RAINTREE COUNTY
Filmed in M-G-M Camera 65
and Color

Lustre-Creme Shampoo, 1957

To him you're just as lovely as a movie star

As far as he's concerned—there's no one else quite as wonderful, quite as lovely as you! And to look your most attractive *always*, be sure your complexion is as fresh and glowing as Kim Novak's. Miss Novak, like 9 out of 10 Hollywood stars, uses new Lux every day . . . and regular Lux care can do as much for your skin as it does for hers.

Cosmetic lather is the secret

New Lux lather has a beneficial cosmetic action on your complexion . . . actually helps your skin maintain the proper moisture balance. It's moisture balance, you know, that helps keep your complexion fresh and glowing.

For the best results, use new Lux this way every day. First, massage the rich, creamy *cosmetic* lather into your skin gently. Rinse with warm, then cool water, and pat dry. The Hollywood stars find new Lux care wonderful —and we think you will, too!

New Lux is sealed in Gold Foil

. . . to protect its cosmetic lather, dazzling whiteness, wonderful fragrance. Only new Lux gives you both cosmetic lather and new Reynolds gold foil protection. You don't have to be a movie star to have a movie star's complexion—that's the beauty of new Lux in Gold Foil!

Kim Novak
starring in
"THE EDDY DUCHIN STORY"
A Columbia Picture in CinemaScope
COLOR BY TECHNICOLOR

Lux Soap, 1956

"My lingerie stays so lovely with LUX care"
SAYS **MAUREEN O'HARA**

Fairy-tale colors stay enchantingly lovely 3 times as long with this gentle care

MAUREEN has a fabulous collection of Belleek china, fragile as eggshells, brought from Ireland . . . loves shamrocks and all shades of green . . . and fragile, feminine lingerie in soft tones that complement her gorgeous red-gold hair.

"I always insist on Lux Flakes care for all my lingerie," Maureen says. "It's so safe for colors, I wouldn't dream of using anything else."

Never before have lingerie shades been so ravishing—gentle care so important! Why take chances with wrong washing methods that may easily fade subtle tints, blur prints or tear fragile lace.

It's no wonder Hollywood stars insist on gentle Lux Flakes. These extra-safe suds refresh slips and nighties in a wink—keep them enchantingly lovely, incredibly new-looking 3 times as long.

No other soap, no other washing product known, leaves colors lovelier. Try this washbowl magic for *your* pretty undies . . . give *all* your nice washables gentle Lux care for that lovely Lux look.

MAUREEN O'HARA
starring in
RKO Radio's
"SONS OF THE MUSKETEERS"
COLOR BY TECHNICOLOR

LUX FLAKES for that **LOVELY LUX LOOK**

Lux Soap Flakes, 1950

Five days of new freedom

Meds Tampons

New Kotex napkins with the Kimlon center
protect better, protect longer. Now Kotex adds the Kimlon center to increase absorbency,
to keep stains from going through. With this inner fabric, the Kotex napkin stays even softer, holds its shape for perfect fit. Choose Kotex — the name you know best — in this smart new package.

KOTEX and KIMLON are trademarks of Kimberly-Clark Corp

Meds Tampons, 1954 ◄   *Kotex Sanitary Napkins, 1958*

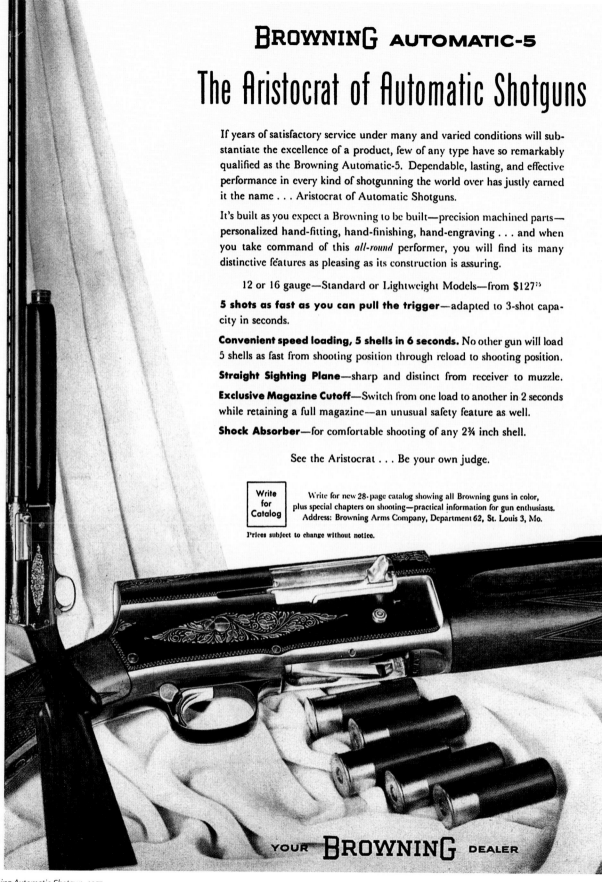

Browning Automatic Shotgun, 1957

for a lifetime of shooting — buy a

PRICED FROM $104.95*

WINCHESTER
TRADEMARK

MODEL 12

Good News! Only $10.95 down and up to 20 months to pay puts the superb Model 12 in your hands. See your local Winchester Time Payment Plan dealer for details.

WINCHESTER
FIREARMS
TIME
PAYMENT
PLAN

No shotgun made anywhere in the world can take it like a Model 12! Built of better materials, to a better design, by craftsmen to whom perfection is the only standard, a Winchester Model 12 is a treasured possession often handed from father to son. For 45 years the Model 12 has been the choice of sportsmen who know the best costs the least in the long run — make the 12 *your* choice, too.

action pictures prove

— that in less than 3/5 of a second a hunter can raise and fire a superbly balanced Model 12. Speed? You bet! The kind you must have for fast, fleet game.

PRICES SUBJECT TO CHANGE WITHOUT NOTICE

25 wear adjustments

Tough Winchester Proof-Steel, machined to exact dimensions gives you years of extra use before any take-up is necessary. Then you can make a slight adjustment and get years more. *No Model 12 has ever used all the adjustment available!* Tough? And how!

WINCHESTER-WESTERN DIVISION · OLIN MATHIESON CHEMICAL CORPORATION · NEW HAVEN 4, CONN.

Winchester Rifle, 1957

▶ *Crosley Electric Range, 1956*

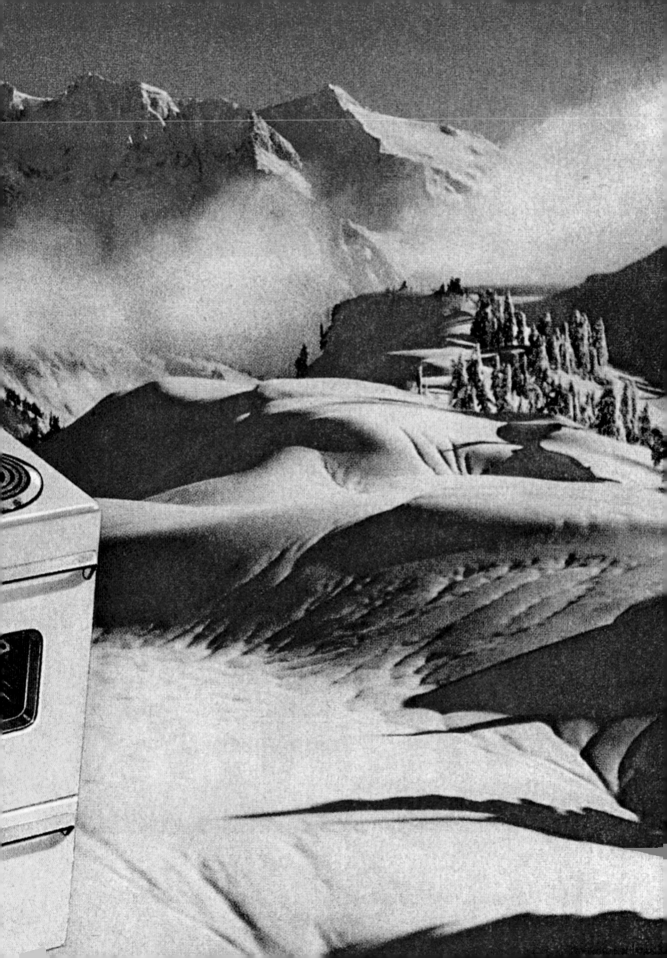

You'll fall in love with the
BRIGHT NEW LOOK
IN HOME APPLIANCES!

Imperial Dual-Temp
ADMIRAL

NOW BROUGHT TO YOU BY
ADMIRAL

Behold the latest of the New Ideas—the "Fashion Front" on Admiral's new Refrigerator-Freezers! See how attractively you can decorate the door panel with wallpaper to match your kitchen! Or, there's a decorator kit of five different color panels optional with your new Dual-Temp. They're shiny, washable—pre-cut to fit—adhesive-backed so you can put them on and peel them off in a wink. Each change is as stimulating as a new hat! So give your kitchen the "Bright New Look"—with Admiral Appliances!

THE NEXT 5 PAGES TELL THE STORY OF **Admiral's** NEW IDEAS IN APPLIANCES...

No "pot-watching"!

MODEL J-408—$4.12 per week after small down payment*

Electric cooking is automatic! *Bake, boil, roast and grill without watching . . . even cook meals while you're away! New unit makes any pan automatic. Oven timer turns oven on and off by itself. Rotisserie barbecues automatically, too.*

MODEL J-408 (*shown above*) is G.E.'s finest range—embodies every G-E advance including: Famous G-E Keyboard Controls • *Two fully automatic ovens* • Master Oven with family-size rotisserie • Electric meat thermometer • Thrifty Companion Oven cooks dinner for six • New automatic surface unit, big removable griddle hold any temperature you set—*automatically!*

GENERAL  ELECTRIC

Admiral, 1956 ◄   *General Electric, 1959*

Aluminum is **Why**

heat jumps out of the fire into the frying pan

If you have ever cooked flapjacks on an aluminum griddle, you know what we mean. They fluff up to an all-over golden brown . . . no burned centers, no uncooked edges.

So it is with *all* aluminum utensils—saucepans, frying pans, kettles. Aluminum conducts heat evenly, quickly. Not only do the bottoms get uniformly hot, but the sides and lids too. No wonder aluminum utensils cook more thoroughly and use less heat than those of any other metal.

Aluminum is food-friendly, too—recommended by leading medical authorities for healthful cooking—widely used in the sparkling kitchens of the better hospitals.

Then there's another reason why the ladies love it. Lustrous, sparkling aluminum utensils enhance the spick-and-span look of modern kitchens. And they're so easy to clean!

ALCOA is **How**

Almost 65 years ago our first salesman interested a manufacturer of cooking utensils in aluminum kettles. Since then, Alcoa technical men have worked constantly with cooking utensil makers—helping them produce pots and pans that can take hard use—finishing them mirror-smooth inside and out—devising handles that stay on and lids that fit. You could say that Alcoa fathered this business through the know-how we have passed on to dozens of companies. ALUMINUM COMPANY OF AMERICA, Pittsburgh 19, Penna.

Refrigerator makers use the cooling efficiency of Alcoa Aluminum in ice trays, freezer chests and vegetable crispers.

Lustrous wall tile made of enameled aluminum can take plenty of abuse and constant moisture. It is light and easy to install.

Your favorite spread wrapped in Alcoa Aluminum Foil stays sweet and pure. Rewrap it in original foil after each use to keep it fresh.

Alcoa Aluminum
ALUMINUM COMPANY OF AMERICA

Alcoa Aluminum Company of America

---

you'll love the way your kitchen looks...
you'll love the way your kitchen works!

HOTPOINT
Quality Appliances
for kitchen and laundry

What a joy it is to please your good taste *and* your good judgment at the same time! Hotpoint lets you do just that. Never were home appliances so beautiful to look at—so automatically convenient to use—so thrifty to own—as are the Hotpoint 1959 models in your choice of four lovely Colortones or classic white. Whether you're planning a complete all-electric kitchen and laundry, or simply replacing a single appliance, visit your Hotpoint dealer and see what he has in store for you!

Hotpoint Appliances, 1959

Look! New Super-Storage Design!

New, Built-To-Last Beauty! New Ice-Blue Trim! New Features Galore!

You'll find them all in FRIGIDAIRE!

See the new De Luxe! New Super-Storage design gives you 9 cu. ft. of storage space—yet this refrigerator takes little more kitchen space than a 5 cu. ft. model of a few years ago! Look outside—at a gleaming Lifetime Porcelain or Durable Dulux finish, rugged steel cabinet, fingertouch Target Latch. Look inside—at lustrous Ice-Blue and golden trim, Full-Width Super-Freezer Chest, full-width plastic Chill Drawer, twin stacking Hydrators! The main food compartment has new, improved Cold-Wall cooling, aluminum shelves that cannot rust. 9 and 10.7 cu. ft. sizes available—frozen storage capacities, 45 and 49 lbs.

Look at it inside! Look at it outside!

You Get New Beauty!
1. New Lustrous Ice-Blue, Gold and White Beauty—sets a new standard for smartness.
2. New Target Door Latch—with finger-tip action—locks cold in.
3. New Streamlined Design—finished in Lifetime Porcelain or Durable Dulux.

You Get New Convenience!
4. Extra Storage Space—in less kitchen space than before.
5. Extra-Large Frozen Storage Space—holds from 15 to 70 lbs.
6. Double-Easy Quickube Ice Trays—trays slide out—cubes released instantly—no melting.
7. New Aluminum Rustproof Shelves—adjustable, sliding—more space between shelves.
8. New, Extra-Deep Porcelain Hydrators—for fruits and vegetables.

You Get New Economy— New Dependability!
9. New Full-Width Plastic Chill Drawer in De Luxe models—ice and ice-cube storage, quick beverage chilling.
10. New Improved Meter-Miser—makes more cold with no more current.
11. Freon-12 Refrigerant—developed by Frigidaire and General Motors.
12. New Improved Cold-Wall Cooling—in all De Luxe and Imperial models.
13. New Sealed-In Mechanism—with 5-Year Protection Plan.
14. This emblem on Frigidaire Refrigerator is your assurance of safe cold from top to bottom, lasting beauty, utmost convenience, proved economy features—plus General Motors' dependability and Frigidaire's 30 years' experience in building more than 12 million refrigerating units.

3 TYPES, 4 SERIES, 10 SIZES
4 to 17 cubic feet—Prices for every purse

Whatever the size of your family, your kitchen, your budget—there's a Frigidaire Refrigerator that fits your needs. You can take your choice of the luxurious Imperial with separate, near-zero Locker-Top—the beautiful De Luxe with spacious Super-Freezer Chest—the big-value Master or low-priced Standard with colder-than-ever Super-Freezer! But whatever you pick, you'll enjoy many time-and-money-saving features found only in Frigidaire—America's No. 1 Refrigerator! Get a demonstration—soon!

You can't match a
FRIGIDAIRE
Refrigerator

See your Frigidaire Dealer for PROOF! Look for his name in Yellow Pages of phone book. Or write Frigidaire Division of General Motors, Dayton 1, Ohio. In Canada, Leaside 12, Ontario.

Refrigerators · Electric Ranges · Automatic Washer · Clothes Dryer
Electric Irons · Food Freezers · Electric Dehumidifier
Electric Water Heaters · Kitchen Cabinets and Sinks · Air Conditioners

IMPERIAL MODEL   MASTER MODEL

Frigidaire Refrigerator

Smart Dining begins with **BROIL-QUIK**

Fully Automatic Infra-Red
BROIL-QUIK CHEF

World's Largest Selling Infra-Red Rotisserie

¶ BARBECUES & ROASTS · Tender roast chicken, exotic shish kebab, juicy "picture" roasts, tempting spare ribs. Fully automatic! It turns itself . . . times itself . . . shuts itself off.

¶ BROILS & TOASTS · Steaks, chops and hamburgers with that incomparable "broiled outdoors" flavor. Fish at its finest. Toasts 8 slices of bread at once!

¶ GRILLS & FRIES · Crackling eggs, ham steaks, tangy melted cheese sandwiches. A perfect food warmer. Top and bottom sections can be used together!

• Exclusive Wall and Tree Tray. Channels all your delicious juices for easy pouring. • Slide-away Glass Spatter Shield. Watch your roast through every stage of cooking. Slides under unit into concealed compartment. • Automatic Self-Timer. Shuts off entire unit and rings a bell when food is done. • 2-Heat Control that really works. A quick-searing heat for perfect broiling . . . a special, controlled heat for barbecuing and roasting.

AC only. Without timer, $59.95; with Chrome (model illustrated) $69.95; other models from $34.95

Fully Automatic BROIL-QUIK
FRYER-COOKER
"A Peerless Product"

¶ DEEP FRIES · French fried potatoes; crisp southern fried chicken; delicious shrimp; fish cakes, fritters; doughnuts extraordinary!

¶ COOKS · Juicy pot roasts; heavenly clam chowder; tender stews and chicken; real old fashioned New England Boiled Dinners; flavor-rich soups.

¶ SERVES · Everything you want to keep tempting hot and delicious. So beautiful in gleaming chrome, you'll be proud to show it off at the dining room table.

AC only $34.95

• Unique Shape. Styled outside, round and tapered inside. Offers greater capacity, uses less shortening!

• Auto-Temp Thermostat. The exact heat you want for as long as you want it. The Thermo-Line signals when correct frying or cooking temperature has been reached.

• Decant-o-Spout. Pours short-cuning quickly, safely.

• Easy-Clean Basket. Made of perforated aluminum (not wire). More efficient, easier to clean.

• Easy-Cook Chart. 40 time and temperature recipes right on the lid.

• Recipe Booklet. 140 kitchen-tested recipes. 72 pages.

...when you buy a BROIL-QUIK, you buy the BEST!

THE BROIL-QUIK COMPANY · 2330 FIFTH AVENUE · NEW YORK 37, N. Y.
World's Largest Manufacturer of Infra-Red Appliances

Broil-Quik, 1953 ▶ *American Gas Association, 1950* ▶▶ *General Electric, 1956*

Beautiful to behold!
And so automatic
you can love it and leave it!

You'll **fall in love** with cooking all over again when you change to a *new* Gas range. It's so *beautiful* you can't stop looking at it . . . yet so *automatic* it cooks a complete meal without a glance from you. Cool, clean, *instantly fast* — it gives *more* than any other modern range—yet costs *less!* Less to buy, install, operate! No wonder millions are choosing new Gas ranges every year!

NEW FREEDOM GAS KITCHEN DESIGN

CHEF "CP" GAS RANGE—ONE OF MANY ALL NEW, ALL AUTOMATIC GAS RANGES BUILT TO "CP" STANDARDS.

Complete clock control!

Any heat-instantly!

Smokeless broiling!

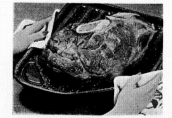

GAS
has got it!

FOR MODERN

COOKING	HOUSE-HEATING
COOKING	AIR-CONDITIONING
REFRIGERATION	CLOTHES-DRYING
WATER-HEATING	INCINERATION

AMERICAN GAS ASSOCIATION

Now...
cooks <u>faster</u>
than gas!

You get one of these new giant Speed-Cooking units on every G-E range

It's new ... it's test-proved! Every G-E range has one of the new Speed-Cooking units that's faster than gas. This 2600-watt unit was tested in G-E laboratories against the large burner of each of four leading gas stoves.

The G-E unit was faster in tests which included four pork chops in an aluminum skillet as illustrated. In addition, two cups, one quart and two quarts of water and a package of frozen peas were brought to a boil faster every time.

All G-E ranges also have big, extra-wide ovens, "Focused Heat" broilers, pushbuttons. Other de luxe models have automatic griddles, electric meat thermometers, automatic units, oven timers to "watch" meals, minute timers and other grand conveniences.

See all the Speed-Cooking ranges at your G-E dealer's ... he's in the classified phone book.

General Electric Company, Appliance Park, Louisville 1, Kentucky.

Progress Is Our Most Important Product

GENERAL ELECTRIC

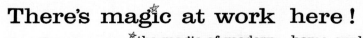

There's magic at work here!

the magic of modern home appliances... (made with Reynolds Aluminum)

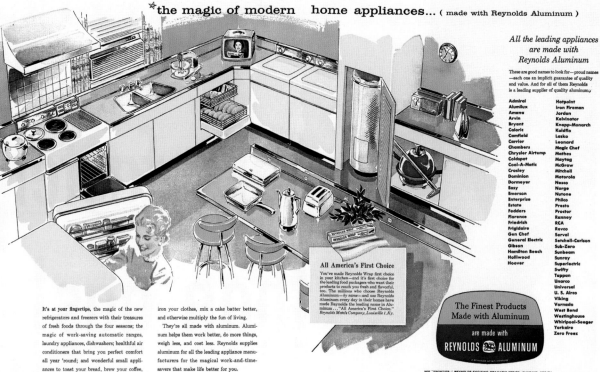

All the leading appliances are made with Reynolds Aluminum

These are good names to look for—proud names—each one an implicit guarantee of quality and value. And for all of them Reynolds is a leading supplier of quality aluminum.

Admiral	Hotpoint
Alumilux	Iron Fireman
Amana	Jordan
Arvin	Kelvinator
Bryant	Knapp-Monarch
Caloric	Koldflo
Camfield	Lasko
Carrier	Leonard
Chambers	Magic Chef
Chrysler Airtemp	Mathes
Coldspot	Maytag
Cool-A-Matic	McGraw
Crosley	Mitchell
Dominion	Motorola
Dormeyer	Nesco
Easy	Norge
Emerson	Nutone
Enterprise	Philco
Estate	Presto
Fedders	Proctor
Florence	Ranney
Friedrich	RCA
Frigidaire	Revco
Gen Chef	Servel
General Electric	Setchell-Carlson
Gibson	Sub-Zero
Hamilton Beach	Sunbeam
Holliwood	Sunray
Hoover	Superlectric
	Swifty
	Tappan
	Unarco
	Universal
	U. S. Airco
	Viking
	Vornado
	West Bend
	Westinghouse
	Whirlpool-Seeger
	Yorkaire
	Zero Freez

All America's First Choice

You've made Reynolds Wrap first choice in your kitchen—and it's first choice for the leading food packagers who want their products to reach you fresh and flavorful, too. The millions who choose Reynolds Aluminum every day in their homes have made Reynolds the leading name in Aluminum ..."All America's First Choice."
Reynolds Metals Company, Louisville 1, Ky.

The Finest Products Made with Aluminum

are made with

REYNOLDS ALUMINUM

SEE "FRONTIER," REYNOLDS EXCITING DRAMATIC SERIES—SUNDAYS, NBC-TV

It's at your fingertips, the magic of the new refrigerators and freezers with their treasures of fresh foods through the four seasons; the magic of work-saving automatic ranges, laundry appliances, dishwashers; healthful air conditioners that bring you perfect comfort all year 'round; and wonderful small appliances to toast your bread, brew your coffee,

iron your clothes, mix a cake batter better, and otherwise multiply the fun of living.

They're all made with aluminum. Aluminum help them work better, do more things, weigh less, and cost less. Reynolds supplies aluminum for all the leading appliance manufacturers and make the magical work-and-time-savers that make life better for you.

Reynolds Aluminum, 1956

Only Westinghouse Refrigerators give you *50* color combinations!

Transform your kitchen without remodeling!

Now you can blend in to look built in . . . transform your present kitchen without remodeling with the completely new 1956 Westinghouse Refrigerator. With five cabinet colors and ten Choose-N-Change color combinations, you choose the Confection Color combination exactly suited to your kitchen. If you redecorate later, the heavy-duty, scratch-resistant vinyl panel can be easily and inexpensively changed to go with your new kitchen colors.

EXCITINGLY NEW INSIDE, TOO!

• **New Stoop-Saver Convenience** keeps the refrigerated foods used most often up top—at reach-in level. No stooping! Shelves roll out, too! Below is the giant 85-lb. freezer with Roll-out Basket for easy access.

• **New Cold-In-Motion** refrigerating system constantly circulates cold from top to bottom of refrigerator section to keep foods uniformly cold—chills them faster to keep them fresher. Completely automatic—no dials to set!

• **Automatic Cycle Defrosting** . . . refrigerator section automatically defrosts itself . . . even the defrost water is disposed of automatically!

• **New Showcase Crisper** at waist level keeps ½ bushel of vegetables dewy-fresh . . . always in view. Tilts down for reach-in convenience . . . lifts out for easy loading. Plus complete specialized storage . . . Meat Drawer, Butter and Cheese Keepers, and Fruit Bin.

There's a Westinghouse in an exciting new style to suit every family . . . in sizes from 8 to 13.2 cu. ft. . . . in 24", 28" or 32" cabinet widths . . . with large Freezer across the top or giant Freezer below . . . with Automatic Cycle Defrosting, Push-Button Automatic Defrosting or Frost-Free! Completely Automatic Defrosting. Prices start as low as $199.95. See your Westinghouse dealer soon. You can be *sure* . . . if it's Westinghouse.

WATCH WESTINGHOUSE!
WHERE **BIG** THINGS ARE HAPPENING FOR **YOU**

*T. M. U.S. Pats. Issued Nos. 2,459,175 and 2,524,509

See TV's Top Dramatic Show . . . Westinghouse Studio One

Westinghouse Refrigerators, 1956

▶ *Glo-Coat Floor Wax, 1950*

15.5 CU. FT. REFRIGERATOR-FREEZER: 34" WIDE, 65½" HIGH, 32 3/16" DEEP, MODEL DI15B

NEW! RCA WHIRLPOOL REFRIGERATOR–FREEZER
with exclusive <u>Air Purifying System</u> keeps food fresher...longer!

CUT FOOD SPOILAGE! Air Purifying System forces air through ultraviolet rays (1); retards growth of air-borne mold and bacteria! Cold, clean air recirculates (2) up the door (3).

END ICE TRAY TROUBLE! No more spilling! New ice tray filler* works with dial *inside* freezer; shuts itself off. New ice ejector zips out cubes, stores ice in server bin!

Imagine! A full-size refrigerator up top with glide-out shelves, twin crispers, a big meat keeper *plus* a new self-filling ice water fountain*! A deep-set door with special food compartments, even shelves for ½-gal. bottles! Plus a 166-lb. freezer with glide-out basket, storage door, true "zero cold"! Backed by 50 years of refrigeration pioneering! Choice of colors, easy terms.

END DEFROSTING MESS! No more pans to empty, buttons to push! Automatic defrost system gets rid of frost and water in refrigerator section almost before it forms!

*optional at small extra cost.

Whirlpool Corporation, St. Joseph, Michigan. (Use of trademarks ® and RCA authorized by trademark owner, Radio Corporation of America.

Hotpoint Refrigerators, 1953 ◄   Whirlpool Refrigerators, 1957

Design for Living ...Graciously

WITH A NEW
ROPER
GAS RANGE

ALLTROL "CENTER-SIMMER" TOP BURNERS ARE MUCH FASTER...MORE EFFICIENT ...IDEAL EVERY WAY

"BAKE-MASTER" OVENS PRE-HEAT FASTER... BAKE AND ROAST WHILE USING LESS FUEL

"ROPER-GLO" BROILER BURNERS BROIL BIG, THICK STEAK IN 10 MINUTES OR LESS

built to "CP" standards

"AMERICA'S FINEST"...PERFORMANCE PROVES IT!

The great new ROPER automatic gas ranges provide a carefree cooking service that's superior in every respect. Utilizing Gas, the nation's favorite fuel, they assure the ultimate in speed, cleanliness, convenience and economy. More than 69 years of gas range manufacturing experience has contributed to the host of exclusive ROPER features you can enjoy today. Choose *your* new ROPER from the most complete line of gas ranges in the industry. Write for Free Folder T. Ask your ROPER retailer about these new beauties. Geo. D. Roper Corporation, Rockford, Illinois.

- **ROPER GAS RANGES • ROPER GAS RANGES IN DECORATOR COLORS**
- **ROPER "arRANGEable" BUILT-IN GAS COOKING UNITS**
- **ROPER "DRY-AIRE" GAS CLOTHES DRYERS**

INDUSTRIAL • COMMERCIAL • RESIDENTIAL • GAS

New way to get big-range cooking in compact space

G-E Spacemaker has oven that holds meal for 24 . . . 4 Hi-Speed top units. Yet it takes up 16 inches less room

Do you need big-range cooking in small space? Or extra counters, storage room in a larger kitchen? This new G.E. is the answer. It has General Electric Speed-Cooking and most of the advantages of de luxe models, including color!

Huge floodlighted oven is so wide one shelf will hold 4 pies. 4 Calrod® pushbutton-controlled surface units give varied heats from barely warm to EXTRA-Hi-Speed. Drip pans and trays lift out to clean. There's a big storage drawer.

A fingertip touch and pushbuttons flick on just the heat you want. So easy even when your hands are full or wet. All surface units are fast-heating; one is General Electric's new giant Hi-Speed 2600-watt unit.

NEW! Oven-and-Minute Timer "watches" meals. Two simple clock settings and dinner cooks, heat goes off "by itself." For shorter baking or boiling jobs, a buzzer lets you know when cooking time's up.

"Charcoal Delicious" steaks, franks are easy with the General Electric "Focused Heat" broiler. It's quick, power-saving. Bake and broil units are fully enclosed. No old-fashioned open coils. Units slide out for easy oven cleaning.

Cooks Faster Than Gas!

It's new . . . it's test-proved! Every General Electric range has one of the new Speed-Cooking units that's faster than gas. This 2600-watt unit was tested in General Electric laboratories against the large burner of each of four leading gas stoves.

The General Electric unit was faster in tests which included four pork chops in an aluminum skillet. In addition, two cups, one quart and two quarts of water and a package of frozen peas were brought to a boil faster every time.

Easily Installed. Your G-E dealer can make arrangements for 220-volt wiring. Cost of range and required wiring can be financed with one low down payment and easy weekly terms.

Start your color-lovely G-E kitchen with this beautiful Speed-Cooking range in a Mix-or-Match color: turquoise green (as shown), canary yellow, cadet blue, petal pink, woodtone brown, satin white. A can of special, matching paint is all you need to "dress up" walls and cabinets.

See all the Speed-Cooking ranges at your G-E dealer's. He's in the classified phone book. General Electric Company, Appliance Park, Louisville 1, Kentucky.

Speed-Cooking ranges . . . so safe . . . so clean . . . so dependable

GENERAL ⓖⓔ ELECTRIC

GREAT NEW KITCHEN IDEA!

the Decorator Refrigerator

by International Harvester

Revolutionary new idea enables you to make your refrigerator a feature of your kitchen decoration. Match it with your curtains—blend it with your color scheme. Use any pattern—any color fabric you choose. And you can change it as often as you change your mind!

COPYRIGHT 1953, INTERNATIONAL HARVESTER COMPANY

Takes just 7 minutes—

and 1¾ yards of fabric—to give your kitchen an "all new" look. For a change of pace, you can leave the fabric off and still have the most beautiful refrigerator you can buy; with handy foot-pedal door control and a handsome plastic push-plate.

Here's the inside story—

It takes 7 different "climates"—from 6° to 55°—to keep all foods in prime condition. You get all 7 of these essential areas of cold (all working at once) in the new IH Decorator Refrigerators—plus Push-button automatic defrosting and many other exciting features for '53. See the newest of the new—now—at your IH dealer's. You'll find his name in the yellow pages of your phone book.

a Fashion First exclusive with

INTERNATIONAL HARVESTER

INTERNATIONAL HARVESTER

International Harvester Company, 180 No. Michigan Ave., Chicago 1... International Harvester also builds Home Freezers... McCormick Farm Equipment and Farmall Tractors... International Trucks... "Big Red" Crawler Tractors

---

General Electric Range, 1956 ◀   *International Harvester Decorator Refrigerator, 1953*

MAGIC CHEF COMBINES COLOR AND CHROME TO BRING A CUSTOMIZED ROOMIER LOOK TO YOUR KITCHEN WITHOUT EXPENSIVE REMODELING

ready-made glamour

At last, a really inexpensive way to modernize your kitchen with the new "decorator" look. Just add the beauty, color and versatility of the new *Magic Chef color-chrome* gas range. Top and sides are Willow Green or Coral Rouge porcelain enamel, with handles in matching color. Entire front and back panel are easy-to-clean gleaming chrome to reflect kitchen decor. This compact 36-inch range has ultra-modern design and famous *Magic Chef* work-saving features.

Magic Chef
color-chrome gas range

—*WORLD LEADER in gas appliances that bring comfort and convenience to millions* MAGIC CHEF, Inc., St. Louis 10, Mo.

RANGES · COMMERCIAL COOKING EQUIPMENT · HEATERS · INCINERATORS · CENTRAL HEATING

Magic Chef Gas Range, 1954

▶ *Deepfreeze, 1950*   ▶▶ *Blackstone Automatic Washer, 1950*

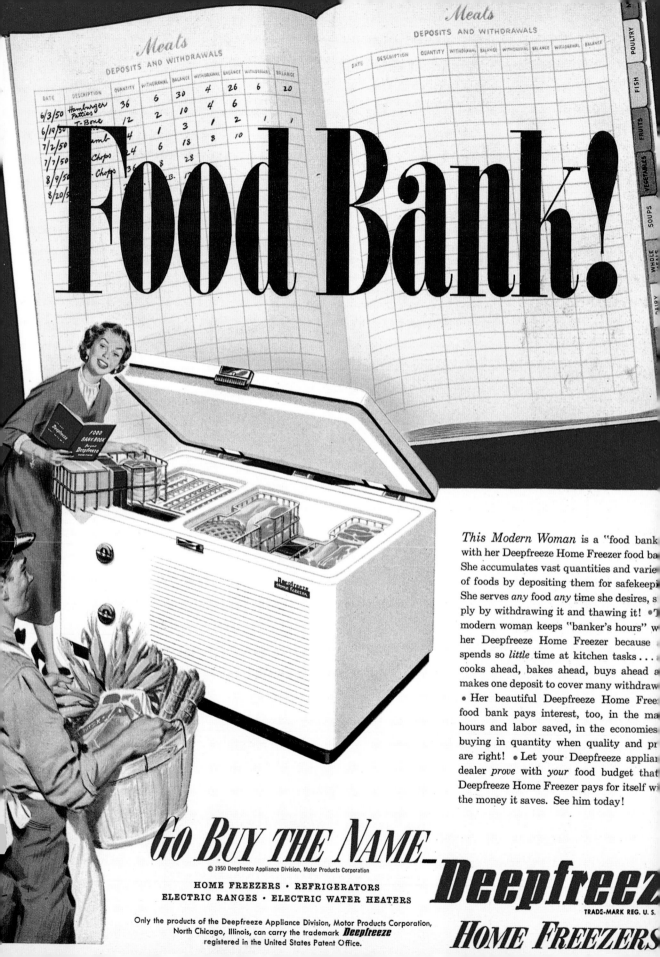

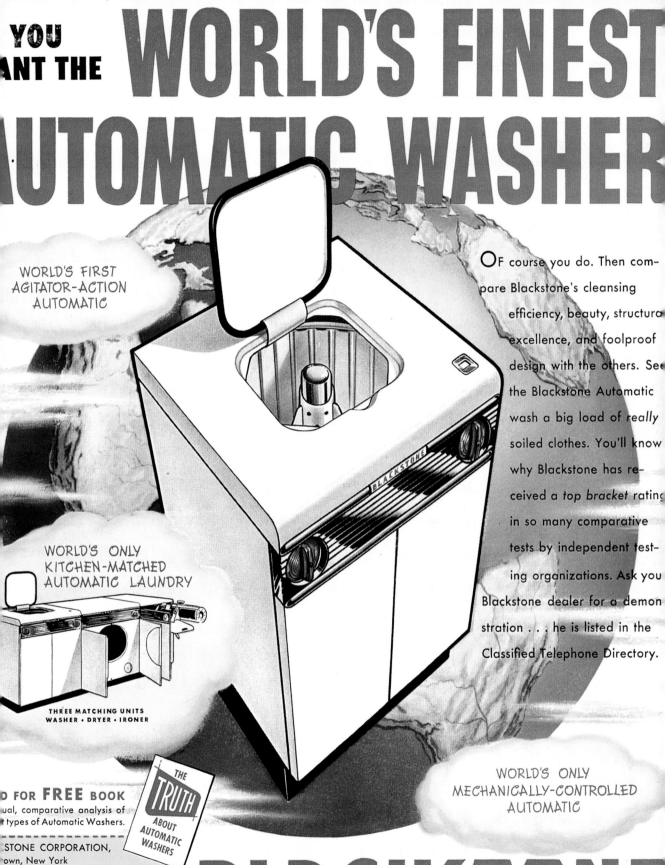

YOU WANT THE WORLD'S FINEST AUTOMATIC WASHER

WORLD'S FIRST
AGITATOR-ACTION
AUTOMATIC

OF course you do. Then compare Blackstone's cleansing efficiency, beauty, structural excellence, and foolproof design with the others. See the Blackstone Automatic wash a big load of *really* soiled clothes. You'll know why Blackstone has received a *top bracket* rating in so many comparative tests by independent testing organizations. Ask your Blackstone dealer for a demonstration . . . he is listed in the Classified Telephone Directory.

WORLD'S ONLY
KITCHEN-MATCHED
AUTOMATIC LAUNDRY

THREE MATCHING UNITS
WASHER · DRYER · IRONER

WORLD'S ONLY
MECHANICALLY-CONTROLLED
AUTOMATIC

THE TRUTH ABOUT AUTOMATIC WASHERS

D FOR **FREE** BOOK
ual, comparative analysis of
t types of Automatic Washers.

STONE CORPORATION,
own, New York
send a copy of your "TRUTH" booklet.

Zone........State..........

BLACKSTONE
WORLD'S OLDEST WASHER MANUFACTURE

Now the luxury of a General Electric Kitchen– at a price to suit your budget

You can own a General Electric Kitchen for as little as $29.00* a month!

You can own all the wonderful new work-saving appliances you want for less per month than typical car payments!

General Electric "Straight-Line" Design custom styling is not merely beautiful—it is planned to conserve your time, your effort; to let you be a lady of leisure in the kitchen. Silent elec-

trical servants make your life in the kitchen easier, faster, more convenient. Pretty enough to entertain in, the General Electric Kitchen shown boasts color-coordinated, built-in appliances.

Ask your General Electric dealer about his Planning Service.
General Electric Company, Appliance Park, Louisville 1, Ky.

*Dream Kitchen illustrated above approx. $69.00 a month. See your General Electric dealer for his exact prices and terms.

Progress Is Our Most Important Product

GENERAL ⊕ ELECTRIC

Visit model homes in your community during National Home Week
Make your house a Medallion home and live better electrically

General Electric Kitchen, 1959

THE BEST GIFTS IN LIFE ARE FREE FOR TOP VALUE STAMPS

Everything you see above is free for Top Value Stamps—and you have hundreds of other wonderful gifts to choose from!

100 FREE Top Value Stamps with every gift!

REDEEM YOUR BOOKS DURING YULE SAVE DAYS...SEPTEMBER 14th THROUGH OCTOBER 31st...FOR THIS SPECIAL BONUS!

At this very moment, America's finest gifts are waiting for you at your Top Value Redemption Store. You'll find a complete selection of wonderful, famous-brand mer-

chandise for all your Christmas gift giving. And as a special bonus for redeeming your books early — during YULE SAVE DAYS—you'll get a certificate worth 100

free Top Value Stamps with every gift. Any one of the thousands of merchants throughout the U.S. who gives Top Value Stamps will exchange your certificate for 100 free

stamps—a good start on your next book.
Visit your Top Value Redemption Store now. Redeem your books for "the best gifts in life." And get this special Christmas bonus.

CHOOSE FROM GIFTS LIKE THESE

Admiral Portable Phonograph. 4-speed. Automatic shut-off. Two-tone case... 13½ books

Regal Automatic Electric Percolator. 24-carat gold-plated. 3 to 10 cup capacity. Detachable cord included. AC only. 7 books

Chrome Cake Caddy. Handsome cover and beautiful glass serving tray lock securely for safe carrying... 2½ books

Bulova "Goddess of Time," 17 jewel, white gold. Matching band... 9½ books
Elgin "Orlando," 19 jewel, shock-resistant. Gold plate case, band. Nite-glo dial. 10½ books

Marlboro "Wash 'n Wear" Dress Shirt. Custom tailored broadcloth with fused, no-wrinkle collar. Sanforized, Button cuff... 1 book

Top Value Stamps Golden Guarantee

Top Value Stamps guarantee each gift you receive to give complete satisfaction or you may return it for replacement or exchange.

Top Value Enterprises, Inc., Dayton 1, Ohio

Top Value Stamps, 1959

in warm air heating . . .

more families buy Lennox
than any other make!

Every day, more new-home buyers discover what long-time homeowners have known for years: *nothing* can compare with Lennox warm air conditioning! Lennox has been the leader in warm air home heating for over 50 years.

If you want to learn new meanings for the words *comfort, heating dependability and fuel econ-*omy, see your Lennox dealer now. Let him give you the complete Lennox story and estimate your heating needs. Consult your classified telephone directory for his name, or write to Lennox direct.

And send for the FREE new booklet, *"How to Select Your Heating System."* Write Dept. S-923, your nearest Lennox office.

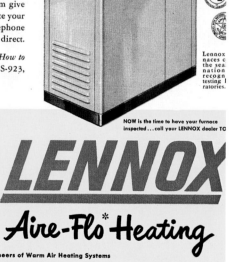

NOW is the time to have your furnace inspected...call your LENNOX dealer TO

Lennox Aire-Flo Heating, 1950

▶ *Spartan Cosmic Eye Television, 1953*

Admiral Television, 1951

Admiral Television, 1951

Admiral Portable TV, 1956

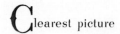

Admiral Television, 1950 ▶ *Admiral Television, 1952* ▶▶ *Admiral, 195_*

only from Admiral!

21" TV

at price of other 17's

43% bigger picture for the same money!

Bigger—yes—but that's not all! You get an amazingly *better* picture, too. Because it's powered by Admiral's extraordinary new "DX-53" chassis—five years in the making. A top quality chassis that outmodes all previous ideas of "fringe area" reception . . . that makes thrilling performance possible in those exasperating "pockets" where rolling countryside or surrounding buildings "blank out" ordinary sets . . . that delivers strikingly superior pictures in *any* location . . . a chassis the like of which has never existed until now! Yours, too, is the proved advantage of *guaranteed* UHF reception, provided by Admiral's famous Cascode Turret Tuner. But—see it! Discover for yourself the host of truly worthwhile advances that await you in Admiral TV for '53. Compare—and you'll *see* why it's a fabulous buy!

Model 121DX11—Admiral 21" TV with new "DX-53" chassis in smart, stain-resistant cabinet.

Model 222DX15—21" TV console . . . Panoramic picture tube. Choice of walnut, mahogany or blonde. In walnut only..$309.95

Model 322DX16—21" TV-radio-phonograph with Panoramic picture tube (245 sq. in.). Beautiful mahogany cabinet....$499.95

$199⁹⁵

NO FINER PICTURE AT __ANY__ PRICE!

Prices slightly higher south and west...subject to change without notice. Fed. Tax and all warranties included.

Admiral...WORLD'S LARGEST TELEVISION MANUFACTURER

8-Transistor Portable Radio. Series 230. 1200 hours battery life. "Rotoscope" antenna. Tan or black. Portables from $29.95.

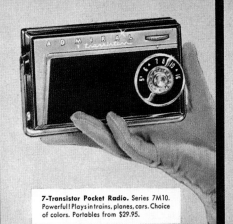

7-Transistor Pocket Radio. Series 7M10. Powerful! Plays in trains, planes, cars. Choice of colors. Portables from $29.95.

DeLuxe FM-AM Table Radio. Series 300. 2 antennas. 4" x 6" speaker. Blonde Oak and Sierra. Radios from $15.95.

FOR CHRISTMAS FROM

Admiral.

SON-R REMOTE CONTROL

Only remote control in the world that adjusts volume to 4 levels! No wires! No batteries! No stirring from your chair! New amazing SON-R also turns TV on-off, changes channels from anywhere in the room!

Look for this Christmas "Best Buy" tag when you shop. It's on specially selected Admiral products, so you can easily spot the Season's Best Gift Values.

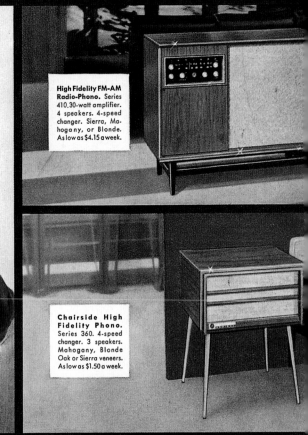

High Fidelity FM-AM Radio-Phono. Series 410. 30-watt amplifier. 4 speakers. 4-speed changer. Sierra, Mahogany, or Blonde. As low as $4.15 a week.

Chairside High Fidelity Phono. Series 360. 4-speed changer. 3 speakers. Mahogany, Blonde Oak or Sierra veneers. As low as $1.50 a week.

DeLuxe Table Radio. Series 270. Extra large 4" x 6" speaker. Completely finished back. White with Red, Turquoise, Gray. Table radios from $15.95.

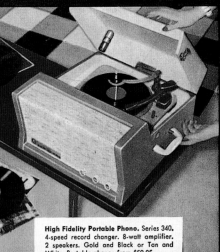

High Fidelity Portable Phono. Series 340. 4-speed record changer. 8-watt amplifier. 2 speakers. Gold and Black or Tan and White. Portable phonos from $59.95.

Prices slightly higher some areas.

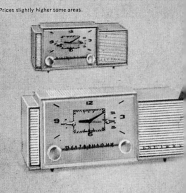

Super DeLuxe Clock Radio. Series 290. Wakes you, reminds you minutes later. Turns on appliances. White with Maroon, Gold, Green. Clock radios from $26.95.

Admiral's new "Thin as a Dime" styling has a glamorous new cabinet barely over 16 inches deep. It's the slimming magic of Admiral's new 110° picture tube. The old-fashioned bulge-in-the-back is gone, too! Your sleek new Admiral fits flush to the wall.

High Fidelity 21" TV, The Seton, Model CH21F54. Hi-Fi 4 speaker system. 8-watt amplifier. Plug in jack for record player. As low as $3.75 a week.

21 in. viewable area, 262 sq. in.

High Fidelity 21" TV, The Exeter, Model LHR21F33, PowerPack. 4 Hi-Fi speakers. Son-R available. As low as $4.20 a week.

BEST BUY

Admiral

BEST BUY for CHRISTMAS

Slimline 21" Table TV, The Asbury, Model TR21E21. Two speakers with up-front sound. Matching base with "Lazy Susan" swivel. Charcoal, Mahogany, Blonde. As low as $2.70 a week. Available with Son-R remote control.

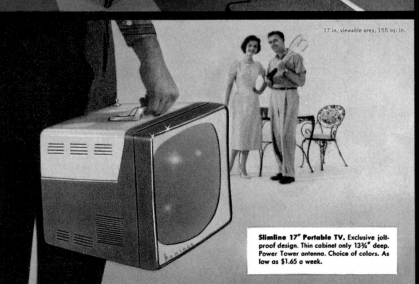

17 in. viewable area, 155 sq. in.

Slimline 17" Portable TV. Exclusive jolt-proof design. Thin cabinet only 13¾" deep. Power Tower antenna. Choice of colors. As low as $1.65 a week.

High Fidelity TV-Radio-Phono. T Canterbury, Model HFR21F42. Son-R Du Remote Control. Mahogany, Blonde Oak, Sierra veneer. As low as $5.40 a wee

General Electric Television, 1950

Crosley Television, 1950

The CAPEHART *"New Amsterdam"... with AM, FM, radio and three-speed phonograph*

IT&T *suggests the finest of family gifts:*

"Years-Ahead"
Television by Capehart

A new Capehart stands in the place of honor—a gift for every member of the family. And *what* a gift—television that's years ahead in clarity and sharpness of picture, years ahead in tonal fidelity. International Telephone and Telegraph Corporation presents Capehart through its associate, *Capehart-Farnsworth Corporation.* See it. Give it! There's a Capehart *just right* for your family, and just right for your pocketbook.

International Telephone and Telegraph Corporation, New York

For full information on Capehart, write to
Capehart-Farnsworth Corporation, Fort Wayne 1, Indiana

New CAPEHART *phonograph-radios with world-famed Capehart tone! (Above)*

Capehart Television, 1950

Sit anywhere in the room

COLUMBIA STEREOPHONIC PHONOGRAPHS
PUT YOU IN THE CENTER OF SOUND

Here is the ultimate in listening—a new Columbia stereophonic phonograph. Turn it on and you're suddenly, dramatically in the Center of Sound—the place where music takes on a third dimension. Turn the remarkable Balanced Listening Control and you shift the Center of Sound wherever you want it. This Columbia engineering exclusive, available on many models, makes it possible for you to enjoy stereophonic sound in perfect proportion —not just in one spot, but *anywhere in the room!* Superb styling and cabinetry make every Columbia Stereo-Fidelity phonograph a truly matchless instrument for your home. Prices begin at only $124.90.

STEREO-FIDELITY PHONOGRAPHS BY COLUMBIA

More to enjoy

MOTOROLA

TV that whispers in your ear! The earphone attachment on our Americana Portable TV lets you enjoy shows anywhere, any time, without disturbing sleepyheads. Has a big loud-speaker voice, too. Plus Motorola's exclusive Magic Mast Antenna that goes way up to pull in stations many other sets can't reach. The handle is to tune with—puts the controls where *you* are—right up front. So much *More to enjoy!*

Motorola TV

Motorola Television, 1951

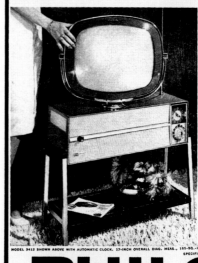

New PHILCO swivel-screen consolette

Predicta

DECORATOR TV PRICED FROM
$199.95
MODEL 3408 WITHOUT CLOCK

Finest performance yet in a TV consolette! Screen swivels a full circle! Beam the picture in any direction. The *Siesta*, shown here, has automatic clock controls. Turns on your favorite programs...turns itself off at night!

Yours, in five fashion-wise colors. Decorator stand included. Complete unit measures just 12 inches deep! Equipped with Perma-Circuits, front sound, fingertip controls, built-in Pivot-Tenna! You can see these fabulous new Predicta Consolettes at your Philco dealer's!

MODEL 3412 SHOWN ABOVE WITH AUTOMATIC CLOCK. 17-INCH OVERALL DIAG. MEAS., 155-SQ.-IN. VIEWABLE AREA.
SPECIFICATIONS SUBJECT TO CHANGE WITHOUT NOTICE.

PHILCO QUALITY FIRST!

★On September 12, Philco brings you the exciting Miss America Pageant—"live" from Atlantic City on CBS-TV.

Philco Television, 1959

the New World by Stromberg-Carlson. Television-radio-phonograph. Because it is designed from a woman's point of view, this superb instrument brings distinctive good looks as well as matchless performance into your home. The exquisite, clean-lined cabinetry is fashioned from lined oak veneer, hand-rubbed to a blond finish that harmonizes so well with other furnishings. And for your entire family:

Big-Picture 17" television...fine AM radio...3-speed automatic record-player providing four hours continuous music. There is generous space for your favorite albums. Truly, "There is nothing finer than a Stromberg-Carlson."

"There is nothing finer than a
STROMBERG-CARLSON."

Stromberg-Carlson television is priced from $289.95 to $975 including excise tax. (Slightly higher in South and West)

Stromberg-Carlson, 1951

TOMORROW IS HERE! General Electric originates a new kind of television styling: the new "Designer" sets. The trim, graceful cabinets look less than a handspan deep. The cheerful colors and smart lines belong in any room. And "Designers" move to any room...easily... with recessed handles.

"Gramercy 17"—17" (overall diagonal) tube—
155 sq. inches of picture area. In a variety of spirited colors.

For all their clean-lined beauty, "Designer" receivers work wherever a console will: each packs a console chassis, full power transformer. More: front-projection speaker, built-in telescoping antenna. The new "Designers" await you...at your General Electric dealer's now.

"Barclay 21"—21" (overall diagonal) tube—262 sq. inches of picture area. Russet leather finish vinyl, and Stargold linen finish vinyl. General Electric Co., Television Receiver Dept., Syracuse, N.Y.

GE BUY NOW FOR EXTRA VALUES!

Progress Is Our Most Important Product
GENERAL ELECTRIC

General Electric Television, 1958

"You bet we bought Motorola TV...we've been a <u>Motorola</u> <u>Family</u> for 20 years!"

THE ANDERSON FAMILY STARTED WITH A MOTOROLA AUTO RADIO 20 YEARS AGO

Since this 1930 Ford there's been a Motorola in every Anderson car!

This First Motorola was the start of a family-wide quality standard.

ONLY MOTOROLA GIVES YOU THESE EXCLUSIVE FEATURES

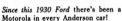

GLARE-GUARD. The curved anti-reflection TV screen that minimizes glare and directs annoying reflections below eye-level.

FASHION AWARD STYLING. Designed and finished with the same care given the finest furniture in your home.

DEPENDA-BILT CHASSIS. Factory-tested under extreme conditions before shipment to assure longer, better performance.

2 SIMPLE CONTROLS. Speedy, easy tuning . . . just turn it on, select your station! That's all there is to do!

"MUSIC LOVER" SOUND. Improved, wider range reception, plus greater fidelity in tone and pitch, of both music and voice.

TWENTY-TWO YEARS OF LEADERSHIP

- World's largest independent manufacturer of auto radios.
- World's largest maker of mobile 2-way radio communications equipment.
- One of the world's four largest manufacturers of television.
- One of the world's largest electronic research and development laboratories.

"WE HAD ONE OF THE FIRST Motorola auto radios," says Albert Anderson, retired Chicago cabinet maker, "and we've been buying Motorola ever since!" Now that the Andersons have a beautiful new Motorola TV in their living room, they're more sold than ever on Motorola quality, value and topnotch performance.

The Andersons chose Model 17K7 because Mrs. Anderson liked the way its Fashion Award cabinet styling harmonized with the furnishings of their home . . . and because Mr. Anderson wanted a screen big enough for his whole family to see at once. Now they enjoy large-as-life snapshot-sharp pictures on the big 17 inch screen.

They're assured of long-life, reliable performance, too, because every Motorola Dependa-Bilt chassis is factory-tested before shipment. They like the Bilt-in-Antenna and quick, two simple control tuning . . . even "Scotty" can tune in his pet programs. The Anderson's enthusiasm has been passed along to their married children who have Motorola TV and radios in their own homes, *and* Motorola auto radios in their cars.

Your family will be just as thrilled with Motorola TV when you get acquainted with Motorola styling, quality and value! See your dealer today.

specifications subject to change without notice

Motorola TV

SEE the 4-STAR REVUE every week on NBC-TV

Motorola Television, 1951

▶ *Zenith Television, 1950*

A new tough face comes to TV

Philco takes the picture tube out of the chassis
...protects it with a face of tough Butyrate plastic

The new line of Philco Predicta TV sets is another example of how Tenite Butyrate plastic can be used to improve the design and sales appeal of products.

Thanks to the toughest "face" on TV—a one-piece molding of clear Tenite Butyrate, tinted to minimize glare—Philco now features a picture tube that is dramatically set apart from the chassis.

Although many factors contributed to the choice of Butyrate here, the basic consideration was its inherent toughness, since a separated picture tube would be exposed to extra hazards.

In Butyrate, Philco engineers found a material with all the toughness and impact resistance they needed. Moreover, this Eastman plastic also satisfied the other requirements involved...light weight...optical clarity...resilience...easy moldability...high dielectric strength.

Incidentally, the color that imparts an eye-easing tint to the face is part of the plastic itself. Philco designers were able to specify the color desired, and Tenite molding com-

pound was supplied to the molder in an exact match. Result: the tinting color is an integral part of the face, not merely a coating that might wear, chip or flake off.

If you are designing or redesigning a product, consider Tenite Butyrate whenever you need a truly tough plastic. Easy to mold, extrude or vacuum-form, Tenite Butyrate is available in clear and colored transparents, translucents, opaques, metallics, and variegations to match your specifications. For more information, write EASTMAN CHEMICAL PRODUCTS, INC., subsidiary of Eastman Kodak Company, KINGSPORT, TENNESSEE.

TENITE
BUTYRATE
an Eastman plastic

Tenite Butyrate Plastic, 1959

▶ *Westinghouse Television, 1953*   ▶▶ *RCA Victor, 1957*

NEW ELECTRONIC EYE ADJUSTS PICTURE
FOR YOUR EYE COMFORT...AUTOMATICALLY

Now you, your family and friends, can enjoy the ultimate in TV viewing comfort. Westinghouse, with electronic eye sensitive to light, does away with irritating glare and washout when room light dims or brightens. Picture automatically keeps the brightness and contrast your eyes like best. So miraculous, you must see it at your Westinghouse dealer's now. Prices of Westinghouse '54 TV begin at a modest $189.95*. Westinghouse Electric Corporation, Television-Radio Division, Metuchen, N. J.

*Prices include Federal Tax and full-year picture tube warranty. Slightly higher in West and Southwest.

ROOM BRIGHT

NO WASHOUT

ROOM DARK

NO GLARE

New for '54! Westinghouse with Exclusive Automatic Brightness Control

PICTURE-PERFECT COMBINATION!
The Charlton (left—790C21), in blond limed oak, has 3-speed record player, powerful radio, 21-inch television. The 21-inch Middleton (above—784K21), in rich mahogany veneer, has matched-grain doors.

TUNE IN EACH WEEK ON TV... WESTINGHOUSE PRO FOOTBALL... WESTINGHOUSE STUDIO ONE

YOU CAN BE SURE...IF IT'S Westinghouse

Look! Portable TV from $129.95.
It's a wonderful Christma.

Easy to see why Santa delivers more RCA Victor TV than any other kind. No other TV offers so many fine features or such a choice of models— 47 of them, completely new inside and out.

New lean, clean and mirror-sharp black-and-white TV. Dramatically slender and clean of line, it fits beautifully where other TV couldn't go at all. Cabinets are up to 9½ inches slimmer! And look at the *variety:* trim table models, TV that rolls, swivels and even fits *in corners.*

Listen to it! That's Balanced Fidelity Sound— the finest! You also get the newest tuning fea-

tures and "One-Touch" on-off control.

New "Flight-Line" Portables. Breezy, easy-going TV to take along, in every popular size. Popular prices, too. Your ideal second set.

Most important, every model gives you RCA Victor's new "Mirror-Sharp" picture for the sharpest, clearest contrasts in TV!

New "Living Color" TV, including the superb new Mark Series. The happiest surprise a Santa could put under any tree, the gift of color! It's *performance-proved*—backed by service records from tens of thousands of homes. The colors

come in bright, natural, with realism tha near startling. Tuning is a snap. The pictu *holds* sure and steady. And you get great co programs every day *plus* all the black-a white shows.

Contact your favorite Santa or TV dealer and ask for RCA Victor TV *soon*—you'll su sure of a wonderful Christmas.

orner TV-lowboys-Living Color!
n RCA Victor land!

COLUMBIA

HIGH FIDELITY

LISTENING IN **DEPTH**

A NEW EXPERIENCE IN "360" HIGH-FIDELITY EXCLUSIVE WITH COLUMBIA

First, Columbia gave you the modern long-playing record. Then, famous "360" sound, which brought high fidelity into your living room. Now, for this Christmas, Columbia research brings you a new adventure in sound. Directed Electromotive Power (D.E.P.*) introduces the miracle of the sealed sound chamber for tonal balance throughout the *entire* listening range. By exploring the whole universe of human hearing, both subconscious and

conscious, Columbia now makes it possible for you and your family to perience the excitement of "Listening in Depth."

There are more than thirty-five 1958 Columbia Phonographs which emb the new characteristics of "360" sound . . . portables, consoles, comb tions, in a wide and attractive price range. As a treasured gift at Christ nothing can match the pleasure of a high-fidelity Columbia Phonogr

THE GREATEST NAME IN SOUND . . . *enjoy the Sound of Genius on Columbia Records . . . protect your valuable records with Columbia Accesso*

from $29.95 to $1,995 . . . COLUMBIA ⊙ PHONOGRAPH:

Hi Ho! Come to the Fair!

GREAT 1958 WEBCOR
HI-FI VALUE FAIR !

Check these red-tag specials for the greatest values in High Fidelity!
Visit your dealer now . . . ask for the Webcor red-tag Hi-Fi values.

Ravinia High Fidelity Fonograf—Aristocrat of consoles! "Magic Mind" Diskchanger. 4 speakers—18 watts—50 to 15,000 cycles. In mahogany, limed oak or cherry. Also available with AM-FM radio.

Overture High Fidelity Fonograf—A marvelous family gift! "Magic Mind" Diskchanger. 3 speakers—8 watts—50 to 15,000 cycles. In mahogany, limed oak or cherry. Also available with AM-FM radio.

Prelude High Fidelity Fonograf—Rich styling . . . magnificent music! "Magic Mind" Diskchanger. 3 speakers—powerful amplifier—50 to 15,000 cycles. In mahogany, limed oak or cherry. Also comes with fine AM radio.

Musicale High Fidelity Fonograf—World's most popular table model! "Magic Mind" Diskchanger. 3 speakers—powerful amplifier—50 to 15,000 cycles. Mahogany, limed oak or cherry. (Matching base extra.)

Musicale High Fidelity Portable—Thrilling music—encased in genuine leather! "Magic Mind" Diskchanger. 3 big speakers—8 watts—50 to 15,000 cycles. In ginger or tan.

Holiday Imperial High Fidelity Portable—Engineered for Console reproduction! "Magic Mind" Diskchanger. 3 speakers—big amplifier—50 to 15,000 cycles. Ebony or tan.

Holiday Coronet High Fidelity Portable—Sensational high fidelity! "Magic Mind" Diskchanger—2 speakers—big amplifier. Ebony and grey or brown and tan.

Holiday High Fidelity Portable—Most popular portable built! "Magic Mind" Diskchanger—2 speakers—wide-range amplifier. Ebony or rust. Also with AM radio.

Imperial Stereofonic Tape Recorder—Unequaled stereo playback of binaural tapes. High fidelity. "No reel-turnover" for monaural record and playback. "Aural Balance" Remote Control. 6-speaker auxiliary sound system (extra). Also available with AM radio.

Royal Coronet Stereofonic Tape Recorder—Superb playback of binaural tapes. High fidelity. Records and plays back monaurally without "reel-turnover." Equipped for "Aural Balance" Remote Control. 3-speaker auxiliary sound system (extra). Ebony or white.

Royal High Fidelity Tape Recorder—Favorite the world over! High fidelity. Frequency range 70 to 7,000 at 3¾ i.p.s.; 50 to 12,000 at 7½ i.p.s. Records and plays back monaurally without "reel-turnover." Ebony or white. Also with AM radio.

Regent Stereofonic Tape Recorder—Thrilling binaural reproduction. Also has all features of the standard monaural models. Plays in vertical or horizontal position—only 31 pounds. 3-speaker auxiliary sound system (extra). Ebony. Also in monaural version.

All Models UL Approved

LISTEN *all music sounds better on a* WEBCOR

Columbia Phonographs, 1957 ◀ Webcor, 1958   ▶ *Motorola Hi-Fi, 1957*

The gift they'll take to their hearts...and everywhere!

General Electric Big-Screen Portable—the portable that—when tested—pulled in a sharp picture 62½ miles from the station.

Here's the most exciting—and most practical—gift you can put under your family's tree! Here's a television set that works wherever a console will, yet goes where a console won't.

It's only 30 pounds (the lightest of big-screen portables). Yet in actual tests in New Jersey, it is brought in a sharp, clear picture 62½ miles from the station, using its own built-in, telescoping antenna.

We do not claim this performance in every locality—it depends on local conditions. At any rate, it works wherever a console will, because the new tetrode tuner gives greater picture power than before.

It's got General Electric's new 110° aluminized picture tube, too. This gives it the new Slim Silhouette—a mere shelf-deep 15 inches. Yet the picture's 11 sq. inches larger than before. The controls are on top—out of the way; the handle's retractable.

Stop in and see it at your dealer's now—you'll settle all your Christmas shopping.

Progress Is Our Most Important Product

GENERAL ELECTRIC

General Electric Television, 1957

The 5th Anniversary of "45" brings many happy returns to you!

Crowning achievement of the "45" system is the *Extended Play Record* which brings you great music for 40% less than you used to pay

Just 5 years ago RCA Victor introduced the "45" RPM system and gave you a reward of new listening pleasure.

With the touch of a button you could sit back and enjoy nearly two hours of your favorite music. There were no changes to make . . . no bulky albums to tote and store . . . and you were rewarded with music that was richer, truer—with all the brilliance of "live" performance.

Moreover, the "45" became the *only* system that played every kind of recorded music—and played them all automatically, selectively.

Today, with the new RCA Victor 45 Extended Play records, you have all these advances, plus one happy financial return: *more music for less money.*

These extraordinary little records bring you the same amount of great music as two 12" old-style records, yet cost little more than half as much.

RCA's continuing program of research in other fields of home entertainment—radio, television, tape-recording, and high fidelity, brings happy returns for millions of Americans.

RCA pioneered and developed compatible color television

RCA RADIO CORPORATION OF AMERICA
World leader in radio—first in television—first in recorded music

RCA, 1954

New design! New distinction

in the world's finest all-transistor pocket radio — Zenith's new Royal 500E!

• Up to 300% more sensitivity from Zenith's specially designed circuit!

• New inverted cone speaker for richer, fuller tone.

• Vernier pin-point tuning; built-in Wavemagnet® antenna.

• Elegantly styled, nonbreakable case in maroon, ebony color or two-tone off white and Brick Red, the Royal 500E $75.00.* Attachment for private listening, optional at extra cost. Other Zenith quality pocket radios from $39.95.*

ZENITH *The quality goes in before the name goes on*

Zenith Radio, 1959

Look at the new Motorola Portables!

The handle is a rotating antenna

You just turn the handle (not the radio) for stronger, clearer reception. Because it's three times as big as other portable antennas, and turns to face signals head-on, you bring in stations you've never heard before on a portable. Sets use AC, DC current or batteries. Shatterproof steel cabinets are covered with scuffproof, stain-resistant miracle fabric.

See them—hear them—at your Motorola dealer.

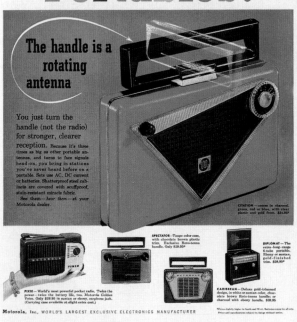

CITATION—comes in charcoal, green, red or blue, with clear plastic and gold front. $34.90*

SPECTATOR—Taupe color case, with chocolate brown plastic trim. Exclusive Roto-tenna handle. Only $29.90*

DIPLOMAT—The extra-long-range 6-tube portable. Ebony or suntan, gold-finished trim. $59.95*

PIXIE—World's most powerful pocket radio. Twice the power—twice the battery life, too. Motorola Golden Voice. Only $39.95 in suntan or ebony, earphone jack. (Carrying case available at slight extra cost.)

CARIBBEAN—Deluxe gold-trimmed design, in white or suntan color, chocolate brown Roto-tenna handle, or charcoal with ebony handle. $39.95

Motorola, Inc., WORLD'S LARGEST EXCLUSIVE ELECTRONICS MANUFACTURER

*Prices slightly higher in South and West. Batteries extra for all sets. Prices and specifications subject to change without notice.

Motorola Radio, 1955

▶ *Philco Television, 1957*

PHILCO

Miss America

MODEL 6624TM

OK AHEAD *and you'll* *choose*

HILCO®

"MISS AMERICA" CONSOLE. Truly the most beautiful, most talented TV of all. Hyper-power touch-panel tuning, Custom De Luxe chassis. Wrap-Around Sound. Phono-jack. Brilliant, 332-sq.-in. picture. Arm Chair remote control optional. Mahogany or blond woods.

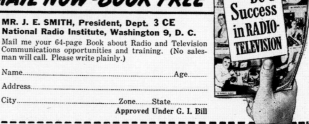

National Radio Institute, 1953

Admiral Television, 1950

DeForest's Training, Inc., 1953

Sprayberry Academy of Radio, 1953

Radio-Television Training Association, 1953

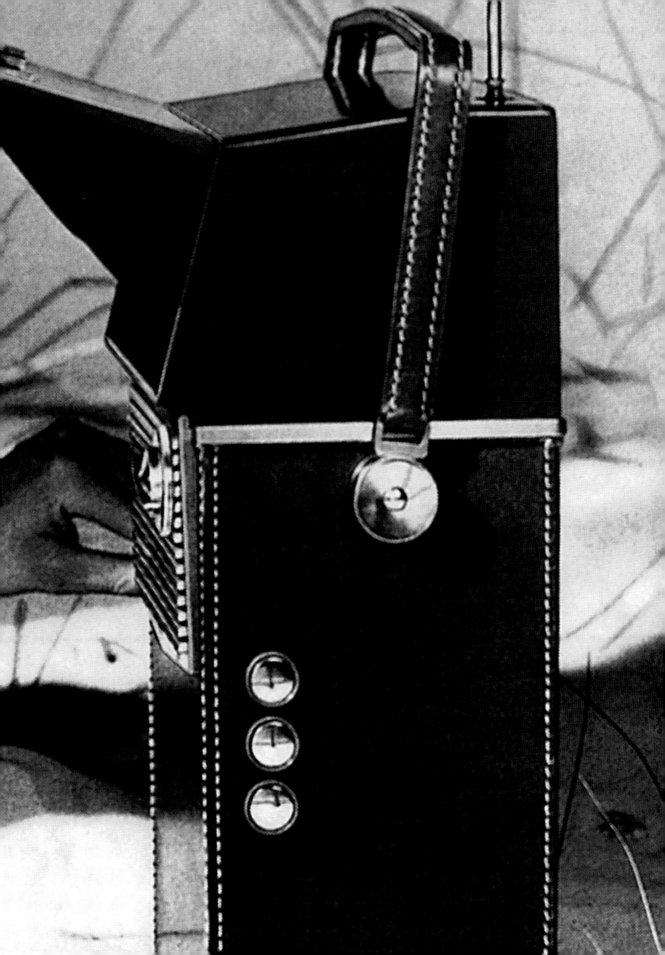

Fabulous *FEDERAL* COOKWARE!

Fabulous *PINK*

Fabulous PRICES

ADVERTISED IN LIFE

99¢

(2 QT. SAUCEPAN WITH COVER)

FEDERAL VOGUE ENAMELED WARE TITANIUM ADDED FOR EXTRA LIFE
FEDERAL ENAMELING & STAMPING CO. PITTSBURGH, U.S.A.

Easy-to-clean PORCELAIN ENAMELED WARE!

Now, have the year's most fashionable cookware color — PINK — and have it at low prices you thought were *out* of fashion! Now, cook, serve, store in the same pot — yet pay *less* than you ever believed possible. No other cookware is so easy-to-clean *completely* — so sanitary. Yesterday's flavors never stay for today; even your most delicate sauces will be cooked to perfection. The price will never be better . . . the color is *right* — and *permanent*. See Federal Vogue PINK enameled ware today!

AT YOUR FAVORITE HOUSEWARES COUNTER

FEDERAL VOGUE ENAMELED WARE *Titanium added for extra life*

FEDERAL ENAMELING AND STAMPING CO.

Windsor shape Open Sauce Pans. Set of three, ⅝, 1, 1½ qts....1.49

Pudding Pan with rolled rim. 1¾ qt. size...49c, 3½ qt....59c

Percolator with aluminum inset. Generous 8 cup size........1.69

Flavor-Saver Covered Pots. Handy 3⅞ qt. size..1.49, 5⅜ qt...1.79

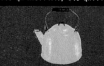

2 qt. Tea Kettle (wood grip)...1.49 Family-style 5 qt. size........1.98

8" Fry Pan. Easy to clean and so attractive to hang on wall.....99c

Oval Dish Pan, 9¼ qt. size...1.39 Round, 8⅜ qt. 1.19 — 11½ qt. 1.39.

Combination Cooker. You can use it five different ways. 2 qt......1.89

Prices may vary slightly according to location

Philco Portable Television, 1959 ◄ *Federal Enameled Ware, 1955*

► *Dixie Cups, 1954*

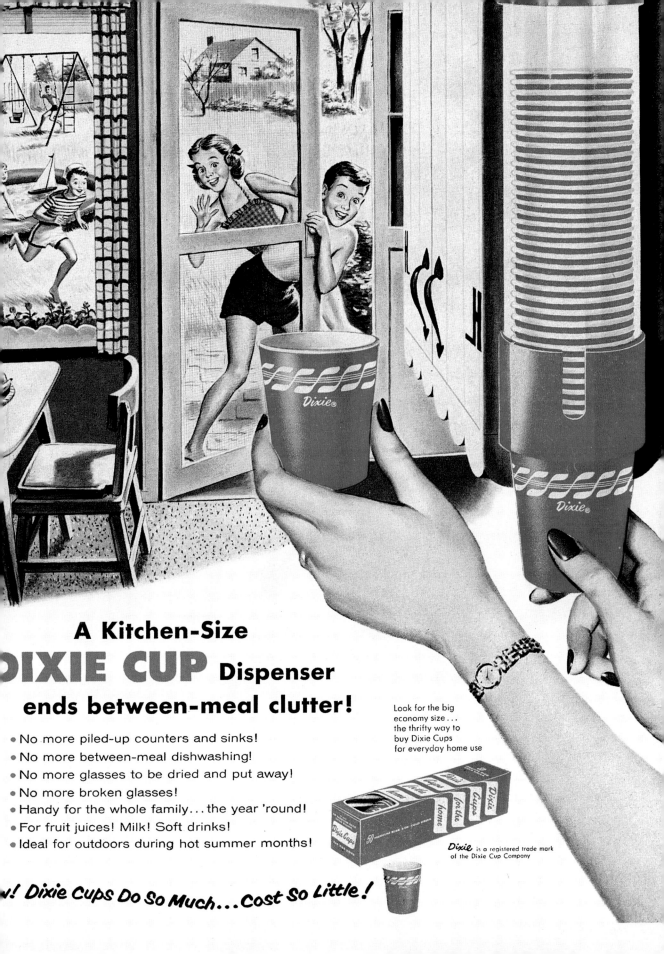

Sunbeam Ironmaster

Sunbeam Mixmaster   ▶ *Sunbeam Mixmaster, 1951*

Osterizer, 1952

Done...with the new Waring Coffee Mill

Waring Coffee Mill, 1957

Stanhome, 1953

Westinghouse, 1950 ▶ Alcoa Aluminum ▶▶ *Lenox China, 1957*

Hors d'oeuvre tree with arrangeable components, salad service and electric casseroles, all of aluminum, designed for the Alcoa collection by Don Wallance Photographed by Becker-Horowitz

FORECAST: THERE'S A WORLD OF ALUMINUM IN THE WONDERFUL WORLD OF TOMORROW . . . where the loveliest pieces on your festive table will be aluminum . . . gay and colorful aluminum . . . anodized, or porcelainized, or brushed to satiny richness . . . aluminum tableware so versatile you will cook in it, serve in it, and create table arrangements as original as a Gauguin canvas. Aluminum Company of America, Pittsburgh.

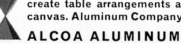 **ALCOA ALUMINUM**

Anchorglass, 1954

Libbey Glass, 1952

Libbey Glass, 1954

Prolon Dinnerware, 1957   ▶ *Servel Electric Wonderbar, 195*

THE YEAR'S MOST EXCITING NEW IDEA FOR MODERN LIVING

SERVEL "Electric Wonderbar"

PORTABLE, SILENT REFRIGERETTE STYLED AS SMART FURNITURE

Silent as a Moonbeam!
Save countless trips upstairs
to a sickroom or nursery!

Holds a Party Full!
Chills all your sodas,
mixers, beer! Handy
removable snack tray!

Executives, Doctors!
Makes gracious hospi-
tality as easy as open-
ing a desk drawer!

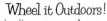

Wheel it Outdoors!
Enjoy it on your porch or patio!
Ideal for boats, too!
Legs or casters optional.

Serve icy drinks right from your own easy chair! So handy while watching TV!

It chills drinks and food! Freezes ice cubes! Rolls indoors or out! Serves as a refreshment center, a snack spot, a portable bar!

Ah!—Cold drinks, snacks, and ice right at your elbow—in a sleek cabinet that's smart in *any* setting! Open the door—there's a big serving shelf! Reach in—you'll find two big trays of ice cubes, plenty of space for food and drink! It's the perfect gift—the perfect servant for entertaining, parties, family fun!

Just plug it in! It's permanently silent. Freezing system has no moving parts to get noisy or wear—and it's covered by a 5-year warranty! Spilled drinks can't mar it. Uses no more current than a 150-Watt bulb. AC or DC, 32 to 230 volts. Mahogany, blond, white. See it wherever fine appliances are sold!

Servel

The name to watch for great advances in
REFRIGERATION and AIR CONDITIONING
GAS—ELECTRIC

Royal Chi-net Paper Plates, 1956

Pyrex, 1954

so lovely...so practical...such...

fashionably-new dinnerware...made of Melamine

What is Melamine? Simply the most amazing material ever developed for dinnerware. Just imagine—the beautiful dinnerware you see here is so durable the manufacturers give you a replacement guarantee. Molded of Melamine, it defies chipping and cracking—stays lustrous and sparkling after repeated dousing in the hottest wash water. That's Melamine —modern plastic as you have never known it before—developed through years of research and testing, fashioned by

leading dinnerware makers and top designers into exciting new shapes, colors and patterns. Take a good look at some of the many styles available. You'll see why dowagers and debutantes agree dinnerware molded of Melamine makes a bright, beautiful setting for a banquet, buffet or Sunday brunch. And before you drop another breakable dish, see... feel... bounce today's new Melamine dinnerware. You'll find it at your favorite store.

Melamine Dinnerware, 1956

▶ American Cynamid Company, 1950

Monsanto reports:

New Colors, New Materials, New Designs for Plastic Housewares

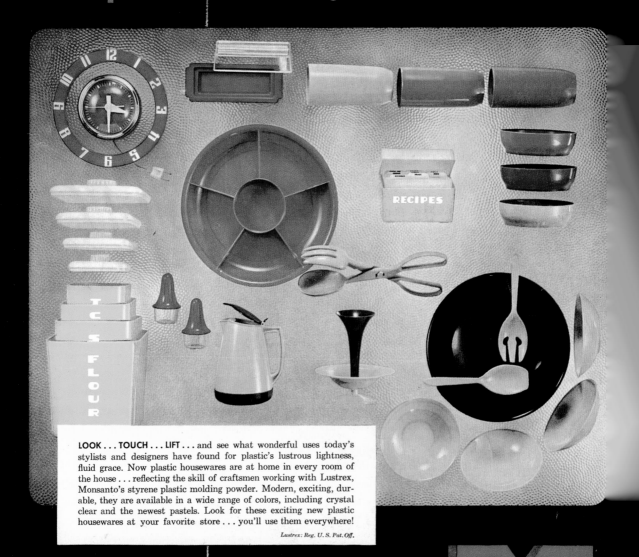

LOOK...TOUCH...LIFT...and see what wonderful uses today's stylists and designers have found for plastic's lustrous lightness, fluid grace. Now plastic housewares are at home in every room of the house...reflecting the skill of craftsmen working with Lustrex, Monsanto's styrene plastic molding powder. Modern, exciting, durable, they are available in a wide range of colors, including crystal clear and the newest pastels. Look for these exciting new plastic housewares at your favorite store...you'll use them everywhere!

Lustrex: Reg. U. S. Pat. Off.

NO MORE "juggling" with new plastic TV snack trays—sectioned, light to handle.

LITTLE HANDS find plastic cup easy to hold, divided plate just right for a beginner.

LEFTOVERS stay together, fit neatly in refrigerator, in this new plastic space-saver.

MONSANTO
CHEMICALS AND PLASTICS

SERVING INDUSTRY...WHICH SERVES MANKIND

IF YOU ARE A MANUFACTURER, call on Monsanto for the latest information on new plastic materials—and suggestions on how plastics can be applied to your own production problems.

Monsanto Plastics, 1953

Russel Wright **american modern***

A tradition that is contemporary . . . and *timeless* — the lasting loveliness of American Modern dinnerware on the tables of fine homes everywhere! For a luxurious New Year's setting, mix the lovely colors created by Steubenville Pottery — at this "little money" price, it's easy to own sets in *several colors!* Sixteen Piece Starter Set — in Black Chutney, Chartreuse, Granite Grey, Coral, White or Seafoam Blue — 4 dinner plates, 4 bread-and-butter plates, 4 cups, 4 saucers, **$7.95** Also in open stock. Write for brochure showing shapes, colors, prices, of complete dinner service. Express charges collect. No C.O.D. orders.

MILWAUKEE, WISC.

*Reg. U.S. Pat. Off.

Also available at

B. ALTMAN, NEW YORK • **NEUSTETER'S,** DENVER • **H & S POGUE,** CINCINNATI • **THE HIGBEE CO.,** CLEVELAND • **MAISON BLANCHE,** NEW ORLEANS

Russel Wright Dinnerware, 1951

...for mother

...because she's always wanted dinnerware
that's beautiful and guaranteed
break-resistant, too!

for the bride...

...because Melmac dinnerware is so smart,
so colorful, so carefree to use
she'll enjoy it happily ever after!

...for yourself

...because you want dinnerware that sets
lovely tables for your important dinners
and brightens up your everyday meals, too!

MELMAC®
dinnerware

Melmac quality melamine dinnerware
is guaranteed by its molders for a full year
against breaking, cracking and chipping.

Melmac is quality molded dinnerware
but not all molded dinnerware is Melmac.

Melmac is found in leading stores
under individual molder's brand names.

Look for the Melmac tag.

CYANAMID

MELMAC®

quality melamine
dinnerware

MELMAC is the registered trade-mark of American Cyanamid
Company, New York 20, N. Y., supplier of molding compounds to manufacturers of quality melamine dinnerware.

Melmac Dinnerware, 1956

▶ *Melmac Dinnerware, 1953* ▶▶ *Montamower, 1950*

LAWN-BOY *modern america's power mower*

Next time you're in Lamar, Missouri, stop in and see the men who make the Lawn-Boy and the way these superb machines are constructed.

If your trips to austral Missouri are rare, you can see a Lawn-Boy right in your own neighborhood. Enterprising merchants have them for sale in every community. Owners will tell you Lawn-Boy is so startlingly different that it is folly to buy any other brand.

The new Lawn-Boy is lightweight, brilliantly designed and styled, staggeringly low in cost. Kitten-quiet but tiger-tough, Lawn-Boy does not one, but four big jobs of lawn maintenance (. . . cuts grass, cuts weeds, trims close, mulches leaves).

And as the crowning feature there's the powerful 2 h.p. Iron Horse, the engine conceived and built exclusively for the new 1955 Lawn-Boy. Here, sir,

there's power and to spare—but quiet as a pair of old sneakers.

Friend, do not buy a power mower carelessly. Talk to men who know them and use them. Seek out your Lawn-Boy dealer (believe us, he's not far). Try it, you'll buy it. *Made only by RPM Manufacturing Company, Lamar, Mo. A subsidiary of Outboard, Marine and Manufacturing Company, makers of Johnson and Evinrude outboard motors.*

Lawn-Boy Power Mower, 1954

Walk or Ride to the smoothest lawn in town

Boy, what a relief—the way LAWN-BOY lightens your lawn chores! No more heavy strain. No more fatigue. But you wind up with an outdoor carpet that's parklike smooth.

Makes a man lawn-proud and makes his neighbors lawn-green with envy.

Running a LAWN-BOY's a cinch. Starts with one pull. Handles easy, too. Because it's aluminum-light, aluminum-strong. It cuts *level,* even over dips and hollows, because the exclusive Activated Pilot Wheel keeps it on an even keel.

Heavy grass? No problem there. Power-packed LAWN-BOY romps through the tallest clumps.

Close trimming a headache? Not with LAWN-BOY. Not even under bushes.

You're the boss when you buy a LAWN-BOY. You have a wide choice of walking or riding models. The Loafer you see here attaches to *any* LAWN-BOY rotary, to the LAWN-BOY reel, and to most other rotaries as well.

And *every* LAWN-BOY, you'll be happy to know, is backed by a nearby authorized service station.

LAWN-BOY

Lamar, Mo., Div. Outboard Marine Corp. *Johnson* and *Evinrude* Outboard Motors. In Canada: LAWN-BOY, Peterborough, Ont.

LAWN-BOY LOAFER

LAWN-BOY DELUXE

Lawn-Boy Power Mower, 1958

Simplicity *built to change your*

4 Great Models for 1954...Best Buys in Garden Tractor History!

New for '54! Simplicity 2½ H. P. MODEL F

ONLY **$199.50** F.O.B. Factory, attachments extra

Lever Gear Shift—6 forward speeds and reverse!

Here's America's peak value garden tractor—unmatched in its outstanding features by any other tractor. All-gear transmission—6 forward speeds and reverse. Speed range ¾ mph. to 6 mph. Dependable Briggs & Stratton engine for plenty of power.

Simplicity Tractors, 1954

Vigoro Seeds, 1956   ► *Sunbeam Rain King Sprinkler, 1954*

The Sprinklers You See on Beautiful Lawns Everywhere

Sunbeam Rain King
The BEST SPRINKLERS MADE

Both Sprinklers Give
EXCLUSIVE
Finger-Tip Control

Set Dial to Sprinkle
5 to 50 FEET *Automatically*

**MERICA'S Sensational NEW
Automatic
TRAVELING SPRINKLER**

ravels any course up to 100
et—Shuts off automatically.
ravels straight or around
orners. Set it . . . Forget it.

utomatically winds up stain-
ss steel tape to pull itself
cross lawn. Shuts itself off.

America's two great automatic lawn sprinklers.

The Sunbeam Rain King on the left travels across the lawn up to 100 feet and shuts off by itself, and the one on the right is non-traveling. Otherwise both sprinklers are the same.

BOTH sprinklers have the automatic finger-tip dial which automatically sets distance and spray. Whether set for small or large areas the spray is always broken up by the speed of the revolving arms to give a natural rain-like shower.

BOTH sprinklers deliver the correct amount of water for deep soil saturation. BOTH offer conveniences found in no other sprinkler. Built-in Sunbeam quality throughout. Automatic non-traveling sprinkler, Model K, $9.25 (Colorado & West, $9.50). Automatic traveling sprinkler, Model K20, $39.50 (Colorado & West, $39.75).

SEE SUNBEAM'S NEW PLASTIC GARDEN HOSE AT YOUR DEALER'S

**AMERICA'S Most Popular
Automatic
NON-TRAVELING SPRINKLER**

Both the non-traveling and traveling sprinklers give deep soil saturation for developing rich, thick, healthy lawns.

These famous sprinklers give a natural rain-like shower best for all kinds of lawns.

MODEL H

Outstanding for any sprinkling job. Ideal for newly seeded areas —throws more water when set with fine spray. Nozzles also adjustable for coarse or medium shower. Revolving or stationary operation. $8.50 (Colorado & West, $8.75)

MODEL D

America's most economical quality sprinkler. Nozzle adjustable for any kind of spray from misty shower to drenching downpour. Can be set to sprinkle circles, narrow strips, or hard-to-reach corners. Revolving or stationary operation, $6.50.

N1A HOSE NOZZLE

Solid brass with lasting beauty of chrome plate. Leakproof. Tarnishproof. Quickly adjustable for any type spray. New type construction permits easier cleaning and repacking. Will discharge 400 gals. per hour on 30 lbs. pressure. $1.50.

Sunbeam
HEDGE TRIMMER

Answers trimming needs of all your shrubbery, hedges, ornamental trees, etc. Saves time, gives professional results. Perfect for side trimming and shaping—cutting weeds, coarse grasses, etc. Sunbeam's "know-how" in building electrical appliances has gone into its design and construction. $49.75 (Colorado & West, $49.95).

**POWERFUL • HIGH SPEED • LIGHTER
EASIER-TO-HANDLE**

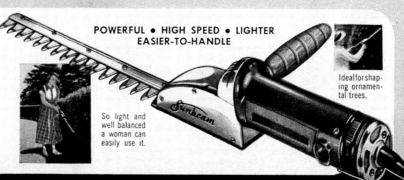

So light and well balanced a woman can easily use it.

Ideal for shaping ornamental trees.

Sunbeam CORPORATION • Dept. 11, 5600 Roosevelt Road, Chicago 50, Illinois • Canada Factory: 321 Weston Road, Toronto 9, Canada
Famous for Sunbeam TOASTER, MIXMASTER, COFFEEMASTER, IRONMASTER, SHAVEMASTER, WAFFLE BAKER

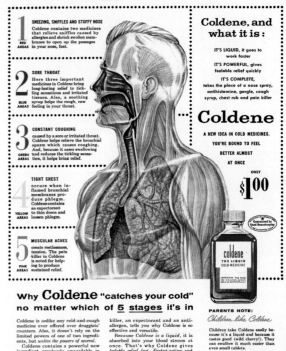

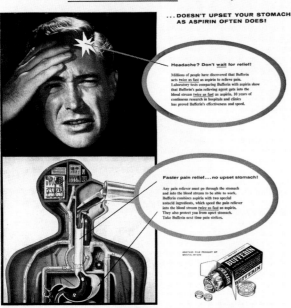

Bufferin, 1956

Coldene, 1957

Lava Soap, 1950

Geritol, 1957   ▶ *Band-Aid, 1956*   ▶▶ *The Home Insurance Company, 1954*

SUPER-STICK

BAND-AID

TRADE MARK

Plastic Strips

WON'T LOOSEN IN WATER

Johnson & Johnson

Now with **SUPER-STICK**. They stick better, protect better.

Free Gift...Hot Handle Holder

for women who clean this easy new way with

Jubilee Kitchen Wax

Takes off dirt in seconds—protects with wax for weeks!

Use Johnson's new Jubilee Kitchen Wax to clean your cabinets, refrigerator, range, woodwork and enameled walls. Here's all you do: Pour out a little Jubilee on a damp cloth and whisk away dirt, fingerprints, greasy cooking films. Then buff lightly and you leave a coat of gleaming wax protection.

Jubilee's creamy blend of detergents and wax is safe for your prized kitchen appliances. It can't scratch enamel—can't dull painted surfaces.

You can "wash" your kitchen with wax for months with a single pint of Johnson's Jubilee. Get a bottle today!

Pictured actual size

No more burned fingers when you have this handy heatproof holder to slip over pan handles. It covers entire handle of any pot or pan. Quilted cotton in gay patterns. Special loop for hanging up. You'll want several!

FREE!
HOT HANDLE HOLDER

TO GET YOUR HOT HANDLE HOLDER USE THIS ORDER FORM OR WRITE TO JOHNSON'S WAX

Stores now have a handy order form for your free Hot Handle Holder wrapped around the neck of each Jubilee bottle. You can use this form—or simply write to Johnson's Wax, Box 12, Racine, Wisconsin. Put your name and address on outside of envelope. Be sure to enclose the little wax paper disc inside the cap of the Jubilee bottle so we'll know you're a Jubilee user.

Another work saver from Johnson's Wax Research

Jubilee Kitchen Wax, 1954

Women tell friends...   mothers tell daughters...   and everyone's telling us...

"There's <u>never</u> been a cleanser like this!"

Procter & Gamble's **new**

Comet fortified with Chlorinol*

Bleaches out stains, wipes out germs as no other cleanser can!

Try this amazing test against any other leading cleanser!

1. Take any stubborn food stain—like tea or coffee makes—and divide in half with a ruler. Then, shake a generous amount of your present cleanser on one side. Above, we call it Cleanser X, but no matter, COMET beats all leading cleansers!

2. Next, shake some COMET on other side. COMET is fortified with Chlorinol,* the most effective form of chlorine bleach. This special ingredient has all the bleaching, stain-removing advantages of chlorine—its disinfecting benefits, too!

3. Using the ruler to keep cleansers divided, rub each side of stain with a different wet sponge. Watch COMET bleach out stains like no other cleanser ever did before! See how COMET foams green. And notice COMET's fresh, clean scent.

4. Rinse and see the proof! Some stain remains on Cleanser X side. With COMET, stain's gone! Sink's whiter than ever! And COMET with Chlorinol* kills up to 99% of household germs—disinfects as no other leading cleanser can!

WHITEST EVER—AND 99% GERM FREE

Comet Cleanser

SURF ADDS BRIGHTNESS

(yes...even to <u>perfect</u> whiteness)

Brightens colors too!

A wash that's merely white is no longer the best you can do. Now all-purpose Surf contains a special brightener that puts ultra-violet rays (like those in sunshine) to work for you. Today's Surf actually <u>adds</u> brightness — even to <u>perfect</u> whiteness. It brightens colors, too. Try Surf and you'll see for yourself. If you don't get the whitest, brightest wash you've ever seen, Lever Brothers will refund every penny you spent.

Surf
with ultraviolet whitener

Black Flag Bug Killer, 1950 ◄   *Surf Laundry Detergent, 1957*

S.O.S cleans white-wall tires really white

S.O.S
magic scouring pads
cleans and shines aluminum

S.O.S. is rugged: Just twist the pad and see. Compact, tightly-interwoven, S.O.S. holds up while cleaning off the toughest curb-marks, grease and ground-in dirt.

S.O.S. has grease-removing soap right in it. Just dampen the pad and squeeze up the suds; that's all you do. An S.O.S. pad is ready to go to work—instantly!

SOS Magic Scouring Pads, 1956

"Nothin' to it... easy as rakin' your lawn"

Nothin' *like* it...the beautiful job you get with

Wizard Masonry Paint

No tedious mixing of powder and water ... just flow it on wet or dry surfaces! Alkali and acid resistant. Will not chalk, peel or blister. Its rubber base formula allows the surface to "breathe". Protects against moisture. Gal. $6.39

FREE! Valuable 48-page booklet at your Western Auto Store

One Coat Seals and Covers
CONCRETE, BRICK
STUCCO AND
ASBESTOS SHINGLES

Wizard Masonry Paint, 1957

"GOTTA PATROL A PLANET, DAD!"

"I'D SAY you're equipped for the assignment, Son. With that modern gadget you'll handle any emergency, and your mission will be successful."

Emergencies in *business*, such as accidents on the job also require special "equipment." They call for workmen's compensation insurance placed with a reliable organization that assures quick, sympathetic service.

Hardware Mutuals rank among the leaders in promptness of paying workmen's compensation claims. This promptness helps speed recovery by relieving financial worry. With the help of Hardware Mutuals loss prevention specialists, employers can eliminate hazards *before* they cause accidents.

Among other benefits of Hardware Mutuals *policy back of the policy®* is friendly, nationwide, day-and-night service. More than $110,000,000 in dividend savings have been returned to policyholders.

For all the facts, simply *call Western Union, ask for Operator 25*, and say you'd like the name and address of your nearest Hardware Mutuals representative.

Insurance for your AUTOMOBILE...HOME...BUSINESS

Hardware Mutuals®

Stevens Point, Wisconsin · Offices Coast to Coast

HARDWARE MUTUAL CASUALTY COMPANY · HARDWARE DEALERS MUTUAL FIRE INSURANCE COMPANY

Hardware Mutual Casualty Company, 1953

▶ *Insurance By North America, 1957*

That's quite a prize you have there, bright eyes. And a pretty picture you make with that colorful yarn and that wide-eyed look. That's how it is with Puss 'N Boots Cats... the Vitamin A gives their eyes sparkle, so makes them extra lovable...

Where'd you get that silky, luxurious fur coat? From a can of Puss 'N Boots can, you say! That's a point! Puss 'N Boots is rich in riboflavin, one of the important nutrients you need to keep your skin healthy—your fur fluffy and full.

Nice kitty! Takes more than a tussle with a ball of yarn to upset your gentle disposition. Thank Puss 'N Boots for the part it plays. It's no vice, in nerve-soothing Vitamin B, it would help tame even a battle-scarred Tom!

This yarn's for you, my pretties!

My what strong bones you have! The better to leap with, of course. It's easy to see you're getting lots of calcium, phosphorus, and Vitamin D. That's no surprise with Puss 'N Boots on your diet. There's a dish worth leaping for!

See what it means...
to be a Puss 'N Boots Cat?

Hey! You're missing the fun! Or are you...Isn't that Puss 'N Boots? 'Nuff said!

Puss 'N Boots adds the Plus!

Yes, all you purry, furry pals have lots in common...health, energy, beauty, and a love for Puss 'N Boots. That's natural, for Puss 'N Boots is finest quality. Fresh-caught whole fish (no by-products or "fillers" ever) plus just the right cereals, cooked in the can and ready to eat. Each feeding of Puss 'N Boots gives you all the food factors found in milk, liver, salmon, and beef... in greater abundance and even better balance. Yet Puss 'N Boots costs your master and mistress far less!

QUALITY MAKES IT... AMERICA'S LARGEST SELLING CAT FOOD

Puss 'N Boots Cat Food, 1951

Your parakeet needs your help to perform his best!

Feed FRENCH'S—the only Parakeet Seed with the new Pep-Up Biscuit

Your parakeet depends on you to keep him happy and playful. Help him perform his best by feeding clean, dependable French's Parakeet Seed! Every package contains a special biscuit that promotes vigor, sharpens appetite, aids digestion. Always feed French's—the only Seed with the pep-up biscuit.

Pet parakeets should have a complete, varied diet—the kind wild parakeets find in nature. French's Natural Feeding Diet is scientifically prepared to provide just such a tasty, balanced menu. Make sure your pet has all the food elements he needs by giving him regularly the "Basic Five"—French's Parakeet Seed and Biscuit, Treat, Conditioning Food, Cuttle Bone, and Gravel.

PROTECT YOUR PARAKEET'S HEALTH
WITH French's
NATURAL FEEDING DIET

YOU CAN DEPEND ON FRENCH'S 54 YEARS OF EXPERIENCE

French's Bird Food, 1956

NEW! From the makers of Ken-L-Ration...

Ken-L-Treats

Not a candy or a sweet
but a biscuit Treat that's good
for your dog to eat!

Fun for you, fun for your dog... and he can eat all he wants and feel better for it, because Ken-L-Treats contain 6 of nature's richest nutrients for dogs

Good as a main meal or between-meal snack. New KEN-L-TREATS contain all the vitamins, minerals, and other nutrients normally found in other good biscuits, and KEN-L-TREATS are supplemented with a unique combination of high-quality proteins that gives them a nutritional balance never before achieved in a dog biscuit. Fun to feed, plus a complete, balanced diet for dogs. Whatever else your dog eats during the day, he needs TREATS, too!

Ken·L Treats
PROTEIN RICH DOG BISCUITS
6 variety shapes... 6 gay colors
MILK, EGG, MEAT, FISH, CHEESE, BONE

6 gay colors... 6 variety shapes!
6 of nature's richest nutrients for dogs in every Ken-L-Treats Biscuit

FISH (Fish Meal)—Vitamins and minerals for which fish is famous.

MEAT (Meat Meal)—high in valuable vitamins and trace minerals.

CHEESE Cheese is a milk derivative—wholesome and appetizing and a basic protein.

EGG Egg with high-protein content to nourish every living cell of your dog's body.

MILK (Milk Solids), the near-perfect food—rich in calcium, high in proteins.

BONE Bone meal rich in calcium for sound bones and teeth—with a contributing amount of proteins.

Teach your dog a new bag of tricks with a box of nutritious Treats!

Ken-L Treats, 1955

Be Smart! Be Thrifty!*
BUY GAINES IN LARGE SIZES

Now Available at Your Grocery Store!

LOWEST PRICES! More and more grocers today are featuring Gaines in a full range of package sizes—including extra-thrifty 25 and 50-pound bags. And regardless of the size you prefer, you'll find that no one sells top-quality dog foods like Gaines for less than your local grocery stores.

SO CONVENIENT! One-stop buying! What could be simpler than buying Gaines at the same time you purchase food for all the family?

ALWAYS CLEAN AND FRESH! In handling quality foods for any member of your family, your grocer's standards of carefulness and cleanliness are similar to those under which Gaines is made. Wholesomeness is further insured by the fact that your grocer buys Gaines so often, sells it so fast. It's America's largest-selling dog food.

*If you own a large dog or more than one dog, you'll find a real saving and extra convenience buying Gaines in 25 or 50-pound bags. The 25-lb. size costs about the same as four 5-lb. packages—giving you a bonus of 5 pounds. Whenever you fail to find the size package you prefer, ask about it. Your grocer can promptly obtain Gaines for you in any of the five handy sizes.

In 2 and 5-lb. cartons; 10, 25, and 50-lb. bags

Gaines MEAL For All Dogs

A Product of General Foods

"Nourishes Every Inch of Your Dog"

Gaines DOG FOODS
America's Largest-Selling Brand

Gaines Dog Food, 1950

► Friskies Dog Food, 1956

another adventure of
the *Ozzie Nelsons...*

"Hey, Big Noise—how's this for a painting? I'm an artist!!"

["This kid's got to go!"]
"Look, Genius—mine's been done for half an hour. C'mon, let's show Mom and Pop."

they paint original

Picture Craft oil paintings

"Yes . . . families everywhere are painting original *Picture Craft!"*

Just like the Ozzie Nelsons . . . you, too, will prefer original Picture Craft. An exclusive process enables you to re-create a true work of art. It's fun, relaxing, you need no experience—and it's GUARANTEED!

The leader for over 15 years, original Picture Craft is the *only* "paint-by-numbers" kit that gives you: true pre-mixed artist's colors . . . a specially treated artist's canvas . . . and an exclusive 4-in-1 brush designed by Picture Craft. It all adds up to the ideal hobby for you . . . the perfect gift for a friend.

Guaranteed by Good Housekeeping

Original Picture Craft bears this seal

Kit includes:
- NUMBERED ARTIST'S CANVAS (16" x 12")
- PRE-MIXED OIL COLORS
- SPECIAL ARTIST'S BRUSH
- SIMPLE PAINTING INSTRUCTIONS

CHOOSE FROM 35 BEAUTIFUL SUBJECTS

ONLY $2.95 COMPLETE KIT

Picture Craft Frames at Slight Extra Cost

At better Department • Art • Hobby • Stationery • Camera and Paint Stores . . . or write to:

PAINT A BEAUTIFUL PICTURE IN OILS
Picture Craft
NO EXPERIENCE · NO LESSONS · NO MIXING

790 N. WATER STREET • DECATUR, ILL.

Enjoy "The Adventures of Ozzie & Harriet" on radio and TV each week on ABC sponsored by Hotpoint and Listerine.

Picture Craft, 1955

Jackets & Jeans
by Blue Ridge Mfg. Co.
Jackets $2.79, Jeans $2.79

Wrist Watches
(Roy Rogers & Dale Evans)
by Bradley Time Corp.
$4.95 plus F.T.
Alarm Clock (not illustrated)
$3.95 plus F.T.

Roy Rogers Hats
by Sackman Bros.
Asst'd colors $1.98

Frontier Shirts
by Rob Roy
Long sleeve $2.95, Short $1.95

A Summer of Fun with
ROY ROGERS
Guaranteed Products

Whenever you get the youngster in your life something "just like Roy's," you can be sure you're getting value for your money. Roy Rogers' "Pledge To Parents" assures you that a leading manufacturer has made a quality product to satisfy *you* as well as your youngster. You can buy Roy Rogers branded merchandise with confidence.

ROY ROGERS GUN & HOLSTER SETS
by Classy Products
Young cowhands "go" for these genuine holsters of hand-worked quality leather. Rust-proof nickel studs, adjustable snaps and Western Buckle.
Upper, deluxe model $7.95
Lower, Two-gun, Deputy style. . . . 5.95
Other models from $1.98 to $10.95

ROY ROGERS T-SHIRTS & SWEAT SHIRTS
by Norwich Mills Inc.
Roy and Trigger design on fine quality cotton, with reinforced seams and interlock collars. In White, Blue or Gold. Guaranteed to take many washings.
Short sleeve T-Shirt. 69c
Long sleeve Sweat Shirt. $1.00

Boots & Felt Slippers
by S. Goldberg & Co., Inc.
All styles $1.99

Boots & Tex-Tans
by Tex Tan of Yoakum
Boots $7.95 up, Tex-Tans $3.79

Roy Rogers "Shootin' Irons"
by Kilgore
(Model left) $1.00
(Model right) 79c

Roy Rogers Lunch Kit
by The American Thermos Bottle Co.
Complete with ½ pint bottle $2.89

ROY ROGERS PLEDGE TO PARENTS

This item of merchandise, bearing my name, has been tested in one of the nation's largest testing bureaus and, in our judgment, equals in quality any merchandise selling in the same price range. You pay no premium for my name. Rather, it is your assurance that this item is an authentic value.

Roy Rogers

Shop your local retailer. He has these items or can get them for you.

ROY ROGERS
1418 North Highland Avenue

ENTERPRISES
Hollywood 28, California

Roy Rogers Enterprises, 1954

Hopalong Cassidy Boots, 1951

Make Him the Happiest Boy in the World this Christmas...with

the Only Train   in the World with

MAGNE-TRACTION
THE NEW SENSATIONAL 1950 LIONEL TRAINS

Lionel Trains, 1950

Lionel Trains, 1954

Insist on
Slinky Toys

AT YOUR NEAREST TOY COUNTER

JAMES INDUSTRIES, PAOLI, PA

SLINKY WORM • SLINKY TRAIN • SLINKY JUNIOR • SLINKY EYES • SLINKY BUCKO

Slinky, 1957

F.W. Woolworth Co., 1950

Comet Gas Model Planes, 1958

OAK Inflatable Play Balls, 1958

Econolite, 1958

Silly Putty, 1958

H. Fishlove & Co., 1958

Tru-Vue, 1958

Walking Doll, 1956

Doctor Dan Story Book, 1951 ▶ *Space Traveler Paint - by - Number Kit, 1958*

...from out of this world!

direct from
TV's hottest
new program,

WALT DISNEY'S
OFFICIAL **MOUSEKETEER** ©

MOUSECAPS*
for Boys and Girls

...designed exactly like the caps to
be worn by the Mouseketeers
every day on Walt Disney's
Mickey Mouse Club TV Program!
Without question, this will be your
biggest children's headwear
promotion of the year!

98¢ retail

©Copyright Walt Disney Productions
* Patent Pending

And...
WALT DISNEY'S
OFFICIAL MOUSEKETEER
"SPECIAL DEPUTY" HATS,

to be worn by the Mouseketeers
(boys and girls) every week
during the program's Western
Talent Round-Up. **$1.98** retail

W1042 T (Girls)

W1075 B (Boys)

Get Ready!
WALT DISNEY'S
MOUSEKETEERS
are Coming!...
on the new
Mickey Mouse Club TV Show
"Breaks" October 3rd!
National ABC-TV Network!
Every week day 5:00-6:00 p.m.!
Estimated 25 Million
Daily Audience!

Order today, for immediate delivery,
from authorized national licensee.

Bailey
OF CALIFORNIA

716 South Los Angeles Street
Los Angeles 14, California

NOTE: Mousecaps; F.O.B. Los Angeles only. Special Deputy Hats F.O.B. Los Angeles—to Western
States; F.O.B. Pennsylvania factory to stores East
of Denver.

Gentlemen: Please ship us following:

	Order	Style No.	Color	Pack	Sizes S-M-L	Cost
dz.	Boys' "Mousecap"	W82	Black	2 dz.	6-12-6	$ 7.25 dz.
dz.	Girls' "Mousecap"	W87	Black	2 dz.	6-12-6	$ 7.25 dz.
dz.	Boys' "Special Deputy"	W1075B	Black	1 dz.	3-6-3	$15.00 dz.
dz.	Girls' "Special Deputy"	W1042T	Tan	1 dz.	3-6-3	$15.00 dz.

☐ Check here for newspaper ad mat.   Terms: 2/10 EOM

Firm Name_____

Buyer_____ Dept._____

Address_____

City_____ State_____

ORDER
TODAY-
USE
THIS
CONVENIENT
ORDER
FORM!

◄

*Patent pending

See us at MAGIC Style Show, Ambassador Hotel, October 23 through 26

Celanese Corporation of America, 1950 ◄ *Mouseketeer Hat, 1955*

481

2 OUT OF 3 CHILDREN IN AMERICA

WILL
WEAR
BENAY-ALBEE
HATS
IN
1958*

SEE WHY AT THE TOY SHOW..HOTEL NEW YORKER..ROOM 1126, 200 FIFTH AVE...ROOM 1118

WESTERN, NOVELTY, CHARACTER AND SUN HATS
BENAY-ALBEE NOVELTY CO. • 52-01 FLUSHING AVE., MASPETH, N. Y.

benay-Albee

Benay-Albee Hats, 1958

Garton Toy Company, 1958

Kusan Pop Gun, 1958

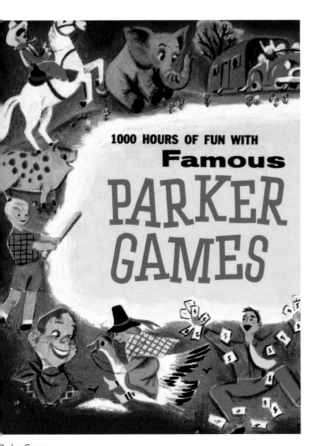

Parker Games

Parker Games

It's Thrifty...it's Smart and so _Easy_ to ride!

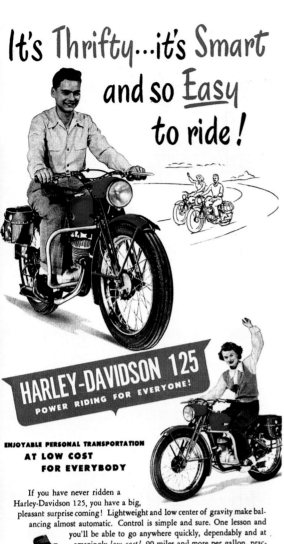

HARLEY-DAVIDSON 125
POWER RIDING FOR EVERYONE!

ENJOYABLE PERSONAL TRANSPORTATION
AT LOW COST
FOR EVERYBODY

If you have never ridden a Harley-Davidson 125, you have a big, pleasant surprise coming! Lightweight and low center of gravity make balancing almost automatic. Control is simple and sure. One lesson and you'll be able to go anywhere quickly, dependably and at amazingly _low cost!_ 90 miles and more per gallon, practically no upkeep, no parking fees. Good looking, too, streamlined, colorful. Smooth, quiet performance with such advanced automotive features as brakes on both wheels, 3-speed transmission, drop-forged steering head, oversize tires, easy-chair saddle, brilliant night lighting. Thousands in use by men, women, boys, girls, for work, business, school, errands, outings. You owe it to yourself to _try_ it. "A penny saved is a penny earned" and think of the _fun_ you can have! Low down payment, easy terms. Phone or see your Harley-Davidson dealer for a FREE ride.

MAIL THE COUPON NOW!

HARLEY-DAVIDSON MOTOR CO., Dept. C, Milwaukee 1, Wisconsin
Send colorful folder and full information about the low-cost Harley-Davidson 125.

Name...
Address..
City.. State.................

DEALERS: Valuable franchises available for the full line of famous Big Twins and the 125 model. Your opportunity to line up with the greatest name in motorcycles. Write or wire for information today.

HARLEY-DAVIDSON 125
POWER RIDING FOR EVERYONE!

Built especially for _YOU!_

YOUNG or old, this is _your_ two-wheeler! So easy to ride, you learn in one lesson! So economical, you get 90 miles and more per gallon. So convenient and dependable, you'll want to ride it everywhere . . . to factory, office, store, school, sports events, outings. Frees you from crowded buses and trolleys. Saves your car. Ends parking problems and traffic troubles. Smartly modern, streamlined, and colorful. Remarkably comfortable with "easy chair" saddle, big tires. Smooth, quiet performance. Built for safety with brakes on both wheels, 3-speed transmission, brilliant lighting. And so easy on your pocketbook! Small down payment and it's yours. Then pay as you ride as you save! Phone or see your dealer today!

MAIL THE COUPON NOW!

HARLEY-DAVIDSON MOTOR CO., Dept. C-2, Milwaukee 1, Wisconsin
Send colorful folder and full information about the NEW, low-cost, economical-to-operate Harley-Davidson 125.

Name...
Address..
City.. State.................

DEALERS: Valuable franchises available for the full line of famous Big Twins and 125 Model. Write today.

Roadmaster Bicycle, 1952 ◄ Harley-Davidson, 1950

Harley-Davidson, 1950

Moo-oo Cow

A new design with mo
than ever! "Moo-oo's" j
real cow as head bob
down. Tail swishes.
12¾" long

AHEAD AGAIN

In Ideas..
In Value..
In Sales !
· · · · · · · · ·

NEW FISHE

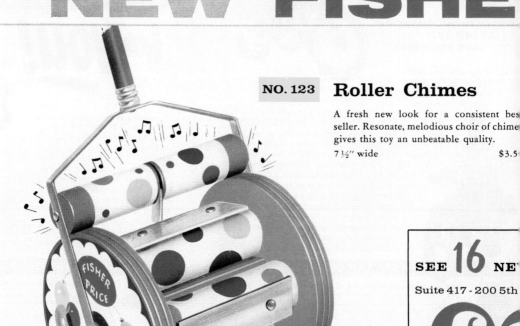

Roller Chimes

A fresh new look for a consistent bes
seller. Resonate, melodious choir of chime
gives this toy an unbeatable quality.
7½" wide $3.5

SEE **16** NE
Suite 417 - 200 5th

FISHER • PRIC

PATENT PENDING

© by Fisher-Price Toys, Inc., East Aurora, N. Y., U. S. A., 1958

Fisher-Price Toys, 1958

O.735 Juggling Jumbo

que new toy idea! Turn the
dle, and colorful balls race
ough Jumbo's unbreakable
ate trunk. A pull toy. A sit
toy!

" long $2.00

CRANK SHOOTS BALLS

PATENT PENDING

Squeaky The Clown

Another new, big-value
toy! All the activity and
color of a three ring circus.
Head bounces up and
down. Arms rotate.
9″ high $1.59

head bobs up and down

SQUEAK

PATENT PENDING

PRICE TOYS

the Original
GIANT SNAP LOCK BEADS

FOR AGES 3 MONTHS TO 4 YEARS

the Original
squeezable,
unbreakable,
GIANT POLYETHYLENE BEADS

"SNAP" TOGETHER   "PULL" APART

Develops finger dexterity,
shape and color perception.

SAFE COLORS

FISHER · PRICE TOYS, INC.

NO. 658   The Original
Giant Snap-Lock Beads

Colorful, new package holds 15 of
these fabulously popular Fisher-
Price polyethylene beads!
10″ x 13½″ $1.00

write for complete new catalog

fp

FISHER · PRICE TOYS
INCORPORATED
EAST AURORA, Erie County, N. Y.

487

designed for **"NO SHOW**
eliminates smears on fir

M552
75mm RADAR AA
SKYSWEEPER

When this kit is cons
only description t
"Jewel-Like." Every
this automatic radar
is faithfully repro
134 precision parts c
of the intricate, fun
tures of the proto
plete model has 34
operating assemblie
gun barrel that actuc
strates recoil action
contains shells wh
loaded or unloaded
ting munition retaine
plete with 5 life-like
bers consisting of C
Radar Operator, Com
ator, Loader and As
Authentic decals incl

Packed: 1 dozen to c
Weight: 10 lbs.

M553
280mm Gun
ATOMIC
CANNON

It takes 279 parts to make up this detailed model of the Army's largest
mobile artillery piece and the specially designed front and rear trucks that
transport it. (Actually 3 kits in 1.) Super-detailed throughout, the finished
model is fully operative...it does everything but fire! Cannon is detachable
from trucks and elevates by hand wheel and gear train. Gun barrel telescopes
6" from travelling position to firing position. Each truck has six free rolling
wheels. Kit complete with 7 lifelike crew members consisting of Commander,
2 drivers, 2 munition haulers with cart and shells, 2 gunners. Authentic decals
included.

Packed: 1/3
Weight: Appr

menting . . .
models!

M551
Self Propelled 8 inch
HOWITZER

Packed: 1 dozen to carton
Weight: Approx 18 lbs.

138 parts that make up the most authentically detailed kit ever offered in any price range. When assembled, the builder has a model that truly captures all the power and excitement of this famous Army weapon. Renwal's engineering insures positive assembly and exclusive "NO SHOW" cementing design eliminates all messy stains. Assembled model has 37 authentic operating parts that include all doors, hatches, gun, turret, engine, tread and wheels. Detailed interior is visible through operating doors. Kit comes complete with 6 lifelike crew members consisting of Commander, Driver, Gunner, Loader, Radio Operator and Technician. Authentic Decals included.

Big Shot

U.S. ARMY ★ 551

U.S. ARMY ★ M553

LITTLE RED SCHOOLHOUSE
Regulation-Size Building Bricks

Sturdy, colorful chest comes filled with 24 rugged regulation-size fibre building bricks all assembled.

Illustrations for basic uses of Bricks and play schoolhouse on inside cover for effective store display.

Take out Bricks and Chest very simply becomes attractive play school-house which can be used in the building scheme.

SPECIFICATIONS -- No. 710
Little Red Schoolhouse Building Bricks

Individual Brick size — 7¾" x 3¾" x 2⅛".

Chest size -- 16" x 11¾" x 9"
24 Bricks per Schoolhouse — weight 7½ lbs. Each in individual mailer.
3 units per master — weight 23 lbs.
Suggested Retail Price — $6.98. Higher in the West.

Tremendous sales appeal in this unique—useful—package.

Each unit in a compact individual mailing carton for factory fresh delivery and easy reshipment.

NATIONAL GAMES INCORPORATED
MAIN OFFICE AND FACTORY
91 CHURCH STREET   WEST SPRINGFIELD, MASSACHUSETTS
NEW YORK SHOWROOM   200 5TH AVENUE

National Games Inc., 1958

▶ *Slinky Toys, 1958*   ▶▶ *Space Missiles, 195*

SLINKY®

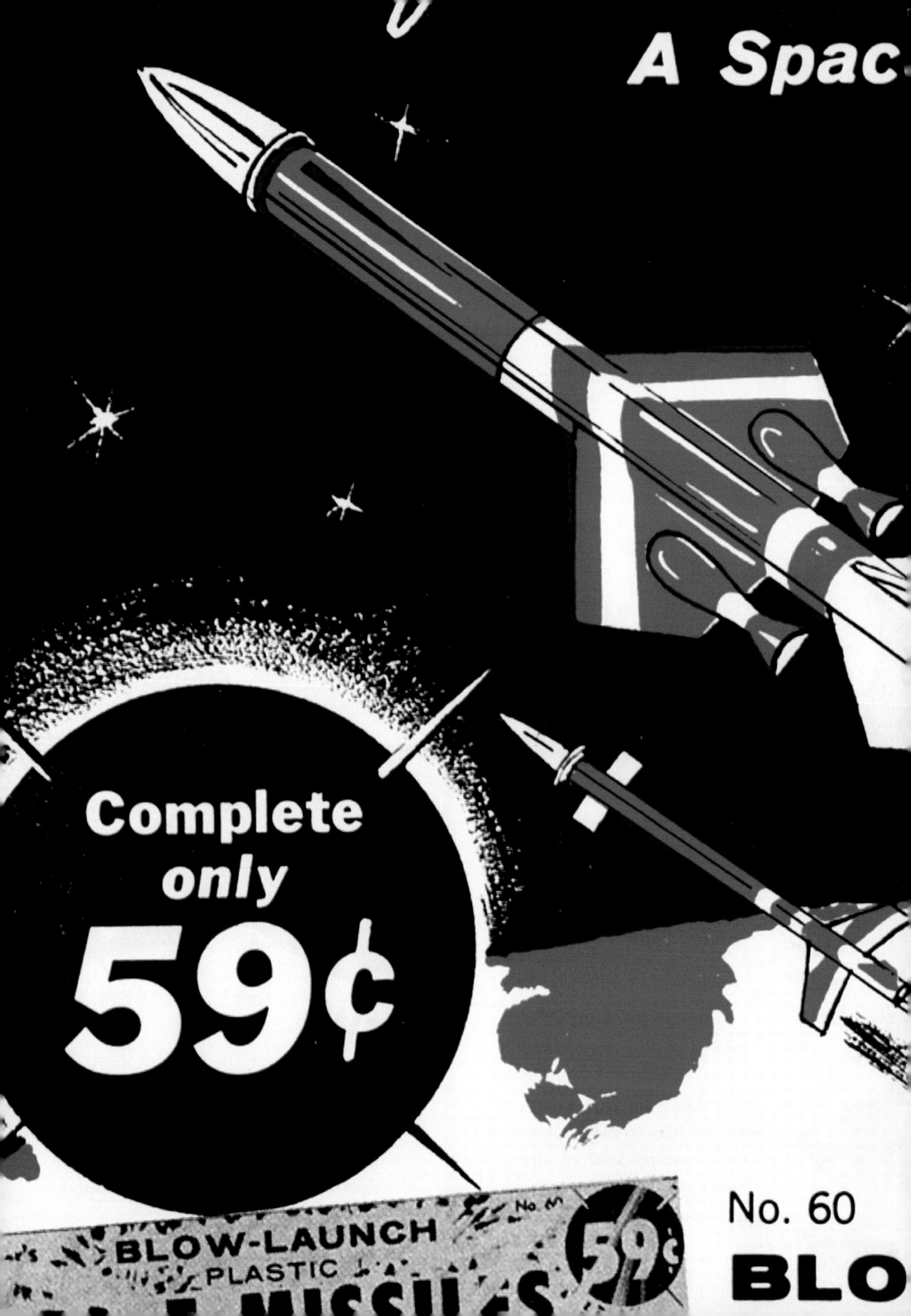
A Spac
Complete
only
59¢
BLOW-LAUNCH
PLASTIC
59¢
No. 60
BLO

Nelson-Hall Co., 1954

497

And the winner is...

Photographs That Give A Realistic Record Of The Scene Of The Crime

Showing crime scenes to sell film? This gruesome photograph was meant to extol the virtues of Ansco film. Unfortunately showing dead bodies on blood soaked snow was a dubious way to get into a consumer's wallet. Hopefully the advertising agency disappeared before the next round of the brainstorming began for the follow-up campaign.

Fotos, die ein realistisches Bild vom Schauplatz des Verbrechens zeichnen

Bilder vom Tatort schrecklicher Verbrechen als Kaufanreiz? Dieses schaurige Foto sollte die hervorragenden Eigenschaften von Ansco-Filmen verdeutlichen. Tote Leiber auf blutgetränktem Schnee zu zeigen, erwies sich jedoch leider nicht gerade als Königsweg ins Portemonnaie der Verbraucher. Hoffen wir, dass die Werbeagentur von der Bildfläche verschwunden war, noch ehe die Brainstorming-Runde für die Nachfolgekampagne in Angriff genommen werden konnte.

Des photographies réalistes du lieu du crime

Montrer des scènes de crime pour faire vendre de la pellicule ? Cette horrible photographie vise à exalter les vertus des films Ansco. Malheureusement, montrer des cadavres sur de la neige ensanglantée est un moyen douteux pour atteindre le portefeuille du consommateur. Heureusement, l'agence de publicité a disparu de la scène avant le déclenchement d'une autre campagne de persuasion.

Color photographs to fight crime!

Law enforcement officers now have a valuable new tool in ANSCO Color Printon ... low cost color photographs that give a realistic record of the scene of a crime or accident. Details in full color show unmistakable evidence, leave less ground for doubt or evasion, confirm and support witnesses' reports. ANSCO Printon will save time in police investigations and court procedure ... save money for litigants and taxpayers.

Printon will also make it possible for local police departments to have color photographs of criminals of record, for easier, more positive identification.

Transparencies taken with ordinary cameras on ANSCO color film, give Printon prints in full color ... can be bought for as little as $3.00 for a large 8 x 10 inch print—*or can be developed in your own darkroom!*

ANSCO research in photography improves film, cameras, processes ... makes picture taking and printing easier for everybody, assures better pictures at lower cost. Five hundred factory tests of ANSCO film are your guaranty of more satisfactory pictures.

MAKING cameras and photographic supplies since 1842, and today a Division of General Aniline & Film, ANSCO is the second largest U. S.

producer of film, photographic papers and cameras ... Another GAF Division at Johnson City, N. Y. makes Ozalid®, the most efficient facsimile copying machine, and sensitized materials ... With large plants at Rensselaer, N. Y. and Grasselli, N. J., General Aniline is this country's largest manufacturer of quality dyestuffs and a large supplier of industrial chemicals *(sold through General Dyestuff Corporation)* ...

General Aniline provides good jobs for more than 7,500 people ... spends more than $35 million a year for wages and salaries, $5 million in research, $12 million in taxes. It's a good company to work for or with, and worth watching.

gaf

General Aniline & Film Corporation

From Research to Reality...230 Park Ave., New York 17, N. Y.

General Aniline & Film Corporation, 1952

HOLLYWOOD, CALIF....

This is the story
of movie writer,
young Joe Gillis,
cub reporter
from Dayton who
always wanted
a Hollywood
swimming pool.

Joe got his pool on
Sunset Boulevard!

But the price
was too high!

! a most
unusual motion
picture

Betty Schaefer...
young and fresh,
loved Joe.

Norma Desmond...
wealthy and
different,
loved him,
too.

A
HOLLYWOOD
STORY!

**SUNSET
BOULEVARD**

starring

WILLIAM
HOLDEN
as Young Joe Gillis

GLORIA
SWANSON
as Norma Desmond

and

ERICH
**VON
STROHEIM**
as Max von Mayerling

with NANCY OLSON • FRED CLARK • LLOYD GOUGH • JACK WEBB

Cecil B.DeMille • Hedda Hopper • Buster Keaton • Anna Q. Nilsson • H. B. Warner • Franklyn Farnum
as themselves

Produced by Charles Brackett • Directed by **BILLY WILDER** • Written by Charles Brackett,
Billy Wilder and D. M. Marshman, Jr. • A Paramount Picture

!

The last time
you saw a pictu
like this, by
Brackett and Wi
it won four
Academy Awards
It was
"THE LOST
WEEKEND"

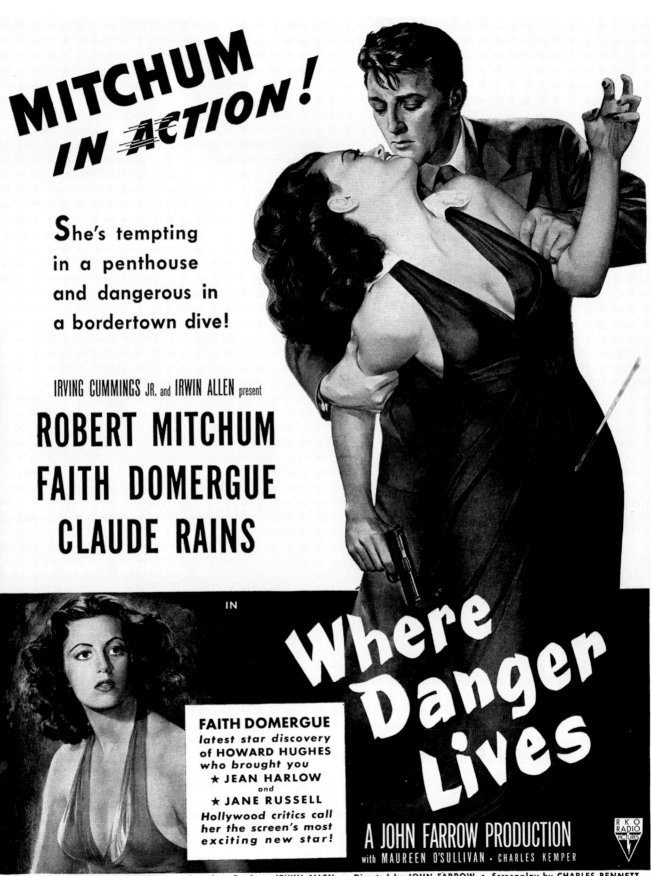

MITCHUM *IN ACTION!*

She's tempting in a penthouse and dangerous in a bordertown dive!

IRVING CUMMINGS JR. and IRWIN ALLEN present

ROBERT MITCHUM
FAITH DOMERGUE
CLAUDE RAINS

IN

FAITH DOMERGUE
latest star discovery
of HOWARD HUGHES
who brought you
★ JEAN HARLOW
and
★ JANE RUSSELL
Hollywood critics call
her the screen's most
exciting new star!

Where Danger Lives

A JOHN FARROW PRODUCTION
with MAUREEN O'SULLIVAN · CHARLES KEMPER

RKO RADIO PICTURES

Produced by IRVING CUMMINGS Jr. · Associate Producer IRWIN ALLEN · Directed by JOHN FARROW · Screenplay by CHARLES BENNETT

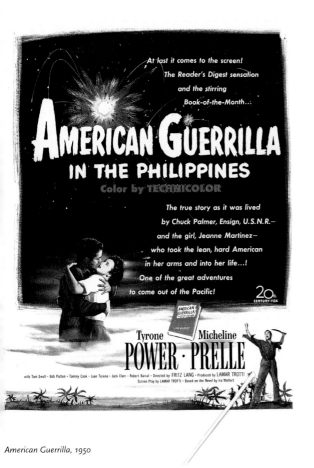

American Guerrilla, 1950

One Minute To Zero, 1952

Jet Pilot, 1957 ◄   American Broadcasting Company, 1951

American Broadcasting Company, 1950

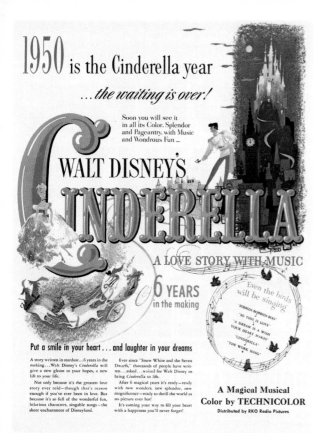

Cinderella, 1950

Alice In Wonderland, 1951

The Great Locomotive Chase, 1956

Annie Get Your Gun, 1950　　　　▶ *Born Yesterday, 1951*

WHO'S WHO in "BORN YESTERDAY"

William Holden
as
PAUL VERRALL
A boy with a nose for news, an ear to the ground, a foot in the door and an eye on a blonde!

Judy Holliday
as
BILLIE DAWN
Pretty, blonde, and pretty dumb. Has a weakness for nice things. Also has other weaknesses.

Broderick Crawford
as
HARRY BROCK
A tycoon who doesn't know what the word means. Has maybe ten million bucks. Also has Billie Dawn —maybe.

COLUMBIA PICTURES
presents

BROADWAY'S

BIGGEST HIT...

BORN YESTERDAY

... Now a Perfectly
Swell Motion Picture

starring

JUDY HOLLIDAY · WILLIAM HOLDEN · Broderick CRAWFORD

Screen Play by Albert Mannheimer · From the Celebrated Stage Play · Produced by S. Sylvan Simon · Directed by GEORGE CUKOR

The Flying Saucer, 1950

▶ The Man In The Grey Flannel Suit, 1950

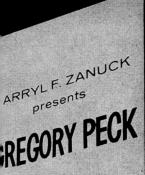

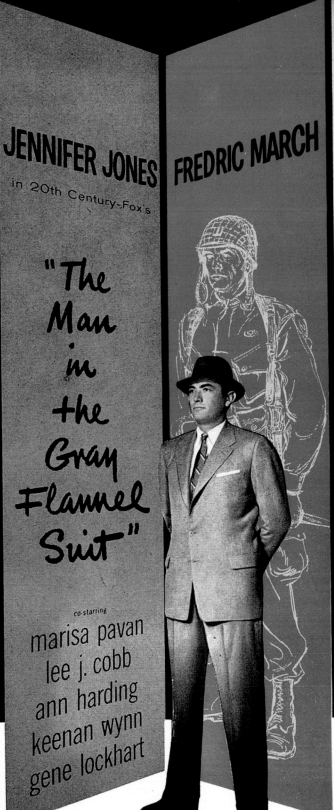

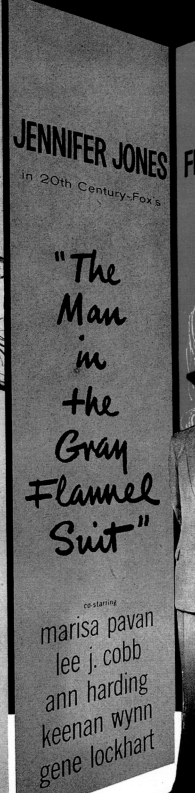

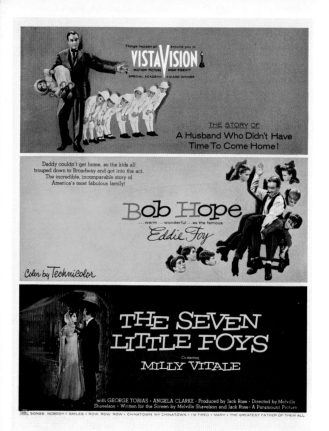

The Seven Little Foys, 1955

Aaron Slick From Punkin Crick, 1952

Mister Roberts, 1955

Trapeze, 1956

▶ *Happy Go Lovely, 1956*

an Adult picture...

no way out

...A great courageous theme

...seven new conceptions
of dramatic portrayal
which reach new heights
of screen dynamics

an ENTERTAINMENT that challenges
your own ability to experience
the emotions of others

a Twentieth Century-Fox picture

Darryl F. Zanuck presents RICHARD WIDMARK · LINDA DARNELL · STEPHEN McNALLY in **NO WAY OUT**
with Sidney Poitier · Mildred Joanne Smith · Harry Bellaver · Stanley Ridges · Dots Johnson
Produced by DARRYL F. ZANUCK · **Directed by JOSEPH L. MANKIEWICZ** · Written by Joseph L. Mankiewicz and Lesser Samuels

No Way Out, 1950

▶ *Vertigo, 1958*

A Paramount Picture in VistaVision® and Technicolor®

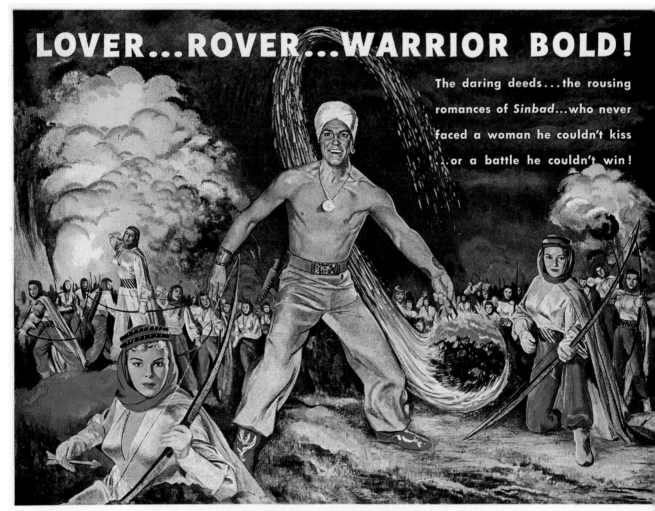

One of the spectacular thrills: the searing siege of Greek Fire! An army of beautiful women . . . against an army of violent men!

Son Of Sinbad, 1950

HOWARD HUGHES presents
JANE RUSSELL
IN UNDERWATER!

ENTER that new, thrilling Underwater World...with Jane Russell as you've never seen her before!

It took 3 years to make...cost $3,000,000!

THE NEW ANAMORPHIC PROCESS
SUPERSCOPE
ON THE GIANT WIDE SCREEN
color by TECHNICOLOR

co-starring
GILBERT ROLAND · RICHARD EGAN · LORI NELSON · Directed by JOHN STURGES · Screenplay by WALTER NEWMAN · Produced by HARRY TATELMAN

Underwater, 1955

Cyrano de Bergerac, 1951

The White Tower, 1950

The Thing From Another World, 1951

Salome, 1953 ▶ *Rancho Notorious, 195*

Gaby, 1956

Tea and Sympathy, 1956

Ivanhoe, 1952

Picnic, 1956

▶ *Cat On A Hot Tin Roof, 1958*

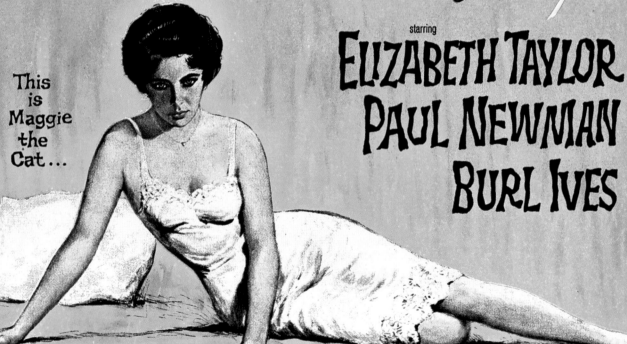

the sultry drama of Tennessee Williams' Pulitzer Prize Play is now on the screen

M·G·M
presents

Cat on a Hot Tin Roof

This is Maggie the Cat...

starring
ELIZABETH TAYLOR
PAUL NEWMAN
BURL IVES

JACK CARSON · JUDITH ANDERSON

Screen Play by RICHARD BROOKS and JAMES POE · Based on the Play "CAT ON A HOT TIN ROOF" by TENNESSEE WILLIAMS

in METROCOLOR · AN AVON PRODUCTION · Directed by RICHARD BROOKS · Produced by LAWRENCE WEINGARTEN

"I am not allowed to love. But I will love you if that is your desire..."

MARLON BRANDO AND AN EXQUISITE NEW JAPANESE STAR. THEY *LIVE* JAMES A. MICHENER'S STORY OF DEFIANT DESIRE. IT IS CALLED

SAYONARA

FILMED IN JAPAN IN TECHNIRAMA® AND TECHNICOLOR®. PRESENTED BY WARNER BROS.

CO-STARRING
PATRICIA OWENS · RED BUTTONS · RICARDO MONTALBAN · MARTHA SCOTT · MIYOSHI UMEKI · JAMES GARNER

AND INTRODUCING MIIKO TAKA

PRODUCED BY · DIRECTED BY · BASED ON THE NOVEL BY · SCREEN PLAY BY
WILLIAM GOETZ · JOSHUA LOGAN · JAMES A. MICHENER · PAUL OSBORN
SONG: SAYONARA WORDS AND MUSIC BY IRVING BERLIN · MUSIC BY FRANZ WAXMAN

Sayonara, 1957

► *Macao, 1952* ►► *Trapeze, 1956*

THE WONDER SH

It Happens There,
In Mid-Air...
In All Its Fire, Flesh And Fury!

TRA

Also Starring
KATY JURADO · **THOMAS GOMEZ** With **JOHN PULEO** · **MINOR WATSON** · Directed by **CAROL RE**

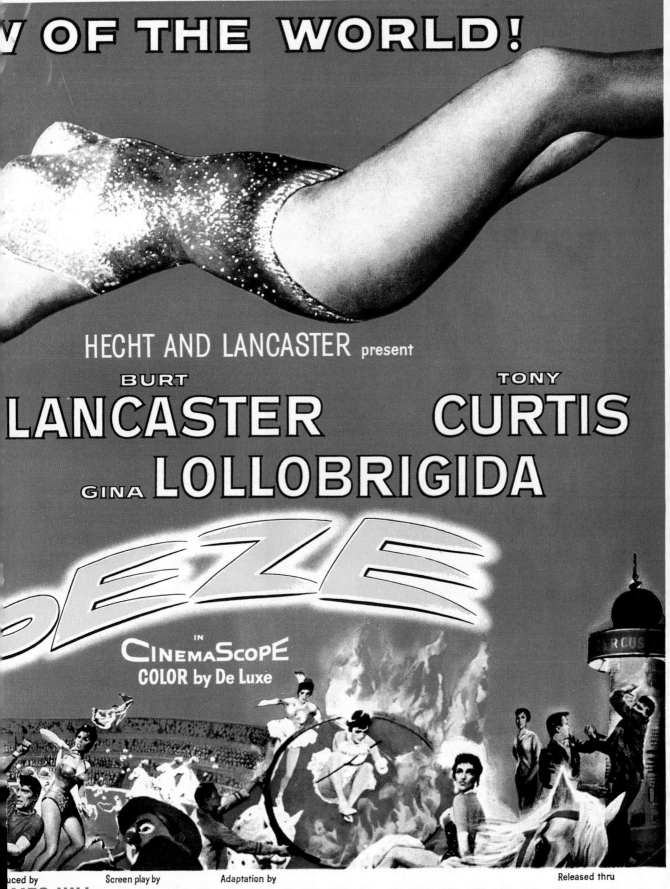

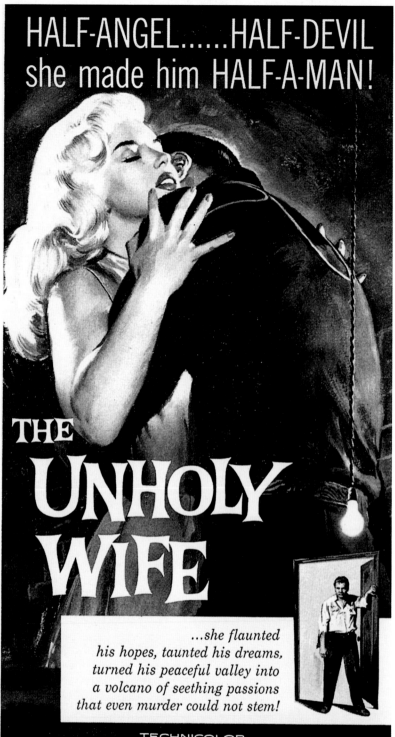

They took what they wanted ... and they wanted the world!

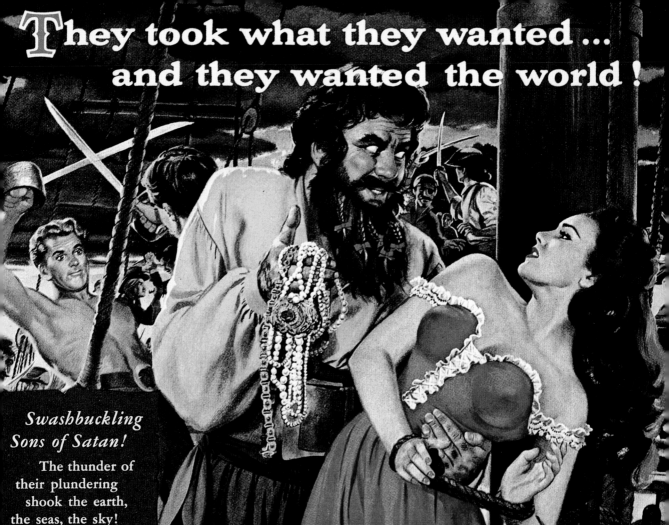

Swashbuckling Sons of Satan! The thunder of their plundering shook the earth, the seas, the sky!

BLACKBEARD THE PIRATE

color by TECHNICOLOR

starring

ROBERT NEWTON
LINDA DARNELL · WILLIAM BENDIX

with KEITH ANDES · ALAN MOWBRAY

AN EDMUND GRAINGER PRODUCTION

Directed by RAOUL WALSH · Screenplay by ALAN Le MAY · Produced by EDMUND GRAINGER

RKO RADIO PICTURES

THE MIGHTY SAGA OF THE WORLD'S MIGHTIEST MAN!

SEE heroic Hercules rip down the Age of Orgy's lavish palace of lustful pleasure!

SEE him crush the savage apemen who guard the shrine of the Golden Fleece!

SEE the Mightiest of Men vs. the Mightiest of Beasts— the killer Cretan Bull!

And more wonders!

SEE the stupendous dragon struck down by Hercules' famed shipmate, Jason!

SEE the dauntless Argonauts dare the pounding perils of wine-dark seas!

SEE the seductive Amazons lure men to voluptuous revels and violent death!

Cast of Thousands...
Cost in Millions!

EASTMAN COLOR by Pathé and in DYALISCOPE!

JOSEPH E. LEVINE PRESENTS

HERCULES

STARRING **STEVE REEVES** SYLVA KOSCINA — FEATURING — GIANNA MARIA CANALE | Fabrizio Mioni · Ivo Garrani · Arturo Dominici | WITH | Mimmo Palmara · Lidia Alfonsi · Gina Rovere | DIRECTED BY PIETRO FRANCISCI O.S.C.A.R. FILM-GALATEA | DISTRIBUTED BY Warner Bros.

SEE IT AT YOUR LOCAL MOTION PICTURE THEATRE!

Hercules, 1959

MIGHTY IN SCOPE

...mighty as this man
whose conquests changed the face
of the world!

When the *great* motion pictures of
1956 are talked about...this one
will be mentioned first!

HOWARD HUGHES presents

JOHN WAYNE · SUSAN HAYWARD

THE
CONQUEROR

CINemaScopE®

PRINT BY
TECHNICOLOR

RKO RADIO PICTURES

2 YEARS IN THE MAKING...AT A COST OF $6,000,000

'THE WORLD?
I WILL
TAKE
IT!'

'THE WOMAN?
I WILL
TAME
HER!'

starring
EDRO ARMENDARIZ · with AGNES MOOREHEAD · THOMAS GOMEZ · JOHN HOYT · WILLIAM CONRAD · TED de CORSIA
A DICK POWELL Production · Written by OSCAR MILLARD · Produced and Directed by DICK POWELL

The Conqueror, 1956

▶ *The Company She Keeps, 1951*

Emotion swept the

like a tidal wave !

M·G·M presents

CARY GRANT

EVA MARIE SAINT

JAMES MASON

THE MASTER OF SUSPENSE WEAVES HIS GREATEST TALE!...

about a
secret that
nobody knew...
a man who
never existed...
and a
love affair
that began
in an
upper berth—
and ended in
screaming
death!

in

ALFRED HITCHCOCK'S

◄NORTH BY NORTHWEST►

VISTA VISION
TECHNICOLOR

Co-starring JESSIE ROYCE LANDIS

Written by ERNEST LEHMAN · Directed by ALFRED HITCHCOCK

SEE IT ONLY ON THE BIG MOTION PICTURE SCREEN

A Place In the Sun, 1951

Imitation Of Life, 1959

North by Northwest, 1959 ◄   *Pillow Talk, 1959*

Gunfight At The O.K. Corral, 1957

Universal-International *proudly announces*

"harvey"

is now a motion picture...

The most wonderful Stage Play
of our time becomes one of
the great Motion Pictures
of all time!

*Concerning the happy
times and funny friends
of Elwood P. Dowd
and his invisible
associate.*

Starring **James STEWART**

with **JOSEPHINE HULL** · CHARLES DRAKE · CECIL KELLAW
JESSE WHITE · VICTORIA HORNE · WALLACE FORD *and* PEGGY DC

From the Pulitzer Prize Play written by **MARY CHASE** and produced by BROCK PEMBERTON · Screenplay by MARY CH
OSCAR BRODNEY · Produced by JOHN BECK · Directed by **HENRY KOS**

South Pacific, 1958

The Benny Goodman Story, 1955

Harvey, 1951 ◄ *Carousel, 1956*

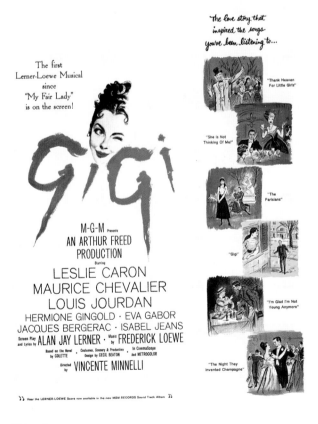

Gigi, 1958

That's My Boy, 1951

Never a Dull Moment!, 1950

Mad Wednesday, 1950　　　▶ *Joe Louis vs Ezzard Charles, 1950*

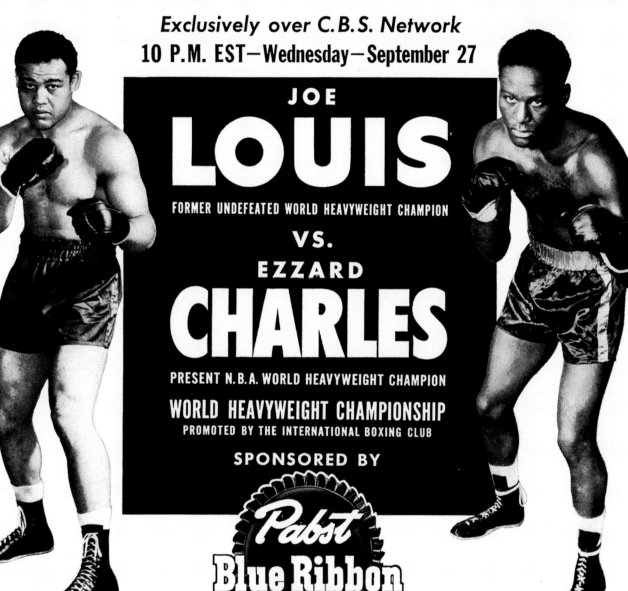

And the winner is...

Trained In An Art As Old As Time

The ultimate grounds for a 1950s divorce. *I Married a Communist* mirrored the anxiety of the McCarthy years. Exploitation cinema at its best, this B movie used every trick in the book to get audiences into the theater including hints of prostitution, violence and death.

Geschult in einer Kunst, die so alt ist wie die Zeit

Ultimative Gründe für eine Scheidung in den Fünfzigern. *I Married a Communist* spiegelte die Furchtsamkeit der McCarthy-Jahre. In bester *exploitation*-Manier ließ dieses B-Movie keinen Trick aus, um die Kinos voll zu bekommen, und spielte auf der Klaviatur von Prostitution, Gewalt und Tod.

Exercice dans l'art le plus vieux du monde.

Le dernier cri comme raison de divorce dans les années 50. *J'ai épousé un communiste* reflète l'inquiétude de la période McCarthy. Exploitation cinématographique maximum, ce film de série B utilise tous les stratagèmes possibles pour attirer les foules, y compris ceux liés à la prostitution, la violence et la mort.

I Married A Communist, 1950

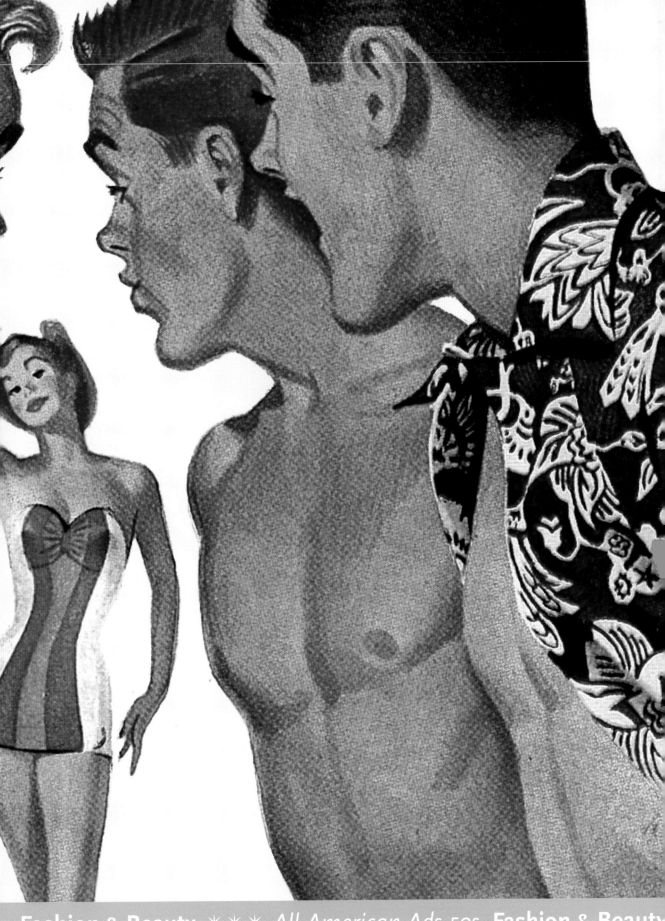

Catalina Swim Suits, 1952

Jantzen Swim Suits, 1956

Jantzen Swim Suits, 1950 ◀◀ Jantzen, 1955 ◀ Catalina Swim Suits, 1955

Catalina Swim Suits, 1958

Catalina Swim Suits, 1954

Jantzen Swim Suits, 1951

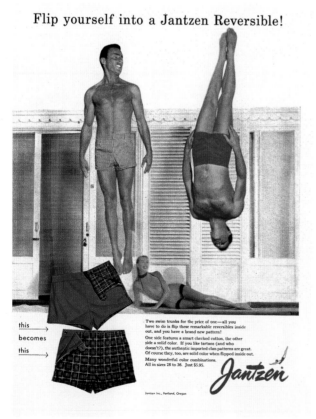

Jantzen Swim Suits, 1956

Jantzen Swim Suits, 1951

Catalina

DESIGNS SWIMSUITS ESPECIALLY FOR YOU

These enhance a small bosom				Beau Catcher Darlin' Daughter Kitty Puff Honey Child
These minimize a large bosom				Golden Pheasant Leading Lady Shipshape Success Story
These slim the upper leg				Fabulous Fit Weskit Scallops Pretty Foxy

Looking for the swimsuit that does *beautiful things for your figure?*

Try a Catalina—one that has been specially designed to call attention to your *good* features . . . draw attention *away* from figure flaws.

Consult the chart above to see which Catalina designs are best for you.

Shown: "Shipshape" (foreground), in color-locked Lastex, $14.95. Background: "Weskit" (far left), in batiste Lastex, $14.95; "Carnation" (center), in elastic shirred cotton, $10.95; "Everything Checks" (right), in laton taffeta, $15.95.

For name of nearest store, write: Catalina, Inc., Div. H, 443 South San Pedro, Los Angeles 13, Calif.

For copy of new folder, "Ten Glamour Tips for the Beach," send 10¢ to above address.

Originators and producers of the *Miss Universe Beauty Pageant.*

© 1954   Suntan by Skol

Catalina Swim Suits, 1954

▶ *Rose Marie Reed Swim Suits, 1958*   ▶▶ *Perma Lift, 1951*

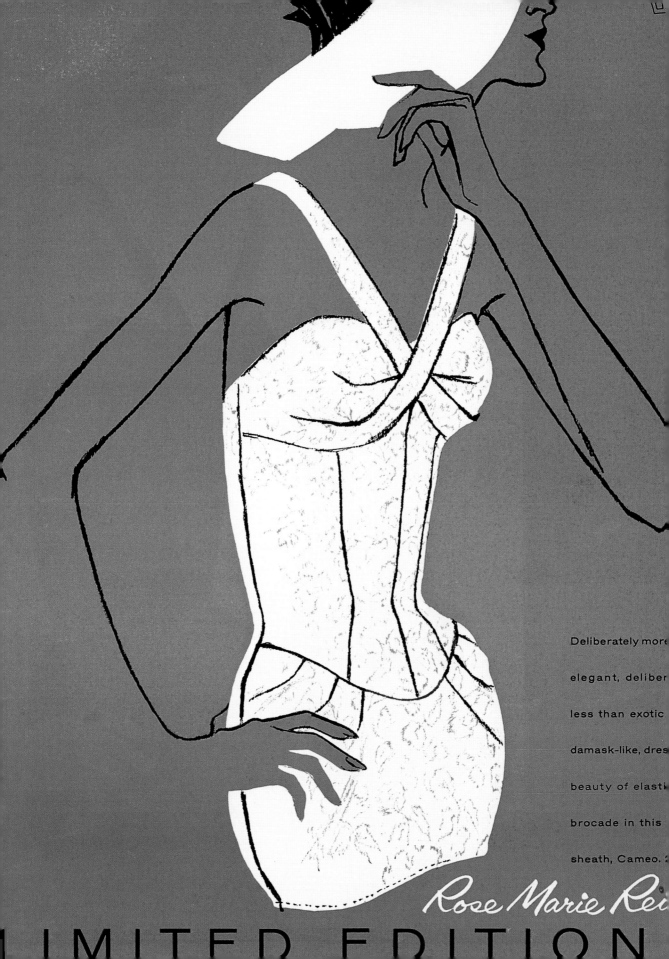

Deliberately more

elegant, deliber

less than exotic

damask-like, dres

beauty of elasti

brocade in this

sheath, Cameo. 2

Rose Marie Rei

LIMITED EDITION

a·lift *Stitched cup*

as, with "The Lift that
er lets you down,"
orify your figure

lift"* stylists have the knack of bra designing
a fine art. Now you can enjoy the compact,
beauty of a Stitched Cup bra with the famous
plift that only "Perma·lift" gives you. In this
ul brassiere, the Magic Insets gently support
ow—the uplift is guaranteed to last the life of
ent no matter how often you wash it or how
wear it. For the only Stitched Cup bra with
t that never lets you down," be fitted in a
lift" Bra today.

otton	$3.00	White
ering Satin	$3.50	White or Pink
ylon	$4.00	White or Pink

"—A trade mark of A. Stein & Company
York–Los Angeles–(Reg. U. S. Pat. Off.)

Perma·lift
GIRDLES
BRASSIERES

Pert and perky is this wispy lit
"Perma·lift" Pantie—fabulous
dainty, yet marvelously stron
So comfortable too, and N
Bones About It—Stays U
Without Stays—the Magic Ins
eliminates annoying bones, y
it can't roll over, wrinkle
bind. Get yours at your favori
corsetiere's today, or write f
name of nearest deale

Power Net Pantie $6.95 White or Pi
Sizes 24 to 30

Power Net Girdle $5.95 White or Pi
Sizes 24 to 30

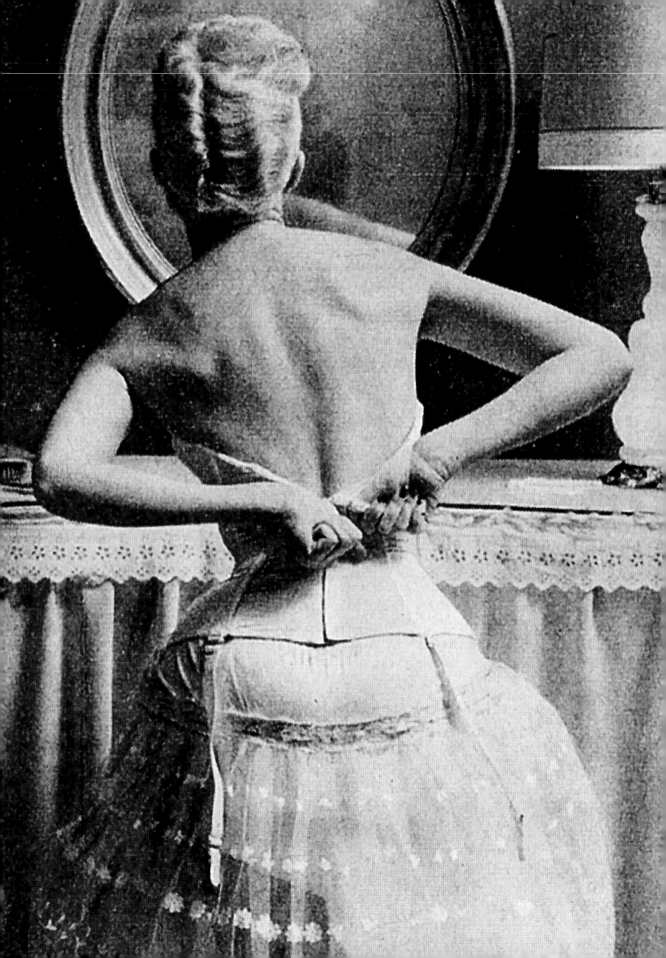

I dreamed I had Spring Fever

in my maidenform bra

For the figure of your fondest day-dreams—Maidenform's lovely new Concerto* gives you curves that are more curvaceous, brings an exciting line to your outline! And it's all accomplished with row upon row of tiny, interlocked stitches! Each stitch catches up an inner cup-lining, pre-shapes this bra just enough to mould a fabulous form! In white stitched broadcloth, lace-margined. AA, A, B and C sizes...2.00

Maidenform Bra, 1956

I dreamed I was a Work of Art in my *maidenform bra*

PORTRAIT OF A LADY in a Maidenform masterpiece: the new Pre-Lude Once-Over Six-Way. Lifts your curves, snugs in your waist, moulds a fabulous figure! With "quick-change" six-way straps, to move or remove for every fashionable neckline. White cotton broadcloth, A, B and C cups...8.95

Maidenform Bra, 1956

Like a glamorous Brandford Model...
you too can look beautiful in an

Exquisite Form
BRASSIERE

AVAILABLE AT YOUR FAVORITE
SPECIALTY SHOP OR
DEPARTMENT STORE

Ask for them by name and number

Style No. 185
Style No. 505
Style No. 225

Free Charm Book for the asking

To help you develop a more attractive personality and an aid to self improvement, Exquisite Form has prepared exclusively for YOU this valuable book. No obligation whatsoever... no purchases... no coupons... no nothing!

Just write - for your Free copy

Exquisite Form CHARM BOOK

Write Direct to EXQUISITE FORM BRASSIERES, INC., Dept. B, 373 Fourth Ave., New York 16, N.Y.

Perma Lift, 1957 ◀   Exquisite Form Brassiere, 1950

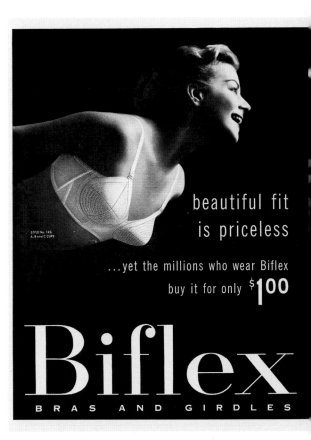

beautiful fit
is priceless

...yet the millions who wear Biflex
buy it for only $1.00

Biflex
BRAS AND GIRDLES

Biflex Bras and Girdles, 1955

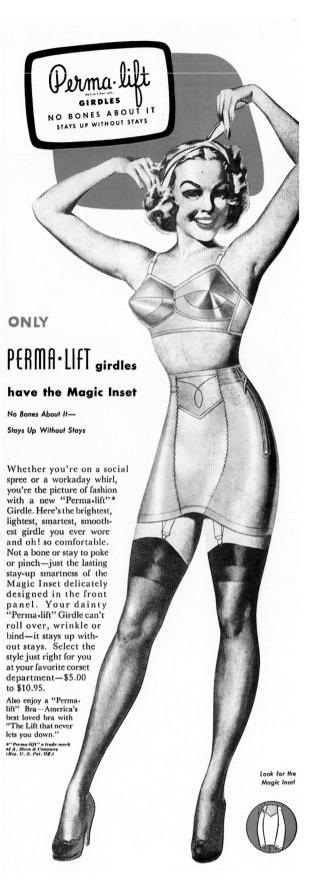

Perma·lift

GIRDLES

NO BONES ABOUT IT
STAYS UP WITHOUT STAYS

ONLY

PERMA·LIFT girdles

have the Magic Inset

No Bones About It—

Stays Up Without Stays

Whether you're on a social spree or a workaday whirl, you're the picture of fashion with a new "Perma·lift"* Girdle. Here's the brightest, lightest, smartest, smoothest girdle you ever wore and oh! so comfortable. Not a bone or stay to poke or pinch—just the lasting stay-up smartness of the Magic Inset delicately designed in the front panel. Your dainty "Perma·lift" Girdle can't roll over, wrinkle or bind—it stays up without stays. Select the style just right for you at your favorite corset department—$5.00 to $10.95.

Also enjoy a "Perma·lift" Bra—America's best loved bra with "The Lift that never lets you down."

*"Perma·lift" a trade-mark of A. Stein & Company (Reg. U. S. Pat. Off.)

Look for the Magic Inset

None

So

Cool

These are the panties that never get clingy, never feel clammy—even on the warmest days. Cool in Summer, comfortable always, because they're naturally absorbent!

the **KNIT** with the **FIT** where you **SIT**

They g-i-v-e with every motion, really fit your figure—they're made for an active life. Easy to care for, they wash and dry quickly, need no ironing. All panty styles.

PANTIES OF

Spun-lo®

RAYON FABRIC

ONLY ABOUT **69¢**

INDUSTRIAL RAYON CORPORATION, Cleveland, Ohio • Producers of Continuous Process Rayon Yarns and ®Tyron Cord for Tires

IT'S A BLOUSE...IT'S A SLIP...ALL IN ONE!

Blue Swan Slipmates

JUST ADD A SKIRT

$2.98

SIZES 32 (dress 9/10) to 40 (dress 17/18)
Also TEEN SIZES for ages 10-12-14

- **ECONOMICAL** ... *Serves a Double Purpose!*
- **FASHIONABLE** ... *Styled For Wear Almost Everywhere!*
- **NEAT** ... *The Blouse Can't Slip Out!*
- **SMOOTH-FITTING** ... *Cut From Exacting Slip Patterns!*
- **PRACTICAL** ... *As Easy To Wash As a Regular Slip!*

Just slip into Slipmates — step into a skirt and you're smartly dressed! Wonderful for wear with a suit too! The blouse top is styled with the popular "bat" sleeves in soft interlock combed cotton jersey with a smart heather effect. Permanently attached is a runproof tricot rayon half slip that beautifully molds to your figure. A clever new idea — at an unbelievably low price.

Hurry to your favorite store for your Slipmates today!

Blouse tops in a choice of lovely heather tones.

GOLDEN ERA YELLOW • DRAMATIC RED • FLIGHT BLUE • GLAMOUR PINK
DYNAMIC GREEN • AUTUMN RUST • FROSTY WHITE

CREATORS OF
Suspants and min

Available at Knit Lingerie Departments and Specialty Shops or write

the genius of Peter Pan shapes a beautiful future!

There's a more exciting summer in store for you! Choose the Peter Pan strapless bra made to make you look your loveliest in all your bare-shoulder fashions:

FREEDOM RING† *(left)*, a new revolutionary *wired* bra that brings you peace of mind—unique spring action takes all irritating pressure off sensitive areas. Comes with Hidden Treasure or Inner Circle cup.

INNER CIRCLE * *(center)*, for the average or full-average bust. The exclusive Dura-form cup guarantees uplift that *keeps up* for the long life of the bra.

HIDDEN TREASURE * *(right)*, the most famous bra in the world, for the small bust or in-between size. The patented Magicup adds fullness *confidentially*, without pads or puffs.

PETER PAN FOUNDATIONS, INC.

FIFTH AVENUE, NEW YORK

MERRY-GO-ROUND OF CANADA. MONTREAL. QUEBEC

* REG. U. S. PAT. OFF. †PATS. PEN

Peter Pan Foundations, Inc., 1954

▶ *Sarong Girdles, 1956*　▶▶ *Whirlpool Bras, 1951*　▶▶▶ *Fredrick's of Hollywood, 195*

Style 124, high-waisted Sarong of light nylon power net and embroidered nylon marquisette. White, black or pink. Sizes 25 to 34. $13.50. Other styles from $7.95.

she's wearing a **sarong**®

the criss-cross girdle that walks and won't ride up

Sarong is completely different from any other girdle — and you'll feel the difference immediately!
There is nothing like a Sarong to fashion your figure with new shapeliness, to make comfort
your personal and permanent possession. Sarong is so wonderfully different!
Its patented, hidden construction lifts and flattens your tummy youthfully. Its exclusive
patented criss-cross feature lets you walk, stand and sit with day-long comfort.
From the moment you slip it on—you'll see and feel your figure improve.
Why not plan to have a Sarong fitted to your figure.

Free! Sarong's new booklet "Facts About Figures".

the registered trademark

sarong
the patented girdle

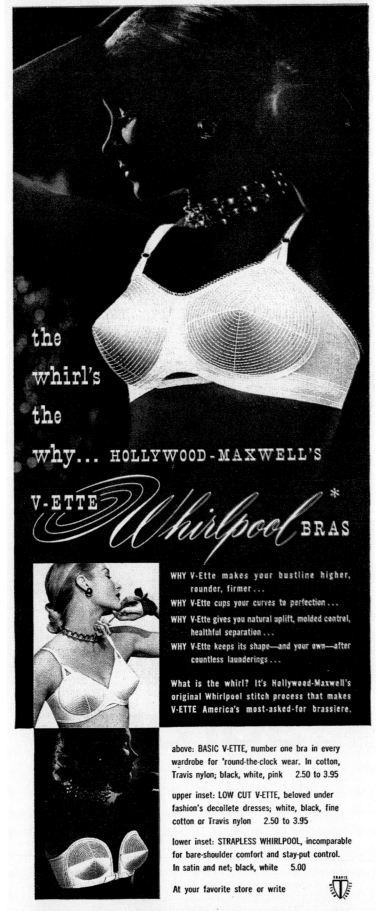

the
whirl's
the
why... HOLLYWOOD-MAXWELL'S

V-ETTE *Whirlpool* BRAS

WHY V-Ette makes your bustline higher,
    rounder, firmer...
WHY V-Ette cups your curves to perfection...
WHY V-Ette gives you natural uplift, molded control,
    healthful separation...
WHY V-Ette keeps its shape—and your own—after
    countless launderings...

What is the whirl? It's Hollywood-Maxwell's
original Whirlpool stitch process that makes
V-ETTE America's most-asked-for brassiere.

above: BASIC V-ETTE, number one bra in every
wardrobe for 'round-the-clock wear. In cotton,
Travis nylon; black, white, pink   2.50 to 3.95

upper inset: LOW CUT V-ETTE, beloved under
fashion's decollete dresses; white, black, fine
cotton or Travis nylon   2.50 to 3.95

lower inset: STRAPLESS WHIRLPOOL, incomparable
for bare-shoulder comfort and stay-put control.
In satin and net; black, white   5.00

At your favorite store or write

DON'T Give These to Your MOTHER *
*if she's over 25!

"Bare-As-You-Dare" LINGERIE from Hollywood

A. "FRENCH LACE" Bra & Panty SET. Filmy all-over lace. Daring! only $7.50

B. "SLEEPY TIME GAL" Pyjamas. Bare midriff; 2-piece. Satin with sheer and lace. NEW! only $11.98

C. "DREAM GIRL" Short nighty in see-thru sheer. Naughty but nice! only $6.98

D. "BEDTIME STORY" Enticing sheer nighty with French Lace trim. only $8.98

ALL STYLES: Finest rayon sheer with imported FRENCH LACE. She'll love them. Colors: Nude–Pink or Black–Mist. Both with BLACK Lace. All Sizes: 32 to 40.

FREDERICK'S of Hollywood
4742 W. Washington Blvd., Dept. 80
Los Angeles 16, California

HOW MANY	STYLE	PRICE	COLOR Nude or Black	Size 32 to 40
	A	$7.50		
	B	$11.98		
	C	$6.98		
	D	$8.98		

Gal's Bust Measure_____ Waist_____
I enclose payment; send postpaid. ☐   Send C. O. D. ☐

Name _____

Address _____

City _____ State _____

EVERY-PENNY-BACK GUARANTEE

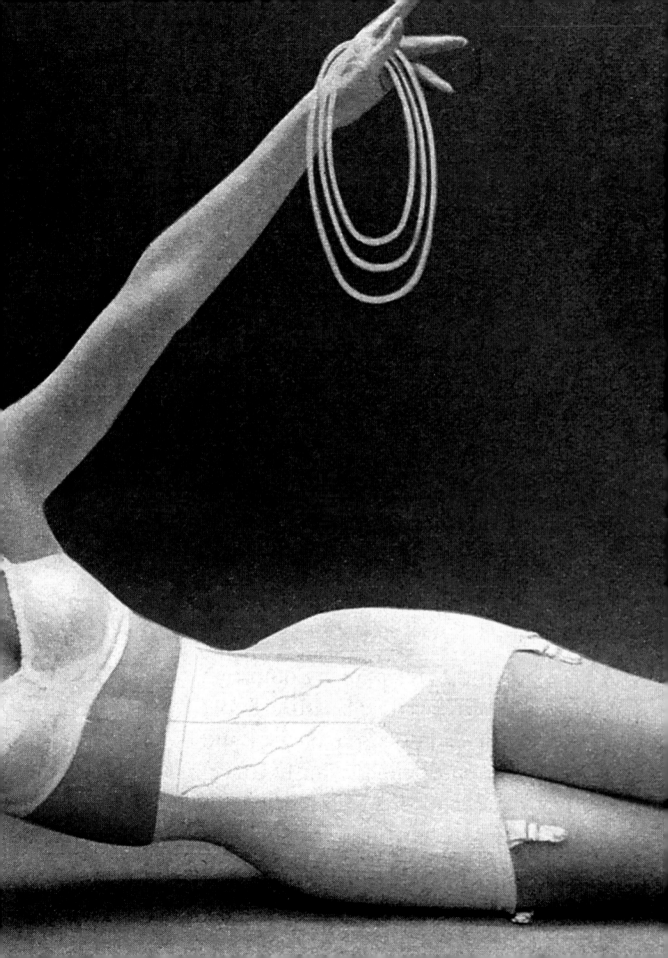

b.

a.

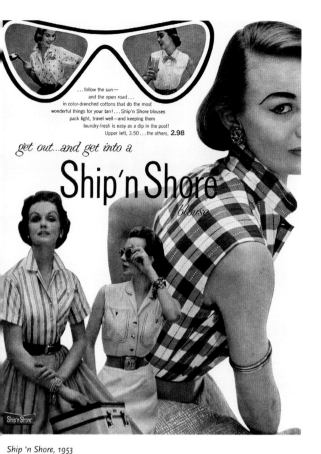

Ship 'n Shore, 1953

Avondale Cottons, 1959

Warner's Underwear, 1956 ◄◄ *Penney's, 1956* ◄ *Jonas Shoppes, 1952*

Gertz, 1952

there is only one
Pendleton Sportswear
always virgin wool

Gather your new Pendleton Skirts

For you... four distinctive virgin wool fabrics colorful as autumn's leaves... four branch-slim skirts tailored in the simple, flattering lines of good fashion that smart women always admire in a genuine Pendleton! Plan to gather this whole new skirt wardrobe soon, each but $12.95... with full-fashioned Pendleton sweaters in companion colors, from $8.95.

For descriptive literature, in full color, on Pendleton Sportswear, write Dept. D-6, Pendleton Woolen Mills • Portland, Oregon

Pendleton Sportswear, 1956

READY
TO WEAR
IN
33 MINUTES

fleece of
caprolan

Like a little girl, fleece of CAPROLAN is so washable. Colorful coats made of CAPROLAN are dry and ready to wear just 33 minutes after you put them in an automatic washer-dryer. They feel so nice, look so smart.

CAPROLAN is made to serve industrial and military uses, too. In tires, rope, conveyor belts and parachutes. Another product for the textile industry from Allied Chemical.

For the whole story on CAPROLAN textile fibers, write Dept. J, Allied Chemical, 261 Madison Avenue, New York.

CAPROLAN is Allied Chemical's trademark for its polyamide fiber

Allied Chemical, 1957

Warm & Sunny
When It's Icy Cold

BORGANA ★★★

...brilliant successor to Borgana. Most luxurious of all the like-furs, and more than ever "more like fur than fur itself." Silkier, softer, richer because it is the only like-fur that blends Darlan® with Orlon®. Seven new colors: Dawn Beige, Dusk Gray, Starlight Taupe, Celestial Blue, Shadow Brown, Night Black, Eclipse Charcoal... in misses, junior and petite sizes. Incomparably fashioned by the makers listed below.

a Borg fabric

Borgana, 1951

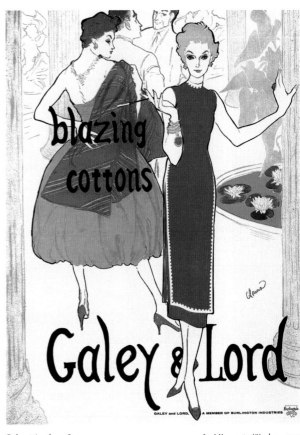

blazing cottons

Galey & Lord

GALEY and LORD, A MEMBER OF BURLINGTON INDUSTRIES

Galey & Lord, 1958   ▶ *Minnesota Woolens, 1959*

SALE! SPECIALLY PRICED! EXCITING NEW COTTONS

PHONE YOUR ORDER TODAY, SUNDAY, 1 P.M. TO 5 P.M. CALL PEnn. 6-5100

#895-201

#895-202

#895-204

#895-198

ALL 80 SQ. PERCALE!

1.99

TWO-PIECE CAPETTE SUNDRESS

2.99

Order Style #895-208

White laurel leaf trim border adds charm to this 80 sq. cotton dress. Detach the cape and you have a sundress. Navy, lavender, green, and luggage. Sizes 12 to 44.

Order Style #895-198

Coat dress, pique novelty collar. Fitted midriff. Red, blue, or green plaid. Sizes 14 to 44. .... 1.99
Same dress, same colors. Sizes 46 to 52. Order #895-200 ... 2.49

Order Style #895-201

Easy on—easy off, backwrap. Rickrack trim. Black ground floral print with lavender, gold or blue flowers. Sizes 14 to 42 ... 1.99

Order Style #895-202

¾ zipper. Rickrack trim. Two big pockets. Check pattern in red, blue, or green. 14 to 44 .... 1.99
Same dress, same colors. Sizes 46 to 52. Order #895-203 ... 2.49

Order Style #895-204

Buttons on shoulder, down side. Multicolor plaid in maize or blue. Sizes 14 to 44. .... 1.99
Same dress, same colors. Sizes 46 to 52. Order #895-205 ... 2.49

Glamorous POP-OVER

1.69

Order Style #895-206

Versatile 80 sq. percale apron smock. Lavender, rose, or blue flowers on a white floral ground print. Small (12 to 14), medium (16 to 18), large (20 to 40).

TWIN DOT ZIPPER HOUSECOAT

2.99

Order Style #895-209

Here's a dot of color and a dash of style you'll love to wear around the house! Red, blue, or green twin dots spark this washable, 80 sq. percale housecoat. Sizes 14 to 44.

Same housecoat, same colors, 46 to 52. Order style #895-210 ... 3.33

MAIL AND PHONE ON 2.01 OR MORE ALLOW TWO WEEKS FOR DELIVERY

GIMBELS BASEMENT, BOX 568, G.P.O., N.Y.C. # 1   NC-FR-2-3
Please send me the following: #895

QUAN.	ORDER #	PRICE	SIZE	COLOR	2nd COLOR

FULL NAME _____

ADDRESS _____ APT. # _____

CITY _____ ZONE # ____ STATE _____

AMT. ENCLOSED _____ CHARGE☐ CHECK☐ M.O.☐ C.O.D.☐
Outside delivery area, add 21c for shipping. For deliveries within N.Y.C. add 3% sales tax. Save high C.O.D. charges by sending check or money order.

SUBURBANITES, CALL HEMPSTEAD 7-2500, MOUNT VERNON 4-2920, HICKSVILLE 5-8250, GARDEN CITY 3-0200, WHITE PLAINS 6-7820 OR GREENWICH 8-4911

Gimbels Basement, 1952

▶ *Ray-Ban Sunglasses, 1954* ▶▶ *American Optical, 1959*

How to buy a pair of Sun Glasses

Off to a flying start...in new school styles from Sears!

Sears own exclusive brands are styled with authority:
BILTWEL · HONEYLANE
KERRYBROOKE · FRATERNITY PREP
GOLD BOND · BOYVILLE
Guaranteed and sold only by Sears

NEW CORDUROY CREATIONS FOR GIRLS!

A. The full-circle sweep of this new Honeylane skirt is even more dramatic in fall's newest color, star sapphire blue. The skirt, in washable fine wale corduroy, also comes in sophisticated black and favorite bright red. Plastic patent belt. Sizes 7-14, **2.49**
Sweet companion is the sissy front white cotton broadcloth blouse with peel johnny collar and tie. Front has 6 rows of crisp nylon pretzie lace, with ruffly lace on sleeves. Washable. Sizes 7-14, **2.49**

B. After-school fun calls for a Honeylane ear-coat jacket with toggle buttons, self-hook closings. Ivy-style patch pockets and a cozy collar that converts to a hood! Matching Italian style pants (note are length) have tapered legs, Ivy-style adjustable buckle back, hand top and zipper fly front ... a smartish side pocket, too! Both coat and pants are Sears fine wale washable corduroy. Mix or match 'em in star sapphire blue, red, or black. Sizes 7-14. Jacket, **4.98** Pants, **2.98**

C. Honeylane "Dutch Boy" suspender skirt can be worn with or without suspenders. Pegged skirt has soft, unpressed pleats. Washable, fine wale corduroy. Star sapphire blue, black, and red. Sizes 7-14, **3.98**
Cuddly Honeylane pullover in washable Orion* has the mock-turtle neck that's making sweater-set news ... plus special stitching to give a full fashioned look. Ribbat neck, cuffs and bottom band. Yellow, white, black, red, turquoise. Sizes 12-18, **2.98**

*DuPont virgin fiber

CLASSIC IVY LOOK STYLES FOR BOYS!

D. The big fellow wears Fraternity Prep Ivy-style trousers in all-wool flannel, with elastic book belt, no-pleats, tapered legs. Cambridge gray or charcoal gray, stripe or solid. Waist sizes 26-32, **6.98**
Classic Ivy-style dress shirt in Sanforized, combed cotton oxford cloth has button-down collar, back button and hand-pleated back. Sizes 6-20, white or blue, **2.49** Handsome Fraternity Prep sweater is washable, high-bulk virgin Orlon*. In 5 colors, sizes 12-18, **3.98**

E. Ivy-style Fraternity Prep trousers is sturdy, 9-oz. polished cotton are machine-washable, need little or no ironing. Flaxltten, book-belt style. Mineralized, Sanforized. Beige or black. Sizes 8-20, **2.98**
The very current long-sleeve Ivy sport shirt has button-down collar. Permo-Smooth finish on yarn-dyed combed cotton requires little or no ironing. In stripes of red, brown, or blue. Sizes 10-20, **2.49** Ivy-style, polished cotton cap to match trousers, **1.69**

F. Big style for little fellows! Boyville trousers of exclusive Orazon (rayon and acetate, 21% nylon sheen gabardine) are crease resistant, spot resistant and water repellent. Matching belt included. In skipper blue, charcoal, dark brown. Sizes 4-10, **2.98**
Ivy-stripes distinguish new Boyville short-sleeve sport shirt with button-down collar. Knit from combed cotton yarns for easy washability. Handsome assortment of styles and colors. Sizes 4-10, **1.79**

BILTWEL HONEYLANE KERRYBROOKE GOLD BOND FRATERNITY PREP BOYVILLE

Mix 'em, Match 'em! Wash 'em, Dry 'em! All girls' styles are designed so that any part of one ensemble will go with any other. Here, in these low-cost ensembles, is a complete school wardrobe...and it's all fully washable, another as clothes can be!

4 easy ways to buy school clothes at Sears—Purchases of $20 or more can be made on Sears Easy Payment Plan. Sears stores feature the Lay-Away Plan, or Credit Purchase Coupon Books you can use like cash. Many stores offer Sears Revolving Charge Accounts, too.

SATISFACTION GUARANTEED OR YOUR MONEY BACK

Shop at Sears and save

You'll enjoy shopping at Sears Stores and Sears Catalog Sales Offices. It's convenient to shop from the Sears Catalog in your home, too, by mail or phone. Sears employees, you know, are the largest owners of the Sears business. They'll do their best to serve you well.

SEARS ROEBUCK AND CO.

Biltwel Ivy-style saddle with smart strap and buckle in back. White with real brown, or black. **3.98**

"Toggle" shoe worn with strap up or colored-down in a pump. Grained leather. Black, red, black patent. **4.98**

Classic Biltwel slip-on mos has long wearing favorite sole. Red, brown or black Kerrybrooke-tenusen, too. **5.98**

Look, Mom, no laces! Boys' Biltwel with Slu-Lok® flap open, closed. Sizes guaranteed 4 months. Black, brown. **7.98**

Carefree, yet correct. Boys' Gold Bond Jelly foil slip-on in long-wearing, polished black or brown leather. **3.98**

Top grain leather. Brand new Biltwel "football toe." Seamless sole for long wear. Black or brown. **6.50**

Indian territory. Keep out!

Got a wild Indian in the upstairs half? Wise mothers save their scalps by keeping Indian braves well supplied with Carter's "TRIGS," well known for their peacemaker abilities. Their gentle fit. Their full coverage. Their soft cotton knit fabric, famous for long wear.
Mothers know, too, how Carter's knits wash without ironing, never stretch out of shape, because papooses are raised on Carter's. Your best wampum value in boys' underwear!

ABOVE: "TRIGS" SUPER T-SHIRT. Neoprene* sleeves. Nylon-set cotton. 2-12 yrs. $1.00. 14-20 yrs. $1.35. "TRIGS" BRIEF. Panel rib knit. Elastic waist. 2-12 yrs. 85¢. 14-20 yrs. 95¢. RIGHT: "TRIGS" MID-LENGTH. 2-12 yrs. $1.10. 14-20 yrs. $1.25. PLAID FRONT PAJAMA. Brushed cotton. Navy/blue. Brown/yellow. Cream/blue. 4-12 yrs. $3.50. 14-20 yrs. $4.00. All are Carter-Soft so won't shrink out of fit.

THE WILLIAM CARTER CO., NEEDHAM HEIGHTS, MASS.

Carter's

Look, mom, she's dancing!

Maybe it's not "Swan Lake," but it does help her express a brimful-of-fun personality! And maybe her new Carter's Ballerina print pajamas have something to do with this enthusiastic point of view. It's that fresh, just-scrubbed look that never needs an iron ... that special softness and warmth ... that gentleness of fit that identify Carter's cotton knits from prom to proms. Why not make your own ballerina dance for joy tomorrow ... over another pair of wonderful Carter's pajamas!

ABOVE: BALLERINA PRINT PAJAMA with solid-color pant. Ruffle trim, elasticized wrists and ankles. Pink, blue. 3-16 years. $4.00. RIGHT: VIOLET PRINT PAJAMA in brushed cotton knit. Pastel cutting trim, all-elastic waist. Blue, pink. 3-14 years. $4.00. All are Carter-Soft so won't shrink out of fit.

THE WILLIAM CARTER CO., NEEDHAM HEIGHTS, MASS.

Carter's

Visual Education~
with a "kick" that gets attention

Titan Tartans
75¢ the pair

Inter woven ®

BY THE LARGEST MANUFACTURER OF MEN'S SOCKS IN THE WORLD

a feast for the eyes!

What more could a man ask for! Just one touch of new, soft, smooth,
Vanuana Sport Shirts and you'll be humming "Sweet Leilani" all
season long. As luxurious and rich-looking as a tropical paradise . . . as
cool and exciting as a night in Waikiki. Sixteen bright, solid, South Sea
colors that dance before your eyes. Short sleeves. **$3.65** or long sleeves. **$4.50.**

Phillips-Jones Corp., N. Y. 1, N. Y., Makers of Van Heusen Shirts • Sport Shirts • Ties • Pajamas • Handkerchiefs • Collars

Van Heusen
REG T. M.
Vanuana sport shirts

McGregor, 1959

Van Heusen, 1951 ◄   Dan River, 1955

Now—Wrangler jeans in 6 exciting colors—wheat, light blue, turquoise, red, gray or charcoal. All color-fast Sanforized denim, sizes 10-18. Blouses, about 1.98

He can rough it in Wranglers! Heaviest denim with jam-proof zipper; sizes 4-16. Shirt, sizes 2-16, 3.49

Trim, tapered, terrific! | Blue Bell | Wrangler
Western jeans for all the family—2.98 to 3.98

Wranglers score with men of action! Bar tacks at points of strain, sizes 27-42. Shirt, sizes 14-17, 4.98

Youngsters live in Wranglers—regular or Dub-L-Knee. Sanforized denim. Shirt, sizes 2-16, 3.49

Champion Cowboys like Jim Shoulders prefer Wrangler jeans, jackets, shirts.

Remember—every Blue Bell garment carries the unconditional Qualitag guarantee

At your favorite store. Blue Bell, Inc., Empire State Bldg., New York—Canada, W. Hewick Mfg. Co., Montreal

Wrangler, 1956

Dickies, 1955

SUNLIGHT GIVES ZEST TO EVERYTHING...from cook-outs to cottons! And Dan River Sunshades seem to have sunlight woven right in! Colors and patterns radiate a special glow you've never seen in cottons. Plaids, checks, stripes and embroideries have fresh new fashion appeal. And these rare cottons are Wrinkl-Shed! Wrinkles hang out overnight; colors stay in for life. Designs are woven in! Ask for Dan River Sunshade cottons in fashions for the whole family, and by the yard. At all fine stores.

DAN RIVER
cottons in radiant new
SUNSHADES
they're Wrinkl-Shed

Bates Fabrics, 1952 ◄   *Dan River, 1957*

Fashion...a man's world, too

We owe a thank-you note to Nassau. Our stylist stopped
off there and was inspired to design these handsome prints for
surf and sand. Patterns like these, on completely washable,
"Sanforized" cotton, show the bold look men favor in their
beach wear. It's no wonder you'll find Arrow Casual Wear
worn at resorts wherever men prize distinctive styling.

Shirt, $3.95, Cabana sun shirt, $3.90, trunks, $5.00, beach jacket, $6.96, trunks, $3.95

ARROW — first in fashion
CASUAL WEAR   Cluett, Peabody & Co., Inc.

Arrow, 1956

How can a shirt that <u>looks</u> so good <u>feel</u> so good!

The answer's in the collar —the sensational new *Arafold* Collar! Here's how it works—

You see, Arafold has no seam, no collar band on the inside. This is for smooth comfort!

This amazing collar slopes so low on your neck you feel almost as free-and-easy as this.

Yet, buttoned, with a tie, Arafold is as smart a looking collar as you've ever worn!

IT'S ARROW'S NEW REVOLUTIONARY Arafold Collar!

You know how good it feels when you get home, loosen your tie and unbutton your collar? Man, that's comfort! Well, you're *practically* that comfortable *all day long* with Arafold! And you *still* have that well-groomed Arrow look.

Drop into your Arrow dealer's soon, ask to see Bi-Way with the Arafold Collar. Let him show you how this supremely comfortable collar works.

You'll find Arafold in a spread collar, a long-point collar, a button-down, a regular-point collar, and a rounded-point collar.

Of course, like all Arrow shirts, Bi-Way with the Arafold Collar is "Sanforized"-labeled, will never shrink out of fit. Buttons are anchored on to stay. Cluett, Peabody & Co., Inc. Arrow Shirts, Sports Shirts, Ties, Handkerchiefs, Underwear.

ARROW'S BI-WAY SHIRT with the new ARAFOLD COLLAR

Arrow, 1951

Washing won't faze this colorful new breed of rayon / **AVISCO** is the reason

This is Van Heusen's sport shirt of the year. It owes its soft sheen and appetite for brilliant colors to Avisco treated rayon.

"Sure," you say, "rayon looks great when it's new, but what happens when you wash it or rough it up?"

Good question. Not too long ago dry cleaning and pampering were the price of rayon's good looks

and fine feel. Avisco treated rayon wipes this costly price off the books for ever and a day. You can wash shirts of this wondrous new yarn week after week, just as you wash ordinary workaday shirts, and they'll come up brilliant of color, true to size and shape.

Avisco treated rayon stays clean longer because it's so hard to soil. There's a new toughness, too, in

these remarkable rayon fibers. Pays off at collar, in seam and around the buttonhole.

How can you be sure the shirts you buy will do all these things? Don't say "I'll take it" until you see the Avisco Integrity Tag. It's your assurance that quality goes all the way back to the fiber. Van Taj sport shirts by Van Heusen $3.95.

SEE VAN HEUSEN SHIRTS WITH THE AVISCO INTEGRITY TAG AT FINE STORES EVERYWHERE

AMERICAN VISCOSE CORPORATION, 350 FIFTH AVENUE, NEW YORK 1, N.Y.

Avisco, 1956

Give your beau an Arrow

This Valentine season, the strategy is the *spirited* approach. Perhaps a bold red is your weapon—crisp and exclusively Arrow in these miniature checks, dots, and stripes. Or, it may be an Arrow white shirt. Either way, he'll be pleased with the soft luxury of fine, Arrow "Sanforized" fabrics. Give your beau all *four* of these Arrows. You'll get his hearty compliment on your good taste and sense...at the very least!

Shirts, $6.00, All-silk Ties, $2.50, Hdkf., $.50 (Other Arrow Shirts $4 to $15.50)

ARROW — first in fashion
Cluett, Peabody & Co., Inc.

Arrow, 1958   ▶ *Arrow, 1951*

Wear an Arrow Shirt
and you'll simply sweep
her off her feet *!*

Smartly Tailored for Smart Relaxing

Look as good as you feel in your "easy-time" clothes!

These distinguished new Arrow Sports Shirts were made to give you casual comfort with the smartest style this side of Bikini. Tailored of a premium all-rayon fabric that's color-fast and WASHABLE, these eye-catching prints come in more color combinations than you can shake a palm leaf at!

Short sleeves, $5. Some with long sleeves, $5.95. Cluett, Peabody & Co., Inc.

Arrow Caribbean Prints

Another smartly styled ARROW SPORTS SHIRT

Arrow, 1953

With a Flair for casual smartness

Want comfort? Want good looks, too? Get yourself an Arrow Dude Ranch sport shirt. This collection includes beautifully tailored neat checks and plaids. It features the regular-length sports shirt collar, or new short points. (The collars on *all* Arrow sports shirts have the new *Arafold* construction that makes them look, fit, feel better.) Fabrics are colorfast, "Sanforized"® cottons. $5.95. Why not pick out a few now. Cluett, Peabody & Co., Inc.

Arrow dude ranch

Another smartly styled ARROW SPORTS SHIRT

Arrow, 1953

Put some romance in your "loaf life"!

ARROW Bali Cay

Whether you're taking a cruise to the Caribbean or just a week-end jaunt to the beach, do it with a splash! Add some *color* to the landscape; pick up an armful of Arrow *Bali Cay!*

These beauties are as colorful as a coral reef ... and just as washable! They come in big, splashy patterns and small, neat designs in both cotton and rayon fabrics. In short or long sleeves. And all have the amazing Arafold Collar. Prices about $4.50 and up. (Subject to government regulation.) See *Bali Cay* at your Arrow dealer's now!

Cluett, Peabody & Co., Inc., Arrow Shirts • Sports Shirts • Ties • Handkerchiefs • Underwear.

Arrow, 1952

Turning leaves splash the Autumn scene with spectacular hues...inspire new shirts with subtle stripes, lavish plaids in the

COLORS OF INDIAN SUMMER

...for the look of the leader

McGregor captures the brilliant changing landscapes of Fall —reaps a harvest of warm, glowing color—in a magnificent new shirt collection of luxurious, washable cotton by Dan River. (left) Kernel III—button-down, back-button, back-pleat Ivy Leaguer. $6.95. (right) Kernel II—new soft roll collar. Fine plaid on distinctive stripes. $6.95. (center) Kernel VI— woven-cotton pullover with fashion-knit collar. $6.95.

Lamb Fleece Cru Sweaters in the colors of Indian Summer. 75% luxurious lambswool for warmth without weight—25% rugged Orlon for washability, authentic crew-neck...terrific colors! Men's $7.95. Wee $4.98. Prep $5.98.

McGREGOR SPORTSWEAR

Also boy-sized, boy-priced
McGregor-Doniger Inc., 303 5th Ave., New York 16, N.Y.   *T.M.

McGregor Sportswear, 1957   ▶ McGregor Sportswear, 1954

c'mon in ... the wearing's fine

Completely washable! They take to water like a mermaid. We're talking about
the new—and we mean *new!*—Van Gab sport shirts. *Gabardine* ... like you've nev
seen! *Silky-smooth gabardine* ... with a new luxurious softness! *Finer-woven gabar*
... that wears and wears and wears! We've tailored this fine fabric with
famous Van Heusen magic sewmanship. Full-cut for action ... figure-tapered for l
Shown here is famous California Lo-No model with exclusive two-way collar
... smart with or without a tie. Completely washable, stays size-right, color-fast. **$**
See Van Gab gabardine in other smart models—$2.95 to $5.95

The ties: Van Heusen Washable Poplin in 100% Nylon, 18 solid-color Sportones...$1.50 each.
Phillips-Jones Corp., New York 1. Makers of Van Heusen Shirts • Ties • Pajamas • Collars • Sport Shirts

...ok at those collars again! California Lo-No with "Fadeaway Collarband". Looks, fits right ... with or without tie.   Season's biggest splash of color with 21 bright, new washable "Aquashades".

| ...nset Red | Sea Clay | Shell Pink | Mermaid Mauve | Mist Grey | Tropi-Tan | Dune Tan | Ocean Blue | Sky Blue | Billow Blue | Pirate Gold | Sand Tan | Beach Beige | Deep Green | Briny Green | Gulf Green | Spray Green | Turtle Green | Sunglow Yellow | Oyster | Foam White |

Van Heusen ®

REG. T. M.

new Van Gab Sport **Shirts** ... *Completely washable* ... $4.95

"Did you say 'Sports Shirts'?"

A 1912 model sportsman exchanges stares with his 1951 counterpart! BOTH are the best-dressed men of their day. BOTH wear Arrow. But what a difference! The early Arrow Collar Man had *Style*. Ditto today's Arrow Sports Shirt Man—with *easy, casual* COMFORT added!

Bali Cay! _Beautiful_, _colorful_ "Island Prints"!

hen the sun is high, men turn to Arrow sports irts! Here are the coolest, most comfortable, ost colorful on the horizon. New leafy patterns . Hawaiian prints . . . brilliant flower designs . and many others inspired by tropical isles. u'll look your best, FEEL your best in these

style-packed Bali Cays—cut free for action and comfort! All completely washable—won't shrink out of fit.

ALL ARROW sports shirts have the revolutionary new Arafold collar. *See* it! *Wear* it! Cluett, Peabody & Co., Inc.

ARROW
Bali Cay
SPORTS SHIRTS

Starting our second 100 years of Style Leadership

Arrow, 1951

Now you can be cooler than she is!

Tri-Tone rayon linen shirt $3.95. Denim walk shorts $2.95.

This is the age of
Wings

LIGHTWEIGHT SPORT SHIRTS FOR MEN AND BOYS

At value minded stores everywhere or write: WINGS • 4 W. 33rd St., New York 1

Wings, 1954

you can't see a
stitch on collar
cuffs and front

Get into the swim . . . get into Van Chick — newest sensation in shirts! Stitches are hidden to give you the coolest, smoothest look in town. And that Van Heusen "Comfort Contour" collar is as refreshing as a morning dip. White, colors, stripes—single or French cuffs. In broadcloth, **$3.95**; in Oxford, **$4.50**

A new shirt free if your Van Heusen shrinks out of size. Tie: Van Heusen Van Chick Shirt-mate, $1.50

Phillips-Jones Corp., N.Y. 1, N.Y., Makers of Van Heusen Shirts • Sport Shirts • Ties • Pajamas Handkerchiefs • Underwear • Swimwear • Collars *. . . and the famous Van Heusen Century Shirt with the soft collar that won't wrinkle ever.*

Van Heusen
"the world's smartest"
shirts

not a stitch in sight . . .
on
the
new
Van Chick

In colors, whites and stripes

Van Heusen, 1950 ◀   Van Heusen, 1952

. . . every day is Father's Day
with
FRUIT OF THE LOOM

DRESS SHIRTS
SPORT SHIRTS
PAJAMAS
NIGHT SHIRTS
TEE SHIRTS
BOXER SHORTS
BRIEFS
UNION SUITS

Guaranteed . . . to make him look and feel his best every day of the year. That's what the Fruit of the Loom label means on your Dad's gift!

Guaranteed . . . to win Dad's smile of approval . . . for color, comfort, styling, wear and washability. For the happiest Father's Day ever, choose Fruit of the Loom, for products of guaranteed quality . . . always sensibly priced.

FRUIT OF THE LOOM
A Family of American Products for the American Family
1450 Broadway, New York 18, N. Y.

GUARANTEE
If this Fruit of the Loom product does not give you satisfaction in use, return it to us and you will receive a new one or a refund of the purchase price.
FRUIT OF THE LOOM INC.
PROVIDENCE, R.I.

Fruit Of The Loom, 1950   ▶ Westminster Socks, 1950

STRIKE!

WESTMINSTER SOCKS
SCORE WITH MEN

for

closer

harmo

new school of design in ties

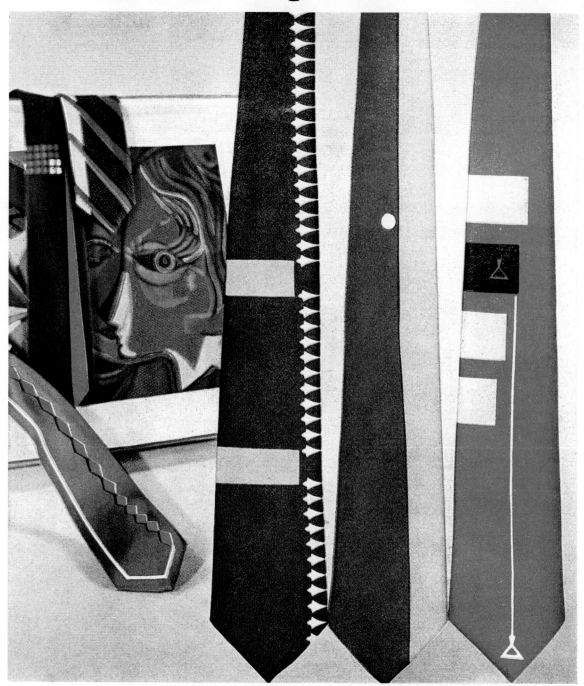

"side glances"

Manhattan combines the conservative and the unusual in a refreshing new note in printed acetate foulard neckwear. These new "Side Glance" ties offer distinctive designs—with the focus of interest on one side of the tie! In a wide array of color combinations—from bright to subdued.

Van Heusen Ties, 1950 ◄ *Manhattan Ties, 1953*　　　　► *Manhattan Ties, 1953* ►► *Haband Ties, 1950*

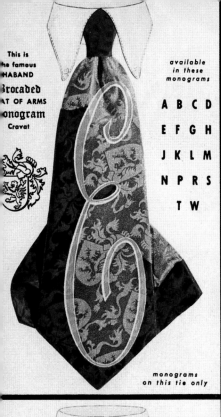

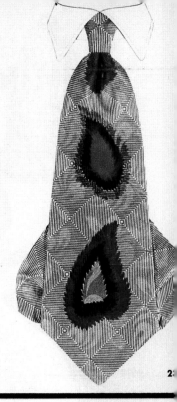

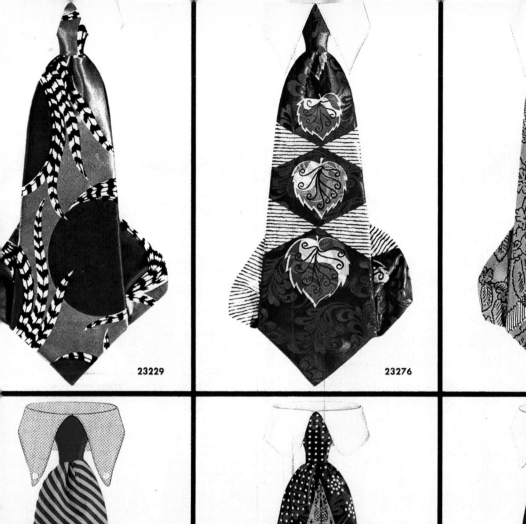

23229

23276

23291

23324

23328

and
SOLID
COLORS
in
NYLON

MAROON — 3
ROYAL — 3
NAVY — 3
BROWN — 3
GREEN — 3
BLACK — 3

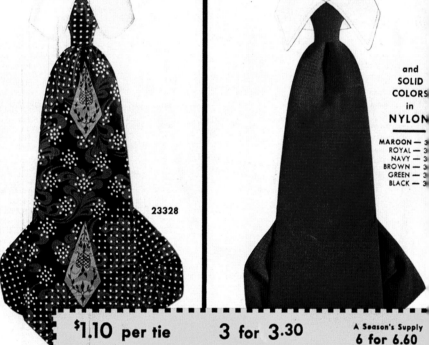
r Jot Down the Numbers you would like to wear and send them to the
with your remittance. The ties will reach you by return mail, bring-
thrill and satisfaction because you will find them more than you
n body fullness, color depth and dollars and cents value—none of
be shown in any picture. But, if for any reason you don't want to
n, you need only send them back to have your money refunded with
atch. Economical handling requires a minimum order of 3 ties. But
season's supply, and receive with that order a timely gift of a 1951
e Desk Calendar. Or, with Christmas coming on, take every tie
2) plus the Desk Piece for only $13.20.

BUY 6 TIES and get this FREE

GIRL DESK CALENDAR—1951 approximately 5½"x6¼"—Easel Type Desk Calendar.
Two tone simulated embossed leather frame. Sep-
r card or page for every month, and on each one a new Esquire Girl picture in full color.
ADVERTISING MATTER OF ANY KIND APPEARS ANYWHERE ON THIS GIFT

For your leisure pleasure

Q: When is a sport coat really a sport coat?

A: When its sporty spirit is definitely defined by good taste. When it doesn't go overboard with bold patterns and wild weaves. When its fabric, color, cut and comfort give you a feeling of well-being at being well-dressed. In short, when it's a sport coat of thoroughbred quality by Hart Schaffner & Marx.

Q: What about prices?

A: Most reasonable...just a trifle more for so much more...the correctness you always get in HS&M sport coats. They're naturals with HS&M slacks, of course. And vice versa!

HART SCHAFFNER & MARX

Hart Schaffner & Marx, 1951

how to weather summer

A lot of men today will say that summers don't seem to be as hot as they were. Could it be that so many of them own Bengaline Dixie Weave® suits? The lightweight fabric has an ingenious twist to its yarns that prevents them from meshing together. On the one hand it is porous and cool. On the other it resists wrinkling and permits fine tailoring.

You will find it only where Hart Schaffner & Marx clothes are sold.

This cool, flattering color is the new "Summer Blue"... shown in the tall, trim TREND model.

HART SCHAFFNER & MARX

Hart Schaffner & Marx, 1953

make like Nero in...

QUO VADIS shorts

...speed up the process by showing your "empress" this page

A minute after she sees this page she'll chariot off to buy you Munsingwear's exclusive QUO VADIS shorts. The gay designs are plucked right out of the dazzling motion picture of spectacular Roman days. Poor toga clad Nero never knew the smart comfort of these full-cut rayon boxer shorts. They're in the happiest patterns you ever saw. If she doesn't come through...get 'em yourself. $2

Inspired by M.G.M's great technicolor motion picture. An authentic QUO VADIS fashion, exclusive fabric by

KNICKERBOCKER *textile corp.*

Eight fiery patterns blazing with color

MUNSINGWEAR
at better stores everywhere

Hart Schaffner & Marx, 1950 ◄ *Munsingwear, 1951*

make like a medicine man

...in **Voodoo Shorts**

Munsingwear gives you a chance to show *her*...you can be just as wild and original with your shorts as she is with her hats. Primitive designs, mysterious as the jungle. Loud, laughing colors that seem to chant a reckless rhythm. Only Munsingwear brings you these Voodoo-Print boxer shorts. In fine rayon, sizes 30-42. $2

1. CROMANTI (jungle dance)—royal blue, red, brown, gray.

2. DJUKA (bushman tribe)—gray, maize, green, wine.

3. VODU (guardian spirit)—red, gray, maize, royal blue, brown.

4. GABUN (primitive masks)—gray, royal blue, brown, red, maize.

MUNSINGWEAR
at better stores everywhere

P.S. *to the ladies...on his day, June 17... give the chief of your tribe Voodoo Print boxer shorts.*

Munsingwear, 1951

You'll steal the show in Plateau—
the suit with the "weightless feel"—$65

Here's a suit that never gives you the weighed-down, restricted feeling that ordinary suits do. Made of rich, lustrous 100% worsted—an exclusive Pacific fabric that has been pre-laxed in the loom to remove tension and give you that "weightless feel." Plateau suits, with "Balanced Tailoring" by Timely Clothes, are available

in nine handsome colors. Ask to see them at leading stores throughout the country.

Free Booklet gives you valuable information about selecting fabrics. Drop a card to Pacific Mills, Worsted Division, Dept. L9, 261 Fifth Avenue, New York 16 or Timely Clothes, Inc., Dept. G9, Rochester 2, New York.

It's a *PACIFIC* fabric BY PACIFIC MILLS...WEAVERS OF FINE WORSTEDS, WOOLENS, COTTONS AND RAYONS

Pacific Fabric, 1950

We took a tip
from an engineer

The soft, fine fibers in this famous *Manhattan* Span Collar are twisted like the steel cables of a bridge. This means greater strength, longer life. In fact, if this collar doesn't outlast the rest of the shirt, *we'll give you a new one free!*

Shirt $3.95* Tie $2.50*

Manhattan
THE MARK OF QUALITY SINCE 1857

Manhattan Shirts, 1951

We'll buy you a new shirt if this "Manhattan" Span Collar doesn't outlast the rest of the shirt

The Span is specially constructed (the fibres are twisted like steel cables) for men who are extra-rough on collars... in a regular point collar style, either fused, or soft with angle stays.

$4.50

Manhattan
THE MARK OF QUALITY SINCE 1857
THE "MANHATTAN" TIE—$1.50

Manhattan Shirts, 1951

Stars in stripes
(and solid hits too!)

Introducing our newest fashion "trio" of woven stripes and solids! They offer three different ways to spotlight your favorite suit. Made of luxurious, long-living broadcloth. Tailored to make you a "headliner." Styled in blue, tan, green and grey. Shirts $4.50* Ties $2.50*

Manhattan

Manhattan Shirts, 1951

HATS—As healthy as they're handsome

RICO TOMASO

THE SOMBRERO—Originally introduced into Latin America by the Spaniards. Its name is taken from the word *sombra*, meaning shade. And a wonderful sun-shade it makes! It's cool, eye- and head-protecting, whether embroidered with colorful threads or decorated with jangling silver.

No MATTER WHERE YOU LIVE—South or North of the Border—the primary purpose of your hat is to *protect* you. In summer, its brim protects your eyes from aching glare; in winter, it protects your head from icy blasts. It guards your hair from the drying effects of the sun's rays, and keeps city soot out of your scalp. More things than sunstroke can happen to men who go bareheaded! Why ask for trouble when one of the handsomest pieces of apparel you can wear is a hat. Your dealer has handsome hats just suited to you. They are *right* for the occasion—wherever you go, or play, or work.

"Wear a Hat—It's as Healthy as It's Handsome!"

HATS — As healthy as they're handsome

THE HAVELOCK—The invention of Sir Henry Havelock of the British Army in India about 1850. Also known as the "kepi" and "forage cap" in other armies. The havelock shown here is worn by a French legionnaire. It's a handsome hat whose primary purpose is protection, to protect the back of the wearer's head and neck from the dangerous direct rays of the tropical sun.

No matter where you live—in New York or New Caledonia—the purpose of your hat is to protect your eyes from glare, your hair from sun and soot, your head from icy blasts. That's the *primary* purpose of a hat. Don't go bareheaded—it simply isn't a very wise thing to do.

It's unkind to your sinuses, and definitely unkind to the hair on your head. There's a handsome hat waiting to improve your appearance—and to protect your head. Styled in shape and color to the moment, there's a *right* hat for the occasion wherever you go, or play, or work.

"Wear a Hat — It's as Healthy as It's Handsome!"

Hats, 1952

HATS — As healthy as they're handsome

THE "TEN GALLON"—The traditional hat of the Western plains has many functions. Its broad brim keeps glare out of the wearer's eyes and the high crown protects his head from the burning sun. It has been used as a pillow, fire-fanner, and drinking cup!

Whether you punch cows or punch a clock, never forget the primary purpose of a hat—to *protect* you. A hat shades your eyes from aching glare, keeps sun and city soot off your hair, and guards your head against icy blasts. That's why when you go bare-headed you're just asking for trouble. It's foolish—especially when there is a handsome, well-styled hat just waiting to improve your appearance. Look in your dealer's window—he has a hat designed *right* for any occasion, wherever you go, or play, or work.

"Wear a Hat — It's as Healthy as It's Handsome!"

Hats, 1952

HATS — As healthy as they're handsome

THE KUFIYAH—The sons of the desert have worn these since time immemorial. The Sheik's headdress pictured here is handsome and costly example, yet primarily, its purpose is protection. The loose folds protect the head from the burning sun. The front part is pulled down to guard the eyes from glare and, on the desert, the folds are wrapped around the face as a protection against flying sand and chill of desert nights.

The primary purpose of *any* hat—Kufiyah or snap-brim—is to *protect* you. It protects your eyes from glare, your head from icy blasts, your hair from burning sun and city soot. As a simple health precaution—*it's wise to wear a hat.* Especially since hats are handsome, too. Look in your dealer's window. There's a styled-to-the-minute hat to complement the clothes you wear. There's a *right* hat for every occasion—wherever you go, or play, or work.

"Wear a Hat — It's as Healthy as It's Handsome!"

Hats, 1952 ◄   *Hats, 1952*

HATS — As healthy as they're handsome

THE SOLA TOPEE—The Indian sun helmet was first developed by the British Army in the early 19th Century. One of the world's most distinguished looking hats, it is white on the outside to reflect the sun, green-lined to help rest the eyes, and is filled with the light, porous pith of the Indian spongewood tree, to insulate against the heat rays of the sun.

Your hat, too, is meant to protect you. It protects your hair from sun and soot, guards your eyes from painful glare, wards off the cold that can chill your head as well as your feet. Just as a practical matter—*it's wise to wear a hat.* It is rewarding, too. There's a healthy, appearance-improving hat waiting for you right now. In color and styling, it's *right* for the occasion—wherever you go, or play, or work.

"Wear a Hat — It's as Healthy as It's Handsome!"

Hats, 1952   ▶ *Jockey Underwear, 1950* ▶▶ *Jockey Underwear, 1950*

Don't Settle for Less!

Feel like a million!

Why accept less when you can be sure of complete comfort with Jockey Underwear! It fits snug as your skin, moves as you move, gives you positive masculine support. Look for the mark, "Y-Front," on the garment— it's your assurance that you're getting the famous Coopers product— and one of many reasons why Jockey gives you a real lift. See your dealer soon—be "Hip-Taped" for perfect fit—then do as millions do —feel like a million in Jockey brand Underwear!

Comfort for Your Every Need—for Every Occasion

Jockey Shorts for active sports

Jockey Midway for everyday wear

Jockey Over-Knee for upper-leg protection

Jockey Longs for full-leg protection

Jockey Bellin for dress-up wear

WEAR
Jockey*
Underwear made ONLY by

Coopers

The Famous Brand of Knit Support Underwear

Also Jockey Brand Underw in Childre Sizes

Christmas just isn't Christmas without a family... of Dobbs hats.

Family man, sportsman, businessman. For all his interests there's the perfect Dobbs hat. Our many-sided man, below, is wearing a Dobbs velour Tyrolean. $20. (Ornaments extra.) There's the new Dobbs Two-Tone* Gamebird. Unique for town and country. $15. For evenings, the sophisticated Dobbs Black Homburg. $13.50 to $20. This year make his Christmas a Dobbs Christmas. Dobbs hats available at fine stores throughout the United States. Also Canada. $10.95 to $100. Dobbs, Park Ave. at 49th St., N.Y.
*U. S. Pat. #2,844,823 and other patents pending.

Dobbs is so easy to give when you give him a Dobbs gift certificate. Let him choose the style and color he wants. Dobbs gift certificates come packaged with unusual miniature Santa Claus cap.

Dobbs Hats, 1958

Cosmopolitan - the man who wears the Stetson with the Mode Edge

Wherever you are you're right in style wearing a Stetson with the famous Mode Edge. It's a sign of fine craftsmanship for those who demand the custom touch. Here you see the Stetson Sussex with the Mode Edge...a hat designed for the trend towards the slimmer, trimmer silhouette. New smart colors with contrasting bands. The Stetson Sussex—$15. Other Stetson styles with the Mode Edge—$15 and $20.

The STETSON is part of the man

The Stetson "Cushioned-To-Fit" leather has been the standard of hat comfort for over 70 years.
Stetson Hats are made only by John B. Stetson Company, and its affiliated companies throughout the world.

Stetson Hats, 1954

the new neat look

Look at it from every angle. The *Stetson Ivy League* gives you that *neat* look—trim, crisp, wide-awake. The face-flattering narrow brim, the tapered crown and the stylish center crease make it the favorite of men with a future.

the STETSON is part of the man

The Stetson "Cushioned-to-fit" leather has been the standard of hat comfort for over 70 years.
Stetson hats are made only by the John B. Stetson Company and its affiliated companies throughout the world.

Stetson Hats, 1953

The Fall American Look

It's a look of unwrinkled neatness and casual comfort

e-x-p-a-n-d-s

ONE SIZE FITS ALL

EXCLUSIVE WITH ESQUIRE SOCKS *"The smartest thing on two feet"*

ORDINARY SOCKS look like this

e-x-p-a-n-d-s socks fit like this . . . forever, because only e-x-p-a-n-d-s all-nylon socks fit as though custom-knit for you alone.

"10-2-14" RIB — The original e-x-p-a-n-d-s rib in a year-round weight. "SENATOR" — Specially patterned clock in flat knit e-x-p-a-n-d-s. "VEEP" — Heavier gauge link 'n link design e-x-p-a-n-d-s.

Individually Gift Boxed
The perfect gift . . . guaranteed for one year against holes caused by wear.

Walk-Over Broadmoor Brogue No. 3490

THE FALL AMERICAN LOOK

DIV. OF CHESTER H. ROTH CO., INC.

ask for the Stetson Ivy League, $10

Crowning touch to the "Neat Look"

For young men with their eyes on the future, here's the hat that says you're going places. Those trim lines, the crisp snap of the narrow brim, the tapered crown, and the stylish center crease give you that wide-awake, alert look. You're on the way up—in the *Stetson Ivy League*. It's Aquanized*, too, to shed showers!

the STETSON is part of the man

The Stetson "Cushioned-to-fit" leather has been the standard of hat comfort for over 70 years.
Stetson hats are made only by the John B. Stetson Company and its affiliated companies throughout the world.

Stetson Hats, 1954

Wembley *fashions*

Sea, Sand and Sun

1^{50} - $2

Each beautiful pattern
in six different
Spring color combinations.

For the Man in Her Life

Wembley

REG. U. S. PAT. OFF.—COPYRIGHT 1951 WEMBLEY, INC.

Wembley Ties are approved for fashion by Men's Fashion Guild ● For name of store nearest you, write Wembley, Inc., Empire State Building, New York

Wembley Ties, 1951

TRY THIS ON FOR SIGHS!

An Arrow Shirt does something for a guy that does something to the gals.

Maybe they figure any man that's so neatly groomed would be just as neat around the house. Maybe that virile Mitoga-tailored fit.

Or maybe they're sure any man who insists on the "Sanforized" label (fabric shrinkage less than 1%), anchored buttons, and the *value* in every Arrow Shirt is sure to be a good provider! Whatever it is, it's *wonderful!*

The shirt being admired is *Par* (above), soft, spread collar...regular or French cuffs. $3.65. If you like a non-wilt collar, you pick *Dart*, $3.65; *Mall* (in finer broadcloth), $3.95; or *Dale* (premium broadcloth), $4.50. *Drew* has medium-short points, low neckband, $3.65.

Tie Note—These shirts will look even handsomer with Arrow's luxurious new *Royalty Satin Ties* (shown) in popular paisley patterns! $2.00 each.

ARROW SHIRTS and TIES

>>>> Cluett, Peabody & Co., Inc., Makers of Arrow Shirts, Ties, Sports Shirts, Handkerchiefs, Underwear.

Arrow Shirts, 1950

GUARANTEED

FRUIT OF THE LOOM
UNDERWEAR

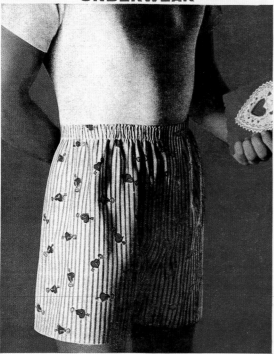

The Short Valentine that lasts so long!

The neat key-in-heart pattern captures the Valentine spirit in these boxer shorts. And Fruit of the Loom's practical features guarantee a satisfied sweetheart: Sanforized high-count cotton broadcloth. Extra-rugged at stress points. Lasting fit through countless washings. Unconditionally guaranteed. Priced so right, too, you'll want to give him a boxful! Win an extra hug — include Fruit of the Loom tee or athletic shirts.

49¢
Athletic Shirts,
Box of 6: $2.90

69¢
Sanforized Shorts, Tee Shirts, Briefs.
Box of 6: $4.10

Boys' Shorts 59c, 6 for $3.50;
Boys' Tee Shirts and Briefs 49c, 6 for $2.90;
Boys' Athletic Shirts 39c, 6 for $2.30. Sizes 2-16

GUARANTEE
If this Fruit of the Loom product does not give you satisfaction in use, return it to us and you will receive a new one or a refund of the purchase price.
FRUIT OF THE LOOM
PROVIDENCE R. I.

More men and boys wear FRUIT OF THE LOOM underwear than any other brand!   EMPIRE STATE BUILDING, NEW YORK 1, NEW YORK

Be well turned out when you turn in

WELDON
PAJAMAS

Fun For ALL...And ALL For Fun

. . . in Weldon's gay . . . colorful . . . happily comfortable "Islander" Pajamas . . . just the ticket for a pleasant evening of playing the Pajama Game together. Everyone looks and feels their free and easy best in these wonderful authentic Caribbean styled pajamas made in fine broadcloth . . . so handsome for lounging . . . so marvelous for sleeping. Multicolor striped shirt tail top with new Caribbean collar . . . solid color red or blue tapered trouser. Available in sizes for the entire family. "Islander" is but one of the many new Weldon Pajama styles . . . inspired by The Pajama Game . . . and now available at your favorite pajama counter . . . popularly priced from $3.95 to $6.95.

"Islander" style illustrated above:
Men's and Women's sizes about $6.95
Boy's and Girl's sizes about $5.00

WELDON PAJAMAS, INC. • EMPIRE STATE BLDG. • NEW YORK 1

Fruit Of The Loom, 1958

Weldon Pajamas, 1957   ▶ *Manhattan Pajamas, 1952*

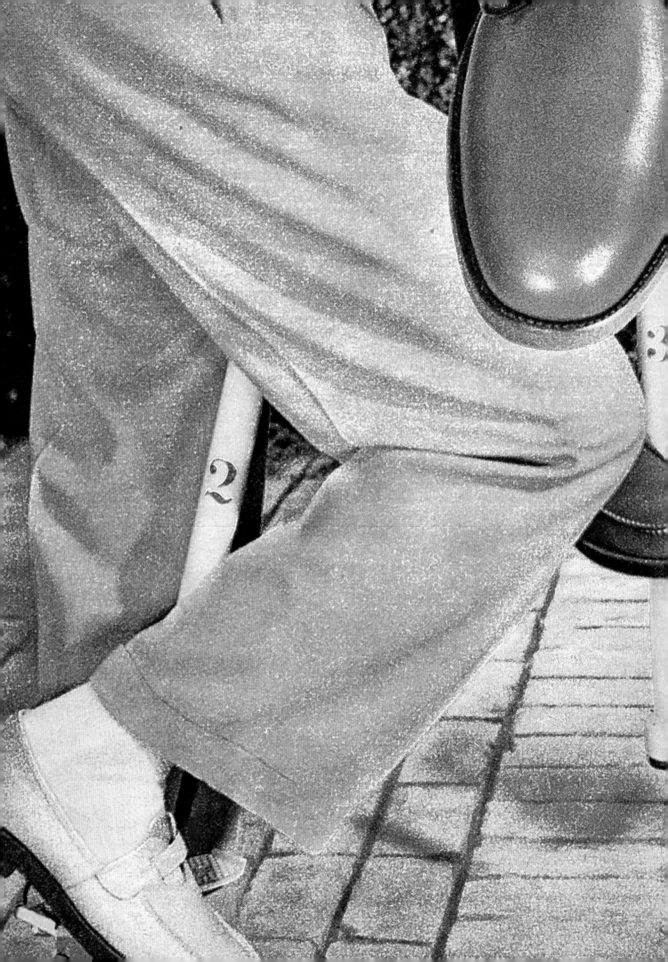

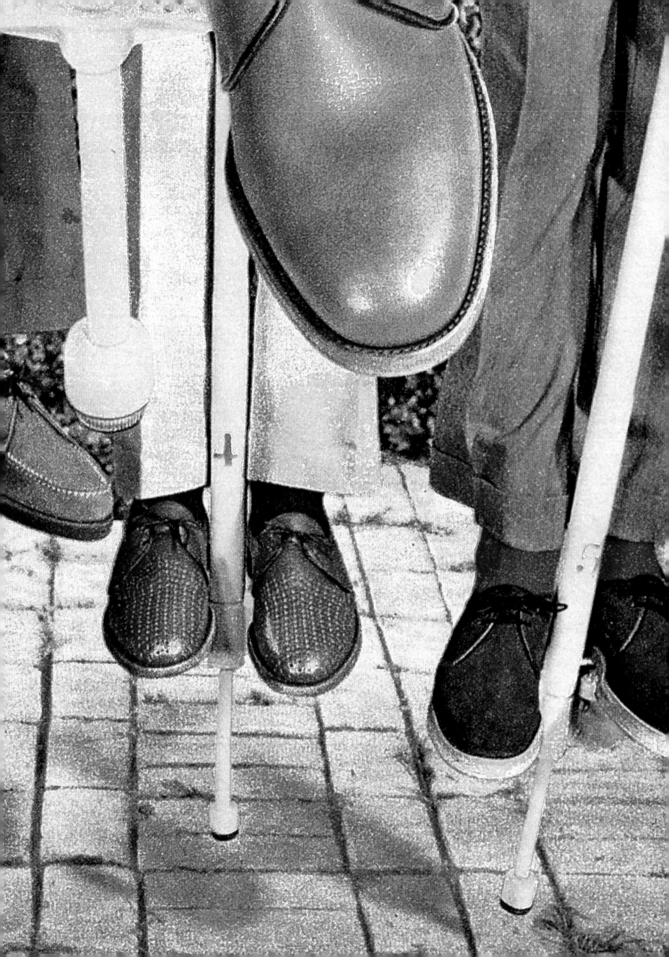

Style #9291
Classic Summer style. Dressy wing tip, with flexible leather sole.

Style #9759
Smart ventilated style. Moccasin toe for extra foot freedom. Fine leather sole.

Style #9610
Genuine Nylon Mesh inlay. Flexible leather sole. Feather-light and wonderfully cool.

Freshen up...

FROM THE GROUND UP...IN

America's No.1 Shoe

Thom McAn's prices for style-right, summer-right shoe values are so down-to-earth that you *can* afford to stride through any summer scene looking and feeling like a cool, cool million! There's a reason for Thom McAn's sensible prices: Thom McAn is America's largest manufacturer-retailer of men's shoes. Huge production brought directly to you through Thom McAn's own retail stores, means big savings which are passed along to *you*. No wonder so many men are buying two pairs of Thom McAns—for less money than they previously spent for only one pair of high-priced shoes.

See them—try them—and you, too, will say:

    "I don't see how they make them for the money."

Thom McAn $7⁹⁵ AND $8⁹⁵

WORN BY MORE MEN THAN ANY OTHER SHOE   **MOST STYLES**

THOM McAN IS A DIVISION OF MELVILLE SHOE CORPORATION

Mansfield Shoes, 1957 ◄   *Thom McAn Shoes, 1951*

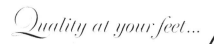

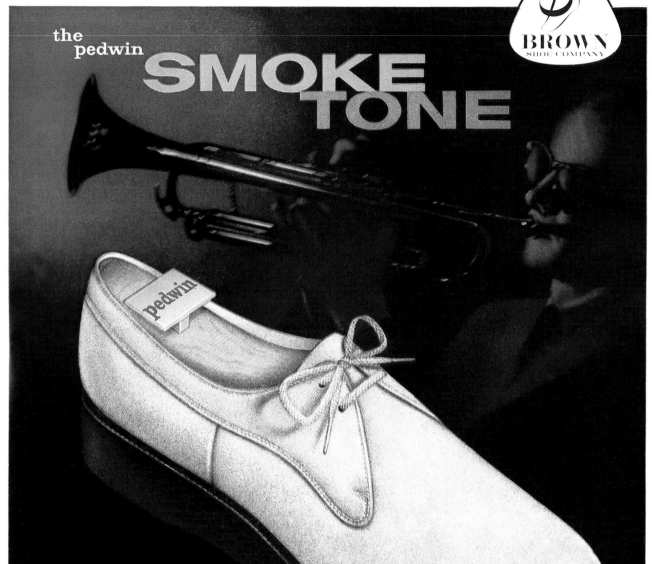

the **pedwin**

SMOKE TONE

Soft casual shoe with a bold look. Comfortable two-eyelet with cushioned crepe wedge sole. Also in Oyster Shag or Dark Grey. Pedwin Division, Brown Shoe Company, St. Louis.

Shoe Illustrated **10.95** Other styles 8.95 to 11.95.

Pedwin, Jrs., for boys, 7.95 to 9.95. All styles Higher Denver West

pedwin®

young ideas in shoes

bobri

In 13000 BC smart women wore nothing.

In 1957 AD smart women wear nothing but **seamless** stockings by *Hanes*

no seams to worry about

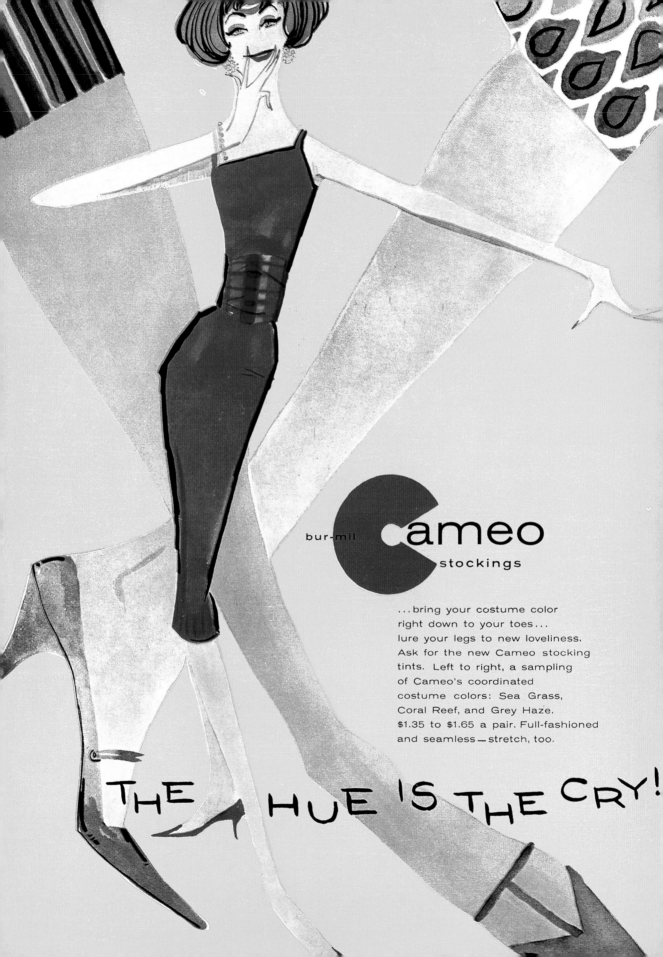

Keds Shoes, 1951

Keds Shoes, 1956

Commodores Shoes, 1952

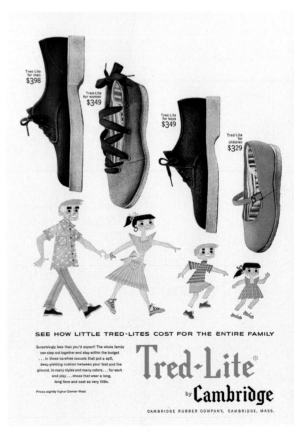

Tred-Lite Shoes, 1954

Soft Illusions... fantastically soft pumps that weigh less than five ounces..... have super-cushioned soles ...and fit like Naturalizers always do.

Soft Illusions
by Naturalizer
High or mid heels in
a variety of colors... in
gossamer-light glacé calf.
Also in Deldi silk suede.

Naturalizer
THE SHOE WITH THE BEAUTIFUL FIT

Naturalizer Shoes, 1958

WALKING SHEER   DRESS SHEER   EVENING SHEER

there's a **time** and a **place**

for all three sheers... in today's lovely stockings of DuPont Nylon

DU PONT

DU PONT NYLON

DuPont Nylon, 1956

Quality at your feet

BROWN
SHOE COMPANY

you can't tell
the mothers from
the daughters in
mother-daughter classics

westports by *life stride*

Life Stride Shoes, 1951

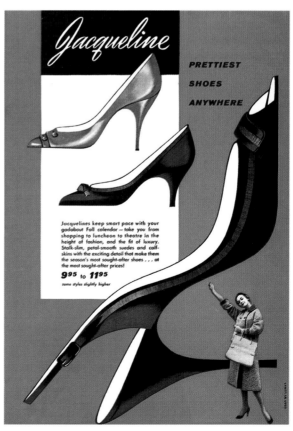

Jacqueline

PRETTIEST
SHOES
ANYWHERE

Jacquelines keep smart pace with your gadabout Fall calendar — take you from shopping to luncheon to theatre in the height of fashion, and the fit of luxury. Stalk-slim, petal-smooth suedes and calf-skins with the exciting detail that make them the season's most sought-after shoes... at the most sought-after prices!
9.95 to 11.95
some styles slightly higher

Jacqueline Shoes, 1956

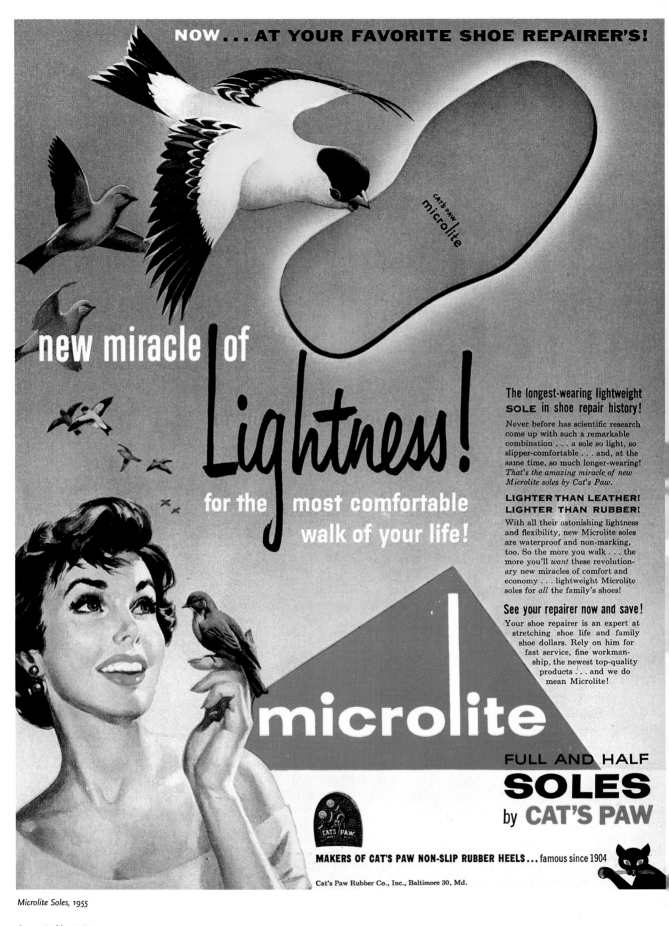

Microlite Soles, 1955

Neolite Soles, 1951

Seamless by

bur-mil Cameo

for natural

beauty

"*Cannon Nylons do something for my legs!*"

says the Cannon Go-Girl

She is a pleasure to paint – Your Cannon Go-Girl. Those Cannon Nylons do, indeed, do something for a girl's legs. I've noticed the smart new shades and pencil-fine profile they give. *Várady*

Go-Radiant—beige, with a dash of sunshine.

A second look? You rate it, every time, in your eye-catching Cannon Nylons.

For Cannon colors sing in soft autumn tones, keyed to fashion's newest spectrum.

And Cannon's *high-twist* thread sleeks your ankle, cleaves tight to your heel in a full-fashioned sheath.

Cannon Nylons wear well, too! No wispy one-day wonders, these.

Gals out in the whirl, out in the world, insist on Cannon Nylons.

Ask for them at your favorite neighborhood shop.

"*on the legs that are on the go*"

Cameo Stockings, 1956 ◀ Cannon Nylons, 1951

And the winner is...

Tugging At A Girdle
Is So Awfully Necessary

Forget taste. When it came to advertising girdles in the 1950s it was anything goes. Pulling your panties in public was justified according to this ad if it meant keeping a creeping girdle in place. The Perma-Lift did just that in a piece of latex straight out of an S&M catalogue.

Es ist so schrecklich –
dass man auch immer an den
Strapsen zupfen muß

Geschmack, was ist das? Die Werbung für Strapse kannte in den Fünfzigern kein Halten mehr. In aller Öffentlichkeit an seinem Höschen zu ziehen, war dieser Reklame nach gerechtfertigt, wenn dadurch ein rutschender Straps an Ort und Stelle blieb. Eben dies leistete der Perma-Lift, und zwar durch ein Latexband geradewegs aus dem S&M-Katalog.

Tirer sur sa gaine,
c'est bon pour la dégaine

Plus question de bon goût. Dans les années 50, quand il s'agit de vanter les vertus de la gaine, il n'y a plus de limite. Remonter sa culotte en public ? Pourquoi pas, s'il s'agit de remettre sa gaine en place. C'est ce que permet la Perma-Lift, grâce à un latex sorti tout droit d'un catalogue sado-maso.

Obviously, the lady doesn't know

Perma·lift's Magic Oval Pantie

CAN'T RIDE UP—EVER!

Perma·lift
PANTIES
NO BONES ABOUT IT
STAYS UP WITHOUT STAYS

Obviously the uncomfortable young shopper on your right doesn't know that "Perma·lift's"* Magic Oval Pantie** Can't Ride Up—Ever! Tugging at a girdle is so awfully necessary with ordinary garments. But this can't happen to you when you wear a "Perma·lift" Magic Oval Pantie, for it's actually guaranteed to remain in place always. Be fitted today.

Pantie 3844—Power Net with front and back control. Only $5.95.
Bra 132—Fine cotton with Magic Insets. $2.50.

*Reg. U. S. Pat. Off. · A product of A. Stein & Company · Chicago—New York—Los Angeles **Pat. No. 2,705,801

Perma-Lift, 1957

WAKE UP

to Aunt Jemima Pancakes!

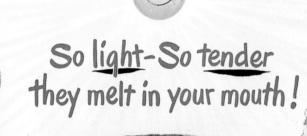

So light-So tender
they melt in your mouth!

No Wonder...

more women prefer Aunt Jemima than all other brands combined!

Let your fork sink into the fluffy lightness of a stack of goldén Aunt Jemima Pancakes. Ever see such fine, fluffy texture? Ever taste such melting tenderness? Now you know why homemakers everywhere choose these better pancakes. Treat your folks to America's favorites tomorrow morning!

AUNT JEMIMA
Pancakes and Waffles

SPECIAL OFFER! Limited Time Only!

Waffles too!
AUNT JEMIMA READY-MIX for **PANCAKES**

Lunch and supper too!
AUNT JEMIMA READY-MIX for **BUCKWHEATS**

3 Piece Aunt Jemima SPICE SET!

For your most-used spices • Nutmeg, Cinnamon, Paprika

Nutmeg *Cinnamon* *Paprika*

TODAY! SEND
only 50c (in coin)
and the top from any
Aunt Jemima Ready-Mix Pkg.
● 4" high!
● Long-Wearing Plastic!
● Washable in Hot Water
MAIL TO: Aunt Jemima
Box D, Dept. 31
Chicago 77, Illinois

Reynolds Aluminum Foil, 1952 ◀ *Aunt Jemima Pancakes & Waffles, 1950* ▶ *Puffin Biscuits, 1957*

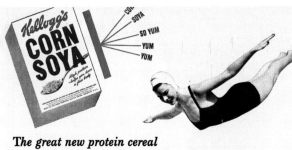

Kellogg's CORN SOYA
SO YUM
YUM
YUM

The great new protein cereal that helps you have

a fine body

ENJOY KELLOGG'S CORN-SOYA,
THE NEW TOASTY-TASTING CEREAL
WITH THE HIGH PROTEIN FACTOR

No other well-known cereal, hot or cold, is so rich in protein—the master body-builder.

You read it, and you wonder. "Can a *cereal* help me have a fine body?"

It can. And it will. This is more than a cereal. Kellogg's Corn-Soya is in the same family of foods as meat and eggs and milk—the master body-builders. For this is the *new protein* cereal.

Protein that helps build firm flesh and solid muscle and fine bodies. Complete, high-quality protein when served with milk. True, Corn-Soya tastes just grand, and has B vitamins, iron and energy value, too. But remember Corn-Soya for protein. The protein that has what it takes to help build a fine body. For you and yours.

Kellogg's Corn Soya Cereal, 1950

REAL NORTH WOODS FLAVOR

LOG CABIN Syrup

A Product of General Foods

Like maple flavor? Then you'll *love* Log Cabin Syrup. It's got that rich, *real maple* taste . . . the result of a delicate, just-right blending of sugar and pure maple sugar syrups. One taste and you'll have visions of "sugarin' off time" in the North Woods! Get Log Cabin—in the familiar tin or handsome "antique" bottle—today.

Just made for each other — Log Cabin 'n Waffles!

Log Cabin Syrup, 1950

"Mom always says — <u>any</u> cereal assortment ... as long as it's Post-Tens!"

DICK SARGENT

MOTHER'S BIGGEST LITTLE HELPER is Post-Tens. Lets you choose just the cereal you want—when you want it. Roasted, toasted, popped or puffed . . . seven delicious cereals, fresh as morning. We say anybody can please *everybody*—with Post-Tens.

"ALL POST CEREALS HAPPEN TO BE JUST A LITTLE BIT BETTER"

 *Post*

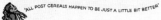 POST-TENS
The Breakfast Foods of General Foods

Post-Tens, 1951

Any corn flakes are <u>real gone</u>... as long as they're Post Toasties

REAL GONE—THAT'S FOR SURE...both the miss and her corn flakes! They're Post Toasties—rolled and toasted a special way that keeps the sweet corn flavor in each curly bit o' crispness. No wonder folks call them the "little bit better" corn flakes. Go ahead—taste 'em yourself!

"ALL POST CEREALS HAPPEN TO BE JUST A LITTLE BIT BETTER"

TOASTIES
CORN FLAKES

 *Post*
The Breakfast Foods of General Foods

Post Toasties, 1951

▶ *Post 40% Bran Flakes, 1950*

Maybe it's something she DIDN'T eat!

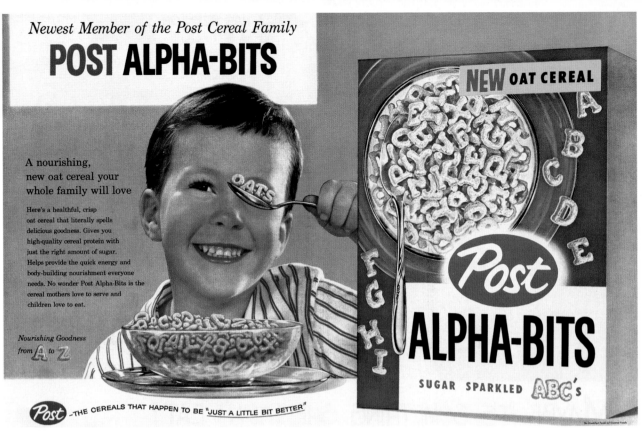

Post Alpha-Bits, 1958

Pillsbury Cinnamon Rolls, 1955

▶ Post Tens, 1955   ▶▶ Wheaties Cereal, 1952

8 A.M. and all's _swell_
when you get your choice

our choice of the world's choicest
eals — in Post Tens!

wouldn't feel terrific at breakfast time—
hat wonderful Post Tens assortment to choose
Miss Freckle Face here leans toward
-Nuts—for more energy per spoonful than any
cereal, cooked or cold! And whatever
ick, all 7 famous Post Cereals are so nutritious,
icious! Give _your_ family a choice and change
day of the week—this convenient Post Tens way!

For _goodness_ sake — get Post Tens!

NEW WHEATIES ARE SUPER-FLAKED!
BIGGER!
SEE THE DIFFERENCE!
TASTE THE DIFFERENCE!
SO CRISP!
BRIGHTER!
BOB FELLER SAYS:
"I grew up on Wheaties and believe me
New WHEATIES®
ARE BETTER THAN EV
WHAT SPARKS A CHAMPION SPARKS YOU—AND CHAMPIONS CHOOSE
"Breakfast of Champions"

AMAZING COFFEE DISCOVERY!

Not a powder! Not a grind! But millions of tiny "FLAVOR BUDS" of <u>real</u> coffee . . . ready to burst instantly into that famous MAXWELL HOUSE FLAVOR!

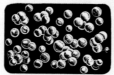

Utterly unlike old-style "instants" . . . just as quick but tastes so different!

In the famous Maxwell House kitchens this superb, roaster-fresh coffee is actually brewed for you. At the exact moment of perfection the water is removed by a special Maxwell House process—leaving the millions of miracle "Flavor Buds"!

100% Pure Coffee—No Fillers Added!

Just add hot water . . . and the bursting "Flavor Buds" flood your cup with coffee as delicious as the best you've ever brewed. One sip and you'll never go back to old ways!

Saves you money, too! The large economy-size jar saves up to 75¢, compared to three pounds of ground coffee!

See how the Flavor Buds "come to life" in your cup!

MAGNIFIED VIEW of new miracle "Flavor Buds" shows how utterly different they are from old-style powders and grinds.

THE INSTANT you add hot water, the "Flavor Buds" burst—releasing flood of rich, delicious Maxwell House flavor!

Reach for the jar with the stars on top!

A Product of General Foods

The only instant coffee with that <u>GOOD-TO-THE-LAST-DROP</u> flavor!

Maxwell House Coffee, 1953

▶ *Pan-American Coffee Bureau, 1953*

THINK BETTER!...Minutes before air-time, newscaster Edward R. Murrow checks his script for CBS Television's *See It Now* — and takes a "Coffee-break"! Delicious, bracing coffee aids clear thinking. A cheerful cup can clear *your* mind for action, too. Whatever your job, keep yourself alert — give yourself a "Coffee-break"!

-give yourself a "Coffee-break"!

WORK BETTER!...TV production is exacting work. That's why *See It Now*'s director and cameraman break... for coffee! Coffee's gentle stimulation makes hard work seem easier. Make a "Coffee-break" part of *your* working day.

FEEL BETTER!... The whole family enjoys Edward R. Murrow's thrilling TV show, and fragrant coffee adds the final touch. Relax often — with coffee "all around." With family, friends, or all by yourself — take a "Coffee-break"!

There's a welcome lift in every cup!

© 1953

Kool-Aid, 1954

Tea, 1952

Tang Breakfast Drink, 1959

G. Washington's Coffee, 1953 ▶ *Hills Brothers Coffee, 1959* ▶▶ *Libby's Juice, 1950*

richer, stronger...pound lasts longer

Selective blending of the finest coffees from all around the world
gives Hills Bros. Coffee rich, vigorous flavor and strength
... more flavor in every cup, more cups from every pound.
It's good strong coffee ... never bitter ... just better.

You'll enjoy WALT DISNEY PRESENTS *every Friday night on ABC-TV.*

Head for the Hills

WEALTHY WITH
Hawaiian Sunshine!
Libby's
PINEAPPLE JUICE
LOOK TO Libby's
FOR PERFECTION!

Kool-Shake makes milk taste like a soda fountain shake!

Shakes up thick and foamy! Just add Kool-Shake to milk and sugar.

kool-SHAKE

MAKES 2 TALL GLASSES

MILK SHAKES

Comes in your favorite milk shake flavors

6¢ PACKAGE MAKES 2 TALL SHAKES

Kool-shake, 1957

ANNOUNCING... the big 3 for thirst!

PING PONG PI-LI

PING — P-I-N for Pineapple G—for Grapefruit A *New* refreshing and healthful drink! **NEW!**

PONG — P—for Pineapple O-N-G—for Orange A *Brand New* drink blend that quenches and refreshes. **NEW!**

Pi-Li — P-I for Pineapple L-I for Lime Pi-Li (say "pie...lie") Delicious *New* drink for meals or snacks **NEW!**

3 DELICIOUS NEW DRINKS BY STOKELY-VAN CAMP! GIVE 'EM ALL THEY WANT! Stokely drinks are rich in Vitamin C. They're non-carbonated. Good for meals, good for thirst, good for all the family.

Stokely-Van Camp Juices, 1959

POWERHOUSE
of Vitamin C

Florida

Terry Brennan, famous Notre Dame football coach, says: "Every coach knows we all need Vitamin C every day. I tell my boys to get it the natural way, in swell-tasting Florida orange juice. That way you get a bonus of seven other health benefits."

One little can of fresh-frozen orange juice makes 4 big glasses. It's a Powerhouse of natural Vitamin C. Saves time! Saves money!

Your body can't store it— you need it every day

Natural Vitamin C is essential to good health. Children, grownups, everyone needs at least one big glass of orange juice from Florida every day. During periods of increased activity, pregnancy, disease or injury, your daily requirements are much higher. And be sure you get Vitamin C in its *natural form* in wonderful tasting orange juice from Florida . . . because with it you get a bonus of other essential nutrients in the balance nature intended. It helps build resistance to disease, promotes growth, helps form bones and teeth, and gives you energy. Orange juice from Florida is a Powerhouse of natural Vitamin C.

FRESH-FROZEN ORANGE JUICE from **Florida**

© FLORIDA CITRUS COMMISSION, LAKELAND, FLORIDA, USA

 Miracle Aid, 1956 ◀ *Florida Orange Juice, 1958*

The Proteins in Milk are one reason

Milk makes Energy!

Refresh with Milk for a lift that lasts

Have a glass of cold, refreshing milk when you need a lift that lasts.

Milk is high in protein. It's a powerhouse of energy.

Recharge—and carry on refreshed, really refreshed, lastingly refreshed.

You never outgrow your need for Milk—and the proteins in Milk.

WOULDN'T A GLASS OF

MILK

TASTE GOOD NOW?

AMERICAN DAIRY ASSOCIATION · Chicago
Representing the dairy farmers in your area
See "The Bob Crosby Show" on NBC-TV

Milk, 1958 ▶ *Ritz Crackers, 1950*

"Nothing tastes as good as RITZ but RITZ!"

Spice, the gift of the magi...

From Spice Islands, eminently suited for Christmas giving ... (left:) Herb Shelf—most appealing, contains 5 useful herbs—with directions. (right:) "Aux Fines Herbes" Salad Set—stunning package of 4 herb-flavored vinegars and 8 vials of salad seasonings, selected for the gourmet touch. Recipes included.

For **free** herb chart and name of nearest store write to:

SPICE ISLANDS COMPANY
Dept. CG, South San Francisco, California

OVEN-READY GAME BIRDS
Since 1922
Prices Prepaid — In Dry Ice

Pheasants 2, Chukars 2, Quail 6............ $29

Pheasants:	2— $9,	6—$25,	or	100—$375
Chukars:	4—$16,	8—$29,	or	100—$350
Quail:	6—$16,	12—$28,	or	100—$200

Your satisfaction guaranteed, as always. . . . Holiday wrapped. . . . Your card enclosed. . . . Send your list, delivery date and check, now!
(Over ½ million game birds shipped.)

M. E. Bogle

527 Ogden Street   San Antonio 2, Texas
Call Capitol 6-9500

Original Pennsylvania-Dutch
HICKORY VALLEY FARM
DELICIOUS SMOKED MEATS BY MAIL
SMOKED TURKEY

Great Chefs, gourmets, famous hostesses acclaim these Hickory Smoked Turkeys as among the true luxury delicacies of the world. The meat is actually pearly pink! Whole Turkeys, Average weight 10 to 20 lbs., @ $1.75 per lb.

. SHERRY-BASTED HAM

This superb Baked Ham is spiced with choicest cloves. It nestles in its distinctive gift package like a great treasure. Hickory Smoked Ham, Average weight 10-18 lbs., @ $1.75 per lb.

Send check or money order along with itemized gift list to:

HICKORY VALLEY FARM   LITTLE KUNKLETOWN
                                STROUDSBURG, PENNA.

Member of Gourmet's Guest Club and Diners' Club. Indicate Account Number to charge.

Spice Island Co., M.E. Bogle, & Hickory Valley Farm, 1955

How long since you've tasted cheese like this?

Wonderful, wonderful Holland Cheese... made as only the Dutch can make it! Exquisitely smooth, surprisingly firm texture. Delectably mellow, subtly elegant flavor. So very good to eat before meals, with meals, after meals, between meals. (For tasty serving ideas, write for our free recipe folders.) Holland Gouda and Holland Edam have a host of imitators, so make sure you get the real thing—always look for the Dutch girl emblem. And remember that the supply of Holland Cheese has been limited by United States import restrictions. If your store can't oblige, be patient. Cheese like this is well worth waiting for. Holland Cheese Exporters Association, 9 Rockefeller Plaza, New York 20, N. Y.

CHEESE OF HOLLAND

Cheese of Holland, 1951

A *new* barbecue sandwich!

It's extra good with a cheese topping of America's finest slices

8 full ounce slices. Easy as peeling a banana!

Vienna Barbecue Sandwiches

For such a handsome topping as this you need *genuine* Kraft De Luxe Slices— the *perfect* slices that separate so easily and always melt beautifully.

For the barbecue sauce blend together and simmer 30 min. 1 c. tomato sauce, ¼ c. catsup, 1 tsp. lemon juice, 1 tsp. salt, ½ tsp. dry mustard, 2 tbsp. brown sugar, 1 tsp. minced onion, a dash each of Tabasco sauce, freshly ground pepper and garlic powder.

Toast two small loaves of French bread and cut lengthwise slices from the tops. Hollow out centers. Heat contents of two 8-oz. cans of Vienna sausage in the barbecue sauce and fill the loaves. Replace the tops.

Cut 6 Kraft De Luxe Slices of pasteurized process American cheese in half diagonally and place 6 overlapping triangles on each sandwich top. Place in moderate, 350° oven until the cheese melts. 4 servings.

Another tested recipe from the Kraft Kitchen

8 SLICES KRAFT De Luxe SLICES PASTEURIZED PROCESS AMERICAN CHEESE

5 KINDS
American • Swiss • Brick • Old English Brand • Pimento
(with full, true pimento flavor) • Pasteurized Process Cheeses

Kraft DE LUXE *Slices*

Kraft De Luxe Slices, 1955

LADIES' HOME JOURNAL

Husky snack for Lent!
Tuna Cheesewiches
topped with America's handiest, best-tasting slices

8 SLICES KRAFT De Luxe SLICES PASTEURIZED PROCESS AMERICAN CHEESE

AMERICAN • PIMENTO • SWISS
BRICK • SHARP OLD ENGLISH BRAND
PASTEURIZED PROCESS CHEESES

FOR FOOD IDEAS! FOR FINE DRAMAS! SEE KRAFT TV THEATRE WED. EVES. NBC TV

Make a salad with one 6½-oz. can flaked tuna, 2 tbsps. pickle relish, ¼ c. diced celery, ¼ c. Kraft Mayonnaise, ¼ tsp. lemon juice, seasonings. Using 8 toast slices (crusts trimmed), make 4 sandwiches filled with salad.

Slit a package of Kraft De Luxe Slices on three sides. You have 8 *perfect* sandwich-size slices—extra delicious. That's because these slices *are not cut* from a loaf but *formed* as the fine process cheese comes from the pasteurizers.

Top each sandwich with a golden Kraft De Luxe Slice. Notice how perfectly these slices separate—"easy as peeling a banana!" Place sandwiches in a 350° oven until the cheese topping melts. Cut the toasted sandwiches diagonally.

Press the wrapper around your remaining Kraft De Luxe Slices so they'll be ready for another cheese treat at a moment's notice. Kraft De Luxe Slices are "extra good keepers" because their surfaces were never roughed up with a knife.

Kraft De Luxe Slices, 1953

Try this trio of fine salad dressings
—made with Spanish Olive Oil

A salad simply isn't a salad unless the dressing is made with pure Spanish olive oil.

Nature blessed Spain with sunny slopes and rich soil, and the tradition of fine olive oil goes back for centuries.

For superb salads, or hot dishes prepared for the taste of a queen, you'll find that Spanish olive oil adds an appealing flavor. Send for our recipe folder* of famous salad dressings. They're by "Gourmet Magazine" and are as easy to make as they are tasty.

Free recipe folder "Key to Salad Dressing"

SPANISH OLIVE OIL INSTITUTE • 500 Fifth Avenue, New York 36, N. Y.

Spanish Olive Oil, 1957

Alcoa Aluminum Foil, 1956

Waxed Paper, 1954

American Dairy Association, 1954 ◄ *Reynolds Wrap, 1956*

Reynolds Wrap, 1950

The Crisp, Cool Touch that Makes the Meal—

Mrs. Fanning's original recipe

The Famous "BREAD and BUTTER" PICKLES

No other pickle adds more flavor, goes so well with so many foods! Not sour, not sweet, just right! CHILL and serve these crisp, spicy slices of sun-ripened cucumbers often. New pack now at your grocer's!

Get a jar soon!

Just what fish needs!

The sandwich-maker's delight!

Secret of successful salads!

Best Foods

FANNING'S BREAD AND BUTTER PICKLES

TRADE-MARK BREAD AND BUTTER REG. U.S.PAT.OFF.
NET WEIGHT 15 OZS.
The BEST FOODS, Inc.
MANUFACTURER
NEW YORK, N.Y.
U.S.A.

The spicy note on cold plates!

Happy touch with hamburgers and most meats!

*TRADEMARK
"BREAD AND BUTTER"
REG U.S. PAT. OFF.

Best Foods Pickles, 1950

Crisco, 1951

French's Instant Mashed Potato, 1959

Minute Rice, 1953

Fritos, 1950

ENJOY "EATING OUT" AT HOME!

重慶

Serve Six for less than $1.00

CHUN KING

CHOW MEIN and CHOP SUEY

Three Choices in BIG New
3 Lb. "Family-Economy" Size............
.... Now at Your Grocers!

Here is Chow Mein at its rich, savory best. And
so quick to fix. Just heat and serve over crisp Chun King Noodles
or Rice. Six good big servings from the new "family-economy" size.
Your choice of Chicken Chow Mein, Beef Chop Suey, Meatless
Chow Mein. For a wonderful family dinner or when guests
drop in—serve Chun King. Tonight? *Any night!*

© CHUN KING SALES, INC.

Also available in 1 lb. cans to serve 2 or
3 persons . . . look for the Chun King
foods section at your grocers.

Chun King, 1953

New! Chef Boy-Ar-Dee Pizza Pie Mix

complete with mellow <u>Italian-style cheese</u> and Chef's incomparable Pizza Sauce!

Imagine — now you can serve this tantalizing Italian dish just as it's served in Naples—sizzling, savory, seasoned to perfection.

It's so easy with Chef Boy-Ar-Dee Pizza Pie Mix! Everything you need comes in one box— complete makings for tender, hearty crust . . . zippy, tomato-rich sauce, ready to use . . . even grated Italian-style cheese to sprinkle on top.

Baking time — only 15 to 20 minutes. Eating time—almost any time!

You'll love Chef Pizza, for example, as a tasty "fill-'em-up" lunch for the youngsters. And as the basis for a real Italian family dinner when you serve it with tossed salad, and fruit for dessert. (Each box makes 5 meal-size servings.)

But above all, try Chef Pizza for company snacks. Cut it in bite-size bits for appetizers. Serve in generous wedges for TV nibbling and late-evening party fare. Guests really gobble it up!

Remember to get a box—or two—tomorrow.

The Joy of Good Eating

LIKE EATING CAKE—Van Camp's Tenderoni . . . as light, white, fluffy as an angel-food cake . . . for Tenderoni is the one and only macaroni product made with egg white. Cooks in only 7 minutes . . . needs no blanching . . . always tender . . . never doughy. Add salt and butter and enjoy . . . or serve with tomato sauce, meat balls, chicken, fish. Tenderoni helps give variety to your Lenten meals.

RICE AND EVERYTHING NICE . . . Van Camp's Spanish Rice . . . blended with tomatoes and peppers and other choice ingredients to give you the colorful, exciting dish that pleases all tastes. Ready to heat, eat, enjoy . . . to serve with shrimp . . . to stuff green peppers and bake. Make Van Camp's Spanish Rice your next adventure in good eating.

MACARONI PRODUCT

Van Camp's TENDERONI

MADE WITH EGG WHITE

Van Camp's TENDERONI
Cook only 7 minutes, do not blanch

Stokely's Finest
BROCCOLI
FROZEN FOODS

Enjoy the Garry Moore Show CBS-TV Network, every Thursday afternoon

Van Camp's

SPANISH RICE

Stokely-Van Camp's • TWO GREAT NAMES IN FOOD *that mean* QUICK MEALS *for you*

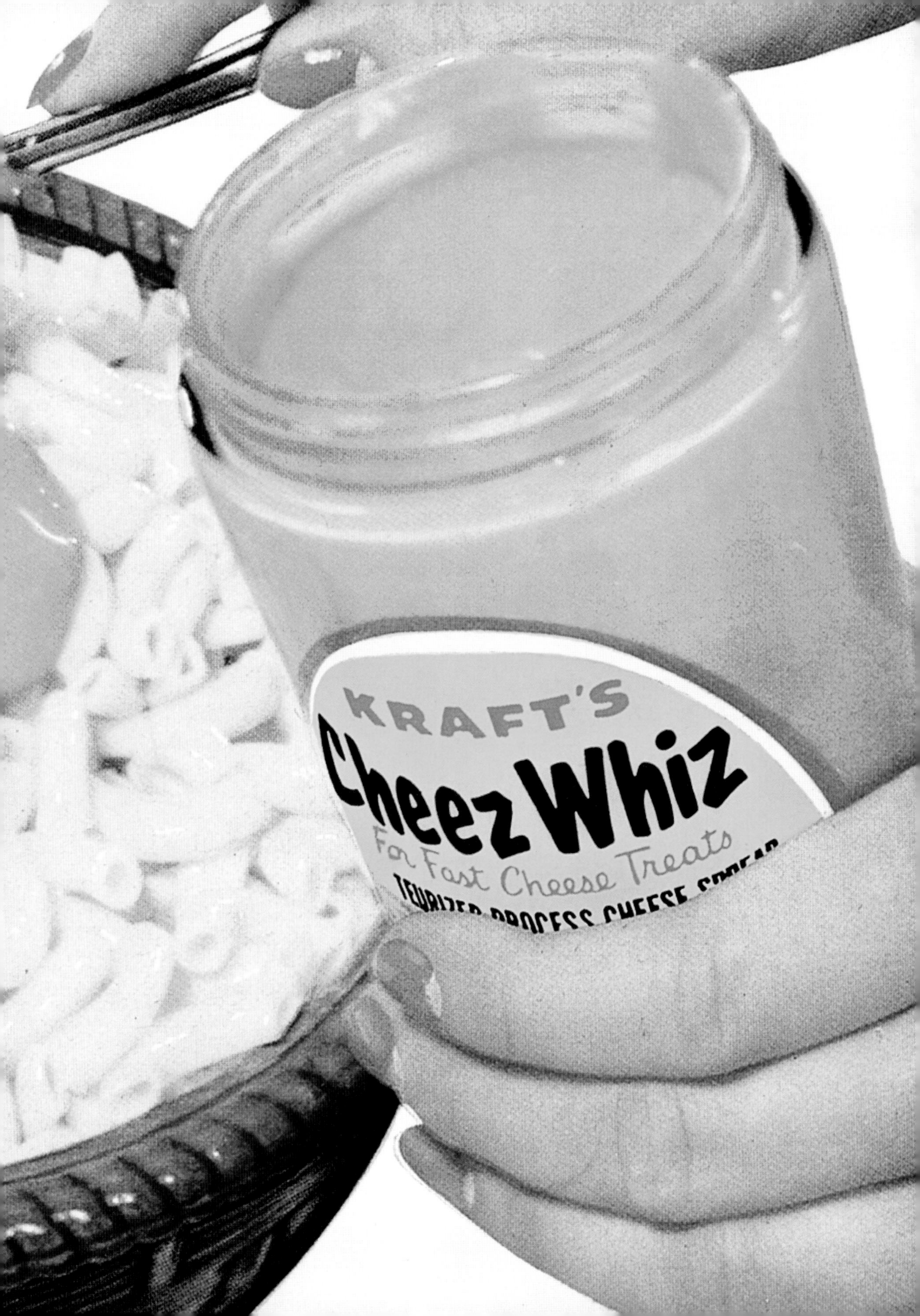
KRAFT'S
Cheez Whiz
For Fast Cheese Treats

Brach's Candy, 1957

Cracker Jack, 1955

Brach's Candy, 1958 ◄ *Brach's Candy, 1950*   ► *Double Bubble Gum, 1953*

STRAWBERRY
CHOCOLATE
BUTTERSCOTCH
MARSHMALLOW
PINEAPPLE
CHERRY
HOT FUDGE

MAIN EVENT

DAIRY QUEEN
SMOOTH...DELICIOUS

Take your choice, folks, from tempting toppings over cool, smooth, delicious DAIRY QUEEN. It's the biggest sundae treat on earth! DAIRY QUEEN is a freshly frozen dairy food. Join the big parade to your nearest gleaming white DAIRY QUEEN store. You'll hurry back for more!

DAIRY QUEEN IS ICE MILK IN THE MAJORITY OF STATES

Advertisement sponsored by members of
DAIRY QUEEN NATIONAL TRADE ASSOCIATION, INC.
DAVENPORT, IOWA

"THE CONE WITH THE CURL ON TOP"

QUARTS AND PINTS FOR HOME DESSERTS

RICH, THICK MALTS AND SHAKES

Dairy Queen Stores Are NATIONALLY KNOWN...LOCALLY OWNED

© 1952 D.Q.N.T.A., INC.

CHOCOLATE
STRAWBERRY
BUTTERSCOTCH
PINEAPPLE
CHERRY
MARSHMALLOW
HOT FUDGE

under the **BIG TOPPING..**

it's **DAIRY QUEEN**
SMOOTH...DELICIOUS

Treat yourself and the whole family to a yummy sundae at your nearest gleaming white DAIRY QUEEN store. DAIRY QUEEN is a freshly frozen dairy food. Stop often for DAIRY QUEEN and order your favorite sundae. It's the biggest treat on earth!

DAIRY QUEEN IS ICE MILK IN THE MAJORITY OF STATES

Advertisement sponsored by members of
DAIRY QUEEN NATIONAL TRADE ASSOCIATION, INC.
DAVENPORT, IOWA

"THE CONE WITH THE CURL ON TOP"

QUARTS AND PINTS FOR HOME DESSERTS

RICH, THICK MALTS AND SHAKES

Dairy Queen Stores Are NATIONALLY KNOWN...LOCALLY OWNED

© 1952 D.Q.N.T.A., INC.

Dairy Queen, 1952

Dairy Queen, 1952

▶ *Dairy Queen, 1956*

In the merry month of May it's the **DAIRY QUEEN**

19¢ SALE
MALTS and SHAKES
May 1st, one day only

Your choice of flavors

HOMOGENIZED AND PASTEURIZED

DAIRY QUEEN

HOME OF
"the cone with the curl on top" ©

NATIONAL DAIRY QUEEN DEVELOPMENT CO., INC.

DAIRY QUEEN...first and largest from coast-to-coast! Your chance to get a famous Dairy Queen malt or shake for only 19¢! In all the world...no other frozen dairy product gives you the smooth texture, richly-satisfying taste and freshly-frozen goodness of Dairy Queen malts and shakes.

Dairy Queen is *frozen just seconds before you taste it!* Learn the pleasure first-hand, of a luscious malt or shake made the Dairy Queen way. Once you do, you'll be back often! Join the millions who enjoy over 300,000,000 Dairy Queen servings yearly.

NATIONAL DAIRY QUEEN DEVELOPMENT CO.
809 Kahl Bldg., Davenport, Iowa

Visit your local Dairy Queen store displaying this sign. It is your invitation to enjoy an Extra Value Dairy Queen Malt or Shake for 19¢ at the home of the "cone with the curl on top®"

DAIRY QUEEN
19¢ SALE
MALTS and SHAKES

Over 3,000 Stores to Serve You!

© 1956, NATIONAL DAIRY QUEEN DEVELOPMENT CO.

Life Savers Candy, 1953

Treat Yourself to the Best-Liked Coconut Candy in All the World

MOUNDS

*Enjoy Luscious, Snowy-White,
Tree-Ripened Coconut
With A Double-Thick,
Rich Chocolate Coating!*

MOUNDS · PETER PAUL'S · DOUBLE BAR · 10¢

You'll Love ALMOND JOY
Peter Paul's Milk Chocolate-Coconut
Bar With Fine Roasted Almonds

TWICE AS MUCH!
TWICE AS GOOD!
TWICE AS FRESH!

IF YOU HAVEN'T yet discovered why Peter Paul's MOUNDS is far and away the world's most popular coconut candy, just open one of these tempting bars! Notice that fresh, inviting fragrance! Bite into that deep, double-thick covering of richly dark and luscious bittersweet chocolate . . . blended to our own exclusive recipe. And then savor fully that center of moist and tender, snowy-white coconut fresh from the finest groves in the Philippines! Every MOUNDS is *filled* with a wealth of this wonderful coconut! And every bar is specially wrapped to preserve its *home-kitchen freshness!*

● **Money can't buy** better candy than MOUNDS—the big *double*-bar for only a dime. Get MOUNDS! See why it's the world's best-loved coconut candy bar!

Masterpieces In Candy From The Kitchens Of

PETER PAUL

PETER PAUL, INC., NAUGATUCK, CONN.

Here it is again!

It's the greatest!

Man, it's real cool!

dig this crazy mixed-up ice cream!

Triple-Treat

it's raspberry, vanilla and orange-pineapple!

MORE PEOPLE ENJOY *Sealtest* THAN ANY OTHER ICE CREAM

Rich red raspberry, so-smooth vanilla, exotic orange-pineapple. All three in one exciting ice cream. A flavor trio that's soon real gone! Only made by Sealtest!

Sealtest TRADE MARK
ICE CREAM

Pillsbury
(as you can see)

Here's a chance to really enjoy an ad. You can sit easy-like right there in your chair. All you are asked to do is to look head-on into the fine, even, luscious texture of these two wonderful cakes. Don't they make easy reading? Now the beauty about this whole thing is that they are almost as easy to make as they are to read about. All you have to remember is that these cakes were made with Pillsbury Cake Mixes. (Milk is all you add.) Pillsbury. (In the neat blue-and-white packages.) Pillsbury. As you can see.

Remember— You and Ann Pillsbury can make a great team

Pillsbury Cake Mixes
WHITE AND CHOCOLATE FUDGE

Milk is all you add – no eggs, flavoring, or extras of any kind required. These are complete mixes.

Pillsbury Cake Mixes, 1951

Red, White and You!

Yes, you're the one we mean. Add milk to a package of Pillsbury White Cake Mix (red cherries and whipped cream for filling and topping) and aren't you wonderful? Pillsbury, the best-selling cake mixes, by far. Why don't you get in on a good thing today?

Cherry filling: Combine ¼ cup sugar, 2 tablespoons corn starch, ¼ teaspoon salt. Stir in 1 cup liquid (juice drained from No. 2 can of red sour cherries plus water). Add ¼ teaspoon red food coloring, if desired. Boil for 5 minutes, stirring constantly. Add cherries; cool. Spread between cooled, baked layers of Pillsbury White Cake Mix. Top with whipped cream.

Pillsbury Cake Mixes
WHITE...CHOCOLATE FUDGE...GOLDEN YELLOW

Milk is all you add

No eggs to buy. No flavorings or extras of any kind required. These are complete mixes. Finest ingredients money can buy.

Sealtest Ice Cream, 1956 ◄ Pillsbury Cake Mixes, 1953

Wonderful way to enjoy Nature's most refreshing flavor

PINEAPPLE UPSIDE DOWN CAKE
So easy to make with.... Canned Pineapple

Just take a can of crushed Pineapple ...or... Pineapple tidbits or chunks ... or sliced Pineapple, and follow your favorite upside-down cake method

PINEAPPLE JUICE CANNED TROPIC-FRESH IS WONDERFUL ANY TIME!

Canned Pineapple, 1953   ► Swans Down Cake Flour, 1955

657

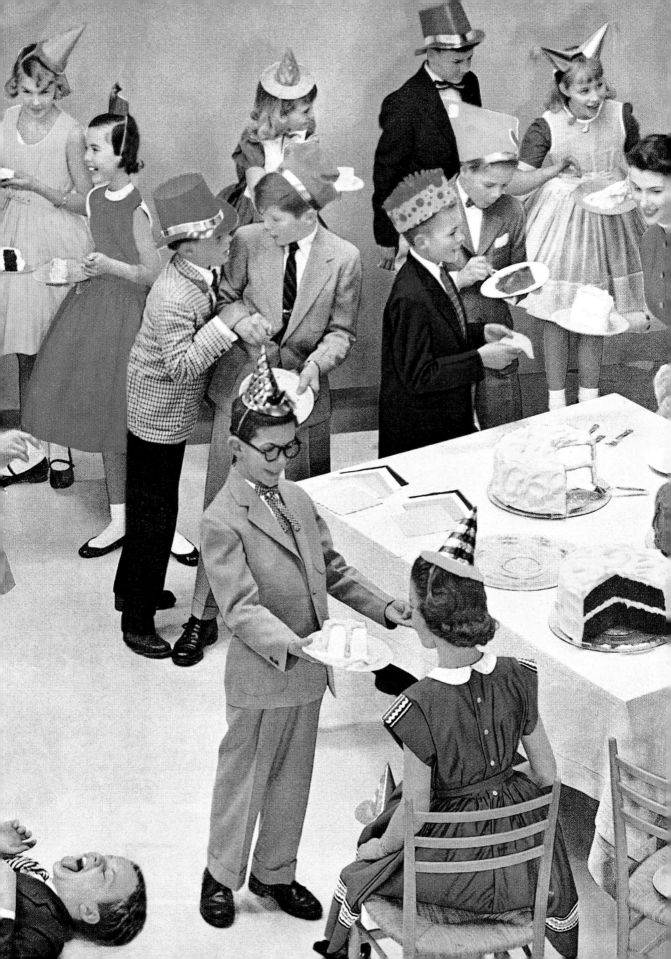

it's CHERRY PIE time

Where in all the world is there a flavor like fresh-made Cherry Pie? . . . spicy fragrance bubbling thru flaky light crust . . . meaty red cherries baked in the tart-sweet essence of their own juices—each taste a tingling experience—each slice a whole-souled token of summer's bounty. And this is the time to enjoy it . . . this is flavor's fiesta . . . this is summer's high holiday . . . *this* is Cherry Pie Time . . . whether you bake it, buy it or enjoy it at your favorite restaurant, now is the time to *revel* in America's best-loved dessert . . . luscious, tempting Cherry Pie!

AT YOUR GROCER'S—BAKER'S—FAVORITE RESTAURANT

it's Cherry Pie Time

NATIONAL RED CHERRY INSTITUTE

The National Red Cherry Institute, 332 S. Michigan Ave., Chicago, Ill., *representing cherry commissions, associations, growers and processors in Colorado, Michigan, New York, Ohio, Oregon, Pennsylvania, Utah, Washington, W. Virginia and Wisconsin.*

National Red Cherry Institute, 1950

All Desserts Become Glamorous with Reddi-wip

Just the touch of your finger turns gelatins, puddings, pies and cakes into party treats

No more dull, plain desserts! Millions of women have found that Reddi-wip turns every day's desserts into exciting, praise-winning treats.

Made with fresh, rich cream that whips itself automatically, Reddi-wip gives the festive touch to all your desserts, yet saves you work at the same time.

Add the glamorous touch of Reddi-wip to quick, easy-to-make gelatin and sliced bananas. See how instantly it becomes a dessert that looks as though it would take hours to prepare. See what Reddi-wip does to chocolate pie or chocolate pudding. Learn how it makes every dessert you serve more delicious—better looking.

Use Reddi-wip for a few days in your home and you will know why it has been welcomed by millions of American housewives in a manner not matched by any other product in recent years. It's so economical with dozens and dozens of servings in every can—and never any waste—that you can use

it on all your desserts. Get Reddi-wip today from your milkman or grocer—keep it on hand in your refrigerator for daily use.

Made with fresh, rich cream. It whips itself!

New! Easy way to frost cake!
It's a great idea acclaimed by women from coast to coast. "Frost" each piece of cake with Reddi-wip when you serve it. Its fresh, delicate flavor brings a new glamor and deliciousness to chocolate, sunshine, angel, pound and all your cakes. (The same fresh, delicate taste that has made whipped cream cakes so popular!) Try it the very next time you bake either ready-mixed or home-mixed cakes.

ASK FOR *Reddi-wip* FROM YOUR MILKMAN OR GROCER

Reddi-Wip, 1950

Only FLUFFO and PET Milk make it rich and colorful as Autumn itself . . .

Golden Harvest Pumpkin Pie

Golden Harvest Pumpkin Pie

FLUFFO'S GOLDEN FLAKY PIE CRUST (9-inch pan)
2½ cups sifted flour
½ teaspoon salt
½ cup Fluffo
3 tablespoons water

Cut Fluffo into flour mixed with ½ teaspoon salt. Stir in water and mix thoroughly. Roll dough ⅛ inch thick into circle 1½ inches larger than top of 9-inch pie pan. Fit dough into pan. Fold edge under and flute. Add filling and bake as directed.

PET'S GOLDEN RICH PUMPKIN FILLING
¾ cup brown sugar
1 tablespoon flour
½ teaspoon salt
2¾ teaspoons pumpkin pie spices
1½ cups canned pumpkin
1⅓ cups Pet Evaporated Milk
1 slightly beaten egg

Mix brown sugar, flour, salt and pumpkin pie spices. Stir in canned pumpkin, add Pet Milk and egg. Stir until smooth. Pour into pastry lined pan. Bake at 375° (350° for glass pan) for one hour unless noted topping is desired. (See below)

FESTIVE NUT TOPPING (optional)
Mix together until crumbly, ½ cup chopped pecans, 1 tablespoon Fluffo, 2 tablespoons brown sugar, 1½ teaspoons grated orange rind. After 45 minutes baking, take pie from oven and spoon mixture around edge. Bake 15 minutes more. Serve warm or cold.

Fluffo and Pet Milk combine to bring you pumpkin pie so exciting it seems to capture the full richness and the golden colors of Autumn. Only Fluffo can make pie crust this golden, flaky and tender. Only Pet Milk can make pumpkin filling this golden rich and creamy smooth —with just one egg. Now is the season . . . treat your family to Golden Harvest Pumpkin Pie.

"PET"—Reg. U.S. Pat. Off.

Fluffo & Pet Milk, 1959   ▶ *Sealtest Ice Cream, 1955*

Kukla and Ollie, top stars of TV
Chorus together in smooth harmony:

Give us Sealtest, boy, oh, boy,
Its creamy flavor is a joy!

Delicious! Mmmm! And so delightful!
Flavor-fine in every biteful!

For ice cream rich with zip and zest,
Get Sealtest. Get the very best!

IT'S HERE

CHICLINES · CHICLINES · CHICLINES · CHICLINES

DELICIOUS Chiclines BUBBLE GUM

BUBBLE GUM

CHICLINES · CHICLINES · CHICLINES · CHICLINES · CHICLINES

25% More Latex!

JOBBERS!
CARLOAD OR CASE LOTS

WHOLESALERS ONLY!

IMMEDIATE DELIVERY!

per BOX of 60-5c Count

*$1 70

(*NOTE 60 COUNT)
Packed 50 BOXES TO CASE
CASE PRICE $85.00 (3000 Pieces)

Only Sold In Case Lots
F.O.B. LAREDO, TEXAS

TERMS: 2%--10 Days to Rated Concerns.
Other Concerns 1/3 Cash,
Balance C.O.D.

FOR BIGGER, BETTER, PINKER BUBBLES AND BIGGER, BETTER, BUBBLE GUM BUSINESS

CHICLINES FOR BIGGER BUBBLES

CHICLINES FOR BETTER BUBBLES

CHICLINES FOR PINKER BUBBLES

FOR BIGGER PROFITS

BUBBLE GUM! Candy Jobbers and Exporters! Chance of a Lifetime! Quantity orders, immediate action! Direct orders attention

LEON 'BUBBLES' KAUFMAN,
Sales Manager
100 S. Flores St.
San Antonio, Texas

GREAT DEMAND! BIG PROFITS! QUICK TURNOVER ORDER TODAY!

KABROS, Inc. Factors and Selling Agents

100 SOUTH FLORES STREET   SAN ANTONIO, TEXAS

Please Rush _____ Cases Chiclines

Railway Express ☐   Rail Freight ☐
Air Freight ☐   Motor Freight ☐

We Are Rated   By Dun & Bradstreet

Name _____

Address _____

City _____

SEE OTHER SIDE

KABROS, Inc., 100 S. Flores St., San Antonio, Texas
FACTORS AND SELLING AGENTS

caught !

that pure orange flavor...

Naturally, "POPSICLE", the king of all cooling refreshments,
is available in a host of other delicious flavors, too!
You'll find them wherever good ice cream is sold...

.in bags with Polka Dots that youngsters save for exciting gifts!

South African Rock Lobster Tails, 1958

Swift Premium Meat, 1958

Swift Premium Meats, 1959

▶ *Morrell Ham, 1953*

EMBER, 1953

MORRELL

MORRELL E-Z-CUT HAM
—Oven dry baked to
perfection just as you
would cook it yourself.
...Fully cooked
when you get it...
shrink is taken out.

PRIDE

Enjoy a Morrell Ham...
give a Morrell Ham
for Christmas. The flavor
you'll remember in the
ham you can't forget!
A product we are proud
to label Morrell.

HAM

MORRELL PRIDE TENDER HAM—ready-to-cook to
your own pet recipe.

MORRELL PRIDE SAVORY CANNED HAM—cooked and
canned in its own luscious juices. Flavor is sealed in.

JOHN MORRELL & CO. SINCE 1827 │ Pork Beef Lamb Ham Bacon Sausage Canned Meats
Ottumwa, Iowa   Sioux Falls, S. D.

The joy of good eating

Fresh-picked ... fresh-packed ... fresh-tasting

—Stokely's Finest Fruits. You will find all your favorites in Stokely's Fruit Festival ... now at your grocer's.

Every meal a picnic ... every picnic all fun ... no work ... with Van Camp's Pork and Beans. Delicious as they come ... or ready to heat ... eat ... enjoy.

Enjoy the Garry Moore Show CBS-TV Network, every Thursday afternoon

Stokely-Van Camp • TWO GREAT NAMES IN FOOD *that mean* QUICK MEALS *for you*

Van Camp's Pork and Beans, 1953

Chiquita Banana, 1951

Morton Salt, 1957

Swift Premium Meats, 1956

PictSweet Strawberries, 1957

only thing missing is the cob

If there's one thing chefs, cookbooks and nutrition experts agree on it's this: Cook vegetables *quick!* That's how you keep the flavor, color and vitamins the good earth put into 'em.

And now the Green Giant has found a way to quick-cook corn. Niblets Brand corn. The corn goes into a dramatically different pressure cooker under split-second automatic control. Zing! It's done.

You get the fun and flavor of a fresh-picked roastin' ear—only thing missing is the cob. New quick-cooked Niblets. Just heat and feast.

NIBLETS BRAND CORN
now quick cooked

Choice of two family sizes:
12-oz. can, serves 4 to 5;
7-oz. can, serves 2 to 3.

Niblets Corn, 1957

NEW PACK!

NIBLETS SWEET CORN

A little horn-tootin' is in order. The Green Giant's done it again! Now in your store is the new, sweeter-than-ever, 1950-model Niblets Brand—the best-eatin' corn ever was. Fill up your arms with cans for the fresh-shucked flavor of tender young corn-on-the-cob without the cob!

Green Giant Company, Headquarters, Le Sueur, Minnesota; Fine Foods of Canada, Ltd., Tecumseh, Ontario.

"Niblets" Brand Reg. U.S. Pat. Off. © A.F.S.

Niblets Corn, 1950

Easy to get cheers for this
BLUE LAKE GREEN BEAN
winner dinner
...with canned tuna and macaroni!

make it in
19 minutes
for only 19¢
a serving!

Winner Dinner
Hot 'n Hearty One-Dish Dinner

From rich garden lands of the West come these wonderful vine-tender

BLUE LAKE *Variety* GREEN BEANS

Once in a blue moon a new adventure in good eating like this: *Blue Lake Green Beans*. Rich soil, gentle climate, years of tending and blending make *Blue Lake beans taste* more delicious, *look* more appetizing . . .

So straight . . . bred to new, exacting standards, these proud young beans pack better, look better, serve better.

So firm and so round . . . each tender, succulent pod is

So green . . . ripened under ideal conditions . . . picked and packed at the height of their youth and tenderness.

So good . . . so delicately flavored . . . from the first forkful you'll say, *"I didn't know beans . . . could taste so wonderful!"*

Be sure to look for the words "Blue Lake" on the label the next time you shop for canned green beans.

Your Favorite Brand of CANNED BLUE LAKE *Variety* GREEN BEANS

Blue Lakes are not a brand, but a type of green bean.

Each can is its own miniature pressure cooker—conserving natural vitamins, minerals, flavor. For best results, just heat and serve. Three years' research at 18 leading universities proves canned food offers the best nutritional value, year 'round, for your money.

The Aristocrat of Green Beans

ASSOCIATED BLUE LAKE GREEN BEAN CANNERS INC.

Blue Lake Green Beans, 1952

"There's our man"—

You can always find the jolly Green Giant
ready to welcome you from the label

The biggest thing about the Green Giant is not his size.
It's the feeling of confidence you get when you see his
picture on a label.

That picture talks. It tells about peas that are still
babies in tenderness. Tall, golden kernels of corn with
summer in every mouthful. Grown with care such as no
peas or corn ever had before. Then *picked and packed at
the fleeting moment of perfect flavor.*

And all this just to make your mealtime life a little
happier. Any wonder he's smiling?

GREEN GIANT PEAS BRAND | **NIBLETS** WHOLE KERNEL **CORN** BRAND

NIBLETS MEXICORN BRAND | **GREEN GIANT** CREAM STYLE **CORN** BRAND

Green Giant Company, headquarters, Le Sueur, Minnesota; Fine Foods of Canada, Ltd., Tecumseh, Ontario.
"Green Giant," "Del Maiz," "Niblets" and "Mexicorn" are trade-marks Reg. U. S. Pat. Off. GGCo. © GGCo.

...enjoy food

Good things to eat
find happy companionship
in ice-cold Coca-Cola.
Here's refreshment,
flavorful and sparkling,
that steps up the enjoyment
of tasty things you like to serve.
Next time you shop,
remember to take *enough* home.

Coca-Cola

REG. U.S. PAT. OFF.

... and now
the *gift* for thirst

Drink
Coca-Cola

Coca-Cola, 1950

Coca-Cola, 1951

Coca-Cola, 1951

Coca-Cola, 1951

Coca-Cola, 1953

Thirst knows no season

Coca-Cola, 1953

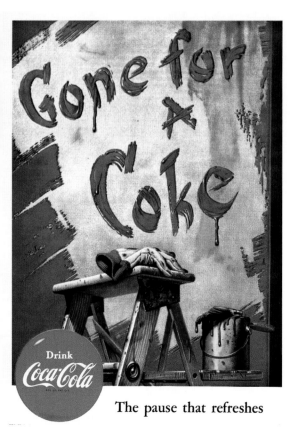

The pause that refreshes

Coca-Cola, 1953

Hospitality can be so easy

Coca-Cola, 1953 ▶ *Coca-Cola, 1959*

Coca-Cola

Pure pleasure!

Seven-Up is so pure...so wholesome!

For a fact, you can even give this sparkling drink to babies—and without any qualms. Lots of mothers do just that!

Just read the ingredients on the 7-Up bottle and you'll see why. We're proud to list them for your inspection, even though regulations don't require this on soft drinks.

Seven-Up has a special fresh, clean taste that appeals to everyone at your house—be he nine months, nine years or ninety. It's the All-Family Drink!

Watch "Soldiers of Fortune" on TV every week. Exciting 7-Up adventure series.

Nothing does it like Seven-Up !

Seven-Up, 1956

Top it off with **HIRES...**

AN ADVENTURE IN REFRESHMENT

When the family takes a voyage in the Treasure Island tradition, Hires has to be aboard. The zesty refreshment of Hires is as out of the ordinary as a chest of pirate treasure, and a whole lot easier to discover. No pirate gold can buy a better beverage. Begin your holiday with an adventure. Cast off with Hires...an adventure in refreshment! Hires...the world's largest selling root beer.

Hires Root Beer, 1959

FOR ANY FAMILY OCCASION...

"*fresh up*" with *Seven-Up !*

BE A "FRESH UP" FAMILY!

Sunday at the zoo! What a family day to remember—Freddie and Kay thrill to the bears' antics. And look what little brother is enjoying! Cheerful, clean-tasting 7-Up takes an active part in family fun at home . . . or anywhere.

Seven-Up is *so pure—so completely wholesome* that even the *very youngest* can "fresh up" just as often as they want . . . and with as much as they want, too.

Seven-Up, the *all-family* drink, is a part of *all-family* fun in millions of homes. So "fresh up" with 7-Up—the *all-family* drink. Order a case where you see those bright 7-Up signs.

You like it . . . it likes you!

FAMILY GAME BOOKLET Family fun suggestions for youngsters and grownups! Send 20¢ in coin to FAMILY FUN, 1722 South 10th Street, St. Louis (4), Missouri, or your local Seven-Up Bottling Company.

BUY A CASE TODAY!

Seven-Up, 1950

Let's have a picnic!

IT'S MORE FUN WITH CANADA DRY... because there's more refreshment to Canada Dry. Once you taste that wonderfully delicious flavor . . . once you enjoy that wholesome, zestful lift . . . you'll never go back to any other drink. Today, have yourself a picnic . . .

Switch to **CANADA DRY** *Ginger Ale!*

See Super Circus on Television

Canada Dry Ginger Ale, 1952   ▶ *Seven-Up, 1958*

Pepsi-Cola, 1953

Canada Dry Ginger Ale, 1951

Pepsi-Cola, 1959

Pepsi-Cola, 1959 ▶ *White Rock Sparkling Water, 1950*

And the winner is...

Not Only Very Good Eating, But Very Wise Eating

Nutrition be damned. The 1950s were all about fun food. And what could be more tempting than a dollop of ice cream on your breakfast cereal first thing in the morning? Even Betty Crocker, the symbol of the American homemaker, endorsed this cholesterol-loaded morning meal.

Nicht nur sehr gutes, sondern auch sehr vernünftiges Essen

Zur Hölle mit der gesunden Ernährung. In den Fünfzigern drehte sich alles um verrückte Speisekreationen. Und was könnte da verlockender sein als ein Klacks Eiskrem auf den Frühstücksflocken, die man morgens als Erstes zu sich nimmt? Sogar Betty Crocker, die amerikanische Vorzeige-Hausfrau, gab dieser cholesterinlastigen Frühmahlzeit ihren Segen.

Manger non seulement bon mais bien

Au diable les principes de nutrition. Mangeons ce qui nous plaît. Et quoi de plus tentant qu'une louchée de glace sur les céréales du petit déjeuner ? Même Betty Crocker, symbole de la ménagère américaine, souscrit à cet afflux de cholestérol matinal.

What d' you know —
a Wheaties Split!

"Spoon right in," Betty Crocker says. "It's still your Breakfast of Champions, but made this time with ice cream (any flavor) and bananas and Wheaties. Not only very *good* eating but very *wise* eating, because wheat is the most popular cereal grain in America. (And full of food energy!) There's a whole kernel of wheat in every Wheaties flake!"

WHEATIES
IN CANADA, TOO!

"BREAKFAST OF CHAMPIONS"

General Mills

Wheaties Cereal, 1956

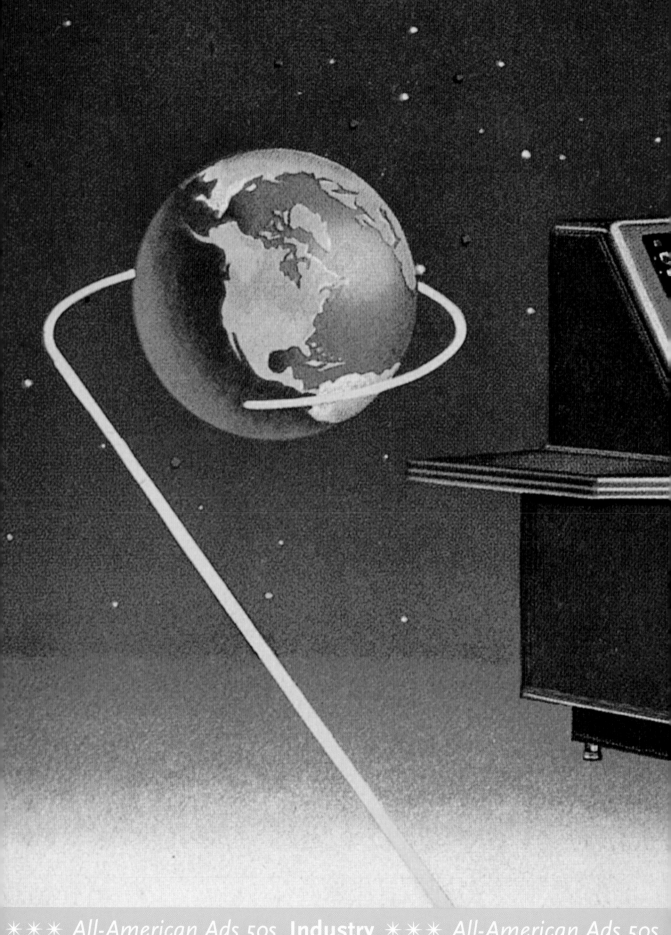

Here's POWER
...to handle YOUR job

This 21-ton tractor (the world's largest) is big enough and rugged enough to give you the advantage on any tractor job.

With a bulldozer, it will tear away a mountainside to uncover a new vein of ore. With a scraper, it will rip off the overburden to open up a seam of coal. With a logging arch, it will drag out of the woods — in one load — logs that will yield lumber for a four-bedroom home.

It fits any dirt-moving job — it's a "get-things-done" tractor! You will like it.

ALLIS-CHALMERS
TRACTOR DIVISION · MILWAUKEE 1, U.S.A.
...Originator of the Torque Converter Tractor

CRAWLER TRACTORS • MOTOR GRADERS • ROAD MACHINERY • ENGINES • FARM AND INDUSTRIAL WHEEL TRACTORS • FARM EQUIPMENT

Allis-Chalmers, 1951

The first dividend is $4,000,000

The engineers for the Illinois Toll Highway Commission had a problem. In fact, they had 200 problems . . . 200 bridges to build in a hurry at a time when steel was in very short supply. They took a good long look at a recent engineering advance in Louisiana, the Lake Pontchartrain Causeway. This causeway, which is really a bridge nearly 25 miles long, was built of precast prestressed concrete members—and therein appeared a possible answer to 200 problems in Illinois.

The engineers for the Illinois Toll Highway Commission built a test bridge with that construction at one of their problem sites. And this is what they found. Not only could long delays in the delivery of steel members be avoided, but the bridges could now be built in half the time required if steel were immediately available. Further, the test showed savings of $20,000 per bridge. Thus, with 200 bridges to build, the first dividend on a new idea from America's engineers is $4,000,000. It will be repeated many times as the nation's system of improved highways expands.

Dietzgen takes pride in telling the achievements of America's engineers.

Dietzgen knows them as few companies do. For more than 70 years we have served them with instruments, equipment and supplies essential to their work. Their dedication to perfection has shaped our standards and has long been our creed. Their achievements have been our constant inspiration. The extent to which the name Dietzgen has won and held their respect has been our most cherished reward.

DIETZGEN
PRECISION EQUIPMENT & SUPPLIES FOR ENGINEERS, ARCHITECTS, DRAFTSMEN, SURVEYORS AND SCIENTISTS

EUGENE DIETZGEN CO., Chicago • New York • San Francisco • New Orleans • Los Angeles • Pittsburgh
Washington • Philadelphia • Milwaukee • Seattle • Denver • Kansas City • Cincinnati • Dealers in All Principal Cities

Dietzgen, 1957

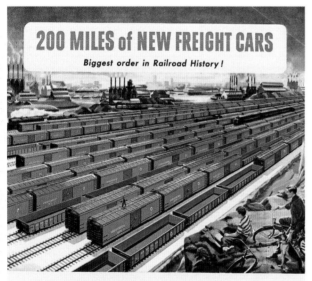

200 MILES of NEW FREIGHT CARS
Biggest order in Railroad History!

20,000 NEW ALL-STEEL FREIGHT CARS . . . enough to form one solid train extending from New York to Baltimore and beyond!

Just what industry is calling for as production speeds up everywhere . . . 8,250 box cars, 11,500 gondolas, 250 flat cars . . . an increase of 5,000 cars since our last report.

Several thousands of these new cars are already in service. Eleven thousand will have been completed and put to work by March 31. The balance will come along at an average of a thousand a month. Freight car builders say this is by far the largest car order ever placed by one railroad. These 20,000 cars will cost $114 million, making a total of $133 million the Pennsylvania Railroad will have spent for newer and better freight cars since January, 1950.

This order to car builders will expand the Pennsylvania Railroad's vast freight fleet to keep pace with the growing demand for railroad transportation by industry and defense.

PENNSYLVANIA RAILROAD
Go by Train . . . Safety—with Speed and Comfort

Keeping Power Costs Low . . .

More Compact Turbine-Generators

This installation represents a milestone in steam turbine design . . . the first close-coupled cross-compound units.

To electric power utilities, this design offers many advantages: Less space means smaller building—single compact foundation—shorter crane span—simplified oil and steam piping.

In other electric power equipment built by Allis-Chalmers —power transformers, circuit breakers, switchgear and auxiliaries—advanced engineering is helping utilities trim costs and keep electric rates low. Allis-Chalmers, Power Equipment Division, Milwaukee 1, Wisconsin.

In Industry After Industry
. . . the needs of each are served with Allis-Chalmers wide range of power generation and distribution equipment and processing machinery designed and manufactured for the particular requirements of that industry.

ALLIS-CHALMERS

U.S. Steel & Univac, ◄ *Pennsylvania Railroad, 1950*

Allis-Chalmers, 1956 ► *Alcoa Aluminum Company of America, 1953*

31 STORIES OF ALUMINUM MAKE NEWS

TURN AN INSPIRED ARCHITECT LOOSE with a contractor who loves aluminum—and a new kind of building starts happening. A building like this 31-story, aluminum-clad Alcoa headquarters office in Pittsburgh. ✓ ✓ ✓ Efficiency through light weight was the purpose of its builders . . . and innovation their method. Outside walls of 6 x 12-foot aluminum panels were simply hung like curtains from within—no scaffolding was required. Aluminum windows pivot on a vertical axis for safe and easy inside cleaning. A year-round aluminum radiant heating and cooling system in the ceiling is paneled with aluminum. Wiring, conduit, water tanks, ducts, elevators—are aluminum, too. *Light-walled*, this building used hundreds of tons less structural steel framing than a conventional building of the same size . . . *Thin-walled*, it yields thousands of feet of extra floor space. It will require no painting—and virtually no maintenance. ✓ ✓ ✓ The innovations which make it a sounder investment and a new, better way of business living were conceived and developed by Alcoa. In fact, the whole American aluminum industry has been built on Alcoa research, which for sixty-four years has worked to give aluminum most usefulness at lowest cost.

ALUMINUM COMPANY OF AMERICA · PITTSBURGH 19, PA.

Alcoa Aluminum

ALUMINUM COMPANY OF AMERICA

Symbolic of the newer chemicals for better living, this Hortonsphere looms up at an entrance to the Wyandotte Glycol plant. Its spherical shape withstands best the great pressures of stored, volatile liquids.

SPHERE OF INFLUENCE

The "sphere of influence" for glycols has spread so widely that, today, these useful chemicals are improving products in nearly every modern industry.

Their personality traits are many. Wyandotte Glycols *are hard to freeze, slow to boil* — so they find uses in *permanent* anti-freezes and coolants. *These versatile chemicals absorb moisture and evaporate slowly* — so they are superb humectants and softening agents for textiles, cellophane, smoking tobacco, inedible gelatin, glue, cork and paper. Glycols are also used in brake fluids, wood stains, perfumes — and as plasticizers for certain resins and as solvents for oils, dyes and other organic compounds.

In making Glycols, more than *half* the ingredients are chemicals which Wyandotte produces from limestone, coal and salt. Vast company-owned resources of these materials help assure dependable deliveries.

Other advantages to customers include Wyandotte's strategic Great Lakes location, for economical transportation by water, rail and truck . . . "know-ahead" research . . . an alert Technical Service Department . . . 60 years of experience. These have made Wyandotte one of the great names in chemicals.

Wyandotte Glycols may well improve your products and save you money. Our Sales Department will be glad to confer with you on their properties and uses.

Wyandotte
REG. U. S. PAT. OFF.

ORGANIC AND INORGANIC CHEMICALS • WYANDOTTE CHEMICALS CORPORATION • Wyandotte, Michigan • Offices in Principal Cities

Wyandotte Chemicals Corporation is one of the world's major producers of soda ash, caustic soda, bicarbonate of soda, chlorine, dry ice and calcium carbonate. Wyandotte produces glycols and related compounds, certain aromatic sulfonic acid derivatives and other organic intermediates. Wyandotte is also the world's largest manufacturer of specialized cleaning compounds for business and industry.

Wyandotte, 1950

▶ *Aluminum from Canada, 1958*

GLASS gives new vision to Science

The first crude microscope opened new vistas to science. The Leyden jar, the retort, and now hundreds of implements of glass let the pioneers of research watch theory become fact. Whatever the next advance in science, it is almost certain to be seen first through glass.

Like the scientist, the shopper, too, wants to see. She prefers foods in glass, drugs in glass, beverages, cleaners —

everything that has quality to put on view. Glass provides so many good things . . . sight, shelter, safety . . . and best of all it is abundant and low in cost.

DIAMOND ALKALI's contribution to the abundance and economy of glass is soda ash of superior quality. To meet growing demand we have enlarged and modernized production facilities . . . to serve industry and you with more and better "Chemicals you live by."

DIAMOND ALKALI COMPANY, Union Commerce Bldg., Cleveland 14, Ohio.

Diamond Chemicals

Diamond Chemicals, 1958

Bloodless plasma...

PVP, polyvinylpyrrolidone . . . *is an acetylene derivative, a white odorless powder. Injected in the blood stream in solution, it has saved thousands of lives.*

This blood plasma substitute has many exciting advantages...needs no blood typing, is low in cost, can be accurately controlled for uniformity, stored indefinitely without deteriorating, is more readily infused than whole blood. Its availability will make it invaluable for military and civilian emergency use.

PVP is not the equivalent of whole blood, or blood plasma...lacks the corpuscles and nutrients of natural blood. *The collection and processing of blood for plasma is still necessary, particularly for military purposes.* PVP will not be in large supply until after approval by the official agencies now evaluating it.

Developed and extensively used abroad, PVP is made in the US by General Aniline. A pilot plant built in 1947 permitted small scale manufacture, and supplied PVP for experiment and research to clinics,

hospitals and laboratories. Present production is limited but a new plant, to be built during the next year, is expected to make ample tonnage available.

THIS acetylene derivative appears to have other valuable properties . . . gives promise of detoxifying dangerous drugs to make them safe... and increase the efficiency of drugs including antibiotics, anaesthetics and others.

General Aniline, with plants at Rensselaer, N. Y. and Grasselli, N.J. is the largest US producer of high quality dyestuffs. The Ansco Division, Binghamton, N. Y. is the country's second largest supplier of cameras, photographic films, and papers. And the Ozalid Division, Johnson City, N. Y. makes Ozalid facsimile reproducing machines and sensitized papers.

For public welfare in peacetime and national security in war...General Aniline is a vital American industry . . . a good company to work for and with, worth knowing and watching.

General Aniline & Film Corporation

...From Research to Reality...
230 Park Avenue, New York 17, N. Y.

General Aniline & Film Corporation, 1951

Building California... *Serving You!*

Every day more than a thousand new people come to California to live. Many follow the example of one-third of the population of this prosperous state and become Bank of America customers. Soon, like their neighbors, they are buying new homes, automobiles—thousands of other consumer goods and commodities. These are the people—this is the economy—that Bank of America serves through 538 California branches. This is banking that is building California and serving you...banking that provides vitally needed credit to one out of every three of your California customers.

Bank of America
NATIONAL TRUST AND SAVINGS ASSOCIATION

A mile ahead...the bank that knows California

Typical of the nation's fastest-growing state is the Miracle Mile in Los Angeles—a bustling stretch of boulevard lined with famous department stores and specialty shops. Typical, too, are the *three* Bank of America branches located on this one-mile strip. For, with 543 branches, Bank of America serves every portion of the giant California market—knows every

phase of its industry, agriculture, and commerce.

Through its system of statewide banking facilities, Bank of America provides its out-of-state customers with a type of service that is unique in California. If you need *local* information concerning new plant sites, land costs, labor supply, on-the-spot estimates of sales and marketing trends—write Bank

of America, 300 Montgomery Street, San Francisco, or 660 South Spring Street, Los Angeles. Attention: Corporation and Bank Relations Department.

With resources of over $8 billion, Bank of America is the world's largest privately owned bank. Its shares are held by more than 200,000 stockholders.

Bank of America
NATIONAL TRUST AND SAVINGS ASSOCIATION

Bank of America, 1953

Bank of America, 1954

Because of Christmas...

Because of Christmas, all of us capture some of the wonder and joy and faith that shine in children's eyes.

Because of Christmas, we feel again the happiness that comes with gift-giving.

Because of Christmas, we shall be a little more patient, and more tolerant and understanding; we shall draw a little closer to our families, our friends and our neighbors.

Because of the magic of Christmas Day, we shall think a little more deeply about the teachings that have survived through the centuries to preserve for us the greatest message of hope and good will the world has ever known.

And, we can take new encouragement from the fact that modern science and industry are doing more today than ever before to give reality to Christmas hopes for a better, happier, and healthier life for millions of people, young and old, throughout the world.

AMERICAN *Cyanamid* COMPANY

30 ROCKEFELLER PLAZA, NEW YORK 20, N. Y.

American Cyanamid Company, 1954

Borg-Warner has been working hand in hand with DEERE & COMPANY through the years

For the famed John Deere line of farm equipment, Borg-Warner supplies many vital operating parts.

Almost every American benefits every day from the 185 products of ***BORG-WARNER*** *created for the automotive, aviation, marine, farm equipment, and home appliance industries.*

Important names in practically every industry are linked with Borg-Warner's World-famous Deere & Company is one of these. For more than a century this firm has been an outstanding factor in helping American farmers feed and clothe more people better.

Of course, it is a matter of daily pride that *all* the foremost builders of farm equipment look to Borg-Warner for a great variety of specialized parts.

Among these are plow discs, harrow teeth, hydraulic pumps, chain drives, universal joints, transmissions, clutches, carburetors, as well as many special types of tillage steels.

Each one is evidence of the B-W determination to "design it better—make it better." B-W's engineering skills and large production facilities help importantly in obtaining for all of us the earth's very best of everything.

Borg-Warner, 1951

▶ *Metropolitan Life Insurance Company, 1957*

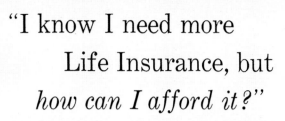

"I know I need more Life Insurance, but *how can I afford it?*"

Have you ever had this thought? Have you ever wondered how your wife could keep the family together if something should happen to you? This question faces most men while their children are growing up.

We believe that you will find the answer to this question in the Metropolitan Family Income Plan. This plan is designed to furnish the extra income needed to take care of your children until they have finished their education or are getting started in life. The plan combines regular insurance with a special income provision which can be fitted to your particular circumstances and family needs. Here are some of its important features:

1. You choose the amount of monthly income needed— $100 a month, $200, $300 or more.

2. If you should die at any time within 20 years—while your children are growing up—the Metropolitan Family Income Plan will provide the income you arrange to be paid to your family each month for the remainder of the 20 years. Then the face amount of the policy will be paid in cash.

3. If you should live beyond the 20 years, when the income provision is no longer in effect, your family will still have continuing protection for the face amount of the policy.

For your own peace of mind, why not get the complete details of the Family Income Plan from your Metropolitan Representative? He will be more than happy to explain it to you, and demonstrate that . . .

**Metropolitan service is as local as Main Street . . .
as close as your phone**

Metropolitan Life Insurance Company
(A MUTUAL COMPANY)
1 MADISON AVENUE, NEW YORK 10, N.Y.

Gurney Miller

University of Virginia; Thomas Jefferson, Architect.

Leaders . . . for tomorrow

"What greater or better gift can we offer the republic than to teach and instruct our youth?"*

"SHOULD I GO TO COLLEGE?" That all-important question is in the minds of many high school students. That they find the right answer is equally important to every one of us . . . and to the future of America.

GREAT GAINS TO YOUTH have been accomplished through education. Still, four out of five of our young people do not go to college. Some of these may have a spark of genius. or leadership talent, that will be wasted through lack of educational opportunity.

400 UNION CARBIDE SCHOLARSHIPS have been provided for through The Union Carbide Educational Fund to encourage able and deserving students toward successful careers in business. Scholarships are now open without special restrictions—through 34 selected liberal arts colleges and technological institutes—to all students of high schools and preparatory schools.

THE PEOPLE OF UNION CARBIDE hope you, too—as you think of the future for your children and other deserving American youth—will do everything you can to encourage their ambitions for adequate education. Also, that you will join in giving co-operation and encouragement to those who guide and teach them.

TO LEARN MORE about the Union Carbide scholarships, their purposes, and the colleges, institutes, and universities in which they have been established, write for booklet Q.

*Cicero

UNION CARBIDE
AND CARBON CORPORATION
30 EAST 42ND STREET   UCC   NEW YORK 17, N.Y.
In Canada: UNION CARBIDE CANADA LIMITED

─────── *UCC's Trade-marked Products include* ───────

LINDE Oxygen	EVEREADY Flashlights and Batteries	NATIONAL Carbons	ACHESON Electrodes	LINDE Silicones
PYROFAX Gas	SYNTHETIC ORGANIC CHEMICALS	PRESTONE Anti-Freeze	UNION CARBIDE	Dynel Textile Fibers
PREST-O-LITE Acetylene	ELECTROMET Alloys and Metals	HAYNES STELLITE Alloys	BAKELITE, VINYLITE, and KRENE Plastics	

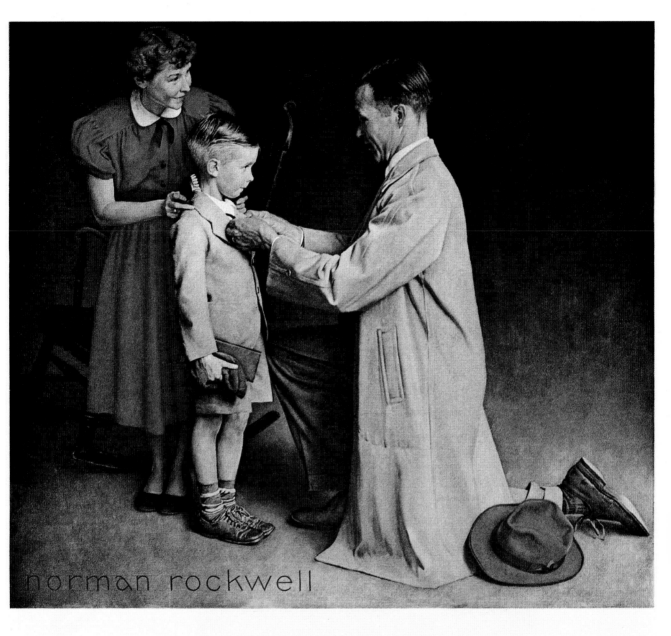

One of the Great Moments of your life... *His First Day At School*

Union Carbide, 1955 ◄   *Massachusetts Mutual Life Insurance Company, 1950*

A better future for you is <u>this</u> close!

Call your Prudential Agent

The PRUDENTIAL
INSURANCE COMPANY OF AMERICA
CARROL M. SHANKS, PRESIDENT

When out-of-town family
or friends have a birthday
Telephone your greetings

It's easy and it's fun to send your birthday wishes across the miles by telephone.

You can share in the thrill and happiness of the day, almost as if you were there in person. And, for the one you call, there's something kind of special about a personal greeting by telephone.

Why not mark your calendar now so that you'll remember the birthday calls you want to make?

BELL TELEPHONE SYSTEM

LONG DISTANCE RATES ARE LOW
Here are some examples:

New York to Philadelphia . . .	40¢
Pittsburgh to Cleveland	45¢
St. Louis to Cincinnati	75¢
Atlanta to Chicago	$105
Seattle to Washington, D. C. .	$200

These are the Station-to-Station rates for the first three minutes, after 6 o'clock every night and all day Sunday. They do not include the 10% federal excise tax.

Call by Number. It's Twice as Fast.

"Visioneering"—unlimited

Turning ideas into sales through the modern magic of molding rubber is the specialty of Goodyear's St. Marys, Ohio Plant. There the vision of designers is combined with the rubber engineering skill and experience of the G.T.M.—Goodyear Technical Man—in the world's largest plant devoted to the molding and extruding of complete assemblies or components for manufacturers throughout industry.

In this huge plant—soon to become even larger—many thousands of

Leakproof — Sanitary — Easily-inserted Sweat-Seal* Vacuum Bottle stopper designed by Aladdin Engineers and the G.T.M. fits Aladdin Hy-Lo, Quality and Economy Vacuum Bottles — gives excellent, heat-and-cold-retaining seal, keeps bottle contents fresh and sweat. Hot water rinse cleanses after use. Won't absorb odors.

*Sweat-Seal—T.M. Aladdin Industries, Inc., Nashville, Tennessee

You can beat—without holding—Revolutionary new Belvedere* Mixing Bowl with Griptite rubber base, precision-molded by Goodyear, that anchors securely to table and holds bowl at any tilt position without use of hands. Now at better housewares stores.

*Belvedere—T.M. Griptite Corp., Lancaster, Ohio

For sports-work-or what have you—Wherever a better grip is important, the new Goodwin* Flange-Wrap Grip—Goodyear produced—is ideal. Easy to apply to sports equipment, hand tools, steering wheels, etc. You'll find these grips on sale in several color designs at Golf Course Pro Shops.

*Goodwin—T.M. Central States Industrial Sales Co., Cleveland, Ohio

Quiet — sanitary — animal proof — The Raymond Loewy Associates-styled Pile-Pail*—a quiet-in-the-night garbage pail with a leak-tight cover and a sanitary readily-cleaned interior—is another of the thousands of molded items building sales for Goodyear customers.

*Pile-Pail—T.M. Reuce Inc., Chicago, Illinois

separate items are being produced to exacting specifications and in quantities to meet production-line requirements. If sub-assemblies or finished articles of rubber — in any of its varied forms — can improve your design or build your sales, it will pay you to consult the G.T.M. Write him at Goodyear, St. Marys, Ohio or Goodyear, Akron 16, Ohio.

GOODYEAR INDUSTRIAL RUBBER PRODUCTS
GTM-Specified
Rubber Molded to Metal
VIBRATION ISOLATER FOR ENGINES
Typical of the hundreds of parts made for manufacturers, featuring the bonding of specific type of rubber to various metals.
FOR HOSE, FLAT BELTS, V-BELTS, MOLDED GOODS, PACKING, TANK LINING, RUBBER-COVERED ROLLS built to the world's highest standard of quality, phone your nearest Goodyear Industrial Rubber Products Distributor.

GOOD/YEAR
THE GREATEST NAME IN RUBBER

Goodyear, 1951

Today, food goes from packer to store to oven to the table in aluminum containers.

Dinners like grandma used to cook come in aluminum now

60 million frozen dinners, 400 million potpies, 75 million fruit and cream pies went to the table last year, most of them packaged in shining aluminum. But that's just part of the story about aluminum's growing role as a super salesman.

Marketing men say aluminum moves goods off the shelves 10 times faster than other wraps. Result—production of foil containers alone pushed well past the billion mark in 1957 and the industry expects this annual volume to triple by 1960 . . . quadruple by 1965.

With packaging taking an ever-increasing share of the aluminum supply, America's need for basic alumi-num will continue to rise steadily. Indeed—it is estimated that the demand for aluminum may well double in the next 10 years.

Fortunately—in neighboring Canada, Aluminium Limited has harnessed water power to create the vast amounts of electricity needed to make aluminum. As in the past, this dependable source will help U.S. businessmen meet their need for more aluminum.

Aluminium Limited sells no consumer products in the U.S. It specializes instead in supplying its customers with high-quality aluminum ingot and technical assistance to help them create new and better products.

Aluminium
Limited
In the U.S.: Aluminium Limited Sales, Inc.
630 Fifth Avenue, New York 20.

Aluminum Limited, 1954

Little man . . .

big business!

He's a youngster on his first job. A big job, too! He helps today's food shopper carry home more than 18 billion dollars worth of food products from self-service stores alone! To compete in this vast market, food processors must offer their products in packaging that wins sales without benefit of salesmen. That's why more and more food products each year are packaged by Marathon—for 40 years the leader in designing, producing and imprinting *packaging that sells food.*

Marathon Corporation, Menasha, Wisconsin: from tree to finished package, Marathon's facilities include—assured pulpwood sources—pulp and paper plants —package-making plants—ink, engraving and printing plants—years of pioneering research, creative design and merchandising experience.

Marathon Corporation
packaging that sells food

Marathon Corporation, 1953

United States Steel, 1955

Budd Transportation, 1951

Budd Transportation, 1951

DOW Chemicals, 1951

Gutta Percha Belting

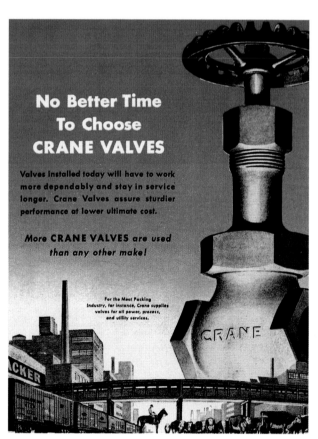

Crane Valves, 1951

DOW Chemicals, 1952   ▶ *DOW Chemicals, 1951*

DETERGENTS "sink the fleet"- but speed the wash

Little Johnny's "Armada" won't stay afloat for long! Mother's handy detergent, spilling into his "ocean", reduces the water's surface tension . . . that well-known tendency of water to form a kind of "tough skin", able to support paper boats . . . and Johnny's ships are doomed to sink.

This ability to make water "wetter" accounts for the exceptional way detergents penetrate and remove soil. Leaving little residue, they cut rinsing operations and are especially well suited for hard water areas.

Detergents depend on caustic soda in their manufacture and Dow, of course, is a prime producer of caustic soda . . . not only for detergents but for soaps and other cleaning

agents. In fact, you are probably a regular customer for many *other* essential products made with Dow caustic soda. This chemical "workhorse" is used to refine petroleum products, process rayons and cottons, refine vegetable oils, plus a host of other uses that contribute to our ever-improving living standards.

To thousands of industrial users of caustic soda Dow offers unequalled, nation-wide distributing facilities enabling them to meet production schedules with dependable service.

THE DOW CHEMICAL COMPANY
MIDLAND, MICHIGAN

What's new at Dow!

Production of caustic soda is being expanded at Dow's Midland, Michigan, Freeport, Texas and Pittsburg, California plants. These installations designed to help meet the country's evergrowing needs are expected to be completed in '52.

DOW

CHEMICALS

This **bryant** furnace can grow on you!

There's an exciting promise in the way this modern comfort maker can grow on you. It's one reason why this Bryant Furnace is going into thousands of homes today. For here is a furnace that gives you an opportunity—better, a practical way—to enjoy *more* than just winter comfort.

It's the famous Bryant "Command-Aire" Furnace (oil or gas)—the superb heating plant that lets you add a "twin" summer air conditioner whenever it suits your convenience. And you can add this extra luxury to your living—and this extra value to your home—without expensive revamping of your duct work, or paying for the complete system all at once.

Whether you plan to build or modernize—air condition or not—ask your Bryant Dealer to show you why the "Command-Aire" Furnace is the wisest, most practical buy today. Call him or use the convenient coupon below.

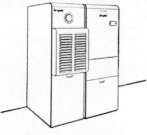

Bryant's "Command-Aire" Twins ... the perfect pair for year 'round comfort.

bryant®

HEATING • AIR CONDITIONING • WATER HEATING

One stands out!

The product with an attractive eye-catching label gets the jump on competition when customers come along. Hands reach out instinctively for the container that looks most inviting. *All Purpose Litho* can add appeal to your product, too. See your Champion merchant.

THE CHAMPION PAPER AND FIBRE COMPANY
HAMILTON, OHIO

*District Sales Offices in New York, Chicago, Philadelphia, Detroit,
St. Louis, Cincinnati, Atlanta, Dallas and San Francisco.*

CHAMPION PAPERS
TRADE-MARK
Symbol of Quality

Champion Papers, 1953

can sinews of glass give your product more "MUSCLE?"

Today there are acetate and paper tapes that match, weight for weight, the strength of toughest metals. Tapes so tough you can't possibly tear them by hand. Industry uses them to make the manufacturers' joint on corrugated boxes, to band bundles of steel rods, and to hold the shipping wrap on heavy metal parts.

What makes these paper tapes so tough? The secret is glass . . . glass in fiber form. And the way it works may suggest an idea for your product.

In these tapes, Fiberglas® Yarns are embedded between layers of paper or in the adhesive. There they contribute enormous strength, without bulk, without rigidity.

The principle of reinforcement with Fiberglas materials has intrigued alert manufacturers in many fields. It is changing old ideas about paper for concrete curing, temporary tarpaulins, furniture wrap. It is increasing the life span of rubber hose and conveyor belting. It is opening new applications for plastics all the way from lampshades to PT boats.

Fiberglas reinforcements may help you to improve your product. Let us discuss it with you. For details, write to Owens-Corning Fiberglas Corporation, 1409 Nicholas Building, Toledo 1, Ohio.

OWENS-CORNING
FIBERGLAS *is in your life..for good!*

Owens-Corning Fiberglas, 1951

Aluminum saves money on production of metal bases of electric lights. Lightness means metal goes farther, cuts material costs. Its workability makes it easy to fabricate, cuts production costs.

Aluminum saves money on chemical storage drums and tanks. Resistance to corrosive action of many chemicals means longer life. Light weight cuts shipping costs every time drums are shipped and returned!

Aluminum saves money on typewriter frames. Production costs are lowered through economical mass production die-casting. And light, strong aluminum reduces weight adding extra value.

Aluminum saves money on service drop cables. Kaiser Aluminum triplex cable combines three wires in one assembly. It needs two-thirds fewer accessories. Takes fewer man hours to install. Can be strung for longer distances.

Aluminum saves money on shoe eyelets. Its combination of advantages makes possible economical mass production, lower material costs—results in eyelets that are strong, rustproof.

New kind of currency

This key is a symbol of money saved—because it's made of *aluminum*.

With aluminum, manufacturers save money on material. They save money on production. And they save money on shipping.

Economy is only one of the outstanding properties of aluminum—which include lightness, strength, corrosion-resistance, workability, heat and light reflectivity.

This unique *combination of advantages* explains why the demands for aluminum are steadily increasing . . . why it is vital to so many products essential to the nation's preparedness program.

To help speed this program, we are operating at peak capacity and are vastly expanding facilities to produce more primary aluminum. In time, our increased production will be shared by everyone.

Kaiser Aluminum & Chemical Corporation, Oakland, California. 63 sales offices and warehouse distributors in principal cities.

Kaiser Aluminum

A major producer in a growing industry

Bryant Furnace, 1954 ◀   *Kaiser Aluminum, 1951*

G-P's new paper mill at Toledo, Ore., with integrated plywood and lumber mills in background.

Rolling on schedule...

Fifteen months ago ground was broken for this new kraft pulp, paper and containerboard mill . . . now in production.

The mountain of wood chips behind the mill is its raw material supply . . . for which not a single additional tree is used. These chips are made from the wood waste of the Georgia-Pacific plywood and lumber mills in the background and are delivered automatically to the new paper mill.

Thus Georgia-Pacific integration moves closer to complete utilization of its huge timber reserves. For new booklet "The Georgia-Pacific Story", write Georgia-Pacific Corporation, 60 East 42nd Street, New York 17, N. Y.

GEORGIA-PACIFIC CORPORATION
GEORGIA-PACIFIC PAPER COMPANY • GEORGIA-PACIFIC PLYWOOD COMPANY

R E S E A R C H . . . R E S O U R C E S . . . R E S O U R C E F U L N E S S

Georgia-Pacific Corporation, 1958

FIRST ORDER OF THE DAY...
PRODUCE!

Today, America's mighty production machine must meet the biggest order in history. It must produce enough to defend freedom and to maintain our economy!

As manufacturers of lubricants—the one product indispensable to *all* industry—our part in this tremendous job is to help your machines run at peak capacity... provide more continuous production, minimize downtime.

Toward this end, we pledge all our resources —offer you...

▶ A complete line of proved quality oils and greases for all your needs.

▶ The services of our staff of lubrication engineers—largest in the industry.

▶ The facilities of our complete research laboratories.

▶ Our lubrication knowledge—acquired through 85 years of experience.

Call on us *any time*.

GARGOYLE
Lubricants

SOCONY-VACUUM OIL CO., INC.,
and Affiliates:
MAGNOLIA PETROLEUM COMPANY
GENERAL PETROLEUM CORP.

SOCONY-VACUUM

Socony-Vacuum
Correct Lubrication
WORLD'S GREATEST LUBRICATION KNOWLEDGE AND ENGINEERING SERVICE

Socony-Vacuum, 1951

Research is our springboard

Tomorrow's more efficient and versatile communications services will be built on new ideas. That's why we are continuously increasing our research and development capabilities.

Today, we have a large and highly-trained staff of scientists and engineers working in many areas of advanced research. In the field of communications, these include—interspacing a number of telephone conversations on one line; controlling industrial processes from a remote point; transmitting business data over a network at high speed.

For America is growing fast, and its appetite for more and better communications is growing faster still.

Our job, as we see it, is to plan and build to meet this need.
General Telephone & Electronics Corporation, 730 Third Avenue, New York 17

GENERAL TELEPHONE & ELECTRONICS

General Telephone, 1958

Steel Is First

To Make

Things Last

When steel puts on its party manners

You don't have to own a country estate to enjoy the fun of parties, steak fries and barbecues right on the home grounds.

With a little imagination—and the right furnishings— any smart couple can transform the area outside their home into an attractively functional site for outdoor living.

You have the imagination—you know what you'd like outside. And the right furnishings are available and agreeably priced. They are made of steel—America's great bargain metal.

Steel outdoor furnishings are handsome as well as hardy. They resist corrosion, rot, fire and warping better than any other paintable material. You know they'll last through years of hard use, years of hard weather.

Steel costs so little... gives so much.
Make steel your standard—and save.

WEIRTON STEEL

Metal sculpture, created in Weirtin—electrolytic zinc-coated steel that resists heat, moisture, rust—demonstrate the exceptional workability of this easily fabricated metal.

WEIRTON STEEL COMPANY
WEIRTON, WEST VIRGINIA

NATIONAL STEEL CORPORATION

National Steel Corporation, 1951

No more "missed" calls while you are out. The Electronic Secretary "answers" the phone, records every message word for word! Write for more information

We're building big on bright ideas
like the Electronic Secretary... product of
America's second-largest telephone system

This "secretary" works overtime and loves it. And so do we! Gen Tel is working overtime to develop new uses for the telephone—making of it a true household appliance, an important tool of business and industry.

That's one reason why we are the nation's second-largest telephone system.

That's one reason why we're growing *fast*—keeping pace with the expanding communities we serve.

We're installing new phones at the rate of 3,750 every week.

We're investing almost $200 million a year in new construction, alone.

We're proud to say it: the only thing brighter than our ideas is our *future!*
General Telephone Corporation, 262 Madison Avenue, New York 16, N.Y.

GENERAL TELEPHONE

General Telephone, 1958   ▶ Everyday Ink   ▶ ▶ Borg-Warner, 1950

Believe It or Not!

GIVING A HAPPY WAG TO ROCKETS' TAILS...FITTING SHOES WITH A NEW LAST...PUTTING EXTRA PULL INTO TRACTORS!

IN SO MANY WAYS, B-W INGENUITY AND SKILL TOUCH THE LIFE OF ALMOST EVERY AMERICAN EVERY DAY.*

FOR EXAMPLE: 19 OUT OF THE 20 MAKES OF MOTORCARS CONTAIN ESSENTIAL PARTS BY **BORG-WARNER**. EVERY COMMERCIAL PLANE AND MANY SHIPS AFLOAT HAVE ABOARD VITAL **B-W** EQUIPMENT. 9 OUT OF 10 FARMS SPEED FOOD PRODUCTION WITH **B-W** EQUIPPED IMPLEMENTS, AND MILLIONS ENJOY THE OUTSTANDING ADVANTAGES OF B-W HOME EQUIPMENT AND APPLIANCES.

4-WHEEL-DRIVE TRACTOR STRETCHES SUMMER!
WITH POWER APPLIED TO **ALL 4 WHEELS**, THIS TRACTOR PULLS WITHOUT SLIPPING ON GROUND STILL TOO WET FOR MOST OTHERS. STEERS WITH LEVERS – LIKE A TANK. LETS FARMERS TILL FIELDS SOONER IN SPRING...LATER IN FALL. CHAIN DRIVES TO THE WHEELS, MADE BY **B-W'S MORSE CHAIN**, GET MORE PULL OUT OF THE ENGINE...GIVE FAR CHEAPER OPERATION. THIS TRACTOR IS ALSO **B-W** EQUIPPED WITH **ROCKFORD CLUTCHES, WARNER GEARS,** AND **MARVEL-SCHEBLER CARBURETER**.

NEW "SHADE" SHUTS OUT SUMMER HEAT AND WINTER COLD!
IT'S **STORM-SHADE**, THE ONLY TRUE ALL-SEASON WEATHER PROTECTION FOR WINDOWS! CREATED BY **B-W'S INGERSOLL**, IT COMBINES PRACTICALLY AIR-TIGHT GLASS PANELS THAT BAR WINTER COLD...AND FAMOUS KOOLSHADE, THE SCREEN THAT REFLECTS SUMMER SUN. YOU SHIFT FROM ONE TO THE OTHER IN MERE SECONDS.

ELECTRONIC "BLOODHOUND" IS CHAMPION SNIFFER!
TO MAKE CERTAIN THAT THE REFRIGERANT IN EVERY **B-W NORGE** REFRIGERATOR IS PERFECTLY SEALED IN, THE COLD-MAKING UNIT IS SEARCHED WITH AN ELECTRONIC BLOODHOUND". SO SENSITIVE IS THIS DEVICE, IT WILL SNIFF OUT MINUTE LEAKS THAT WOULD LOSE AS LITTLE AS AN OUNCE OF REFRIGERANT IN 100 YEARS.

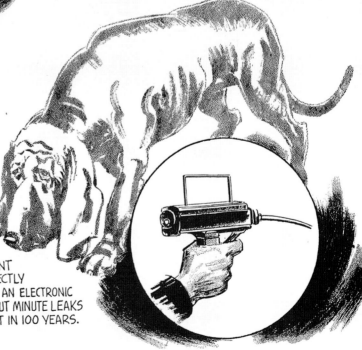

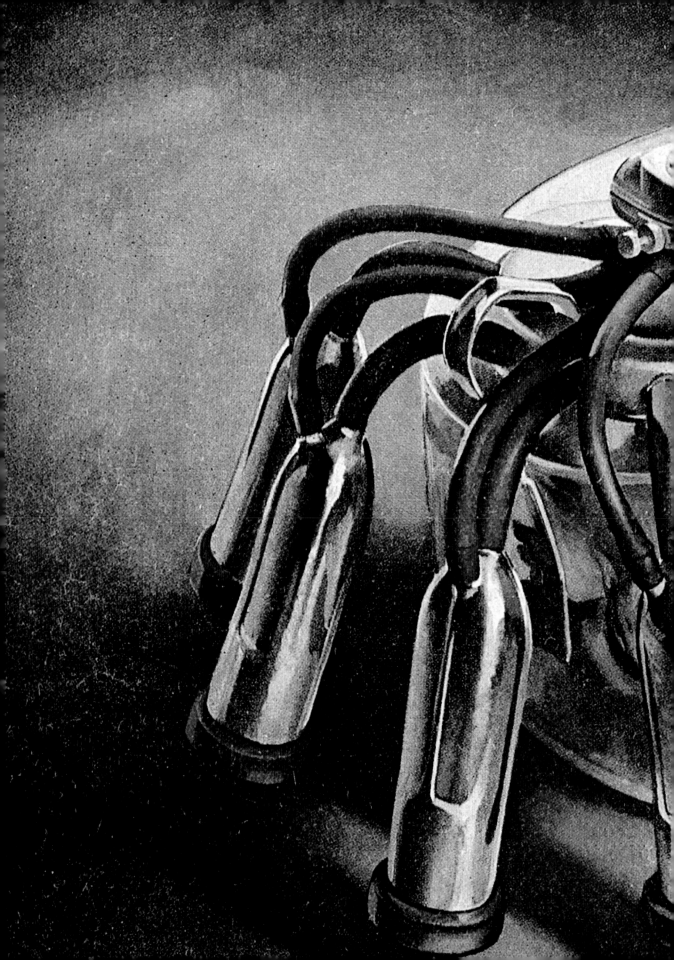

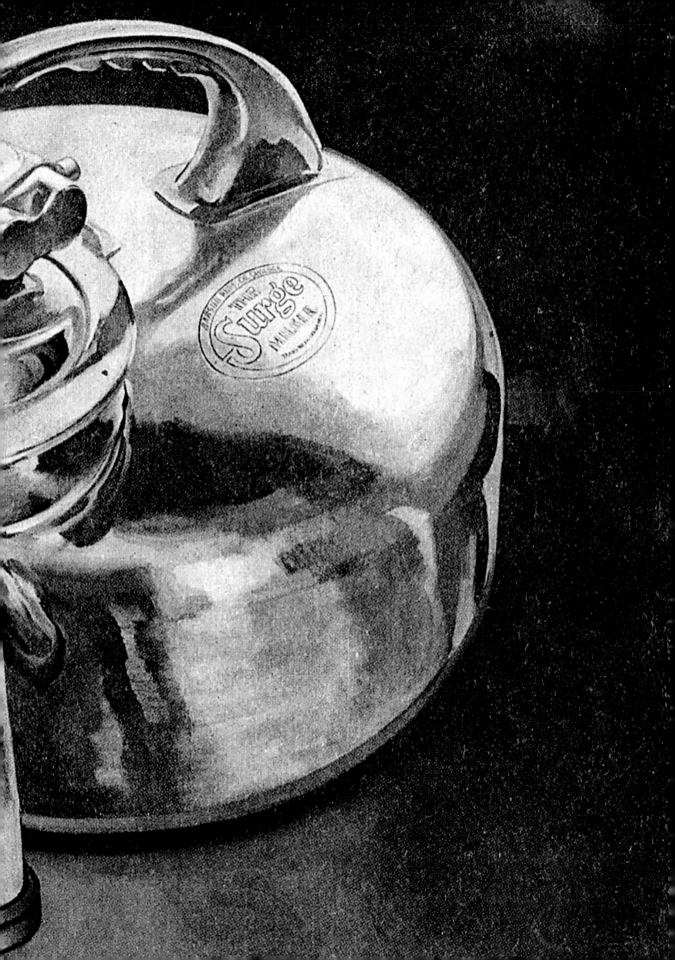

How to buy Crop Insurance... for $5,000 less!

Growing problem for many farmers in the Southwest is round-the-clock irrigation. A few hours under blistering sun without water can ruin the healthiest crops. Such was the case with one Arizona farmer who relied on deep wells to keep his fields green.

Trouble was the heart of his system—a 3,000-gallon-per-minute pump—constantly kicked over its traces. Its drive was too short for ordinary flat belts to handle its rugged quarter-turn. *No belt lasted over four months.* And to redesign the drive to avoid breakdown during the nine-month season would cost $5,000.

How to insure the crop, without this expenditure, was the problem given the G.T.M.—Goodyear Technical Man.

After studying the drive, the G.T.M. recommended the revolutionary new COMPASS HD Transmission Belt — the world's first flat belt built with endless, Triple-Tempered (3-T) Cord, developed by Goodyear Research.

16 months later, *after four times the average service,* the belt finally failed and was replaced with another COMPASS HD Belt. 3-T Cord thoroughly proved it could resist the heavy load and the torturous twisting and flexing to the point where the belt gave trouble-free operation.

3-T Cord is the result of an exclusive, triple-action tempering process, involving Tension, Temperature and Time, which sets synthetic cord at its maximum strength and resiliency. It makes possible a COMPASS HD Belt that's up to 20% thinner, up to 60% stronger than other flat belts. For details on how it cuts drive costs to the bone, see the G.T.M., your Goodyear Distributor or write Goodyear, Industrial Products Division, Akron 16, Ohio.

YOUR GOODYEAR DISTRIBUTOR can quickly supply you with Hose, Flat Belts, V-Belts, Packing or Rolls. Look for him in the yellow pages of your Telephone Directory under "Rubber Products" or "Rubber Goods."

GOODYEAR INDUSTRIAL PRODUCTS
Specified
COMPASS HD TRANSMISSION BELT
for heavy-duty, high-shock-load drives

GOOD/YEAR
THE GREATEST NAME IN RUBBER

Goodyear, 1955

The "pillow" that nestles a Queen

New speed queen of the Atlantic, the S.S. United States makes its New York home at a completely reconditioned pier. One bump against the corner of the pier could deform the plates of the ship—cause costly repairs and expensive delays—and damage the pier as well. Yet, in docking, the great ship is safely warped around the end of the pier by a combination of wind, tide and tugs as her side rests against the dock.

Secret of safe dockings is a huge dock fender that "pillows" the bulk of the liner. It's built around special extruded rubber tubing—15" in diameter, compounded to resist pressure, abrasion, and constant immersion in salt water. The designing engineers and contractors who installed this bumper, the Geo. W. Rogers Construction Corporation, knew what was needed in general—and called in the G.T.M.—Goodyear Technical Man—for specific engineering and compounding of these huge rubber fender parts.

Meeting exacting demands with parts molded or extruded from rubber is a specialty of the G.T.M. For he knows rubber in all its forms far better than anyone else. In large parts or small, simple or extremely complex in design, he can specify compounds to deliver exactly the service you need — and in the process, simplify your problems of product design or parts procurement.

Unrivaled anywhere, the facilities of the world's largest molded goods plant—Goodyear St. Marys—are available to the G.T.M. to insure delivery of the parts and subassemblies needed to meet your production line requirements. Even more important, you get outstanding service from Goodyear St. Marys — the backing of a trained staff of engineers, chemists, sales engineers and an experienced production staff. You get complete service—from product design, in cooperation with your own staff—through production—to in-the-field follow-up.

Doesn't it add up to this? Wherever molded or extruded rubber may be the answer to problems of new product design or old product improvement, it will pay you to come to Molded Goods Headquarters *first*—by consulting the G.T.M., or writing direct to Goodyear, Molded Goods Department, St. Marys, Ohio or Los Angeles 54, California.

YOUR GOODYEAR DISTRIBUTOR can quickly supply you with Hose, Flat Belts, V-Belts, Molded Goods, Packing, Tank Lining, Rubber-Covered Rolls. He's listed in the yellow pages of your telephone directory under "Rubber Products" or "Rubber Goods." Or write Goodyear, Mechanical Goods Division, Akron 16, Ohio.

GOODYEAR INDUSTRIAL RUBBER PRODUCTS
Specified EXTRUDED RUBBER DOCK FENDER TUBES
for George W. Rogers Construction Corp.

GOOD/YEAR
THE GREATEST NAME IN RUBBER

We think you'll like "THE GREATEST STORY EVER TOLD" *Every Sunday—ABC Network*

Babson Bros. Co., 1950 ◀ *Goodyear, 1952*

Cities Service, 1950

National City Bank of New York, 1955

St. Regis Paper Company, 1957

▶ Armstrong's Industrial Insulations, 1950

FAST FEEDING FOR THIRSTY FIGHTERS

Speeding "meal-time" for carrier planes was once a major problem for our Navy. Vital minutes were wasted because refueling hoses for aircraft were stiff, heavy and awkward to handle on a carrier's crowded flight deck. Furthermore, the hoses were deteriorating rapidly due to the destructive action of gasoline on the natural rubber.

A new kind of hose was indicated. Countless materials were tried without success until Hewitt-Robins Neoprene hose was tested aboard the carriers *Saratoga* and *Lexington* in 1932. The first *synthetic* rubber gasoline hose ever manufactured . . . it immediately proved

successful. It was lightweight, flexible, tough, cut down refueling time drastically, and was completely resistant to the action of gasoline and oil.

The next step was obvious—Hewitt-Robins synthetic oil-resistant hose was a "natural" for the entire oil industry. Today, from oil well to service station, it has become an instinctive choice for handling liquid petroleum products.

Whatever you must handle—from gasoline to grout—you will find a Hewitt-Robins hose to meet your most particular needs. Hewitt-Robins has offices and distributors in all major cities.

Hewitt-Robins Synthetic Oil-Resistant Hose is specially designed to withstand deterioration and flaking from liquid petroleum products. It is lightweight, easy-to-handle . . . one of 1,000 types of specialized hose we manufacture.

HEWITT ROBINS

Executive Offices: 370 Lexington Avenue, New York 17, N. Y.

HEWITT RUBBER DIVISION: Belting, hose and other industrial rubber products
ROBINS CONVEYORS DIVISION: Conveying, screening, sizing, processing and dewatering machinery
ROBINS ENGINEERS DIVISION: Designing and engineering of materials handling systems
HEWITT RESTFOAM DIVISION: Restfoam® mattresses, pillows and comfort-cushioning

Hewitt-Robins is participating in the management and financing of Kentucky Synthetic Rubber Corporation

Hewitt Robins, 1951

FIREWORKS AT 20 FATHOMS

Burning metal on the bottom with an oxy-hydrogen cutting torch has speeded up undersea salvage operations. For now the flaming finger of the torch slices through steel in a matter of minutes, where hack saws once took hours.

Making fire work under water calls for a special type of cutting torch, with three hose lines instead of two . . . one for oxygen, one for hydrogen, while a third carries high pressure air to blast water away from the cutting flame.

Hewitt-Robins Twin-Weld Hose is a natural for this operation. It makes hose handling easier—halves the danger of snagging and snarling, because Twin-Weld combines the oxygen and hydrogen lines into one integral hose unit.

Wherever hose must withstand unusual pressures or service, industry turns to Hewitt-Robins. We make over 1000 different types of rubber hose, natural and synthetic . . . a hose to meet every industrial need.

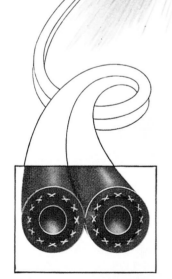

Hewitt-Robins Twin-Weld® Hose is easily identified by the green oxygen line and the red hydrogen line. One stroke of a knife separates the connecting fin for quick and easy coupling to equipment.

Hewitt Robins, 1951

HEWITT **HR** ROBINS

Executive Offices: Stamford, Connecticut

HEWITT RUBBER DIVISION: Belting, hose and other industrial rubber products

ROBINS CONVEYORS DIVISION: Conveying, screening, sizing, processing and dewatering machinery

ROBINS ENGINEERS DIVISION: Designing and engineering of materials handling systems

HEWITT RESTFOAM DIVISION: Restfoam® pillows and comfort-cushioning

Hewitt-Robins is participating in the management and financing of Kentucky Synthetic Rubber Corporation

HOSE HARNESS
FOR THE IRON HORSE

Airpower replaced manpower for railroad braking with the adoption of the automatic air brake. But for almost 40 years after its invention by George Westinghouse in 1869, failures plagued air brake users.

Source of the trouble lay, not in the brake, but in the system's "life-line" — the coupling hoses that carried the airline from car to car. Existing hose couldn't stand the strain of constant flexing, sudden strong pressures, weathering and ballast scuffing.

Improving airline performance became a challenge to Hewitt-Robins. By investigating all the causes of coupling

hose failures, we succeeded in designing the *first* hose that solved the problem. Hewitt-Robins Air Brake Hose made history . . . it was the first rubber product ever scientifically designed to meet a specific industrial need.

Developing better rubber products for industry to facilitate the handling of gases, fluids and solids has been the specialty of Hewitt-Robins for almost a century.

If you have a hose problem — or any bulk materials handling problem — have Hewitt-Robins solve it for you. Hewitt-Robins maintains offices and has distributors in all major cities.

HEWITT **HR** ROBINS

Executive Offices: 370 Lexington Avenue, New York 17, N. Y.

HEWITT RUBBER DIVISION: Belting, hose and other industrial rubber products
ROBINS CONVEYORS DIVISION: Conveying, screening, sizing, processing and dewatering machinery
ROBINS ENGINEERS DIVISION: Designing and engineering of materials handling systems
HEWITT RESTFOAM DIVISION: Restfoam® mattresses, pillows and comfort-cushioning

Hewitt-Robins is participating in the management and financing of Kentucky Synthetic Rubber Corporation

For air brake coupling, or any other application . . . wherever hose is used in industry . . . Hewitt-Robins has designed over 1,000 types. You'll find one to meet your most exacting needs.

Hewitt Robins, 1951

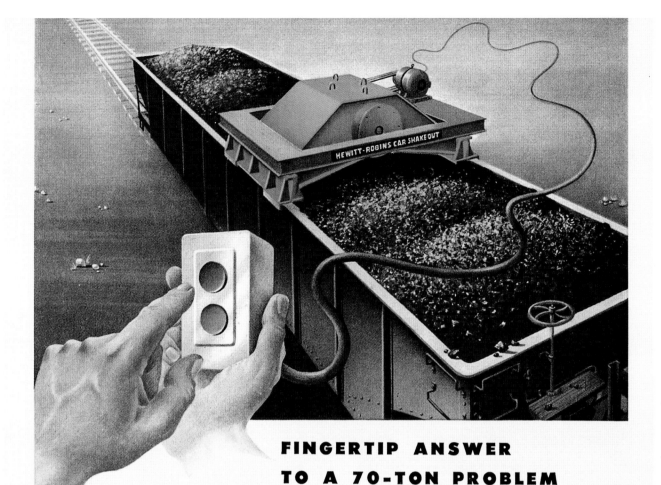

FINGERTIP ANSWER
TO A 70-TON PROBLEM

One touch of a button . . . and a 70-ton hopper car empties itself in as little as 90 seconds!

One touch of a button . . . and even hard-packed loads come free, leaving the car "broom clean"!

For coal, stone, ore, grain—*whatever bulk material you must unload*—the Hewitt-Robins Car Shakeout is the *modern* answer. You save time, money and labor by reducing demurrage charges . . . by cutting unloading crews from as many as twelve to as few as two, even one. You end damage to cars, danger to workmen . . . make a tedious, expensive operation quick, simple, safe.

Over *four hundred million tons* of free-flowing bulk materials have been moved "down the hopper" by Hewitt-Robins Car Shakeouts.

Like so many other notable advances in bulk materials handling, the Car Shakeout is a Hewitt-Robins "first". The *controlled vibration* that makes it so efficient is an old story to us; we've put precisely controlled vibration to work in a long line of time-tested equipment for screening, sizing, feeding, conveying, grading, purifying, dewatering or otherwise processing everything from bits to boulders . . . from pumice to pyrites.

If you have a screening problem . . . *whatever it is* . . . why not make it ours?

THE HEWITT-ROBINS CAR SHAKEOUT is made in two models: Model GS, for plants unloading 15 cars or less daily, and Model HD for continuous, heavy-duty service.

HEWITT (HR) ROBINS

Executive Offices: 370 Lexington Avenue, New York 17, N. Y.

HEWITT RUBBER DIVISION: Belting, hose and other industrial rubber products

ROBINS CONVEYORS DIVISION: Conveying, screening, sizing, processing and dewatering machinery

ROBINS ENGINEERS DIVISION: Designing and engineering of materials handling systems

HEWITT RESTFOAM DIVISION: Restfoam® mattresses, pillows and comfort-cushioning

Hewitt-Robins is participating in the management and financing of Kentucky Synthetic Rubber Corporation

Merchandising's most modern methods work best in National's Long-Span Multiple Buildings

When the time came to pick a building design for suburban Cleveland's modern new Meadowbrook Mart, the most logical choice—from every standpoint—was a Stran-Steel Long-Span 50 Multiple building, 152 feet wide and 642 long.

First consideration was floor space, and the choice was strongly influenced by the Long-Span's provision of a maximum amount of unobstructed interior area—in the Mart's case, over 91,000 square feet . . . enough for the more than 100 retail businesses that make it an outstanding service and shopping center.

Second was construction costs. Long-Spans go up rapidly and easily, so the Mart's owners made appreciable savings in time and money by their choice. And finally, Long-Span was chosen because it easily lends itself to adaptation and modern treatment, as shown by the illustration of the Mart above.

The Long-Span Multiple, a product of the Stran-Steel division of Great Lakes Steel, fits into any site or any application—farm, industrial, or commercial —as readily as it did for the Meadowbrook Mart. Straight sturdy sidewalls and arch roof give a maximum amount of unobstructed space. Arch ribs and trusses of famous N-A-X High-Tensile Steel make for long life, strength and economy.

All-steel buildings are but one of the many special and standard National Steel products that serve many industries in many ways . . . that make National Steel one of America's leading producers of steel.

NATIONAL STEEL CORPORATION
GRANT BUILDING — PITTSBURGH, PA.

SERVING AMERICA BY SERVING AMERICAN INDUSTRY

SEVEN GREAT DIVISIONS WELDED INTO ONE COMPLETE STEEL-MAKING STRUCTURE

GREAT LAKES STEEL CORP. Detroit, Mich. A major supplier of standard and special carbon steel products for a wide range of applications in industry.

WEIRTON STEEL COMPANY Weirton, W. Va. World's largest independent manufacturer of tin plate. Producers of many other important steel products.

STRAN-STEEL DIVISION Ecorse, Mich. and Terre Haute, Ind. Exclusive manufacturer of famous Quonset building and Stran-Steel nailable framing.

HANNA IRON ORE COMPANY Cleveland, Ohio. Producer of iron ore from extensive holdings in the Great Lakes area.

THE HANNA FURNACE CORP. Buffalo, New York. Blast furnace division for production of various types of pig iron.

NATIONAL MINES CORP. Supplies high grade metallurgical coal for the tremendous needs of National Steel mills.

NATIONAL STEEL PRODUCTS CO. Houston, Texas. Warehouse and distribution facilities for steel products in the Southwest.

NATIONAL STEEL

National Steel, 1954

NATIONAL STEEL

This is National Steel

Producing Quonsets–the "world's most useful buildings"–to help America swell production

Born at the Stran-Steel Division of Great Lakes Steel Corporation in the stress of World War II, the versatile Quonset has since proved itself the "world's most useful building" in many different fields of America's production and distribution.

On the farm, Quonsets are helping to increase livestock yields, save crops, preserve machinery. In commerce, everything from banks to bowling alleys—from service stations to super markets—are being housed in easy-to-adapt Quonsets! In industry, these all-steel structures are providing urgently needed factory and warehouse space with speed and economy.

National Steel products serve many industries in many ways. In addition to National's large output of standard steel products, its diversified operations provide special carbon steels for the automotive industry; tin plate for the canning industry; zinc-coated steel for the home appliance industry; low-alloy sheets and fabricated steel flooring for the railroad and trucking industries; steel framing for the building industry.

All these products are National Steel from ore to customer. All are the result of the complete integration, the continual expansion that make National Steel one of America's steel production leaders.

NATIONAL STEEL CORPORATION
GRANT BUILDING — PITTSBURGH, PA.

SERVING AMERICA BY SERVING AMERICAN INDUSTRY

SEVEN GREAT DIVISIONS WELDED INTO ONE INTEGRATED STEEL-MAKING STRUCTURE

GREAT LAKES STEEL CORP. Detroit, Mich. A major supplier of standard and special carbon steel products for a wide range of application in industry.

WEIRTON STEEL COMPANY Weirton, W. Va. World's largest independent manufacturer of tin plate. Producer of many other important steel products.

STRAN-STEEL DIVISION Ecorse, Mich. and Terre Haute, Ind. Exclusive manufacturer of world-famed Quonset building and Stran-steel nailable framing.

HANNA IRON ORE COMPANY Cleveland, Ohio. Producer of iron ore from extensive holdings in the Great Lakes region.

THE HANNA FURNACE CORP. Blast furnace division located in Buffalo, New York.

NATIONAL MINES CORP. Supplier of high grade metallurgical coal for National Steel's tremendous needs.

NATIONAL STEEL PRODUCTS CO. Houston, Texas. Warehouse and distribution facilities for steel products in the Southwest.

National Steel, 1952

▶ *Pittsburgh Plate Glass Company, 1958*

PPG AT THE SHOWPLACES OF AMERICA
Lambert Airport, St. Louis
Architects: Hellmuth, Yamasaki & Leinweber

SOARING ARCHES with acres of PPG glass give St. Louis one of the world's most modern airports. Colorful aircraft, trimmed and protected with PPG finishes, wing into Lambert Field . . . keep passengers comfortable with PPG fiber glass insulation.

PPG opens new horizons in this golden age for building things

We can build airports to express the beauty of flight because PPG glass comes in sizes, shapes and kinds to do it. We can build sleek airliners of aluminum because Columbia-Southern soda ash refines raw ore to make this light, wonder metal. We can build powerful engines that speed planes farther and faster because of today's high-octane fuels made with Columbia-Southern chemicals. Progress all around us—and practically everything we see and use keeps up to date with glass or paint made by PPG, or chemicals made by Columbia-Southern, subsidiary of PPG. PITTSBURGH PLATE GLASS COMPANY, Pittsburgh.

The Power Authority of the State of New York turns water pressure into electricity with the help of Shell Research.

Watts up at the St. Lawrence

SURGING through the world's second largest hydroelectric power plant, the St. Lawrence River will soon be producing 1.8 million kilowatts of low-cost electricity for the U. S. and Canada.

This electricity, coming from turbine generators embedded deep in the new St. Lawrence Power Dam, will serve farms, factories and homes. Only the most precise lubrication, however, will keep the 2,000,000-pound turbine rotors whirling trouble-free. A product of Shell Research was selected to help keep trouble away.

Shell Turbo® Oil was chosen for its ability to cool, resist rust and avoid foaming, plus its ability to protect bearings and shafts during the critical start-up period. These qualities assure economical operation for many years to come.

Developing premium lubricants that safeguard turbines over longer periods of time is another example of the way Shell Research works to assure you of better products, more for your money, wherever you see the Shell name and trademark.

Leaders in Industry rely on Shell Industrial Products

© 1959, SHELL OIL COMPANY

Shell Industrial Products, 1959

At one of Morton's Midwestern plants, 100,000-gallon tanks are used in the chemical processing of high quality brine before converting it to high purity evaporated salt.

Only Morton offers salt service to industry everywhere in America

Morton, the only nation-wide salt company, has salt sources, sales offices and warehouses from coast to coast. This means Morton can offer you complete salt service whether you have just one plant or several plants in different states.

To tailor-make salt for the many special needs of industry, Morton starts with high purity salt from one of its sources. With the aid of gigantic processing, refining and screening equipment, plus constant quality checks, Morton can produce and package salt to meet exacting specifications for any user—from mammoth canneries to small cheese companies.

Morton produces nearly 100 different grades of salt for industry. Morton delivers salt by boat, barge, truck and rail. This means you can get fast delivery on a bag to thousands of tons, anywhere in the country.

Morton sales representatives are backed by the services of their own ultra-modern salt research laboratory—the most complete laboratory of its kind in the world. This means you can get complete technical assistance on any problem relating to salt. This service help alone may be worth thousands of dollars to you every year.

▲ Salt Sources   ▲ Warehouses   ▲ Sales Offices

MORTON SALT COMPANY
INDUSTRIAL DIVISION
110 N. Wacker Drive, Chicago 6, Illinois, Telephone FI 6-1500

Morton Salt Company, 1959

Your letterhead is as much a part of your business personality as your receptionist. MEAD BOND for stationery and envelopes lends correspondence the authority and substance it deserves. Whatever the printing process, MEAD BOND assures a clear, flawless impression. For other office uses, there are MEAD MIMEO,

MEAD DUPLICATOR, and MEAD LEDGER. Each type carries the distinctive Mead watermark. Each type is a specialist without peer.

Your printer or lithographer—and, behind him, America's leading paper merchants—knows that Mead Papers mean business. Ask for convincing evidence.

THE MEAD CORPORATION "Paper Makers to America"   **MEAD papers**

Sales Offices: The Mead Sales Co., 118 W. First St., Dayton 2 · New York · Chicago · Boston · Philadelphia · Atlanta

Mead Paper Co.

Take a page  *from the official military report† on transistors...*

1 OUT OF 3 IS MADE BY PHILCO* EXCLUSIVELY

Transistors play a key role in the space age! Millions upon millions are earmarked for vital military applications. In the significant types, more than one out of every three is designed and produced exclusively by Philco and its licensees ... dramatic proof of Philco pioneering leadership in transistor research and development! The same reliable performance demanded in critical military applications also makes Philco Transistors first choice for industrial and commercial use. To meet your transistor needs ... or for assistance in transistorizing your product .. consult Philco first.

PHILCO / LANSDALE TUBE DIVISION / LANSDALE, PENNSYLVANIA

PHILCO. TRANSISTOR CENTER U.S.A.

†Official report of the Electronics Production Resources Agency of the Department of Defense, projecting military transistor requirements through 1961.   *and Philco licensees

Philco, 1959

ELECTRONICS
is giant industry in the Philadelphia area, where you'll find such names as General Electric, Philco, RCA, Westinghouse and others. If electronics means business to you, you'll benefit from the "on-the-spot" contact provided by The Philadelphia National.

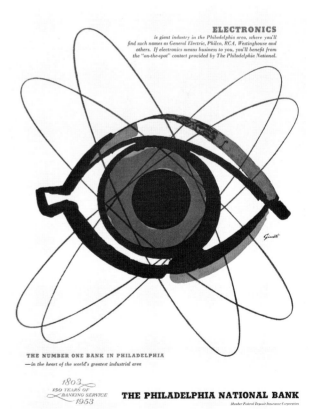

THE NUMBER ONE BANK IN PHILADELPHIA
—in the heart of the world's greatest industrial area

1803
150 YEARS OF BANKING SERVICE
1953

THE PHILADELPHIA NATIONAL BANK
Member Federal Deposit Insurance Corporation

The Philadelphia National Bank, 1953

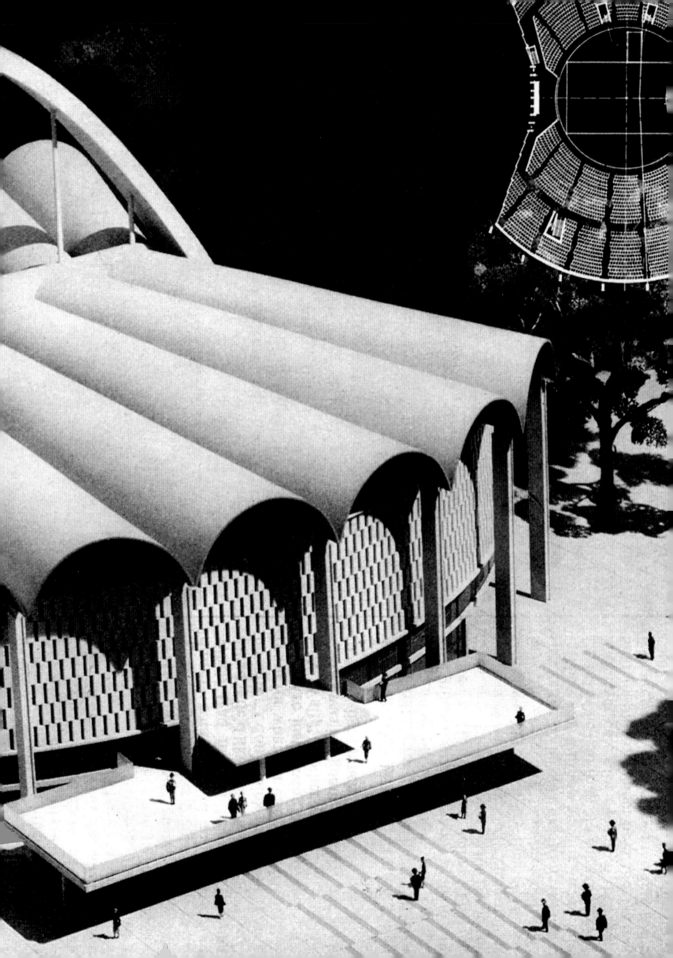

THE TAYLORMAN BRINGS AN ARCHITECT'S DREAM TO LIFE FOR THE EXCITING NEW "LA CONCHA" IN PUERTO RICO

1 A complex form of wood and plywood is created in the shape of the familiar conch shell found on Caribbean beaches.

2 The form is reinforced with steel bars and covered with Gunite cement mixture applied through high-pressure hoses.

3 A unique supper club emerges with a roof that gives "La Concha" its name and a distinctive indigenous personality.

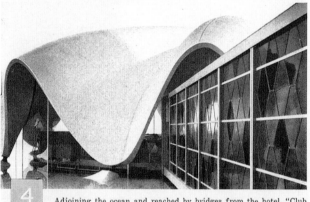

4 Adjoining the ocean and reached by bridges from the hotel, "Club La Concha" emulates a giant half shell set in a lovely tropical lagoon.

5 Inside the room two hundred guests view the sea through cathedral-like windows and dine in air-conditioned sound-absorptive comfort.

6 "La Concha" represents a triumph in construction logistics. The Taylorman co-ordinated materials and workmen from stateside and many foreign countries to build this 266-room, 12-story hotel and dramatic dining room...and he did it all on schedule!

The Taylorman ...symbol of the construction experts assigned to supervise every Taylor project... and a solid reason why anybody contemplating a major building effort should *talk to Taylor*.

TAYLOR
CONSTRUCTION COMPANY

A DIVISION OF

NEW YORK   Taylor INTERNATIONAL CORP   MIAMI
LOS ANGELES   SAN JUAN, P.R.

Universal Cements, 1956 ◄   *Taylor Construction Company, 1959*

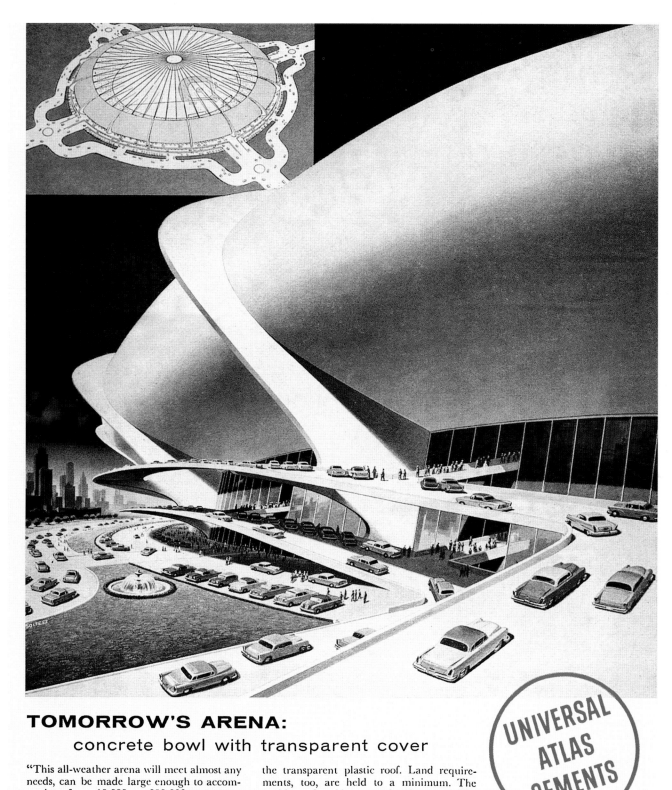

TOMORROW'S ARENA:
concrete bowl with transparent cover

"This all-weather arena will meet almost any needs, can be made large enough to accommodate from 10,000 to 200,000 spectators. The design principles call for a minimum of structural materials, costly excavation and foundation work, since the prestressed concrete bowl is bound together into a unified structure by the steel cables that also support the transparent plastic roof. Land requirements, too, are held to a minimum. The problem of parking space is taken care of by the spacious multideck parking ramps that are an integral part of the underside of the bowl. This simple, practical arena design is made possible by the versatility of concrete."

LEV ZETLIN, *Consulting Engineer*

■ When such concrete structures of tomorrow are built, Universal Atlas will supply, as now, a major share of the essential building material—cement.

UNIVERSAL ATLAS CEMENTS

Universal Atlas Cements, 1958

▶ *Western Electric, 1950*

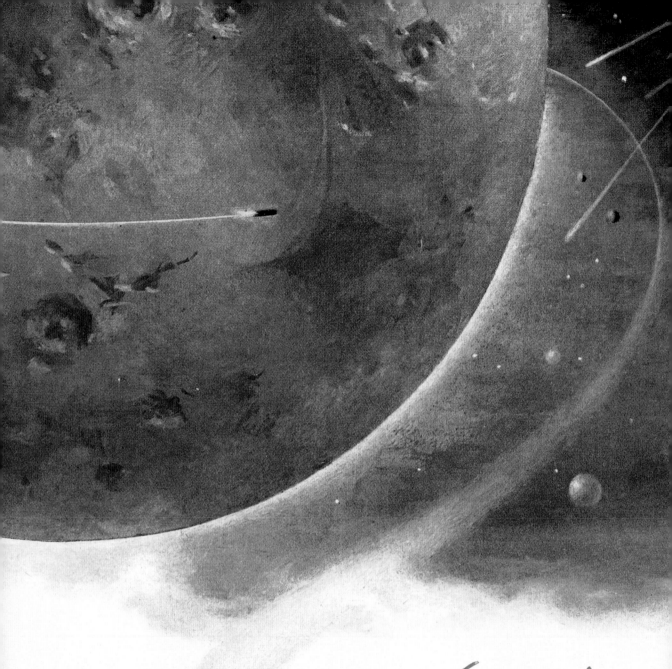

GETTING CLOSER TO *Infinity!*

Businessmen, engineers, and scientists now are solving accounting and research problems which, a few years ago, would have been considered well-nigh infinite.

IBM Electronic Business Machines are making an important contribution to this progress. These machines accomplish once-overwhelming tasks with incredible speed and accuracy . . . freeing thousands of valuable minds for creative effort.

Memory in the millions...

You are looking inside the world's most remarkable business machine . . . the IBM Electronic Calculator. It solves accounting and research problems faster than any other commercial calculator in general use.

GETTING YOUR ANSWERS

. . . at electronic speed!

IBM's vast engineering know-how is helping American business, industry and the Armed Forces get the answers . . . fast. Through its leadership in applying electronic principles to calculators and other types of punched card business machines, IBM has given greater speed, accuracy and economy to the nation's vital processes of calculating and accounting.

Already thousands of IBM Electronic Business Machines are in everyday use. We are continuing to manufacture them in quantity . . . as fast as quality production will permit.

 **INTERNATIONAL BUSINESS MACHINES**
590 MADISON AVENUE · NEW YORK 22, N. Y.

International Business Machines, 1952 ◀◀ *IBM, 1956* ◀ *IBM, 1951* ▶ *International Business Machines, 1951*

PIERCING THE UNKNOWN

This IBM electronic tube assembly cuts through the unknown like a rocket through the stratosphere.

It probes the mysteries of the atom's core; predicts critical wing flutter of fast aircraft; traces paths of light through a lens system; calculates trajectories of guided missiles; plots the course of planets for the navigator.

It calculates payrolls, inventories, costs; points out savings of time and money.

These compact, pluggable units are the heart of IBM Electronic Calculators.

IBM

IBM Electronic Business Machines are vital defense weapons in the hands of our nation's industrial engineers and scientists.

INTERNATIONAL BUSINESS MACHINES

DOES **UNIVAC 120** REALLY <u>THINK</u>?

Many executives who use today's most advanced punched-card computer say..."Yes!"

Because . . ."It makes dozens of record-keeping decisions and calculations every second". . ."It figures out the complete story on our profit changes while the facts are still useful". . ."It simplifies and solves our most complicated payroll, production and billing problems."

The Remington Rand Univac 120 actually *does* replace routine human thinking. Take time-keeping for example. Univac 120 arrives at pay hours while allowing for thousands of variations in shift time, pre- and post-shift time, lunch hours, etc.—checks its own computations—and flags obvious human recording errors.

Does Univac 120 eliminate intelligence? Certainly not. But it does free your skilled personnel for creative thinking. Wherever you pay for clerical chores that involve analyzing, classifying, making logical decisions, comparing and calculating . . . Univac 120 electronic methods will earn their way over and over in speed, accuracy and efficiency. Put it squarely up to us to show you *how* and *where*.

MANAGEMENT ENGINEERED

Engineered to meet the major demands of modern management, the Bendix G-20 data processing system is designed to increase profits in an era of critically spiralling costs. ■ Specifically designed as a central, integrated system, the G-20 is capable of concurrently handling the computer workloads of all of your company's major departments: accounting, marketing, engineering, manufacturing, administration, warehousing and distribution. ■ Bendix G-20 automatic programming and linear programming systems open the door to a vast range of applications. For instance, a Bendix G-20 in a typical business organization could, at this moment, be performing these functions: *design automation and cost analysis, inventory control, budget analysis, production and facility control, sales analysis and forecasting, raw material flow, market research and product planning, order processing, advertising planning, and operations research*...all these in addition to more standard business and scientific applications. As workloads increase, G-20 modularity allows you to expand your system without reprogramming. ■ Backing up the proven hardware-software capabilities of the Bendix G-20 is a nationwide team of experienced applications specialists, providing systems support in depth...from preliminary evaluation through systems analysis, programming, installation and on-site maintenance and service. ■ Your nearby Bendix Computer representative will be glad to introduce you to the Bendix G-20 solution to swiftly rising costs: or write for the brochure, "A Solution to the Profit Squeeze," Bendix Computer Division, 5630 Arbor Vitae Street, Los Angeles 45, California, Dept. AF-39.

Bendix Computer Division

THE BENDIX G-20 COMPUTING SYSTEM

Bendix Computing System, 1952

Announcing UNIVAC 120
for punched-card electronics

The new electronic computer that cuts operating costs — tightens management controls.

You've heard of Univac, the data-processing system that eats up mountains of paperwork in a flash of electrons. Now here's Univac 120, the advanced *punched-card* computer that makes hundreds of calculations and logical decisions in a fraction of a second.

See how Univac 120 races through complicated problems of production control and engineering design. How it saves machine steps on payrolls and cost records. How it saves manpower on billing, accounting, sales analysis and other records.

What's more, with Univac 120 you can afford to get many special reports that take guesswork out of management decisions. It will dig out basic facts and figures that up to now have cost too much or taken too long.

Why not put it squarely up to us to show you how punched-card electronics can pay its way several times over in your organization? Room 2101, 315 Fourth Avenue, New York 10.

Remington Rand
Electronic Systems

Remington Rand & Univac, 1954

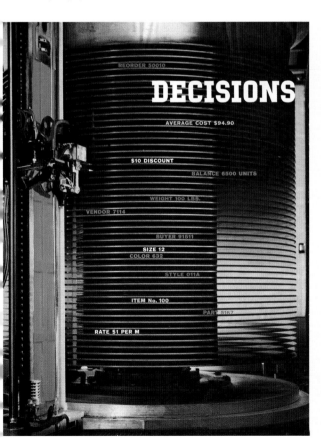

Remington Rand & Univac, 1955 ◄   IBM, 1956

DON'T HAVE TO WAIT!

IBM RAMAC® 305 ORGANIZES FACTS FOR FAST EXECUTIVE ACTION

Immediacy is the order of the day with the IBM RAMAC 305! Current, timely facts for management decisions are always at hand, instantly accessible, and up to date.

RAMAC 305 automatically posts and updates all records related to a single transaction simultaneously. These records are stored in a lightning-fast disk "memory" with a capacity that recent IBM advances have increased to 20-million characters. Data for management review is immediately available; and it can be delivered in complete form at the RAMAC 305 or selectively at a remote "inquiry" station, conveniently located.

The only system of its kind, the IBM RAMAC 305 is bringing dramatic, yet practical benefits to a wide range of businesses today. In transportation, for example, railroads enjoy the many advantages of "electronic storekeeping" including complete, up-to-date management facts and elimination of costly out-of-stock situations. Airlines, too, find RAMAC 305 invaluable in coping with the complexities of reservations as well as conventional accounting problems.

RAMAC 305 can help you gain up-to-the-minute facts for profitable decision-making. For more information, call your local IBM representative.

DATA PROCESSING IBM®

J.W. Clement Co., 1956 ►

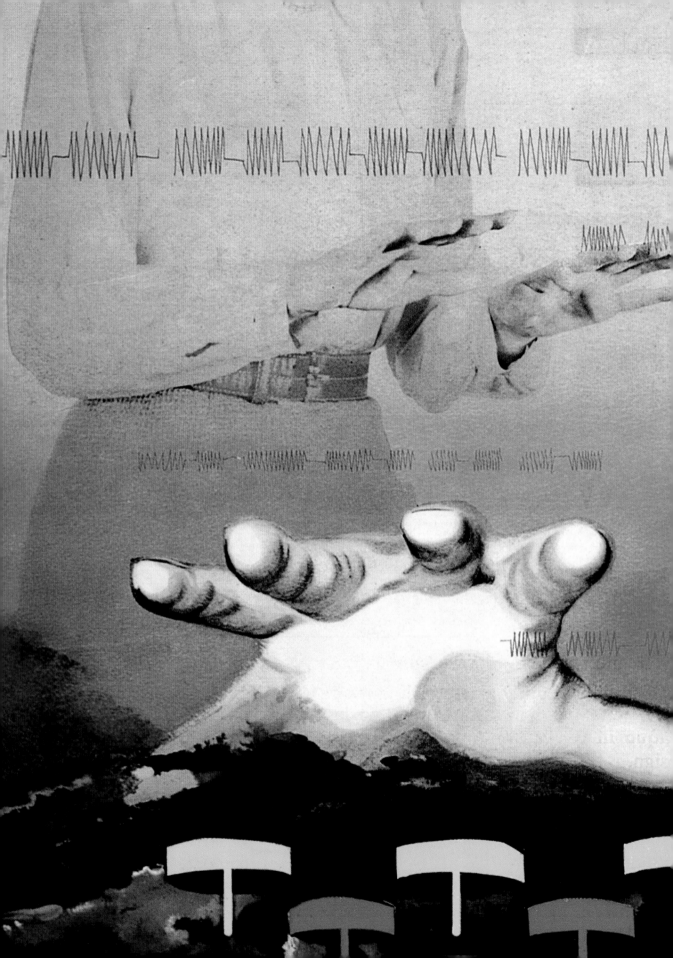

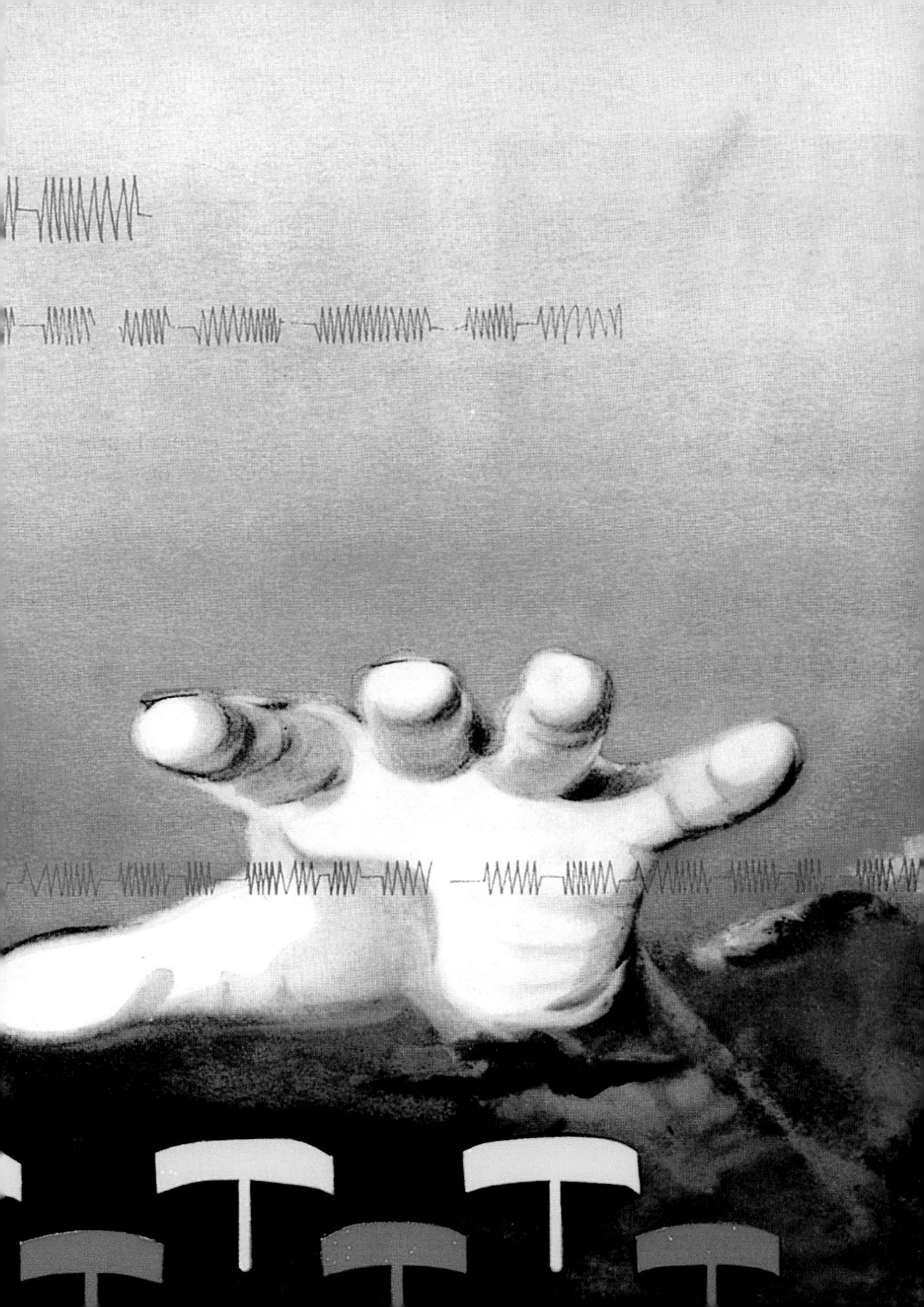

Both are medicine . . .

A carved stick is as logical a medicine to a Colombian Indian as an antibiotic is to us. His knowledge of the cause and cure of disease depends on isolated experience and the memory of the medicine man; ours on the recorded and organized experience of many scientists over many years. This increasing accumulation of knowledge makes continued improvement of our medicines possible.

Medicine . . . Produced with care . . . Designed for health

© 1952 The Upjohn Company, Kalamazoo, Michigan

Upjohn

Upjohn, 1952

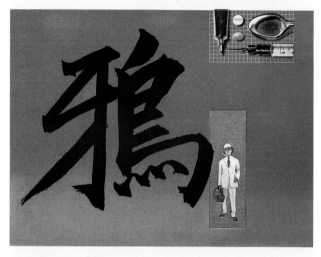

A Chinese crow, a missionary, and . . .

Even before Doctors Minot and Murphy discovered the value of liver in the treatment of pernicious anemia, a missionary in China had learned from an old Chinese doctor that crow's liver cured this disease and he tried it successfully in one case. The long search for this anti-anemia substance in liver resulted recently in the discovery of the red crystals of vitamin B_{12}. Further research established that the most practical source of this vitamin is not liver but a by-product of streptomycin—an antibiotic.

Development and constant improvement of new medicine may often take an unpredictable and challenging course. A drug, at first worth many times its weight in gold, becomes cheap and consequently available to all as a result of improved production methods. The investment of the millions necessary for research and development is therefore both sound business and sound humanitarianism.

Medicine . . . Produced with care . . . Designed for health

© 1952 The Upjohn Company, Kalamazoo, Michigan

Upjohn

Upjohn, 1952

angry young computer

Our B 200 can outdo any computer in its class. Any computer, regardless of name or initials. So naturally, when it sees a system being bought or leased on the basis of name or initials, the B 200 gets angry. Because it knows it can do a better job for fewer dollars. If you know anybody who's considering a computer, do him a favor. Mention the Burroughs B 200. The same goes for anybody who's angry at his present computer. And we hear a lot of people are. Burroughs—TM

Burroughs Corporation
See a Burroughs computer in action, Election Night, ABC-TV.

Burroughs Corporation

CORNER, FROM DETROIT, MICHIGAN

Our B 200 wants a shot at your computer. (Or that computer you were thinking of making yours.) Why? To settle once and for all just who can flatten your dataload fastest. For less money.

Burroughs Corporation
DETROIT, MICHIGAN 48232

Burroughs Corporation

Industry

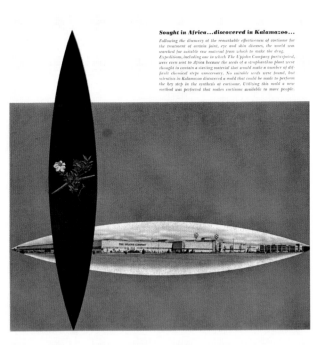

Upjohn, 1952

Upjohn, 1954

Chemstrand Nylon, 1959

IBM

G. Washington

on foreign policy

... it is a maxim founded on the universal experience of mankind that
no nation is to be trusted farther than it is bound by its interest.

Container Corporation of America, 1955

The new revolution in business ... packaging

Ingenious packages sell consumers,
speed manufacturing ... with bank aid

Everything from biscuits to ball bearings comes pre-packed today. Vegetables, girdles, hardware, even complete dinners are marketed in an amazing assortment of glass, metal, plastic, wood, paper, foil, or fiber packages.

Automation in the factory, self-service in the market, and an endless stream of new, highly competitive products have built packaging into a $12 billion industry that is developing new techniques and materials at an amazing rate.

Only a few years ago, plastic squeeze bottles, aerosol cans, pull-tab cartons, and plastic pouches were unheard of. Today, they put convenience on every household shelf, save manufacturers large sums in production, handling, and shipping. Even some industrial prod-

ucts, such as bolt-and-screw sets, come neatly packed in plastic "blisters."

Functional packaging is also helping to speed manufacturing. Component parts come in special packages that can be fed right into the assembly line. Resistors, for example, are sealed in individual plastic pockets on belts of pressure-sensitive tape. Grease fittings are strip-packaged and fed into the line from a reel in the carton.

In factories and processing plants, marvelous new machines simplify packaging operations. Filling lines that han-

dle 1,000 cans per minute, accumulating tables, and automatic carton unloaders are some recent developments.

First National City helps keep this packaging parade on the march by supplying seasonal and interim credit to producers of raw materials for containers, and to processors and fabricators of all types of finished containers.

The creative banking services offered by First National City can benefit your own business. Consult us for the many advantages of having a *banker* instead of just a bank account.

The First National City Bank of New York

Handsome is as ...

There is no good reason why a plant can't be both efficient *and* handsome.

Proper layout and design will provide swift, smooth-flowing production and a truly functional plant that is attractive and an asset to the community.

Austin-designed plants are that kind of plant. Designed from the inside out as fine production machines, they look efficient because they are efficient.

Owners like their flexible layout; their low cost of operation. They like, too, the *plus* value of their attractive appearance which Austin provides at no premium in cost.

And regardless of the type of project, or its location, the Austin Method, which combines and co-ordinates engineering and construction under a single contract, saves the Owner time, money and complications.

A discussion of this Austin approach involves no obligation on your part.

THE AUSTIN COMPANY ⬠ **ENGINEERS AND BUILDERS · CLEVELAND**
OFFICES COAST TO COAST · NEW YORK · PHILADELPHIA · WASHINGTON · PITTSBURGH · CLEVELAND · DETROIT
INDIANAPOLIS · CHICAGO · ST. LOUIS · HOUSTON · LOS ANGELES · OAKLAND · PORTLAND · SEATTLE · TORONTO

The Austin Company, 1951

Paper and the Good Earth

From the time the slip is planted in its Hawaiian soil, it takes nearly two years to grow a pineapple. But that growth is improved, and made more certain, because of the black mulch paper through which the slips are planted. ■ Pineapple mulch paper, which Crown Zellerbach helped to develop, keeps the soil warmer, conserves moisture and defends against

weeds. The result: a richer harvest, and a better product for your table. ■ This is but one of many kinds of paper which Crown Zellerbach produces to help the grower, packer, shipper, retailer and consumer of fruits and vegetables. Just as it serves all other industries, Paper serves Agriculture in an increasing variety of useful ways.

Paper serves every person and every industry

CROWN ZELLERBACH 👑
PAPER AND PAPER PRODUCTS SINCE 1870   San Francisco 19

Crown Zellerbach, 1955 ▶ *Marathon, 1952*

This year shoppers will make over six billion trips to grocery stores. Most every trip, they'll take home food in packages made by Marathon.

Marathon Corporation, Menasha, Wisconsin: from tree to finished package, Marathon's facilities include—assured pulpwood sources—pulp and paper plants—package-making plants—ink, engraving and printing plants—years of creative design and merchandising experience.

Marathon
packaging that sells food

Bower Roller Bearings, 1955

Western Electric, 1959

Western Electric, 1950

Western Electric, 1951

Television waves travel better
on the world's tiniest ball bearings . . .

Electric currents zigzag up to 216 million times a second through the radio frequency coil of the typical FM radio or television circuit. The quality of reception of any set is largely determined by this coil.

The heart of the best radio frequency coil is a small cylinder . . . of insulated, compressed carbonyl iron powder.

Carbonyl iron powder is 98.0% chemically pure iron, in almost perfect spheres—feels finer than a woman's face powder. This form of iron retains its inductive and magnetic properties indefinitely, is stable to temperature extremes, does not deteriorate with use.

Carbonyl iron powder is formed and purified under carefully controlled heats and pressures . . . a difficult and complex process . . . and in this country is made by General Aniline . . . supply source to manufacturers of electronic equipment and television sets.

Today carbonyl iron powder is finding new uses for pharmaceuticals, iron tonics, and the enrichment of bread and other food products.

And carbonyl iron powder is only one of approximately four thousand products of General Aniline . . . whose laboratories make a major contribution to public welfare.

GENERAL ANILINE plants at Rensselaer, N.Y. and Grasselli, N. J. lead the US production of high quality dyestuffs (sold through General Dyestuff Corporation, NYC) . . . the Ansco division at Binghamton, N.Y. is the oldest maker of photographic equipment, cameras, and films . . . the Ozalid division at Johnson City, N. Y. makes facsimile reproducing machines and sensitized papers...Antara Products in New York City develops new product applications.

In a big industry essential to our national economy, General Aniline is a good company to work for and with, buy from and sell to . . . worth knowing and watching!

Under a microscope magnifying 750 times, the carbonyl iron powder shows spherical shape.

Electronic wave trap (below) has carbonyl iron powder core.

GENERAL
ANILINE & FILM CORPORATION
...From Research to Reality...

230 Park Avenue, New York 17, N. Y.

General Aniline & Film Corporation

▶ Moore Business Forms, Inc., 1952

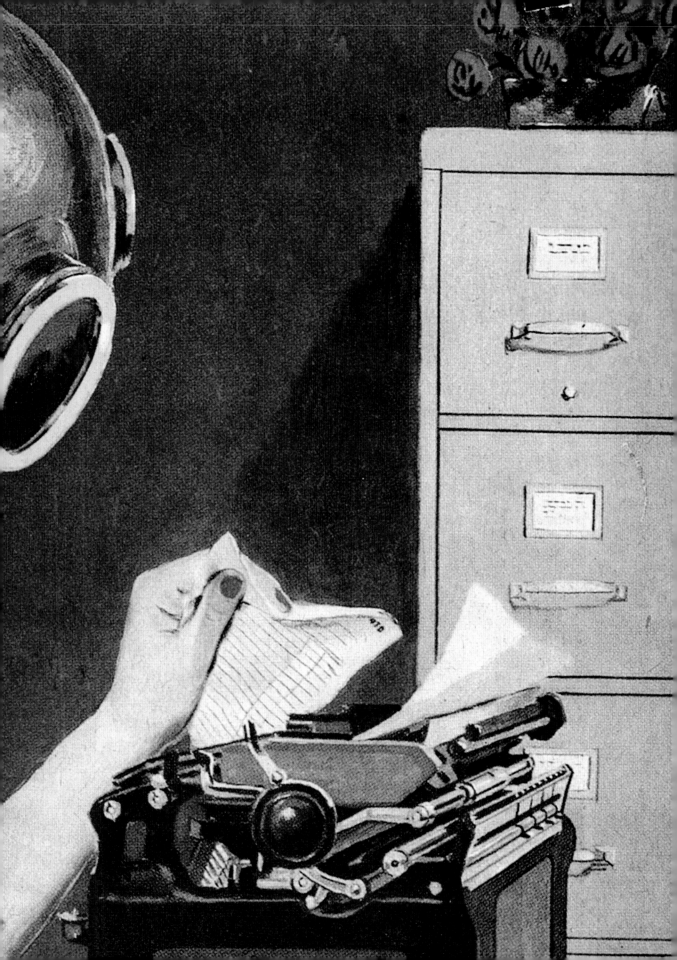

Now, your choice of colors ...in the Royal Portable!

Sport coats, telephones, houses, refrigerators and now Royal Quiet De Luxe® Portable Typewriters give you the chance to express your personality in color.

And think what fun it's going to be to get better marks in school when you type your work on one of these gorgeous new Royals . . . the Standard typewriter in Portable size. Educators tell us that marks go up when work is typed. The work looks neater . . . is easier to read and grade. Spelling improves. Sentences become sharper and clearer.

You pay only $9.95 down. 18 months to pay the balance. Liberal trade-ins at your Royal Portable dealer's. *Remember: More students want Royal Portables than the next three makes combined.*

Based on a nationwide survey among more than 4000 high school students of both sexes living in 30 cities located in 22 states.

Now in color—the new rugged  portable

Royal Typewriter Company, *Division of Royal McBee Corporation*

Gilbert Papers, 1955 ◀   *Royal Portable Typewriters, 1955*

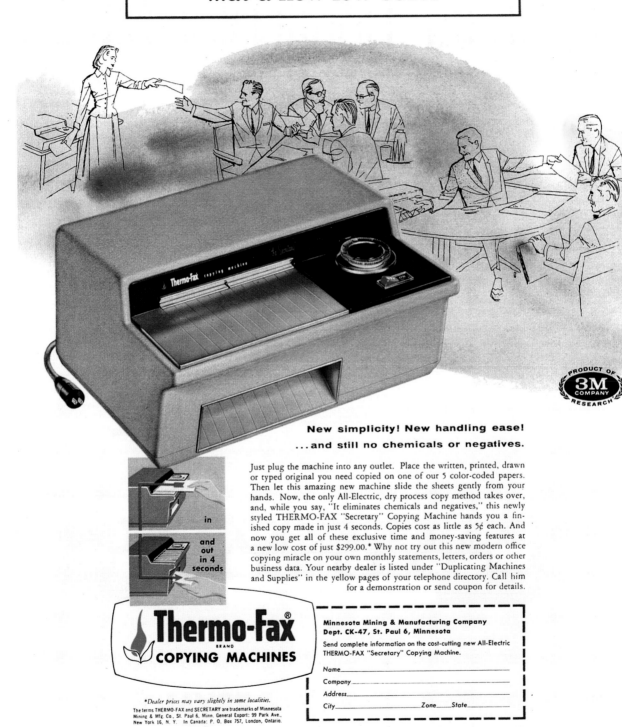

Announcing: A new "Thermo-Fax" Copying Machine for

4-second copying speed
...at a new low cost!

New simplicity! New handling ease!
...and still no chemicals or negatives.

Just plug the machine into any outlet. Place the written, printed, drawn or typed original you need copied on one of our 5 color-coded papers. Then let this amazing new machine slide the sheets gently from your hands. Now, the only All-Electric, dry process copy method takes over, and, while you say, "It eliminates chemicals and negatives," this newly styled THERMO-FAX "Secretary" Copying Machine hands you a finished copy made in just 4 seconds. Copies cost as little as 5¢ each. And now you get all of these exclusive time and money-saving features at a new low cost of just $299.00.* Why not try out this new modern office copying miracle on your own monthly statements, letters, orders or other business data. Your nearby dealer is listed under "Duplicating Machines and Supplies" in the yellow pages of your telephone directory. Call him for a demonstration or send coupon for details.

in
and out in 4 seconds

Thermo-Fax®
BRAND
COPYING MACHINES

Dealer prices may vary slightly in some localities.
The terms THERMO-FAX and SECRETARY are trademarks of Minnesota Mining & Mfg. Co., St. Paul 6, Minn. General Export: 99 Park Ave., New York 16, N. Y. In Canada: P. O. Box 757, London, Ontario.

Minnesota Mining & Manufacturing Company
Dept. CK-47, St. Paul 6, Minnesota

Send complete information on the cost-cutting new All-Electric THERMO-FAX "Secretary" Copying Machine.

Name_____
Company_____
Address_____
City_____ Zone____ State_____

Thermo-Fax Copying Machines, 1957

If your typewriters are used
more than 2¼ hours a day
you need new Royal electrics

This new kind of electric typewriter can increase production up to 14%.

It can free 1 typist out of 8 for other work. Even if you increase production only 6%, figures show that you are justifying the additional expense.

We have the stop watch. You have the old typewriters. Here's what we want to do:

1. Time your production and see if we can save you money. **2.** Show you the extraordinary new Royal Electric. **3.** Let you try the new Royal Electric right in your own office, so you can prove to yourself how it can save you money.

A telephone call will bring the Royal Representative, and he may save you money.

World's largest manufacturer of typewriters...  electric · portable
standard
roytype business supplies

Royal Typewriter Company, *Division of Royal McBee Corporation*

Royal Electric Typewriters, 1956

The show goes home on the dotted line

Televising a show takes talent, technic[al] genius and paper forms—*plenty* of the[m].

Programs, for example, are arranged an[d] talent screened with paper forms. Salari[es] are paid, advertisers billed and checks, in[-] voices, statements typed on paper. Form[s] even buy factory parts, check inventor[y] see a set assembled, then deliver it.

Moore's DOTTED LINE helps keep all the[se] operations grooved and swift-moving. It [is] the perforation on forms made by Moore— and an *idea*, a time-saving, cost-cutti[ng] system that puts snap into the work of [a] single employee or a company.

Here—in Moore's DOTTED LINE—you ha[ve] an invisible force that runs through a[n] organization saving profit *where profit* [is] *often lost.* Forms may vary from a simp[le] stock Order Pad to a 14-part continuo[us] Order-Invoice giving many departmen[ts] full instructions from one quick writing.

Let a Moore representative show yo[u] how (1) system is improved and (2) co[st] controlled in businesses *like* yours. Or wri[te] any factory: Niagara Falls and Elmir[a,] N. Y.; St. Paul, Minn.; Denton, Tex.; L[os] Angeles and Emeryville, Calif.; Salem, Or[e.]

1 Sales Books for Every Business Operation

2 Continuous Interleaved Typewriter Forms

3 Continuous Register Forms and Registers

4 Fanfold Billing Machine Forms

5 Speedisets for Fast Carbon Extraction

6 Marginal Punched Business Machine Forms

MOORE

BUSINESS FORMS, IN[C]

Offices in over 200 cities. Regional factories and dis[tri-] bution points in Canada also ✱ ✱ ✱ THE RIG[HT] BUSINESS FORM FOR EVERY FORM OF BUSINES[S]

Pushbutton DICTATION

MODERN!   LOWEST COST!

Paperwork f-l-o-w-s with new pushbutton dictation. You pick up a phone, push a button and dictate. It's as simple as that! And you do it at your convenience. Handling paperwork becomes a new experience in timesaving efficiency never before thought possible. And with PhonAudograph III you get new, premium features at *lowest cost ever!* For an eye-opening demonstration showing how Gray PhonAudograph III can be effectively applied to your paperwork problems . . . save you money as no other system can — call your Audograph dealer today. The Gray Manufacturing Company, Hartford 1, Connecticut.

New GRAY PHONAUDOGRAPH III

Moore Business Forms, Inc., 1950 ◄   *Gray PhonAudograph III, 1954*

A woman's scarf: *or how to boost typing production*

OFF-BEAT as this statement may appear, nevertheless the scarf weighs *more* than the amount of weight it takes to depress one key on the new Royal Electric.

In fact, the new Royal Electric is 13 times easier to operate than a non-electric typewriter—*which simply means a big boost in typing production.*

How big a boost? In your case, it involves these factors: Typists' salaries, days worked per year, hours typed per day, and production rates.

When you and your Royal Representative talk over these factors, he'll be able to calculate the expected savings when you install new Royal Electrics.

ROYAL® *electric · standard · portable*
Roytype® business supplies

Products of Royal McBee Corporation

Royal Electric Typewriters, 1956

▶ *Burroughs Corporation, 1953*

A new rugged Royal portable...

ROYALITE*

Price? Just $69.95 *Plus applicable taxes.*

Only 3 inches high
...with full-sized keyboard
Gives sharp, clear typing
Mighty durable, too!

Even a dachshund could straddle the new Royalite. It's only 3 inches high and weighs a mere 8 pounds.

But it's got a full-sized, grown-up keyboard and it turns out wonderful, professional-looking work. And rugged? It's in the rugged Royal tradition. Just the portable for students, travellers, professional people and those who type at home.

Did you realize that more students prefer Royal Portable than the next 3 makes combined?† Hurry down to your local Royal Portable dealer and try it. Ask him about his low, low budget plan.

choice of case in red, green or tan

ROYAL

Royal Typewriter Company, Division of Royal McBee Corporation

"Royalite is a trade-mark of the Royal McBee Corporation.

Royalite Portable Typewriter, 1956

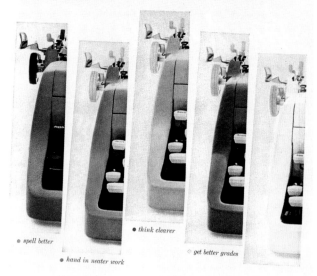

# of colors
Royal Portable!

- spell better
- think clearer
- hand in neater work
- get better grades

$9.95 down. 18 months to pay. Liberal trade-ins.

Royal Portable Typewriter, 1955

<u>this</u> is the new IBM Electric

IBM

It's <u>new</u>—inside and out, with 28 engineering achievements that bring you typing at its finest! Your secretary will love its alive, eager response. You'll admire its styling and high-volume output. For this—is the most handsome, efficient typewriter made.

IBM Electric Typewriter, 1959

Increase production as much as 14%
with this new kind of electric typewriter

If you increase typing output 14%, you're saving money per typist.

Or, you're freeing one typist out of eight for other work.

Even if you only increase production 6% with the new Royal Electric, figures show you are justifying the additional expenditure.

In fact, if the typewriters in your office are in use more than two and a quarter hours per day, you need new Royal Electric typewriters. We'd like to put a stop watch against your typing production for three reasons:

1. To see if we can save you money.
2. To show you the extraordinary new Royal Electric.
3. To sell you new Royal Electrics if the figures justify the expenditure.

Why not call your Royal Representative?

World's largest manufacturer of typewriters... *electric · portable standard roytype business supplies*

Royal Electric Typewriter, 1954   ▶ *IBM Electric Typewriter, 1953*

SECRETARY

To busy executive. Interesting work. Pleasant surroundings, modern office, including IBM Electric Typewriter. Write Box M2345.

"*that's the job for me!*"

Other things being equal, what girl wouldn't prefer a job that includes an IBM Electric Typewriter? It's so easy to use and turns out such beautiful letters and reports.

With an IBM, you'll do your typing almost effortlessly, and with no errors due to fatigue.

To the executive, an IBM means faster typing, and better-looking letters that are a pleasure to sign.

For illustrated brochure, write or telephone your nearest IBM office.

IBM *Electric Typewriters*

INTERNATIONAL BUSINESS MACHINES   590 Madison Avenue, New York 22, N. Y.
In Canada: Don Mills Road, Toronto 6, Ont.

Now! each key its own motor bar...

...saves up to 50% hand motion

"LIVE" KEYBOARD
National adding machine

now you can forget the motor bar!

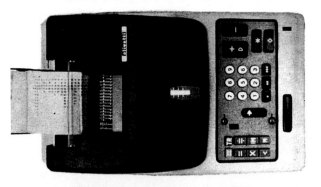

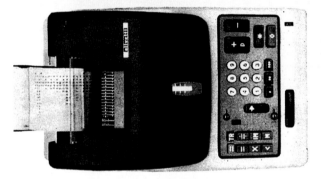

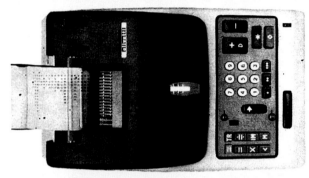

olivetti

The Olivetti Divisumma 24, with its simplified keyboard and unique automatic constant and "memory," combines the many parts of a business figurework problem into a single running calculation, thus saving time and eliminating re-entries. There's an Olivetti branch or dealer near you. Olivetti Corporation of America, 375 Park Ave., New York 22.

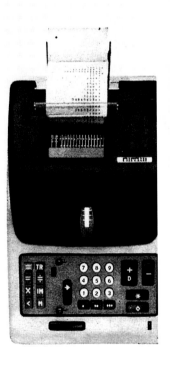

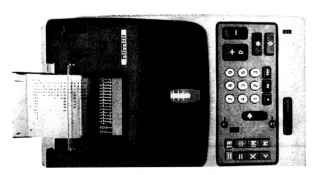

National Adding Machine ◄   *Olivetti Corporation of America, 1959*

MOST HONORED! MOST WANTED!
...and MOST FOR YOUR MONEY, TOO!

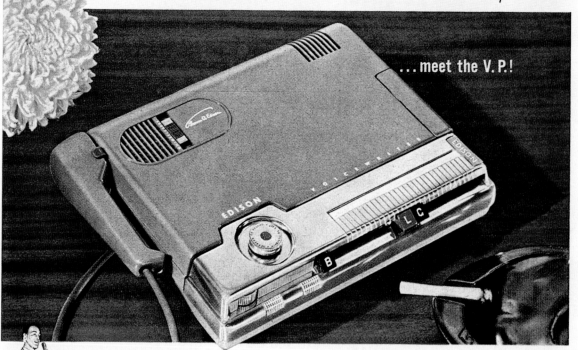

...meet the V.P.!

TINY BUT TOUGH! A dozen luxurious features have won the new V.P. EDISON VOICEWRITER its unmatched popularity, including: unique Master Control, automatic disc positioning, twice-as-accurate indexing. It's EDISON-engineered to take the most rugged daily desk use!

SMALLEST, LIGHTEST! Book-shape, book-size, the handsome V.P. is the most carryable instrument on the market! You can tuck it under your arm! And only the "Veep" permits *transcribing* as well as dictating... a *complete* dictation service in one!

TWICE AS USEFUL! Cross-town or cross-country, the versatile V.P. slips right into your bag or briefcase... goes home with you... or on trips... to meetings or conferences! It's a double-duty marvel, years ahead of the field... yet priced *below* it!

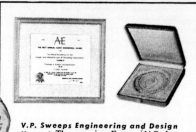

V.P. Sweeps Engineering and Design Honors! The amazing EDISON V.P. has won the Audio Engineering Award, while its styling has won for famed designer Carl Otto the National Designers' Institute Medal. Make this prize-winning performer your *personal* dictating instrument!

FREE! 12-page full-color booklet "GET ACTION ON THE GO!" Just clip coupon to your letterhead and sign. Or phone local EDISON VOICEWRITER representative.

Thomas A. Edison
INCORPORATED

THE EDISON VOICEWRITER V.P.

EDISON, 43 Lakeside Avenue, West Orange, N. J.
O.K., send me "GET ACTION ON THE GO!"—no obligation.

NAME _____ TITLE _____

COMPANY _____

ADDRESS _____

CITY _____ ZONE _____ STATE _____

Edison Voicewriter

▶ *Marchant Calculators, 1955*

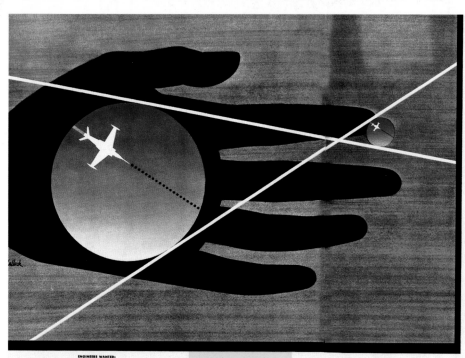

From Crosley— new dimensions for the electronic age

As electronics works its magic for defense and industry, scientists of Avco's Crosley Division reckon with the problem of making already reliable electronic systems more flexible— to give them greater usefulness in navigation, communication, national defense. Now, out of intensive study of electronics and related areas—thermodynamics, optics, aerodynamics, human factors—has emerged the knowledge necessary to achieve this critical goal. Working closely with the military, outstanding Crosley scientists have changed the dimensions of many electronic systems: lightening them, compressing them, "miniaturizing" them. Now—improved radar, communications receivers, navigational aids and scores of other systems are coming off the Crosley lines and performing their miracles in smaller space, with less weight, requiring less power. Through "miniaturization" in electronics, as well as advances in air-frame assemblies, Crosley brings the findings of research to practical fulfillment—for defense, for peace.

If your plans are linked to advanced electronics, find out how Crosley's capabilities and knowledge can be brought to bear on your specific problems. Wire, phone or write for Miniaturization Booklet to Avco Defense and Industrial Products, Stratford, Conn.

FOR A COPY OF THIS HALLOCK ILLUSTRATION, SUITABLE FOR FRAMING, WRITE TO PUBLIC RELATIONS DEPT., AVCO DEFENSE AND INDUSTRIAL PRODUCTS STRATFORD, CONN.

Crosley avco defense and industrial products

Avco Defense and Industrial Products combine the scientific skills, and production facilities of 9 Avco divisions: Crosley; Avco Advanced Development; Lycoming — to produce power plants, electronics, air-frame components, precision parts at: Boston; Cincinnati; Dayton; Everett, Mass.; Los Angeles; Nashville, Tenn.; Stratford, Conn.; Washington, D. C.; Williamsport, Pa.

Crosley, 1955

New frontiers for electronics

Bringing the "magic" of electronics to the control of industry's equipment and processes demands rare combinations of talent and experience. Two types of engineers are required. One group must know electronics and contribute its unique benefits to industry and science. The other must know industrial control, the service it must perform and the conditions it must meet. Only through the teamwork of such engineers is progress possible . . . and this has been the way to new frontiers for electronics at Cutler-Hammer. No electronics engineers anywhere are held in higher regard than those of Cutler-Hammer's A.I.L. Division. And no control engineers have won greater respect for their industrial experience and achievements than those of Cutler-Hammer, pioneers in control.

The amazing new radar at New York's Idlewild Airport once again demonstrates the electronics leadership of Cutler-Hammer A.I.L. Division engineers. Day and night, in fair weather or foul, this radar shows control tower operators runways and taxiways with profiles of aircraft and vehicles for new safety and fewer delays. So needed with the steady gain in traffic and the advent of jets, ten more are now being built for major airports from coast to coast.

CUTLER·HAMMER

Cutler-Hammer Inc., Milwaukee, Wis. • Division: Airborne Instruments Laboratory. • Subsidiary: Cutler-Hammer International, C. A.
Associates: Canadian Cutler-Hammer, Ltd.; Cutler-Hammer Mexicana, S. A.; Intercontinental Electronics Corporation.

Cutler-Hammer, 1959

The finest tires are made with NYLON cord

Whether you're driving on high-speed highways or city streets, the extra strength of nylon tire cord gives you extra protection.

Nylon cord tires resist bruise damage, run cooler than ordinary tires. And nylon's toughness absorbs the added strains put on today's tires by power getaway, power steering, power braking.

Nylon tire cord was first developed to take the terrific landing impact of heavy bombers. Today nylon cord tires are standard equipment on commercial airliners. And billions of miles of use in heavy-duty trucking have proved the superiority of nylon cord tires.

You'll find that nylon cord tires give priceless extra protection to you and your family —yet cost very little more.

Du Pont produces the nylon fiber. Leading tire manufacturers make nylon cord tires —in tubeless or conventional types.

DU PONT
REG. U.S. PAT. OFF.

BETTER THINGS FOR BETTER LIVING...THROUGH CHEMISTRY

November is National Tire Safety Month. For utmost protection, equip your car with nylon cord tires. See your tire dealer today!

Du Pont, 1955   ▶ *Avisco Cellophane, 1955*   ▶▶ *Wellington Sears, 1956*

GROW WITH
AVISCO*
CELLOPHANE

It's our business to help other business
grow.

And. because we feel that way about
our salesmen do a lot more than se
cellophane.

The AVISCO cellophane man gets
know your business. He works with y
to be sure that you use our cellophane
the very best advantage.

The AVISCO cellophane man likes sm
businesses, especially. He can put ma
services to work for you—package d
velopment aid, marketing researc
technical help and advice.

And whether your order is big or sma
you can be sure of delivery as promise
with special attention if you need it.

What's the result of this personal servic
About 3 out of every 9 products wrapp
in cellophane are packaged in AVISC
cellophane. And our sales are still gro
ing! Film Division, American Visco
Corporation, 1617 Pennsylvania Bou
vard, Philadelphia 3, Pennsylvania.

*Trade mark of American Viscose Corporation

AVISCO
CELLOPHANE

Housed in the huge bubbles of the off-shore Texas Tower is radar equipment to warn against enemy attack. These pressurized "radomes" are made of rubberized nylon, now being used in a variety of radically new applications.

Wellington Sears fabrics find

A roller bearing in a steel rolling mill must withstand tremendous stress and pressure. Here it is made of a plastic laminate reinforced with heavy cotton duck, one of many laminating fabrics provided by Wellington Sears.

Collapsible liquid field-storage tanks, capable of being dropped by air, make use of strong rubberized nylon fabric. Similar materials go into fuel cells for military vehicles.

Protective coverings of all kinds are being made with "Welkote" nylon as the base fabric for vinyl or neoprene coating. Lightness, high strength, long life are a few of the many important advantages.

Beneath the colorful surface, Wellington Sears woven fabrics strengthen and lengthen the life of handbags, luggage, upholstery, countless other products. "Lantuck" non-woven fabrics and "Knitkote" knitted fabrics, coated with plastic, are also used here.

new uses in sound "Mergers"

Big things happen when fabric teams with other materials. Wholly new products are created, some to do old jobs better, others to help bring to life radically new ideas. A coastline, for instance, is better guarded against attack . . . fuel is moved and stored more quickly, more safely . . . building construction is accelerated . . . end processes are simplified.

Examples shown here are of "base" fabrics in various combinations with rubber and plastics. Some are fabrics coated with these other materials; some are fabrics in "sandwich-type" laminates. But they all represent just a handful of the areas served by these "fabrics plus" . . . and just a small part of the long list of fabrics supplied to all industry by Wellington Sears for over a century.

With this record of experience, Wellington Sears is the logical place to turn for help in solving your fabric problem. Call on us, for direct assistance, or for contact with the leading suppliers and fabricators who distribute and use our fabrics.

Wellington Sears

FIRST In Fabrics For Industry

WELLINGTON SEARS COMPANY, 65 WORTH STREET, NEW YORK 13, N. Y.

What does age 9 care about cement? Just nothin'!

• But his parents do. As taxpayers, concerned with the cost of highways, school construction, building maintenance. As mothers and fathers, concerned with their children's safety and health. As citizens, concerned with providing school facilities which attract good teachers.

It's amazing how *taken-for-granted* concrete influences the fortunate lives of all of us in America. In our homes. Our work. Our transportation. Everything that comprises our abundant living. Without concrete we would still have cobbled streets, rutted roads, covered bridges ... and the little red school house.

Lehigh Portland Cement Company is a major producer of cement—the basic ingredient of concrete—which helps make modern living possible and daily improves it.

Our job, of course, involves the many figures on costs and earnings, orders and shipments. But it also provides abundant opportunities to help make dreams come true.

Lehigh Portland Cement Company, Allentown, Pa.

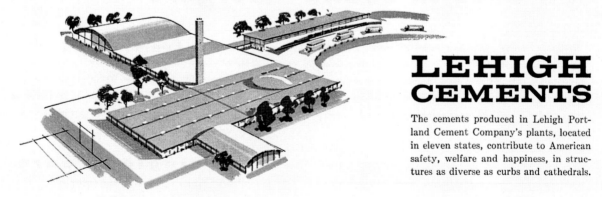

LEHIGH CEMENTS

The cements produced in Lehigh Portland Cement Company's plants, located in eleven states, contribute to American safety, welfare and happiness, in structures as diverse as curbs and cathedrals.

Lehigh Cements, 1959

▶ *Otis Elevator, 1952*　▶▶ *Alcoa Aluminum*

And the winner is...

Instantaneous Access To 24,000 Alphabetic or Numerical Characters

Forget about personal computers. This Univac unit took a room, not a lap, to occupy. This cumbersome dinosaur reveals how quickly technology has progressed.

Sofortzugriff auf 24.000 alphabetische oder numerische Zeichen

An PCs oder gar Laptops war noch gar nicht zu denken. Diese Univac-Anlage konnte man nicht auf den Knien balancieren, sie beanspruchte nämlich einen ganzen Raum. An solch sperrigem Dinosaurier wird deutlich, wie schnell die technologische Entwicklung vorangeschritten ist.

Accès instantané à 24.000 caractères alphabétiques ou numériques

Pas question d'ordinateurs individuels et encore moins de portables. Pour un Univac, c'est une pièce entière qu'il faut. Cet encombrant dinosaure montre à quelle rapidité la technologie a progressé.

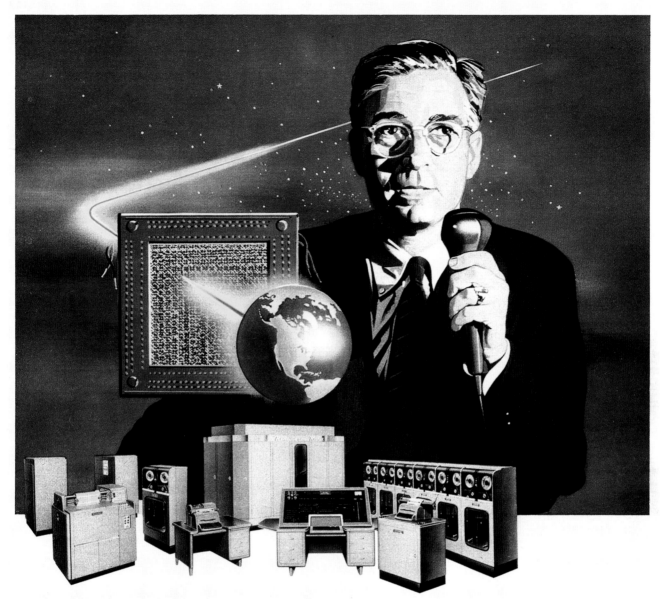

…now Univac's speed is doubled!

The famous Univac® of Remington Rand has widened still further its lead over other electronic business computing systems. Univac is still the *only* completely self-checked system . . . the only one which can read, write, and compute simultaneously without extra equipment. And now, the Univac II adds to these superior features the speed of a magnetic-core memory.

The Remington Rand magnetic-core mem-

ory is more than a laboratory promise. It has been in actual customer use for over a year, passing all tests with flying colors in the first commercially available electronic computer to use core storage successfully.

The capacity of the internal memory of Univac has also been doubled, giving instantaneous access to 24,000 alphabetic or numeric characters. If needed, this can be even further increased to 120,000 characters.

Univac's external memory — magnetic tape — now has greater capacity, too, increasing input and output to 20,000 characters per second . . . the equivalent of reading or writing every character on this page more than 1,000 times a minute.

These new Remington Rand developments can be incorporated into any existing Univac installation to double its speed of operation and to increase its economy still further.

ELECTRONIC COMPUTER DEPARTMENT ***Remington Rand*** ROOM 2205, 315 FOURTH AVENUE, NEW YORK 10, NEW YORK
DIVISION OF SPERRY RAND CORPORATION

Remington Rand & Univac, 1955

PASCOE

KN

RISOM ←

MILLER →

ALUMINUM CHAIRS DESIGNED FOR THE ALCOA COLLECTION BY PAUL McCOBB. PHOTOGRAPHED BY BECKER-HOROWITZ.

Forecast:

A place for work, quiet reflection, and informal meetings: such an environment helps you to make the right decisions. Herman Miller's

Executive Group shown here in the Seagram Building is displayed by 113 selected dealers who can show you how this versatile group

will answer your working needs. Write Dept. F259 for name of nearest dealer. Herman Miller Furniture Company, Zeeland, Michigan.

Carroll Sagar & Associates, 1950 ◄◄   *Alcoa Aluminum, 1951* ◄   *Herman Miller, 1959*

A NEW GROUP OF UPHOLSTERED WIRE CHAIRS DESIGNED BY CHARLES EAMES

FOR LOW-COST SEATING COMFORT IS NOW AVAILABLE FOR IMMEDIATE DELIVERY.

FRANK BROS. HAS THE COMPLETE LINE. A WIDE VARIETY OF MODELS

STARTING AT 25.00 INCLUDE THE TWO SIDE CHAIRS AS SHOWN.

ALL CHAIRS ARE AVAILABLE WITH FABRIC OR LEATHER UPHOLSTERY

WITH ONE PIECE OR TWO PIECE COVERS.

FRANK BROS

2400 AMERICAN AVE., LONG BEACH, CALIFORNIA, LONG BEACH 4-8137—NEVADA 6-3709

OPEN MONDAY & FRIDAY EVENINGS UNTIL 9:00

NO CHARGE FOR SHIPPING ANYWHERE IN THE UNITED STATES

Frank Bros, 1952

▶ *Herman Miller, 1952*

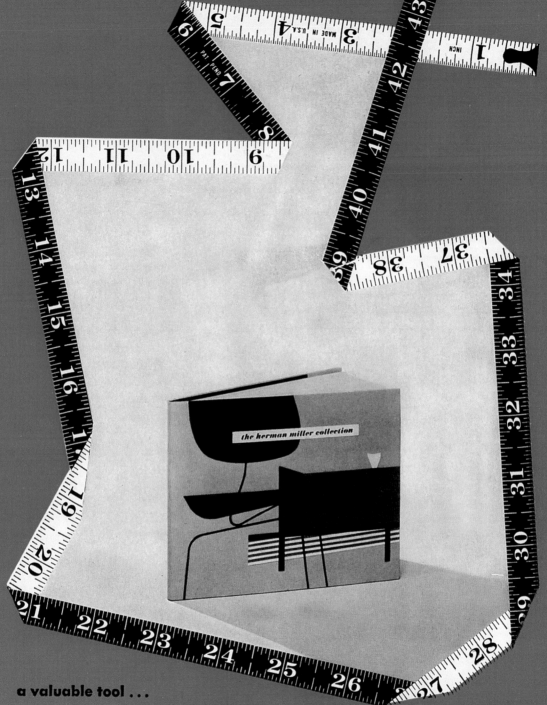

harper

the herman miller collection

a valuable tool . . .

the second edition of "The Herman
Miller collection" to be published in April,
1952, will prove extremely helpful to interior
designers and architects in working on public,
commercial and residential projects. Entirely
revised and much enlarged——116 pages with over
200 photographs, diagrams and specifications.
Depicts complete current selection of designs by
George Nelson, Charles Eames, Isamu Noguchi and
Hvidt and Nielsen, truly "America's foremost
collection of modern furniture." Price $5.
Send your check or money order to Dept. I-3,

herman ⋀ **iller** Zeeland, Mich.

NEW
PATTERN
VERSATILITY

Corona del Mar residence Architect: Smith & Gray, AIA

PLUS STRUCTURAL SOUNDNESS!

"We're witnessing another great trend here in Southern California... a trend to extensive residential use of Concrete Block. In the past few years, block manufacturers have produced new shapes and designs that have practically transformed Concrete Block into a new building material. Tremendous pattern versatility and structural soundness are obtained with ease and economy when Concrete Block is used... and these features help to explain its fast-growing popularity"... J. Merrill Gray of Smith & Gray, A.I.A.

A non-profit Association of Southern California's leading Concrete Block manufacturers, QUALITY BLOCK PRODUCERS will be happy to supply information or literature on New Concrete Block. If you haven't received your free copy of the new "Protective Coatings For Exterior Surfaces of Concrete Masonry Walls in Southern California," write today.

New Concrete Block also adds elegance to bathroom of same home.

Quality Block Producers, 1959

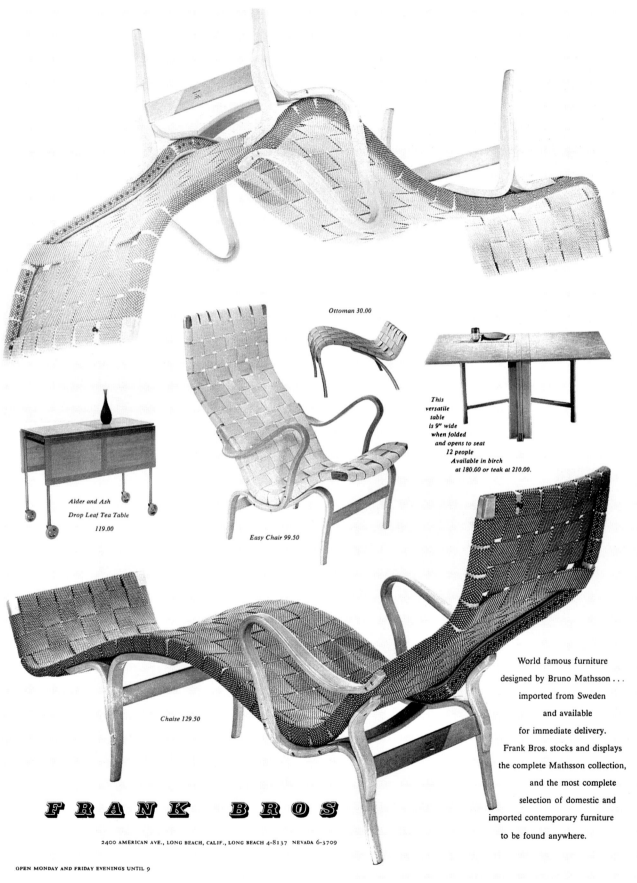

Ottoman 30.00

*This
versatile
table
is 9" wide
when folded
and opens to seat
12 people
Available in birch
at 180.00 or teak at 210.00.*

*Alder and Ash
Drop Leaf Tea Table
119.00*

Easy Chair 99.50

Chaise 129.50

World famous furniture
designed by Bruno Mathsson . . .
imported from Sweden
and available
for immediate delivery.
Frank Bros. stocks and displays
the complete Mathsson collection,
and the most complete
selection of domestic and
imported contemporary furniture
to be found anywhere.

F R A N K   B R O S

2400 AMERICAN AVE., LONG BEACH, CALIF., LONG BEACH 4-8137 NEVADA 6-3709

OPEN MONDAY AND FRIDAY EVENINGS UNTIL 9

Frank Bros, 1953

779

REEL LIGHT

Catalog
Number
GL5

GENERAL LIGHTING COMPANY

8336 West Third Street
Los Angeles 48 California
WYoming 2275

General Lighting Company, 1950

general merchandise
WRITE OR VISIT
HERON · TEAK
FURNITURE AND ACCESSORIES · 989 EAST GREEN STREET · PASADENA 1, CALIFORNIA · RYAN 1-8918

Heron Teak, 1953

New designs by George Nelson
solve the need for a
guest room set-up that's
complete in one unit.
Here's everything most guests
need: luggage rack, ample
drawer space, a desk, and
cosmetic compartments.
Ideal for hotels, too.
Professional discounts, of course.

herman miller, zeeland, mich.

showrooms: one park ave., new york
622 merchandise mart, chicago
exhibitors' bldg., grand rapids
8810 beverly blvd., los angeles

Herman Miller, 1950

NEW ARRIVALS ARE CONSTANTLY COMING IN TO OUR LOS ANGELES SHOWROOM... TO BE INSTALLED IN SETTINGS DESIGNED BY CHARLES EAMES

come in soon to see how expertly your furniture needs can be met when you choose from "america's foremost collection of modern furniture"

8806
BEVERLY BOULEVARD

herman miller, zeeland, michigan

showrooms —
new york, chicago, grand rapids, los angeles

professional discounts, of course

you are invited to bring or send your clients

Herman Miller, 1950

Is there an ⩗ in your future? The best way to find out is to visit a Herman Miller showroom or connect with our catalogue. You will be surprised by the number of furniture needs (and whims) in both home and office we can cope with.

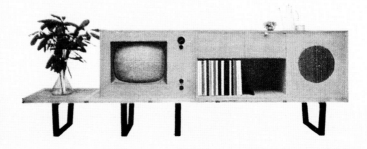

Herman Miller was the first to introduce a complete modular line of storage units. With the special cabinets shown above you can now make any hi-fi go even higher. Incidentally, the reason people buy so many slat benches is that they use them for practically everything. In this arrangement the controls are up where you can get at them.

George Nelson's home desk, launched almost a decade ago in considerable trepidation, continues to surprise everyone (except us) by remaining a best seller. People like it because it has space for what they need: portable typewriter, storage, and a ventilated file for high temperature correspondence. Upholstered desk chair by Charles Eames.

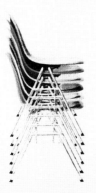

The stacking chair is the newest version of Charles Eames' comfortable, colorful fiberglas shells. Architects and decorators have been specifying them in carload lots for their best commercial and institutional jobs. If you ever have an extra four at bridge they are not bad at home either. (They hook together to make rows too).

Unless you are in Gwen Verdon's class we don't recommend this use of the slat bench for more than five minutes at a stretch. We don't know if the bench is a favorite of Miss Verdon's, or if it was just lying around the photographer's studio, but we were glad to see it used on her latest RCA Victor album.

George Nelson's steelframe seating is not a piece of furniture but a surprisingly flexible system. Seats and table units ride a pair of steel rails and can be arranged and rearranged in any way you like. How do you like?

For those very special storage requirements Herman Miller's miniature cases may interest you. Lots of little drawers in teak with porcelain pulls stack vertically and horizontally with or without bases. For decorative storage of small things (in living room, dining room, bedroom, study) you might try several in assorted arrangements.

A ring and the book ($5.00 for the complete catalog) are all you need to start furnishing with Herman Miller. If you lack a decorator, architect or dealer, call our nearest showroom for the names of dealers in your area.

HERMAN ⩗ILLER FURNITURE CO., ZEELAND, MICH.

Showrooms: New York, Boston, Chicago, Dallas, Grand Rapids, Kansas City, Los Angeles, Pittsburgh (Hende-Jon), Minneapolis (Midwest Furniture Showrooms), Philadelphia (Robert Le Fort Co.), San Francisco (K.I.P. Showroom), Canada (Robin Bush Assoc., Vancouver and Toronto)

Herman Miller, 1956

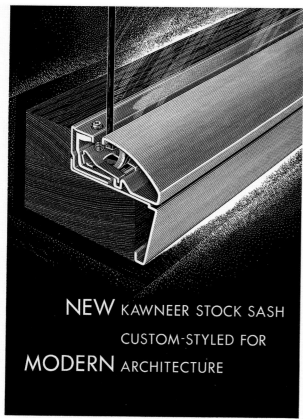

NEW KAWNEER STOCK SASH

CUSTOM-STYLED FOR

MODERN ARCHITECTURE

UNEQUALED IN PRECISION ENGINEERING AND WORKMANSHIP

Striking simplicity in styling and sound construction make this Kawneer Assembly one of today's truly outstanding architectural metals.

The graceful curve of the sash, the dramatic shadow-line, and the clean plane of the sill create a visual unit which meets the highest standards of contemporary design.

Like all other Kawneer Glazing Assemblies, this Sash incorporates the famous Kawneer resilient-grip principle which insures maximum safety and reliability. The resilient steel spring-clip

minimizes breakage due to sudden blows, strong winds, and normal structural settling.

For further information and details, write The Kawneer Company, Department AA-60, 1105 North Front Street, Niles, Mich., or Department AA-60, 930 Dwight Way, Berkeley, California.

THE
Kawneer
COMPANY
ARCHITECTURAL METAL PRODUCTS
Store Front Materials
Aluminum Roll-Type Awnings · Modern Entrances
Aluminum Facing Materials · Flush Doors

Kawneer Company, 1950

LEHIGH

LEHIGH'S FLEXIBLE GROUP CREATES ENDLESS POSSIBILITIES FOR INVENTIVE SPACE ARRANGEMENTS.

one-two-three-four unit frames in black steel, chrome or brass. table tops in travertine, marble, colored or woodgrain Melamite plastic tops. cushions may be fixed or free.
write, on your letterhead, for catalogue.
LEHIGH FURNITURE CORPORATION
18 east 53rd street, new york 22, n.y., plaza 5-2048
factory: 407-13 east 91st street, n.y. 28

Herman Miller, 1950 ◄   Lehigh, 1955

AGAINST HEAT AND COLD — KNOLL TEXTILES — INSULATED WITH MILIUM

provides new control of indoor temperature,
new protection against fading.
Use as a drapery fabric or lining.
Swatches on request.
"Fresco Milium" matching in solid colors.
"Triad" in a three-tone design by Eszter Haraszty, first Award winner, A.I.D. design competition.

KNOLL TEXTILES, INC., 575 MADISON AVENUE, NEW YORK

BOSTON · CHICAGO · DALLAS · DETROIT · MIAMI · WASHINGTON

Knoll Textiles, 1955   ► The Kawneer Company, 1950

W ALL-ALUMINUM
EER FLUSH DOORS!
EQUALED
NDSOME, MODERN APPEARANCE
GED, INTEGRATED CONSTRUCTION

For Stores, Shops, Institutions, Schools, Hospitals, Hotels, Theatres, Restaurants, Apartment Buildings, Offices, Factories, etc.

Striking in their simplicity of styling and their lustrous alumilited finish, Kawneer All-Aluminum Flush Doors will add a unique and modern keynote to any interior or exterior. They combine good taste in design with the strong, eye-appeal of gracefully-fluted aluminum.

Their remarkable rigidity and durability are based on a new exclusive Kawneer method of construction (Patent Pending) which locks the two door faces to the interior framework, thus forming a rugged integral unit which assures long-term service and minimum maintenance.

Precision-made and correctly balanced, Kawneer Flush Doors will operate smoothly year after year. Their ease of operation is further increased by their unusual light weight—for example, the 3 foot by 7 foot size weighs only about 50 pounds without hardware.

In addition to the Standard Style shown at right above, Flush Doors can be ordered with one or more lights of glass or louvers. Single-acting or double-acting doors are available as single units or in pairs. Hardware is installed at the factory to assure accurate fitting.

For detailed information, write The Kawneer Company, Dept. AA 49, 1105 North Front St., Niles, Mich., or Dept. AA 49, 930 Dwight Way, Berkeley, Cal.

THE
Kawneer
COMPANY
ARCHITECTURAL METAL PRODUCTS
Store Front Metals
Aluminum Roll-Type Awnings • Modern Entrances
Aluminum Facing Materials • Flush Doors

Good Reason for a Celebration!

You can hardly blame our rising young executive for declaring a night-on-the-town to celebrate his latest promotion. Just look at his handsome new office! And who could resist treating his wife to an after-hours preview . . . especially when it includes a look at his new Executive Model *"Correlation"* Desk by Steel Age. This distinguished desk was designed to offer the utmost in efficiency and comfort to the man who makes achievement a habit.

There are *Correlation* models to meet virtually every desk need in your office. Each combines dynamic styling with complete adaptability to your changing space requirements. We urge you to call a Steel Age dealer for a demonstration of this exciting new concept in modern office furniture. *Corry-Jamestown Mfg. Corp., Corry, Pa.*

Have your secretary send for your copy of this interesting "Correlation" Brochure. Features full-color photographs of model offices. Write to Dept. C-3.

"The Quality Choice of Modern Offices"

Branch Offices: Atlanta • Boston • Chicago • Dallas • Detroit • New York • Oakland • Philadelphia • Seattle

---

Steel Age Office Furniture, 1957

▶ *Yawman and Erbe Office Furniture, 1953*

Offices for Living START WITH FURNITURE BY STANDARD

Office Planned for the Tempo of today — You can tell at a glance that this is the office of a man other men emulate, a man whose every possession reflects the beauty, richness and superlative craftsmanship to be found only in fine wood furniture.

You can tell, too, that everything in this distinguished office is geared to help you speed the transition from idea to reality. The desk and the service unit of your Continental Omega Executive Suite form a closely-knit "team" capable of handling any assignment you give it. And, with two broad decks like these at your command, you've all the convenience, all the privacy, all the clutter-free work space a fast-paced executive could require.

To see this and some of the many other "custom-planned" arrangements available, visit your nearby Standard dealer soon. You'll find his address in the Yellow Pages, or write: The Standard Furniture Company, Herkimer, New York.

SEND FOR FREE SKETCHBOOK OF IDEAS to help you plan your own color-coordinated 'Office for Living.' Contains a variety of furniture designs and plans for executive, junior executive, secretarial and general offices — in a wide range of prices.

CONTINENTAL OMEGA EXECUTIVE FURNITURE, CHAIRS, DESK ACCESSORIES AND CONTINUITY PLANS ARE EXCLUSIVE WITH STANDARD DEALERS

Standard SINCE 1866, THE WORLD'S LARGEST MAKER OF EXECUTIVE OFFICE FURNITURE

Standard Office Furniture, 1957

Furniture upholstery coated with BAKELITE Brand Vinyl Resins lasts longer, keeps bright colors brighter longer. Other advantages include ease of cleaning, superior scratch and scuff resistance. Wall coverings surfaced with vinyl resins provide easily-maintained, luxurious room decoration.

For style, service, beautiful designs and colors, and long years of easy upkeep, flooring made of BAKELITE Brand Vinyl Resins is the new standard. Tough for long wear, resilient for comfort underfoot, it's the type of flooring preferred by those who want the most in beauty teamed up with economy.

First in the world of plastics

DID YOU KNOW? The intricate 3-dimensional map on the wall above is made of BAKELITE Rigid Vinyl Plastic by vacuum-forming . . . a process that offers great benefits for many types of products. BAKELITE Resins are also in the finish for the wall paneling, make the unbreakable recording discs in the dictating machine and are used in glass fiber reinforced plastic chairs.

BAKELITE COMPANY, A Division of Union Carbide and Carbon Corporation UCC 30 East 42nd Street, New York 17, N.Y.
The term BAKELITE and the Trefoil Symbol are registered trade-marks of UCC.

Bakelite Plastics, 1954

Good looks...good taste...good business

Furnishing the modern office calls for the distinctive styling of ASE furniture with its sleek silhouette, clean sculptured lines and soft, rich colors. But even more important is the fact that ASE furniture is built to keep its good looks for years . . . with bonderite treated finish that will not chip or peel . . . honeycomb top construction for extra strength, permanent smoothness and quietness . . . smoothly rounded corners . . . and dozens of other equally important advantages. Only ASE can give you all these plus values. Yet it costs no more. See your ASE dealer or write for catalog.

 ALL-STEEL EQUIPMENT Inc.
Aurora, Illinois

All-Steel Equipment Inc., 1959

STATUS

Give your executives the status they deserve
...an Italic-Styled office by GF Studios

Consider for a moment a man of exceptional ability —a man who has worked his way to the top. Naturally he deserves an environment that reflects his own achievement. But how does he find an office that is personally his—that is right in every detail—that shows imagination and flair, subtly, and with flawless taste?

We sincerely believe you'll find all that in Italic Styling from GF Studios. It's a new concept in executive environment that provides everything you need:

skillful planning, a superb new design in executive furniture, decorating with exclusive custom-made accessories. GF Studios does the whole job and tailors it to the precise character of your business — and to the personality and taste of the executive involved.

To learn more about Italic Styling, call your GF dealer or branch, or write for your full-color Italic Styling brochure. GF Studios, Inc., Dept. T-22, Youngstown 1, Ohio. Division of The General Fireproofing Company.

Italic Styling by **GF STUDIOS, INC.**
A DIVISION OF **THE GENERAL FIREPROOFING CO.**

GF Studios, Inc., 1959   ▶ *Carrier Air Conditioning, 1954*

THE NEW SILHOUETTE *ROOM AIR CONDITIONER*

BUILT BY THE PEOPLE WHO KNOW AIR CONDITIONING BEST. CARRIER CORPORATION, SYRACUSE, NEW YORK

Valentine Seaver Originals

PRODUCT OF **KROEHLER**

DESIGNS
OF
DISTINCTION

CLASSICALLY
CONTEMPORARY...
YET SO VERY COMPATIBLE

Exemplifying the French Riviera influence in modern styling, the new de Ville Group is notable for the grace of its sweeping slender lines ... rare compatibility with either traditional or contemporary living rooms.

Notable, too, is the luxurious comfort of foam rubber cushioning ... the excitement of fresh new linen-like fabric in turquoise, gold, coral and many other interesting decorator colors.

Kroehler, 1957

a sectional grouping from The Sonata Collection

KROEHLER

Exquisite furniture
Delightfully designed
Thoughtfully priced

VALENTINE SEAVER *Originals*

Kroehler, 1951

Bright New Living begins with this fashionable new furniture

- Superb new styling!
- Metallic nylon fabrics in exciting new colors!
- Durable Cushionized' construction!
- New arrangeability for modern living!

The new "Boulevard" Group by **KROEHLER**

WORLD'S LARGEST FURNITURE MANUFACTURER
General Offices: Chicago 11, Ill. • In Canada: Stratford, Ontario

Kroehler, 1955

▶ *Pittsburgh Plate Glass Company, 1951*

NEVER A DULL MOMENT! That's the cheerful prospect for any room that has a big expanse of clear Plate Glass to let in floods of daylight and frame your nicest view. Whether you choose Pittsburgh Picture Windows or Window Walls . . . regular Plate Glass or Twindow, the insulated window . . . you'll make your home a brighter home, a pleasanter place to live.

More light, more life, more loveliness

WITH PITTSBURGH GLASS

GLASS IS GETTING LOVELIER all the time! Why not give your bathroom or kitchen the benefit of it, with walls or wainscot of colorful Carrara Glass? Carrara walls stay young and beautiful indefinitely, never fade or stain or craze. 10 colors to choose from, including the Forest Green shown here. Ideal for remodeling as well as new homes.

LUCKY IS THE LADY who sees herself as others see her. And you can . . . head to toe . . . with the help of several full-length Pittsburgh Door Mirrors in your home. They're useful to every member of the family . . . and they cheer up your rooms a lot, too. Easy to install . . . you can do it yourself in just a few minutes.

MADE FROM
PITTSBURGH
PLATE GLASS

THIS LABEL identifies products made of genuine Pittsburgh Plate Glass.

NEW FREE BOOKLET! 24 pages of practical suggestions for effective use of glass in your home. Illustrated in color. Ideas for new homes and old. Send the coupon for your free copy.

- - - - - - - - - - - - PLEASE PRINT - - - - - - - - - - - -

Pittsburgh Plate Glass Company
2043-1 Grant Building, Pittsburgh 19, Pa.

Please send me, without obligation, your free, illustrated booklet, "How to give your home Glamour with Glass."

Name . . . .

Street . . . .

City . . . .

County . . . . State . . . .

PAINTS • GLASS • CHEMICALS • BRUSHES • PLASTICS

PITTSBURGH PLATE GLASS COMPANY

Dunbar Furniture Corporation, 1951

Drexel Furniture Company, 1956

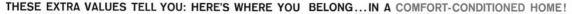

Owens-Corning Fiberglas, 1959

Startling!

This fabulously lovely carpet is ORADEL, one of the rayon-wool blends pioneered by Beattie. Because it is a blend of man-made and natural fibers, it takes a lovelier color, wears better . . . and, surprise of surprises, sells for only about $10.95 per square yard! Remember . . . Beattie blended carpets are backed by a mill that has woven quality rugs for 111 years! Other Beattie blended carpets from about $6.95 per square yard.

Beattie
The Beattie Manufacturing Company, 295 Fifth Avenue, New York

Beattie Carpet, 1951

The Duchess of Elm Street recommends carpet

Carpet is a great help to a Duchess these days.

Carpet's softness and warmth keep her comfortable when she's doing homework or consulting with friends on the phone. Carpet's quietness muffles her footsteps when she's going to see if there's any cake left, and carpet's safe footing saves mother many anxious moments when the Duchess takes stairs two or three at a time.

In fact, carpet is as indispensable to her parents as it is to the Duchess.

For carpet not only brings quiet, comfort and safety to a house—it brings richness and beauty, too. Yet, for all its richness and beauty, for all it does to decorate a room or a home, carpet asks so little in time, care and money. Just once around with a vacuum keeps carpet looking lovely . . . and prices are far lower than you'd expect.

You can probably carpet two rooms for what you'd imagine one would cost. Stop in at your store this week—see the wonderland of new styles and variety of exciting colors waiting for you.

Don't just look at the carpet you want. Enjoy it—while you pay for it. Take advantage of the budget terms offered by retailers who represent these American manufacturers

ARTLOOM · BEATTIE · BIGELOW · CABIN CRAFTS-NEEDLETUFT · DOWNS · FIRTH · GULISTAN
HARDWICK & MAGEE · HIGHTSTOWN · HOLMES · KARASTAN · LEES · MAGEE · MASLAND · MOHAWK
NYE-WAIT · PHILADELPHIA CARPET · ROXBURY · SANFORD · ALEXANDER SMITH
CARPET INSTITUTE, INC. · 350 FIFTH AVENUE, NEW YORK 1, N.Y.

Home means more with carpet on the floor—*more comfort · quiet · safety · beauty · easier care*

Carpet, 1956

M *brand new and beautiful aristocrats*
MARTEX

Kitchen Linens
. . . 100% pure Irish linen

Breakfast TIME *Tea* TIME *Party* TIME

Time-savers all, they're the gayest collection of towels that ever decked your kitchen. And so irresistibly pretty, you'll want to convert them into cocktail aprons, place mats, tray cloths, and gifts for all your friends. Loomed by Martex right here in the U.S.A. these fine Irish linen towels will do the very best job on your dishes. 17" x 30", $1.29 each, at stores listed. Martex, 65 Worth St., New York 13.

Martex Kitchen Linens, 1957

▶ *Owens-Corning Fiberglas, 1956*

Herbert Matter

For natural beauty in your home

there's nothing in the world like WOOD

Beauty so stirring it invites your caress. Touch it! Enjoy the natural beauty of a living material . . . yours in unending variations of tones and textures. Only wood conveys such elegance. Only wood offers such *livability* . . . warmth and intimacy no other building material can hope to duplicate.

Inherently versatile, wood *belongs* indoors and out . . . responds to good design in any application. So rich, so *right*, you never tire of it. For has it not been said that a thing of beauty is a joy forever?

NATIONAL LUMBER MANUFACTURERS ASSOCIATION

Live, Work, Build Better with Wood

Consult your architect, building contractor or lumber dealer for more information on wood. And for your free copy of the colorful new 20 page booklet, "Livability Unlimited," write to WOOD, P. O. Box 1816, Washington 13, D. C.

National Lumber Manufacturers Association, 1959

▶ *Leather Industries of America, 1950*

The Leather Look
afoot for Spring

The "Leather Look" is the look of beauty for spring! All across the country the "Leather Look" leads in fashion . . . and for good reason. Its lustrous tones and exciting textures infuse leather with the sparkle and spirit of spring. Remember, nature never makes two pieces of leather exactly alike. That's why leather can give you that touch of individuality. In shoes, clothes, handbags, gloves, belts, luggage — and a host of other fashions, leather means quality, value and a lasting look of beauty. You'll look smarter in leather! Join "The Leather Look" afoot for spring! *LEATHER INDUSTRIES OF AMERICA*

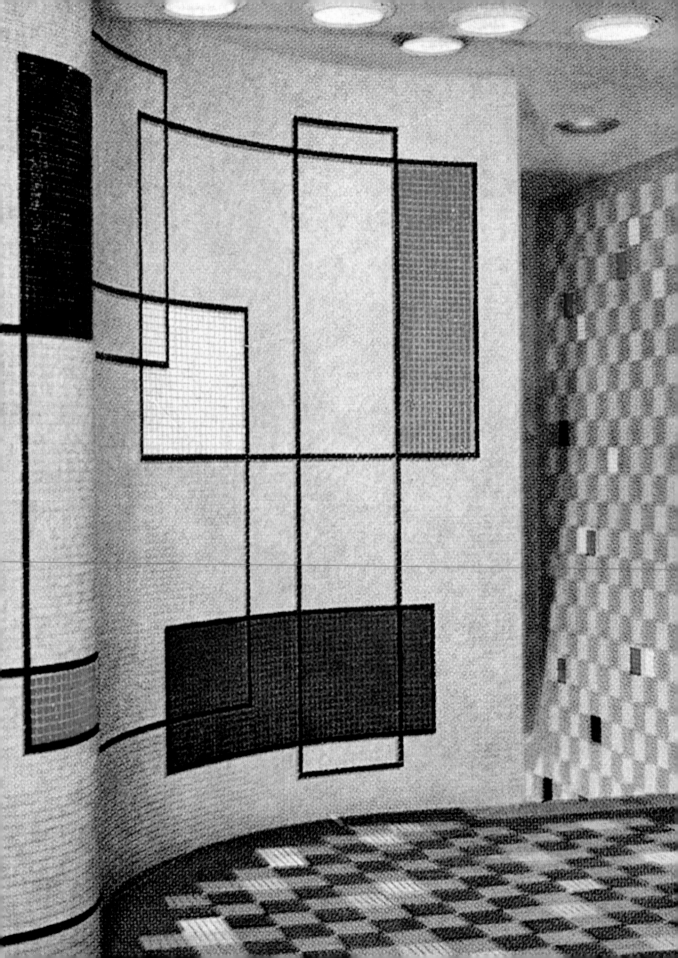

how (MOSAIC) tile helped make

THE PACESETTER HOUSE OF 1951

a spectacular success

The editors of "House Beautiful" have pioneered some unusually practical uses for Mosaic Tile in modern residences, where easier, more carefree living is the growing pattern.

The "House Beautiful" Pacesetter House of 1951, at Dobbs Ferry, New York.

Suntile, 1955 ◄   *Mosaic Tile, 1951*

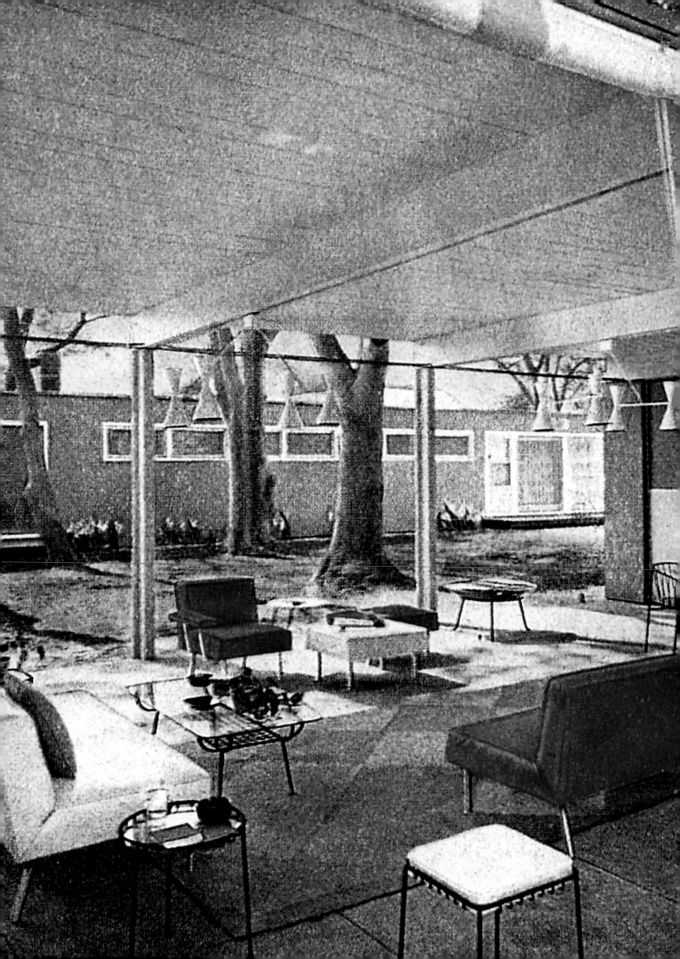

How rayon makes your home say "Come on in!"

Why is it that some homes have a wonderful "come-hither" look while others leave you cold?

It's a wide-open secret! Many a modern homemaker will point out that the lively, lovely, live-withable rayon draperies, and the new rayon decorative fabrics, make it easy for her to put warmth and charm into a house.

That's because rayon, being man-made, gives fabrics an endless variety of colors, textures, patterns and draping qualities such as grandma never dreamed of.

Today, rayon is wearing a special new feather in its cap—beautiful new rayon carpets. Homemakers everywhere are welcoming their brighter, crisper colors, their fresh new surface effects . . . and their astonishingly low prices. And where could you find a better place for rayon's utmost scorn for moths!

Look into these exquisite rayon fabrics, and the well-nigh magic rayon carpets, that years of Avisco rayon research have helped to make so useful.

American Viscose Corporation, 350 Fifth Avenue, New York 1, N. Y.

AMERICAN VISCOSE CORPORATION

WORLD'S LARGEST PRODUCER OF MAN-MADE FIBERS

Naugahyde, 1951 ◄   *American Viscose Corporation, 1952*   ► *Knoll, 1959*

Duco® Enamel
Semi-Gloss
Jonquil Yellow

Duco Enamel
Spray Magic
Primrose Yellow

Flow Kote®
Wall Paint
Periwinkle Blue

Custom Color
Semi-Gloss
No. 1318

Look under "Paint" in the Classified Telephone Directory for your nearest Du Pont Paint Dealer

If you're painting something new, or renewing something old...

the beauty _lasts_ when you paint with the finest ... DU PONT paints

REG. U.S. PAT. OFF

Better Things for Better Living...through Chemistry

Armstrong's Linoleum, 1954 ◄   *Du Pont, 1958*

ALL-AMERICAN CHOICE!

BATES "TOMORROW" bedspread and matching draperies, approved by Princeton students Eben Hardie and All-American tackle Holland Donan. The most popular plaid on every campus...tan background squared off in the colors shown below.

Bates are the bedspreads and draperies you see in most dormitories and fraternity houses...the right kind for college. Their colors and patterns are casual and correct...their quality gives you more than your money's worth. They resist wrinkles, won't shed lint, don't fade...and washing only improves them. At good stores everywhere ...and it's a good idea to get yours early!

CAMPUS TESTED! • CAMPUS APPROVED!
Bates
BEDSPREADS AND MATCHING DRAPERIES

BATES FABRICS, INC., 80 WORTH STREET, NEW YORK 13

Bates Fabrics, 1951

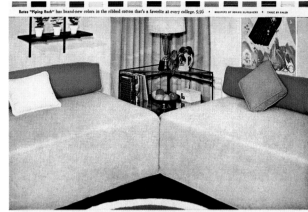

Bates "Piping Rock" has brand-new colors in the ribbed cotton that's a favorite at every college. 9.95

The right room-mates for college

Easy to see why nothing but Bates will do for college! They're the campus-correct bedspreads and draperies that give four walls a warm, inviting dorm look in nothing flat. Bates new college line has ten perfect patterns in 63 color combinations! And smart students have found what an economical buy Bates is...in mussproof easy care and years of rugged wear. So pick room-mates you know are right: pick a college pattern by Bates.

Bates BEDSPREADS • MATCHING DRAPERIES
CAMPUS-TESTED • CAMPUS-APPROVED.

Bates "Royal Tartan" a campus classic in cheery color combinations is the choice of Bill Chapman, graduate student of New York University. 8.95

Cash prizes for undergraduates in Bates "PLAN A COLLEGE ROOM" CONTEST. Write for your entry blank to Dept. 7, Bates Fabrics, Inc.
112 West 34th Street, New York 1

Bates Fabric, 1956

GLOSHEEN* "MatchMakers"
FOR STRIKING NEW COLOR SCHEMES!

Draperies, "Larkspur Bouquet," Bedspread skirt and pillow covers in multicolor "Match-Maker" stripe. Coverlet and cornice in matching quilted solid color.

Wondrous *GLOSHEEN* — with its lustrous satiny finish that's woven in so it won't wear out — now in a new group of breathtakingly beautiful floral and geometric patterns — each with its own "made-to-match" stripe, plaid or solid.

It's the decorating idea of the year — and so inexpensive. Choose from a large assortment — backed by the Waverly Bond that guarantees complete satisfaction even after countless washings or exposure to sunlight.

WAVERLY *Bonded* **FABRICS**
Division of F. Schumacher & Co.

We aim to produce the best possible merchandise at the lowest possible price.

SEND FOR 24 PAGE DECORATING BOOKLET!

Waverly Bonded Fabrics, Division of F. Schumacher & Co.
60 West 40th Street, New York 18, N. Y.

I enclose 10c for booklet "Color Your Home With Fabrics" that includes money saving decorating hints.

NAME
ADDRESS
CITY_____ZONE___STATE

*Reg. U.S. Pat. Off.

"DAISY CHAIN" with MATCH-MAKER OMBRE STRIPE

"HEIRLOOM DOCUMENT" with MATCH-MAKER MULTICOLOR STRIPE

Waverly Fabrics, 1951

Today's Modern

Furniture For Your Bedroom

Today's Modern is so carefully planned that it literally fits in any size room. Sizes and choice of pieces are optional. Double or twin size beds are available. Chests may be used simply in pairs. For master bedroom, children's room, or guest room there is just the right combination to choose from.

Today's Modern is both exclusive and original in design. It is created with imagination for the amateur decorator seeking something attractively different within reasonable budget limits.

The color is oyster-white on natural grained ash, achieved by a special baked-on lacquer process, giving a smooth high luster, easy to clean and polish. Raised center panels on dressers and chests are inlaid with gold tooled ivory leather and serve as drawer pulls. Interiors are finished to eggshell smoothness.

UNITED *Furniture Corporation*
LEXINGTON, NORTH CAROLINA

ON DISPLAY AT BETTER FURNITURE AND DEPARTMENT STORES

United Furniture Corporation, 1951 ▶ *Ficks Reed Co., 1951*

Caribbean Casual

RATTAN FURNITURE...CORRELATED FABRICS

Every home a tropical wonderland! That's our motto and it will be yours too, once you've seen how this blithe-spirited furniture (dramatized by our own exotic prints) can change your living-dining area into a romantic showspot. See the Ficks Reed display at a fine store near you or, consult your decorator. Write for interesting folder.

The Chaise Units are covered in "Palm Thatch," one of 16 tropical prints designed exclusively for Ficks Reed Co. Furniture and fabrics designed by John Wisner.

Ficks Reed Co.

424 Findlay Street • Cincinnati 14, Ohio

Santa Claus presents six beautiful BarcaLoungers!

A wonderfully comfortable BarcaLounger is the perfect gift for hard-working Mother or Dad... in fact it's a gift the whole family will enjoy. New improved "Floating Comfort" makes the BarcaLounger different from any other chair. The back-rest, seat and leg-rest are synchronized to cradle your body automatically in any position from upright sitting to reclining—without knobs or levers. You just sit down and lean back. The BarcaLounger gives you a welcome rest before or after meals. Puts you in just the relaxed mood for a sound night's sleep. For hand-crafted beauty, quality and head-to-toe relaxation, the BarcaLounger is in a class by itself.

See the many styles, sizes and coverings at your favorite department or furniture store now! Write for free illustrated booklets and name of nearest dealer. Barcalo Manufacturing Co., Dept. S10, Buffalo 4, N.Y.

THE ONE AND ONLY BarcaLounger

BarcaLounger, 1953

Gold Seal NAIRON STANDARD TILE

...for lovely, personalized vinyl floors and walls

Here are all the amazing qualities of vinyl plastics in tile form. With Nairon Standard tiles—and a little imagination—the homemaker can achieve wonderful effects...even continue a floor design right up a wall. This tile is so flexible...so easy to cut with knife or scissors...that the man or woman of the house can easily install it.

Nairon Standard colors are bright and clear and the satin-smooth surface seals out dirt, grease and spills. It is unharmed by household acids and alkalies...wipes clean with a damp mop. Made of the finest quality vinyls, Gold Seal Nairon Standard tile will give years of trouble free wear. Also available by-the-yard.

RECOMMENDED USES:
- above-grade floors of wood, concrete or ceramic tile
- on-grade floors of concrete or ceramic tile (may be used with radiant heating)
- below-grade—not recommended
- walls—according to specifications

windswept white
also 6 ft. wide

Nairon Standard Tile

High fashion furniture! Thrifty low price!
Long wear and easy care!

It's Daystrom's new black dining group—steel-strong for long wear, light in weight for easy care. Cheerfully at home in kitchen, dining or living room—even the patio! Foam-cushioned chairs have contour-curved backs for easy comfort. Table is trimly topped in rich wood-grain Daystromite® that shrugs off scratches, stains, heat!

See this and other easy-to-live-with Daystrom dining groups at better stores everywhere. All decorator-designed for every purse and home, in black, golden bronze or chrome finishes. In many handsome styles from drop-leaf tables for tiny rooms to big family tables that seat twelve.

Table shown (top 35" x 62", including one 12" leaf), wood-grain and other decorator patterns in yellow, gray, chartreuse, limed oak, black, white. Chairs in yellow, flamingo, white, pink, blue, chartreuse, red, green, grey. All tables and chairs completely washable. (Serving cart also by Daystrom.)

DAYSTROM

Daystrom, 1954

BIG VALUES FOR LITTLE BUDGETS!

Pennies work harder

when you spend them for this light-hearted dinette set that's designed to make mealtimes merry. Yes, the table seats six with ease, opens to a hospitable 52 inches. It's topped with Daystromite, that work-sparing, hard-wearing plastic. The husky chairs are comfortably padded, and cheerily upholstered in washable Pantex "Fantasy" designed by Raymond Loewy. Look for the name "Daystrom"—and be sure of high value at low prices. Other Daystrom sets from $49.95* to $199.50*.

Set, about $69.95*—in red, blue, green, yellow or grey

Short of space?

Then this versatile little table has extra inches built in! Closed, it takes up little room, only 21 inches by 30. But two generous leaves snap up to give you a full 51-inch length when company comes! Every inch is washable—the Daystromite wonder top, the sleek chromed surfaces, even the Duran upholstery. At furniture and department stores, in five fiesta colors, with matching or contrasting chairs.

Table, 2 chairs, about $64.95*; with 4 chairs, about $84.95*

—it's DAYSTROM furniture!

Awarded the Fashion Academy Gold Medal for 1950

THE TABLES WITH THE WONDER TOP

Daystrom Corporation, Olean, N.Y.
Daystrom-Balboa Corporation, Fullerton, Calif.

DAYSTROMITE RESISTS HEAT! — DAYSTROMITE RESISTS SCARS! — DAYSTROMITE RESISTS STAINS!

Daystrom, 1950

▶ *Gold Seal Congoleum Rugs*

Gold Seal

CONGOLEUM® RUGS

...a sparkling, colorful floor in minutes

The choice of budget minded homemakers everywhere! Gold Seal "Congoleum", enameled surface, rugs add new life and sparkle to any room . . . costs only a few dollars for a room size rug . . . gives outstanding wear.

No installation expense—simply unroll your rug and lay it over the floor. Made with G-10 plastic—for a brighter, smoother finish, the surface resists dirt, grease and surface moisture . . . cleans easily.

These rugs are styled by experts to give you the newest designs and colors. Colors that are bright and clear—highly fade-resistant.

RECOMMENDED USES: *Gold Seal "Congoleum" rugs may be installed over above grade floors of wood, concrete or ceramic tile.*

Don't get us wrong! Actually, this new room Joey needed so badly is all paid for. But we're going to get all our money back . . . in big savings on our fuel bills!

There was only one place to add the new room—up in the attic. And Joey *had* to have it. He'd grown right out of his old small room. But how to pay for a new one?

"You'll save up to 25% a year on fuel by insulating with Gold Bond Rock Wool!" said our Gold Bond lumber and building material dealer.

With his "how-to-do-it" instructions, it was easy to staple the fireproof Gold Bond Rock Wool "blankets" right between the studs!

We nailed up panels of Gold Bond Gypsum Wallboard for a smooth sturdy wall. Our Gold Bond dealer showed us how to conceal the joints . . . with the Gold Bond Tape Joint System.

Decorating the walls and woodwork was a cinch with Gold Bond Velvet, the new latex-base paint that almost flows on by itself. The wonderful part is, Velvet is scrubable! Even crayon marks wash off with soap and water!

See your Gold Bond dealer! There are over 150 Gold Bond Products, including Gold Bond Gypsum Lath and Plaster. (Gold Bond Velvet is available at leading paint stores too.)
NATIONAL GYPSUM COMPANY, BUFFALO 2, N. Y.

FIREPROOF WALLBOARDS • DECORATIVE INSULATION BOARDS • LATH • PLASTER • LIME • SHEATHING • WALL PAINTS • TEXTURES • MASONRY PAINTS • ROCK WOOL INSULATION • METAL LATH • SOUND CONTROL PRODUCTS

We're not going to pay for this room!

ADD·A·ROOM NOW!
with **Gold Bond**

Gold Bond, 1953

George Cooper Rudolph, A.I.A.

a Girl's bedroom
MALARKEY HOUSE

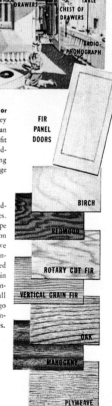

Even though your new home may be delayed by credit and building restrictions, you can still *modernize your present home*. Why not remodel a room, add a wing, or finish an unused attic? For example, your growing daughter would like a room as shown above. Feminine, yet functional, this room can grow up with the girl, thanks to foresighted design made possible by use of Malarkey doors and plywoods. It can be adapted to the needs of any girl from 6 to 26.

Plenty of convenient built-ins and closets inspire neatness and encourage pride in taking care of clothing and possessions. Behind the wardrobe closet doors, for instance, are various size drawers and clothes rod that can be raised as the girl grows. The Malarkey one panel door was selected so that a full length mirror could be mounted on the inside. This door is one of Malarkey's wide variety of beautiful detail fir doors at economical stock door prices.

In correct styles for every type of architecture, and in sizes to fit every opening.

Malarkey doors and plywoods are the perfect materials for creating individual rooms, allowing you to have the full enjoyment of your home. They can be finished to your liking. You can modernize without upsetting the household. There's no fuss . . . no mess with Malarkey plywood and doors. A home carpenter can often do the work.

Your architect, interior decorator, builder or lumber dealer will help you select the Malarkey doors and plywoods for your remodeling or building job.

Send 10c for plans of wardrobe closet shown in Girl's Bedroom above. Includes detailed drawings, specifications and complete bill of materials. Easy for you or your builder to follow. M and M Wood Working Company, 2301 N. Columbia Boulevard, Portland 17, Oregon.

Modernize present rooms or add new ones. With Malarkey plywoods and doors you can "tailor" your rooms to fit your needs. In this girl's bedroom a regulation-size dressing table is provided to encourage good grooming.

Handy Wardrobe Closet
Drawers of wardrobe are graduated to store various foldables. Toy chest can be used as hope chest later, doll collection shelf for books. Attractive plywood valances give soft indirect lighting over the bed and dressing table. The built-in radio-phonograph provides entertainment for girls of all ages. Convenient built-ins go clear to the floor, reduce cleaning and maintenance chores.

Malarkey plywoods and doors

Look for the Malarkey red diamond trademark

Malarkey Plywoods and Doors, 1951

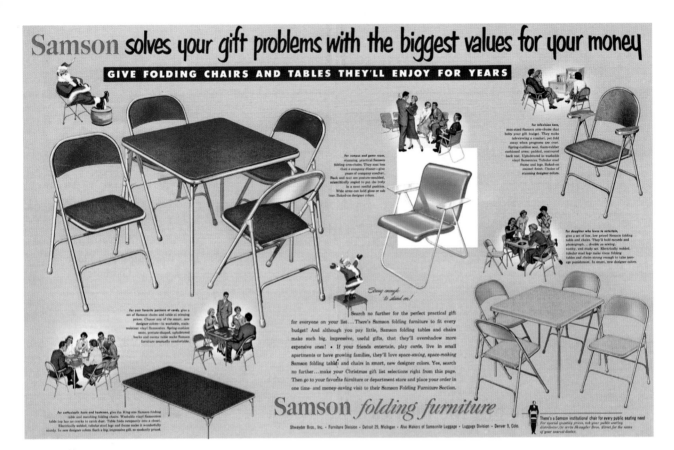

Samson solves your gift problems with the biggest values for your money

GIVE FOLDING CHAIRS AND TABLES THEY'LL ENJOY FOR YEARS

Search no further for the perfect practical gift for everyone on your list...There's Samson folding furniture to fit every budget! And although you pay little, Samson folding tables and chairs make such big, impressive, useful gifts, that they'll overshadow more expensive ones! • If your friends entertain, play cards, live in small apartments or have growing families, they'll love space-saving, space-making Samson folding tables and chairs in smart, new designer colors. Yes, search no further...make your Christmas gift list selections right from this page. Then go to your favorite furniture or department store and place your order in one time- and money-saving visit to their Samson Folding Furniture Section.

Samson *folding furniture*

Shwayder Bros., Inc. • Furniture Division • Detroit 29, Michigan • Also Makers of Samsonite Luggage • Luggage Division • Denver 9, Colo.

Samson Folding Furniture, 1950

it's always a "good morning" here

Getting up and making breakfast is almost fun when you're greeted by a cheerful kitchen like this. It's bright and sunny even on gray, chilly mornings, because the color scheme is warm with yellows and reds chosen from the gay floor of Armstrong Spatter Linoleum. But the floor gives this room even more than beauty. It adds wonderful practicality, too. There's hardly a seam...hardly a place where dust can hide. Of course, the floor can't prevent an occasional grease splash or muddy footprint...such things will happen. But this clever Spatter design does help conceal them until you have a free moment to whisk them away with a sponge mop. No wonder Spatter is such a popular design in Armstrong Linoleum—a modern floor that's a favorite all through the house.

SEND FOR FREE BOOK, "Decorating Ideas for Today's Living." You also receive sketch plan of this lovely kitchen dining area. Write Armstrong Cork Company, 3702 Scott Drive, Lancaster, Pa.

Armstrong
THE MODERN FASHION IN
FLOORS

LINOLEUM • PLASTIC CORLON® • EXCELON® VINYL-ASBESTOS TILE • CUSTOM CORLON PLASTIC TILE • RUBBER TILE • CORK TILE • ASPHALT TILE • LINOTILE®

Armstrong Floors

BEGIN WITH A BEAUTIFUL BACKGROUND *of plastic wall tile*

IDEA! A panel of blues in classic design on a wall of white Styron plastic tile.

Play up a divider wall! This cheerful contemporary kitchen began with plastic wall tile made of Styron®. Creamy yellow and white squares for walls and counter facings...king-size blue squares to accent the divider wall with its butterfly motif in white triangles. The dozens of decorator-styled Styron colors and varied tile shapes will inspire decorating ideas that are as practical as they are beautiful for your whole house. For your certified dealer can guarantee the quality of Styron plastic wall tile and installation. Whether you're building, remodeling or decorating, see your dealer soon . . . and begin with a beautiful background of Styron plastic wall tile. Send 10¢ for a colorful portfolio of designs in plastic wall tile. Plastics Sales Dept. PL 1564G, THE DOW CHEMICAL COMPANY, Midland, Michigan.

YOU CAN DEPEND ON **DOW**

Interior designs by John and Earline Brier.

DOW, 1957

Damage-resistant Natcolite "Nevamar" tops are an extra-value feature of all Lloyd Chrome Plated Dinette tables.

Lloyd

New Convenience—New Beauty! This beautiful "bow-end" table No. 161½ (the chairs are No. 108) with Chrome Plated or Enameled skirt stores its extra leaf—ready to seat six in a jiffy.

This new Lloyd table stores its own leaf ready for instant use.

Leaf unfolds, extending table with no change in height of top!

Chrome Plated Furniture

Smart Space-Saver—*Another Lloyd "first" is this drop-leaf table No. 557 which folds so compactly for use as a console table.*

Gay choice for moderns who look ahead

The bright, gay beauty of Lloyd Chrome Plated Furniture gives a festive note to the simplest breakfast—or a "company-best" dinner. And the Lloyd tag on every piece is your assurance of the *right* choice for years of usefulness as well. For Lloyd Chrome Plating is noted for its extra quality. Lloyd experience brings you table tops that resist damage from wear and tear, alcohol, boiling water—even cigarette burns. The smartly designed chairs have plastic coverings in a wide range of patterns which keep their gleaming beauty through long, long service. You'll find extra pleasure, too, in the *smooth* trouble-free action of extension and drop-leaf tables—and it's a joy to know that every gleaming, damage-resistant surface will swish bright and clean in a jiffy!

See the wide variety of Lloyd dinette and kitchen furniture at your favorite department or furniture store today. Lloyd Manufacturing Company, makers of Outdoor Furniture and the famous Rock-A-Feller Chair. Menominee. Mich.

Lloyd Chrome Plated Furniture, 1951

Tommi Parzinger calls

Amtico Rubber Flooring "Designer's Delight!"

HOMEMAKER'S DELIGHT, TOO—Noted designer, Tommi Parzinger, frequently completes the decor of the distinguished rooms that he creates with Amtico Rubber Flooring. Amtico keeps its just-installed lustre and rich, clear colors through a lifetime of rugged wear. Springy underfoot as a golf green, it's quiet, fire-resistant, cleanable in minutes. Choose Amtico Rubber Flooring for your home to combine elegance with effortless housekeeping.

Amtico Rubber Flooring, 1951

▶ *Armstrong Asphalt Tile, 1953*

Low-cost decorating ideas can build a restaurant's business

OU don't have to spend a lot of money to give a restaurant an air of elegance. Imaginative handling of inexpensive ɪstruction materials and attention to decorative details produce an interior that will compete favorably with re lavishly furnished establishments.

ɪn this restaurant, for example, inexpensive sheets of dboard were formed to make a gracefully curved wall. ten strips cover the joints and produce a pleasing panel ct. Ordinary dinner plates hung on the wall reflect the ɪkering candlelight to give the room an air of special charm distinction.

ʰe colorful buffet table in the center of the room is a orative extra that more than pays its way. It not only ɪts appetites for the cold meats, appetizers, and salads it ɪlays but also speeds service. To center attention on the ɪet, an unusual design was created in the handsome floor Armstrong's Asphalt Tile. Black and white tiles were ɪnged to set the table area apart from the rest of the floor. ɪe this floor is laid block by block, such special effects possible at no extra cost.

ɪrmstrong's Asphalt Tile also meets the requirements of practical low-cost decoration in many other ways. While surprisingly inexpensive, this floor offers all the toughness and durability needed to take concentrated traffic. The colors go all the way through each tile, so they can't wear off. The handsome swirl marbleization is an Armstrong exclusive that adds strength as well as beauty.

Spilled foods or beverages wipe up from Armstrong's Asphalt Tile quickly and easily. Even cigarette burns can be removed without leaving a trace. A minimum of maintenance keeps it looking clean and attractive for years.

You can use Armstrong's Asphalt Tile over any type of subfloor, even in basements or on grade-level concrete. Unlike most floors, it's not harmed by the alkaline moisture found in concrete slabs in direct contact with the ground.

Ask your Armstrong flooring contractor for full information on Armstrong's Asphalt Tile. He'll gladly show you samples and give you a cost estimate without obligation.

Which floor for your business? Because no one floor can meet every need, Armstrong makes several types of resilient floors—Armstrong's Linoleum, Corlon®, Asphalt Tile, Linotile®, Rubber Tile, Cork Tile, Excelon Tile, and Custom Corlon Tile. Each of these is unequaled in quality, and each has its own special advantages which make it particularly effective for certain kinds of installations. Your choice of the Armstrong Floor that's best suited to your own needs depends upon the effect you want to create, the amount of money you wish to spend, and the type of subfloor over which the installation is to be made.

Send for free booklet. "Which Floor for Your Business?", a 20-page, full-color booklet, will help you select the resilient flooring best suited to your needs. Write Armstrong Cork Co., 5310A Madison St., Lancaster, Pennsylvania. Ⓐ

ARMSTRONG'S ASPHALT TILE

See the New —
Callaway Towels and Rugs

Callaway Towels and Rugs, 1954

WASHABLE TWO-TONE SANFORIZED* CRETONNE SLIPCOVERS

Gimbels Basement, 1950

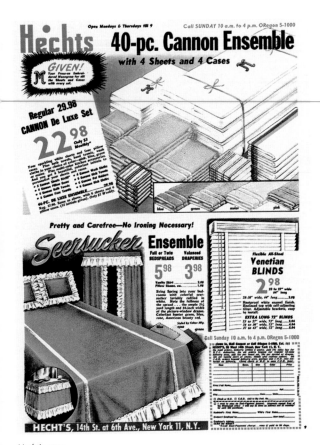

Hecht's, 1952

Hecht's, 1952 ▶ *Eljer, 1953* ▶▶ *Crane Plumbing Fixtures, 1950*

ELJER

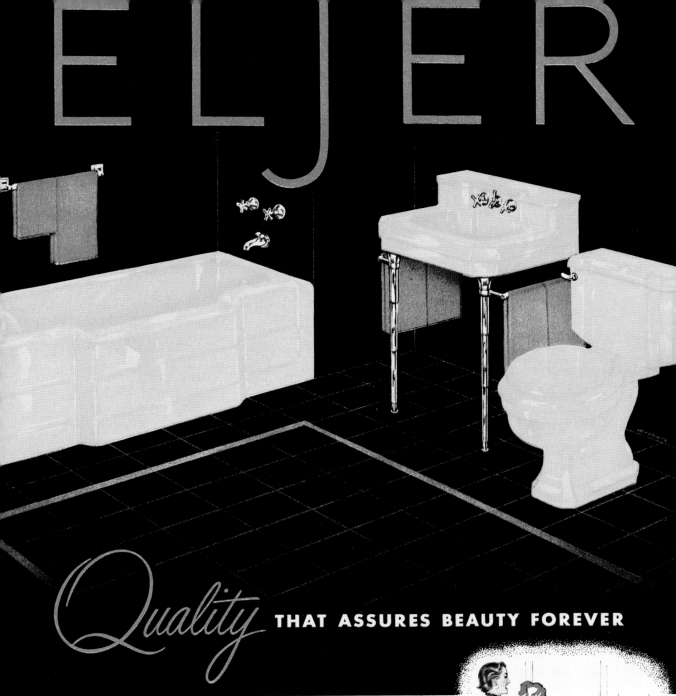

Quality **THAT ASSURES BEAUTY FOREVER**

You can expect Eljer's Fine Plumbing Fixtures to stay beautiful and new-looking for a lifetime, with ordinary care. Whether you choose a lovely pastel color or Eljer's *snow white*, the finish *cannot* fade. Bathtubs and Kitchen Sinks have an extra-thick coating of glass-like enamel . . . fused to a cast-iron base. Vitreous China Lavatories and Closet Combinations resist stains and are impervious to all ordinary acids . . . because they are *real* china. Eljer Fixtures wipe sparkling clean with a damp cloth. For free booklet, write Eljer Co., Box 192, Ford City, Pennsylvania.

THE HEART OF YOUR PLUMBING SYSTEM . . . Pipes bring in fresh water and carry the waste away, but for satisfactory service, you want faucets that work smoothly and efficiently . . . without dripping. So, in kitchen, bathroom or laundry, specify Eljer Fittings, quality-built for long, trouble-free service. All wearing parts are easily renewable.

CRANE

the preferred plumbing

THE KITCHEN PRIDE SINK
VAILABLE IN WHITE OR IN COLORS.
CRANE-LINE STEEL CABINETS
RMIT IDEAL STORAGE ARRANGEMENT.

PLUMBING AND HEATING · VALVES · FITTINGS · PIPE

CRANE
the preferred plumbing

DREXEL
LAVATORY

BASEBOARD RADIATION

Crane fixtures bring you beauty in design
—maximum utility—highest quality throughout. Typical of the many convenience features
are *Dial-ese* Controls which operate at a
finger's touch. See Crane Preferred Plumbing
at your Crane Dealer or Crane Branch. For
sale by the Crane Dealer in your locality.

"Our bathroom is our beauty secret"

K OHLER SPRUCE GREEN has a clear, fresh beauty—lasting in appeal as Kohler fixtures and fittings are durable in use. Like all Kohler pastel shades it fits into varied decorative effects with individuality and charm.

Time-tested materials and careful workmanship guided by unexcelled engineering experience make Kohler plumbing a sound investment in health-protection and lasting satisfaction.

The smooth, lustrous Kohler enamel finish of the Cosmopolitan Bench Bath is glass-hard,

easy-to-clean—and free from effects of stress and strain because it's fused to a base of non-flexing iron, cast for rugged strength. The Gramercy vitreous china lavatory is typical of the beauty and practicality of Kohler design.

Kohler chromium-plated brass fittings work easily, with lasting efficiency. Be sure to specify them for all your Kohler fixtures. Consult your Kohler dealer on selections for bathroom, washroom, kitchen or laundry. Kohler Co., Kohler, Wisconsin. Established 1873.

TO HELP YOU PLAN
Send for our new free booklet C-2, showing practical arrangements of fixtures and fittings in modern settings. Illustrated in full color.

KOHLER OF KOHLER

PLUMBING FIXTURES • HEATING EQUIPMENT • ELECTRIC PLANTS • AIR-COOLED ENGINES

Kohler Plumbing Fixtures, 1950

▶ *Clay Tile, 1951*

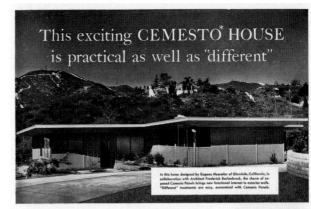

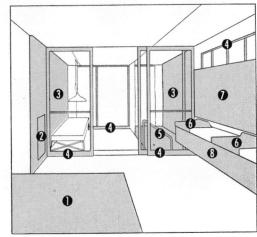

Marvin Culbreth Styles a Bathroom That Features Steel

The tile Culbreth specified in this bathroom design is made of Weirzin, the electrolytically zinc-coated steel that resists heat, moisture and rust . . . that forms a lasting bond with its finish. And, it whisks clean in seconds.

The key below shows the many ways in which steel dresses up this room. So remember, for the luxury-look . . . for strength . . . for beauty . . . use steel.

1. *Table framework* 2. *Heater* 3. *Wall tile* 4. *Steel framework* 5. *Bathtub and hand-rail* 6. *Sink* 7. *Cabinet* 8. *Drawers.*

"When you're after beauty on a budget you'll score a success with steel," says Marvin Culbreth, noted designer and consultant. "This room takes its whole character from steel. It's the focal point in the decor.

"I enjoy using steel wall tile for its jewel-like beauty that masks its modest price . . . its durability . . . ease of application (you can install it yourself)."

Weirton Steel Company, 1955

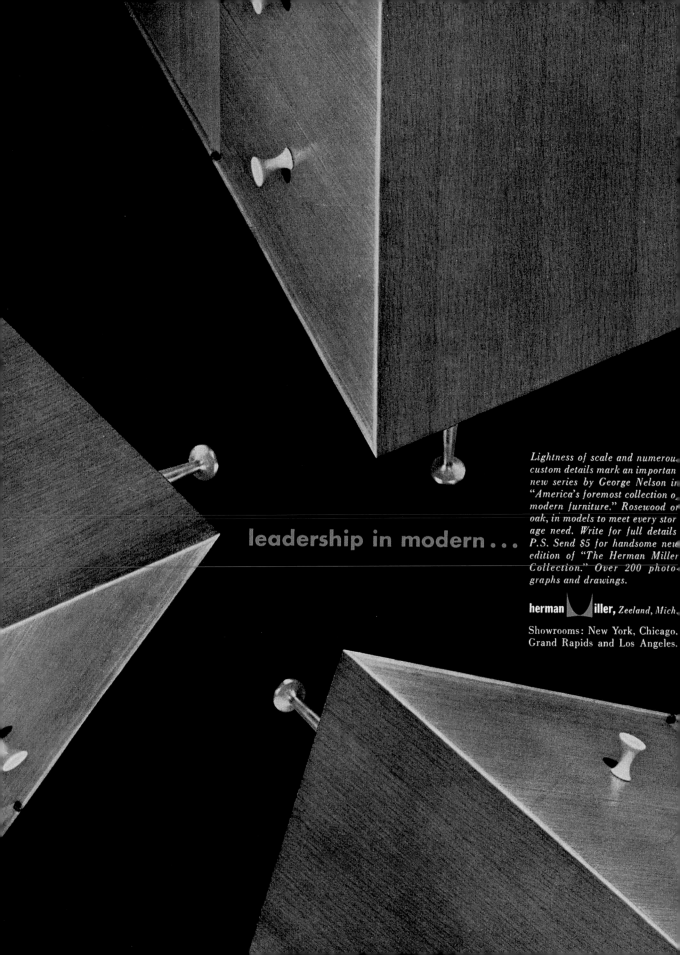

leadership in modern . . .

Lightness of scale and numerou[s]
custom details mark an importan[t]
new series by George Nelson i[n]
"America's foremost collection o[f]
modern furniture." Rosewood o[r]
oak, in models to meet every stor[age]
age need. Write for full details
P.S. Send $5 for handsome ne[w]
edition of "The Herman Miller
Collection." Over 200 photographs and drawings.

herman ᴍiller, Zeeland, Mich.

Showrooms: New York, Chicago,
Grand Rapids and Los Angeles.

NEW DIMENSIONS IN TILE FROM

HERMOSA

new, exclusive
GEM *tile*

...another dimension in tile expression...gleaming "gems" of tile-on-tile...made possible now by a new glazing discovery at Gladding, McBean & Co. Raised about ¼-inch from the surface of the tile, "Gem" adds a touch of color...a note of fashion...a new decorative idea to tile. Available in a wide array of color combinations. Send for "Gem" detail and specifications data today.

HERMOSA *glazed ceramic* **TILE**
a product of **GLADDING, McBEAN & CO.**
2901 LOS FELIZ BOULEVARD, LOS ANGELES, CALIFORNIA
SALES OFFICES IN SAN FRANCISCO, SEATTLE, PORTLAND, SPOKANE AND PHOENIX

Herman Miller, 1953 ◄ *Hermosa Ceramic Tile, 1959*

ANTHONY BROS. POOL FOR CASE STUDY HOUSE #17
PHOTO BY JASON HAILEY

ANTHONY BROS., INC.

HAS BEEN *Merit Specified* BY

CRAIG ELLWOOD ASSOCIATES

TO PERFORM SPECIAL ENGINEERING AND CONSTRUCTION
OF THE POOL FOR . . .

CASE STUDY HOUSE #18

for ARTS & ARCHITECTURE magazine

Anthony Bros., Inc. is now recognized as the Southland's largest pool builder. Outstanding among the reasons for Anthony's success is the unique swimming pool filter system utilized. It has recently been improved to incorporate an all brass pump and lint strainer, making the complete filter rust proof.

Another reason so many are insisting on an Anthony Pool is the fact that the firm builds most of the pool parts in its South Gate plant. Anthony also owns all its own equipment, and Anthony's crews do all the various construction phases.

An Anthony pool can be built to any size and shape, with the Gunite method of construction. Anthony also manufactures preformed one-piece Fiberglas pools that can be enclosed as part of the living area—ideal for the smaller yard.

Write for full information on:
- Gunite Pools
- Fiberglas Pools
- Swimming Pool Equipment

5871 FIRESTONE BLVD., SOUTH GATE
LUdlow 3-6371 • TOpaz 2-4102 • TOpaz 2-5804
"ASK THE FAMILY WHO OWNS ONE"

Visit our model pools

Many unusual ideas for swimming pool landscaping are featured at Anthony's three model pools in South Gate. Display is open daily until 8 p.m.

Anthony Bros. Inc., 1957

ANTHONY BROS. POOL FOR CASE STUDY HOUSE #17
PHOTO BY JASON HAILEY

ANTHONY BROS., INC.

HAS BEEN *Merit Specified* BY

CRAIG ELLWOOD ASSOCIATES

TO PERFORM SPECIAL ENGINEERING AND CONSTRUCTION
OF THE POOL FOR . . .

CASE STUDY HOUSE #18

for ARTS & ARCHITECTURE magazine

Anthony Bros., Inc. is now recognized as the Southland's largest pool builder. Outstanding among the reasons for Anthony's success is the unique swimming pool filter system utilized. It has recently been improved to incorporate an all brass pump and lint strainer, making the complete filter rust proof.

Another reason so many are insisting on an Anthony Pool is the fact that the firm builds most of the pool parts in its South Gate plant. Anthony also owns all its own equipment, and Anthony's crews do all the various construction phases.

An Anthony pool can be built to any size and shape, with the Gunite method of construction. Anthony also manufactures preformed one-piece Fiberglas pools that can be enclosed as part of the living area—ideal for the smaller yard.

Write for full information on:
  • Gunite Pools   • Fiberglas Pools   • Swimming Pool Equipment

Anthony Bros. inc.

5871 FIRESTONE BLVD., SOUTH GATE
LUdlow 3-6371 • TOpaz 2-4102 • TOpaz 2-5804

"ASK THE FAMILY WHO OWNS ONE"

Visit our model pools

Many unusual ideas for swimming pool landscaping are featured at Anthony's three model pools in South Gate. Display is open daily until 8 p.m.

Anthony Bros. Inc., 1957

Davidson Brick Co., 1954

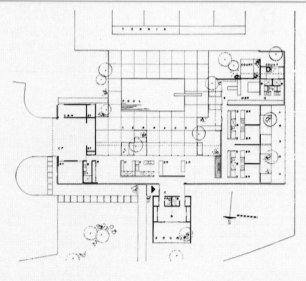

Davidson Brick Co., 1954

multalum

a new concept in furniture flexibility

KM/2

KM/HI-BAC

KM/3tc

KM/26

designed by George Kasparian

A birds-eye view of a multiple seating unit with corner table arrangement, one of the many variations possible with the Multalum structure design. As an extension of the basic seating variations, Multalum offers the lounge and Hi-Bac chairs shown, a bench, coffee and end table, conference table, shoe fitting stools and a host of advantages that may be derived from this easily maintained, brilliantly flexible design. This aluminum and walnut structure, with your choice of upholstery, is the answer to an interior planner's dream. A request on your letterhead (please), is the only step necessary to bring the complete story of Multalum to you. KASPARIANS, 7772 Santa Monica Boulevard, Los Angeles 46, California. You may see Multalum now at any of the wholesale showrooms listed below.

KK

KASPARIANS

Wholesale Showrooms: Bacon & Perry, Dallas, Texas / Contract Interiors, Denver, Colorado / Carroll Sagar & Associates, Los Angeles, California

Kasparians, 1959

Miller sliding glass doors and windows offer complete freedom in modern architectural design

Automatic weatherstripping

Quality hardware

Can be installed after plastering

The increasing specification of Miller doors and windows on the drawing boards of leading architects throughout the West is proof that the excellence of the product has been attained through the use of disciplined designed skills.

Immediate delivery.
Please write for pictorial brochure.

FRANK B. Miller MFG. CO., INC.

3216 Valhalla Drive
Burbank, California

Miller Mfg. Co., 1953

a design study for The Mosaic Tile Company to illustrate uses for ceramic tile in an automobile showroom

by Victor Gruen, A.I.A.
8640 Santa Monica Boulevard
Hollywood, California

As colorful showroom walls.

As time-defying, weatherproof out-of-door planting beds.

Areas where Mosaic Tile performs a major selling and service job in a truly-modern automobile showroom!

As showroom floors of lifetime beauty and utility.

As intriguing, moisture-resistant decorative panels at service and receiving entrance.

As trouble-free facing, traffic directional insets, drive and walkways.

As attractive curb areas defining drive and walkway.

SALES

SERVICE ENTRANCE

Showroom

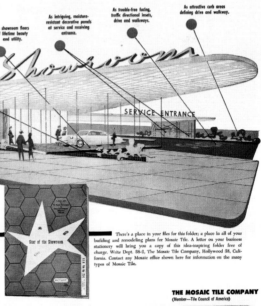

Star of the Showroom

Yesterday, ceramic tile was but a *bit* player on the automotive stage! Today, ceramic tile can be the "Star of the Showroom" . . . play a major sales role in present and future automobile merchandising plans.

Why? Simply because Mosaic Tile gives an amazing combination of beauty, color, permanence and "rock-bottom" maintenance expense . . . plus that much sought-after atmosphere of quality and prestige!

Models change . . . but Mosaic Tile — never! It's a hard-as-nails material with qualities of permanence and low-maintenance ideally suited for walls and floors in sales, service, maintenance and lubritorium areas. The smooth, pit-and-pore free surface of Mosaic Tile resists the penetration of dirt and grease . . . is easily cleaned by conventional methods. And, the *first cost* is literally the *last cost*, for Mosaic Tile won't burn, warp, crack or fade —it wears and wears but doesn't wear out!

How Mosaic Tile may assume a star's role in the automotive field is revealed by this design study, made by Victor Gruen, A. I. A., Hollywood, California.

The results, including sketches and floor plan, have been incorporated into a six-page, full-color folder which is available to you now. For details on how to receive your *free copy,* see the adjoining page!

Send for this folder TODAY!

There's a place in your files for this folder; a place in all of your building and remodeling plans for Mosaic Tile. A letter on your business stationery will bring you a copy of this idea-inspiring folder free of charge. Write Dept. S8-2, The Mosaic Tile Company, Hollywood 58, California. Contact any Mosaic office shown here for information on the many types of Mosaic Tile.

Branch Offices:

Hollywood 38, California
829 North Highland Avenue
Phone: Hillside 5238

Portland 14, Oregon
45 S. E. Salmon Street
Phone: Fillmore 3717

Salt Lake City 9, Utah
560 Gale Street
Phone: 9-8295

San Francisco, California
345 Leavis Street
Phone: Valencia 6-3924

Seattle 4, Washington
538 First Avenue, So.
Phone: Mutual 2213

Factories:

Jordan Tile and Manufacturing Company
Corona, California

General Tile Corporation
El Segundo, California

Representatives:

Denver 7, Colorado
Phone: Dexter 2618

THE MOSAIC TILE COMPANY
(Member—Tile Council of America)

MOSAIC

Offices, Showrooms and Warehouses across the nation.
Over 4000 Tile Contractors to serve you

Mosaic Tile Company, 1952

Low-cost feature that gives homes an *extra quality* look

Many prospective home buyers don't understand the principles of sound design and construction. But they all recognize the value of built-in telephone facilities . . . the neater appearance of concealed wiring, the added convenience of extra outlets. These "extra-quality" features encourage people to buy. Yet, they cost so little.

Why not take advantage of Pacific Telephone's free Architects and Builders service. Let us help you plan the kind of home telephone facilities every buyer wants.

Put built-in telephone facilities in your plans

Pacific Telephone

Matching Cove in a Full Range of beautiful Sunset Colors

Sunset RUBBER TILE

Equal in quality to the best . . . Custom color runs on special orders . . . Samples on Request.

BURKE RUBBER CO.
402 Sunol St., San Jose, California

SOFA AND CHAIR DESIGNED IN DENMARK BY PETER HVIDT FOR JOHN STUART INC.

MIRO

Modern and traditional furniture for bedroom, dining room and living room.

JOHN STUART INC.
FOURTH AVE. AT 32nd ST. NEW YORK 16

John Stuart furniture is sold only by architects, decorators and select stores.

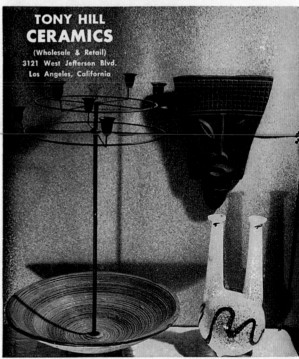

TONY HILL CERAMICS
(Wholesale & Retail)
3121 West Jefferson Blvd.
Los Angeles, California

LAMP & MASK AS ABOVE   **VASES, ASHTRAYS, ETC.**

Pacific Telephone, (top) Sunset Rubber Tile, 1954

John Stuart Inc., (top) Tony Hill Ceramics, 1954   ▶ *Hermosa Ceramic Tile, 1953*

Hospital with a Bright Future: Architects H. C. Chambers and Lester Hibbard used Hermosa 6 x 4¼ Tile to create this handsome Hydrotherapy Room at Los Angeles' new Shriners' Crippled Children's Hospital. Fairy Tale murals by Malcolm Cameron were reproduced on tile by Gladding, McBean. Contractor: Pozzo Construction Co. Tile installation: Bruner Marble and Tile Co.

And the winner is...

Today's Decorating Trend Is To Fiberglass

Fiberglass? Asbestos? Our chemical friends were changing lives for the better in the 1950s. Or so this ad suggested. Fill your modern living room with the best that chemistry has to offer. The future never looked lovelier. Or deadlier.

Der Ausstattungsstrend geht heute zur Glasfaser

Glasfaser? Asbest? Unsere chemischen Freunde wendeten unser Leben in den Fünfzigern nur zum Besseren. Zumindest dieser Werbung zufolge. Richte deinen modernen Wohnraum mit dem Besten ein, was die Chemie zu bieten hat. Nie schaute die Zukunft freundlicher aus. Oder tödlicher.

De nos jours, la tendance est à la fibre de verre

Fibre de verre ? Amiante ? Dans les années 50, nos amis chimistes changent notre vie pour l'embellir. C'est ce que dit la pub. Meublez votre séjour avec ce que la chimie offre de mieux. Jamais l'avenir n'a été si beau. Ou si mortel.

Dramatically effective in a glass-walled living room is FIBRA . . . a new Fiberglas no-iron drapery pattern, its color repeated in a decorative screen.

Fiberglas GRAPHIC . . . a heavily textured no-iron fabric adds an exciting ornamental note to a modern dining room. Used as a room-dividing screen and drapery.

New interest for a modern bedroom—a wall of color and design woven of Fiberglas *Aerocor* yarns. The striking no-iron fabric is named HONEYCOMB. About $3.00 a yd.

Richard Himmel, A.I.D., Winnetka, Illinois, created these rooms using new Fiberglas fabrics with the modern-classic look. Write Fiberglas for Richard Himmel's decorating hints.

NEW LIVING IDEAS: MODERN CLASSICS WITH PERFECTLY WASHABLE FIBERGLAS

Refreshing point of view in decorating . . . Modern influenced by classic design, in magnificent fabrics woven of Fiberglas*. All are perfectly beautiful, perfectly washable, absolutely no-iron. Rehang them damp; they dry wrinkle-free, fresh as new. See Fiberglas fabrics to match *all* of today's top decorating trends . . . in new patterns and textures at fine stores everywhere, or ask your decorator. Owens-Corning Fiberglas Corporation, Dept. 10S-15, 598 Madison Avenue, New York 22, N. Y.

TODAY'S DECORATING TREND IS TO FIBERGLAS

OWENS·CORNING
FIBERGLAS

makes the fibers, not the fabrics
*T.M. (Reg. U.S. Pat. Off.) O·C·F· Corp.

Owens-Corning Fiberglas, 1958

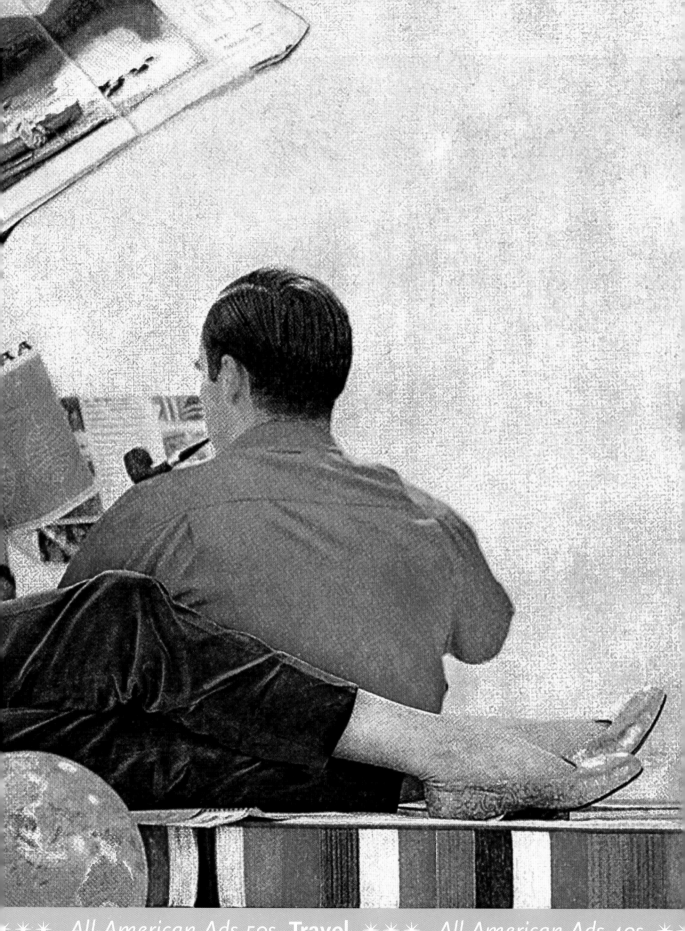

Panagra Airways, 1953

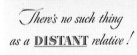

Don made the Trip
—TOO LATE AGAIN

John made the Sale
— HE TOOK THE PLANE

America's Leading Airline **AMERICAN AIRLINES** INC.

THE CHARMING SETTING for your luxury flight overseas is the smart interior of your Air France Constellation. Limited number of "skylounger" chairs provide the most spacious accommodations in air travel for your individual comfort. You are served in the inimitable French manner by friendly English-speaking stewards and hostess.

Fly in Luxury **UNEXCELLED IN AIR TRAVEL —AT NO EXTRA COST!** *Fly Air France!*

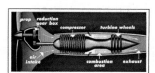

VETERAN PILOTS—many of whom have logged more than a million miles in the air—fly the new-type AIR FRANCE Constellations. Seasoned world-travelers know and respect the world-famed AIR FRANCE reputation for regularity and dependability. They know, too, that AIR FRANCE offers the ultimate in gracious living aloft—luxury unequalled in air travel. Gourmet cuisine, prepared by masters of the art of French cooking. Champagne, too, or a vintage wine...a liqueur after dinner, of course. Your entire trip by AIR FRANCE is an adventure in living as *only* the French know how!

THE WORLD'S LARGEST NETWORK of AIR ROUTES Serving 76 Countries on 6 Continents

FRANCE

SPAIN

INDIA

SEE YOUR TRAVEL AGENT

"THE PARISIAN"—Luxury trans-Atlantic air travel—an experience in gracious living. Departures from New York, Boston, and Montreal to Paris, Frankfurt, Berlin, Rome.

"THE PARISIAN SPECIAL"—The world-famous ultra-de-luxe AIR FRANCE flight—non-stop overnight from New York to Paris. Ten dollars additional fare.

NEW TOURIST SERVICE. New York-Paris round-trip $522 April 1-October 31, $453 November 1-March 31. New Type constellations. Meals obtained at moderate prices.

AIR FRANCE
THE LUXURY WORLD-WIDE AIRLINE

AIR FRANCE, 683 Fifth Avenue, New York 22, PLaza 9-7000
Offices in Boston, Chicago, Cleveland, Dallas, Los Angeles, San Francisco, Washington, D. C., Bogota, Caracas, Havana, Mexico, Montreal.

Air France, 1952

The World's Largest Airline

Air France puts the world before you. 145,000 miles of routes linking the 6 continents are at your service. You will enjoy the fleetness and luxury of the Air France travel mode. Wherever your overseas destination, fly Air France! New-type Constellations flown by million-mile pilots... the special charm of French elegance... the World's Largest Airways System.

AIR FRANCE
The Luxury World-wide Airline

"The Parisian" luxury service from N.Y., Boston and Montreal to Paris — gateway to all Europe.

"The Parisian Special"...famous non-stop overnight flight from New York to Paris. Extra fare.

"Tourist Service" by Constellations, the most powerful in tourist service to Europe.

Air France: New York, Boston, Chicago, Cleveland, Detroit, Philadelphia, Dallas, Los Angeles, San Francisco, Washington, D. C., Bogota, Caracas, Havana, Montreal, Toronto, Mexico.

Air France, 1953

A new kind of Air Travel is in the making

New military engine—soon to undergo first tests in civilian transport— promises smoother, faster, quieter, more pleasant air travel

HOW THE TURBO-PROP ENGINE OPERATES

The Turbo-Prop Engine is a gas turbine engine, like the well-known Turbo-Jet.

But in the Turbo-Prop, as the diagram shows, the turbine is connected through a drive shaft and reduction gears to a special type Aeroprop propeller. Air enters the compressor, which feeds it under high pressure into the combustion chamber, where it is mixed with fuel and ignited. The thrust of this hot gas drives the turbine which generates the power to operate both compressor and propeller. The small amount of energy remaining in the exhaust gas is used as jet thrust.

The Allison T38 Turbo-Prop Engine develops 2,750 horsepower, yet weighs only 1,250 pounds—2.2 horsepower for every pound of weight. This is more than twice the power per pound of weight developed by the best reciprocating type aviation engines used in World War II.

Allison also produces the J33 and J35 Turbo-Jet Engines which power today's Shooting Stars, Thunderjets, Panthers, Scorpions and other near-sonic-speed jet fighters.

WITHIN a short time the first American commercial airliner ever to be powered by turbine engines will be delivered to the Allison Division of General Motors.

The power plants in this Convair are new Allison Model "501" Turbo-Props—commercial version of the Navy T38. They are geared to a new high-performance propeller especially designed and built for high-engine-power characteristics by the Aeroproducts Division of General Motors.

The "501" is lighter, smaller, smoother and quieter than any other propeller-type engine of equal horsepower—and much more efficient than a jet, up to near-sonic speeds.

Developed for military use, the Allison Turbo-Prop engine with Aeroproducts Propellers has already set new performance targets in multi-engine aircraft as large as the Navy's giant 60-ton Convair XP5Y flying boat and also in a high-performance, carrier-based Navy attack plane, the XA2D. So the next step is to adapt this new type of power to commercial use.

No one is better fitted to do this than General Motors with its great technical ability and long experience in all types of engine and propeller development.

As soon as this experimental Turbo-Prop transport is delivered, General Motors-Allison engineers will start putting it through a long and comprehensive series of flight tests.

In cooperation with the airlines it will be flown under all types of operating conditions—in all kinds of weather. It will be given the works, checked and rechecked many times over, until all its performance characteristics are definitely evaluated.

This is in accordance with General Motors' policy of sponsoring to the public only products that have been thoroughly proved in advance. It is GM's task to demonstrate for airplane manufacturers, airline operators

Allison "501" Turbo-Prop engines fit in nacelles of present commercial transports.

and the Civil Aeronautics Authority that Turbo-Prop power is as safe and practical as it is economical and comfortable.

Such an all-out test program may take a year or more. But it will be well worth it, in view of the fact that present military experience indicates that Turbo-Prop power should bring the following benefits to commercial aviation:

Ability to use low-cost, low-octane fuels, without increased consumption.

Faster speed—up to maximum limit permitted by airframe design.

Very low engine weight—less than half—increasing range or pay load.

Much improved take-off and climb—permitting use of shorter runways, with greater safety and better schedules.

Smoother operation—for passenger comfort; also lower maintenance and overhaul costs.

Quieter operation—more restful and pleasant travel.

Usable in present aircraft—no costly modifications in changing over to turbine power.

When General Motors is satisfied with its tests of these engines and they are approved for commercial use by the C.A.A., it will be possible to convert present airlines to smoother turbine power without further delay—giving America very high-speed, low-cost, regular airline service.

The development of the Allison Turbo-Prop engine, America's first axial flow propeller-type turbine engine, together with Aeroproducts Propellers, is another example of General Motors progress—and who serves progress, serves the nation.

Your key to Better Power

"MORE AND BETTER THINGS FOR MORE PEOPLE"

GENERAL MOTORS

ALLISON AIRCRAFT ENGINES • AEROPRODUCTS PROPELLERS • CHEVROLET • PONTIAC • OLDSMOBILE
BUICK • CADILLAC • BODY BY FISHER • GMC TRUCK & COACH

General Motors, 1950

▶ *American Airlines, 1951*

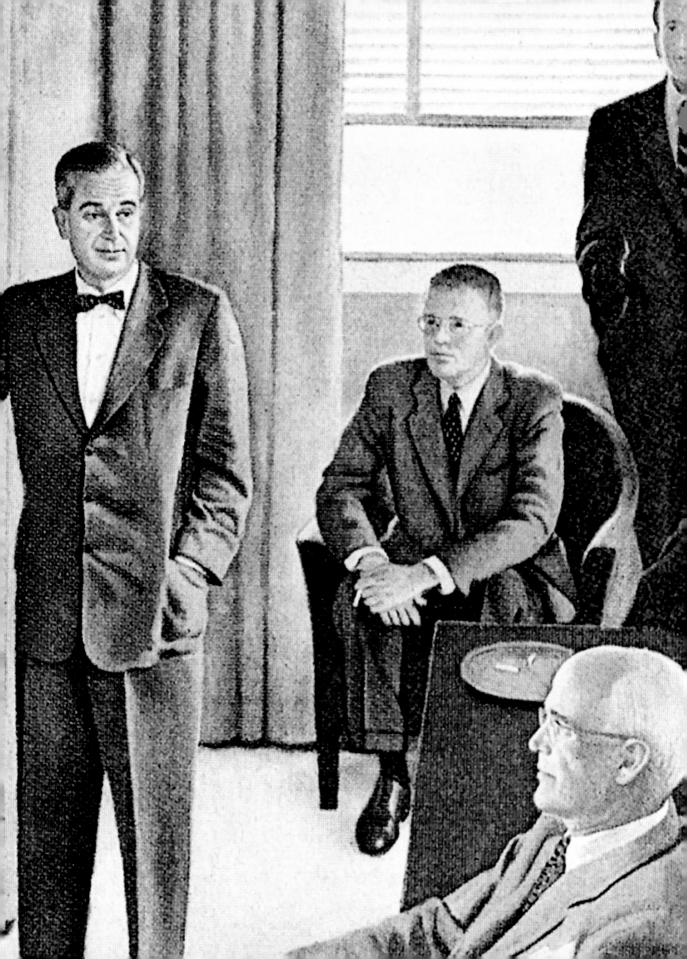

ONE MILLION

passengers have now flown the Boeing 707 jetliner!

These airlines have ordered 707 or shorter-range 720 jetliners: AIR FRANCE • AIR-INDIA INTERNATIONAL • AMERICAN AIRLINES • BRANIFF INTERNATIONAL AIRWAYS • BRITISH OVERSEAS AIRWAYS CORPORATION • CONTINENTAL AIR LINES • CUBANA DE AVIACION • IRISH AIR LINES • LUFTHANSA GERMAN AIRLINES • PAN AMERICAN WORLD AIRWAYS • QANTAS EMPIRE AIRWAYS • SABENA BELGIAN WORLD AIRLINES • SOUTH AFRICAN AIRWAYS • TRANS WORLD AIRLINES • UNITED AIR LINES • VARIG AIRLINES OF BRAZIL • *Also the* MILITARY AIR TRANSPORT SERVICE

BOEING 707 and 720

Boeing, 1959

▶ *American Airlines, 1950* ▶▶ *American Airlines, 1954*

American's New DC-7 Lead

In 1954 YOU'LL FLY THE MOST MODERN FLEET OF

TRANSPORT AIRCRAFT IN THE WORLD ON THE ROUTE OF THE FLAGSHIPS

In 1954 American's new DC-7 is leading the finest Flagship Fleet in history. It includes such outstanding passenger carriers as the popular inter-city Convair and the famous long range DC-6 and DC-6B Flagships as well as the DC-6A, the biggest, fastest cargo plane in operation today.

American's magnificent new Turbo Compound DC-7 Flagship is the *first* plane especially designed for NONSTOP transcontinental travel and the *only* aircraft capable of nonstop coast-to-coast service under 8 hours.

This means that American now offers the fastest service between New York and Los Angeles and New York and San Francisco. The addition of the DC-7 also enables American to greatly expand its nonstop service between major cities on its 10,800 miles of routes.

So welcome aboard the Flagship Fleet for '54. Welcome *to* the most modern fleet of transport aircraft in the world. And welcome *from* American's 17,000 trained personnel whose friendly attentive service has long set the standard for air transportation.

AMERICAN AIRLINES INC.

America's Leading Airline

the Finest Flagship Fleet Ever

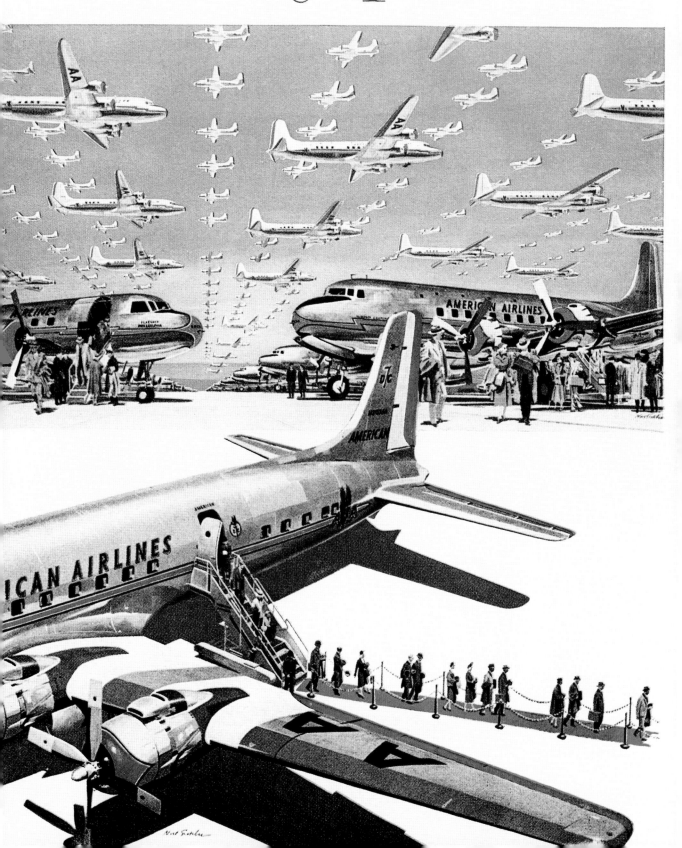

NO CHARGE for the First Billion Miles

You don't pay extra for Braniff experience and safety. They're yours without charge...yet Braniff's background of 22 years, and more than one billion passenger miles flown in complete safety, add much to your travel enjoyment.

All that you could ask for—really more than you can imagine—in speed, comfort and niceties of service is yours, too.

Braniff's famous "El Conquistador" flights to Cuba, Panama, Lima, Rio and Buenos Aires are the last word in luxury aloft. With deep-cushioned, reclining seats for daytime lounging, cocktails or cards and bed-size berths for nighttime, with gourmet meals and music, this is truly travel de luxe. Extra-fine, extra-fast, but *no* extra fare.

For the budget-minded, Braniff offers fine, fast, four-engine service on its "El Intercontinental" tourist liners at a 25% savings under standard fares.

At home or abroad, when you fly Braniff, you fly the best.

Aboard El Conquistador

The minutes and the miles slip away as you enjoy the friendly atmosphere of the luxury lounge, the special drinks and dishes of the countries over which you fly, the unsurpassed scenery of Braniff Express Routes...it's air travel at its Braniff best.

BRANIFF
International AIRWAYS

Offices in principal cities throughout the Americas. Or, your favorite Travel Agent.

Braniff Airways, 1950

address: WASHINGTON

Here in the Nation's Capital—world center of free Government and keystone of Democracy—is the home of Capital Airlines.

From "address: Washington," Capital directs the operation of its vast system of 73 cities—from the Atlantic to the West, from the Great Lakes to the Gulf. One of the nation's leading carriers, Capital last year served nearly a million and a half passengers. And Capital's 23 years of experience is your assurance of *greater comfort, greater safety* and *better service.*

450 flights daily serving these Capital Cities...

*Washington • New York • Pittsburgh • Cleveland • Detroit • Chicago • Milwaukee • Minneapolis • St. Paul
New Orleans • Atlanta • Mobile • Birmingham • Knoxville • Memphis • Akron • Canton • Asheville
Hendersonville • Baltimore • Saginaw • Bay City • Midland • Bristol • Kingsport • Johnson City • Buffalo
Niagara Falls • Greensboro • High Point • Burlington • Charleston, W. Va. • Charlotte • Chattanooga
Cheboygan • Pellston • Petoskey • Harbor Springs • Clarksburg • Elmira • Corning • Raleigh • Durham
Elizabeth City • Erie • Flint • Grand Rapids • Harrisburg • Huntsville • Lansing • Morgantown
Muskegon • Newark • Norfolk • Virginia Beach • Portsmouth • Newport News • Williamsburg
Philadelphia • Reading • Richmond • Rochester • Rocky Mount • Youngstown • Sharon • Warren
Wheeling • Strabenville • Sault Ste. Marie • Toledo • Traverse City • Williamsport • Winston-Salem*

Capital
AIRLINES

Capital Airlines, 1950

What airline gives you Red Carpet* Service?

It's "Red Carpet" luxury all the way...

aboard United's special nonstop DC-7s!

Inviting lounge, superlative service...

de luxe meals and refreshments!

Games, kits, scores of travel items...

many other "extras" at no extra cost!

Copr. 1956, United Air Lines

United Air Lines, 1956

Ever watch this great team in action?

Perhaps you've wondered how United Air Lines holds so closely to its schedules. Here's part of the answer — a scene that's enacted thousands of times yearly at United terminals, with the teamwork of competent people — the precision of careful planning.

You see the great Mainliner taxi from the runway and pivot on its loading station. Even before it stops rolling, you notice that lift trucks, tankers, ramps and other ground units are moving toward it.

There are dozens of things to do in the next few minutes. Fuel, mail, express, freight, luggage, meal service, mechanical inspections...these are just a few. You're conscious of great activity. But as you watch you see no confusion...no waste motion.

You see efficiency, thoroughness and consideration for the passengers. You see the Mainliner take off on time. Then it comes to you that here are many of the qualities that make United such a fine and dependable way of travel. You've been watching, in miniature, a great airline at work.

THE NATION'S NUMBER 1 COAST-TO-COAST AIRLINE

† Today Mainliner fares are often less than the cost of first class surface travel.
◊ For reservations, call or write United or see an Authorized Travel Agent.

UNITED
AIR LINES

PASSENGERS • MAIL • EXPRESS
FREIGHT • AIR PARCEL POST

United Air Lines, 1951

THE NATION'S NUMBER 1 COAST-TO-COAST AIRLINE

United carries more coast-to-coast passengers than any other airline. It is U. S. Air Mail Route No. 1, officially—and the pioneer in many great advances.

For example, United was the first airline to carry passengers from coast to coast. It was the first major airline to centralize operations control for better on-time performance. First to offer stewardess service. And, backed by such experience, United's leadership continues in improvements for the present and the future.

One of the latest of such forward strides has been the success of United's program to increase the year-round schedule dependability of air travel.

Yet, while the dependability, comfort and speed of Mainliner travel have increased steadily, the cost of your ticket is only about 4% above 1941. This is in contrast to increases that are several times that amount for other forms of transportation.

Today United Mainliner travel often costs less than standard 1st class rail plus lower berth, tips, and meals en route! In *value, too,* The Main Line Airway leads the way.

For reservations call or write United or an Authorized Travel Agent
PASSENGERS • MAIL • EXPRESS • FREIGHT • AIR PARCEL POST

RECIPIENT OF THE
1950 FASHION ACADEMY
GOLD MEDAL AWARD
FOR STYLING AND LUXURY

UNITED
AIR LINES

ONLY COAST-TO-COAST ALL RADAR FLEET
IT COULD ONLY BE ONE AIRLINE

UNITED
AIR LINES

You're sure of more on-time arrivals and smoother, more comfortable flights on United's radar-equipped Mainliners®. United, the Radar Line, is the only coast-to-coast airline with radar on every plane. Radar "X-rays" weather up to 150 miles ahead, shows where storm centers are, helps the pilot

United Air Lines, 1958

United Air Lines, 1950

The air is yours...
use it
to travel **above** the bad weather

IN these uncertain times it is more important than ever to save time when you travel. Businessmen are finding that modern airliners can fly around or over bad weather in any season. They save precious hours, and often days, in reaching their destination. Ask any airline representative or travel agent to tell you more about the speed and dependability of air travel.

United Aircraft
CORPORATION
EAST HARTFORD, CONNECTICUT

Makers of Pratt & Whitney Engines, Hamilton Standard Propellers, Chance Vought Aircraft and Sikorsky Helicopters for the U. S. Armed Forces and the Finest Airlines in the World.

United Air Lines, 1950

UNITED
AIR LINES

A JET AGE "FIRST" IN EXTRA CARE

United Air Lines is the first—and only—airline with an electronic jet "airplane," the DC-8 flight simulator, built by Link Aviation, Inc. The simulator shown below realistically duplicates every phase of jet flight, with actual instruments, controls, sound, motion and an airport panorama that unfolds before pilots as they "land" and "take off." United flight crews trained in the simulator will be expert in all jet flight procedures before they actually fly new DC-8 Jet Mainliners. United's captains average 3,000,000 miles in the air, yet they regularly "fly" in flight simulators for extra skills. United is the world's largest airline user of these electronic devices for jet and piston-engine aircraft—another reason for that extra care you enjoy on United Air Lines.

YOU GET EXTRA CARE AT THE REGULAR FARE—ON UNITED, THE RADAR LINE

UNITED

United Air Lines, 1958

▶ *Pan American Air Lines, 1959*

Only seven hours to brush up on your French

The superb Boeing 707 jet airliner goes into service first across the Atlantic, and within weeks across the United States.

You'll be delighted with the feeling of solid security you get from flight aboard this swift new skyliner. It begins the moment of take-off, as abundant, jet-smooth power lifts the 707 effortlessly to cruising altitude. You'll fly serenely through high, weatherless skies.

In just 60 minutes, you're almost 600 miles out of New York. In scarcely six hours you'll be trotting out your best French for the *douanier* at Paris.

The spacious cabin is peaceful and quiet, and completely free from vibration. There is only luxurious comfort, and a sense of exhilaration from the almost magical ease and smoothness of 707 flight.

Even if you're a veteran airline traveler you'll find flight in the 707 truly exciting—and secure. The 707 is the most thoroughly flight-tested aircraft ever to enter commercial service.

These airlines have ordered 707s or shorter-range 720s:
AIR FRANCE • AIR-INDIA INTERNATIONAL • AMERICAN AIRLINE
BRANIFF INTERNATIONAL AIRWAYS • BRITISH OVERSEAS
AIRWAYS CORPORATION • CONTINENTAL AIR LINES
CUBANA DE AVIACION • LUFTHANSA GERMAN AIRLINES
PAN AMERICAN WORLD AIRWAYS • QANTAS EMPIRE AIRWAYS
SABENA BELGIAN WORLD AIRLINES • SOUTH AFRICAN AIRWAYS
TRANS WORLD AIRLINES • UNITED AIR LINES • VARIG AIRLINES
OF BRAZIL • *Also the* MILITARY AIR TRANSPORT SERVICE

BOEING 707 and 720

Boeing, 1958

That first meal is the hardest

...*but not for You!*

You are looking at a meal in a mock-up. The Stewardess serving dinner is a *trainee*. She is going to BOAC's school in Heston, near London, for 12 weeks...before being allowed to serve her first meal in a BOAC aircraft.

At the moment, she is facing her most critical "passengers"...her own fellow Stewards and Stewardesses. They themselves are veterans. They know every move she should make in serving. They will catch her out in the slightest error.

Maybe now she's flustered by their scrutiny. Maybe she's taken aback by their questions in French or Italian. (She must know at least one extra language.)

Some day, all the strict training will be behind her. Some day, *she* will have made a hundred crossings!

Some day, she, too, will be a veteran.

You will find her...when she serves *you*...competent, cheerful, courteous to a fault.

BOAC's British cabin-attendance is not indoctrinated in a day. You will not forget it in a long time!

No other airline can provide it.

Equipment: BOAC flies you in the most modern aircraft, including "DC-7C's", jet-prop "Britannias" and pure jet "Comet 4's".

Classes of Fares...BOAC tickets cost exactly the same as those of other scheduled airlines. Round-trip, New York to London, they are de Luxe $873, First Class $783, Tourist $567, Economy $453.60. (Subject to change after April 1st.)

Travel Agents' requests for your reservations are honored at all BOAC offices. They can give you travel and tour literature, timetables and answers to your individual questions.

B·O·A·C

WORLD LEADER IN JET TRAVEL
BRITISH OVERSEAS AIRWAYS CORPORATION
Flights from New York, Boston, Chicago, Detroit, San Francisco, Montreal. Offices also in Atlanta, Dallas, Los Angeles, Miami, Philadelphia, Pittsburgh, Washington, Toronto, Vancouver, Winnipeg.

BOAC, 1959

Dad's *favorite* chair

Comfort and complete relaxation! Dad's found both in his TWA Skyliner seat ... and lots more. He's found the magic key to covering territory, arriving fresher, and quite often, first. Best of all—and how the family loves this—a Skyliner lets Dad spend most of his evenings where he wants to be most—in his *other* favorite chair—at home!

ACROSS THE U.S. AND OVERSEAS ... YOU CAN DEPEND ON **TWA**
TRANS WORLD AIRLINES
U.S.A · EUROPE · AFRICA · ASIA

Listen to Cary Grant and Betsy Drake as "Mr. & Mrs. Blandings" every Sunday PM, NBC.

TWA, 1951

Delta to Miami ... **trunk line to Sunshine**

While your DC-7 doesn't really taxi up to your hotel's poolside, there is no faster, no finer way to sunny Miami than these giant Golden Crown DC-7's non-stop from such cities as Chicago, Cincinnati and Atlanta. Delta also provides DC-7 through service from the Midwest to the Caribbean and South America, via New Orleans. For unsurpassed speed, unforgettable hospitality, fly Delta Golden Crown DC-7's and DC-7B's to Miami and the Caribbean.

General Offices
Atlanta Airport 7, Atlanta, Ga

Serving 60 cities in the U.S.A. and Caribbean

Delta Air Lines, 1958

Springboard...
to cool MIAMI BEACH and the Caribbean

Today the Midwest looks South to the seashore. Just beyond the steps of the big Delta DC-6 lies the most magnificent, the most complete holidayland in all the world – cool, luxurious, inviting. A winter mecca for millionaires, in summer it's a dream-come-true for budget-wise Americans.

Palatially impressive, yet hospitable in the Southern tradition, this vacation land is another business success story served by Delta.

Inquire about Delta's Millionaire Dream Vacation to MIAMI BEACH

FREE folder describes this summer's greatest travel bargain—7 days including hotel and air fares—tax extra from Chicago—$130.00 from Cincinnati—$119.80 Special excursion rates until Oct. 31st.

Ask your Travel Agent or write

Capital Air Lines, 1953 ◄   *Delta Air Lines, 1952*

"DC" MEANS DOUGLAS ... builder of the famous DC-3 and DC-4 ... the ultra-modern DC-6 and DC-6B ... tomorrow's DC-7. Next time, go by air! Ask for reservations on a dependable *Douglas*.

In the next <u>hour</u>—5 times around the world!

Every day, Douglas "DC" airplanes fly about 3,126,500 miles for 160 airlines. That is more than five times around the world *every hour!* Douglas airplanes link all the continents, and they span the seven seas.

Navy's "Skyknight" has twin-jet speed, radar eyes, rocket punch!

Douglas builds the sleek Skyknight for use on aircraft carriers. With its two big jet engines, it flies near the speed of sound. Its radar pinpoints targets in any weather, day or night. 84% of Douglas production is military.

Each Douglas builds all four airplane types: j[e]t-prop, turbo-prop, jet, rocket ... and guided missiles, too.

"Picture window" is right! Windows in the Douglas DC-6 and DC-6B are big ... 16 by 18 inches ... to display the magnificent views below. Made of clear, heavy plastic, the windows have an "air-sandwich" construction that prevents formation of mist or frost.

"Queen of the fleet" on these leading airlines of the world is the giant, modern Douglas DC-6 or DC-6B:
AA Argentina • "ALITALIA Italy • AMERICAN U. S. • BOPA Australia New Zealand
BRANIFF U. S. • CMA Mexico • CONTINENTAL U. S. • OPAL Canadian • DELTA U. S.
*FLYING TIGER U. S. • KLM Netherlands • LAI Italian • NATIONAL U. S.
PAL Philippine • PANAGRA U. S. • PAN AMERICAN U. S. • SABENA Belgian
SAS Danish Norwegian Swedish • SLICK U. S. • SWISSAIR Swiss • *TAI French
TRANSOCEAN U. S. • UNITED U. S. • WESTERN U. S.   *Prop*

Twice as many people fly **DOUGLAS**
as all other airplanes <u>combined</u>

Douglas Aircraft, 1953   ► *TWA, 1950*

Explore colorful, cosmopolitan San Francisco and Hollywood. Or simply loaf in the sun along beautiful Pacific shores, enjoying the extra time TWA gives you.

Your camera lens captures unbelievable colors in the glorious Southwest, where outdoor fun reigns in the wide-open spaces of dude ranches and resorts.

For wonderful fishing, fly TWA to Chicago and head North to the pine-forested lake country. There's camping, resort life, golfing, swimming and sailing.

Look for the new, the old, the smart and unique in New York — served by more than 25 TWA flights daily. It's a vacation full of memorable sights and experiences.

New England holds a treasure of Americana, cool salt breezes along Cod sand dunes and sparkling fresh lakes nestled in the mountains.

Where in the world can you go on just 2 weeks' vacation?

Here's an easy way to measure your own new horizons along the HIGH ways of TWA.

You pick the places you'd *like* to go, then check the TWA time-map below.* Possibilities are TWA can save you so much travel time you actually *can* go . . . even with limited vacation time off! And TWA fares are surprisingly easy on your budget.

So forget the old, usual vacation haunts. This year, follow the TWA highway to the Great Southwest, to the east or west coast; to the mountains; to the seashores; to the Golden Gate or the Grand Canyon or the canyons of New York. You pick it—you measure it—you can make it, easily, probably in mere hours from where you are right now!

But perhaps your eyes are on the Old World . . . way, way overseas. How far is it by TWA? Look at the map again and see what a vast distance one single day's flight can cover. Yes, you *can* go to Paris on a two weeks' vacation. You can go to Switzerland; to Rome; to Cairo; to Lisbon; to Madrid. You can take your pick of these and many other famed holiday centers and resort lands along TWA's direct world routes and *still keep well within the practical time limits of a short vacation!*

If *you* have been dreaming about a certain trip, don't put it off this year due to a short vacation. Plan to use the speed of Skyliner travel to bridge the distance and make that dream come true. Your travel agent will be glad to help with all the answers to your trip questions. Or call TWA.

* *All flying times shown are approximate. Check your travel agent or TWA for exact schedules.*

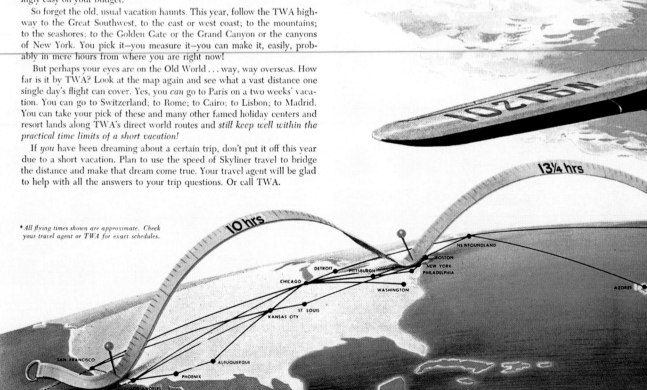

...mer in Ireland is a season of color-...scenes and fun-filled events . . . from ...it fairs and fine racing to the famous ...lin Horse Show in August.

For leisurely sight-seeing, try the quiet lanes of provincial France. For gaiety and sidewalk cafes—there's nothing like Paris! 16 TWA flights weekly from the U. S.

Like luxurious living? Then take a 300-mph TWA Skyliner to the Mediterranean area. You'll find the finest hotels and smart casinos on the world-famous Riviera.

Motoring offers rich rewards in the Swiss Alps, where breath-taking new scenes await you at every turn. And car rentals are reasonable in Europe.

Magnificent monuments and ancient art masterpieces are everywhere in Rome, scene of the Holy Year observances. Less than a day from the U. S. by TWA.

Part of the pleasure on your vacation will be the few pleasant hours en route, when you travel by world-proved 300-mph TWA Skyliner. As soon as you board, the thoughtful TWA hostess sees that you're comfortably settled in a deep, reclining seat. She'll bring you magazines, playing cards, writing material . . . serve you delicious hot meals when it's time to eat. As you relax and rest, your dependable Skyliner speeds you to your destination in *hours* instead of days.

Across the U.S. and overseas . . . you can depend on

TWA
TRANS WORLD AIRLINE
U. S. A. · EUROPE · AFRICA · ASIA

Ship almost anything anywhere by TWA Air Cargo—fast, dependable, low-cost! For mail and small packages, use air mail and air parcel post.

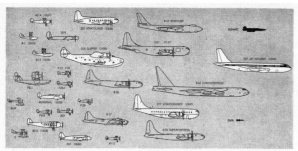

From Boeing have come the pioneering passenger planes . . . the mighty fortresses . . . the flying boats . . . all part of the family tree of America's first jet airliner, the incomparable Boeing 707.

Aboard the Boeing 707 you'll enter the age of jet travel in a plane flight-tested three years . . . cruise across continents and seas . . . in luxurious comfort and quiet . . . at 600 miles an hour.

BOEING 707

Boeing, 1957

On most of the world's leading airlines it's

"Queen of the fleet"

The Douglas DC-6 and DC-6B, above, are the choice of most major airlines for their big four-engine airplanes. Hundreds are now in service. They are also the 2-to-1 choice of experienced air *travelers*, according to a nationwide survey.

Jet "Skyray" has rocket stingers! Douglas builds the batlike Skyray interceptor for use on aircraft carriers. Today, 89% of Douglas production is military.

Only Douglas builds all four airplane types: piston-engine, turbo-prop, jet, rocket . . . and guided missiles, too.

DC-6 air conditioning is even smoker-proof! In the Douglas DC-6 and DC-6B, the temperature and humidity of the cabin air are controlled for perfect comfort—and the air is *completely replaced* every three minutes with fresh outside air. Make *your* next trip a Douglas "DC" airplane; see your airline or travel agent.

Twice as many people fly **DOUGLAS** as all other airplanes combined

Douglas Aircraft, 1953

Your fastest way to tropic sun—fly DC-7

Whatever your reason for getting there faster...

Nothing beats the DC-7—world's *fastest* airliner

You go up to *50 mph faster* in the new DC-7 than in any other airliner—its top speed is 410! You fly in luxury, too, with scores of new comforts, new conveniences.

Next time, be sure to go by DC-7. See why twice as many people fly Douglas as all other airplanes *combined.*

HOLIDAY/NOVEMBER

Douglas Aircraft, 1953 ◄ *Douglas Aircraft, 1956*

MAUREEN O'SULLIVAN and her 7 attractive children leaving for Ireland on the World's Most Experienced Airline

Q. Which airline carries the most passengers to Europe?

A. PAN AMERICAN, the only airline that has completed over 48,000 Atlantic crossings . . . and the only airline that can fly you direct to so many European cities.

Pan American Air Lines, 1955

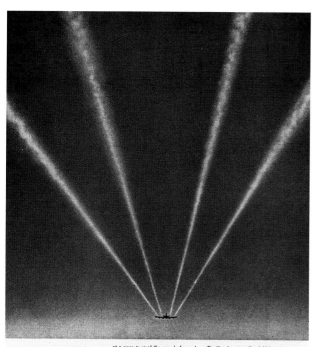

THE NEW BLUE HIGHWAY

Eight miles higher than you stand, in the peaceful purple-blue of the stratosphere, a flawless open road is almost ready for you.

So soon now, you'll skim along this wide blue highway in the DC-8 jetliner

at a pace to rival the speed of sound, with the whims of weather far below.

On this endlessly beautiful celestial thoroughfare in the DC-8, distance will all but surrender. The earth, so small now, will shrink a good deal more. Time will tick at a different tempo.

But your rewards in the jet age will be measured by more than time and space.

Startling beauty will unfold for you . . . spectacles from the universe of stars and moon and sun, never so close to you before. And for your spirit, an unearthly sense of serenity.

It will soon be yours, this magic highway. And on its way to lift you to this thrilling new realm of flight is . . . the Douglas DC-8 Jetliner.

These fourteen airlines already have purchased DC-8's: Delta Air Lines • Eastern Air Lines • Japan Air Lines • KLM Royal Dutch Air Lines National Airlines • Olympic Airways • Pan American World Airways • Panagra • Scandinavian Airlines System • Swissair • Trans-Canada Air Lines Transports Aeriens Intercontinentaux • Union Aeromaritime de Transport • United Air Lines

Douglas Aircraft, 1951

The DC-8, now in flight, will soon carry you to new heights of luxurious air travel.

DC-8 introduces you to Her Serene Highness—the Stratosphere

Beneath the outstretched wings of the DC-8, the world falls swiftly below. The sky you climb into turns from blue to purple, and as you reach new heights, there comes over you a sense of serenity you've never known before.

Cradled in your pressurized cabin in the Douglas Jetliner eight miles high, with the sun and moon your neighbors, you gaze down on the toylike towns and peaks and waters of the world. Tranquility suspend-

ed in the clear quiet of the stratosphere, you experience no sense of speed, no vibration, no engine's roar . . . nothing but a beautiful peace of mind and body.

But the DC-8 offers you more than speed and serenity. It brings you a family history of experience, dependability and comfort unmatched in the annals of flight. It is this—and more—which makes passengers and pilots look up to Douglas. You'll sense it all when you take your first flight in the fabulous . . .

DOUGLAS DC-8 JETLINER

Built by the most respected name in aviation

These famous air lines already have purchased the DC-8: ALITALIA-Linee Aeree Italiane • DELTA AIR LINES • EASTERN AIR LINES • JAPAN AIR LINES • KLM ROYAL DUTCH AIR LINES NATIONAL AIRLINES • OLYMPIC AIRWAYS • PANAGRA • PANAIR DO BRASIL • PAN AMERICAN WORLD AIRWAYS • SCANDINAVIAN AIRLINES SYSTEM • SWISSAIR TRANS-CANADA AIR LINES • TRANS CARIBBEAN AIRWAYS • TRANSPORTS AERIENS INTERCONTINENTAUX • UNION AEROMARITIME DE TRANSPORT • UNITED AIR LINES

Douglas Aircraft, 1958

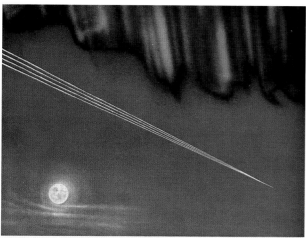

The Douglas DC-8 in flight, newest bearer of the most respected name in aviation

Look up to the DC-8 . . . world's _newest_ jetliner!

Into the skies—from the Northern Lights to the Southern Cross—flies the Douglas DC-8. And with this flight, travel by air reaches a new high level of performance and comfort.

In the still, blue stratosphere, the miles tick away on the wings of this most modern of passenger planes. The earth's masses of land and water, awesome as they are, yield to the murmuring power of the

DC-8 jet engines. Cradled in peace and luxury, you now can reach the world's farthest corners in less time than it takes the sun to go full circle.

But speed alone is not what distinguishes Douglas from all other names in aviation. The DC-8—like each of its world-famous predecessors—takes to the skies a family tradition of experience, dependability and com-

fort unrivalled in the annals of flight. It is this—and more—which makes passengers and pilots look up to Douglas . . . reveals, in part, why more people and more airlines fly Douglas than all other airplanes combined.

Your own personal introduction to the jet age is not far off. Like so many others, you will experience it in the nonpareil of the upper air, the fabulous . . .

DOUGLAS DC-8 JETLINER

Built by the most respected name in aviation

These famous airlines already have purchased the DC-8: ALITALIA-Linee Aeree Italiane • DELTA AIR LINES • EASTERN AIR LINES • JAPAN AIR LINES • KLM ROYAL DUTCH AIR LINES NATIONAL AIRLINES • OLYMPIC AIRWAYS • PANAGRA • PANAIR DO BRASIL • PAN AMERICAN WORLD AIRWAYS • SCANDINAVIAN AIRLINES SYSTEM • SWISSAIR TRANS-CANADA AIR LINES • TRANS CARIBBEAN AIRWAYS • TRANSPORTS AERIENS INTERCONTINENTAUX • UNION AEROMARITIME DE TRANSPORT • UNITED AIR LINES

Douglas Aircraft, 1958

John B. Huarisa, Executive Vice President of Admiral Corp., says—

Special Jobs require a Specialist's Attention

we use **Flying Tigers**

NOW SERVING THE PACIFIC NORTHWEST! With Regularly Scheduled Service to and from Seattle, Washington; Tacoma, Washington; and Portland, Oregon.

FLYING TIGERS . . . ANOTHER BUSINESS BUILT ON 'CAN DO'

Write for "THE AIR FREIGHT WAY TO LOWER COSTS AND BETTER SERVICE"

The Flying Tiger Line Inc.

OFFICES IN PRINCIPAL CITIES • GENERAL OFFICES: LOCKHEED AIR TERMINAL, BURBANK 8, CALIFORNIA • CABLE: FLYTIGER

The Flying Tiger Line Inc., 1952

Convair, 1958

American Airlines, 1958

▶ *SAS Air Lines, 1954*

Leadership demands constant achievement

20 Distinguished World Airlines
have selected
THE CONSTELLATION & SUPER CONSTELLATION

On every continent of the world leading airlines fly the famous Constellation. Today more people fly over more oceans and continents on the Constellations of these great airlines than on *any other modern airplane*. It is also the leader on the most traveled route, the

North Atlantic. This successful operation by international airlines established the Constellation's record for dependable performance—leading to the development of the new Super Constellation, today's finest transport airplane. Altogether 20 distinguished

airlines have selected the Constellation and Super Constellation. Whenever or wherever you travel, insist on the dependable service of these airline leaders.* If there is no local airline office, see your travel agent.
Listed above on travel posters.

LOCKHEED
AIRCRAFT CORPORATION · BURBANK, CALIFORNIA, AND MARIETTA, GEORGIA

Lockheed, 1955

This is Florida—Sunshine, U.S.A.—where everything you do and every place you go are filled with glorious adventure.

This year take it *all* in—the brilliance of Florida's palm-fringed beaches and sun-warmed surf; the tingling excitement of landing that first, or *hundred*-and-first, big-game fish; the thrill of driving one down the middle of velvet-green fairway. This year discover for yourself the splendor of Florida's scenic landmarks; the glamour of its renowned spectator events; the romance of its nights under the stars. And this year see with your own eyes why so many millions agree, there's no place like Florida for sunny pleasure, healthful relaxation, and sheer good living.

Plan it today—your sparkling Winter with Sunshine in Florida—the vacation adventure you'll remember a lifetime.

Florida

MAIL THIS COUPON TODAY

STATE OF FLORIDA,
2201 COMMISSION BUILDING, TALLAHASSEE.

Please send at once new, free 48-page booklet in full color: "Florida, the Sunshine State."

Name_____

Street and No._____

City_____ Zone____ State_____

Florida, 1950

▶ *Northwest Airlines, 1955*

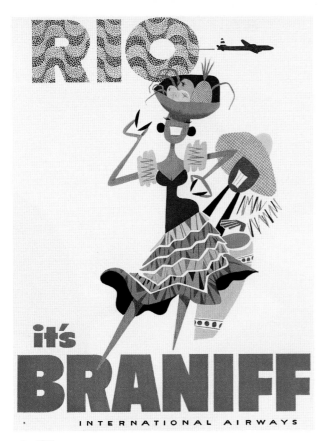

Braniff Airways, 1953

Lockheed, 1951

Lockheed, 1955

Northwest Orient Airlines, 1955

Come aboard and see NORTHWEST *Orient* AIRLINES great new SUPER CONSTELLATIONS
(World's finest overseas airliners)

Huge cabins create restful atmosphere of spaciousness. Big, wide, comfortable seats, and altitude-conditioning, invite complete relaxation. Northwest's Super Constellations are coming soon . . . on both the famous "Hawaiian Express" and "Orient Express."

New look, new luxury is typified by the smart modern lounge, providing an intimate club atmosphere. Appointments throughout are styled to make your flight a gala occasion. Comfortable, low-cost Tourist service, as well as luxurious First Class, available.

Tempting meals are served in the grand manner, with the finest china and silverware. You can enjoy your favorite beverage, too! Thoughtful attention to your comfort makes your Super Constellation trip to Honolulu or the Orient the finest you've ever had!

Shortest, fastest to the Orient. Fly Northwest's short-cut route from cities coast to coast . . . to Alaska, Tokyo, Korea, Okinawa, Formosa, Manila . . . and to Hong Kong via Hong Kong Airways. Only Northwest offers this one-airline through service.

Northwest Airlines, 1955

Grandmother and child on way to rejoin "Mommy" in Santiago, Chile . . . photographed in a corner of "Fiesta Lounge" aboard El InterAmericano

"When your mommy was just your age—*we* flew in South America with Panagra!"

Like this grandmother who's introducing the 3rd generation to the world's friendliest airline, many of our passengers have been flying with us since 1928 . . . when Panagra pioneered air service on South America's West Coast.

Today, Panagra offers ten flights weekly to South America . . . all by latest-type pressurized planes. Choose deluxe *El InterAmericano*, daily DC-6, or thrifty *El Pacifico*, DC-6B tourist service. Call your Travel Agent or Pan American World Airways, U.S. Sales Agent for—

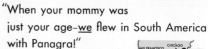

PANAGRA
Pan American-Grace Airways

We're proud of our clock-watchers at TWA!

TWA Captain Thomas Lynch brings in Flight 1

It takes *team* work to send the mighty Jetstreams' winging to their destinations all over the world, departing *on schedule*, arriving *on time!* And it takes a *big* team of clock-watchers to do it – maintenance men, weather analysts, flight dispatchers,

operating crews. TWA is proud of them. You'll understand why . . . when, after the smoothest, most luxurious flight you've ever had . . . *your* TWA plane taxis in *on time!* For reservations, telephone your travel agent or nearest TWA office today.

FLY THE FINEST . . . FLY TWA TRANS WORLD AIRLINES

Jetstream is a service mark owned exclusively by TWA.

TWA, 1958

4 corners of the earth
. . . only hours apart

NORTHWEST AIRLINES

EXCLUSIVE STRATOCRUISERS COAST TO COAST . . . HAWAII . . . ALASKA . . . THE ORIENT
THE ONLY ONE-CARRIER SERVICE ALL THE WAY!

Northwest Airlines, 1952

Vacation Corner of the Delta-C&S Golden Triangle

Golden Crown DC-7's - Fastest to

Miami Beach and the Caribbean

Royal Biscayne .. **CHICAGO-MIAMI** .. 3⅔ hrs. Non-Stop
Royal Hibiscus . **CINCINNATI-MIAMI** . 3 hrs. Non-Stop
Royal Poinciana .. **ATLANTA-MIAMI** ... 2 hrs. Non-Stop

Also the Royal Ranger, **Chicago-St. Louis-Houston**
Coming in April, DC-7 service, **Atlanta-Birmingham-Dallas-West Coast**
and **Chicago-New Orleans-Havana-Montego Bay-Caracas**

**Fly Now—Pay Later
No Down Payment**

Delta-C&S Flies on Seth Thomas Time

Delta-C&S AIR LINES

General Offices:
Atlanta, Georgia

Delta Air Lines, 1955

MIAMI is calling...

It's not hard to hear Miami's call these chilly days, even a thousand or more miles away. But that's not surprising because Miami is remarkably—and *comfortably*—close to all the Midwest and the South by fast-moving Delta-C&S. Call one of the local phone numbers shown on the map, or any Delta-C&S office—Miami's closer than you think.

Island-hopping in the modern Caribbean makes a delightful tropic holiday, now that Delta-C&S has twice daily service from New Orleans. Ask at any Delta office for maps and guide book.

Call Delta-C&S

Delta-C&S AIR LINES   General Offices: Atlanta, Georgia

Delta Air Lines, 1954

▶ *TWA*, 1953

"El Presidente"

Step aboard at New York
and step out at Rio de Janeiro
in 20⅔ hours...fly on to
Buenos Aires in 6⅓ hours.
This is a deluxe all-sleeper
service with double-decked
"Strato" Clippers.

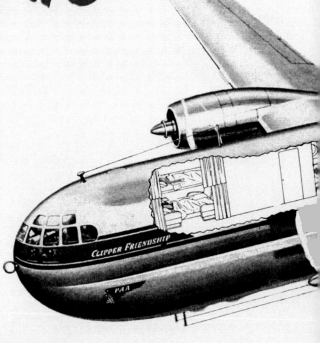

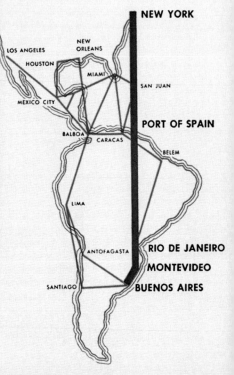

This is the way to travel! "El Presidente" leaves New York, Mondays, Thursdays and Saturdays, at 11:00 A.M. Your first stop is Port-of-Spain early the same evening. 9:40 the next morning you step out, fresh as a daisy, at Rio de Janeiro—or continue on to Buenos Aires, arriving there at 5 in the afternoon.

The BLUE RIBBON AIR SERVICE

PAN AMERICAN

WORLD'S MOST EXPERIENCED AIRLINE

The Sleeperette* is Pan American's exclusive, foam-soft easy chair which reclines to almost horizontal so you can sleep *lying down. No extra charge is made for Sleeperettes.*

On "El Presidente" nobody sits up at night! You have your choice of a Sleeperette seat (above) at no extra charge, or of fifteen upper berths at $10 and two lower berths at $20. Berths are big, wide and comfortable.

—And there are many, many other luxuries aboard "El Presidente." This is, without question, the Blue Ribbon service of the Western Hemisphere!...You are served a 7-course Continental dinner with vintage wines ...You are waited on by extra cabin attendants—and there's even Lanvins' *Arpège* perfume for the ladies!

No wonder a blue carpet is rolled out for every departure of "El Presidente"! It climaxes 23 years of Pan American service between the U.S.A. and Latin America. Yet the surcharge all the way from New York to Rio is only $10; to Buenos Aires, only $20. For reservations call your Travel Agent or Pan American's nearest office.

*Trade Mark, Reg. U.S. Pat. Off.

Borg-Warner, 1954

Pan American Air Lines, 1958

Pan American Air Lines, 1950 ◄◄   Sheraton Hotels, 1955 ◄   American Air Lines, 1952

American Airlines, 1953

"That's the 5:15 – from Paris"

Kids are kids same as ever . . . though time has changed the scene. Today they love to watch a giant TWA Skyliner as it glides in right on schedule after a smooth, comfortable overseas flight. And their heroes are the men who fly the planes . . . the skilled TWA crews who, in logging more than 20,000 Atlantic crossings, have helped TWA set standards of transoceanic service unsurpassed by any other airline in the world.

Where in the world do you want to go? For information and reservations, call TWA or see your travel agent.

ACROSS THE U.S. AND OVERSEAS . . . YOU CAN DEPEND ON **TWA**
TRANS WORLD AIRLINES
U.S.A. · EUROPE · AFRICA · ASIA

TWA, 1951

Paris in the Spring... *love, John*

Mary was a little dazed at first, and then she remembered. Her thoughts raced back to the dreamy days of their engagement when John had ventured, "Someday I'll take you on a trip to Paris . . . in the Spring . . ."

And now it was all coming true. Paris, London, Rome. She dabbed her eyes and looked at the Giftrip certificate again. The gift of travel – how wonderfully different! And then she noticed something else. Only her John would have thought of it. There in the envelope was a third ticket – the gift that meant Mother could come to stay with the children while she and John were abroad.

Perhaps the TWA Giftrip . . . the gift of travel . . . is the unusual idea you've been looking for. It's easy to arrange a Skyliner trip to any long-dreamed-of place–in this country or overseas. Or you can arrange to bring loved ones to join you for the holidays. Call TWA or your travel agent, and avoid shopping crowds.

ACROSS THE U.S. AND OVERSEAS . . . YOU CAN DEPEND ON **TWA**
TRANS WORLD AIRLINES
U.S.A. · EUROPE · AFRICA · ASIA

TWA, 1950   United Air Lines, 1958   ▶▶ United Air Lines, 1952

UNITED A

IN SAN FRANCISCO MAINTENANCE BASE

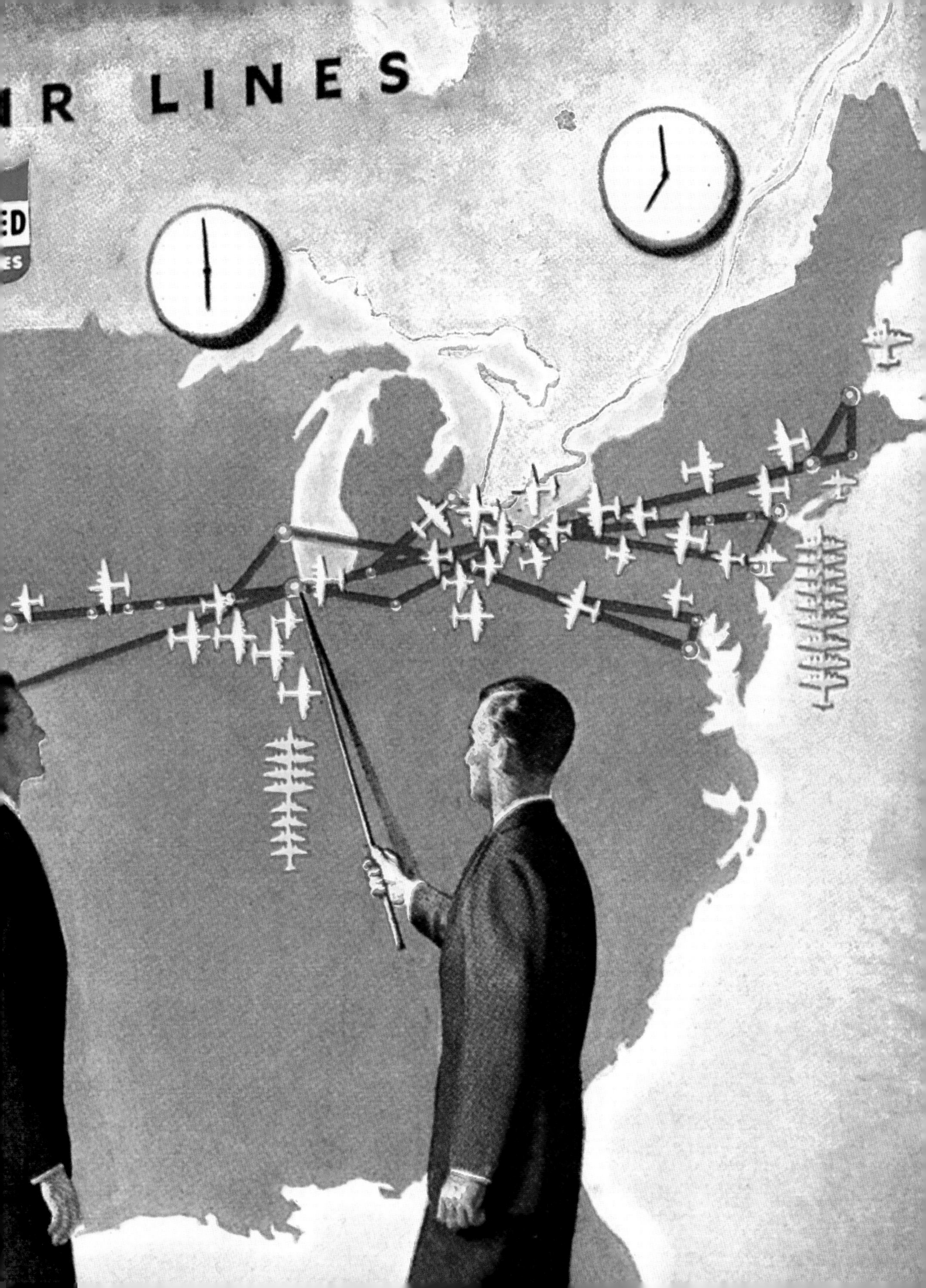
IR LINES
ED
ES

Leave New York at noon—reach Los Angeles before 5 p.m.
on United Air Lines' *DC-7s*, nonstop coast to coast!

ALREADY OFFERING your fastest flights, nonstop between San Francisco and New York—United's de luxe DC-7 Mainliners® now are also flying nonstop between New York and Los Angeles. You can leave New York at noon on "the Continental" at noon, arrive in Los Angeles at 4:55 p.m. (local times). Eastbound it's only 7½ hours nonstop!

And starting July 1: nonstop DC-7 service between Chicago and these cities: San Francisco, Los Angeles, New York. You can enjoy the finest coast-to-coast travel in history on United Air Lines' DC-7s—including the only nonstop flights from San Francisco to New York, fastest by over an hour, and the fastest service, also, from Manhattan to the Golden Gate.

Along with this magic speed—superb comfort! Full-course meals prepared by United's famous chefs . . . beverages and other enjoyable "extras" . . . extra-fast baggage delivery from a special baggage compartment adjoining the main cabin (a United exclusive) . . . many other new ideas that make United's DC-7s the finest in the sky!

FOR RESERVATIONS CALL OR WRITE UNITED OR AN AUTHORIZED TRAVEL AGENT

The Main Line Airway—to 80 Cities

UNITED AIR LINES

United Air Lines, 1954

The air is yours... **use it**

to save yourself trouble, time and money

If you've flown on the airlines recently, you know what a fast, easy way it is to travel. When you fly, you have more time to spend at your destination. And, nowadays, it frequently costs you *less*, too. Ask any airline or travel agent to tell you more.

United Aircraft
CORPORATION
EAST HARTFORD, CONNECTICUT

Makers of Pratt & Whitney Engines, Hamilton Standard Propellers, Chance Vought Aircraft and Sikorsky Helicopters for the U. S. Armed Forces and the Finest Airlines in the World.

United Aircraft Corporation, 1950

How many of these famous places have you visited?

You can visit the far-off, exciting places you've always dreamed about —even on a short vacation—if you travel by air. You'll have more time to enjoy yourself at your destination, thanks to today's fast flights and frequent schedules. Modern air travel is convenient, clean, and comfortable. The cost may be less than you think, with family travel plans or air coach rates. Any airline representative or travel agent will be glad to offer suggestions about flying to new places this year to help you get the most out of your precious vacation.

The air is yours—use it!

UNITED AIRCRAFT CORPORATION *East Hartford, Conn. • In Canada: Canadian Pratt & Whitney Aircraft Co., Ltd.*
Designers and builders of: PRATT & WHITNEY AIRCRAFT *engines,* HAMILTON STANDARD *propellers and turbine aircraft equipment, and* SIKORSKY AIRCRAFT *helicopters—for our armed forces and the finest airlines in the world.*

United Aircraft Corporation, 1957 ▶ *United Air Lines, 1951* ▶▶ *Lockheed, 1955*

United Air Lines is the

only airline linking the East,

the Middle West, all major

Pacific Coast cities and Hawaii.

Wherever you travel,

fly United's Main Line Airway—

truly the Nation's

No. 1 Coast-to-Coast Airline.

© U.A.L. 1951

FOR RESERVATIONS, CALL OR WRITE UNITED OR AN AUTHORIZED TRAVEL AGENT. PASSENGERS • MAIL • EXPRESS • FREIGHT • AIR PARCEL POST

MOST COMFORTABLE WAY
TO GET THERE FAST

QUIET LUXURY TO MAKE THE TIME FLY – NEW SPEED TO SHORTEN THE DISTANCE

Largest, Roomiest
Airliner in the World

*Far Quieter for
Greater Comfort*

Wider Aisles & Seats

Larger Windows

Finest Air Conditioning

Restful 5-Cabin Privacy

Congenial
Starlight Lounge

Henry Dreyfuss Interiors

The Fastest
Constellation Ever Built

For all the speed, and quiet comfort, too, fly Super Constellations over every ocean and continent on these 20 leading airlines: AIR FRANCE • AIR-INDIA INTERNATIONAL
AVIANCA • CUBANA • DEUTSCHE LUFTHANSA
EASTERN AIR LINES • FLYING TIGER LINE • IBERIA
KLM • LAV • NORTHWEST ORIENT AIRLINES
PAKISTAN INTERNATIONAL • QANTAS
SEABOARD & WESTERN • SLICK AIRWAYS • TAP
THAI AIRWAYS • TRANS-CANADA AIR LINES
TWA–TRANS WORLD AIRLINES • VARIG

LOCKHEED SUPER CONSTELLATION

Look to Lockheed for Leadership

Leadership demands constant achievement

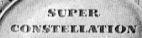

SUPER
CONSTELLATION

Lockheed Presents The

Super Constellation

*An even finer version of the World's Most
Experienced Airliner*

Lockheed's new Super Constellation combines the unmatched record
of experience and dependability of the world-famous Constellation with
greater speed, greater range, greater comfort and greater size~unquestion-
ably the finest airliner in the world.

Now in service for Eastern Air Lines and soon in service for Trans
World Airlines, Air France, KLM Royal Dutch Airlines, Pakistan
International, Qantas, Trans-Canada Air Lines, and other leading airlines.

LOCKHEED

AIRCRAFT CORPORATION, BURBANK, CALIFORNIA

Look to Lockheed for Leadership

Lockheed sets the new world standard of Quality

New Super Constellation designed for non-stop international and over-ocean travel

Here is an airliner so different you'll be eager to fly on it again and again—fast, dependable, spacious and luxuriously beautiful—the world's finest airliner. Counseled by famous industrial designer Henry Dreyfuss, Lockheed has created a completely new interior atmosphere for airliners catering to world travelers who appreciate non-stop schedules.

In service in 1953 between America and Europe on KLM, Air France and Trans-Canada Air Lines—will also span the world's other oceans for Air India, AVIANCA, Braathens, Iberia, LAV, Pakistan International and Qantas. At your first opportunity insist on *Super Constellation* service.

LEADERSHIP

DEMANDS

CONSTANT

ACHIEVEMENT

Forward Cabin—Cabin No. 1 has fully reclining, adjustable chairs—deep cushioned, roomy, relaxing. As throughout the plane here is the comfort appreciated in non-stop travel.

Main Cabin—Cabin No. 2 with its extra wide aisle and broad ceiling affords unusual spaciousness. Beauty of line and color matches that of the other cabins.

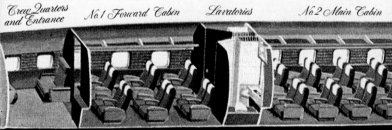

Crew Quarters and Entrance   *No 1 Forward Cabin*   *Lavatories*   *No 2 Main Cabin*

The Super Constellation is the longest, largest, finest airliner ever built—with 4 superbly appointed passenger cabins, a luxurious lounge, galley and bar, 4 lavatories, crew's quarters, pilot's cabin—all air conditioned. Compartmentization creates a solid feeling of sturdiness never before achieved in any airliner.

LOCKHEED
Super Constellation

Club Lounge—Cabin No. 3 is far the most unique, attractive and comfortable lounge designed for any airliner. Variety of seating allows privacy for 4 couples or mingling of groups.

No 3 Club Lounge   *No 4 Entrance and Galley*   *No 5 Rear Cabin*   *Lavatories*

The Super Constellation is the most flexible airliner ever built. Converts in a few hours from first class accommodations to a high density tourist transport or partial cargo carrier.

LOCKHEED AIRCRAFT CORPORATION
BURBANK, CALIFORNIA, AND MARIETTA, GEORGIA

LOOK TO LOCKHEED FOR LEADERSHIP

Galley and Bar—Cabin No. 4 has ample space for several attendants, assuring quick service. Can be curtained off when used as entrance way.

Rear Cabin—Cabin No. 5 offers a full length view of the plane's beautiful interior with its mahogany paneling, modern lines and restful color harmony.

Hertz rents the kind of cars you like to drive!

What's your pleasure? A Cadillac, maybe? Hertz rents Cadillacs. Hertz rents big Buicks and Oldsmobiles, too. Thousands of new Chevrolets and other fine cars. Station wagons, convertibles, sports cars. Take your pick at most Hertz offices.

They're all in A-1 condition, expertly maintained, more dependable, cleaner cars. More with power steering. That's The Hertz Idea. You'll get the kind of car you like to drive at over 1,250 Hertz offices in more than 900 cities—world-wide. That's *more* offices by far where you can *rent* a car. *More* cities by far where you can *leave* a car. *More* locations where you can make a *reservation* for a car!

Just show your driver's license and proper identification. The national average rate for a new Powerglide Chevrolet Bel Air is only $7.85 a day plus 8 cents a mile. And that includes the cost of *all* the gasoline and oil you use en route...and proper insurance. In addition to the Hertz charge card, we honor all air, rail, Diners' Club and hotel credit cards.

To be sure of a car at your destination—anywhere—use Hertz' more efficient reservation service. Call your local Hertz office for fast, courteous service. We're listed under "Hertz" in *alphabetical* phone books everywhere! Hertz Rent A Car, 218 South Wabash Avenue, Chicago 4, Illinois.

More people by far...use **HERTZ** Rent a car

"Rent it here...Leave it there" Now, nation-wide at no extra charge! (on rentals of $25.00 or more).

Hertz Rent a Car, 1957

Now... you always know the way to go, when you rent a car from Hertz!

Only Hertz Rent A Car shows you the way to go wherever you are, wherever you're going. And only Hertz, with over 1,750 offices, makes it so easy to reserve a car, so fast to rent a car and so convenient to pick up a car at one Hertz office and leave it at another. Our low rates cover everything, too—all gasoline, oil and proper insurance. Just call your local Hertz office or see your travel agent to reserve a new Chevrolet or other fine car anywhere. It will be waiting for you on arrival. And so will a free Hertz Direction Finder Kit.

Hertz Rent a Car, 1959

America's choice

You and your family will always find a friendly welcome at Howard Johnson's...a pleasant atmosphere...good food at sensible prices served by a waitress trained to bring you the best in courteous, efficient, friendly service...no matter where you travel!

HOWARD JOHNSON'S
RESTAURANTS · MOTOR LODGES
Ice Cream · Candies · Take-Home Frozen Foods
"Landmark for Hungry Americans"

Lockheed, 1952 ◄◄ *Lockheed, 1952* ◄ *Howard Johnson's, 1958*

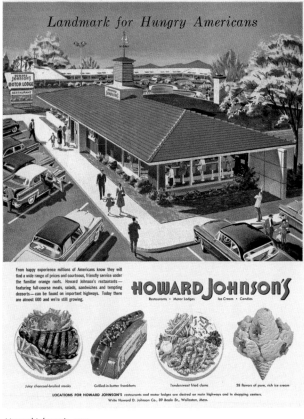

Landmark for Hungry Americans

From happy experience millions of Americans know they will find a wide range of prices and courteous, friendly service under the familiar orange roofs. Howard Johnson's restaurants—featuring full-course meals, salads, sandwiches and tempting desserts—can be found on important highways. Today there are almost 600 and we're still growing.

HOWARD JOHNSON'S
Restaurants · Motor Lodges · Ice Cream · Candies

Howard Johnson's, 1957

Hilton and Statler Hotels select  Rent-a-Car for their guests

These 28 distinguished hotels will deliver you a fine, new car from Avis ... or reserve one for you when you reserve your room.

For they know the discriminating traveler wants the freedom and comfort of a personal car wherever he stays ... on business or pleasure. And they know that Avis provides cars you are proud to drive ... new models, sparkling clean, fully insured and serviced.

It's easy to reserve an Avis car. Call any Avis Office or Hilton-Statler—or ask your plane or train ticket agent. You can reserve a car almost anywhere in the world at Avis' 800 offices. They honor credit cards from Avis, Hilton-Statler, and many others.

Next time you travel have a new Avis car available wherever you go ... for as long as you need it. And ask about the convenient "Rent it here—leave it there" service.

AVIS
RENT-a-CAR
AWAY OR AT HOME...
A CAR OF YOUR OWN

At the beautiful new Beverly Hilton, Beverly Hills, California, the transportation desk provides a guest with a new Plymouth or other fine car from Avis for $7 a day and 8¢ a mile ... including gas, oil and insurance. (There is never an extra charge for extra passengers.)

Avis Rent a Car, 1956

▶ *Hertz Rent a Car, 1959*

BUSINESS   TRAVEL   VACAT

1959

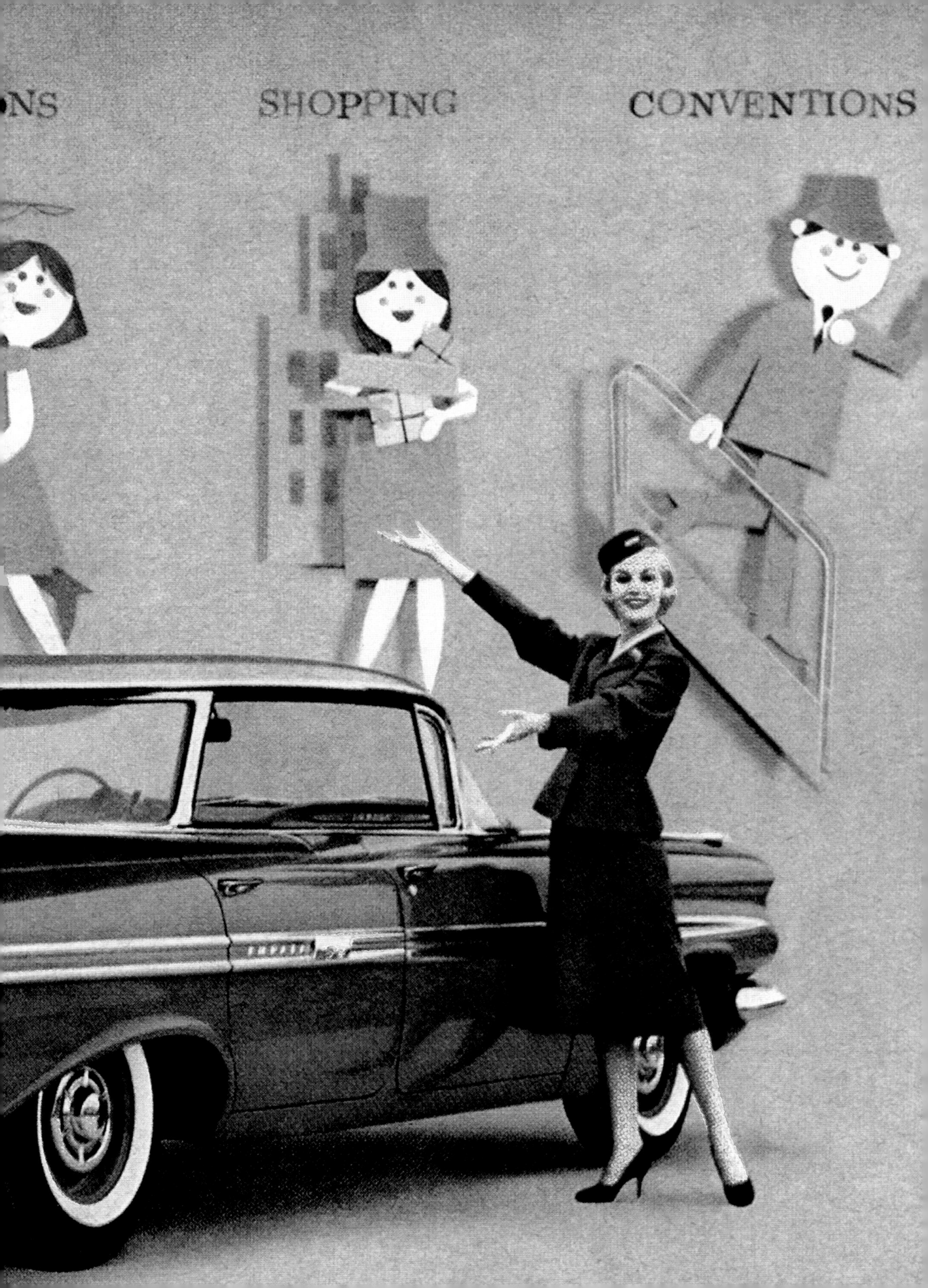

NS
SHOPPING
CONVENTIONS

Cunard, 1954

Cunard, 1956

Cunard, 1953

Cunard, 1953　　　　　▶ *Cunard, 1953*

GETTING THERE IS HALF THE FUN

Crossing to Europe or cruising to faraway places...
don't miss the joy of going Cunard! Days and nights
of enchanted relaxation ... laughter, music,
sparkling companionship ... and the sheer wizardry of master chefs
... make your voyage a brilliant holiday in itself.

*See your Cunard-authorized
travel agent and ...* **GO CUNARD**

BURR TILLSTROM, KUKLA AND OLLIE, whimsical, lovable stars of NBC television trade their five nights a week spotlight for days of sunlight on their recent Mediterranean holiday aboard the great new Sun-Liner Independence.

Every voyage a Gay Cruise...

When you sail the Sun-Lane to Europe, it's not just a trip from one port to another but an exciting voyage that touches upon the loveliest lands of the Mediterranean. And liberal stop-over privileges make all of these garden spots yours to sample if you're in a hurry, or to linger in if you wish.

On the great new Sun-Liners of American Export Lines, you enjoy "Modern American Living at Sea"...a gay, friendly,

carefree informality amid every comfort and service that American ingenuity can provide.

Even the weather on the Sun-Lane conspires to lift your spirits. Fall, winter and spring average 87 per cent rain-free days, and through the summer the gentle trade winds cool your smooth path to a perfect 71 degrees average. When you enter the Continent from the sunny, southern side you'll find much of the best of Europe all around you . . . the rest of Europe just hours away.

SEE YOUR TRAVEL AGENT OR **AMERICAN EXPORT LINES** 39 BROADWAY, N.Y. 6, N.Y.

INDEPENDENCE · CONSTITUTION ☆ EXETER · EXCALIBUR · EXOCHORDA · EXCAMBION

American Export Lines, 1952

HOT 'n HANDSOME
NEW 1957 CHRIS·CRAFT SHOWBOATS

Chris-Craft now brings you the greatest fleet in history — with dazzling new styling, new color combinations, luxuriously appointed interiors. For a limited time only, you can buy your new Chris-Craft Showboat and deduct 10% for fall delivery! Take advantage of this opportunity NOW! Your Chris-Craft will be built of finest materials under ideal conditions. See your dealer today before fall production schedules are filled. Buy now and

DEDUCT 10% FOR FALL DELIVERY!

BOAT DIVISION, CHRIS-CRAFT CORPORATION, ALGONAC, MICHIGAN

WORLD'S LARGEST BUILDERS OF MOTOR BOATS

Chris Craft, 1956

The lovely new *Andrea Doria*

These men have built a ship...

What gives a ship that thing called personality? From where come those qualities

Into every detail of this lovely vessel have gone the skill and pride of the great-

The completely air conditioned *Andrea Doria* enters transatlantic service to York in January. *Special West I*

Italian Lines, 1952

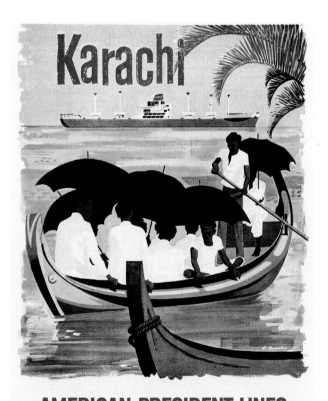

Karachi

AMERICAN PRESIDENT LINES
GRAND FLEET OF THE PACIFIC AND 'ROUND THE WORLD

American President Lines, 1951

EVERY VOYAGE *a cruise*

every cruise a **GAY HOLIDAY**

Fortnightly sailings all year from New York by

s.s. *Brazil* · s.s. *Uruguay* · s.s. *Argentina*

for TRINIDAD · RIO DE JANEIRO · SANTOS · SAO PAULO · MONTEVIDEO · BUENOS AIRES

Sailing on regular schedules essential to business travel . . . offering the most glamorous of holidays to those who travel for pleasure . . . the Good Neighbor Liners make a voyage for any purpose a relaxing and merry vacation. Planned and staffed for your enjoyment . . . offering congenial companion-ship . . . gay parties . . . deck sports . . . big outdoor swimming pools . . . complete comfort and the finest of food and service. *Consult your Travel Agent or*

TRAVEL ARRANGEMENTS TO MEET EVERY REQUIREMENT—*for business*—One-way pas-sages to any port · Round-trip passages with liberal stopovers and travel connections for all parts of South America · Combination sea-air round trips via East or West Coast of South America . . . *for pleasure*—38-DAY CRUISES (Buenos Aires and return) · 24-DAY CRUISES (Rio de Janeiro and return) · Round trips with stopover privileges in all ports of call · 'Round South America Cruise Tours (all sea or sea-air) and extended South American Tours.

MOORE-McCORMACK *Lines*

Five Broadway   New York 4

Moore-McCormack Lines, 1952

Light-hearted Latin gayety...vivid foreign charm—
in nearby
CUBA
"HOLIDAY ISLE OF THE TROPICS"

Matson doubles its sailings to the Islands

"Hawaii hears a new aloha"

Now it's easier than ever to know the thrill of Hawaii's world-famed Aloha welcome to the LURLINE and MATSONIA. Even two-week vacationers can enjoy a round trip on Matson's famous companion ships and 5 glorious days in the Islands. Or stay as long as you like. There's a Matson sailing every week to stretch your Hawaiian vacation all the way back to California. You'll love the spacious decks, sun-splashed pool, air-conditioned staterooms and lounges of the LURLINE and MATSONIA. And Matson is famous for cuisine and service. It's round-trip thrift, round-trip fun when you go Matson...the smart way to Hawaii. Call your Travel Agent today.

Matson Lines, 1957

A chapter in your life you'll never forget

ALL too few are the occasions in life so gloriously, immeasurably perfect in every way that one cherishes their memory for a lifetime. Yet, the moment you step aboard your luxurious Italian Line flagship you'll know in your heart that *this* trip will be one of them.

You sail away from worry and care into another world of leisurely living . . . gracious service . . . superb cuisine . . . exciting visits to fascinating lands. You return rested, refreshed . . . rich in experiences you will treasure always, as you relive them in memory again and again.

COMING SOON! *The new 25,000-ton luxury liner s.s. ANDREA DORIA. Completely air conditioned. Fine, spacious accommodations.*

Italian Line
"ITALIA" SOCIETA di NAVIGAZIONE, GENOVA

Italian Lines, 1952

So close...
So enticing! *Hawaii*

A vacation costs so little in these magical tropic isles!

■ The colorful fun of famous Waikiki . . . the music and dancing and feasts of old Polynesia . . . the romance of ancient life on dreamy island shores . . . these are the fabric of your adventure in Hawaii. Air and steamship lines link Hawaii with San Francisco, Los Angeles, Portland, Seattle, Vancouver. Short flights take you from Honolulu on OAHU to the grandeur of Haleakala on MAUI . . . to the acres of orchids of HAWAII . . . the unspoiled loveliness of KAUAI. Let your Travel Agent help you arrange to see all their scenic splendor.

Cuba, 1950 ◀ *Hawaii Visitors Bureau, 1950*

TRAILWAYS 4 STAR THRU no change **BUSES** GIVE YOU MORE TRAVEL ADVANTAGES AT THE SAME LOW FARES!

★ **IMPROVED SCHEDULES** Best routes. No connection worries. Saves time en route.

★ **FINEST EQUIPMENT** New, modern Silverliners. Foam rubber reclining seats. Safe, courteous drivers.

★ **NO CHANGE OF BUS** Same seat straight-thru. No change of buses. No transfer of baggage.

★ **SAME LOW FARE** Lowest cost luxury travel. No extra fare. Save more—buy round trip.

TRAILWAYS bright, new 4-star THRU no change BUSES now serve you with more and more straight-thru, no change travel to destinations both near and far. For example TRAILWAYS THRU BUSES now go all the way from coast-to-coast at scenery-level with just one change the whole way. Enjoy the extra comfort plus the big, money-saving difference over any other form of transportation—on your next trip take the best, take TRAILWAYS.

For information on all TRAILWAYS low fares, convenient THRU-BUS schedules, and Pleasure Planned Tours, consult the phone book for your friendly local TRAILWAYS agent or mail the coupon below to NATIONAL TRAILWAYS BUS SYSTEM, Dept. 24-C, 185 N. Wabash Avenue, Chicago 1, Illinois.

Buses Available for Charter Groups

NATIONAL **TRAILWAYS** BUS SYSTEM

Trailways Serves the Nation at "Scenery Level"

Trailways, 1950 ▶ *Samsonite Luggage & Greyhound, 1956*

General Motors Locomotives, 1951

New York Central, 1950

Sunset Limited, 1951

Great Northern Railway, 1951

Samsonite Luggage, 1953

Samsonite Luggage, 1951

Samsonite Luggage, 1953

Hilton Hotels, 1959

NEW YORK STATE SIGNPOSTS

You'll always remember a visit to Niagara Falls. For mighty Niagara is truly one of Nature's wonders—a breath-taking spectacle that attracts more than three million people every year.

A boat ride on the "Maid of the Mist," a tour through the Cave of the Winds, a trip by cable car over Devil's Whirlpool—these are a few of Niagara's unique attractions. All contribute to the wonder of Niagara and to your enjoyment of this outstanding vacationland.

Niagara Falls is but one of the many attractions in friendly New York State. There's an endless variety of things to see and do—vacation fun to suit every taste and travel budget. For an introduction to New York State's fifteen vacation areas, mail the coupon below.

Finger Lakes Region—Sailboating and scenic beauty have made this region a favorite vacationland.

Saratoga-Lake George—See America's most famous spa, its oldest race track, and 30-mile-long Lake George.

Hudson-Taconic Region—Here you'll enjoy superb scenery, West Point, Hyde Park, and Bear Mountain State Park.

Adirondacks—Whiteface Mountain and historic Lake Champlain are outstanding features of this famous summer playground.

Central New York—Visit the Baseball Hall of Fame, the Farmer's Museum at Cooperstown, or relax on drives through quiet countrysides.

Chautauqua-Allegany Region—Chautauqua offers summer programs of music and education. Allegany, the state's largest park, is here.

FREE BOOKLET "New York State Vacationlands" gives you a preview of the many things to see and do in New York State. Contains 196 pages, 100 maps and drawings, 81 full-color photos. Send for your copy today!

More people find more to see and do in
New York State
the Vacation Empire

New York State Department of Commerce
Room 757, 112 State Street, Albany 7, New York

Send "New York State Vacationlands." I am interested in: A ( ) resort hotel, B ( ) city hotel, C ( ) bungalow colony, D ( ) tourist home, E ( ) summer cottage, F ( ) campsite, G ( ) children's camp, H ( ) dude ranch. I would like information sent from resort areas checked:

1. ☐ Adirondacks	6. ☐ Finger Lakes	11. ☐ Hudson-Taconic
2. ☐ New York City	7. ☐ Saratoga-Lake George	12. ☐ Genesee Region
3. ☐ Catskills	8. ☐ Long Island	13. ☐ Chautauqua-Allegany
4. ☐ 1000 Islands-St. Lawrence	9. ☐ Mohawk Valley	14. ☐ Capital District
5. ☐ Niagara Frontier	10. ☐ Central New York	15. ☐ Southern Tier

Name_____
(PLEASE PRINT)

Address_____

City_____ Zone_____ State_____

New York State, 1953

▶ *American Express Travelers Checks, 1950*

Fairyland in Stone! Carlsbad Caverns National Park is one of the world's great natural wonders. It dwarfs all other caverns in size—contains 2¾ miles of lighted paths. Its formations are the most spectacular of all. Your entire family will be thrilled. Easy conducted tours. Three elevators for your convenience.

EXCITING AS A FOREIGN LAND!
COMFORTABLE AS HOME!

Come enjoy a really different vacation this summer in high, cool New Mexico!

Mission Church, Isleta Pueblo. New Mexico's many interesting landmarks are closer than you think. Wherever you live in the U.S., you can drive here, tour state and return home, all within 2 weeks.

See Navaho Indians driving wagons on side roads near the main highways. Visit pueblos and reservations. Watch Indians make pottery—bake bread in outdoor ovens.

Sightseeing is fun here! New Mexico's 7000 miles of paved highways lead you to modern cities, national monuments, state parks and vast national forests.

Quaint shops, galleries, museums and distinctive architecture give Santa Fe a continental flavor.

Aztec Ruins—remnants of a culture that thrived long before Columbus discovered America.

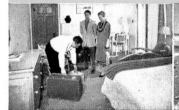

Hospitality Plus! You'll find good lodgings in New Mexico's more than 1600 hotels, motels, resorts and ranches. Fine restaurants here, too.

Elephant Butte Lake, tops for bass fishing. Northern lakes and streams offer trout. Excellent hunting and skiing in season.

Ride, camp, picnic in New Mexico's 8½ million acres of national forests. Days are clear, sunny. Nights cool, starlit.

NEW MEXICO
LAND OF ENCHANTMENT

FREE BOOKLETS AND MAPS! Write New Mexico State Tourist Bureau, Box 5530-B, Santa Fe, New Mexico

how to work up an appetite
for what's cooking in Caracas

Pirates had to eat, too, but they never had it so good as modern-day guests of the Hotel Tamanaco in Caracas, Venezuela, on the Ancient Spanish Main.

Whether you're licking your chops at the "groaning board" or "loafing it up" beside the sun-drenched swim-

ming pool, you'll find yourself heir to the best of two worlds: the adventure of foreign travel, the comfort of American care.

From the food to the accommodations and entertainment, American attention to detail tempers Latin imagination. For that is what an Interconti-

nental vacation holds for you: service and efficiency blended with traditions of hospitality that are centuries old.

So if you've been looking for a vacation spot that's tailor-made for good times and good eating, the Hotel Tamanaco is your kind of place. Even without pirates, it's the most exciting place in Caracas.

Phone your travel agent or write Intercontinental Hotels, Chrysler Bldg., New York 17, N.Y. (If you prefer, call STillwell 6-5858 in New York.)

Elegant service — that's just one specialty of the house

INTERCONTINENTAL HOTELS

What's cooking?

A completely different holiday recipe — glorious sunshine, ever-changing scenery, amazing contrasts in breath-taking, adventurous South Africa! Make South Africa your travel adventure of a lifetime . . . see your Travel Agent or SATOUR for free and friendly information.

SOUTH AFRICA

SATOUR

SOUTH AFRICAN TOURIST CORPORATION
475 Fifth Avenue, New York 17, N. Y.
I would like to know more about a South African holiday.

NAME_____

STREET_____

CITY_____ZONE_____STATE_____

My Travel Agent is_____

IN CHICAGO IT'S THE
SHERATON
HOTEL

NOW OPEN...LATIN AMERICA'S TALLEST, LARGEST HOTEL

habana H hilton

HAVANA, the glamorous, gay capital of Cuba, provides a sophisticated setting for the new 30-story high Habana Hilton. Overlooking Havana, historic Morro Castle and the harbor, this spectacular, completely air-conditioned hotel offers 630 lavishly appointed rooms and suites, each with a large private balcony, plus all the facilities of a magnificent resort. A swimming pool, colorful cabanas, an exciting Trader Vic's restaurant and a roof top cocktail lounge, the Sugar Bar, are just a few of the many outstanding features at Latin America's largest hotel, the fabulous new Habana Hilton.

Reservations: See Travel Agent or call New York, LOng-acre 3-6900 • Chicago, FInancial 6-2772 • San Francisco, YUkon 6-0576 • Miami, FRanklin 9-3427 • Pittsburgh, COurt 1-5600 • Toronto, EMpire 8-2911 • Montreal, UNiversity 1-3301 • Havana, F-3296 or any Hilton Hotel.

EXECUTIVE OFFICES THE CONRAD HILTON CHICAGO 5, ILL.

Hilton Hotels
Conrad N. Hilton, President

Hilton Hotels, 1958

The Largest and Finest Hotel In The Caribbean

Within Hotel Nacional's fabulous 13 gardened acres, you find a vacation land complete to meet your moods under the sun and moon. In Havana on this island paradise, you have at hand an unlimited variety of sights, scenes, places and things to do. Hotel Nacional bids you a cordial welcome. Please see your Travel Agent for literature and information or call the Kirkeby Hotel nearest to you.

KIRKEBY HOTELS

New York THE GOTHAM • HAMPSHIRE HOUSE • THE WARWICK
Upper Saranac Lake, N. Y. SARANAC INN
Philadelphia THE WARWICK • Chicago THE BLACKSTONE
Beverly Hills, Calif. BEVERLY WILSHIRE
Hollywood, Calif. SUNSET TOWER
Miami Beach THE KENILWORTH
Havana HOTEL NACIONAL de CUBA
Panama City, R. P. EL PANAMA

Miami office, Roper Building, phone Miami 9-7612.

Hotel Nacional de Cuba
HAVANA
A Kirkeby Hotel

Hotel Nacional de Cuba, 1953

REBELS RIOT, SHOOT UP TOWN
U.S. LAUNCHES ITS FIRST SATELLITE
48 KILLED AS PLANES COLLIDE
FRENCH BOMB-RAID, 100 TUNISIANS
SNOWSTORM PARALYZES EAST U.S.
WORST RAIN IN YEARS HITS HAWAII
SEATO NATIONS HANDED THREAT
INDONESIA REBEL ISLAND INVADED
BACTERIA KILLS 16, INFECTS 81
5000 FLEE WEST COASTAL FLOODS
HANDS OFF HUNGARY, REDS WARN
DELINQUENCY TO DOUBLE BY 1962
INDONESIA NAVY READY TO ATTACK
TITO WARNS RUSS, NOT INTERFERE
OFFICIAL STONED, FLAG RIPPED
RUSS LAUNCH 1½-TON SPUTNIK
U.S. SHIPS RUSH TOWARD LEBANON
FRENCH LEADERS FEAR CIVIL WAR
HUNGARY REVOLT 'CHIEF EXECUTED
WORLD CRISIS FEARED IN LEBANON
RUSS ON MOVE, POLES EYE THREAT
370 TRAFFIC DEATHS MAR HOLIDAY
TIDAL WAVE HITS SOUTHERN ALASKA
THOR COMBAT MISSILE TO BE FIRED
IRAQ KING FEISAL KILLED IN COUP
PARATROOPERS LAND IN JORDAN
ROME STIRRED BY COMMUNIST RIOT
RUSS REJECT SUMMIT PROPOSAL
U.N. ORDERS EMERGENCY SESSION
RUSS WARNS U.S. OF DESTRUCTION
FEARS OF JORDAN COUP INCREASE
TERRORISTS STRIKE IN FRANCE
REDS THREATEN QUEMOY INVASION
ATLAS ICBM ON 3000 MILE TEST
RUSS WARN WILL JOIN CHINA REDS
WILL FIGHT FOR QUEMOY, U.S. SAYS
INTEGRATION CRISIS NEARS
REDS HURL 8000 SHELLS AT QUEMOY
TRAIN DIVES OFF DRAWBRIDGE
GUN BATTLES SWEEP BEIRUT
POPE PIUS XII ON DEATH BED
SUPREME COURT WARNS SOUTH
JEWISH SYNAGOGUE DYNAMITED

BE NOT AFRAID

for behold I bring you good tidings of great joy to all people, for this day in the city of David is born to you a Savior... to enlighten them that sit in darkness and in the shadow of death: to direct our feet into the way of peace.

Hilton Hotels
CONRAD N. HILTON, president

Sheraton Hotels, 1954 ◄ *Hilton Hotels, 1958*

The Key to Delightful Dining

Hilton guests around the world enjoy a wide variety of fine food served in attractive settings, ranging from popular priced coffee houses to distinguished dining rooms. With their high culinary standards, superb service, comfortable accommodations and convenient addresses, Hilton Hotels offer the utmost in perfection. Although each hotel possesses its own character and individuality, the quality and hospitality are traditionally the same throughout the entire group.

Sketched in the Victorian Room of the Palmer House

A HILTON GUEST ENJOYS THE BEST

In New York
THE WALDORF-ASTORIA
THE PLAZA
THE ROOSEVELT
THE NEW YORKER

In Washington, D. C.
THE MAYFLOWER

In St. Louis, Mo.
THE JEFFERSON

In Columbus, Ohio
THE DESHLER HILTON

In Fort Worth
and El Paso, Texas
THE HILTON HOTEL

In San Bernardino, Cal.
ARROWHEAD SPRINGS

In Chicago
THE CONRAD HILTON
THE PALMER HOUSE

In Los Angeles
THE TOWN HOUSE

In Dayton, Ohio
THE DAYTON BILTMORE

In Albuquerque, New Mexico
THE HILTON HOTEL

In San Juan, Puerto Rico
THE CARIBE HILTON

In Madrid, Spain
THE CASTELLANA HILTON

In Istanbul, Turkey
THE ISTANBUL HILTON
(Opens this Fall)

Hilton Hotels
Conrad N. Hilton, President

Hilton Hotels, 1954

Beverly Hilton, 1955

Hilton Inns, 1959

Sherton Hotels, 1955

Sheraton Hotels, 1959

BOSTON'S SHERATON PLAZA FROM PUBLIC LIBRARY, COPLEY SQUARE. TRINITY CHURCH AND JOHN HANCOCK BUILDING IN BACKGROUND.

World Renowned!

Social center of the city, and host to distinguished visitors from this country and abroad, the Sheraton Plaza enjoys a fame that is shared by only a few of the world's really great hotels. In twenty-one cities experienced travelers prefer Sheraton. For each Sheraton has its own special personality —quiet dignity at the Sheraton Plaza—rich modernity in Detroit's Sheraton-Cadillac—friendly charm at the Sheraton-Gibson in Cincinnati— metropolitan atmosphere in New York's Park Sheraton. Just call your nearest Sheraton Hotel for prompt Teletype reservations.

SHERATON HOTELS

IN THE U. S. A.		IN CANADA
BOSTON	WASHINGTON	MONTREAL—Sheraton-Mt. Royal
PROVIDENCE	DETROIT	—The Laurentien
NEW YORK	CINCINNATI	TORONTO—King Edward
BALTIMORE	CHICAGO	WINDSOR—Prince Edward
PHILADELPHIA	ST. LOUIS	HAMILTON—Royal Connaught
PITTSBURGH	WORCESTER	NIAGARA FALLS—Sheraton-Brock
BUFFALO	PITTSFIELD, Mass.	
ROCHESTER	SPRINGFIELD, Mass.	

Sheraton Hotels

Santa Fe, 1952

Santa Fe, 1952

Santa Fe, 1955

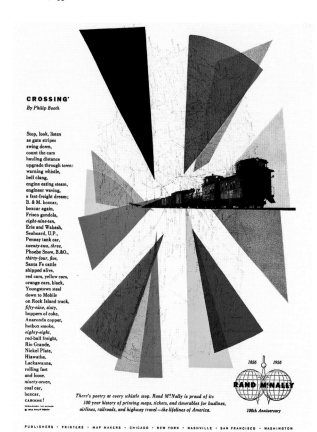

Rand McNally, 1956   ▶ Santa Fe, 1957   ▶▶ Santa Fe, 1951

Step aboard the

Let us show you around the

You can see at a glance it's different, because it's so tall and sleek, but you won't realize how different—how quiet and smooth—until you actually ride it. So step aboard this new kind of all-coach train, and let us show you around.

Santa Fe

new Hi-level train

gher, quieter, smoother El Capitan

Ever see such roomy baggage racks? The porter keeps your baggage here, on the lower level of your car, out of your way. And isn't it nice to be able to travel with *all* the luggage you need?

There's always a "show" going on. It's right outside your window. And when you go Hi-Level, you're up where you can see it all ... as you relax in your stretch-out sleeper seat.

A picture window 2,224 miles long. No place like this dome lounge to see the sights—or just to relax over cool refreshments, conversation or a hand of gin rummy.

Coffee-break in the Kachina Lounge. Make yourself comfortable in the quiet, intimate Kachina coffee shop in the lower lounge for a quick snack. Service from dawn to midnight.

You dine Hi-Level, too. Feast your eyes on the scenery—and yourself on the famous Fred Harvey budget meals. With soft music and impeccable service, dinner becomes an event. Why not go Hi-Level your next trip?

$66.12

(plus tax)
one way between
Chicago-Los Angeles,
including extra fare.
Lower with Family Fares.

*For reservations, consult
the nearest railroad or travel agent.*

New **HI-LEVEL**

El Capitan

CHICAGO-LOS ANGELES

Be carefree, be comfortable and enjoy a
New World

Standard in Travel
The new Santa Fe
Super Chief

Advanced ideas for your travel luxury...new cradled smoothness in the ride...daily between Chicago and Los Angeles

From the flanges on the wheels to the tip of the Pleasure Dome, the Super Chief is new—entirely new.

To give you the smoothest ride of your life on rails, this new Super Chief glides on cushioned springs ... revises any ideas you ever had about any train.

The keynote is comfort.

You find it in the distinctive Turquoise Room in the lounge car—a delightful place to relax, enjoy a cocktail or entertain your friends at dinner—the first time such a room has been provided on any train.

You find it in the Pleasure Dome—"top of the Super, next to the stars"—that brings you an unobstructed view of wonderful southwestern scenery.

You find it in the new dining cars where Fred Harvey chefs present new and exciting menus.

Accommodations in this beautiful all-room train are designed to pamper you every mile of the way. "Push-button" radio or music in your room when you *want* it ... beds you just can't help sleeping in ... charming apartments by day.

From the engineers who glide you across this great country to the porter who answers your bell, this is the train of thoughtful service.

For your next trip between Chicago and Los Angeles say "Super Chief." Now, more than ever, it is America's train of trains. Just consult your local ticket agent.

SANTA FE SYSTEM LINES
Serving the West and Southwest

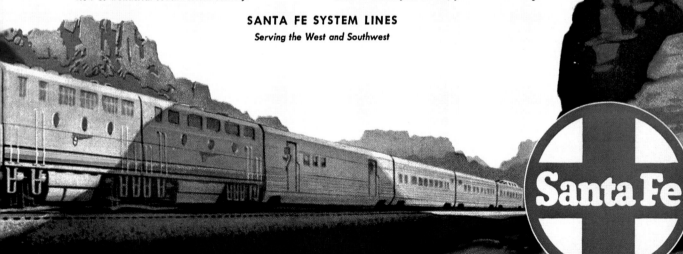

Santa Fe

And the winner is...

Watch The Blast From The Comfort Of Your Favorite Casino!

"There's always something going on in Las Vegas!" Sure. Like a nuclear explosion. In a push to boost tourism, Las Vegas advertised heavily about its proximity to testing sights. Visitors were encouraged to view the blasts from the middle of town and on the rooftops of the casinos. Compulsive gamblers barely noticed the rumble and afterglow.

Verfolgen Sie die Detonation in der komfortablen Umgebung Ihres Lieblingskasinos!

»In Las Vegas ist immer etwas los!« Na klar. Zum Beispiel eine Atomexplosion. Um den Tourismus anzuheizen, warb Las Vegas mächtig mit seiner Nähe zu den Testgeländen. Besucher wurden dazu ermuntert, die Zündungen aus der Stadtmitte oder von den Dachterrassen der Kasinos herab zu beobachten. Eingefleischte Spieler allerdings nahmen vom Dröhnen und vom Nachglühen des Atomblitzes kaum Notiz.

Admirez l'explosion depuis votre casino préféré !

« Il se passe toujours quelque chose à Las Vegas ! » Pour sûr. Par exemple, une explosion nucléaire. Dans le désir de promouvoir son tourisme, Las Vegas met en avant sa proximité avec les terrains d'essais nucléaires. Les visiteurs sont encouragés à assister aux déflagrations depuis le centre-ville et le toit des casinos. Les joueurs invétérés remarquent à peine le bruit et la fureur qui s'ensuivent.

Las Vegas, 1952

Index

...for the funniest movie ever made
Everybody likes it hot!

"In the old days, when cinemaphilia was still hip, everyone dreamed of a perfect book about film. Movie fans are fetishists—you can sell them anything, if you come on right.

... And now comes this absolutely direct, headstrong, unwaveringly passionate declaration of love to everyone's favorite comedy—a book that behaves as if the *foreign affair* that celluloid once conducted with art paper had never fallen apart. As an overture to the coming attraction: the first fascinating color photos on the black-and-white film. A tantalizing, bigger-than-life impression!"
—*Frankfurter Rundschau*, Frankfurt

"Anyone who purchases this book will no doubt be faced with an immediate quandary: Do I read it, eat it or make love to it? To call the book luscious and sexy is barely hyperbole. In fact, it is inconceivable that there is a more alluring book on the market today." —*Variety.com*

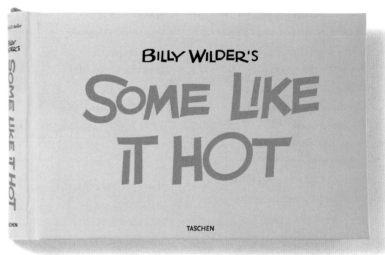

Billy Wilder's SOME LIKE IT HOT Ed. Alison Castle / Interviews by Dan Auiler
English/German/French / With an original cartoon Billy Wilder bookmark and a facsimile-reprint of Marilyn Monroe's personal promptbook / Padded cover, format: 39.8 x 24.9 cm (15 ³/₈ x 9 ³/₄ inches), 384 pp., 843 ills. / US$ 150 / £ 100 / DM 300 / € (F) 150 / PES 30.000 / ¥ 20,000

"...Some Like It Hot is essentially a love letter to one of the author's most revered films." —*New York Post, New York*

***Extra special bonus:** Marilyn Monroe's personal promptbook (with her handwritten comments), which recently sold at auction for $60,000, is provided in facsimile as a pull-out booklet!

The complete guide to Billy Wilder's masterpiece!! Find out everything you could ever want to know (and more) about the movie voted best comedy of the century by the American Film Institute. A daring tale of cross-dressing from a time when the subject was all but taboo, *Some Like It Hot* (1959) tells the story of two jazz musicians who are forced to go undercover in an all-girls' band to escape from the mob. With an ingenious screenplay by I.A.L. Diamond and Billy Wilder, and flawless performances by Tony Curtis, Jack Lemmon and the famously difficult Marilyn Monroe, *Some Like It Hot* is the embodiment of comic perfection.

Includes:
— Interviews with Billy Wilder, Tony Curtis, Jack Lemmon, and others
— Complete facsimile of the screenplay with film stills from every scene
— Excerpts from the script's first draft
— Behind-the-scenes photos
— Original promotional materials from all around the world
— Annotated/illustrated Billy Wilder filmography

The editor: **Alison Castle** studied philosophy as an undergraduate at Columbia University and went on to receive her graduate degree in photography and film from the New York University/International Center of Photography masters program. She is currently based in Paris and works as an artist and writer.
The interviewer: **Dan Auiler** is the author of *Hitchcock's Notebooks* (HarperCollins/Bloomsbury) and *Vertigo: The Making of a Hitchcock Classic* (St. Martin's Press). His books on Martin Scorsese's *Taxi Driver* and *Goodfellas* (Putnam/Bloomsbury) will be published in 2002. He lives in Long Beach, California.

YOU ARE CORDIALLY INVITED TO "SULKA'S WEDDING" AND "TABOO"

The ins and outs of XXX

The Christy Report Introduction by Kim Christy / Text by John Quinn / Postscript by Dian Hanson / English/German/French / Hardcover, 608 pp., 1,092 ills.
US$ 50 / £ 30 / DM 75 / € (F) 45 / PES 6.995

To make this magazine appropriate for the whole family, we have included these conveniently placed smilies. The actual book is completely ☺-free!

-rated culture. Everything you ever wanted to know about sex . . .

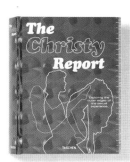

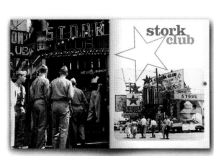

Penetrate the world of the 20th-century adult underground with publisher, film producer, and archivist Kim Christy. Compiled from extensive private collections, *The Christy Report* brings you a plethora of images tracing the evolution of porn as we know it, from beginnings in early photography, illustration, and film, through the glory days of the 70s porn explosion, up to today's expanded digital-age market. A history book unlike any you ever had in school, *The Christy Report* is more than eye candy, it's also educational (wink, wink)!

Kim Christy spent several years dancing and performing in night clubs before working for the Eros Publishing Company on such titles as *Eros, Mode Avantgarde, Hooker* and *Exposé*. Christy has since produced and directed several feature films, including *Sulka's Wedding, Squalor Motel,* and *Corrupt Desires.*